Y0-DYJ-056

Bibliographies for Biblical Research

New Testament Series

in Twenty-One Volumes

General Editor

Watson E. Mills

Bibliographies for Biblical Research

New Testament Series

in Twenty-One Volumes

Volume II

The Gospel of Mark

Compiled by
Watson E. Mills

Lewiston/Queenston/Lampeter

Library of Congress Cataloging-in-Publication Data
(Revised for vol. 2)

Bibliographies for biblical research.

Includes index.
Contents: v. 1. The Gospel of Matthew / compiled by Watson E. Mills -- v. 2. The Gospel of Mark / compiled by Watson E. Mills.
1. Bible. N.T.--Criticism, interpretation, etc.--Bibliography. I. Mills, Watson E.
Z7772.L1B4 1993 [BS2341.2] 016.2262'06 93-30864
ISBN 0-7734-2347-8 (v. 1)
ISBN 0-7734-2349-4 (v. 2)

This is volume 2 in the continuing series
Bibliographies for Biblical Research
New Testament Series
Volume 2 ISBN 0-7734-2349-4
Series ISBN 0-7734-9345-X

A CIP catalog record for this book is available from the British Library.

The Edwin Mellen Press
Box 450
Lewiston, New York
USA 14092

The Edwin Mellen Press
Box 67
Queenston, Ontario
CANADA L0S 1L0

Edwin Mellen Press, Ltd.
Lampeter, Dyfed, Wales
UNITED KINGDOM SA48 7DY

Printed in the United States of America

Dedication

To Ruth Cheves

with appreciation and affection

Contents

Introduction to the Series ix

Preface xi

Abbreviations xiii

Part 1 Citations by Chapter and Verse 1

Part 2 Citiations by Subjects 277

Part 3 Commentaries 485

Author Index 501

Introduction to the Series

This volume is the second in a series of bibliographies on the books of the Hebrew and Christian Bibles as well as the deutero-canonicals. This ambitious series calls for 21 volumes covering the New Testament alone over the next 4-6 years complied by practicing scholars from various traditions.

Each author (compiler) of these volumes is working within the general framework adopted for the series, i.e., citations are to works published within the twentieth century that make important contributions to the understanding of the text and backgrounds of the various books.

Obviously the former criterion is more easily quantifiable than the latter, and it is precisely at this point that an individual compiler makes her/his specific contribution. We are not intending to be comprehensive in the sense of definitive, but where resources are available, as many listings as possible have been included.

The arrangement for the entries, in most volumes in the series, consists of three divisions: scriptural citations; subject citations; commentaries. In some cases the first two categories may duplicate each other to some degree. Multiple citations by scriptural citation are also included where relevant.

Those who utilize these volumes are invited to assist the compilers by noting textual errors as well as obvious omissions that ought to be taken into account in subsequent printings. Perfection is nowhere more elusive than in the citation of bibliographic materials. We would welcome your assistance at this point.

We hope that these bibliographies will contribute to the discussions and research going on in the field among faculty as well as students. They should serve a significant role as reference works in both research and public libraries.

I wish to thank the staff and editors of the Edwin Mellen Press, and especially Professor Herbert Richardson, for the gracious support of this series.

Watson E. Mills, Series Editor
Mercer University
Macon GA 31211
July 1993

Preface

This Bibliography on the Gospel of Mark provides an index to the journal articles, essays in collected works, books and monographs, dissertations, commentaries, and various encyclopedia and dictionary articles published in the twentieth century through 1992 (a few titles for the early months of 1993 are included when these were available for verification). Technical works of scholarship, from many differing traditions constitute the bulk of the citations though I have included some selected works that intend to reinterpret this research to a wider audience.

Four extant bibliographies on the Gospel of Mark proved most helpful in the preparation of this text: Günter Wagner, *An Exegetical Bibliography of the New Testament: Matthew and Mark* (Mercer University Press, 1983); Paul-Émile Langevin, *Bibliographie biblique* (Les Presses de l'Université Laval, 1972, 1978, 1985); Hugh M. Humphrey, *A Bibliography for the Gospel of Mark 1954-1980* (Edwin Mellen Press, 1981); and Frans Neirynck, et al., *The Gospel of Mark: A Cumulative Bibliography 1950-1990* (Louvain: Peeters Press, 1992). The first covers a wide representative of traditions and confessions (especially from Europe) but contains listings only by scriptural citation; the second is heavily slanted toward Catholic publications but particularly the third volume begins to move toward a more balanced perspective. Langevin's work is very heavy in citations to French literature, but is meticulously indexed by scriptural citation as well as subject and contains detailed indexes. Humphrey's is a helpful compilation of over 1,600 entries and Neirynck's massive volume covers materials published since 1950. This latter volume is easily the most definitive.

Building the database necessary for a work of this magnitude was a tedious and time-consuming task. I acknowledge the administration of Mercer University for granting me a sabbatical leave during the 1991-1992 academic year. Also, I acknowledge with gratitude the Education Commission of the Southern Baptist Convention which provided funds for travel to overseas libraries.

I want to express my gratitude to the staff librarians at the following institutions: Baptist Theological Seminary (Rüschlikon, Switzerland); Oxford University (Oxford, UK); Emory University (Atlanta, GA); Duke University (Durham, NC); University of Zürich (Zürich, Switzerland); Southern Baptist Theological Seminary (Louisville, KY).

I wish to thank especially, Virginia L. Cairns, Reference Librarian, Mercer University Library, for her cheerful assistance in verifying citations in this work. Finally, I gratefully acknowledge the invaluable assistance given me in technical aspects of this work by my long-time associate Ms. Irene Palmer.

Watson E. Mills
Mercer University
Macon GA 31211
January 1994

Abbreviations

ABR	Australian Biblical Review (Melbourne)
AbrN	Abr-Nahrain (Louvain)
ACEBT	Amsterdanse Cahiers voor exegese en bijbelse theologie (Kampen)
ACR	Australian Catholic Record (Manly)
AfER	African Ecclesial Review (Masaka, Uganda)
AfTJ	African Theological Journal (Tanzania)
AJET	African Journal of Evangelical Theology (Arusha, Tanzania)
AL	Archiv für Liturgiewissenschaft (Regensburg)
ALB	Adyar Library Bulletin (Adyar)
AmER	American Ecclesiastical Review (Washington, DC)
AMEZQR	AME Zion Quarterly Review (Philadelphia)
AnaCal	Analecta calasanctiana (Salamanca)
AnBib	Analecta Biblica (Rome)
AnBoll	Analecta Bollandiaa (Brussels)
Ant	Antonianum (Rome)
AsiaJT	The Asia Journal of Theology (Singapore)
AsSeign	Assemblées du Seigneur (Paris)
AsSem	Asbury Seminarian (Wilmore, KY)
ASV	Anales del Seminario de Valencia (Valencia)
ATR	Anglican Theological Review (Evanston, IL)
AugR	Augustinianum (Rome)
BA	Biblical Archaeologist (Ann Arbor, MI)
BAR	Biblical Archaeology Review (Washington, DC)

BASP	Bulletin of the American School of Papyrology (Waqshington)
BB	Bible Bhashyam: An Indian Biblical Quarterly (Vadavathoor)
BETL	Bibliotheca ephemeridum theologicarum lovaniensium (Louvain)
Bib	Biblica (Rome)
BibFe	Biblia y fe: Revista de teologia bíblica (Madrid)
BibL	Bibel und Leben (Düsseldorf)
BibN	Biblische Notizen: Beiträge zur exegetischen Diskussion (Munich)
BibO	Bibbia e Oriente (Brescia)
BibOr	Bibliotheca orientalis (Leiden)
BibTh	Biblical Theology (Belfast)
BibTo	Bible Today (Collegeville, MN)
Bij	Bijdragen: Tijdschrift voor Filosofie en Theologie (Nijmegen)
BJRL	Bulletin of the John Rylands University Library (Manchester, UK)
BK	Bibel und Kirche (Stuttgart)
BL	Bibel und Liturgie (Vienna)
BLE	Bulletin de Littérature Ecclésiastique (Paris)
BLOS	Bulletin de liaison sur l'origine des Synoptiques (Orléans)
BLT	Brethren Life and Thought (Oak Brook, IL)
BogV	Bogoslovni vestnik (Ljubljana)
BQ	Baptist Quarterly (Oxford, UK)
BR	Biblical Research (Chicago)
BRev	Bible Review (Washington)
BSac	Bibliotheca Sacra (Dallas, TX)
BSS	Bulletin of Saint Sulpice (Paris)
BT	Bible Translator (Aberdeen, UK)
BTAf	Bulletin de théologie africaine (Kinshasa)
BTB	Biblical Theology Bulletin (St. Bonaventure, NY)
BTF	Bangalore Theological Forum (Bangalore)
BTS	Bible et Terre Sainte (Paris)
Bur	Burgense: Collectanea Scientifica (Burgos)

BVC	Bible et Vie Chretienne (Paris)
BZ	Biblische Zeitschrift (Paderborn)
CANZTR	Colloquium: The Australian and New Zealand Theological Review (Auchland)
Cath	Catholica: Vierteljahresschrift für ökumenische Theologie (Münst)
CBG	Collationes Brugenses et Gandavenses (Gent)
CBQ	Catholic Biblical Quarterly (Washington, DC)
CC	Christian Century (Chicago)
CCER	Cahiers du cercle Ernest Renan pour libres recherches d'historie du christianisme (Paris)
Chr	Christus (Paris)
ChrSo	Le Christianisme Social (Paris)
CICR	Communico: International Catholic Review (Spokane, WA)
CiTom	Ciencia tomista (Salamanca)
CivCatt	La Civiltà Cattolica (Rome)
CJ	Concordia Journal St. Louis, MO)
CJT	Canadian Journal of Theology (Toronto)
CL	Communautés et liturgies (Ottignies)
ClerR	Clergy Review (London)
CollBQ	College of the Bible Quarterly (Lexington KY)
CollM	Collectanea Mechliniensia (Mechelen)
CollT	Collectanea Theologica (Warsaw)
Communio	Communio: Commentarii internationales de ecclesia et theologia (Seville)
Comp	Compostellanum (Santiago de Compostela)
Conci	Concilium (New York)
ConRel	Conoscenza Religiosa (Firenze)
CQ	Covenant Quarterly (Chicago)
CQR	Church Quarterly Review (London)
Crit	Criterion (Chicago, IL)
CrNSt	Cristianesimo nella Storia (Bologna)
Crux	Crux (Vancouver)
CS	Chicago Studies (Chicago)

CT	Christianity Today (Des Moines, IA)
CThM	Currents in Theology and Mission (Chicago)
CTM	Concordia Theological Monthly (St. Louis, MO)
CTQ	Concordia Theological Quarterly (Fort Wayne, IN)
CuBí	Cultura Bíblica (Madrid)
CVia	Communio Viatorum (Prague)
DBM	Deltío Biblikôn Meletôn (Athens)
Dia	Dialog (Minneapolis, MN)
Did	Didascalia (Otterburne, Canada)
Div	Divinitas (Laterano, Italy)
DivT	Divus Thomas (Piacenza)
DR	Downside Review (Bath, UK)
DTT	Dansk Teologisk Tidsskrift (Copenhagen)
DunR	Dunwoodie Review (Yonkers, NY)
DWort	Dienst am Wort (Freiburg)
EB	Estudios Bíblicos (Madrid)
ECarm	Ephemerides Carmelitical (Rome)
ÉCB	Évangile. Cahiers bibliques (Paris)
EcumRev	Ecumenical Review (Geneva)
ED	Euntes docet (Rome)
EE	Estudios Eclesiásticos (Madrid)
EGLMBS	Eastern Great Lakes and Midwest Biblical Society (no place of publication cited)
ÉgT	Église et théologie (Ottawa, Canada)
Emmanuel	Emmanuel (New York)
Enc	Encounter (Indianapolis, IN)
Ent	Entschluss (Vienna)
EpRev	The Epworth Review (London)
EQ	Evangelical Quarterly (Exeter, UK)
ErAu	Erbe und Auftrag (Beuron)
EstAg	Estudios agustiniano (Valladolid)
EstFr	Estudios franciscanos (Barcelona)
EstT	Estudios Teológicos (Guatemala City)
ET	Expository Times (Edinburgh, UK)
ETL	Ephemerides Theologicae Lovanienses (Louvain)

ÉTR	Études Théologiques et Religieuses (Montpellier)
Études	Études (Paris)
ÉtudF	Études Franciscaines (Barcelona)
EV	Esprit et Vie (Langres)
EvErz	Der evangelische Erzieher (Frankurt/M)
EvT	Evangelische Theologie (Stuttgart)
EX	Ecclesiastica Xaveriana (Bogata)
ExA	Ex Auditu (Princeton)
FilN	Filologia Neotestamentaria (Córdoba)
FM	Faith and Mission (Wake Forest, NC)
Forum	Forum (Sonoma, CA)
FT	La foi et le temps (Tournai)
FV	Foi et Vie (Paris)
FundJ	Fundamentalist Journal (Lynchburg, VA)
FZPT	Freiburger Zeitschrift für Philosophie und Theologie (Freiburg)
GCAJS	Gratz College Annual of Jewish Studies (no place of publication cited)
GeistL	Geist und Leben (Würzburg)
GOTR	Greek Orthodox Theological Review (Brookline, MA)
GR	Gordon Review (Boston)
Greg	Gregorianum (Rome)
GTJ	Grace Theological Journal (Winona Lake, IN)
GTT	Gereformeered Theologisch Tijdschrift (Kampen, Neth)
HartQ	Hartford Quarterly (Hartford, CT)
HBT	Horizons in Biblical Theology: An International Dialogue (Pittsburg, PA)
HeyJ	Heythrop Journal (London)
HJ	Hibbert Journal (London)
Hokhmah	Hokhmah (Bordeaux)
Horizons	Horizons: The Journal of the College Theology Society (Villanova, PA)
HTR	Harvard Theological Review (Cambridge, MA)
HTS	Hervormde Teologiese Studies (Pretoria)

HUCA	Hebrew Union College Annual (New York)
Hum	Humanitas (Pittsburg, PA)
IBS	Irish Biblical Studies (Belfast)
IEJ	Israel Exploration Journal (Jerusalem)
IJT	Indian Journal of Theology (Calcutta)
IKaZ	Internationale Katholische Zeitschrift "Communio" (Frankfurt/M)
Immanuel	Immanuel: A Bulletin of Religious Thought and Research in Israel (Jerusalem)
IndES	Indian Ecclesiastical Studies (Bangalore)
Int	Interpretation (Richmond, VA)
IRM	International Review of Mission (Geneva)
ITQ	Irish Theological Quarterly Kildare, Ireland)
ITS	Indian Theological Studies (Bangalore)
JAAR	Journal of the American Academy of Religion (Atlanta, GA)
JBL	Journal of Biblical Literature (Atlanta, GA)
JBR	Journal of Bible and Religion (Philadelphia, PA)
Je	Jeevadhara (Kerala, India)
JES	Journal of Ecumenical Studies (Philadelphia, PA)
JETS	Journal of the Evangelical Theological Society (Jackson, MS)
JNES	Journal of Near Eastern Studies (Chicago)
JPC	Journal of Pastoral Care (Decatur, GA)
JQR	Jewish Quarterly Review (Philadelphia, PA)
JR	Journal of Religion (Chicago)
JRAS	Journal of the Royal Asiatic Society of Great Britian and Ireland (London)
JRT	Journal of Religious Thought (Washington, DC)
JSNT	Journal for the Study of the New Testament (Sheffield, UK)
JSS	Journal of Semitic Studies (Oxford, UK)
JTS	Journal of Theological Studies (Oxford, UK)
JTSA	Journal of Theology for Southern Africa (Cape Town)
Judaism	Judaism (New York)

K	Kairos (Salzburg)
KatB	Katechetische Blätter (Münich)
KathG	Der Katholische Gedanke (Augsburg)
KathGed	Der Katholische Gedanke (Regensburg)
KD	Kerygma and Dogma (Göttingen)
KerkT	Kerk en theologie (Den Haa)
KingsTR	King's Theological Review (London)
KIsr	Kirche und Israel: Theologische Zeitschrift (Neukirchen)
Klerusblatt	Klerusblatt (Praha)
KRS	Kirchenblatt für die Reformierte Schweiz
Lat	Lateranum (Rome)
Laur	Laurentianum (Rome)
LB	Linguistica Biblica (Bonn)
List	Listening: Journal of Religion and Culture (Romeoville, IL)
LivL	The Living Light (Huntington, IN)
LouvS	Louvain Studies (Louvain)
LQ	Lutheran Quarterly (Milwaukee, WI)
LQHR	London Quarterly and Holbon Review (London)
LR	Lutherische Rundschau (Stuttgart)
LTK	Lexikon für Theologie und Kirche (Freiburg)
LTP	Laval théologique et philosophique (Quebec)
LV	Lumen Vitae (Brussells)
LVie	Lumière et Vie (Lyon)
LZ	Lebendiges Zugnis (Paderborn)
Marianum	Marianum: Ephemerides Mariologiae (Rome)
MarSt	Marian Studies (Dayton, OH)
May	Mayéutica (Marcilla)
MC	Modern Churchman (Oxford)
MD	Maison-Dieu (Paris)
MeliT	Melita Theologia (Rabat, Malta)
MillSt	Milltown Studies (Dublin)
MiscFranc	Miscellanea Franciscana (Rome)
MQR	Mennonite Quarterly Review (Goshen, IN)
MThSt	Marburger theologische Studien (Marburg)

MTZ	Münchener theologische Zeitschrift (München)
NatGrac	Naturaleza y gracia (Salamanca)
NBlack	New Blackfriars (London)
NC	Nouveaux Cahiers (no place of publication cited)
NedTT	Nederlands theologisch tijdschrift (Gravenhage, Neth)
Neo	Neotestamentica: Journal of the New Testament Society of South Africa (Pretoria)
Nexus	Nexus: Spiritual Resource for Ministry (Boston)
NovT	Novum Testamentum (Leiden, Neth)
NovVet	Nova et Vetera (Fribourg)
NRT	Nouvelle revue théologique (Tournai)
NTheoR	New Theology Review (Collegeville, MN)
NTS	New Testament Studies (Cambridge, UK)
NTT	Norsk teologisk tidsskrift (Oslo)
Numen	Numen: International Review for the Study of Religions (Leiden)
NZSTR	Neue Zeitschrift für systematisch Theologie und Religionsphilosophie (Berlin)
OCP	Orientalia christiana periodica (Rome)
OPTAT	Occassional Papers in Translation and Textlinguistics (Dallas, TX)
Or	Orientalia (Rome)
OrBibLov	Orientalia et Biblica Louvaniensa (Louvain)
OrChr	Oriens Christianus (Rome)
Orient	Orientierung (Zürich)
OSide	The Other Side (Philadelphia, PA)
P&P	Priests & People (Philadelphia, PA)
Pacifica	Pacifica: Australian Theological Studies (Brunswick, East, Victoria, Australia)
PalCl	Palestra del Clero (Rovigo)
Paradigms	Paradigms (Louisville, KY)
ParaM	Parabola Magazine
ParSpirV	Parola, spirito e vita: Quaderni di lettura biblica (Bologna)

PatByzR	Patristic and Byzantine Review (Kingston, NY)
PEQ	Palestine Exploration Quarterly (London)
Persp	Perspective (no place of publication cited)
PerT	Perspectiva Teológica (Belo Horizonte, Brazil)
PIBA	Proceedings of the Irish Biblical Association (Dublin)
PJ	Perkins Journal (Dallas, TX)
Pneuma	Penuma: The Journal of the Society for Pentecostal Studies (Gaithersburg, MD)
POC	Proche Orient Chrétien (Jerusalem)
PRS	Perspectives in Religious Studies (Lewiston, NY)
Protest	Protestantesimo (Rome)
PV	Parole di vita (Torino)
QR	Quarterly Review: A Journal of Theological Resources for Ministry (Nashville, TN)
RAfT	Revue Africaine de Théologie (Alger)
RB	Revue biblique (Paris)
RBib	Rivista Biblica (Bologna)
RBR	Ricerche Bibliche e Religiose (Milan)
RCA	Revue du clergé Africain (Mayidi)
RCB	Revista de Cultura Bíblica (San Paulo)
RCT	Revista Catalana de Teología (Barcelona)
RechSR	Recherches de science religieuse (Paris)
REd	Religious Education (New Haven, CT)
Reformatio	Reformatio: (Evangelische Zeitschrift für Kultur, Politik, Kirche (Zürich)
RET	Revista española de teología (Madrid)
RevB	Revista Biblica (Buenos Aires)
RevBB	Revista bíblica brasileira (Fortaleza)
RevExp	Review and Expositor (Louisville, KY)
RevQ	Revue de Qumran (Paris)
RevRef	Revue réformée (Saint-Germain-en-Laye)
RevRel	Review for Religious (St. Mary's. KS)
RevSR	Revue des sciences religieuses (Strasbourg Cedex)
RevTL	Revista Teológica Limense (Lima)

RHPR	Revue d'historie et de philosophie religieuses (Strasbourg Cedex)
BibRev	Biblical Review (Washington)
RIDA	Revue Internationale des Droits de l'Antiquité (Brussels)
RivSO	Rivista degli studi orientali (Rome)
RL	Religion in Life (Nashville, TN)
RoczTK	Roczniki Teologiczno-Kanoniczne (Lublin)
RQ	Restoration Quarterly (Abilene, TX)
RR	Reformed Review (Holland, MI)
RSB	Religious Studies Bulletin (Calgary)
RSLR	Rivista di storia e letteratura religiosa (Firenze)
RSPT	Revue des sciences philosophiques et théologiques (Paris)
RSR	Religious Studies Review (Valapariso, IN)
RSRel	Rivista di scienze della religione (Molletta)
RT	Revue Thomiste (Paris)
RTAM	Recherches de Théologie Ancienne et Médiévale (Louvain)
RTL	Revue théologique de Louvain (Louvain)
RTP	Revue de Théologie et de Philosophie (Geneva)
RTR	Reformed Theological Review (Hawthorne, Australia)
RuchB	Ruch biblijny (Krakow)
RUO	Revue de l'université d'Ottawa (Ottawa)
RW	Reformed World (Geneva)
SacD	Sacra Doctrina (Bologna)
Sale	Salesianum (Rome)
Salm	Salmanticensis (Salamanca)
SBFLA	Studii Biblici Franciscani Liber Annuus (Jerusalem)
SBLSP	Society of Biblical Literature Seminar Papers (Atlanta)
SBT	Studia Biblica et Theologica (Pasadena, CA)
ScC	Scuola cattolica: Rivista di scienze religiose (Milan)
ScE	Science et Esprit (Montreal)
Schrift	Schrift (Landstichting, Neth)
Scr	Scripture (Scripture Bulletin after 1968; London)
ScrB	Scripture Bulletin (London)
ScripT	Scripta theologia (Pamplona, Spain)

ScrSA	Scriptura: Journal of Bible and Theology in South Africa (Stellenbosch, South Africa)
SE	Sciences Ecclésiastiques: Revue philosophique et théologique (Montreal)
SEÅ	Svensk Exegetisk Årsbok (Lund)
SEAJT	South East Asia Journal of Theology (Manila)
SecCent	Second Century (Abilene, TX)
SelTeol	Selecciones de teología (Barcelona)
SémBib	Sémiotique et Bible (Lyon)
Semeia	Semeia (Atlanta, GA)
Semitica	Semitica (Paris)
Servitium	Servitium, quaderni de spiritualità (Casale Monferrato)
SJT	Scottish Journal of Theology (Edinburgh, UK)
SLJT	Saint Luke's Journal of Theology (Sewanee, TN)
SM	Studia Missionalia (Rome)
SMR	Saint Mark's Review (Canberra)
SNTU-A	Studien zum Neuen Testament und seiner Umwelt (series A) (Linz)
Soj	Sojourners
SouJT	Southwestern Journal of Theology (Fort Worth, TX)
SR	Studies in Religion/Sciences religieuses (Waterloo, Ontario)
StCan	Studia Canonica: Revue canadienne de droit canonique (Ottawa)
SThV	Studia theologica Varsaviensia (Warsaw)
StOvet	Studium Ovetense (Oviedo)
StPa	Studia Patavina: Revista di scienze religiose (Padova)
StTheol	Studia theologica: Scandinavian Journal of Theology (Lund)
StudE	Studia evangelica (Berlin)
StudL	Studium Legionense (León)
StudPat	Studia Patristica (Berlin)
SVTQ	St. Vladimir's Theological Quarterly (Crestwood, NY)
TAik	Teologinen Aikakauskrija (Helsinki)
TB	Theologische Berichte (Zürich)

TBe	Theologische Beiträge (Wuppertal)
TBT	Theologische Bibliothek Töpelmann (Berlin)
TD	Theology Digest (Duluth, MN)
TGeg	Theologie der Gegenwart (Münster)
Teología	Teología (Brescia)
TexteK	Texte und Kontexte: Exegetische Zeitschrift (Berlin)
TGl	Theologie und Glaube (Paderborn)
Themelios	Themelios (Leicester, UK)
Theok	Theokratia: Jahrbuch des Instiutum Delitzschianum (Leiden)
Theologica	Theologica (Braga)
Theology	Theology (London)
TheoP	Theologie und Philosophie (Freiburg)
TheoR	Theologische Revue (Münich)
TheoV	Theologische Versuche (Berlin)
ThEv	Theologia evangelica (Pretoria)
Thomist	Thomist (Washington, DC)
TijT	Tijdschrift voor Theologie (Nijmegen)
TJT	Toronto Journal of Theology (Toronto)
TLZ	Theologische Literaturzeitung (Leipzig)
Touch	Touchstone: Heritage and Theology in a New Age (Winnipeg)
TPQ	Theologische-praktische Quartalschrift (Linz)
TQ	Theologische Quartalschift (Tübingen)
TR	Theologische Rundschau (Tübingen)
Trans	Transformation: An International Evangelical Dialogue on Mission and Ethics (Exeter)
TS	Theological Studies (Washington, DC)
TSFB	Theological Students' Fellowship Bulletin (Baltimore, MD)
TT	Theology Today (Princeton, NJ)
TTZ	Trierer Theologische Zeitschrift (Trier)
Tugn	Tugónian Ecumenical Journal of Discussion and Opinion (Manila)
TVia	Theologia Viatorum (Berlin)
TW	Am Tisch des Wortes (Stuttgart)
TynB	Tyndale Bulletin (London)

TyV	Teología y vida (Santiago)
TZ	Theologische Zeitschrift (Basel)
UnSa	Una Sancta (Freising)
URM	Ultimate Reality and Meaning (Toronto)
USQR	Union Seminary Quarterly Review (New York)
UUC	Unitarian Universalist Christian (Boston)
VC	Vigiliae Christianae (Amsterdam)
VD	Verbum Domini (Rome)
VerbC	Verbum Caro: Revue théologique et oecuménique (Neuchâtel)
VoxE	Vox evangelica (London)
VS	La vie spirituelle (Paris)
WesTJ	Wesleyan Theological Journal (Marion, IN)
WD	Wort und Dienst: Jahrbuch der theologischen Schule Bethel (Bielefeld)
Worship	Worship (Collegeville, MN)
WTJ	Westminster Theology Journal (Philadelphia)
WW	Word and World (St. Paul, MN)
ZAW	Zeitschrift für die alttestamentliche Wissenschaft (Berlin)
ZDPV	Zeitschrift des Deutschen Palästina-Vereins (Wiesbaden)
ZKT	Zeitschrift für Katholische Theologie (Innsbruck)
Zion	Zion (Jerusalem)
ZKG	Zeitschrift für Kirchengeschichte (Stuttgart)
ZMiss	Zeitschrift für Mission (Basel)
ZNW	Zeitschrift für die neutestamentliche Wissenschaft (Berlin)
ZPE	Zeitschrift für Papyrologie und Epigraphik (Bonn)
ZRGG	Zeitschrift für Religions- und Geistesgeschichte (Erlangen)
ZTK	Zeitschrift für Theologie und Kirche (Tübingen)

PART ONE

Citations by Chapter and Verse

1:1-8:26

0001 R. C. Stedman, *The Servant Who Rules*. Waco TX: Word Books, 1976.

0002 Frans Neirynck, "Mark and His Commentators: Mk 1,1-8,26," *ETL* 65 (1989): 381-89.

1:1-3:36

0003 Eduard Schweizer, "Die theologische Leistung des Markus," *EvT* 24 (1964): 337-55.

1:1-3:35

0004 Marvin F. Cain, "An Analysis of the Sources of Mark 1:1-3:35 and Parallels," doctoral dissertation, Duke University, Durham NC, 1971.

1:1-15

0005 J. F. Seitz, "Praeparatio Evangelica in the Markan Prologue," *JBL* 82 (1963): 201-206.

0006 Leander E. Keck, "The Introduction to Mark's Gospel," *NTS* 12 (1965-1966): 352-70.

0007 Rudolf Pesch, "Anfang des Evangeliums Jesu Christi: Eine Studie zum Prolog des Markusevangeliums (Mk 1,1-15)," in Günther Bornkamm and Karl Rahner, eds., *Die Zeit Jesu* (festschrift for Heinrich Schlier). Freiburg: Herder, 1970. Pp. 108-44.

0008 John M. Gibbs, "Mark 1,1-15; Matthew 1,1-4,16; Luke 1,1-4,30; John 1,1-51: The Gospel Prologues and Their Function," *StudE* 6 (1973): 154-88.

0009 Hugolinus Langkammer, "Tradycja i redakcja w prologu Ewangelii Marka (1,1-15)," *RoczTK* 20 (1973): 37-57.

00010 Gerhard Dautzenberg, "Die Zeit des Evangeliums. Mk 1,1-15 und die Konzeption des Markusevangeliums," *BZ* 21 (1977): 219-34.

00011 Gerhard Dautzenberg, "Die Zeit des Evangeliums. Mk 1,1-15 und die Konzeption des Markusevangeliums [Pt. 2]," *BZ* 22/1 (1978): 76-91.

0012 Cornelis J. den Heyer, "Markus 1,1-15: De proloog van het Markus-evangelie," *ACEBT* 1 (1980): 76-84.

0013 Robert A. Guelich, "The Beginning of the Gospel," *BR* 27 (1982): 5-15.

0014 Robert A. Guelich, "The Gospel Genre," in Peter Stuhlmacher, ed., *Das Evangelium und die Evangelien.* Tübingen: Mohr, 1983. Pp. 183-219.

0015 John Drury, "Mark 1:1-15: An Interpretation," in A. E. Harvey, ed., *Alternative Approaches to New Testament Study*. London: Latimer, 1985. Pp. 25-36.

0016 M. Eugene Boring, "Mark 1:1-15 and the Beginning of the Gospel," *Semeia* 52 (1990): 43-81.

0017 Klauspeter Blaser, "Der Stärkere: biblische Besinnung zu Mk 1:1-15 par," *ZMiss* 17/1 (1991): 3-7.

0018 Jan Lambrecht, "John the Baptist and Jesus in Mark 1:1-15: Markan Redaction of Q?" *NTS* 38 (1992): 357-84.

<u>1:1-14</u>

0019 Vernon K. Robbins, "Interpreting the Gospel of Mark as a Jewish Document in a Greco-Roman World," in P. V. M. Flesher, ed., *New Perspectives on Ancient Judaism. 5: Society and Literature in Analysis*. Lanham MD: University Press of America, 1990. 5:47-72.

<u>1:1-13</u>

0020 J. J. C. Willemse, "God's First and Last Word: Jesus (Mark 1,1-13 and John 1,1-18," in Pierre Benoit and Roland E. Murphy, eds., *The Human Reality of Sacred Scripture,* David T. LeFort, trans. Concilium #10. New York: Paulist Press, 1965. Pp. 75-95.

0021 Richard T. France, "The Beginning of Mark," *RTR* 49 (1990): 11-19.

<u>1:1-8</u>

0022 Harald Sahlin, "Zwei Fälle von harmonisicrendem Einfluss des Matthausevangeliums auf das Markus-Evangelium," *StTheol* 13 (1959): 166-79.

0023 Rudolf Pesch, "Ausrichtung auf den 'Kommenden' (Mk 1,1-8)," *TW* 101 (1969): 57-64.

0024 Paul Ternant, "Le ministere de Jean, commencement de l'Evangile, Mc 1,1-8," *AsSeign* 6 (1969): 41-53.

0025 Rámon Trevijano Etcheverría, *Comienzo del Evangelio. Estudio sobre el Prólogo de San Marcos*. Publicaciones de la Facultad de Teológica del Norte de España. Sede de Burgos 26. Burgos: Ediciones Aldecoa, 1971.

0026 Albert Fuchs, "Die Überschneidungen von Mk und 'Q' nach B. H. Streeter und E. P. Sanders und ihre wahre Bedeutung (Mk 1,1-8 Par.)," in Wilfrid Haubeck and W. Bachmann, eds., *Wort in der Zeit: Neutestamentliche Studien* (festschrift for K. H. Rengstorf). Leiden: Brill, 1980. Pp. 28-81.

0027 A. Radaelli, "I racconti dell'infanzia nel contesto del prologo all'Evangelo," *RBR* 15 (1980): 7-26.

0028 Gert Lüderitz, "Rhetorik, Poetik, Kompositionstechnik im Markusevangelium," in Hubert Cancik, ed., *Markus-Philologie*. Tübingen: Mohr, 1984. Pp. 165-203.

1:1-6

0029 Ernest C. Colwell, "The Significance of Grouping New Testament Manuscripts," *NTS* 4 (1957-1958): 73-92.

1:1-3

0030 Wolfgang Feneberg, *Der Markusprolog: Studien zur Formbestimmung des Evangeliums*. Studien zum Alten und Neuen Testament 36. Münich: Kösel, 1974.

1:1

0031 J. A. Emerton, "Some New Testament Notes," *JTS* 11 (1960): 329-36.

0032 Paul Lamarche, " 'Commencement de l'Evangeleide Jesus, Christ, Fils de Dieu' (Mc I,1)," *NRT* 92/10 (1970): 1024-36.

0033 Mario Galizzi, "Vangelo di Gesu Cristo, figlio di Dio (Mc 1,1)," *PV* 18 (1973): 51-70.

0034 Mark E. Glasswell, "The Beginning of the Gospel: A Study of St. Mark's Gospel with Regard to its First Verse," in

Mark E. Glasswell and Edward W. Fashole-Luke, eds., *New Testament Christianity for Africa and the World: Essays in Honour of Harry Sawyerr*. London: SPCK, 1974. Pp. 36-43.

0035 Gerhard Arnold, ''Mk 1:1 und Eröffnungswendungen in griechischen und lateinischen Schriften,'' *ZNW* 68 (1977): 123-27.

0036 J. Slomp, ''Are the Words 'Son of God' in Mark 1.1 Original?'' *BT* 28 (1977): 143-50.

0037 André Feuillet, ''Le 'Commencement' de l'économie chrétienne d'après He ii.3-4; Mc i.1 et Ac i.1-2,'' *NTS* 24 (1977-1978): 163-74.

0038 Mario Galizzi, ''Inizio del Vangelo di Gesù il Cristo, il Figlio di Dio,'' *PV* 26 (1981): 404-18.

0039 Alexander Globe, ''The Caesarean Omission of the Phrase 'Son of God' in Mark 1:1,'' *HTR* 75 (1982): 209-18.

0040 Hans Weder, ''Evangelium Jesu Christi (Mk 1,1) und 'Evangelium Gottes' (Mk 1,14),'' in Ulrich Luz and Hans Weder, eds., *Die Mitte des Neuen Testaments: Einheit and vielfalt neutestamentlicher theologie* (festschrift for Eduard Schweizer). Göttingen: Vandenhoeck & Ruprecht, 1983. Pp. 399-411.

0041 Detlev Dormeyer, ''Die Kompositionsmetapher 'Evangelium Jesu Christi, des Sohnes Gottes' Mk 1:1: ihre theologische und literarische Aufgabe in Markus,'' *NTS* 33/3 (1987): 452-68.

0042 Eugene A. LaVerdiere, ''Looking Ahead to the Year of Mark,'' *Emmanuel* 93 (1987): 494-501.

0043 Donald H. Juel and Patrick R. Keifert, ''A Markan Epiphany: Lessons from Mark 1,'' *WW* 8 (1988): 80-85.

0044 David Flusser, ''Die Versuchung Jesu und ihr jüdischer Hintergrund,'' *Jud* 45 (1989): 110-28.

0045 Peter M. Head, ''A Text-Critical Study of Mark 1:1: 'The Beginning of the Gospel of Jesus Christ','' *NTS* 37 (1991): 621-29.

1:2-15

0046 Joachim Schüling, *Studien zum Verhältnis von Logienquelle und Markusevangelium.* Würzburg: Echter, 1991.

1:2-13

0047 Eugene A. LaVerdiere, ''Mark's Gospel in Miniature,'' *Emmanuel* 93 (1987): 546-53.

0048 John Wright, ''Spirit and Wilderness: The Interplay of Two Motifs within the Hebrew Bible as a Background to Mark 1:2-13,'' in Edgar W. Conrad and Edward G. Newing, eds., *Perspectives on Language and Text* (festschrift for Francis Andersen). Winona Lake IN: Eisenbrauns, 1987. Pp. 269-98.

0049 Frank J. Matera, ''The Prologue as the Interpretative Key to Mark's Gospel,'' *JSNT* 34 (1988): 3-20.

1:2-8

0050 Otto Betz, *What Do We Know About Jesus?* M. Kohl, trans. London: SCM, 1968.

0051 Juan Dobládez, ''La apocaliptica como origen del género literario evangelio,'' *EstFr* 76 (1975): 131-57.

0052 R. P. Merendino, ''Testi anticotestamentari in Mc 1,2-8,'' *RBib* 35 (1987): 3-25.

1:2-6

0053 M.-É. Boismard, ''Évangile des Ébionites et problème synoptique (Mc. I,2-6 et par.),'' *RB* 73 (1966): 321-52.

0054 Frans Neirynck, ''Une nouvelle theorie synoptique (À propos de Mc. I,2-6 et par.). Notes critiques,'' *ETL* 44 (1968): 141-53.

1:2-4

0055 Heinrich Lausberg, *Minuscula philologica.* III. *Die prooemiale Periode des Evangeliums nach Markus.* Göttingen: Vandenhoeck & Ruprecht, 1979.

1:2-3

0056 Klyne R. Snodgrass, "Streams of Tradition Emerging from Isaiah 40:1-5 and Their Adaptation in the New Testament," *JSNT* 8 (1980): 24-45.

0057 Augustin del Auga-Pérez, "El 'deras' cristológico," *ScriptT* 14 (1982): 203-17.

0058 Gaëtan Minette de Tillesse, "Uma tradiçâo batista?" *RevBB* 7 (1990): 213-48.

1:2

0059 C. T. Ruddick, "Behold, I Send My Messenger," *JBL* 88 (1969): 381-417.

0060 Michael D. Goulder, "On Putting Q to the Test," *NTS* 24 (1977-1978): 218-34.

0061 J. M. Ross, "The 'Harder Reading' in Textual Criticism," *BT* 33 (1982): 138-39.

0062 Christopher M. Tuckett, "On the Relationship between Matthew and Luke," *NTS* 30 (1984): 130-42.

1:3-4

0063 Alfonso Ortega, "Nueva vision de Marcos I,3-4," *Salm* 9 (1962): 599-607.

1:3

0064 Carlo Buzzetti, "Parallels in the Synoptic Gospels: A Case Study," *BT* 34 (1984): 425-431.

1:40-3:6

0065 Mario Galizzi, "Gesù ha scelto l'uomo (Mc 1,40-3,6)," *PV* 21 (1976): 31-37.

1:4-14

0066 Michal F. Czalkowski, "Solidarność Boga z nami (Mk 1,4-14)," *SThV* 12/1 (1974): 201-209.

1:4-11

0067 Donald H. Juel and Patrick R. Keifert, "A Markan Epiphany: Lessons from Mark 1," *WW* 8 (1988): 80-85.

1:4-8

0068 Christian Wolff, "Zur Bedeutung Johannes des Täufers im Markusevangelium," *TLZ* 102 (1977): 857-65.

1:4-5

0069 Rámon Trevijano Etcheverría, "La tradiciáon sobre el Bautista en Mc. 1,4-5 y par.," *Bur* 12 (1971): 9-39.

1:4

0070 Hartwig Thyen, "Baptisma metanoias eis aphesin hamartiōn (Mc 1,4=Lc 3,3)," in Erich Dinkler, ed., *Zeit und Geschichte* (festschrift for Rudolf Bultmann). Tübingen: Mohr, 1964. Pp. 97-125.

0071 Herman Ljungvik, "Randanmärkningar till 1963 års bibelkommités översättningsförslag," *SEÅ* 34 (1969): 147-69.

0072 J. K. Elliott, "Ho baptizōn and Mark i.4," *TZ* 31 (1975): 14-15.

0073 T. Mueller, "An Application of Case Grammar to Two New Testament Passages," *CTQ* 43 (1979): 320-25.

0074 Paul Ellingworth, "Translating Parallel Passages in the Gospels," *BT* 34 (1983): 401-407.

1:5

0075 Ernest C. Colwell, "Method in Locating a Newly-Discovered Manuscript," *StudE* 1 (1959): 757-77.

0076 John S. Kloppenborg, "City and Wasteland: Narrative World and the Beginning of the Sayings Gospel (Q)," *Semeia* 52 (1990): 145-60.

1:6-11

0077 Edmond Jacquemin, "Le baptême du Christ. Mt 3,13-17; Mc 1,6b-11; Lc 3,15s.21s.," *AsSeign* 12 (1969): 48-66.

1:7-8

0078 Oscar Cullmann, "Ὁ ὀπίσω μου ἐρχόμενος," in A. J. B. Higgins, ed., *The Early Church*. London: SCM, 1956. Pp. 177-82.

0079 Paul Hoffmann, "Markus und Q," in *Studien zur Theologie der Logienquelle*. Münster: Aschendorff, 1970. Pp. 19-22.

0080 François Martin, "Le baptême dans l'Esprit: Tradition du Nouveau Testament et vie de l'Église," *NRT* 106 (1984): 23-58.

0081 Balembo Buetubela, "Le message de Jean Baptiste en Mc 1,7-8," *RAfT* 9 (1985): 165-73.

1:7

0082 Francis L. Andersen, "The Diet of John the Baptist (Mc 1,7)," *AbrN* 3 (1961-1962): 60-74.

0083 W. R. Weeks, "Mark 1:7," *ET* 73 (1961-1962): 54.

0084 René Kieffer, "A Christology of Superiority in the Synoptic Gospels," *RSB* 3/2 (1983): 61-75.

1:8

0085 F. J. Botha, "Ἐβάπτισα in Mark i.8," *ET* 64 (1952-1953): 286.

0086 J. E. Yates, "The Form of Mark 1:8b: 'I Baptized You with Water; He Will Baptize You with the Holy Spirit'," *NTS* 4 (1957-1958): 334-38.

0087 Norman K. Bakken, "Uma nova criaçao: o Cristo para o nosso tempo," *EstT* 24/2 (1984): 118-28.

0088 Bas M. F. van Iersel, "He Will Baptize You with the Holy Spirit (Mark 1,8)," in Tjitze Baarda, ed., *Text and Testimony: Essays on New Testament and Apocryphal Literature* (festschrift for A. F. J. Klijn). Kampen: Kok, 1988. Pp. 132-41.

0089 J. D. Charles, " 'The Coming One'/'Stronger One' and His Baptism: Matthew 3:11-12, Mark 1:8, Luke 3:16-17," *Pneuma* 11 (1989): 37-50.

0090 Simon Légasse, "L'autre 'baptême' (Mc 1,8; Mt 3,11; Lc 3,16; Jn 1,26.31-33)," in F. Van Segbroeck, et al., eds., *The Four Gospels 1992* (festschrift for Frans Neirynck). BETL #100. 3 vols. Louvain: Peeters Press, 1992. 1:257-73.

1:9-14

0091 Pietro Zarrella, "Il battesimo di Gesù nei Sinottici (Mc. 1,9-14; Mt. 3,13-17; Lc. 3,21-22," *ScC* 97 (1969): 3-29.

1:9-13

0092 Ernest C. Colwell, "Method in Locating a Newly-Discovered Manuscript," *StudE* 1 (1959): 757-77.

0093 Eugene A. LaVerdiere, "The Baptism of the Lord," *Emmanuel* 94 (1988): 6-13, 21.

1:9-11

0094 T. Nicklin, "The Messiah's Baptism and the Holy Ghost," *CQR* 149 (1950): 127-37.

0095 Herbert Braun, "Entscheidende Motive in den Berichten über die Taufe Jesu von Markus bis Justin," *ZTK* 50 (1953): 39-43.

0096 C. E. B. Cranfield, "The Baptism of Our Lord: A Study of St. Mark 1:9-11," *SJT* 8 (1955): 53-63.

0097 André Feuillet, "Le Baptême de Jésus d'après l'Évangile selon Saint Marc (1,9-11)," *CBQ* 21 (1959): 468-90.

0098 Placide Roulin and Giles Carton, "Le Baptême du Christ," *BVC* 25 (1959): 39-48.

0099 S. Lewis Johnson, "The Baptism of Christ," *BSac* 123 (1966): 220-29.

0100 Dieter Zeller, "Jesu Taufe—ein literarischer Zugang zu Markus 1,9-11," *BK* 23 (1968): 90-94.

0101 Lars Hartman, "Dop, ande och barnaskap. Några traditionshistoriska överväganden till Mk 1:9-11 par," *SEÅ* 37/38 (1972): 88-106.

0102 Giuseppe Segalla, "La predicazione dell'amore nella tradizione presinottica," *RBib* 20 (1972): 481-528.

0103 Anton Vögtle, "Die sogenannte Taufperikope Mk 1,9-11. Zur problematik der Herkunft und des ursprünglichen Sinns," in *Evangelisch-Katholisher Kommentar zum Neuen*

Testament. Vorarbeiten 4. Neukirchen-Vluyn: Neukirchener Verlag, 1972. Pp. 105-39.

0104 Antonio Vargas-Machuca, "La narración del bautismo de Jesus (Mc 1,9-11) y la exégesis reciente. ¿Visión real o 'género didáctico'?" *CuBí* 30 (1973): 131-41.

0105 George Richter, "Zu den Tauferzahlungen Mk 1:9-11 und Joh 1:32-34," *ZNW* 65 (1974): 43-56.

0106 A. Tosato, "Il battesimo di Gesu e alcuni passi trascurati dello Pseudo-Filone," *Bib* 56 (1975): 405-409.

0107 Stephen Gero, "The Spirit as a Dove at the Baptism of Jesus," *NovT* 18 (1976): 17-35.

0108 Paul Garnet, """The Baptism of Jesus and the Son of Man Idea," *JSNT* 9 (1980): 49-65.

0109 Gerhard Barth, *Die Taufe in frühchristlicher Zeit*. Neukirchen-Vluyn: Neukirchener Verlag, 1981.

0110 Eugen Ruckstuhl, "Jesus als Gottessohn im Spiegel des markinischen Taufberichts [Mk 1:9-11]," in Ulrich Luz and Hans Weder, eds., *Die Mitte des Neuen Testaments: Einheit and vielfalt neutestamentlicher theologie* (festschrift for Eduard Schweizer). Göttingen: Vandenhoeck & Ruprecht, 1983. Pp. 193-220.

0111 Gerhard Sellin, "Das Leben des Gottessohnes: Taufe und Verklärung Jesu als Bestandteile eines vormarkinischen 'Evangeliums'," *K* 25/3-4 (1983): 237-53.

0112 Augustin del Auga-Pérez, "El procedimiento derásico que configura el relato del bautismo de Jesús (Mc 1,9-11): Estudio de crítica literaria," in Domingo Muñoz León, ed., *Salvación en la palabra: Targum - Derash - Berith* (festschrift for Alejandro Díez Macho). Madrid: Cristiandad, 1986. Pp. 593-609.

0113 Sigfred Pedersen, "Die Gotteserfahrung bei Jesus," *StTheol* 41 (1987): 127-56.

0114 Ernst L. Schnellbächer, "Sachgemässe Schriftauslegung," *NovT* 30 (1988): 114-31.

0115 James R. Edwards, "The Baptism of Jesus According to the Gospel of Mark [1:9-11]," *JETS* 34 (1991): 43-57.

0116 Donald H. Juel, "The Baptism of Jesus," *WW* Supplement 1 (1992): 119-26.

<u>1:9-10</u>

0117 Helmut Gollwitzer, "Zur Frage der 'Sündlosigkeit Jesu," *EvT* 31 (1971): 496-506.

<u>1:9</u>

0118 Theodor Lorenzmeier, "Wider das Dogma von der Sündlosigkeit Jesu," *EvT* 31 (1971): 452-71.

0119 Jean-Marie van Cangh, "La Galilée dans l'évangile de Marc: un lieu théologique?" *RB* 79 (1972): 59-75.

<u>1:10-11</u>

0120 Jean Delorme, "Le discours de l'intertextualité dans le discours exégétique," *SémBib* 15 (1979): 56-62.

0121 Silvia Schroer, "Der Geist, die Weisheit und die Taube: Feministisch-kritische Exegese eines neutestamentlichen Symbols auf dem Hintergrund seiner altorientalischen und hellenistisch-fruhjüdischen Traditionsgeschichte," *FZPT* 33 (1986): 197-225.

<u>1:10</u>

0122 Herman Ljungvik, "Randanmärkningar till 1963 års bibelkommités översättningsförslag," *SEÅ* 34 (1969): 147-69.

0123 Michael FitzPatrick, "The Structure of St. Mark's Gospel: With a Reconsideration of the Hypothesis of Pre-Markan Collections in Mk 1-10," doctoral dissertation, University of Louvain, Louvain, 1975. 2 vols.

0124 Paul Ellingworth, "Translating Parallel Passages in the Gospels," *BT* 34 (1983): 401-407.

0125 Carlo Buzzetti, ''Parallels in the Synoptic Gospels: A Case Study,'' *BT* 35 (1984): 425-31.

0126 Ernst M. Dörrfuss, ''Wie eine Taue: Uberlegungen zum Verständnis von Mk 1:10,'' *BibN* 57 (1991): 7-13.

0127 David Ulansey, ''The Heavenly Veil Torn: Mark's Cosmic Inclusio [linking 1:10 and 15:38]'' *JBL* 110 (1991):123-25.

1:11

0128 W. Dekker, ''De 'geliefde Zoon' in de synoptische evangeliën,'' *NTT* 16 (1961-1962): 94-106.

0129 George D. Kilpatrick, ''The Order of Some Noun and Adjective Phrases in the New Testament,'' *NovT* 5 (1962): 111-14.

0130 P. G. Bretscher, ''Exodus 4:22-23 and the Voice from Heaven,'' *JBL* 87 (1968): 301-11.

0131 Antonio Gaboury, ''Deux fils uniques: Isaac et Jésus. Connexions vétérotestamentaires de Mc 1,11 (et parallèlles),'' *StudE*: 4 (1968): 198-204.

0132 I. Howard Marshall, ''Son of God or Servant of Yahweh? A Reconsideration of Mark 1:11,'' *NTS* 15 (1968-1969): 326-36.

0133 C. H. Dodd, ''New Testament Translation Problems II,'' *BT* 28 (1977): 101-16.

0134 Alfredo Scattolon, ''L'ἀγαπητός sinottico nella luce della tradizione giudaica,'' *RBib* 26 (1978): 3-32.

0135 Gerhard Schneider, ''Christologische Aussagen des 'Credo' im Lichte des Neuen Testaments,'' *TTZ* 89 (1980): 282-92.

0136 Norman K. Bakken, ''Uma nova criaçao: o Cristo para o nosso tempo,'' *EstT* 24/2 (1984): 118-28.

1:12-15

0137 Françoise Smyth-Florentin, ''Jésus, le Fils du Père, vainqueur de Satan. Mt 4,1-11; Mc 1,12-15; Lc 4,1-13,'' *AsSeign* 14 (1973): 56-75.

1:12-13

0138 A. Dondorp, *De verzoekingen van Jezus Christus in de woestijn*. Kampen: Kok, 1951.

0139 Peter Doble, "The Temptations," *ET* 72 (1960-1961): 91-93.

0140 Raymond E. Brown, "Incidents That Are Units in the Synoptic Gospels but Dispersed in St. John," *CBQ* 23 (1961): 143-60.

0141 André Feuillet, "L'épisode de la Tentation d'après l'Évangile selon Saint Marc (I,12-13)," *EB* 19 (1960): 49-73. See also *TD* 12 (1964): 79-82.

0142 Jacques Dupont, "L'origine du récit des tentations de Jésus au désert," *RB* 73 (1966): 30-76.

0143 Birger Gerhardsson, *The Testing of God's Son (Matt 4:1-11 & Par.): An Analysis of an Early Christian Midrash*. Lund: Gleerup, 1966.

0144 J. I. Gonzalez Faus, "Las tentaciones de Jesus y la tentacion cristiana," *EE* 47 (1972): 155-88.

0145 Antonio Vargas-Machuca, "La tentacion de Jesus segun Mc. 1,12-13, ¿Hecho real o relato de tipo haggadico?" *EE* 48 (1973): 163-90.

0146 C. Bombo, "As Tentaçôes de Jesus nos Sinóticos," *RCB* 10 (1973): 83-102.

0147 Henryk Muszyński, "Kuszenie Chrystusa w tradycji synoptycznej," *CollT* 46/3 (1976): 17-41.

0148 Frans Neirynck, "Réponse à P. Rolland," *ETL* 60/4 (1984): 363-66.

0149 Philippe Rolland, "L'arrière-lond sémitique des évangiles synoptiques," *ETL* 60 (1984): 358-62.

0150 Michel Gourgues, *Le défi de la fidélité: L'expérience de Jésus*. Paris: Cerf, 1985.

0151 Ben Hemelsoet, ''De verzoeking van Jezus in de woestijn,'' *ACEBT* 9 (1988): 97-116.

0152 Donald M. McKinnon, ''The Evangelical Imagination,'' in James P. Mackey, ed., *Religious Imagination*. Edinburgh: Edinburgh University Press, 1986. Pp. 175-85.

0153 Bruce D. Chilton, *Profiles of a Rabbi: Synoptic Opportunities in Reading about Jesus*. Atlanta: Scholars Press, 1989.

0154 David Flusser, ''Die Versuchung Jesu und ihr jüdischer Hintergrund,'' *Jud* 45 (1989): 110-28.

0155 Curtis C. Mitchell, ''The Practice of Fasting in the New Testament,'' *BSac* 147 (1990): 455-69.

1:12

0156 Ulrich W. Mauser, *Christ in the Wilderness: The Wilderness Theme in the Second Gospel and Its Basis in the Biblical Tradition*. Studies in Biblical Theology 39. Naperville IL: Allenson, 1963.

0157 J. B. Livio, ''Face a face dans le desert (Mc 1,12s),'' *BTS* 127 (1971): 2-5.

0158 Otto Betz, ''Early Christian Cult in the Light of Qumran,'' *RSB* 2 (1982): 73-85.

0159 Wilhelm Wilkens, ''Die Versuchung Jesu Hach Matthaus,'' *NTS* 28/4 (1982): 479-89.

0160 René Kieffer, ''A Christology of Superiority in the Synoptic Gospels,'' *RSB* 3/2 (1983): 61-75.

0161 Klaus-Peter Koppen, ''The Interpretation of Jesus' Temptations (Mt. 4,1-11; Mk. 1,12f.; Lk. 4,1-3) by the Early Church Fathers,'' *PatByzR* 8/1 (1989): 41-43.

1:13

0162 W. A. Schulze, ''Der Heilige und die wilden Tiere. Zur Exegese von Mk 1,13b,'' *ZNW* 46 (1955): 280-83.

0163 Hans P. Rüger, "Die lexikalischen Aramaismen im Markusevangelium," in Hubert Cancik, ed., *Markus-Philologie*. Tübingen: Mohr, 1984. Pp. 73-84.

0164 Erich Grässer, "Kai en meta thon therion (Mk 1,13b): Ansätze einer theologischen Tierschutzethik," in Wolfgang Schrage, ed., *Studien zum Text und zur Ethik des Neuen Testaments* (festschrift for Heinrich Greeven). Berlin: de Gruyter, 1986. Pp. 144-57.

1:14-8:30

0165 Eugene A. LaVerdiere, "Jesus the Christ," *Emmanuel* 94 (1988): 74-81.

1:14-8:26

0166 Geert Van Oyen, *De summaria in Marcus en de compositie van Mc 1,14-8,26*. Louvain: Peeters Press, 1987.

1:14-3:6

0167 Patrick Simpson, "Reconciliation in the Making: A Reading of Mark 1:14-3:6," *AfER* 17 (1975): 194-203.

0168 Eugene A. LaVerdiere, "Jesus and the Call of the First Disciples," *Emmanuel* 94 (1988): 154-59, 173.

0169 Scaria Kuthirakkattel, *The Beginning of Jesus' Ministry according to Mark's Gospel*. Analecta Biblica #123. Rome: Biblical Institute Press, 1990.

1:14-45

0170 Eugene A. LaVerdiere, "Jesus and the Call of the First Disciples: A New Teaching with Authority," *Emmanuel* 94 (1988): 190-97.

1:14-20

0171 Herman Ljungvik, "Randanmärkningar till 1963 års bibelkommités översättningsförslag," *SEÅ* 34 (1969): 147-69.

0172 Jean Brière, "Jésus agit par ses disciples. Mc 1,14-20," *AsSeign* 34 (1973): 32-46.

0173 John H. Reumann, "Mark 1:14-20," *Int* 32 (1978): 405-10.

0174 Vernon K. Robbins, "Mark 1:14-20: An Interpretation at the Intersection of Jewish and Graeco-Roman Traditions," *NTS* 28 (1982): 220-36.

1:14-15

0175 James L. Mays, "Jesus Came Preaching: A Study and Sermon on Mark 1:14-15," *Int* 26 (1972): 30-41.

0176 Karl-Georg Reploh, " 'Evangelium' bei Markus. Das Evangelium des Markus als Anruf an die Gemeinde zu Umkehr und Glaube (1,14-15)," *BK* 27 (1972): 110-14.

0177 P.-É. Langevin, "Les artisans du Royaume: Perspectives des évangiles synoptiques," *LTP* 29 (1973): 143-64.

0178 J. J. A. Kahmann, "Marc 1,14-15 en hun plaats in het geheel van het Marcusevangelie," *Bij* 38 (1977): 84-98.

0179 John E. Alsup, "Mark 1:14-15," *Int* 33 (1979): 394-98.

0180 Franz Mussner, "Jesu Ansage der Nähe der eschatologischen Gottesherrschaft nach Markus 1,14.15: Ein Beitrag der modernen Sprachwissenschaft zur Exegese," in J. Auer, et al., eds., *Gottesherrschaft - Weltherrschaft* (festschrift for Rudolf Graber). Regensburg: Pustet, 1980. Pp. 33-49.

0181 Klemens Stock, "La venuta del Regno," *ParSpirV* 8 (1983): 103-18.

0182 Heinrich Baarlink, "Vervulling en voleinding volgens de synoptische evangeliën," in Heinrich Baarlink and W. S. Duvekot, eds., *Vervulling en voleinding. De toekomstverwochting in hel Nieuwe Testament*. Kampen: Kok, 1984. Pp. 95-220.

0183 Augustine Stock, "Hinge Transitions in Mark's Gospel," *BTB* 15 (1985): 27-31.

0184 Heinrich Baarlink, *Die Eschatologie der synoptischen Evangelien*. Stuttgart: Kohlhammer, 1986.

0185 Rinaldo Fabris, "San Pietro apostolo nella prima chiesa," *SM* 35 (1986): 41-70.

0186 Andreas Lindemann, "Erwägungen zum Problem einer 'Theologie der synoptischen Evangelien'," *ZNW* 77/1-2 (1986): 1-33.

0187 Donald H. Juel and Patrick R. Keifert, "A Markan Epiphany: Lessons from Mark 1," *WW* 8 (1988): 80-85.

0188 Jean Delorme, "Text and Context: 'The Gospel' according to Mark 1:14-15,"in Theodore W. Jennings and Hendrikus Boers, eds., *Text and Logos: The Humanistic Interpretation of the New Testament.* Atlanta: Scholars Press, 1990. Pp. 273-87.

0189 Gustavo Gutiérrez, "Mark 1:14-15," *RevExp* 88 (1991): 427-31.

<u>1:14</u>

0190 Franz Mussner, "Die Bedeutung von Mk 1,14f. fur die Reichsgottesverkündigung," *TTZ* 66 (1957): 257-75.

0191 Franz Mussner, "Gottesherrschaft und Sendung Jesu nach Mk 1,14f.: Zugleich ein Beitrag über die inner Struktur des Markusevangeliums," in Franz Mussner, ed., *Praesentia Salutis: Gesammelte Studien zu Fragen und Themen des Neuen Testaments.* Düsseldorf: Patmos-Verlag, 1967. Pp. 81-98.

0192 Jean-Marie van Cangh, "La Galilée dans l'évangile de Marc: un lieu théologique?" *RB* 79 (1972): 59-75.

0193 Matthew Vellanickal, "Faith and Conversion," *BB* 8 (1982): 29-41.

0194 Hans Weder, "Evangelium Jesu Christi (Mk 1,1) und 'Evangelium Gottes' (Mk 1,14)," in Ulrich Luz and Hans Weder, eds., *Die Mitte des Neuen Testaments: Einheit and vielfalt neutestamentlicher theologie* (festschrift for Eduard Schweizer). Göttingen: Vandenhoeck & Ruprecht, 1983. Pp. 399-411.

<u>1:15</u>

0195 Matthew Black, "The Kingdom of God Has Come," *ET* 63 (1951-1952): 289-90.

0196 Herbert Braun, "'Umkehr' in spatjudisch-häretischer und in frühchristlicher Sicht," *ZTK* 50 (1953): 243-58.

0197 Robert F. Berkey, "ΕΓΓΙΖΕΙΝ, ΦΘΑΝΕΙΝ, and Realized Eschatology," *JBL* 82 (1963): 177-87.

0198 James C. G. Greig, "The Problem of the Messianic Interpretation of Jesus' Ministry in the Primitive Church," *StudE* 6 (1973): 197-220.

0199 Lars Hartman, "Baptism 'Into the Name of Jesus' and Early Christology: Some Tentative Considerations," *StTheol* 28 (1974): 21-48.

0200 Rainer Stuhlmann, *Das eschatologische Maß im Neuen Testament*. Göttingen: Vandenhoeck & Ruprecht, 1983.

0201 Norman K. Bakken, "Uma nova criaçao: o Cristo para o nosso tempo," *EstT* 24/2 (1984): 118-28.

0202 John Drury, "Mark 1:1-15: An Interpretation," in A. E. Harvey, ed., *Alternative Approaches to New Testament Study* . London: Latimer, 1985. Pp. 25-36.

0203 John M. McDermott, "Gegenwärtiges und kommendes Reich Gottes," *IKaZ* 15/2 (1986): 142-44.

0204 George R. Beasley-Murray, "Jesus and the Kingdom of God," *BQ* 32 (1987): 141-46.

0205 Joel Marcus, " 'The Time Has Been Fulfilled!' (Mark 1.15)," in Joel Marcus and Marion L. Soards, eds., *Apocalyptic and the New Testament* (festschrift for J. Louis Martyn). Sheffield: JSOT Press, 1989. Pp. 49-68.

0206 Paul S. Pudussery, "'Repent and Believe in the Gospel' (Mk 1:15)," *BB* 16 (1990): 95-113.

1:16-2:17

0207 Juan I. Alfaro, "Exegesis Pastoral, Mc 1:16-2:17: Un desafío para hoy," *RevB* 50/2-3 (1988): 171-82.

1:16-39

0208 Michael D. Goulder, "On Putting Q to the Test," *NTS* 24 (1977-1978): 218-34.

0209 Christopher M. Tuckett, "On the Relationship between Matthew and Luke," *NTS* 30 (1984): 130-42.

1:16-20

0210 Rudolf Schnackenburg, "Zur formgeschichtlichen Methode in der Evangelienforschung," *ZKT* 85 (1963): 16-32.

0211 Rudolf Pesch, "Berufung und Sendung, Nachfolge und Mission. Eine Studie zu Mk 1,16-20," *ZKT* 91 (1969): 1-31.

0212 Albert L. Descamps, "Aux origines du ministère: La pensée de Jesus," *RTL* 2 (1971): 3-45; 3 (1972): 121-59.

0213 James Donaldson, " 'Called to Follow': A Twofold Experience of Discipleship in Mark," *BTB* 5 (1975): 67-77.

0214 Luigi Di Pinto, "Seguitemi, vi farò diventare pescatori di uomini (Mc 1,16-20)," *ParSpirV* 2 (1980): 83-104.

0215 Francis J. Moloney, "The Vocation of the Disciples in the Gospel of Mark," *Sale* 43 (1981): 487-516.

0216 Michel Cornillon, "De l'appel du Christ à l'appel de l'Église: trois récits du Nouveau Testament," *BSS* 10 (1984): 107-50.

0217 Samuel O. Abogunrin, "The Three Variant Accounts of Peter's Call: A Critical and Theological Examination of the Texts," *NTS* 31 (1985): 587-602.

0218 Claude Coulot, "Les figures du maître et de ses disciples dans les premières communautés chrétiennes," *RevSR* 59/1 (1985): 1-11.

0219 Raffaele Giuliano, "Pescatori di uomini, per raccogliere i dispersi," *RSRel* 1 (1987): 13-32.

1:16-18

0220 James R. Butts, "The Voyage of Discipleship: Narrative, Chreia, and Call Story," in Craig A. Evans and William F. Stinespring, eds., *Early Jewish and Christian Exegesis* (festschrift for William H. Brownlee). Atlanta: Scholars Press, 1987. Pp. 199-219.

1:16

0221 Sebastián Bartina, "La red esparavel del Evangclio (Mt 4.18; Mc 1,16)," *EB* 19 (1960): 215-27.

0222 J. Duncan M. Derrett, "ἦσαν γάρ ἁλιεῖς (Mk. 1,16). Jesus' Fishermen and the Parable of the Net," *NovT* 22 (1980): 108-37.

0223 Paul Ellingworth, "Translating Parallel Passages in the Gospels," *BT* 34 (1983): 401-407.

0224 Carlo Buzzetti, "Parallels in the Synoptic Gospels: A Case Study," *BT* 35 (1984): 425-31.

0225 Lars Lode, "The Presentation of New Information," *BT* 35 (1984): 101-108.

1:17-18

0226 Jeremiah Crosby, "The Call to Discipleship in Mark 1:17-18," *TBT* 27 (1966): 1919-22.

0227 Helmut Gollwitzer, "Zur Frage der 'Sündlosigkeit Jesu'," *EvT* 31 (1971): 496-506.

1:17

0228 Jindrich Mánek, "Fishers of Men," *NovT* 2 (1957-1958): 138-41.

0229 J. B. Livio, "Pécheurs d'hommes," *BTS* 192 (1977): 22.

0230 E. C. B. MacLaurin, "The Divine Fishermen," *SMR* 94 (1978): 26-28.

1:18

0231 Otto Betz, "Donnersöhne, Menschenfischer und der Davidische Messias," *RevQ* 3 (1961): 41-70.

1:20

0232 Günther Schwarz, ''Καὶ εὐθὺς ἐκάλεσεν αὐτούς (Markus 1:20a),'' *BibN* 48 (1989): 19-20.

1:21-3:19

0233 David L. Dungan, ''Synopses of the Future,'' *Bib* 66/4 (1985): 457-92.

1:21-3:6

0234 C. C. Marcheselli, ''La ricerca di Dio nei segni dei tempi: la struttura tematico-letteraria di Mc 1,21-3,6 parr,'' in François Bovon, et al., eds., *Analyse structurale et exégèse biblique: Essais d'interprétation*. Neuchâtel: Delachaux et Niestlé, 1972. Pp. 289-313.

0235 J. S. Allsop, ''The Development of the Gospel Miracle Tradition: With Special Reference to Mark 1.21-3.6; 4.35-5.43; 6.30-8.26,'' doctoral dissertation, University of Nottingham, Nottingham UK, 1978.

0236 Miguel de Burgos Nuñez, ''La acción liberadora de Jesús en la jornada de Cafarnaún,'' *Communio* 19 (1986): 323-41.

1:21-2:12

0237 David E. Garland, '' 'I Am the Lord Your Healer': Mark 1:21-2:12,'' *RevExp* 85/2 (1988): 327-43.

1:21-45

0238 T. A. Burkill, ''Evidence of the Fact in Word and Deed,'' in *Mysterious Revelation: An Examination of the Philosophy of St. Mark's Gospel*. Ithaca NY: Cornell University Press, 1963. Pp. 28-40.

0239 Dany Dideberg and Pierre Mourlon Beernaert, '' 'Jésus vint en Galilée.' Essai sur la structure de Marc 1,21-45,'' *NRT* 98 (1976): 306-23.

1:21-39

0240 Perry V. Kea, ''Perceiving the Mystery: Encountering the Reticence of Mark's Gospel,'' *EGLMBS* 4 (1984): 181-94.

1:21-34

0241 Rudolf Pesch, "Ein Tag vollmachtigen Wirkens Jesu in Kapharnaum (Mk 1,21-34, 35-39)," *BibL* 9 (1968): 114-28, 177-95, 261-77.

1:21-28

0242 Rudolf Pesch, " 'Eine neue Lehre aus Macht.' Eine Studie zu Mk 1,21-28," in Johannes Baptist Bauer, ed., *Evangelienforschung. Ausgewählte AufsätzeDeutscher Exegeten.* Graz/Köln: Verlag Styria, 1968. Pp. 241-76.

0243 Jean Brière, "Le cri et le secret. Signification d'un exorcisme. Mc 1,21-28," *AsSeign* 35 (1973): 34-46.

0244 Aloysius M. Ambrozic, "Obsedenec v Kafarnaumu," *BogV* 36 (1976): 53-61.

0245 Miguel de Burgos Nuñez, "Le enseñanza liberadora de Jesús desde la Sinagoga. Ensayo de semiótica narrativa en Marcos 1,21-28," *Communio* 9 (1976): 201-19.

0246 A. Viard, "Quatrième Dimanche (Mc 1,21-28)," *EV* 86 (1976): 8-10.

0247 Evelin Albrecht, *Zeugnis durch Wort und Verhalten untersucht an ausgewahlten Texten des Neuen Testaments.* Basel: Reinhardt, 1977.

0248 Helge K. Nielsen, "Ein Beitrag zur Beurteilung der Tradition über die Heilungstätigkeit," *SNTU-A* 4 (1979): 5-26.

0249 Georges Casalis, "Jesús, el exorcista," *BibFe* 6 (1980): 28-40.

0250 Pierre Guillemette, "La Forme des Recits d'Exorcisme de Bultmann: Un Dogme a Reconsiderer," *EgT* 11/2 (1980): 177-93.

0251 Paul J. Achtemeier, "The Ministry of Jesus in the Synoptic Gospels," *Int* 35 (1981): 157-69.

0252 Walter Kern and L. Kuld, ''Somatische Handlungen Jesu: Überlegungen zu einer erfahrungsbezogenen Didaktik der Wundergeschichten,'' *KatB* 109 (1984): 43-53.

0253 Alfred Suhl, ''Überlegungen zur Hermeneutik an Hand von Mk 1:21-28,'' *K* 26/1-2 (1984): 28-38.

0254 D. Boythe, ''Battling the Demons,'' *CQ* 43/3 (1985): 17-20.

0255 Bruce D. Chilton, ''Exorcism and History: Mark 1:21-28,'' in David Wenham and Craig Blomberg, eds., *Gospel Perspectives*: 6. *The Miracles of Jesus*. Sheffield: JSOT Press, 1986. 6:253-71.

0256 Enzo Bianchi, ''Esei da costui!'' *ParSpirV* 19 (1989): 109-38.

0257 Heinz Giesen, ''Dämonenaustreibungen - Erweis der Nähe der Herrschaft Gottes: Zu Mk 1.21-28,'' *TGeg* 32 (1989): 24-37.

0258 Ulrich Busse, ''Metaphorik in neutestamentlichen Wundergeschichten? Mk 1,21-28; Joh 9,1-41,'' in Karl Kertelge, ed., *Metaphorik und Mythos im Neuen Testament*. Freiburg: Herder, 1990. Pp. 110-34.

<u>1:21</u>

0259 Robert H. Stein, ''The 'Redaktionsgeschichtlich' Investigation of a Markan Seam (Mc 1:21f.),'' *ZNW* 61 (1970): 70-94.

0260 Hans P. Rüger, ''Die lexikalischen Aramaismen im Markusevangelium,'' in Hubert Cancik, ed., *Markus-Philologie*. Tübingen: Mohr, 1984. Pp. 73-84.

<u>1:22-27</u>

0261 L. I. J. Stadelmann, ''A Autoridade como una Caracteristica do Ministerio de Jesus. Estudo Exegetico de Mc 1,22.27,'' *PerT* 5 (1973): 173-84.

<u>1:22</u>

0262 H. J. Flowers, ''Ὡς ἐξουσίαν ἔχων,'' *ET* 66 (1954-1955): 254.

0263 D. F. Hudson, "Ὡς ἐξουσίαν ἔχων," *ET* 67 (1955-1956): 17.

0264 A. W. Argyle, "The Meaning of ἐξουσία in Mark 1:22, 27," *ET* 80 (1969-1970): 343.

0265 William R. Domeris, "The Office of the Holy One," *JTSA* 54 (1986): 35-38.

1:23-28

0266 Léopold Sabourin, "The Miracles of Jesus (II). Jesus and the Evil Powers," *BTB* 4 (1974): 115-75.

0267 J. González-Faus, "Jesus y los demonios: Intróducción cristológica a la lucha por la justicia," *EE* 52 (1977): 487-519.

0268 Peter Pimentel, "The 'Unclean Spirits' of St. Mark's Gospel," *ET* 99 (1987-1988): 173-75.

1:24-31

0269 Roy M. Liuzza, "The Yale Fragments of the West Saxon Gospels," in Peter Clemoes, et al., eds., *Anglo-Saxon England*. Cambridge: Cambridge University Press, 1988. 7:67-82.

1:24-25

0270 Rámon Trevijano Etcheverría, "El trasfondo apocalípticode Mc. 1,24.25; 5,7.8 y par.," *Bur* 11 (1970): 117-33.

1:24

0271 Franz Mussner, "Ein Wortspiel in Mk 1:24?" *BZ* 4/2 (1960): 285-86.

0272 Eduard Schweizer, " 'Er wird Nazoräer heissen' (zu Mc 1:24, Mt 2:23)," in Walther Eltesteu, ed., *Judentum, Urchristentum, Kirche* (festschrift for Joachim Jeremias). Berlin: Töplemann, 1960. Pp. 90-93.

0273 Ernest Best, "Mark's Preservation of the Tradition," in M. Sabbe, ed., *L'évangile selon Marc: Tradition et rédaction*. BETL #34. Gembloux/Louvain: Duculot/Louvain University, 1974. Pp. 21-34.

0274 Otto Bächli, " 'Was habe ich mit dir zu schaffen?' Eine formelhafte Frage im Alten Testament und Neuen Testament," *TZ* 33 (1977): 69-80.

0275 Pierre Guillemette, "Mc 1,24 est-il une formule de defense magique?" *ScE* 30 (1978): 81-96.

0276 A. Marcello Buscemi, "La prolessi nel Nuovo Testamento," *SBFLA* 35 (1985): 37-68.

0277 William R. Domeris, "The 'Holy One of God' as a Title for Jesus," *Neo* 19 (1985): 9-17.

0278 Francis Watson, "The Social Function of Mark's Secrecy Theme," *JSNT* 24 (1985): 49-69.

0279 Klaus Berger, *Einführung in die Formgeschichte*. Tübingen: Francke, 1987.

1:25

0280 B. Kollmann, "Jesu Schweigegebote an die Dämonen," *ZNW* 82 (1991): 267-73.

1:27

0281 A. W. Argyle, "The Meaning of ἐξουσία in Mark 1:22, 27," *ET* 80 (1968-1969): 343.

0282 Aloysius M. Ambrozic, "New Teaching with Power (Mk 1:27)," in Joseph Plevnik, ed., *Word and Spirit: Essays in Honor of David Michael Stanley on his 60th Birthday*. Willowdale, Ont.: Regis College, 1975. Pp. 113-49.

0283 William R. Domeris, "The Office of the Holy One," *JTSA* 54 (1986): 35-38.

0284 Roland Minnerath, *Jésus et le pouvoir*. Le point theologique #46. Paris: Beauchesne, 1987.

1:28-41

0285 J. Harold Greenlee, *Nine Uncial Palimpsests of the Greek New Testament*. Salt Lake City: University of Utah, 1968.

1:29-39

0286 Gilles Gaide, "De l'admiration à la foi. Mc 1,29-39," *AsSeign* 36 (1974): 39-48.

1:29-34

0287 Thomas R. W. Longstaff, *Evidence of Conflation in Mark? A Study in the Synoptic Problem.* Society of Biblical Literature Dissertation Series 28. Missoula MT: Scholars Press, 1977.

0288 Angelo Lancellotti, "La Casa Pietro a Cafarnao nel Vangeli Sinottici. Redazione e Tradizione," *Ant* 58/1 (1983): 48-69.

1:29-31

0289 Alfred Suhl, *Die Wunder Jesu: Ereignis und Überlieferung.* Gütersloh: Mohn, 1968.

0290 M. L. Rigato, "Tradizione e redazione in Mc. 1,29-31 (e paralleli). La guarigione della suocera di Simon Pietro," *RBib* 17 (1969): 139-74.

0291 Rainer Riesner, "Wie sicher ist die Zwei-Quellen-Theorie?" *TBe* 8 (1977): 49-73.

0292 Albert Fuchs, "Entwicklungsgeschichtliche Studie zu Mk 1,29-31 par Mt 8,14-15 par Lk 4.38-39: Macht über Fieber und Dämonen," *SNTU-A* 6-7 (1981-1982): 21-76.

0293 Josef Blank, "Frauen in den Jesusüberlieferungen," in Gerhard Dautzenberg, et al., eds., *Die Frau im Urchristentum.* Freiburg: Herder, 1983. Pp. 9-91.

0294 Carlo Buzzetti, "Parallels in the Synoptic Gospels: A Case Study," *BT* 35 (1984): 425-31.

1:30-4:35

0295 Ched Myers, "Binding the Strong Man: Jesus's First Campaign of Nonviolent Direct Action, Mark 1:30-4:35," *Soj* 16 (1987): 28-32.

1:30-32

0296 Helmut L. Egelkraut, "The Triple Tradition and Its Variants in the Travel Narrative," in *Jesus' Mission to*

Jerusalem: A Redaction Critical Study of the Travel Narrative in the Gospel of Luke. Bern: Lang, 1976. Pp. 62-133.

1:30

0297 George Howard, "Stylistic Inversion and the Synoptic Tradition," *JBL* 97 (1978): 375-89.

1:32-34

0298 T. W. Kowalski, "Les sources pré-synoptiques de Marc 1,32-34 et parallèles. Phénomenes d 'amalgame et independance mutuelle immédiate des évangélistes synoptiques," *RechSR* 60 (1972): 541-73.

0299 Gert Lüderitz, "Rhetorik, Poetik, Kompositionstechnik im Markusevangelium," in Hubert Cancik, ed., *Markus-Philologie*. Tübingen: Mohr, 1984. Pp. 165-203.

0300 Jozef Verheyden, "Mark 1:32-34 and 6:53-56: Tradition or Redaction?" *ETL* 64/4 (1988): 415-28.

1:34

0301 Klemens Stock, "La conoscenza religiosa nel Nuovo Testamento (i demoni, Mc 1,34)," *ParSpirV* 18 (1988): 93-112.

1:35-42

0302 Roy M. Liuzza, "The Yale Fragments of the West Saxon Gospels," in Peter Clemoes, et al., eds., *Anglo-Saxon England*. Cambridge: Cambridge University Press, 1988. 7:67-82.

1:35-39

0303 R. H. Lightfoot, "A Consideration of Three Passages in St. Mark's Gospel," in Werner Schmauch, ed., *In Memoriam Ernst Lohmeyer*. Stuttgart: Evangelisches Verlagswerk, 1951. Pp. 110-15.

0304 Rudolf Pesch, "Ein Tag vollmachtigen Wirkens Jesu in Kapharnaum (Mk 1,21-34, 35-39)," *BibL* 9 (1968): 114-28, 177-95, 261-77.

0305 Manfred Wichelhaus, "Am ersten Tage der Woche. Mk. i,35-39 und die didaktischen Absichten des Markus-Evangelisten," *NovT* 11 (1969): 45-66.

0306 Robert Schlarb, "Die Suche nach dem Messias: ζητέω als Terminus technicus der markinischen Messianologie," *ZNW* 81 (1990): 155-70.

1:35

0307 Walter Kirchschlager, "Jesu Gebetsverhalten als Paradigma zu Mk 1,35," *K* 20 (1978): 303-10.

0308 Gregory Murray, "Did Luke Use Mark?" *DR* 104 (1986): 268-71.

0309 Benny R. Crockett, "The Function of Mathetological Prayer in Mark," *IBS* 10 (1988): 123-39.

1:38

0310 Günther Schwarz, " 'Auch den anderen Städten'? (Lukas iv.43a)," *NTS* 23 (1976-1977): 344.

0311 D. O. Wretlind, "Jesus' Philosophy of Ministry: A Study of a Figure of Speech in Mark 1:38," *JETS* 20 (1977): 321-23.

1:39-45

0312 Rainer Dillmann, "Die Bedeutung neuerer exegetischer Methoden für eine biblisch orientierte Pastoral: Aufgezeigt an Mk 1,39-45 - der Heilung eines Aussatzigen," *TGl* 80 (1990): 116-30.

0313 Edwin K. Broadhead, "Christology as Polemic and Apologetic: The Priestly Portrait of Jesus in the Gospel of Mark," *JSNT* 47 (1992): 21-34.

1:39

0314 Jean-Marie van Cangh, "La Galilée dans l'évangile de Marc: un lieu théologique?" *RB* 79 (1972): 59-75.

0315 J. K. Elliott, "The Relevance of Textual Criticism to the Synoptic Problem," in David L. Dungan, ed., *The Interrelations of the Gospels*. Louvain: Peeters Press, 1990. Pp. 348-59.

1:40-2:15

0316 William R. Domeris, ''Historical Materialist Exegesis,''in Patrick J. Hartin and J. H. Petzer, eds., *Text and Interpretation: New Approaches in the Criticism of the New Testament*. Leiden: Brill, 1991. Pp. 299-311.

1:40-45

0317 Charles C. Ryrie, ''The Cleansing of the Leper,'' *BSac* 113 (1956): 262-67.

0318 Charles Masson, ''La guérison du lepreux,'' in Charles Masson, ed., *Vers les sources d'eau vive: Études d'exégèse et de théologie du Nouveau Testament*. Lausanne: Payot, 1961. Pp. 11-19.

0319 André Paul, ''La guérison d'un lépreux: Approche d'un récit de Marc,'' *NRT* 92 (1970): 592-604.

0320 Gilles Gaide, ''Guérison d'un lépreux: Mc 1,40-45,'' *AsSeign* 4/37 (1971): 53-61.

0321 M. H. Marco, ''La curación de un leproso según San Marcos (Mc 1,40-45),'' *EB* 31 (1972): 399-433.

0322 C. H. Cave, ''The Leper: Mark 1:40-45,'' *NTS* 25 (1978-1979): 245-50.

0323 André Fossion, ''From the Bible Text to the Homily: Cure of a Leper,'' *LV* 35 (1980): 279-90.

0324 M.-É. Boismard, ''La guérison du lépreux (Mc 1,40-45 et par.),'' *Salm* 28 (1981): 283-91.

0325 Vittorio Fusco, ''Il segreto messianico nell'episodio del lebbroso (Mc. 1,40-45),'' *RBib* 29 (1981): 273-313.

0326 Lars Lode, ''The Presentation of New Information,'' *BT* 35 (1984): 101-108.

0327 Frans Neirynck, ''Papyrus Egerton 2 and the Healing of the Leper,'' *ETL* 61/1 (1985): 153-60.

0328 John J. Pilch, ''Understanding Biblical Healing: Selecting the Appropriate Model,'' *BTB* 18 (1988): 60-66.

0329 Michal Wojciechowski, "The Touching of the Leper (Mark 1:40-45) as a Historical and Symbolic Act of Jesus," *BZ* 33/1 (1989): 114-19.

0330 C.-B. Amphoux, "Étude synoptique: La purification du lépreux (Mt 8,2-4 / Mc 1,40-45 / Lc 5,12-16 / Egerton 2)," *BLOS* 4 (1990): 3-12.

0331 Jon B. Daniels, "The Egerton Gospel: Its Place in Early Christianity," doctoral dissertation, Claremont Graduate School, Claremont CA, 1990.

0332 Dominique Hermant, "La purification du lépreux (Mt 8,1-4; Mc 1,40-45; Lc 5,12-16)," *BLOS* 4 (1990): 13-22.

0333 Philippe Rolland, "Préliminaires à la premiere multiplication des pains," *BLOS* 3 (1990): 12-18.

0334 Philippe Rolland, "Propos intempestifs sur la guérison du lépreux," *BLOS* 4 (1990): 23-27.

0335 Carl Kazmierski, "Evangelist and Leper: A Socio-Cultural Study of Mark 1:40-45," *NTS* 38 (1992): 37-50.

1:40-44

0336 Samuel T. Lachs, "Hebrew Element in the Gospels and Acts," *JQR* 71 (1979-1980): 31-43.

0337 Gregory Murray, "Five Gospel Miracles," *DR* 108 (1990): 79-90.

1:41

0338 Kenneth W. Clark, "The Theological Relevance of Textual Variation in Current Criticism of the Greek New Testament," *JBL* 85 (1966): 1-16.

1:45

0339 Frederick W. Danker, "Mark 1:45 and the Secrecy Motif," *CTM* 37 (1966): 492-99.

0340 J. K. Elliott, "The Conclusion of the Pericope of the Healing the Leper and Mark i.45," *JTS* 22 (1971): 153-57.

0341 J. K. Elliott, "Is ὁ ἐξελθὼν a Title for Jesus in Mark 1:45?" *JTS* 27 (1976): 402-405.

0342 James Swetnam, "Some Remarks on the Meaning of ὁ δὲ ἐξελθὼν in Mark 1:45," *Bib* 68/2 (1987): 245-49.

0343 George D. Kilpatrick, "Mark i.45," in *The Principles and Practice on New Testament Textual Criticism*. BETL #96. Louvain: Peeters Press, 1990. Pp. 282-85.

0344 George D. Kilpatrick, "Mark i.45 and the Meaning of λόγος," in *The Principles and Practice on New Testament Textual Criticism*. BETL #96. Louvain: Peeters Press, 1990. Pp. 280-81.

<u>2:1-3:6</u>

0345 Walter E. Keller, "The Authority of Jesus as Reflected in Mk 2,1-3,6: A Contribution to the History of Interpretation," doctoral dissertation, Harvard University, Cambridge MA, 1967.

0346 Cesare Bissoli, "Le cinque controversie galilaiche," *PV* 15/3 (1970): 217-32.

0347 Joanna Dewey, "The Literary Structure of the Controversy Stories in Mark 2:1-3:6," *JBL* 92/3 (1973): 394-401.

0348 Pierre Mourlon Beernaert, "Jésus controversé: Structure et théologie de Marc 2,1-3,6," *NRT* 95 (1973): 129-49.

0349 David J. Clark, "Criteria for Identifying Chiasm," *LB* 35 (1975): 63-72.

0350 Werner Thissen, *Erzáhlung der Befreiung: Eine exegetische Untersuchung zu Mk 2:1-3:6*. Forschung zur Bibel 21. Würzburg: Echter Verlag, 1976.

0351 Joanna Dewey, *Markan Public Debate: Literary Technique, Concentric Structure and Theology in Mark 2:1-3:6*. Chico CA: Scholars Press, 1978.

0352 Ronald J. Kernaghan, "History and Redaction in the Controversy Stories in Mark 2:1-3:6," *SBT* 9 (1979): 23-47.

0353 Ulrich B. Müller, "Zur Rezeption Gesetzes-Kritischer Jesusuberlieferung im Fruhen Christentum," *NTS* 27/2 (1980-1981): 158-85.

0354 Darrell J. Doughty, "The Authority of the Son of Man," *ZNW* 74/3-4 (1983): 161-81.

0355 James D. G. Dunn, "Mark 2:1-3:6: A Bridge Between Jesus and Paul on the Question of the Law," *NTS* 30/3 (1984): 395-415.

0356 E. W. Stegemann, "From Criticism to Enmity: An Interpretation of Mark 2:1-3:6," in Willy Schottroff and E. W. Stegemann, eds., *God of the Lowly: Socio-Historical Interpretation of the Bible*. Maryknoll NY: Orbis, 1984. Pp. 104-17.

0357 Jarmo Killunen, *Die Vollmacht im Wuderstreit: Untersuchungen zum Werdegang von Mk 2,1-3,6*. Annales Academiae Scientiarum Fennicae: Dissertationes Humanarum Litterarum #40. Helsinki: Suomalainen Tiedeakatemia, 1985.

0358 Benoît Standaert, "La rhétorique ancienne dans saint Paul," in Albert Vanhoye, ed., *L'Apôtre Paul: personnalité, style et conception du ministère*. Louvain: Louvain University Press, 1986. Pp. 78-92.

0359 Eugene A. LaVerdiere, "Jesus and the Call of the First Disciples: Conflict with the Scribes and Pharisees," *Emmanuel* 94 (1988): 264-69, 272-73, 292.

<u>2:1-28</u>

0360 Verner Hoefelmann, "O caminho da paixao de Jesus na perspectiva do evangelista Marcos," *EstT* 26/2 (1986): 99-119.

<u>2:1-17</u>

0361 Jean Calloud, "Toward a Structural Analysis of the Gospel of Mark," *Semeia* 16 (1979): 133-65.

<u>2:1-13</u>

0362 Jean Delorme, "Les évangiles dans le texte," *Études* 35/3 (1980): 91-105.

0363 Jean Delorme, "Marc 2,1-13—ou l'ouverture des frontières," *SémBib* 30 (1983): 1-14.

0364 Edwin K. Broadhead, "Christology as Polemic and Apologetic: The Priestly Portrait of Jesus in the Gospel of Mark," *JSNT* 47 (1992): 21-34.

2:1-12

0365 Allen Cabaniss, "A Fresh Exegesis of Mark 2:1-12," *Int* 11 (1957): 324-27.

0366 R. T. Mead, "The Healing of the Paralytic—A Unit?" *JBL* 80 (1961): 348-54.

0367 G. G. Gamba, "Considerazioni in margine alla poetica di Mc 2,1-12," *Sale* 28 (1966): 324-49.

0368 Robert J. Maddox, "The Function of the Son of Man according to the Synoptic Gospels," *NTS* 15 (1968-1969): 45-74.

0369 Gilles Gaide, "Le paralytique pardonné et guéri: Mc 2,1-12," *AsSeign* 4/38 (1970): 79-88.

0370 Alfred Blenker, "Tilgivelse i Jesu forkyndelse," *DTT* 34 (1971): 105-109.

0371 Ingrid Maisch, *Die Heilung des Gelähmten. Eine exegetisch-traditionsgeschichtliche Untersuchung zu Mk 2.1-12*. Stuttgarter Bibelstudien 52. Stuttgart: Katholisches Bibelwerk, 1971.

0372 Alfons Auer, "Sünde und Vergebung in der Botschaft Jesu," *KathG* 29 (1973): 14-17, 76-79.

0373 Detlev Dormeyer, " 'Narrative Analyse' von Mk 2,1-12," *LB* 31 (1974): 68-88.

0374 Léopold Sabourin, "The Miracles of Jesus (II). Jesus and the Evil Powers," *BTB* 4 (1974): 115-75.

0375 Bo Reicke, "The Synoptic Reports on the Healing of the Paralytic: Matt. 9:1-8 with Parallels," in J. K. Elliott, ed.,

Studies in New Testament Language and Text (festschrift for George D. Kilpatrick). Leiden: Brill, 1976. Pp. 319-29.

0376 Hans-Josef Klauck, "Die Frage der Sundenvergebung in der Perikope von der Heilung des Gelahmten Mk 2,1-12 Parr," *BZ* 25/2 (1981): 223-48.

0377 Rudolf Frieling, "Heilungen," in *Christologische Aufsätze*. Stuttgart: Urachhaus, 1982. Pp. 189-246.

0378 Otfried Hofius, "Vergebungszuspruch und Vollmachtsfrage: Mk 2,1-12 und das Problem priesterlicher Absolution im antiken Judentum," in H.-G. Geyer, et al., eds., *"Wenn nicht jetzt, wann dann?"* (festschrift for Hans-Joachim Kraus). Neukirchen-Vluyn: Neukirchener Verlag, 1983. Pp. 115-27.

0379 Carlo Buzzetti, "Parallels in the Synoptic Gospels: A Case Study," *BT* 35 (1984): 425-31.

0380 Wolfgang Lipp, "Der rettende Glaube: Eine Untersuchung zu Wundergeschichten im Markusevangelium," doctoral dissertation, University of Marburg, Marburg, 1984.

0381 Lars Lode, "The Presentation of New Information," *BT* 35 (1984): 101-108.

0382 Charles P. Anderson, "The Trial of Jesus as Jewish-Christian Polarization: Blasphemy and Polemic in Mark's Gospel," in P. Richardson and D. Granskou, eds., *Anti-Judaism in Early Christianity:* 1. *Paul and the Gospels*. Waterloo, Ont.: Wilfrid Laurier University Press, 1986. 1:107-25.

0383 Jonathan Bishop, "Parabole and Parrhesia in Mark," *Int* 40/1 (1986): 39-52.

0384 Peder Borgen, "John and the Synoptics: Can Paul Offer Help?" in Gerald F. Hawthorne and Otto Betz, eds., *Tradition & Interpretation in the New Testament* (festschrift for E. Earle Ellis). Grand Rapids: Eerdmans, 1987. Pp. 80-94.

0385 Mechthild von Heusinger, "The Meaning of Disease in Relation to Sin and Forgiving," in J. Leibowitz and S. S. Kottek, eds., *Koroth*: 9. *Proceedings of the Third International Symposium on Medicine in Bible and Talmud, Jerusalem, 1987*. Jerusalem: Israel Institute of History and Medicine, 1988. 9:73-83.

0386 Albert Fuchs, "Offene Probleme der Synoptikerforschung: Zur Geschichte der Perikope Mk 2,1-12 par Mt 9,1-8 par Lk 5,17-26," *SNTU-A* 15 (1990): 73-99.

0387 Isabelle Parlier, "L'autorité qui révèle la foi et l'incrédulite: Marc 2/1-12," *ÉTR* 67/2 (1992): 243-47.

2:1-10

0388 Paul J. Achtemeier, "The Ministry of Jesus in the Synoptic Gospels," *Int* 35 (1981): 157-69.

2:1-3

0389 Pierre Mourlon Beernaert, "Jésus Controversé: Structure et Théologie de Marc 2,1-3, 6," *NRT* 95/2 (1973): 129-49.

2:1-2

0390 John Vannorsdall, "Mark 2:1-2," *Int* 36/1 (1982): 58-63.

0391 Ivor Bailey, "The Cripple's Story," *ET* 99 (1987-1988): 110-12.

2:2-12

0392 Gregory Murray, "Five Gospel Miracles," *DR* 108 (1990): 79-90.

2:3-11

0393 F. C. Synge, "A Matter of Tenses—Fingerprints of an Annotator in Mark," *ET* 88 (1976-1977): 168-71.

2:3-5

0394 Emilio Rasco, " 'Cuatro' y 'la fe': ¿quiénes y de quién? (Mc 2,3b.5a)," *Bib* 50 (1969): 59-67.

2:3

0395 Michael D. Goulder, "On Putting Q to the Test," *NTS* 24 (1977-1978): 218-34.

0396 Christopher M. Tuckett, "On the Relationship between Matthew and Luke," *NTS* 30 (1984): 130-42.

2:4

0397 Herman Ljungvik, "Randanmärkningar till 1963 års bibelkommités översättningsförslag," *SEÅ* 34 (1969): 147-69.

0398 David A. Black, "Some Dissenting Notes on R..Stein's *The Synoptic Problem* and Markan 'Errors'," *FilN* 1 (1988): 95-101.

0399 Günther Schwarz, "ἀπεστέγασαν τὴν στέγην (Markus 2:4c)," *BibN* 54 (1990): 41.

2:5-10

0400 Johann Michl, "Sündenvergebung in Christus nach dem Glauben der fruhen Kirche," *MTZ* 24 (1973): 25-35.

2:5-7

0401 Paul Ellingworth, "Translating Parallel Passages in the Gospels," *BT* 34 (1983): 401-407.

2:5

0402 Harvie Branscomb, " 'Son, Thy Sins are Forgiven' (Mark 2:5)," *JBL* 53 (1934): 53-60.

0403 Jan W. Doeve, "Le rôle de la tradition orale dans la composition des Évangiles synoptiques," in J. Heuschen, ed., *La formation des évangiles: Problème synoptique et Formgeschichte*. Paris: Desclée, 1957. Pp. 70-84.

0404 E. M. Sidebottom, "The So-Called Divine Passive in the Gospel Tradition," *ET* 87 (1975-1976): 200-204.

0405 Marius Reiser, "Der Alexanderroman und das Markusevangelium," in Hubert Cancik, ed., *Markus-Philologie*. Tübingen: Mohr, 1984. Pp. 131-63.

2:6-12

0406 Joseph Keller, "Jesus and the Critics: A Logico-Critical Analysis of the Marcan Confrontation," *Int* 40/1 (1986): 29-38.

2:6

0407 Pierre Mourlon Beernaert, "Jésus Controversé: Structure et Théologie de Marc 2,1-3, 6," *NRT* 95/2 (1973): 129-49.

2:7

0408 John Thorley, "Aktionsart in New Testament Greek: Infinitive and Imperative," *NovT* 31 (1989): 290-315.

2:8-11

0409 Gert Lüderitz, "Rhetorik, Poetik, Kompositionstechnik im Markusevangelium," in Hubert Cancik, ed., *Markus-Philologie*. Tübingen: Mohr, 1984. Pp. 165-203.

2:8-9

0410 Ronald Ross, "Was Jesus Saying Something or Doing Something? (Mark 2:8-9)," *BT* 41 (1990): 441-42.

2:8

0411 Philippe Rolland, "L'arrière-lond sémitique des évangiles synoptiques," *ETL* 60 (1984): 358-62.

0412 Philippe Rolland, "Jésus connaissait leurs pensées," *ETL* 62 (1986): 118-21.

2:9

0413 Ulrich Luck, "Was wiegt leichter? Zu Mk 2,9," in Hubert Frankemölle, ed., *Vom Urchristentum zu Jesus* (festschrift for Joachim Gnilka). Freiburg: Herder, 1989. Pp. 103-108.

2:10-28

0414 André Feuillet, "L'ἐξουσία du Fils de l'homme (d'après Mc, 2:10-28 et par.)," *RechSR* 42 (1954): 161-92.

0415 Christopher M. Tuckett, "The Present Son of Man," *JSNT* 14 (1982): 58-81.

2:10

0416 George H. Boobyer, "Mark 2:10a and the Interpretations of the Healing of the Paralytic," *HTR* 47 (1954): 115-20.

0417 Jacques Duplacy, "Marc 2,10. Note de syntaxe," in *Mélanges bibliques rédigés en l'honneur de André Robert*. Travaux de l'Institut Catholique de Paris #4. Paris: Bloud et Gay, 1957. Pp. 420-27.

0418 Christian P. Ceroke, "Is Mark 2:10 a Saying of Jesus?" *CBQ* 22 (1960): 369-90.

0419 I. Howard Marshall, "The Synoptic Son of Man Sayings in Recent Discussion," *NTS* 12 (1965-1966): 327-51.

0420 L. S. Hay, "The Son of Man in Mark 2:10 and 2:28," *JBL* 89 (1970): 69-75.

0421 Carsten Colpe, "Traditionsüberschreitende Argumentationen zu Aussagen Jesu über sich selbst," in Gert Jeremias, Heinz-Wolfgang Kung, and Hartmut Stegemann, eds., *Tradition und Glaube: das frühe Christentum in seiner Umwelt* (festschrift for Karl Georg Kuhn). Göttingen: Vandenhoeck & Ruprecht, 1971. Pp. 230-45.

0422 Karl Kertelge, "Die Vollmacht des Menschensohnes zur Sündenvergebung (Mk 2,10)," in Paul Hoffmann, ed., with Norbert Brox and Wilhelm Pesch, *Orientierung an Jesus: Zur Theologie de Synoptiker: Für Josef Schmid.* Freiburg/Basel/Vienna: Herder, 1973. Pp. 205-13.

0423 Lars Hartman, "Baptism 'Into the Name of Jesus' and Early Christology: Some Tentative Considerations," *StTheol* 28 (1974): 21-48.

0424 P. Maurice Casey, "The Son of Man Problem," *ZNW* 67/3 (1976): 147-54.

0425 George Howard, "Stylistic Inversion and the Synoptic Tradition," *JBL* 97 (1978): 375-89.

2:11-16

0426 Herman Ljungvik, "Randanmärkningar till 1963 års bibelkommités översättningsförslag," *SEÅ* 34 (1969): 147-69.

2:11-12

0427 Frans Neirynck, "Les accords mineurs et la rédaction des évangiles: L'épisode du paralylique," *ETL* 50 (1974): 215-30.

2:11

0428 José O'Callaghan, "Tres casos de armonización en Mt 9," *EB* 47 (1989): 131-34.

2:12-3:21

0429 Bonifatius Fischer, *Die lafeinischen Evangelien bis zum 10. Jahrhundert. 11. Varianten zu Markus*. Freiburg: Herder, 1989.

2:12

0430 Martin J. Higgins, "New Testament Result Clauses with Infinitive," *CBQ* 23 (1961): 233-41.

0431 Angelo Lancellotti, "La Casa Pietro a Cafarnao nel Vangeli Sinottici: Redazione e Tradizione," *Ant* 58/1 (1983): 48-69.

0432 Lars Lode, "Narrative Paragraphs in the Gospels and Acts," *BT* 34/3 (1983): 322-35.

2:13-17

0433 B. M. F. van Iersel, "La vocation de Lévi 5 Mc II,13-17; Mt IX,9-13; Lc V,27-32," in I. de la Potterie, ed., *De Jésus aux Évangiles: Tradition et Rédaction dans les Évangiles synoptiques* (festschrift for Iosepho Coppens). BETL #25. Gembloux/Paris: Duculot/Lethielleux, 1967. Pp. 212-32.

0434 G. G. Gamba, "Considerazioni in margine alla redazione di Mc 2,13-17," *DivT* 72 (1969): 201-26.

0435 Paul Lamarche, "The Call to Conversion and Faith. The Vocation of Levi (Mark 2:13-17)," *LV* 25 (1970): 301-12.

0436 Albert L. Descamps, "Aux origines du ministère: La pensée de Jesus," *RTL* 2 (1971): 3-45; 3 (1972): 121-59.

0437 Paul Lamarche, "L'appel de Levi. Marc 2,13-17," *Chr* 23 (1976): 107-18.

0438 Michael Theobald, "Der Primat der Synshronie vor der Diachronie als Grundaxion der Literaturkritik. Methodische Erwagungen an Hand von Mk 2,13-17, Mt 9,9-13," *BZ* 22/2 (1978): 161-86.

0439 Martin Völkel, " 'Freund der Zöllner und Sünder'," *ZNW* 69 (1978): 1-10.

0440 Balembo Buetubela, "La vocation de Lévi et le repas avec les pécheurs (Mc 2,13-17)," *RAfT* 3 (1979): 47-60.

0441 Dietrich-Alex Koch, "Jesu Tischgemeinschaft mit Zöllnern und Sündern: Erwägungen zur Entstehung von Mk 2,13-17," in Dietrich-Alex Koch, et al., eds., *Jesu Rede von Gott und ihre Nachgeschichte im frühen Christentum* (festschrift for Willi Marxsen). Gütersloh: Gütersloher Verlag, 1989. Pp. 57-73.

<u>2:13-14</u>

0442 Francis J. Moloney, "The Vocation of the Disciples in the Gospel of Mark," *Sale* 43 (1981): 487-516.

0443 Jean Magne, "La vocation de Matthieu," *BLOS* 3 (1990): 3-6.

<u>2:13</u>

0444 Enzo Bianchi, "Gesù alla tavola dei peccatori, amico dei pubblicani e delle prostitute: Mc 2,13ss e par," *ParSpirV* 20 (1989): 127-50.

<u>2:14-17</u>

0445 John R. Donahue, "Tax Collectors and Sinners: An Attempt at Identification," *CBQ* 33 (1971): 39-61.

<u>2:14-16</u>

0446 Fritz Herrenbrück, "Wer waren die 'Zöllner'?" *ZNW* 72 (1981): 178-94.

0447 Fritz Herrenbrück, "Zum Vorwurf der Kollaboration des Zöllners mit Rom," *ZNW* 78 (1987): 186-99.

<u>2:14</u>

0448 Rudolf Pesch, "Levi-Matthäus (Mc 2,14 / Mt 9,9; 10,3): Ein Beitrag zur Lösung eines alten Problems," *ZNW* 59 (1968): 40-56.

0449 Demetrios Trakatellis, "*Akolouthei moi*—Follow Me (Mk 2:14): Discipleship and Priesthood," *GOTR* 30 (1985): 271-85.

0450 Beltran Villegas, "Peter, Philip and James of Alphaeus," *NTS* 33 (1987): 292-94.

2:15-3:5

0451 Jan Lambrecht, "Gesetzesverständnis bei Paulus [Gal 3:10-14]," in Karl Kertelge, ed., *Das Gesetz im Neuen Testament*. Freiburg: Herder, 1986. Pp. 88-127.

2:15-17

0452 C. H. Dodd, *The Parables of the Kingdom*. Rev. ed. London: Nisbet, 1961.

0453 Rudolf Pesch, "Das Zöllnergastmahl (Mk 2,15-17)," in Albert Descamps and André de Halleux, eds., *Mélanges bibliques: en hommage au R. P. Béda Rigaux*. Gembloux: Éditions J. Duculot, 1970. Pp. 63-87.

0454 Herbert Braun, "Gott, die Eröffnung des Lebens für Nonkonformisten. Erwägungen zu Markus 2,15-17," in Gerhard Ebeling, Eberhard Jüngel, and Gerd Schunack, eds., *Festschrift für Ernst Fuchs*. Tübingen: Mohr/Siebeck, 1973. Pp. 97-101.

0455 Paul De Maat, "Hoe Krijst Marcus 2:15-17 betekenis?" *Bij* 44/2 (1983): 194-207.

0456 Robert G. Bratcher, "Unusual Sinners," *BT* 39 (1988): 335-37.

0457 James D. G. Dunn, "Pharisees, Sinners and Jesus," in Jacob Neusner, et al., eds., *The Social World of Formative Christianity and Judaism* (festschrift for Howard Clark Kee). Philadelphia: Fortress Press, 1988. Pp. 264-89.

0458 Jean Magne, "Le repas avec les pécheurs," *BLOS* 5 (1990): 17-20.

2:15-16

0459 H.-W. Bartsch, "Zur Problematik eines Monopoltextes des Neuen Testaments. Das Beispiel Markus 2, Vers 15 und 16," *TLZ* 105 (1980): 91-96.

0460 Carlo M. Martini, "Were the Scribes Jesus' Followers? (Mk 2:15-16): A Textual Decision Reconsidered," in M.

Brecht, ed., *Text-Wort-Glaube: Studien zur Überlieferung, Interpretation und Autonisienung biblischer Texte Kurt Alund gewidmet*. New York: de Gruyter, 1980. Pp. 31-39.

0461 H.-W. Bartsch, "Ein neuer Textus Receptus für das griechische Neue Testament?" *NTS* 27 (1980-1981): 585-92.

2:15

0462 Elizabeth Struthers Malbon, "Τῇ οἰκίᾳ αὐτοῦ: Mark 2:15 in Context," *NTS* 31/2 (1985): 282-92.

2:16-17

0463 José Alonso Díaz, "La parábola del médico en Mc. 2,16-17," *CuBí* 16 (1959): 10-12.

2:16

0464 Donald E. Cook, "A Gospel Portrait of the Pharisees," *RevExp* 84 (1987): 221-33.

0465 J. K. Elliott, "The Relevance of Textual Criticism to the Synoptic Problem," in David L. Dungan, ed., *The Interrelations of the Gospels*. Louvain: Peeters Press, 1990. Pp. 348-59.

0466 George D. Kilpatrick, "Two Studies of Style and Text in the Greek New Testament," *JTS* 41 (1990): 94-98.

2:17

0467 Jan W. Doeve, "Le rôle de la tradition orale dans la composition des Évangiles synoptiques," in J. Heuschen, *La formation des évangiles: Problème synoptique et Formgeschichte*. Paris: Desclée, 1957. Pp. 70-84.

0468 John J. Vincent, "The Parables of Jesus as Self-Revelation," *StudE* 1 (1959): 79-99.

0469 G. M. Lee, " 'They that are Whole Need Not a Physician'," *ET* 76 (1964-1965): 254.

0470 Carlo Buzzetti, "Parallels in the Synoptic Gospels: A Case Study," *BT* 35 (1984): 425-31.

2:18-28

0471 David Daube, "Responsibilities of Master and Disciples in the Gospels," *NTS* 19 (1972-1973): 1-15.

0472 Jean Calloud, "Toward a Structural Analysis of the Gospel of Mark," *Semeia* 16 (1979): 133-65.

0473 Maria Waibel, "Die Auseinandersetzung mit der Fasten- und Sabbatpraxis Jesu in urchristlichen Gemeinden," in Gerhard Dautzenberg, et al., eds., *Zur Geschichte des Urchristentums*. Freiburg: Herder, 1979. Pp. 63-96.

2:18-22

0474 Harvey K. McArthur, "The Dependence of the Gospel of Thomas on the Synoptics," *ET* 71 (1959-1960): 286-87.

0475 Juan Fernández y Fernández, "La cuestión de ayuno (Mt 9,14-17; Mc 2,18-22; Lu 5,33-39)," *CuBí* 19 (1962): 162-69.

0476 John O'Hara, "Christian Fasting. Mk 2,18-22," *Scr* 19 (1967): 82-95.

0477 Gottfried Schille, "Was ist ein Logion?" *ZNW* 61 (1970): 172-82.

0478 Richard A. Batey, *New Testament Nuptial Imagery*. Leiden: Brill, 1971.

0479 Gilles Gaide, "Question sur le jeûne. Mc 2,18-22," *AsSeign* 39 (1972): 44-54.

0480 Robert Banks, "Jesus and Custom," *ET* 84 (1972-1973): 265-69.

0481 J. A. Ziesler, "The Removal of the Bridegroom: A Note on Mark 2:18-22 and Parallels," *NTS* 19 (1972-1973): 190-94.

0482 Gottfried Schille, *Osterglaube*. Arbeiten zur Theologie #51. Stuttgart: Calwer, 1973.

0483 John B. Muddiman, "Jesus and Fasting: Mark ii.18-22," in J. Dupont, ed., *Jésus aux origines de la christologie*. BETL #40. Louvain: Louvain University Press, 1975. Pp. 271-81.

0484 Luciano Fanin, "L'interrogazione sul digiuno: Mc 2,18-22," *MiscFranc* 76 (1976): 93-107.

0485 John B. Muddiman, "The Fasting Controversy in Mark: A Historical and Exegetical Study," doctoral dissertation, Oxford University, Oxford, 1976.

0486 Rainer Riesner, "Wie sicher ist die Zwei-Quellen-Theorie?" *TBe* 8 (1977): 49-73.

0487 Pieter J. Maartens, "Mark 2:18-22: An Exercise in Theoretically-Founded Exegesis," *ScrSA* 2 (1980): 1-54.

0488 Philippe Rolland, "Les Prédécesseurs de Marc: Les Sources Présynoptiques de Mc II,18-22 et Paralleles," *RB* 89/3 (1982): 370-405.

0489 R. S. Good, "Jesus, Protagonist of the Old, in Luke 5:33-39," *NovT* 25/1 (1983): 19-36.

0490 Curtis C. Mitchell, "The Practice of Fasting in the New Testament," *BSac* 147 (1990): 455-69.

0491 Knut Backhaus, *Die 'Jungerkreise' des Täufers Johannes: Eine Studie zu den religionsgeschichtlichen Ursprungen des Christentums*. Paderborn: Schoningh, 1991.

2:18-20

0492 André Feuillet, "La controverse sur le jeûne (Mc 2,18-20; Mt 9,14-15; Lc 5,33-35)," *NRT* 90 (1968): 113-36; 252-77.

0493 T. A. Burkill, "Should Wedding Guests Fast? A Consideration of Mark 2:18-20," in T. A. Burkill, ed., *New Light on the Earliest Gospel: Seven Markan Studies*. Ithaca NY: Cornell University Press, 1972. Pp. 39-47.

0494 Frans Neirynck, "Les expressions doubles chez Marc et le problème synoptique," *ETL* 59/4 (1983): 303-30.

2:18

0495 Frederico Dattler, "A mixná no Nôvo Testamento," in J. Salvador, ed., *Alualidades Bíblicas* (festschrift for F. J. J. Pedreira de Castro). Petrópolis: Vozes, 1971. Pp. 395-402.

0496 José O'Callaghan, "Tres casos de armonización en Mt 9," *EB* 47 (1989): 131-34.

2:19-20

0497 Ruderic Dunkerley, "The Bridegroom Passage," *ET* 64 (1952-1953): 303-304.

0498 Augustin George, "Comment Jésus a-t-il perçu sa propre mort?" *LV* 101 (1971): 34-59.

0499 J. C. O'Neill, "The Source of the Parables of the Bridegroom and the Wicked Husbandmen," *JTS* 39 (1988): 485-89.

2:19

0500 Franz G. Cremer, " 'Die Söhne des Brautgemachs' (Mk 2,19 parr) in der griechischen und lateinischen Schrifterklärung," *BZ* 11 (1967): 246-53.

2:20-22

0501 Paul Ellingworth, "Translating Parallel Passages in the Gospels," *BT* 34 (1983): 401-407.

2:20

0502 Karl T. Schäfer, " '. . . und dann werden sie fasten, an jenem Tage'," in Josef Schmid and Anton Vögtle, eds., *Synoptische Studien* (festschrift for Alfred Wikenhauser). Münich: Zink, 1953. Pp. 124-47.

0503 Franz G. Cremer, *Die Fastenansage Jesu. Mk 2:20 und Parallelen in der Sicht der patristischen und scholastischen Exegese*. Bonner Biblische Beiträge 23. Bonn: Hanstein, 1965.

0504 José O'Callaghan, "Dos retoques antioquenos: Mt 10,10; Mc 2,20," *Bib* 68/4 (1987): 564-67.

2:21-22

0505 Johannes Herz, "Die Gleichnisse der Evangelien Matthaus, Markus und Lukas in ihrer geschichtlichen Überlieferung und ihrem religiös-sittlichen Inhalt," in E.-H. Amberg and U. Kühn, eds., *Bekenntnis zur Kirche* (festschrift for Ernst Sommerlath). Berlin: Evangelische Verlagsanstalt, 1960. Pp. 52-93.

0506 L. Paul Trudinger, "The Word on the Generation Gap. Reflections on a Gospel Metaphor," *BTB* 5 (1975): 311-15.

0507 Vernon K. Robbins, "Picking Up the Fragments: From Crossan's Analysis to Rhetorical Analysis," *Forum* 1 (1985): 31-64.

2:21

0508 J. M. Bover, "La parábola del Remiendo (Mt. 9,16; Mc. 2,21; Lc. 5,36)," in A. Metzinger, ed., *Miscellanea Biblica et Orientalia*. Rome: Orbis Catholicus, 1951. Pp. 327-39.

0509 John Hargreaves, *Guide to the Parables*. 2nd ed. London: SPCK, 1970.

0510 Ferdinand Hahn, "Die Bildworte vom neuen Flicken und vom jungen Wein (Mk. 2,21f. parr)," *EvT* 31 (1971): 357-75.

0511 Michael G. Steinhauser, "Neuer Wein braucht neue Schläuche. Zur Exegese von Mk 2,21f. par.," in Helmut Merklein and Joachim Lange, eds., *Biblische Randbemerkungen: Schülerfestschrift für Rudolf Schnackenburg zum 60. Geburtstag*. Würzburg: Echter-Verlag, 1974. Pp. 113-23.

2:22

0512 David Flusser, "Do You Prefer New Wine?" *Immanuel* 9 (1979): 26-31.

2:23-6:6

0513 Eugene A. LaVerdiere, "Jesus and the New Israel," *Emmanuel* 94 (1988): 322-29.

2:23-3:6

0514 Henri Troadec, "Le Fils de l'Homme est Maitre même du sabbat (Marc 2,23-3,6)," *BVC* 21 (1958): 73-83.

0515 Antoine Duprez, "Deuz affrontements un jour de sabbat. Mc 2:23-3:6," *AsSeign* 40 (1972): 43-53.

0516 E. A. Russell, "Mark 2,23-3,6—A Judaean Setting," *StudE* 6 (1973): 466-72.

<u>2:23-28</u>

0517 Eduard Lohse, "Jesu Worte über den Sabbat," in Walther Eltester, ed., *Judentum, Urchristentum, Kirche* (festschrift for Joachim Jeremias). BNZW #26. 2nd ed. Berlin: Töplemann, 1964. Pp. 79-89.

0518 Joseph A. Grassi, "The Five Loaves or the High Priest," *NovT* 7 (1964-1965): 119-22.

0519 Arland J. Hultgren, "The Formation of the Sabbath Pericope in Mark 2:23-28," *JBL* 91/1 (1971): 38-43.

0520 Herbert Braun, "Erwägungen zu Markus 2,23-28 Par.," in Hermann Horn, ed., *Entscheidung und Solidarität: Festschrift für Johannes Harder. Beiträge zur Theologie. Politik Literatur und Erziehung*. Wuppertal: Hammer, 1973. Pp. 53-56.

0521 J. Duncan M. Derrett, "Judaica in St. Mark," *JRAS* (1975): 2-15.

0522 Bernard Jay, "Jesus et le sabbat. Simples notes a propos de Marc 2/23-28," *ÉTR* 50 (1975): 65-68.

0523 Hermann Aichinger, "Quellenkritische Untersuchung der Perikope vom Ährenraufen am Sabbat: Mk 2,23-28 par, Mt 12,1-8 par, Lk 6,1-5," *SNTU-A* 1 (1976): 110-53.

0524 G. G. Gamba, "Struttura letteraria e significato dottrinale di Marco 2,23-28 e 3,1-6," *Sale* 40 (1978): 529-82.

0525 Andreas Lindemann, " 'Der Sabbat ist um des Menschen willen geworden. . .': Historische und theologische Erwägungen zur Traditionsgeschichte der Sabbatperikope Mk 2,23-28 parr.," *WD* 15 (1979): 79-105.

0526 Lars Lode, "The Presentation of New Information," *BT* 35 (1984): 101-108.

0527 Luise Schottroff and Wolfgang Stegemann, "The Sabbath Was Made for Man: The Interpretation of Mark 2:23-28," in Willy Schottroff and W. Stegemann, eds., *God of the Lowly: Socio-Historical Interpretation of the Bible*. Maryknoll NY: Orbis, 1984. Pp. 118-28.

0528 Stanley N. Olson, "Christ for All of Life: Mark's Miracle Stories for 1985," *CThM* 12 (1985): 90-99.

0529 Peder Borgen, "John and the Synoptics: Can Paul Offer Help?" in Gerald F. Hawthorne and Otto Betz, eds., *Tradition & Interpretation in the New Testament* (festschrift for E. Earle Ellis). Grand Rapids: Eerdmans, 1987. Pp. 80-94.

0530 Michel Gourgues, "Halakâh el Haggadâh chrétiennes: Les indications de Marc 2.23-28 et parallèles (les épis arrachés) sur le 'sens chrétien de l'Ancien Testament'," in *La vie de la Parole: De l'Ancien au Nouveau Testament* (festschrift for Pierre Grelot). Paris: Desclée, 1987. Pp. 195-209.

0531 P. Maurice Casey, "Culture and Historicity: The Plucking of the Grain in Mark 2:23-28," *NTS* 34/1 (1988): 1-23.

0532 George J. Brooke, "The Temple Scroll and the New Testament," in George J. Brooke, ed., *Temple Scroll Studies*. Sheffield: JSOT Press, 1989. Pp. 181-99.

0533 J. H. van Halsema, "Aren plukken op de sabbat," *KerkT* 42 (1991): 210-17.

0534 Edwin K. Broadhead, "Christology as Polemic and Apologetic: The Priestly Portrait of Jesus in the Gospel of Mark," *JSNT* 47 (1992): 21-34.

0535 Luise Schottroff and Wolfgang Stegemann, "The Sabbath Was Made for Man: The Interpretation of Mark 2:23-28," in Willy Schottroff and W. Stegemann, eds., God of the Lowly: Socio-Historical Interpretation of the Bible [cf1]. Maryknoll, NY: Orbis, 1984. Pp. 118-28.

<u>2:23-26</u>

0536 Damià Roure, *Jésus y la fgura de Daldd en Mc 2,23-26: Trasfondo bíblico, intertestamentario rabínico*. Rome: Editrice Pontificio Biblico, 1990.

<u>2:23</u>

0537 H.-J. Schoeps, "Jesus et la Loi juive," *RHPR* 33 (1953): 1-20.

2:24

0538 Donald E. Cook, ''A Gospel Portrait of the Pharisees,'' *RevExp* 84 (1987): 221-33.

2:25

0539 John A. T. Robinson, ''Did Jesus Have a Distinctive Use of Scripture?'' in *Twelve More New Testament Studies*. London: SCM, 1984. Pp. 35-43.

2:26

0540 Alan D. Rogers, ''Mark 2:26,'' *JTS* 2 (1951): 44.

0541 Jan W. Doeve, ''Le rôle de la tradition orale dans la composition des Évangiles synoptiques,'' in J. Heuschen, *La formation des évangiles: Problème synoptique et Formgeschichte*. Paris: Desclée, 1957. Pp. 70-84.

0542 Nigel Turner, ''The Minor Verbal Agreements of Mt. and Lk. against Mk.,'' *StudE* 1 (1959): 223-34.

0543 C. S. Morgan, '' 'When Abiathar Was High Priest,' (Mark 2:26),'' *JBL* 98 (1979): 409-10.

0544 J. H. van Halsema, ''Het raadsel als literaire vorm in Marcus en Johannes,'' *GTT* 83/1 (1983): 1-17.

0545 Craig A. Evans, ''Patristic Interpretation of Mark 2:26: 'When Abiathar was High Priest','' *VC* 40/2 (1986): 183-86.

2:27-28

0546 Félix Gils, '' 'Le sabbat a été fait pour l'homme et non l'homme pour le sabbat' (Mc II,27). Réflexions à propos de Mc II,27-28,'' *RB* 69 (1962): 506-23.

0547 J. M. Casciaro Ramírez, ''General, Generic and Indefinite: The Use of the Term 'Son of Man' in Aramaic Sources and in the Teaching of Jesus,'' *JSNT* 29 (1987): 21-56.

2:27

0548 T. W. Manson, ''Mark 2:27f.,'' in *Coniectanea neotestamenties, XI, in honorem Antonii Fridrichsen sexagenarii*. Lund: Gleerup, 1947. Pp. 138-46.

0549 Félix Gils, " 'Le sabbat a été fait pour l'homme et non l'homme pour le sabbat' (Mc II,27). Réflexions à propos de Mc II,27-28," *RB* 69 (1962): 506-23.

0550 Frans Neirynck, "Jesus and the Sabbath: Some Observations on Mark 2,27," in J. Dupont, ed., *Jésus aux origines de la christologie*. BETL #40. Louvain: Louvain University Press, 1975. Pp. 227-70.

0551 Luise Schottroff, "Anti-Judaism in the New Testament," G. Harrison, trans., in Elisabeth Schüssler-Fiorenza and David Tracy, eds., *The Holocaust as Interruption*. Edinburgh: T. & T. Clark, 1984. Pp. 53-59.

0552 Rüdiger Bartelmus, "Mk 2:27 und die ältesten Fassungen des Arbeitsruhegebotes im AT: biblisch-theologische Beobachtungen zur Sabbatfrage," *BibN* 41 (1988): 41-64.

<u>2:28</u>

0553 L. S. Hay, "The Son of Man in Mark 2:10 and 2:28," *JBL* 89 (1970): 69-75.

0554 P. Maurice Casey, "The Son of Man Problem," *ZNW* 67/3 (1976): 147-54.

0555 Douglas J. Moo, "Jesus and the Authority of the Mosaic Law," *JSNT* 20 (1984): 3-49.

<u>3:1-4:20</u>

0556 James R. Edwards, "Markan Sandwiches: The Significance of Interpolations in Markan Narratives," *NovT* 31 (1989): 193-216.

<u>3:1-12</u>

0557 Benito Marconcini, "La predicazione del Battista in Marco e Luca confrontata con la redazione di Matteo," *RBib* Supp. 20 (1972): 451-66.

<u>3:1-7</u>

0558 Edwin K. Broadhead, "Christology as Polemic and Apologetic: The Priestly Portrait of Jesus in the Gospel of Mark," *JSNT* 47 (1992): 21-34.

<u>3:1-6</u>

0559 Josef Schmid, "Markus und der aramäische Matthaus," in Josef Schmid and Anton Vögtle, eds., *Synoptische Studien* (festschrift for Alfred Wikenhauser). Münich: Zink, 1953. Pp. 75-118.

0560 Jean Levie, "L'évangile araméen de S. Matthieu est-il la source de l'évangile de S. Marc?" *NRT* 76 (1954): 689-715, 812-43.

0561 Cyril S. Rodd, "Are the Ethics of Jesus Situation Ethics?" *ET* 79 (1967-1968): 167-70.

0562 Pierre Géoltrain, "La violation du sabbat: Une lecture de Marc 3,1-6," *FV* 69/3 (1970): 70-90.

0563 Léopold Sabourin, "The Miracles of Jesus (III): Healings, Resuscitations, Nature Miracles," *BTB* 5 (1975): 146-200.

0564 J. Smit Sibinga, "Text and Literary Art in Mark 3:1-6," in J. K. Elliott, ed., *Studies in New Testament and Text* (festschrift for George D. Kilpatrick). Leiden: Brill, 1976. Pp. 357-65.

0565 Evelin Albrecht, *Zeugnis durch Wort und Verhalten untersucht an ausgewahlten Texten des Neuen Testaments.* Basel: Reinhardt, 1977.

0566 Thomas R. W. Longstaff, *Evidence of Conflation in Mark? A Study in the Synoptic Problem.* Society of Biblical Literature Dissertation Series 28. Missoula MT: Scholars Press, 1977.

0567 Léopold Sabourin, *The Divine Miracles Discussed and Defended.* Rome: Catholic Book Agency, 1977.

0568 Christian Dietzfelbinger, "Vom Sinn der Sabbatheilungen Jesu," *EvT* 38 (1978): 281-98.

0569 G. G. Gamba, "Struttura letteraria e significato dottrinale di Marco 2,23-28 e 3,1-6," *Sale* 40 (1978): 529-82.

0570 Jürgen Sauer, "Traditionsgeschichtliche Überlegungen Zu Mk 3,1-6," *ZNW* 73/3-4 (1982): 183-203.

0571 J. Duncan M. Derrett, ''Christ and the Power of Choice: Mark 3:1-6,'' *Bib* 65/2 (1984): 168-88.

0572 Lars Lode, ''The Presentation of New Information,'' *BT* 35 (1984): 101-108.

0573 Wolfgang Feneberg, ''Das Neue Testament: Sprache der Liebe—Zum Problem des Antijudaismus,'' *ZKT* 107 (1985): 333-40.

0574 P.-G. Klumbies, ''Die Sabbatheilungen Jesu nach Markus und Lukas,'' in D.-A. Koch, et al. eds., *Jesu Rede von Gott und ihre Nachgeschichte im fruhen Christentum: Beitrage zur Verkundigung Jesu und zum Kerygma der Kirche* (festschrift for Willi Marxsen). Gütersloh: Mohn, 1989. Pp. 165-78.

3:2

0575 A. Marcello Buscemi, ''La prolessi nel Nuovo Testamento,'' *SBFLA* 35 (1985): 37-68.

0576 Lino Cignelli, ''La grecità biblica,'' *SBFLA* 35 (1985): 203-48.

3:4

0577 John Thorley, ''Aktionsart in New Testament Greek: Infinitive and Imperative,'' *NovT* 31 (1989): 290-315.

3:6

0578 H.-J. Schoeps, ''Jesus et la Loi juive,'' *RHPR* 33 (1953): 1-20.

0579 Constantin Daniel, ''Les 'Herodiens' du Nouveau Testament sont-ils des Esseniens?'' *RevQ* 6 (1967): 31-53.

0580 W. J. Bennett, ''The Herodians of Mark's Gospel,'' *NovT* 17/1 (1975): 9-14.

0581 Augustine Stock, ''Jesus, Hypocrites, and Herodians,'' *BTB* 16/1 (1986): 3-7.

3:7-19

0582 Lucien Cerfaux, ''La mission de Galilée dans la tradition synoptique,'' *ETL* 27 (1951): 369-89; 28 (1952): 629-47.

3:7-12

0583 Leander E. Keck, "Mark 3:7-12 and Mark's Christology," *JBL* 84/4 (1965): 341-58.

0584 T. A. Burkill, "Mark 3:7-12 and the Alleged Dualism in the Evangelist's Miracle Material," *JBL* 87/4 (1968): 409-17.

0585 Wilhelm Egger, "Die Verborgenheit in Mk 3,7-12," *Bib* 50 (1969): 466-90.

0586 Eugene C. Szarek, "Markan Ecclesiology and Anthropology: A Structural Analysis of Mark 3:7-12," doctoral dissertation, Marquette University, Milwaukee WI, 1975.

0587 Alois Stöger, "Sohn Gottes im Markusevangelium (II). Meditation (Mk 3,7-12; 5,1-12)," *BL* 49 (1976): 112-15.

0588 M.-É. Boismard, "Réponse aux deux autres hypothèses: 1: La théorie des deux sources: Mc 3:7-12 et parallèles; 2: La 'two-Gospel hypothesis'," in David L. Dungan, ed., *The Interrelations of the Gospels: A Symposium Led by M.-É. Boismard, W. R. Farmer, F. Neirynck, Jerusalem 1984*. Louvain: Peeters Press, 1990. BETL #95. Pp. 259-88.

3:7-8

0589 George Howard, "Stylistic Inversion and the Synoptic Tradition," *JBL* 97 (1978): 375-89.

3:8

0590 George D. Kilpatrick, "Two Studies of Style and Text in the Greek New Testament," *JTS* 41 (1990): 94-98.

3:9

0591 Günther Schwarz, "Ἵνα πλοιάριον προσκαπτερῇ αὐτῷ: Markus 3.9," *NTS* 33/1 (1987): 151-52.

3:10

0592 Martin J. Higgins, "New Testament Result Clauses with Infinitive," *CBQ* 23 (1961): 233-41.

3:13-19

0593 Albert L. Descamps, "Aux origines du ministère: La pensée de Jesus," *RTL* 2 (1971): 3-45; 3 (1972): 121-59.

0594 Francis J. Moloney, "The Vocation of the Disciples in the Gospel of Mark," *Sale* 43 (1981): 487-516.

0595 Michel Cornillon, "De l'appel du Christ à l'appel de l'Église: trois récits du Nouveau Testament," *BSS* 10 (1984): 107-50.

3:13-16

0596 J. Sudbrack, "Berufung, Gebet, Sendung: Die Einsetzung der zwölf Apostel nach Markus 3,13-16," *GeistL* 50 (1977): 387-90.

3:13

0597 Lino Cignelli, "La grecità biblica," *SBFLA* 35 (1985): 203-48.

3:14

0598 Ernest Best, "Mark's Use of the Twelve," *ZNW* 69/1-2 (1978): 11-35.

0599 Roland Minnerath, *Jésus et le pouvoir*. Le point theologique #46. Paris: Beauchesne, 1987.

3:15-32

0600 J. Harold Greenlee, *Nine Uncial Palimpsests of the Greek New Testament*. Salt Lake City: University of Utah, 1968.

3:16-19

0601 Michael D. Goulder, "On Putting Q to the Test," *NTS* 24 (1977-1978): 218-34.

0602 Christopher M. Tuckett, "On the Relationship between Matthew and Luke," *NTS* 30 (1984): 130-42.

3:16-17

0603 Harald Sahlin, "Emendationsvorschläge zum griechischen Text des Neuen Testaments I," *NovT* 24 (1982): 160-79.

3:17

0604 S. Grill, "Die Donnersöhne Mk 3.17 nach dem syrischen Text," *BL* 23 (1955-1956): 137-38.

0605 Otto Betz, "Donnersöhne, Menschenfischer und der Davidische Messias," *RevQ* 3 (1961): 41-70.

0606 Randall Buth, "Mark 3:17· **BONEPEΓEM** and Popular Etymology," *JSNT* 10 (1981): 29-33.

3:18-19

0607 J.-A. Morin, "Les deux derniers des Douze: Simon le Zelote et Judas Iskariôth," *RB* 80 (1973): 332-58.

3:18

0608 Beltran Villegas, "Peter, Philip and James of Alphaeus," *NTS* 33 (1987): 292-94.

0609 Roger L. Omanson, "Lazarus and Simon," *BT* 40 (1989): 416-19.

3:19-30

0610 O. Lamar Cope, "The Beelzebul Controversy, Mark 3:19-30 and Parallels: A Model Problem in Source Analysis," *SBLSP* 1/1 (1971): 251-56.

3:19-21

0611 Anthony O. Nkwoka, "Mark 3:19b-21: A Study on the Charge of Fanaticism against Jesus," *BB* 15 (1989): 205-21.

3:19-20

0612 Frans Neirynck, "The Order of the Gospels and the Making of a Synopsis," *ETL* 61/1 (1985): 161-66.

3:19

0613 Yoël Arbeitman, "The Suffix of Iscariot," *JBL* 99 (1980): 122-23.

3:20-4:34

0614 Jan Lambrecht, *Marcus Interpretator. Stijl en boodschap in Mc. 3,20-4,34*. Utrecht: Desclée de Brouwer, 1969.

3:20-35

0615 Jan Lambrecht, "Ware Verwantshasp en Eeuwige Zonde: Onstaan en Structuur van Mc. 3:20-35," *Bij* 29/2 (1968): 114-50.

0616 Gilles Gaide, "Les deux 'maisons': Mc 3,20-35," *AsSeign* 21/41 (1971): 39-53.

0617 David M. May, "Mark 3:20-35 from the Perspective of Shame/Honor," *BTB* 17/3 (1987): 83-87.

0618 Sharyn E. Dowd, *Prayer, Power, and the Problem of Suffering: Mark 11:22-25 in the Context of Markan Theology*. Atlanta: Scholars Press, 1988.

0619 Eugene A. LaVerdiere, "Teaching for the New Israel," *Emmanuel* 94 (1988): 383-89.

3:20-30

0620 Franklin I. Gamwell, "The House Divided," *Crit* 27 (1988): 15-18.

3:20-25

0621 Heikki Räisänen, *Die Mutter Jesu im Neuen Testament*. Helsinki: Suomalainen Tiedeakatemia, 1969.

0622 John Dominic Crossan, "Mark and the Relatives of Jesus," *NovT* 15 (1973): 81-113.

3:20-21

0623 P. J. Gannon, "Could Mark Employ αὐτός in 3,21 Referring to ὄχλος in 3,20?" *CBQ* 15 (1953): 400-61.

0624 Francesco Spadafora, "Lo studio della koinè nella esegesi. Mc. 3:20-21," *RBib* 4 (1956): 93-113, 193-217.

0625 José Alonso Díaz, "El pasaje evangélico del conflicto de Jésus con sus parientes (Mc 3,20-21,31-35 y par.) en su dimensión mariológica," *Theologica* 4/4 (1969): 425-36.

0626 Lorenz Oberliner, *Historische Überlieferung und christologische Aussage. Zur Frage der "Bruder Jesu" in der Synopse*. Stuttgart: Katholisches Bibelwerk, 1975.

0627 Martin Avanzo, "María en las primeras tradiciones evangelicas," *RevB* 38 (1976): 49-57.

0628 Angelo Lancellotti, "La Casa Pietro a Cafarnao nel Vangeli Sinottici. Redazione e Tradizione," *Ant* 58/1 (1983): 48-69.

0629 Detlev Dormeyer, "Die Familie Jesu und der Sohn der Maria im Markusevangelium," in Hubert Frankemölle, ed., *Vom Urchristentum zu Jesus* (festschrift for Joachim Gnilka). Freiburg: Herder. 1989. Pp. 109-35.

0630 Robert Schlarb, "Die Suche nach dem Messias: ζητέω als Terminus technicus der markinischen Messianologie," *ZNW* 81 (1990): 155-70.

0631 Detlev Dormeyer, "Dialogue with the Text: Interactional Bible Interpretation," *ScrSA* 33 (1990): 55-64.

0632 Meinrad Limbeck, "Hindernisse fürs Christein: Zur Verkündigung des Markusevangeliums," *BL* 64 (1991): 164-68.

3:20

0633 Martin J. Higgins, "New Testament Result Clauses with Infinitive," *CBQ* 23 (1961): 233-41.

0634 Francesco Spadafora, "Il greco degli Evangeli, esegesi di Mc 3,20s," *Lat* 28 (1962): 126-47.

0635 Ernest Best, "Mark 3:20, 21, 31-35," *NTS* 22/3 (1975-1976): 309-19.

0636 Klemens Stock, "La familia di Gesù se vergogna di lui: Mc 3,20s," *ParSpirV* 20 (1989): 105-26.

3:21

0637 Anselm Schulz, *Nachfolgen und Nachahmen: Studien über das Verhältnis der neutestamentlichen Jüngerschaft zur urchristlichen Vorbildethik*. Münich: Kösel, 1962.

0638 Henry Wansbrough, "Mark iii.21—Was Jesus Out of His Mind?" *NTS* 18 (1971-1972): 233-35.

0639 David Wenham, "The Meaning of Mark III.21," *NTS* 21/2 (1974-1975): 295-300.

0640 Ernest Best, "Mark 3:20, 21, 31-35," *NTS* 22/3 (1975-1976): 309-19.

0641 Schuyler Brown, "Mk 3,21: A Forgotten Controversy?" in F. Paschke, et al., eds., *Überlieferungsgeschichtliche Untersuchungen.* Berlin: Akademie-Verlag. 1981. Pp. 99-108.

0642 George E. Rice, "Is Bezae a Homogeneous Codex [Variants to Codex B]," *PRS* 11 (1984): 39-54.

0643 George E. Rice, "Is Bezae a Homogeneous Codex?," in Charles H. Talbert, ed., *Perspectives on the New Testament* (festschrift for Frank Stagg). Macon GA: Mercer University Press, 1985. Pp. 39-54.

<u>3:22-30</u>

0644 Roland Meynet, "Qui Donc Esr 'Le Plus Fort'? Analyse Rhetorique de Mc 3,22-30; Mt 12,22-37; Luc 11,14-26," *RB* 90/3 (1983): 334-50.

0645 Douglas E. Oakman, "Rulers' Houses, Thieves, and Usurpers: The Beelzebul Pericope," *Forum* 4 (1988): 109-23.

0646 G. Chico, "Jesús y Beelzebul: La presencia del Reino en un cuadro polémico," *Communio* 22 (1989): 41-52.

<u>3:22-29</u>

0647 Joachim Schüling, *Studien zum Verhältnis von Logienquelle und Markusevangelium.* Würzburg: Echter, 1991.

<u>3:22-27</u>

0648 Bruce D. Chilton, *Profiles of a Rabbi: Synoptic Opportunities in Reading about Jesus.* Atlanta: Scholars Press, 1989.

<u>3:22-26</u>

0649 J. Duncan M. Derrett, "Trees Walking, Prophecy, and Christology," *StTheol* 35/1 (1981): 33-54.

<u>3:22-23</u>

0650 Lars Lode, "The Presentation of New Information," *BT* 35 (1984): 101-108.

3:22

0651 Alfred Suhl, *Die Wunder Jesu: Ereignis und Überlieferung*. Gütersloh: Mohn, 1968.

0652 Meinrad Limbeck, "Beelzebul—eine ursprüngliche Bezeichnung fur Jesus?" in Helmut Feld and J. Nolte, eds., *Wort Gottes in der Zeit* (festschrift for Karl H. Schelkle). Düsseldorf: Patmos, 1973. Pp. 31-42.

0653 E. C. B. MacLaurin, "Beelzeboul," *NovT* 20/2 (1978): 156-60.

0654 Daniel R. Schwartz, " 'Scribes and Pharisees, Hypocrites': Who Were the Scribes?" *Zion* 50 (1985): 121-32.

0655 Philippe Rolland, "Jésus connaissait leurs pensées," *ETL* 62 (1986): 118-21.

3:23-30

0656 Chrys C. Caragounis, "Kingdom of God, Son of Man and Jesus' Self-Understanding," *TynB* 40 (1989): 3-23; 223-38.

3:23-27

0657 Johannes Herz, "Die Gleichnisse der Evangelien Matthaus, Markus und Lukas in ihrer geschichtlichen Überlieferung und ihrem religiös-sittlichen Inhalt," in E.-H. Amberg and U. Kühn, eds., *Bekenntnis zur Kirche* (festschrift for Ernst Sommerlath). Berlin: Evangelische Verlagsanstalt, 1960. Pp. 52-93.

3:27

0658 H.-W. Bartsch, "Das Thomas-Evangelium und die synoptischen Evangelien. Zu G. Quispel's Bemerkungen zum Thomas-Evangelium," *NTS* 6 (1959-1960): 249-61.

0659 Simon Légasse, " 'Homme Fort' de Luc XI,21-22," *NovT* 5 (1962): 5-9.

3:28-30

0660 Robert J. Maddox, "The Function of the Son of Man according to the Synoptic Gospels," *NTS* 15 (1968-1969): 45-74.

<u>3:28-29</u>

0661 Owen E. Evans, "The Unforgiveable Sin," *ET* 68 (1956-1957): 240-44.

0662 Robin Scroggs, "The Exaltation of the Spirit by Some Early Christians," *JBL* 84/4 (1965): 359-73.

0663 M. Eugene Boring, "The Unforgivable Sin Logion Mark 3:28-29/Matt 12:31-32/Luke 12:10: Formal Analysis and History of the Tradition," *NovT* 18/4 (1976): 258-79.

0664 James D. G. Dunn, "Prophetic 'I'-Sayings and the Jesus Tradition: The Importance of Testing Prophetic Utterances within Early Christianity," *NTS* 24 (1977-1978): 175-98.

0665 M. Eugene Boring, *Sayings of the Risen Jesus: Christian Prophecy in the Synoptic Tradition*. SNTSMS #46. Cambridge: Cambridge University Press, 1982.

0666 P. Maurice Casey, "Aramaic Idiom and Son of Man Sayings," *ET* 96 (1984-1985): 233-36.

0667 P.-R. Berger, "Zum Aramäischen der Evangelien und der Apostelgeschichte," *TheoR* 82 (1986): 1-17.

<u>3:28</u>

0668 Evald Lövestam, "Logiet om hädelse mot den helige Ande (Mark. 3:28f. par. Matt. 12:31f.; Luk. 12:10)," *SEÅ* 33/34 (1968): 101-17.

0669 Evald Lövestam, *Spiritus Blasphemia. Eine Studie zu Mk 3,28f par Mt 12,31f, Lk 12,10*. Scripta Minora Regiae Societatis Humaniorum Litterarum Lundensis, 1966-1967: 1. Lund: Gleerup, 1968.

0670 Faustino Salvoni, "Bestemmia contro lo Spirito Santo (Mc 3,28s par)," *RBR* 5 (1970): 365-81.

0671 M. Eugene Boring, "How May We Identify Oracles of Christian Prophets in the Synoptic Tradition? Mark 3:28, 29 as a Test Case," *JBL* 91/4 (1972): 501-20.

0672 Robert Holst, "Re-examining Mark 3:28f. and its Parallels," *ZNW* 63 (1972): 122-24.

3:29

0673 William C. Nolting, "The Sin against the Holy Ghost," doctoral dissertation, Lutheran University, Waterloo, Ont., 1952.

0674 Carsten Colpe, "Der Spruch von der Lästerung des Geistes," in Eduard Lohse, ed., *Der Ruf Jesu und die Antwort der Gemeinde: Exegetische Untersuchungen* (festschrift for Joachim Jeremias). Göttingen: Vandenhoeck & Ruprecht, 1970. Pp. 63-79.

0675 M. Eugene Boring, "How May We Identify Oracles of Christian Prophets in the Synoptic Tradition? Mark 3:28, 29 as a Test Case," *JBL* 91/4 (1972): 501-20.

0676 Ernest Best, "An Early Sayings Collection," *NovT* 18/1 (1976): 1-16.

0677 J. C. O'Neill, "The Unforgivable Sin," *JSNT* 19 (1983): 37-42.

0678 Baird Tipson, "A Dark Side of 17th Century English Protestantism: The Sin Against the Holy Spirit," *HTR* 77/3-4 (1984): 301-30.

0679 Byron L. Rohrig, "You Cannot Be Too Bad to Be Forgiven," *CC* 105 (1988): 863.

3:30-5:20

0680 H. E. Klinger, *One Day in the Life of Christ.* Bryn Mawr PA: Dorrance, 1987.

3:30

0681 Francesco Spadafora, "Entusiasmo della folla frenato dagli apostolie proposito energico dei parenti di Gesù (Mc 3,30s)?" *RBib* 4 (1956): 98-113.

3:31-35

0682 Paul Gaechter, "Die 'Brüder' Jesu," *ZKT* 75 (1953): 458-59.

0683 Roger Mercurio, "Some Difficult Marian Passages in the Gospels," *MarSt* 11 (1960): 104-22.

0684 Georgius R. Castellino, "Beata Virgo Maria in Evangelio Marci (Mc 3,31-35)," in *Maria in sacra Scriptura. Acta Congressus mariologicimariani in Republica Dominicana anno 1965 celebrati.* 4: *De Beata Virgine Maria in Evangeliis Synopticis*. Rome: Pontificia Academia mariana internationalis, 1967. 4:519-28.

0685 José Alonso Díaz, "El pasaje evangélico del conflicto de Jésus con sus parientes (Mc 3,20-21,31-35 y par.) en su dimensión mariológica," *Theologica* 4/4 (1969): 425-36.

0686 Ekkart Sauser, "Ungewohnte Väterilussagen über Maria," *TTZ* 79 (1970): 306-13.

0687 Guy Lafon, "Qui est dedans? Qui est dehors? Une lecture de Marc 3,31-35," *Chr* 21 (1974): 41-47.

0688 Ernest Best, "Mark 3:20, 21, 31-35," *NTS* 22/3 (1975-1976): 309-19.

0689 Martin Avanzo, "María en las primeras tradiciones evangelicas," *RevB* 38 (1976): 49-57.

0690 Bertrand Buby, "A Christology of Relationship in Mark," *BTB* 10/4 (1980): 149-54.

0691 Angelo Lancellotti, "La Casa Pietro a Cafarnao nel Vangeli Sinottici: Redazione e Tradizione," *Ant* 58/1 (1983): 48-69.

0692 Robert W. Funk, "From Parable to Gospel: Domesticating the Tradition," *Forum* 1/3 (1985): 3-24.

0693 Enzo Bianchi, "La nuova famiglia di Gesù," *ParSpirV* 14 (1986): 179-92.

0694 Detlev Dormeyer, "Dialogue with the Text: Interactional Bible Interpretation," *ScrSA* 33 (1990): 55-64.

0695 Robert Schlarb, "Die Suche nach dem Messias: ζητέω als Terminus technicus der markinischen Messianologie," *ZNW* 81 (1990): 155-70.

0696 M. H. Smith, "Kinship Is Relative: Mark 3:31-35 and Parallels," *Forum* 6 (1990): 80-94.

0697 Meinrad Limbeck, "Hindernisse fürs Christein: Zur Verkündigung des Markusevangeliums," *BL* 64 (1991): 164-68.

<u>3:33-35</u>

0698 Josef Blinzler, "Jesus und seine Mutter nach dem Zeugnis der Evangelien: Das Wort über die wahren Verwandten," *Klerusblatt* 47 (1967): 144-75.

<u>3:33</u>

0699 M. Philip Scott, "Chiastic Structure: A Key to the Interpretation of Mark's Gospel," *BTB* 15 (1985): 17-26.

<u>3:34-35</u>

0700 George Howard, "Harmonistic Readings in the Old Syriac Gospels," *HTR* 73 (1980): 473-91.

<u>3:34</u>

0701 Anselm Schulz, *Nachfolgen und Nachahmen: Studien über das Verhältnis der neutestamentlichen Jüngerschaft zur urchristlichen Vorbildethik*. Münich: Kösel, 1962.

<u>4:1-8:26</u>

0702 Norman R. Petersen, "The Composition of Mark 4:1-8:26," *HTR* 73 (1980): 185-217.

<u>4:1-34</u>

0703 D. W. Riddle, "Mark 4:1-34: The Evolution of a Gospel Source," *JBL* 56 (1937): 77-90.

0704 Ernst Percy, "Liknelseteorien i Mark 4,11f och kompositionen av Mark 4,1-34," in *Professor Johannes Lindblom: på hans 65-årsdag den 7 juni 1947*. Uppsala: Wretmans, 1948. Pp. 242-62.

0705 C. H. Cave, "The Parables and the Scriptures," *NTS* 11 (1964-1965): 374-87.

0706 Eduard Lohse, "Die Gottesherrschatt in den Gleichnissen Jesu," *EvT* 18 (1958): 145-57.

0707 George H. Boobyer, "The Redaction of Mark 4:1-34," *NTS* 8 (1961-1962): 59-70.

0708 Birger Gerhardsson, "The Parable of the Sower and Its Interpretation," *NTS* 14 (1967-1968): 165-93.

0709 David Wenham, "The Synoptic Problem Revisited: Some New Suggestions about the Composition of Mark 4:1-34," *TynB* 23 (1972): 3-38.

0710 James C. Little, "Redaction Criticism and the Gospel of Mark with Special Reference to Mark 4:1-34," doctoral dissertation, Duke University, Durham NC, 1973.

0711 Sigfred Pedersen, "Is Mark 4,1-34 a Parable Chapter?" in Elizabeth A. Livingstone, ed., *StudE* 6 (1973): 408-16.

0712 R. P. Merendino, "Gleichnisrede und Wortliturgie. Zu Mk 4,1-34," *AL* 16 (1974): 7-31.

0713 R. P. Merendino, "Ohne Gleichnisse redete er nicht zu Ihnen (Zu Mk 4.1-34)," in L. Alvarez Verdes and E. J. Alonso Hernandez, eds., *Homenaie a Juan Prado: miscelánea de estudios bíblicos y hebraicos*. Madrid: Consejo Superior de Investigaciones Cientificas, 1975. Pp. 341-71.

0714 Diego A. Losada, "Las parábolas de crecimiento en el evangelio de Marcos," *RevB* 38 (1976): 113-25.

0715 Madeleine I. Boucher, *The Mysterious Parable. A Literary Study*. CBQMS #6. Washington DC: Catholic Biblical Association, 1977.

0716 Gerhard Sellen, "Allegorie und 'Gleichnis': Zur Formenlehre der synoptischen Gleichnisse," *ZTK* 75 (1978): 281-335.

0717 Vittorio Fusco, *Parola e regno: La sezione delle parabole (Mc. 4.1-34) nella prospettiva marciana*. Aloisiana 13. Brescia: Morcelliana, 1980.

0718 C. C. Marcheselli, "Le parabole del vangelo di Marco," *RBib* 29 (1981): 405-15.

0719 Gerhard Sellin, ''Textlinguistische und Semiotische Erwagungen zu Mk. 4:1-34,'' *NTS* 29/4 (1983): 508-30.

0720 Klaus Berger, *Einführung in die Formgeschichte*. Tübingen: Francke, 1987.

0721 John R. Donahue, ''The Parables in Mark,'' in *The Gospel in Parable: Metaphor, Narrative, and Theology in the Synoptic Gospels*. Philadelphia: Fortress Press, 1988. Pp. 28-62.

0722 Eugene A. LaVerdiere, ''Teaching in Parables,'' *Emmanuel* 94 (1988): 439-45, 453.

0723 Christopher M. Tuckett, ''Mark's Concerns in the Parables Chapter (Mark 4,1-34),'' *Bib* 69/1 (1988): 1-26.

0724 Paul Beauchamp, ''Paraboles de Jésus, vie de Jésus: L'encadrement évangélique et scripturaire des paraboles,'' in J. Delorme, ed., *Les paraboles évangéliques: perspectives nouvelles*. Paris: Cerf, 1989. Pp. 151-70.

0725 Greg Fay, ''Introduction to Incomprehension: The Literary Structure of Mark 4:1-34,'' *CBQ* 51/1 (1989): 65-81.

0726 Vittorio Fusco, ''Mc 4,1-34: la section des paraboles,'' in Jean Delorme, ed., *Les paraboles évangéliques: perspectives nouvelles*. Paris: Cerf, 1989. Pp. 219-34.

0727 Jean-Claude Giroud, ''La parabole ou l'opacité incontournable: a propos de Mc 4,1-34,'' in Jean Delorme, ed., *Les paraboles évangéliques: perspectives nouvelles*. Paris: Cerf, 1989. Pp. 235-46.

0728 Gerhard Dautzenberg, ''Mk 4:1-34 als Belehrung über das Reich Gottes: Beobachtungen zum Gleichniskapitel,'' *BZ* 34/1 (1990): 38-62.

0729 Philip H. Sellew, ''Oral and Written Sources in Mark 4:1-34,'' *NTS* 36 (1990): 234-67.

0730 Fritzleo Lentzen-Deis, ''Handlungsorientierte Exegese der 'Wachstums-Gleichnisse' in Mk 4,1-34: pragmalinguistische Aspekte bei der Auslegung fiktionaler Texte,'' in Johannes

Degenhardt, *Die Freude an Gott: Unsere Kraft* (festschrift for Otto B. Knoch). Stuttgart: Verlag Katholisches Bibelwerk, 1991. Pp. 117-34.

4:1-20

0731 Max A. Chevalier, ''Notes bibliques de prédication pour les dimanches après l'Epiphanie,'' *VerbC* 14 (1960): 369-76.

0732 M. Gertner, ''Midrashim in the New Testament,'' *JSS* 7 (1962): 267-92.

0733 Elizabeth A. Bogert, ''The Parable and the Greenhouse: Mark 4:1-20,'' *HartQ* 4 (1964): 61-64.

0734 Charles C. McDonald, ''The Relevance of the Parable of the Sower,'' *BibTo* 26 (1966): 1822-27.

0735 Eduard Schweizer, ''Du texte à la prédication. Marc 4:1-20,'' *ÉTR* 43 (1968): 256-64.

0736 Marcel Didier, ''La parabole du semeur,'' in *Au service de la parole de Dieu* (festschrift for André-Marie Charue). Gembloux: Éditions J. Duculot, 1969. Pp. 21-41.

0737 C. F. D. Moule, ''Mark 4:1-20 Yet Once More,'' in E. Earle Ellis and Max Wilcox, eds., *Neotestamentica et Semitica* (festschrift for Matthew Black). Edinburgh: T. & T. Clark, 1969. Pp. 95-113.

0738 T. K. Seim, ''Apostolat og forkynnelse. En studie til Mk. 4.1-20,'' *DTT* 35 (1969): 206-22.

0739 Christian Dietzfelbinger, ''Das Gleichnis vom ausgestreuten Samen,'' in Eduard Lohse, ed., *Der Ruf Jesu und die Antwort der Gemeinde: Exegetische Untersuchungen* (festschrift for Joachim Jeremias). Göttingen: Vandenhoeck & Ruprecht, 1970. Pp. 80-93.

0740 John Drury, ''The Sower, the Vineyard, and the Place of Allegory in the Interpretation of Mark's Parables,'' *JTS* 24/2 (1973): 367-79.

0741 John W. Bowker, ''Mystery and Parable: Mark 4:1-20,'' *JTS* 25/2 (1974): 301-17.

0742 Eduard Schweizer, "From the New Testament Text to the Sermon. Mk 4:1-20," *RevExp* 72 (1975): 181-88.

0743 Eugene E. Lemcio, "External Evidence for the Structure and Function of Mark IV.1-20, VII.14-23, and VIII.14-21," *JTS* 29/2 (1978): 323-38.

0744 Craig A. Evans, "On the Isaianic Background of the Parable of the Sower," *CBQ* 47/3 (1985): 464-68.

0745 James R. Edwards, "Markan Sandwiches: The Significance of Interpolations in Markan Narratives," *NovT* 31 (1989): 193-216.

0746 Michael Stahl, "Vom Verstehen des Neuen Testaments in der einen Welt," *ZMiss* 16/4 (1990): 224-35.

4:1-9

0747 John Horman, "The Source of the Version of the Parable of the Sower in the Gospel of Thomas," *NovT* 21/4 (1979): 326-43.

0748 Ingo Baldermann, "Engagement und Verstehen: Politische Erfahrungen als Schlüssel zu biblischen Texten," *EvErz* 36 (1984): 147-157.

0749 Ingo Baldermann, "Hoffnung gegen die Gewalt: Das Gleichnis vom viererlei Acker," *KatB* 110 (1985): 862-65.

0750 Bernard B. Scott, *Hear Then the Parable: A Commentary on the Parables of Jesus*. Minneapolis: Fortress Press, 1989.

0751 Patrick J. Hartin, "Disseminating the Word: A Deconstructive Reading of Mark 4:1-9 and Mark 4:13-20," in Patrick J. Hartin and J. H. Petzer, eds., *Text and Interpretation: New Approaches in the Criticism of the New Testament*. Leiden: Brill, 1991. Pp. 187-200.

4:3-20

0752 I. Howard Marshall, "Tradition and Theology in Luke 8:5-15," *TynB* 20 (1969): 56-75.

4:3-9

0753 Augustin George, "Le sens de la parabole des semailles (Mc 4,3-9 et parallèles)," in J. Coppens, et al., eds., *Sacra Pagina. Miscellanea biblica Congressus Internationalis Catholici de re Biblica*. Paris: J. Gabalda, 1959. Pp. 163-69.

0754 Johannes Herz, "Die Gleichnisse der Evangelien Matthaus, Markus und Lukas in ihrer geschichtlichen Überlieferung und ihrem religiös-sittlichen Inhalt," in E.-H. Amberg and U. Kühn, eds., *Bekenntnis zur Kirche* (festschrift for Ernst Sommerlath). Berlin: Evangelische Verlagsanstalt, 1960. Pp. 52-93.

0755 Francis J. McCool, "The Preacher and the Historical Witness of the Gospels," *TS* 21 (1960): 517-43.

0756 C. H. Dodd, *The Parables of the Kingdom*. Rev. ed. London: Nisbet, 1961.

0757 Domenico Ellena, "Thematische Analyse der Wachstumsgleichnisse," *LB* 23/24 (1973): 48-62.

0758 Rudolf Bultmann, "Die Interpretation von Mk 4,3-9 seit Jülicher," in E. Earle Ellis and Erich Grässer, eds., *Jesus und Paulus* (festschrift for Werner Georg Kümmel). Göttingen: Vandenhoeck & Ruprecht, 1975. Pp. 30-34.

0759 H.-J. Geischer, "Verschwenderische Güte. Versuch über Markus 4,3-9," *EvT* 38 (1978): 418-27.

0760 Madeleine I. Boucher, *The Parables*. Wilmington DE: Glazier, 1981.

0761 Paul Garnet, "The Parable of the Sower: How the Multitudes Understood It," in Edward J. Furcha, ed., *Spirit within Structure* (festschrift for George Johnston). Allison Park PA: Pickwick, 1983. Pp. 39-54.

0762 Helmut Koester, "Three Thomas Parables," in A. H. B. Logan and A. J. M. Wedderburn, eds., *The New Testament and Gnosis* (festschrift for Robert McL. Wilson). Edinburgh: T. & T. Clark, 1983. Pp. 195-203.

0763 Gerhard Lohfink, ''Die Metaphorik der Aussaat im Gleichnis vom Sämann,'' in Françios Refoulé, ed., *À cause de l'Evangile: Études sur les synoptiques et les Actes* (festschrift for Jacques Dupont). Paris: Cerf, 1985. Pp. 211-28.

0764 Gerhard Lohfink, ''Das Gleichnis vom Sämann: Mk 4,3-9,'' *BZ* 30/1 (1986): 36-69.

0765 Gerhard Lohfink, ''Die Not der Exegese mit der Reich-Gottes-Verkündigung Jesu,'' *TQ* 168 (1988): 1-15.

4:3-8

0766 William Neil, ''Expounding the Parables: II. The Sower (Mark 4:3-8),'' *ET* 77 (1965-1966): 74-77.

0767 Joachim Jeremias, ''Palästinakundliches zum Gleichnis vom Säemann (Mark. IV.3-8 Par.),'' *NTS* 13 (1966-1967): 48-53.

0768 Ferdinand Hahn, ''Das Gleichnis von der ausgestreuten Saat und seine Deutung (Mk iv.3-8, 14-20),'' in Ernest Best and R. McL. Wilson, eds., *Text and Interpretation* (festschrift for Matthew Black). New York: Cambridge University Press, 1979. Pp. 133-42.

0769 Ulrich Busse, ''Der verrückte Bauer: Mk 4,3-8—Gotteserfahrung in der Jesustradition,'' *K* 29 (1987): 166-75.

0770 Sigfred Pedersen, ''Die Gotteserfahrung bei Jesus,'' *StTheol* 41 (1987): 127-56.

4:3

0771 John Thorley, ''Aktionsart in New Testament Greek: Infinitive and Imperative,'' *NovT* 31 (1989): 290-315.

4:4-7

0772 José O'Callaghan, ''Dos vartantes en la parábola del sembrador,'' *EB* 48 (1990): 267-70.

4:4

0773 Nigel Turner, ''The Minor Verbal Agreements of Mt. and Lk. against Mk.,'' *StudE* 1 (1959): 223-34.

0774 H.-W. Bartsch, "Das Thomas-Evangelium und die synoptischen Evangelien. Zu G. Quispel's Bemerkungen zum Thomas-Evangelium," *NTS* 6 (1959-1960): 249-61.

0775 J. A. L. Lee, "Some Features of the Speech of Jesus in Mark's Gospel," *NovT* 27 (1985): 1-26.

4:5-6

0776 Michal Wojciechowski, "Une autre division de Mc 4:5-6," *BibN* 28 (1985): 38.

4:6

0777 Harald Sahlin, "Emendationsvorschläge zum griechischen Text des Neuen Testaments I," *NovT* 24 (1982): 160-79.

4:7

0778 José O'Callaghan, "La Variante 'Ahogaron' en Mt 13,7," *Bib* 68/3 (1987): 402-403.

4:8-26

0779 John Hargreaves, *Guide to the Parables*. 2nd ed. London: SPCK, 1970.

4:9

0780 Eric F. F. Bishop, "Ἀκούειν ἀκουέτω: Mark 4:9, 23," *BT* 7 (1956): 38-40.

0781 Clemens Roggenbuck, "Mk 4:9: eine Weck-Formel?" *BibN* 3 (1977): 27-32.

0782 F. Gerald Downing, " 'Ears to Hear'," in Anthony E. Harvey, ed., *Alternative Approaches to New Testament Study*. London: SPCK, 1985. Pp. 97-121.

4:10-13

0783 William R. Myers, "Disciples, Outsiders, and the Secret of the Kingdom: Interpreting Mark 4:10-13," doctoral dissertation, McGill University, Montreal, 1961.

4:10-12

0784 William Manson, "The Purpose of the Parables: A Re-Examination of St. Mark 4:10-12," *ET* 68 (1956-1957): 132-35.

0785 E. F. Siegman, "Teaching in Parables (Mk 4,10-12; Lk 8,9-10; Mt 13,10-15)," *CBQ* 23 (1961): 161-81.

0786 John Coutts, " 'Those Outside' (Mk 4:10-12)," *StudE* 2 (1964): 155-57.

0787 G. V. Jones, *The Art and Truth of the Parables: A Study in their Literary Form and Modern Interpretation.* London: SPCK, 1964. Pp. 225-30.

0788 Ingeborg Gottschalk, "Die evangelische Parabeltheorie: Markus 4,10-12," in C. Bourbeck, ed., *Gleichnisse aus Altem und Neuem Testament.* Stuttgart: Klotz, 1971. Pp. 120-25.

0789 Peter Lampe, "Die markinische Deutung des Gleichnisses vom Samann Markus 4:10-12," *ZNW* 65 (1974): 140-50.

0790 K. H. Schelkle, "Der Zweck der Gleichnisreden (Mk 4,10-12)," in Joachim Gnilka, ed., *Neues Testament und Kirche* (festschrift for Rudolf Schnackenburg). Freiburg: Herder, 1974. Pp. 71-75.

0791 Léopold Sabourin, "The Parables of the Kingdom," *BTB* 6 (1976): 115-60.

0792 J. R. Kirkland, "The Earliest Understanding of Jesus' Use of Parables: Mark 4:10-12 in Context," *NovT* 19/1 (1977): 1-21.

0793 F. C. Synge, "A Plea for the Outsiders: Commentary on Mark 4,10-12," *JTSA* 30 (1980): 53-58.

0794 G. K. Falusi, "Jesus' Use of Parables in Mark with Special Reference to Mark 4:10-12," *IJT* 31 (1982): 35-46.

0795 Perry V. Kea, "Perceiving the Mystery: Encountering the Reticence of Mark's Gospel," *EGLMBS* 4 (1984): 181-94.

0796 Joel Marcus, "Mark 4:10-12 and Markan Epistemology," *JBL* 103/4 (1984): 557-74.

0797 Vincent Parkin, "Mark Chapter 4:10-12: An Exegesis," *IBS* 8 (1986): 179-82.

0798 S. Goan, "To See or Not to See. . . Mark 4:10-12 Revisited," *MillSt* 25 (1990): 5-18.

0799 Michael D. Goulder, "Those Outside (Mark 4:10-12)," *NovT* 33 (1991): 289-302.

0800 Chris L. Mearns, "Parables, Secrecy and Eschatology in Mark's Gospel," *SJT* 44 (1991): 423-42.

<u>4:10-11</u>

0801 Angelo Lancellotti, "La Casa Pietro a Cafarnao nel Vangeli Sinottici: Redazione e Tradizione," *Ant* 58/1 (1983): 48-69.

<u>4:10</u>

0802 Peter H. Igarashi, "The Mystery of the Kingdom (Mark 4:10ff.)," *JBR* 24 (1956): 83-89.

0803 Anselm Schulz, *Nachfolgen und Nachahmen: Studien über das Verhältnis der neutestamentlichen Jüngerschaft zur urchristlichen Vorbildethik.* Münich: Kösel, 1962.

0804 Robert P. Meye, "Mark 4:10: 'Those about Him with the Twelve'," *StudE* 2 (1964): 211-18.

0805 D. E. Dozzi, "Chi sono 'Quelli attorno a Lui' di Mc 4,10?" *Marianum* 36 (1974): 153-83.

0806 Ernest Best, "Mark's Use of the Twelve," *ZNW* 69/1-2 (1978): 11-35.

0807 Philippe Rolland, "L'arrière-lond sémitique des évangiles synoptiques," *ETL* 60 (1984): 358-62.

<u>4:11-12</u>

0808 Günter Haufe, "Erwägungen zum Ursprung der sogenannten Parabeltheorie Markus 4,11-12," *EvT* 32 (1972): 413-21.

0809 Michel Hubaut, "Le 'mystère' révélé dans les paraboles (Mc 4,11-12)," *RTL* 5 (1974): 454-61.

0810 Mary Ann Beavis, *Mark's Audience: The Literary and Social Setting of Mark 4.11-12*. Sheffield: JSOT Press, 1989.

0811 Gerhard Sellin, "Einige symbolische und esoterische Züge im Markus-Evangelium," in Dietrich-Alex Koch, et al., eds., *Jesu Rede von Gott und ihre Nachgeschichte im frühen Christentum* (festschrift for Willi Marxsen). Gütersloh: Gütersloher Verlag, 1989. Pp. 74-90.

0812 J. M. Casciaro Ramírez, "Parábola, hipérbola y mashal en los sinópticos," *ScripT* 25 (1993): 15-31.

4:11

0813 Ernst Percy, "Liknelseteorien i Mark 4,11f och kompositionen av Mark 4,1-34," in *Professor Johannes Lindblom: på hans 65-årsdag den 7 juni 1947*. Uppsala: Wretmans, 1948. Pp. 242-62.

0814 W. von Loewenich, "Luther und die Gleichnistheorie von Mc 4,11s," *TLZ* 77 (1952): 483-88.

0815 J. Arthur Baird, "A Pragmatic Approach to Parable Exegesis: Some New Evidence on Mark 4:11, 33-34," *JBL* 76 (1957): 201-207.

0816 Béda Rigaux, "Révélation des mystères et perfection à Qumran et dans le Nouveau Testament," *NTS* 4 (1957-1958): 237-62.

0817 Klaus Haacker, "Erwagungen zu Mc IV,11," *NovT* 14/3 (1972): 219-25.

0818 Schuyler Brown, "The Secret of the Kingdom of God," *JBL* 92/1 (1973): 60-74.

0819 Rudolph Obermüller, "Hablar de la revelación según el Nuevo Testamento: Un estudio terminológico," *RevB* 39 (1977): 117-27.

0820 Vittorio Fusco, "L'accord mineur Mt 13,11a / Lc 8,10a contre Mc 4,11a," in Joël Delobel, ed., *Logia: Les Paroles de Jésus* (festschrift for Joseph Coppens). BETL #59. Louvain: Peeters Press, 1982. Pp. 355-61.

0821 Robert Hill, "Synoptic 'basileia' and Pauline 'mysterion'," *EB* 45/3-4 (1987): 309-24.

4:12

0822 A. Soldatelli, "Ne quando convertantur, Mc 4,12," *PalCl* 34 (1955): 534-43.

0823 C. H. Peisker, "Konsekutives ἵνα in Markus 4:12," *ZNW* 59 (1968): 126-27.

0824 C. A. Moore, "Mark 4:12: More Like the Irony of Micaiah than Isaiah," in Howard N. Bream, Ralph D. Heim, and Carey A. Moore, eds., *A Light unto My Path: Old Testament Studies in Honor of Jacob M. Meyers*. Gettysburg Theological Studies IV. Philadelphia: Temple University Press, 1974. Pp. 335-44.

0825 Craig A. Evans, "A Note on the Function of Isaiah, vi,9-10 in Mark, iv," *RB* 88 (1981): 234-35.

0826 Kazimierz Romaniuk, "Exégèse du Noveau Testament et Ponctuation," *NovT* 23/3 (1981): 195-209.

0827 Michal Wojciechowski, "Sur hina dans Mc 4:12 [trad de subjonctif]," *BibN* 28 (1985): 36-37.

4:13-20

0828 Félix Casá, "Parabolas y catequesis," *RevB* 38 (1976): 97-111.

0829 Paul Garnet, "The Parable of the Sower: How the Multitudes Understood It," in Edward J. Furcha, ed., *Spirit within Structure* (festschrift for George Johnston). Allison Park PA: Pickwick, 1983. Pp. 39-54.

0830 Patrick J. Hartin, "Disseminating the Word: A Deconstructive Reading of Mark 4:1-9 and Mark 4:13-20," in Patrick J. Hartin and J. H. Petzer, eds., *Text and Interpretation: New Approaches in the Criticism of the New Testament*. Leiden: Brill, 1991. Pp. 187-200.

0831 Meinrad Limbeck, "Hindernisse fürs Christein: Zur Verkündigung des Markusevangeliums," *BL* 64 (1991): 164-68.

4:13

0832 Juan Mateos, ''Algunas notas sobre el Evangelio de Marcos (part 1,'' *FilN* 3 (1989): 197-204

0833 Juan Mateos, ''Algunas notas sobre el Evangelio de Marcos (part 2),'' *FilN* 3 (1990): 159-66.

4:14-20

0834 Francis J. McCool, "The Preacher and the Historical Witness of the Gospels,'' *TS* 21 (1960): 517-43.

0835 Joachim Gnilka, ''Das Christusbild einer alten Passionsgeschichte,'' in *Jesus Christus nach frühen Zeugnissen des Glaubens*. Münich: Kösel, 1970. Pp. 95-110.

0836 Ferdinand Hahn, ''Das Gleichnis von der ausgestreuten Saat und seine Deutung (Mk iv.3-8, 14-20),'' in Ernest Best and R. McL. Wilson, eds., *Text and Interpretation: Studies in the New Testament Presented to Matthew Black*. New York/London: Cambridge University Press, 1979. Pp. 133-42.

4:15

0837 Herman Ljungvik, ''Översättningsförslag och språkliga förklingar till skilde ställen i Nya Testamentet,'' *SEÅ* 30 (1965): 102-20.

0838 Harald Sahlin, ''Emendationsvorschläge zum griechischen Text des Neuen Testaments I,'' *NovT* 24 (1982): 160-79.

4:17-19

0839 John A. McGuckin, ''The Vine and the Elm Tree: The Patristic Interpretation of Jesus' Teachings on Wealth,'' in W. J. Sheils and Diana Wood, eds., *The Church and Wealth*. New York: Blackwell, 1986. Pp. 1-14.

4:18-19

0840 Hans Kosmala, ''The Three Nets of Belial: A Study in the Terminology of Qumran and the New Testament,'' *ASTI* 4 (1965): 91-113.

4:19-20

0841 Nigel Turner, ''The Minor Verbal Agreements of Mt. and Lk. against Mk.,'' *StudE* 1 (1959): 223-34.

4:21-25

0842 Ernest Best, "Mark's Preservation of the Tradition," in M. Sabbe, ed., *L'évangile selon Marc: Tradition et rédaction*. BETL #34. Gembloux/Louvain: Duculot/Louvain University, 1974. Pp. 21-34.

0843 Jacques Dupont, "La transmission des paroles de Jésus sur la lampe et la mesure dans Marc 4,21-25 et dans la tradition Q," in Joël Delobel, ed., *Logia: Les Paroles de Jésus* (festschrift for Joseph Coppens). BETL #59. Louvain: Peeters Press, 1982. Pp. 201-36.

4:21

0844 J. M. Bover, " 'Nada hay encubierto que no se descubra' (Mc 4,21 par)," *EB* 13 (1954): 319-23.

0845 W. G. Essame, "Καὶ ἔλεγεν in Mark 4:21, 24, 26, 30," *ET* 77 (1965-1966): 121.

0846 J. Duncan M. Derrett, "The Lamp which Must Not be Hidden (Mc iv.21)," in J. Duncan M. Derrett, *Law in the New Testament*. London: Darton, Longman & Todd, 1970. Pp. 189-207.

0847 Gerhard Schneider, "Das Bildwort von der Lampe. Zur Traditionsgeschichte eines Jesus-Wortes," *ZNW* 61 (1970): 183-209.

4:22-24

0848 José O'Callaghan, "Posible identificación de P^{44} C *recto* b como Mc 4,22-24," *Bib* 52 (1971): 398-400.

4:23

0849 Eric F. F. Bishop, "Ἀκούειν ἀκουέτω: Mark 4:9, 23," *BT* 7 (1956): 38-40.

4:24-34

0850 A. Marcello Buscemi, "La prolessi nel Nuovo Testamento," *SBFLA* 35 (1985): 37-68.

4:24-29

0851 Franz Mussner, "Gleichnisauslegung und Heilsgeschichte. Dargetan am Gleichnis von der wachsenden Saat (Mc 4,24-29)," *TTZ* 64 (1955): 257-66.

0852 Michael McCormick, "Two Leaves from the Lost Uncial Codex 0167: Mark 4:24-29 and 4:37-41," *ZNW* 70/3-4 (1979): 238-42.

4:24-25

0853 Howard A. Hatton, "Unraveling the Agents and Events," *BT* 37/4 (1986): 417-20.

0854 Pieter J. Maartens, "Sign and 'Significance' in the Theory and Practice of Ongoing Literary Critical Interpretation with Reference to Mark 4:24 and 25: A Study of Semiotic Relations in the Text," in Patrick J. Hartin and J. H. Petzer, eds., *Text and Interpretation: New Approaches in the Criticism of the New Testament*. Leiden: Brill, 1991. Pp. 63-81.

4:24

0855 Léon Vaganay, "Existe-t-il chez Marc quelques traces du Sermon sur la Montagne?" *NTS* 1 (1954-1955): 193-200.

0856 Jan W. Doeve, "Le rôle de la tradition orale dans la composition des Évangiles synoptiques," in J. Heuschen, *La formation des évangiles: Problème synoptique et Formgeschichte*. Paris: Desclée, 1957. Pp. 70-84.

0857 W. G. Essame, "**Καὶ ἔλεγεν** in Mark 4:21, 24, 26, 30," *ET* 77 (1965-1966): 121.

0858 Hans P. Rüger, " 'Mit welchem Mass ihr meßt, wird euch gemessen werden'," *ZNW* 6 (1969): 174-82.

0859 Johannes B. Bauer, "Et Adicietur Vobis Credentibus Mark 4,24f.," *ZNW* 71/3-4 (1980): 248-51.

0860 Carlo Buzzetti, "Parallels in the Synoptic Gospels: A Case Study," *BT* 34 (1984): 425-31.

4:25

0861 Paul Glaube, "Einige Stellen, die Bedeutung des Codex D charakterisieren," *NovT* 2 (1957-1958): 310-15.

0862 Juan Mateos, "Algunas notas sobre el Evangelio de Marcos," *FilN* 3 (1990): 159-66.

4:26-34

0863 Jacques Dupont, "Deux paraboles du Royaume. Mc 4,26-34," *AsSeign* 2/42 (1970): 50-59.

4:26-32

0864 Nils A. Dahl, "Parables of Growth," *StTheol* 5 (1951): 132-66.

0865 Johannes Herz, "Die Gleichnisse der Evangelien Matthaus, Markus und Lukas in ihrer geschichtlichen Überlieferung und ihrem religiös-sittlichen Inhalt," in E.-H. Amberg and U. Kühn, eds., *Bekenntnis zur Kirche* (festschrift for Ernst Sommerlath). Berlin: Evangelische Verlagsanstalt, 1960. Pp. 52-93.

0866 Bernard B. Scott, *Jesus, Symbol-Maker for the Kingdom.* Philadelphia: Fortress Press, 1981.

4:26-30

0867 Bernard B. Scott, *Hear Then the Parable: A Commentary on the Parables of Jesus*. Minneapolis: Fortress Press, 1989.

0868 Jacques Dupont, " 'Le royaume des cieux est semblable à . . .'," *BibO* 6 (1964): 247-53.

4:26-29

0869 Heinrich Baltensweiler, "Das Gleichnis von der selbstwachsenden Saat (Markus 4,26-29) und die theologische Konzeption des Markusevangelisten," in Felix Christed, ed., *Oikonomia: Heilsgeschichte als Thema der Theologie. O. Cullmann zum 65. Geburtstag gewidmet.* Hamburg-Bergstedt: Reich, 1967. Pp. 69-75.

0870 Jacques Dupont, "La parabole de la semence qui pousse toute seule (Marc 4,26-29)," *RechSR* 55 (1967): 367-92.

0871 Richard Eckstein, "Die von selbst wachsende Saat. Markus 4,26-29," in C. Bourbeck, ed., *Gleichnisse aus Altem und Neuem Testament*. Stuttgart: Klotz, 1971. Pp. 139-45.

0872 Ingeborg Gottschalk, "Das Gleichnis vom Samann. Markus 4,26-29," in C. Bourbeck, ed., *Gleichnisse aus Altem und Neuem Testament*. Stuttgart: Klotz, 1971. Pp. 125-32.

0873 Rainer Stuhlmann, ''Beobachtungen und Uberlegungen zu Markus IV.26-29,'' *NTS* 19/2 (1972-1973): 153-62.

0874 Domenico Ellena, ''Thematische Analyse der Wachstumsgleichnisse,'' *LB* 23/24 (1973): 48-62.

0875 P.-É. Langevin, ''Les artisans du Royaume: Perspectives des évangiles synoptiques,'' *LTP* 29 (1973): 143-64.

0876 Jacques Dupont, ''Encore la parabole de la Semence, qui pousse toute seule (Mc 4,26-29),'' in E. Earle Ellis and Erich Grauasser, eds., *Jesus und Paulus: Festschrift für Werner Georg Kümmel zum 70. Geburtstag*. Göttingen: Vandenhoeck & Ruprecht, 1975. Pp. 96-108.

0877 Harald Sahlin, ''Zum Verständnis der christologischen Anschauung des Markusevangeliums,'' *StTheol* 31 (1977): 1-19.

0878 Ingo Baldermann, ''Engagement und Verstehen: Politische Erfahrungen als Schlüssel zu biblischen Texten,'' *EvErz* 36 (1984): 147-57.

0879 Otto Betz, ''Jesu Tischsegen: Psalm 104 in Lehre und Wirken Jesu,'' in *Jesus: Der Messias Israels*. Tübingen: Mohr, 1987. Pp. 202-31.

0880 Claude N. Pavur, ''The Grain is Ripe: Parabolic Meaning in Mark 4:26-29,'' *BTB* 17/1 (1987): 21-23.

0881 Ekkehard W. Stegemann, ''Das Gleichnis vom Leben im Aufschub,'' *EvErz* 41 (1989): 375-78.

0882 J. Duncan M. Derrett, ''Ambivalence: Sowing and Reaping at Mk 4,26-29,'' *EB* 48 (1990): 489-510.

0883 George Aichele, ''Two Theories of Translation with Examples from the Gospel of Mark,'' *JSNT* 47 (1992): 95-116.

<u>4:26</u>

0884 W. G. Essame, ''**Καὶ ἔλεγεν** in Mark 4:21, 24, 26, 30,'' *ET* 77 (1965-1966): 121.

4:27

0885 C. H. Dodd, "The Sayings," in *Historical Tradition in the Fourth Gospel*. Cambridge: Cambridge University Press, 1963. Pp. 315-405.

4:28

0886 E. J. Vardaman, "The Earliest Fragments of the New Testament," *ET* 83 (1971-1972): 374-76.

0887 Maurice Baillet, "Les manuscrits de la Grotte 7 de Qumrân et le Nouveau Testament," *Bib* 53 (1972): 508-16.

0888 Pierre Benoit, "Note sur les fragments grecs de la grotte 7 de Qumrân," *RB* 79 (1972): 321-24.

0889 Eugene Fisher, "New Testament Documents among the Dead Sea Scrolls?" *BibTo* 61 (1972): 835-41.

0890 Joseph A. Fitzmyer, "A Qumran Fragment of Mark?" *America* (New York) 126 (1972): 647-50.

0891 Lucien Legrand, "The New Testsment at Qumran?" *IndES* 11 (1972): 157-66.

0892 José O'Callaghan, "Notas sobre 7Q tomadas en el 'Rockefeller Museum' de Jerusalén," *Bib* 53 (1972): 517-33.

0893 C. H. Roberts, "On Some Presumed Papyrus Fragments of the New Testament from Qumran," *JTS* 23 (1972): 446-47.

0894 Léopold Sabourin, "A Fragment of Mark at Qumran?" *BTB* 2 (1972): 308-12.

0895 Ernst Vogt, "Entdeckung neutestamentlicher Texte beim Toten Meer?" *Orient* 36 (1972): 138-40.

4:30-32

0896 Otto Kuss, "Zur Senfkorn-Parabel," *TGl* 41 (1951): 40-46.

0897 Ernst Fuchs, "Was wird in der Exegese des Neuen Testaments interpretiert?" *ZTK* 56 (1959): 31-48.

0898 Otto Kuss, "Zum Sinngehalt des Doppelgleichnisses vom Senfkorn und Sauerteig," *Bib* 40 (1959): 641-53.

0899 Franz Mussner, "1QHodajoth und das Gleichnis vom Senfkorn (Mk 4:30-32 Par)," *BZ* 4/1 (1960): 128-30.

0900 C. H. Dodd, *The Parables of the Kingdom*. Rev. ed. London: Nisbet, 1961.

0901 Bernhard Schultze, "Die ekklesioklogische Bedeutung des Gleichnisses vom Senfkorn," *OCP* 27 (1961): 362-86.

0902 Jacques Dupont, "Les paraboles du sénevé et du levain," *NRT* 89 (1967): 897-913.

0903 Ernst Fuchs, *Jesus: Wort und Tat*. Tübingen: Mohr, 1971.

0904 H.-P. Hertzsch, "Jésus herméneute. Une étude de Mc 4,30-32," *FV* 70 (1971): 109-16.

0905 Domenico Ellena, "Thematische Analyse der Wachstumsgleichnisse," *LB* 23/24 (1973): 48-62.

0906 Robert W. Funk, "The Looking-Glass Tree Is for the Birds. Ezekiel 17:22-24; Mark 4:30-32," *Int* 27 (1973): 3-9.

0907 Alberto Casalegno, "La parabola del granello di senape (Mc. 4,30-32)," *RBib* 26 (1978): 139-61.

0908 Olof Linton, "Coordinated Sayings and Parables in the Synoptic Gospels: Analysis versus Theories," *NTS* 26 (1979-1980): 139-63.

0909 Giuseppe Pace, "La senapa del vangelo," *BibO* 22 (1980): 119-23.

0910 John A. Sproule, "The Problem of the Mustard Seed," *GTJ* 1/1 (1980): 37-42.

0911 Richard Bauckham, "The Parable of the Vine: Rediscovering a Lost Parable of Jesus," *NTS* 33/1 (1987): 84-101.

4:30

0912 H.-W. Bartsch, "Eine bisher übersehene Zitierung der LXX in Mark 4,30," *TZ* 15 (1959): 126-28.

0913 W. G. Essame, "**Καὶ ἔλεγεν** in Mark 4:21, 24, 26, 30," *ET* 77 (1965-1966): 121.

4:32

0914 Martin J. Higgins, "New Testament Result Clauses with Infinitive," *CBQ* 23 (1961): 233-41.

4:33-34

0915 J. Arthur Baird, "A Pragmatic Approach to Parable Exegesis: Some New Evidence on Mark 4:11, 33-34," *JBL* 76 (1957): 201-207.

0916 Gerhard Sellin, "Einige symbolische und esoterische Züge im Markus-Evangelium," in Dietrich-Alex Koch, et al., eds., *Jesu Rede von Gott und ihre Nachgeschichte im frühen Christentum* (festschrift for Willi Marxsen). Gütersloh: Gütersloher Verlag, 1989. Pp. 74-90.

4:33

0917 Einar Molland, "Zur Auslegung von Mc 4,33 **καθὼς ἠδύναντο ἀκούειν**," in E. Molland, ed., *Opuscula Patristica*. Oslo: Universitets-förlaget, 1970. Pp. 1-8.

4:35-9:49

0918 Lionel A. Whiston, *Power of a New Life: Relational Studies in Mark*. Waco TX: Word Books, 1976.

4:35-8:30

0919 L. F. Rivera, "La liberación en el éxodo. El éxodo de Marcos y la revelación del líder (4,35-8,30)," *RevB* 33 (1971): 13-26.

4:35-8:26

0920 Paul J. Achtemeier, "Toward the Isolation of Pre-Markan Miracle Catenae," *JBL* 89/3 (1970): 265-91.

0921 Paul J. Achtemeier, "The Origin and Function of the Pre-Marcan Miracle Catenae," *JBL* 91 (1972): 198-221.

0922 Robert P. Meye, "Psalm 107 as 'Horizon' for Interpreting the Miracle Stories of Mark 4:35-8:26," in Robert A. Guelich, ed., *Unity and Diversity in New Testament Theology: Essays in Honor of George E. Ladd.* Grand Rapids: Eerdmans, 1978. Pp. 1-13.

4:35-8:21

0923 Ched Myers, "The Miracle of One Loaf [Mk 4:35-8:21; pt 3 on Gospel of Mark]," *Soj* 16 (1987): 31-34.

4:35-6:6

0924 Walter Schmithals, *Wunder und Glaube. Eine Auslegung von Markus 4,35-6,6a.* Biblische Studien 59. Neukirchen-Vluyn: Neukirchener Verlag, 1970.

4:35-5:43

0925 J. S. Allsop, "The Development of the Gospel Miracle Tradition: With Special Reference to Mark 1.21-3.6; 4.35-5.43; 6.30-8.26," doctoral dissertation, Nottingham University, Nottingham UK, 1978.

0926 K. M. Fisher and W. C. von Wahlde, "The Miracles of Mark 4:35-5:43: Their Meaning and Function in the Gospel Framework," *BTB* 11/1 (1981): 13-16.

0927 Francesco Mosetto, "I miracoli di Gesù prima del vangelo di Marco: 'Chi è costui'?" *PV* 27 (1982): 187-207.

0928 Mark F. S. C. McVann, "Dwelling among the Tombs: Discourse, Discipleship, and the Gospel of Mark 4:35-5:43," doctoral dissertation, Emory University, Atlanta, 1984.

0929 Mark F. S. C. McVann, "Destroying Death: Jesus in Mark and Joseph in 'The Sin Eater'," in Robert Detweiler and W. G. Doty, eds., *The Daemonic Imagination: Biblical Text and Secular Story.* Atlanta: Scholars Press, 1990. Pp. 123-35.

0930 Mark F. S. C. McVann, "Baptism, Miracles, and Boundary Jumping in Mark," *BTB* 21 (1991): 151-57.

4:35-5:20

0931 Eugene A. LaVerdiere, "Journey to the Gentiles," *Emmanuel* 94 (1988): 554-61.

4:35-41

0932 Eric F. F. Bishop, "Jesus and the Lake," *CBQ* 13 (1951): 398-414.

0933 Paul J. Achtemeier, "Person and Deed: Jesus and the Storm-Tossed Sea," *Int* 16 (1962): 169-76.

0934 Gottfried Schille, "Die Seesturmerzählung Markus 4:35-41 als Beispiel neutestamentlicher Aktualisierung," *ZNW* 56 (1965): 30-40.

0935 C. Milo Connick, "Auslegung von Markus 4,35-41 par; Markus 8,31-37 par; Römer 1,3f.," *EvErz* 20 (1968): 249-60.

0936 Ferdinand Staudinger, "Die neutestamentlichen Wunder in der Verkündigung," *ErAu* 44 (1968): 355-66.

0937 Jozef Bulckens, "Het stillen van de storm," *CollM* 54 (1969): 453-71.

0938 Paul Lamarche, "La tempête apaisée," *AsSeign* 43 (1969): 43-53.

0939 T. M. Suriano, " 'Who Then Is This?' . . . Jesus Masters the Sea," *BibTo* 79 (1975): 449-56.

0940 F. C. Synge, "A Matter of Tenses—Fingerprints of an Annotator in Mark," *ET* 88 (1976-1977): 168-71.

0941 Léopold Sabourin, *The Divine Miracles Discussed and Defended.* Rome: Catholic Book Agency, 1977.

0942 Ulrich Ruegg, H. Stotzer-Klos, and M. Voser, "Zum Vertrauen befreit, Jesus mit seinen Jüngern im Sturm (Markus 4,35-41). Ein Rettungswunder," in Anton Steiner, ed., *Wunder Jesu.* Bibelarbeit in der Gemeinde 2. Basel/Zürich: Reinhardt/Benziger, 1978. Pp. 113-26.

0943 B. M. F. van Iersel and A. J. M. Linmans, "The Storm on the Lake, Mk iv,35-41 and Mt viii,18-27 in the Light of Form Criticism, '*Redaktionsgeschichte*' and Structural Analysis," in T. Baarda, A. F. J. Klihn, and W. C. van Unnik, eds., *Miscellanea Neotestamentica*. Novum Testamentum Supplement 48. Leiden: Brill, 1978. 2:17-48.

0944 G. M. Soares Prabhu, "And There Was a Great Calm: A 'Dhvani' Reading of the Stilling of the Storm (Mark 4,35-41)," *BB* 5 (1979): 295-308.

0945 Rudolf Frieling, "Der Weg des Christus," in *Christologische Aufsätze*. Stuttgart: Urachhaus, 1982. Pp. 1-186.

0946 Wolfgang Lipp, "Der rettende Glaube: Eine Untersuchung zu Wundergeschichten im Markusevangelium," doctoral dissertation, University of Marburg, Marburg, 1984.

0947 Gert Lüderitz, "Rhetorik, Poetik, Kompositionstechnik im Markusevangelium," in Hubert Cancik, ed., *Markus-Philologie*. Tübingen: Mohr, 1984. Pp. 165-203.

0948 Craig L. Blomberg, "The Miracles as Parables," in David Wenham and Craig L. Blomberg, eds., *Gospel Perspectives*. Sheffield: JSOT Press, 1986. 6:327-59.

0949 Franz Schnider, "Rettung aus Seenot: Ps 107,23-32 und Mk 4,35-41," in E. Hagg, et al., eds., *Freude an der Weisung des Herrn: Beiträge zur Theologie der Psalmen* (festschrift for Heinrich Groß. Stuttgart: Katholisches Bibelwerk, 1986. Pp. 375-93.

0950 Xavier Alegre, *Los sinópticos hoy*. Madrid: Fundación Santa Maria, 1989.

0951 Albert Fuchs, "Die 'Seesturmperikope' Mk. 4:35-41 par im Wandel der urkirchlichen Verkündigung," *SNTU-A* 15 (1990): 101-33.

0952 Meinrad Limbeck, "Hindernisse fürs Christein: Zur Verkündigung des Markusevangeliums," *BL* 64 (1991): 164-68.

4:35-39

0953 Pamela Thimmes, "The Biblical Sea-Storm Type-Scene: A Proposal," *EGLMBS* 10 (1990): 107-22.

4:36

0954 Philippe Rolland, "L'arrière-lond sémitique des évangiles synoptiques," *ETL* 60 (1984): 358-62.

4:37-41

0955 Michael McCormick, "Two Leaves from the Lost Uncial Codex 0167: Mark 4:24-29 and 4:37-41," *ZNW* 70/3-4 (1979): 238-42.

0956 Victor Bobb, "Asleep in the Storm," *FundJ* 5/3 (1986): 59.

4:37

0957 George D. Kilpatrick, "The Order of Some Noun and Adjective Phrases in the New Testament," *NovT* 5 (1962): 111-14.

4:38

0958 Rainer Riesner, "Das Boot vom See Gennesaret," *BK* 41 (1986): 135-38.

4:39

0959 Lino Cignelli, "La grecità biblica," *SBFLA* 35 (1985): 203-48.

4:40

0960 Johannes B. Bauer, "Procellam cur sedarit Salvator," *VD* 35 (1957): 89-96.

4:41

0961 David A. Black, "Some Dissenting Notes on R. Stein's *The Synoptic Problem* and Markan 'Errors'," *FilN* 1 (1988): 95-101.

5:1-43

0962 Helge K. Nielsen, "Ein Beitrag zur Beurteilung der Tradition über die Heilungstätigkeit," *SNTU-A* 4 (1979): 5-26.

0963 Mark F. S. C. McVann, "Markan Ecclesiology: An Anthropological Experiment," *List* 23/2 (1988): 95-105.

0964 Gail R. O'Day, "Hope beyond Brokenness. A Markan Reflection on the Gift of Life," *CThM* 15 (1988): 244-51.

5:1-21

0965 Tullio Aurelio, "Mistero del regno e unione con Gesù: Mc 5:1-21," *BibO* 19 (1977): 59-68.

5:1-20

0966 T. Hawthorn, "The Gerasene Demoniac: A Diagnosis (Marc 5:1-20 and Luke 8:26-39)," *ET* 66 (1954-1955): 79-80.

0967 J. P. Louw, "De bezetene en de kudde, Marc. 5:1-20. Een hypothese," *NedTT* 13 (1958): 59-61.

0968 Charles Masson, "Le demoniaque de Gerasa," in Charles Masson, *Vers les sources d'eau vive: Études d'exégèse et de théologie du Nouveau Testament.* Lausanne: Payot, 1961. Pp. 20-37.

0969 Harald Sahlin, "Die Perikope vom gerasenischen Besessenen und der Plan des Markusevangeliums," *StTheol* 18 (1964): 159-72.

0970 Christian Hartlich, "Der Besessene von Gerasa (Mk 5:1-20)," *EvErz* 20 (1968): 345-54.

0971 Alfred T. Hennelly, "The Gerasene Perikope (Mk 5:1-20): A Study in Redaction-Criticism," doctoral dissertation, Marquette University, Milwaukee WI, 1968.

0972 Paul Lamarche, "Le possédé de Gérasa," *NRT* 90 (1968): 581-97.

0973 Jan Lambrecht, "Le possédé et le troupeau (Mc 5,1-20)," *RCA* 33 (1968): 557-69.

0974 John Bligh, "The Gerasene Demoniac and the Resurrection of Christ," *CBQ* 31 (1969): 383-90.

0975 Ernest C. Colwell, "Method in the Study of the Gospel Lectionaries," in Ernest C. Colwell, *Studies in Methodology* *in Textual Criticism of the New Testament.* Leiden: Brill, 1969. Pp. 84-95.

0976 Cyrille Argebti, ''A Meditation on Mark 5:1-20,'' *EcumRev* 23 (1971): 398-408.

0977 M. de Mello, ''The Gerasene Demoniac: The Power of Jesus Confronts the Power of Satan,'' *EcumRev* 23 (1971): 409-18.

0978 Rudolf Pesch, ''The Markan Version of the Healing of the Gerasene Demoniac,'' *EcumRev* 23 (1971): 349-76.

0979 Jean Starobinski, ''An Essay in Literary Analysis—Mark 5,1-20,'' *EcumRev* 23 (1971): 377-97.

0980 Karl Gatzweiler, ''La guérison du démoniaque gérasénien,'' *FT* 2 (1972): 460-76.

0981 Franz J. Leenhardt, ''Essai exégétique: Marc 5:1-20,'' in François Bovon, et al., eds., *Analyse structurale et exégèse biblique: Essais d'interprétation.* Neuchâtel: Delachaux et Niestlé, 1972. Pp. 95-121.

0982 Rudolf Pesch, *Der Besessene von Gerasa. Entstehung und Überlieferung einer Wundergeschichte.* Stuttgarter Bibelstudien 56. Stuttgart: Katholisches Bibelwerk, 1972.

0983 Jean Starobinski, ''Le démoniaque de Gérasa. Analyse de Mc 5,1-20,'' in Roland Barthes, et al., eds., *Analyse structurale et exégèse biblique.* Neuchâtel: Delachaux & Niestlé, 1972. Pp. 63-94.

0984 Jean Starobinski, ''The Struggle with Legion: A Literary Analysis of Mark 5:1-20,'' *NLH* 4 (1972): 331-56.

0985 Miguel de Burgos Nuñez, ''El poseso de Gerasa (Mc 5,1-20): Jesús portador de una existencia liberadora,'' *Communio* 6 (1973): 103-18.

0986 Léopold Sabourin, ''The Miracles of Jesus (II). Jesus and the Evil Powers,'' *BTB* 4 (1974): 115-75.

0987 Franz Annen, *Heil für die Heiden: Zur Bedeutung und Geschichte der Tradition vom Besessenen Gerasener (Mk 5.1-20 parr.)*. Frankfurter Theologische Studien 20. Frankfurt: Knecht, 1976.

0988 Jean-Noël Aletti, "Une lecture en questions," in Xavier Léon-Dufour, ed., *Les miracles de Jésus selon le Nouveau Testament*. Paris: Éditions du Seuil, 1977. Pp. 189-208.

0989 Louis Beirnaert, "Approche psychanalytique," in Xavier Léon-Dufour, ed., *Les miracles de Jésus selon le Nouveau Testament*. Paris: Seuil, 1977. Pp. 183-88.

0990 Jean Calloud, et. al., "Essai d'analyse sémiotique," in Xavier Léon-Dufour, ed., *Les miracles de Jésus selon le Nouveau Testament*. Paris: Seuil, 1977. Pp. 151-81.

0991 J. González-Faus, "Jesus y los demonios: Intróducción cristológica a la lucha por la justicia," *EE* 52 (1977): 487-519.

0992 Helmut Harsch, "Psychologische Interpretation biblischer Texte. Ein Versuch zu Mk 5,1-20: Die Heilung des Besessenen von Gerasa," *UnSa* 32 (1977): 39-45.

0993 J. Duncan M. Derrett, "Contributions to the Study of the Gerasene Demoniac," *JSNT* 3 (1979): 2-17.

0994 Sjef van Tilborg, "Het strukturalisme binnen de exegese: een variant van het burgerlijke denken," *Bij* 40 (1979): 364-79.

0995 Georges Casalis, "Jesús, el exorcista," *BibFe* 6 (1980): 28-40.

0996 Pierre Guillemette, "La Forme des Recits d'Exorcisme de Bultmann: Un Dogme a Reconsiderer," *EgT* 11/2 (1980): 177-93.

0997 Ulrich B. Müller, "Zur Rezeption Gesetzes-Kritischer Jesusuberlieferung im Fruhen Christentum," *NTS* 27/2 (1980-1981): 158-85.

0998 Andrea Strus, ''Cristo, Liberatore Dell'Uomo, Nella Catechesi di Pietro, Secondo Mc 5:1-20,'' *Sale* 44/1 (1982): 35-60,

0999 A. J. R. Uleyn, ''Dieptestructuren in het evangeliesatieproces,'' in J. A. van der Ven, ed., *Toekomst voor de kerk* (festschrift for Frans Haarsma). Kampen: Kok, 1985. Pp. 302-16.

1000 A. J. R. Uleyn, ''The Possessed Man of Gerasa: A Psychoanalytic Interpretation of Reader Reactions,'' in J. A. van Belzen and J. M. van der Lars, eds., *Current Issues in Psychology of Religion*. Amsterdam: Rodopi, 1986. Pp. 90-96.

1001 Peter Pimentel, ''The 'Unclean Spirits' of St. Mark's Gospel,'' *ET* 99 (1987-1988): 173-75.

1002 D. S. Arnold, ''Hidden Since the Foundation of the World: Girard, Turner and Two Mythic Readings,'' in Robert Detweiler and W. G. Doty, eds., *The Daemonic Imagination: Biblical Text and Secular Story*. Atlanta: Scholars Press, 1990. Pp. 137-48.

1003 M. Burdette, ''Sin Eating and Sin Making: The Power and Limits of Language,'' in Robert Detweiler and W. G. Doty, eds., *The Daemonic Imagination: Biblical Text and Secular Story*. Atlanta: Scholars Press, 1990. Pp. 159-67.

1004 William G. Doty, ''Afterword: Sacred Pigs and Secular Cookies: Mark and Atwood Go Postmodern,'' in Robert Detweiler and W. G. Doty, eds., *The Daemonic Imagination: Biblical Text and Secular Story*. Atlanta: Scholars Press, 1990. Pp. 191-207.

1005 Dorothy Figueira, ''The Redemptive Text,'' in Robert Detweiler and W. G. Doty, eds., *The Daemonic Imagination: Biblical Text and Secular Story*. Atlanta: Scholars Press, 1990. Pp. 149-58.

1006 Ken Frieden, ''The Language of Demonic Possession: A Key-Word Analysis,'' in Robert Detweiler and W. G. Doty, eds., *The Daemonic Imagination: Biblical Text and Secular Story*. Atlanta: Scholars Press, 1990. Pp. 41-52.

1007 René Girard, "The Demons at Gerase," in Robert Detweiler and W. G. Doty, eds., *The Daemonic Imagination: Biblical Text and Secular Story*. Atlanta: Scholars Press, 1990. Pp. 77-98.

1008 David Jasper, "Siding with the Swine: A Moral Problem for Narrative," in Robert Detweiler and William Doty, eds., *The Daemonic Imagination: Biblical Text and Secular Story*. Atlanta: Scholars Press, 1990. Pp. 65-75.

1009 Carol S. LaHurd, "Biblical Exorcism and Reader Response to Ritual in Narrative," in Robert Detweiler and W. G. Doty, eds., *The Daemonic Imagination: Biblical Text and Secular Story*. Atlanta: Scholars Press, 1990. Pp. 53-63. Cf. *BTB* 20 (1990): 154-60.

1010 Carol S. LaHurd, "Reader Response to Ritual Elements in Mark 5:1-20," *BTB* 20 (1990): 154-60.

1011 A.-J. Morey, "The Old In/Out," in Robert Detweiler and W. G. Doty, eds., *The Daemonic Imagination: Biblical Text and Secular Story*. Atlanta: Scholars Press, 1990. Pp. 169-79.

1012 Gregory Murray, "Five Gospel Miracles," *DR* 108 (1990): 79-90.

5:1-12

1013 Alois Stöger, "Sohn Gottes im Markusevangelium (II). Meditation (Mk 3,7-12; 5,1-12)," *BL* 49 (1976): 112-15.

5:1-3

1014 Zan Holmes, "Getting It All Together," *PJ* 38 (1985): 56-59.

5:1

1015 Tjitze J. Baarda, "Gadarenes, Gerasenes, Gergesenes and the 'Diatessaron' Traditions," in E. Earle Ellis and M. Wilcox, eds., *Neotestamentica et Semitica* (festschrift for Matthew Black). Edinburgh: T. & T. Clark, 1969. Pp. 181-97.

5:2-20

1016 Juan Mateos, ''Términos relacionados con 'Légion' en Mc 5:2-20,'' *FilN* 1 (1988): 211-16.

5:7-8

1017 Rámon Trevijano Etcheverría, ''El trasfondo apocalípticode Mc. 1,24.25; 5,7.8 y par.,'' *Bur* 11 (1970): 117-33.

1018 David A. Black, ''Some Dissenting Notes on R. Stein's *The Synoptic Problem* and Markan 'Errors',' *FilN* 1 (1988): 95-101.

5:7

1019 T. A. Burkill, ''Concerning Mark 5:7 and 5:18-20,'' *StTheol* 11 (1957): 159-66.

1020 Otto Bächli, '' 'Was habe ich mit dir zu schaffen?' Eine formelhafte Frage im Alten Testament und Neuen Testament,'' *TZ* 33 (1977): 69-80.

5:10

1021 Günther Schwarz, '' 'Aus der Gegend' (Markus v.10),'' *NTS* 22 (1975-1976): 214-15.

5:13

1022 Kamila Blessing, ''Call not Unclean: The Pigs in the Story of the Legion of Demons,'' *EGLMBS* 10 (1990): 92-106.

5:16-40

1023 J. Harold Greenlee, *Nine Uncial Palimpsests of the Greek New Testament.* Salt Lake City: University of Utah, 1968.

5:18-20

1024 T. A. Burkill, ''Concerning Mark 5:7 and 5:18-20,'' *StTheol* 11 (1957): 159-66.

5:20

1025 S. Thomas Parker, ''The Decapolis Reviewed,'' *JBL* 94 (1975): 437-41.

5:21-43

1026 C. H. Dodd, "The Sayings," in *Historical Tradition in the Fourth Gospel*. Cambridge: Cambridge University Press, 1963. Pp. 315-405.

1027 Willi Marxsen, "Bibelarbeit über Mk 5,21-43 / Mt 9,18-26," in *Der Exeget als Theologe: Vorträge zum Neuen Testament*. Gütersloh: Mohn, 1968. Pp. 171-82.

1028 Alfred Suhl, *Die Wunder Jesu: Ereignis und Überlieferung*. Gütersloh: Mohn, 1968.

1029 Jean Potin, "Guérison d'une hémorroisse et résurrection de la fille de Jaïre. Mc 5,21-43," *AsSeign* 44 (1969): 38-47.

1030 Liliane Dambrine, "Guérison de la femme hémorroïsse et résurrection de la fille de Jaïre. Un aspect de la lecture d'un texte: Mc 5:21-43; Mt 9:18-26; Lc 8:40-56," *FV* 70 (1971): 75-81.

1031 Léopold Sabourin, "The Miracles of Jesus (III): Healings, Resuscitations, Nature Miracles," *BTB* 5 (1975): 146-200.

1032 J. Duncan M. Derrett, "Mark's Technique: The Haemorrhaging Woman and Jairus' Daughter," *Bib* 63/4 (1982): 474-505.

1033 Josef Blank, "Frauen in den Jesusüberlieferungen," in Gerhard Dautzenberg, et al., eds., *Die Frau im Urchristentum*. Freiburg: Herder, 1983. Pp. 9-91.

1034 Geert Hallbäck, *Strukturalisme og eksegese: Modelanalyser af Markus 5,21-43*. Copenhagen: Gad, 1983.

1035 Vincenzo Scippa, "Ricerche preliminari per uno studio su Mc 5,21-43 secondo la Redaktionsgeschichte," *RBib* 31 (1983): 385-404.

1036 Michel Gourgues, "Deux miracles, deux démarches de foi (Marc 5,21-43 par.)," in Françios Refoulé, ed., *À cause de l'Evangile: Études sur les synoptiques et les Actes* (festschrift for Jacques Dupont). Paris: Cerf, 1985. Pp. 229-49.

1037 James R. Edwards, "Markan Sandwiches: The Significance of Interpolations in Markan Narratives," *NovT* 31 (1989): 193-216.

1038 Eugene A. LaVerdiere, "Women in the New Israel," *Emmanuel* 95 (1989): 34-41, 56.

1039 Liz L. McCloskey, "Hearing and Healing Hedda Nussbaum: A Reflection on Mark 5:21-43," *CC* 106 (1989): 178-79.

1040 Lone Fatum, "En kvindehistorie om tro og køn," *DTT* 53 (1990): 278-99.

1041 Gregory Murray, "Five Gospel Miracles," *DR* 108 (1990): 79-90.

1042 Tom Shepherd, "Intercalation in Mark and the Synoptic Problem," *SBLSP* 30 (1991): 687-97.

5:21-24

1043 Léopold Sabourin, *The Divine Miracles Discussed and Defended.* Rome: Catholic Book Agency, 1977.

5:22-43

1044 F. C. Synge, "A Matter of Tenses—Fingerprints of an Annotator in Mark," *ET* 88 (1976-1977): 168-71.

1045 Dominique Hermant, "La femme au flux de sang et la fille de Jaïre (Mt 9,18-26; Mc 5,22-43; Lc 8,41-56)," *BLOS* 5 (1990): 8-16.

5:22-24

1046 Jean Martucci, "Les récits de miracle: influence des récits de l'Ancien Testament sur ceux du Nouveau," *SE* 27 (1975): 133-46.

5:22

1047 Rudolf Pesch, "Jarius (Mk 5:22/Lk 8:41)," *BZ* 14/2 (1970): 252-56.

5:24-34

1048 James L. Bailey, "Comparing the Contributions of the Synoptic Writers," *BibTh* 18 (1968): 54-57.

1049 Marla J. Selvidge, "Woman, Cult, and Miracle Recital: Mark 5:24-34," doctoral dissertation, St. Louis University, St. Louis MO, 1980.

1050 Jean Delorme, "Mise en discours et structures narratives ou le dynamisme du récit," in H. Parret and H. G. Ruprecht, eds., *Exigences et perspectives de la sémiotique* (festschrift for A. J. Greimas). Amsterdam: Benjamins, 1985. Pp. 709-18.

1051 Vernon K. Robbins, "The Woman Who Touched Jesus' Garment: Socio-rhetorical Analysis of the Synoptic Accounts," *NTS* 33 (1987): 502-15.

1052 Mary Ann Beavis, "Women as Models of Faith in Mark," *BTB* 18 (1988): 3-9.

5:25-34

1053 Marla J. Selvidge, "Mark 5:25-34 and Leviticus 15:19-20: A Reaction to Restrictive Purity Regulations," *JBL* 103 (1984): 619-23.

1054 Jean Delorme, "Jésus et l'hémorroïsse ou le choc de la rencontre (Marc 5,25-34)," *SémBib* 44 (1986): 1-17.

1055 John S. Reist, "Telling the Truth: A Biblical View of Personality," in Thomas J. Burke, ed., *Man and Mind: A Christian Theory of Personality*. Hillsdale MI: Hillsdale College Press, 1989 Pp. 149-70.

1056 Dieter Nestle, " 'Tochter, du hast dich getraut!' Zum Umgang mit Evangelium nach Markus 5,25-34," *EvErz* 42 (1990): 396-401.

5:30-31

1057 Enzo Bianchi, " 'Chi dite che io sia?' Per una nuova conoscenza di Gesù di Nazareth," *Servitium* 6 (1972): 53-68, 205-18.

5:30

1058 Robert H. Thouless, "Miracles and Physical Research," *Theology* 72 (1969): 253-58.

1059 A. Marcello Buscemi, "La prolessi nel Nuovo Testamento," *SBFLA* 35 (1985): 37-68.

5:33

1060 Harald Sahlin, "Emendationsvorschläge zum griechischen Text des Neuen Testaments I," *NovT* 24 (1982): 160-79.

5:33-43

1061 Jean Martucci, "Les récits de miracle: influence des récits de l'Ancien Testament sur ceux du Nouveau," *SE* 27 (1975): 133-46.

5:34

1062 Georg Braumann, "Die Schuldner und die Sunderin Luk. VII.36-50," *NTS* 10/4 (1963-1964): 487-93.

5:35-43

1063 Léopold Sabourin, *The Divine Miracles Discussed and Defended.* Rome: Catholic Book Agency, 1977.

5:35-42

1064 Stephen M. Reynolds, "The Zero Tense in Greek: A Critical Note," *WTJ* 32 (1969): 68-72.

5:39

1065 R. E. Ker, "St. Mark v.39," *ET* 65 (1953-1954): 315-16; 66 (1954-1955): 125.

1066 W. Powell, "St. Mark v,39," *ET* 66 (1954-1955): 61, 215.

5:41

1067 Enrique López-Dóriga, "Y cogiendo la mano de la niña le dice: Talitha koumi (Mc 5,41). Nota exegético-filológica," *EE* 39 (1964): 377-81.

5:42

1068 Jeremy Moiser, " 'She Was Twelve Years Old' (Mk 5.42): A Note on Jewish-Gentile Controversy in Mark's Gospel," *IBS* 3 (1981): 179-86.

5:43

1069 James M. Efird, "Note on Mark 5:43," in James M. Efird, ed., *The Use of the Old Testament in the New and Other*

Essays (festschrift for William F. Stinespring). Durham NC: Duke University, 1972. Pp. 307-309.

<u>6</u>

1070 E. Schott, "Die Aussendungsrede Mt 10. Mc 6. Lc 9. 10," *ZNW* 7 (1906): 140-150.

<u>6:1-8</u>

1071 Michael D. Goulder, "Mark 6:1-8 and Parallels," *NTS* 24/2 (1977-1978): 235-40.

<u>6:1-6</u>

1072 Charles Masson, "Jésus à Nazareth," in Charles Masson, *Vers les sources d'eau vive: Études d'exégèse et de théologie du Nouveau Testament*. Lausanne: Payot, 1961. Pp. 38-69.

1073 Erich Grässer, "Jesus in Nazareth (Mark 6:1-6a): Notes on the Redaction and Theology of St. Mark," *NTS* 16 (1969-1970): 1-23.

1074 David Hill, "The Rejection of Jesus at Nazareth: Luke 4:16-30," *NovT* 13/3 (1971): 161-80.

1075 John Dominic Crossan, "Mark and the Relatives of Jesus," *NovT* 15 (1973): 81-113.

1076 Charles Perrot, "Jésus à Nazareth. Mc 6,1-6," *AsSeign* 45 (1974): 40-49.

1077 Lorenz Oberliner, *Historische Überlieferung und christologische Aussage. Zur Frage der "Bruder Jesu" in der Synopse*. Stuttgart: Katholisches Bibelwerk, 1975.

1078 Martin Avanzo, "María en las primeras tradiciones evangelicas," *RevB* 38 (1976): 49-57.

1079 R. L. Sturch, "The 'Πατρίς' of Jesus," *JTS* 28 (1977): 94-96.

1080 Otto Betz, "Jesus in Nazareth. Bemerkungen zu Markus 6,1-6," in G. Müller, ed., *Israel hat dennoch Gott zum Trost* (festschrift for Schalom Ben-Chorin). Trier: Paulinus, 1978. Pp. 44-60.

1081 Bernhard Mayer, "Uberlieferungs-und Redaktionsgeschichtliche Uberlegungen zu Mk 6,1-6a," *BZ* 22/2 (1978): 187-98.

1082 Bertrand Buby, "A Christology of Relationship in Mark," *BTB* 10/4 (1980): 149-54.

1083 Sijbolt J. Noorda, "Jesus in zijn vaderstad; coherentie en incoherentie in Marcus 6.1-6," in E. Talstra, et al., eds., *Segmenten: Studies op het gebied van de theologie*. II: *Exegetica*. Amsterdam: Vrije Universiteit Boekhandel, 1981. Pp. 55-82.

1084 Jacques Dupont, "Jésus devant l'incrédulité de ses concitoyens," Casale C. Marcheselli, ed., *Parole e Spirito* (festschrift for Settimio Cipriani). 2 vols. Brescia: Paideia, 1982. 1:195-210.

1085 Eugene A. LaVerdiere, "Jesus' Native Place and the Apostolic Mission," *Emmanuel* 95 (1989): 74-79.

<u>6:2-7</u>

1086 Michael D. Goulder, "On Putting Q to the Test," *NTS* 24 (1977-1978): 218-34.

1087 Christopher M. Tuckett, "On the Relationship between Matthew and Luke," *NTS* 30 (1984): 130-42.

<u>6:3-44</u>

1088 Joseph Knackstedt, "De duplici miraculo multiplicationis panum," *VD* 41 (1963): 39-51, 140-53.

<u>6:3</u>

1089 Alexander Jones, "Reflections on a Recent Dispute," *Scr* 8 (1956): 13-22.

1090 Josef Blinzler, "Die Brüder Jesu," *TGeg* 10 (1967): 8-15.

1091 Ethelbert Stauffer, "Jeschu ben Mirjam. Kontroversgeschichtliche Anmerkungen zu Mk 6:3," in E. Earle Ellis and Max Wilcox, eds., *Neotestamentica et Semitica* (festschrift for Matthew Black). Edinburgh: T. & T. Clark, 1969. Pp. 119-28.

1092 Antonio Salas, "Jesús 'Ben Myriam' (Mc 6,3). Anotaciones criticas sobre el origen de Jesus en la tradición sinóptica," *EstAg* 12 (1977): 87-97.

1093 Jacques Dupont, "Jésus et la famille dans les évangiles," *CL* 62/6 (1980): 477-91.

1094 Richard A. Batey, "Is Not This the Carpenter?" *NTS* 30 (1984): 249-58.

1095 Martin Hengel, "Entstehungszeit und Situation des Markusevangeliums [Mk 6:3; 7:24; 8:27ff; 13; 15:21]," in Hubert Cancik, ed., *Markus-Philologie*. Tübingen: Mohr, 1984. Pp. 1-45.

6:4

1096 Brian A. Mastin, " 'Jesus Said Grace'," *SJT* 24 (1971): 449-56.

6:6-13

1097 E. N. Testa, "Studio di Mc 6,6b-13 secondo il metodo della storia della tradizione," *DivT* 75 (1972): 177-91.

1098 John Bradshaw, "Oral Transmission and Human Memory," *ET* 92 (1980-1981): 303-307.

1099 Dale C. Allison, "The Pauline Epistles and the Synoptic Gospels: The Pattern of the Parallels," *NTS* 28/1 (1982): 1-32.

1100 J. Duncan M. Derrett, "Peace, Sandals and Shirts," *HeyJ* 24 (1983): 253-65.

1101 Sylvester Lamberigts, "De zendingsrede volgens Marcus," in *Wie is Hij toch? De Bijbel leren lezen om Jezus te kennen*. Tielt-Weesp: Lannoo, 1984. Pp. 166-70.

1102 Eugene A. LaVerdiere, "The Apostolic Mission: A New Exodus," *Emmanuel* 95 (1989): 138-44.

6:6

1103 Philippe Rolland, "Le sommaire de Marc 6,6b et l'envoi des Douze en mission," *BLOS* 5 (1990): 21-23.

6:7-13:30

1104 Lucien Cerfaux, ''La mission de Galilée dans la tradition synoptique,'' *ETL* 27 (1951): 369-89; 28 (1952): 629-47.

6:7-30

1105 James R. Edwards, ''Markan Sandwiches: The Significance of Interpolations in Markan Narratives,'' *NovT* 31 (1989): 193-216.

6:7-13

1106 Rudolf Schnackenburg, ''Zur formgeschichtlichen Methode in der Evangelienforschung,'' *ZKT* 85 (1963): 16-32.

1107 Jean Delorme, ''La mission des Douze en Galilée. Mc 6,7-13,'' *AsSeign* 46 (1974): 43-50.

1108 James Donaldson, '' 'Called to Follow': A Twofold Experience of Discipleship in Mark,'' *BTB* 5 (1975): 67-77.

1109 Gregory Murray, ''Did Luke Use Mark?'' *DR* 104 (1986): 268-71.

6:7-12

1110 Eugene A. LaVerdiere, ''Take Nothing on the Journey,'' *Emmanuel* 91 (1985): 382-85.

6:7

1111 Nigel Turner, ''The Minor Verbal Agreements of Mt. and Lk. against Mk.,'' *StudE* 1 (1959): 223-34.

1112 Ernest Best, ''Mark's Use of the Twelve,'' *ZNW* 69/1-2 (1978): 11-35.

6:8-11

1113 M. Eugene Boring, *Sayings of the Risen Jesus: Christian Prophecy in the Synoptic Tradition.* SNTSMS #46. Cambridge: Cambridge University Press, 1982.

6:8-9

1114 Lucien Legrand, ''Bare Foot Apostles? The Shoes of St. Mark (Mk. 6:8-9 and Parallels),'' *ITS* 16 (1979): 201-19.

6:8

1115 Tjitze J. Baarda, " 'A Staff Only, Not a Stick': Disharmony of the Gospels and the Harmony of Tatian," in J.-M. Sevrin, ed., *The New Testament in Early Christianity: La réception des écrits néotestamentaires dans le christianisme primitif.* BETL #86. Louvain: Peeters Press, 1989. Pp. 311-33.

6:10-11

1116 John Thorley, "Aktionsart in New Testament Greek: Infinitive and Imperative," *NovT* 31 (1989): 290-315.

6:10

1117 G. M. Lee, "Two Notes on St. Mark," *NovT* 18/1 (1976): 36.

6:11

1118 George B. Caird, "Uncomfortable Words: II. Shake Off the Dust from Your Feet," *ET* 81/2 (1969-1970): 40-43.

1119 Édouard Delebecque, "Secouez la Poussiere de vos Pieds . . . sur l'Hellenisme de Luc IX,5," *RB* 89/2 (1982): 177-84.

1120 Silvia Schroer, "Konkretionen zum Vaterunser," *UnSa* 45 (1990): 110-13.

6:12-13

1121 A. R. C. Leaney, "Dominical Authority for the Ministry of Healing," *ET* 65 (1953-1954): 121-23.

6:14-8:30

1122 Frank J. Matera, "The Incomprehension of the Disciples and Peter's Confession (Mark 6,14-8,30)," *Bib* 70/2 (1989): 153-72.

6:14-29

1123 Jacques Schwartz, "Récits bibliques et moeurs perses," in A. Caquot, et al., eds., *Hellenica et Judaica* (festschrift for Valentin Nikiprowetzky). Louvain: Peeters Press, 1986. Pp. 267-77.

1124 Gaëtan Minette de Tillesse, "Uma tradiçâo batista?" *IRevBB* 7 (1990): 213-48.

6:14-22

1125 Jakob Jervell, "Herodes Antipas og hans plass i evangelieoverleveringen," *NTT* 61 (1960): 28-40.

1126 Joseph B. Tyson, "Jesus and Herod Antipas," *JBL* 79 (1960): 239-46.

1127 K.-S. Krieger, "Die Herodianer im Markusevangelium: Ein Versuch ihrer Identifizierung," *BibN* 59 (1991): 49-56.

6:14-16

1128 Klaus Berger, *Die Auferstehung des Propheten und die Erhöhung des Menschensohnes: Traditionsgeschichtliche Untersuchungen zur Deutung des Geschickes Jesu in frühchristlichen Texte*. Göttingen: Vandenhoeck & Ruprecht, 1976.

1129 Johannes M. Nützel, "Zu Schicksal der eschatologischen Propheten," *BZ* 20 (1976): 59-94.

1130 J. Roberts, "Galilean Resurrection," *EpRev* 15 (1988): 44-46.

1131 Eugene A. LaVerdiere, "Herod and John the Baptizer," *Emmanuel* 95 (1989): 202-208.

1132 Frans Neirynck, "Marc 6:14-16 et par.," *ETL* 65/1 (1989): 105-109.

1133 S. J. Nortje, "John the Baptist and the Resurrection Traditions in the Gospels," *Neo* 23 (1989): 349-58.

1134 Philippe Rolland, "La question synoptique demande-t-elle une résponse compliquée?" *Bib* 70/2 (1989): 217-23.

1135 Knut Backhaus, *Die 'Jungerkreise' des Täufers Johannes: Eine Studie zu den religionsgeschichtlichen Ursprungen des Christentums*. Paderborn: Schoningh, 1991.

6:14-15

1136 Richard A. Horsley, "Like One of the Prophets of Old: Two Types of Popular Prophets at the Time of Jesus," *CBQ* 47 (1985): 435-63.

6:14

1137 Gottfried Schille, "Prolegomena zur Jesusfrage," *TLZ* 93 (1968): 481-88.

1138 Sasagu Arai, "Zum 'Tempelwort' Jesu in Apostelgeschichte 6:14," *NTS* 34/3 (1988): 397-410.

1139 Frans Neirynck, "**ΚΑΙ ΕΛΕΓΟΝ** en Mc 6,14," *ETL* 65/1 (1989): 110-18.

6:15

1140 Norman Perrin, " 'Un prophète comme l'un des prophètes'," in Maurice Carrez, et al., eds., *De la Tôrah au Messie* (festschrift for Henri Cazelles). Paris: Desclée, 1981. Pp. 417-23.

6:16

1141 Heinrich Greeven, "Erwägungen zur synoptischen Textkritik," *NTS* 6 (1959-1960): 282-96.

6:17-29

1142 Ignace de la Potterie, "Mors Johannis Baptistae (Mc 6,17-29)," *VD* 44 (1966): 142-51.

1143 Joachim Gnilka, "Das Martyrium Johannes' des Täufers (Mk 6,17-29)," in Paul Hoffmann, ed., *Orientierung an Jesus: Zur Theologie der Synoptiker* (festschrift for Josef Schmid). Freiburg: Herder, 1973. Pp. 78-92.

1144 Diego A. Losada, "La muerte de Juan el Bautista. Mc 6,17-29," *RevB* 39 (1977): 143-54.

1145 Roger D. Aus, *Water into Wine and the Beheading of John the Baptist: Early Jewish-Christian Interpretation of Esther 1 in John 2:1-11 and Mark 6:17-29*. Atlanta: Scholars Press, 1988.

1146 Eugene A. LaVerdiere, "The Death of John the Baptizer," *Emmanuel* 95 (1989): 374-81, 402.

1147 Knut Backhaus, *Die 'Jungerkreise' des Täufers Johannes: Eine Studie zu den religionsgeschichtlichen Ursprungen des Christentums*. Paderborn: Schoningh, 1991.

6:17-25

1148 E. W. Deibler, "Translating from Basic Structure," *BT* 19 (1968): 14-16.

6:17-20

1149 George Aichele, "Two Theories of Translation with Examples from the Gospel of Mark," *JSNT* 47 (1992): 95-116.

6:17

1150 Willem S. Vorster, "Concerning Semantics, Grammatical Analysis, and Bible Translation," *Neo* 8 (1974): 21-41.

6:18

1151 Paul Ellingworth, "Translating Parallel Passages in the Gospels," *BT* 34 (1983): 401-407.

1152 Lino Cignelli, "La grecità biblica," *SBFLA* 35 (1985): 203-48.

6:20

1153 Giuseppe Ghiberti, " 'Uomo giusto e santo' (Mc. 6,20). Tracce di agiografia nel Nuovo Testamento?," in *Testimonium Christi. Scritti in onore di Jacques Dupont.* Brescia: Paideia, 1985. Pp. 237-55.

1154 David Alan Black, "The Text of Mark 6:20," *NTS* 34/1 (1988): 141-45.

6:21-29

1155 Frédéric Manns, "Marc 6,21-29 à la lumière des dernières fouilles du Machéronte," *SBFLA* 31 (1981): 287-90.

6:22

1156 William Lillie, "Salome or Herodias," *ET* 65 (1953-1954): 251.

1157 J. M. Ross, "The 'Harder Reading' in Textual Criticism," *BT* 33 (1982): 138-39.

1158 Rykle Borger, "NA^{26} und die neutestamentliche Textkritik," *TR* 52 (1987): 1-58.

6:25

1159 Ronald A. Kittel, ''John the Baptist in the Gospel according to Mark,'' doctoral dissertation, Graduate Theological Union, Berkeley CA, 1977.

6:30-8:27

1160 A.-M. Denis, ''Une théologie de la vie chrétienne chez saint Marc (VI,30-VIII,27),'' *VS* 41 (1959): 416-27.

6:30-8:26

1161 A.-M. Denis, ''La section des pains selon S. Marc (6,30-8,26), une théologie de l'Eucharistie,'' *StudE* 4 (1968): 171-79.

1162 J. S. Allsop, ''The Development of the Gospel Miracle Tradition: With Special Reference to Mark 1.21-3.6; 4.35-5.43; 6.30-8.26,'' doctoral dissertation, Nottingham University, Nottingham UK, 1978.

1163 Corina Combet-Galland, ''Analyse structurale de Marc 6,30 à 8,26,'' *FV* 77 (1978): 34-46.

1164 Walter Wink, ''The Education of the Apostles: Mark's View of Human Transformation,'' *REd* 83/2 (1988): 277-90.

6:30-8:21

1165 F. C. Synge, ''Common Bread. The Craftsmanship of a Theologian,'' *Theology* 75 (1972): 131-35.

6:30-8:10

1166 John E. Phelan, ''Rhetoric and Meaning in Mark 6:30-8:10,'' doctoral dissertation, Northwestern University, Evanston IL, 1985.

6:30-7:30

1167 P.-E. Bonnard, ''La méthode historico-critique appliquée à Marc 6,30 à 7,30,'' *FV* 77 (1978): 6-18.

6:30-46

1168 Rámon Trevijano Etcheverría, ''Crisis mesiánica en la multiplicacion de los panes (Mc 6,30-46 y Jn 6,1-15),'' *Bur* 16 (1974): 413-39.

1169 Rámon Trevijano Etcheverría, "La multiplicación de los panes (Mc 6,30-46; 8,1-10 y par.)," *Bur* 15 (1974): 435-65.

1170 Jean Martucci, "Les récits de miracle: influence des récits de l'Ancien Testament sur ceux du Nouveau," *SE* 27 (1975): 133-46.

6:30-45

1171 Andreas Pangritz, "Die Speisung der Fünftausend: Ammerkungen zu Markus 6:30-45," *TexteK* 6 (1979): 5-40.

1172 Karl P. Donfried, "The Feeding Narratives and the Marcan Community: Mark 6,30-45 and 8,1-10," in Dieter Lührmann and Georg Strecker, eds., *Kirche* (festschrift for Günther Bornkamm). Tübingen: Mohr, 1980. Pp. 95-103

6:30-44

1173 Austin M. Farrer, "Loaves and Thousands," *JTS* 4 (1953): 1-14.

1174 Jean Levie, "L'évangile araméen de S. Matthieu est-il la source de l'évangile de S. Marc?" *NRT* 76 (1954): 689-715, 812-43.

1175 Henri Clavier, "La multiplication des pains dans le ministère de Jesus," *StudE* 1 (1959): 441-57.

1176 Georg Ziener, "Die Brotwunder im Markusevangelium," *BZ* 4 (1960): 282-85.

1177 Alan Shaw, "The Marcan Feeding Narratives," *CQR* 162 (1961): 268-78.

1178 Giovanni Giavini, "Le due moltiplicazioni di pane nel vangelo di S. Marco," in *Miscellanea Carlo Figini*. Milano: La scuola cattolica, 1964. Pp. 31-46.

1179 Gabriel A. Herbert, "History in the Feeding ot the Five Thousand," *StudE* 2 (1964): 65-72.

1180 Eero Repo, "Viisi leipaa ja kaksi kalaa," *TAik* 73 (1968): 331-42.

1181 R. Dross, "Die Bedeutung didaktischer Konzeptionen für die Interpretation biblischer Texte, dargestellt an Mk 6,30-44," in Klaus Wegenast, ed., *Theologie und Unterricht: über die Repräsentanz des Christlichen in der Schule. Festgabe für Hans Stock zu seinem 65. Geburtstag.* Gütersloh: Güterslohen Verlagshaus Gerd Mohn, 1969. Pp. 65-78.

1182 E. Schuyler English, "A Neglected Miracle," *BSac* 126 (1969): 300-305.

1183 Jean-Marie van Cangh, "Le thème des poissons dans les récits évangéliques de la multiplication des pains," *RB* 78 (1971): 71-83.

1184 G. Ory, "Des pains, des poissons et des hommes," *CCER* 18 (1971): 21-28.

1185 T. M. Suriano, "Eucharist Reveals Jesus: The Multiplication of the Loaves," *BibTo* 58 (1972): 642-51.

1186 Jean-Marie van Cangh, "La multiplication des pains dans l'évangile de Marc: Essai d'exégèse globale," in M. Sabbe, ed., *L'évangile selon Marc: Tradition et rédaction.* BETL #34. Louvain: Louvain University Press, 1974. Pp. 309-46.

1187 Ignace de la Potterie, "Le sens primitif de la multiplication des pains," in J. Dupont, ed., *Jésus aux origines de la christologie.* BETL #40. Louvain: Louvain University Press, 1975. Pp. 303-29.

1188 Rámon Trevijano Etcheverría, "Historia de milagro y cristolo gía en la multiplicacion de los panes," *Bur* 17 (1976): 9-38.

1189 Lamar Williamson, "An Exposition of Mark 6:30-44," *Int* 30 (1976): 169-73.

1190 Giuseppe Pace, "La prima moltiplicazione dei pani. Topografia," *BibO* 21 (1979): 85-91.

1191 Sarrae Masuda, "The Good News of the Miracle of the Bread: The Tradition and Its Markan Redaction," *NTS* 28 (1982): 191-219.

1192 Donald P. Senior, "The Eucharist in Mark: Mission, Reconciliation, Hope," *BTB* 12 (1982): 67-72.

1193 Ulrich H. J. Körtner, "Das Fischmotiv im Speisungswunder," *ZNW* 75/1 (1984): 24-35.

1194 Jouette M. Bassler, "The Parable of the Loaves," *JR* 66/2 (1986): 157-72.

1195 Fritz Neugebauer, "Die wunderbare Speisung (Mk 6:30-44 parr) und Jesu Identität," *KD* 32/4 (1986): 254-77.

1196 A. G. Van Aarde, "Die wonderbaarlike vermeerdering van brood (Matt 14:13-21 en par): Historiese kritiek in perspektief," *HTS* 42 (1986): 229-56.

1197 Ignace de la Potterie, "The Multiplication of the Loaves in the Life of Jesus," *Communio* 16 (1989): 499-516.

1198 Joseph A. Grassi, *Loaves and Fishes: The Gospel Feeding Narratives*. Collegeville: Liturgical Press, 1991.

1199 Gerhard Lohfink, "Wie werden im Reich Gottes die Hungernden satt? zur Erzählintention von Mk 6,30-44," in Johannes Degenhardt, *Die Freude an Gott: Unsere Kraft* (festschrift for Otto B. Knoch). Stuttgart: Verlag Katholisches Bibelwerk, 1991. Pp. 135-44.

<u>6:30-43</u>

1200 Robert M. Fowler, *Loaves and Fishes: The Function of the Feeding Stories in the Gospel of Mark*. Chico CA: Scholars Press, 1981.

<u>6:30-34</u>

1201 Jean Delorme, "Jésus, les apôtres et la foule: Mc 6,30-34," *AsSeign* 2/47 (1970): 44-58.

1202 Frans Neirynck, "The Matthew-Luke Agreements in Matt 14:13-14 and Lk 9:10-11 (par Mk 6:30-34): The Two-Source Theory behind the Impasse," *ETL* 60/1 (1984): 25-44.

1203 Michael Pettem, "Le premier récit de la multiplication des pains et le problème synoptique," *SR* 14/1 (1985): 73-83.

6:30

1204 Hugh W. Montefiore, "Revolt in the Desert? (Mark 6:30ff.)," *NTS* 8 (1961-1962): 135-41.

1205 Giuseppe Frizzi, "L'ἀπόστολος delle tradizioni sinottiche (Mc, Q, Mt, Lc. e Atti)," *RBib* 22 (1974): 3-37.

1206 P.-E. Bonnard, "La méthode historico-critique appliquée à Marc 6,30 à 7,30," *FV* 77 (1978): 6-18.

6:31-8:26

1207 Lucien Cerfaux, "La section des pains," in Josef Schmid and Anton Vögtle, eds., *Synoptische Studien* (festschrift for Alfred Wikenhauser). Münich: Zink, 1953. Pp. 64-77.

1208 T. A. Burkill, "Mark 6:31-8:26. The Context of the Story of the Syrophoenician Woman," in L. Wallach, ed., *The Classical Tradition: Literary and Historical Studies in Honor of Harry Caplan.* Ithaca NY: Cornell University Press, 1966. Pp. 329-44.

6:31-7:37

1209 L. H. Jenkins, "A Marcan Doublet: Mark 6.31-7.37, and 8.1-26," in Ernest A. Payne, ed., *Studies in History and Religion: Presented to Dr. H. Wheeler Robinson.* London: Lutterworth, 1942. Pp. 87-111.

6:31-44

1210 Gerhard Friedrich, "Die beiden Erzählungen von der Speisung in Mark 6,31-44; 8,1-9," *TZ* 20 (1964): 10-22.

1211 Francis J. Moloney, "Reading the Eucharist Texts in Mark," *PIBA* 14 (1991): 7-24.

6:31

1212 Lino Cignelli, "La grecità biblica," *SBFLA* 35 (1985): 203-48.

6:32-15:47

1213 Morton Smith, "Mark 6:32-15:47 and John 6:1-19:42," *SBLSP* 8/2 (1978): 281-88.

6:32-56

1214 Siegfried Mendner, ''Zum Problem 'Johannes und die Synoptiker','' *NTS* 4 (1957-1958): 282-307.

6:32-44

1215 Rudolf Schnackenburg, ''Hermeneutik und Exegese. Mt 14,2.-33; Mk 6,32-44,'' in G. Stachel, ed., *Existenziale Hermeneutik: Zur Diskussion des fundamentaltheologischen und religionspädagogischen* (festschrift for H. Halbfas). Einsiedeln-Koln: Benziger, 1969. Pp. 140-59.

1216 Konrad Raiser, ''Bibelarbeit über Markus 6,32-44,'' in Hansgeorg Kraft and Hans Mayr, eds., *Botschafter von der Versöhnung* (festschrift for Walter Arnold). N.p., 1979. Pp. 115-21.

1217 Craig L. Blomberg, ''The Miracles as Parables,'' in David Wenham and Craig L. Blomberg, eds., *Gospel Perspectives*. Sheffield: JSOT Press, 1986. 6:327-59.

6:33-38

1218 Philippe Rolland, ''L'arrière-lond sémitique des évangiles synoptiques,'' *ETL* 60 (1984): 358-62.

6:34-44

1219 Alan Richardson, ''The Feeding of the Five Thousand: Mark 6:34-44,'' *Int* 9 (1955): 144-49.

1220 Alkuin Heising, ''Exegese und Theologie der alt- und neutestamentlichen Speisewunder,'' *ZKT* 86 (1964): 80-96.

1221 Alkuin Heising, ''Das Kerygma der wunderbaren Fischvermehrung (Mk 6,34-44 parr),'' *BibL* 10 (1969): 52-57.

1222 Léopold Sabourin, *The Divine Miracles Discussed and Defended*. Rome: Catholic Book Agency, 1977.

6:34

1223 Ethelbert Stauffer, ''Zum apokalyptischen Festmahl in Mk 6,34ff.,'' *ZNW* 46 (1955): 264-66.

1224 Wilfred Tooley, ''The Shepherd and Sheep Image in the Teaching of Jesus,'' *NovT* 7 (1964-1965): 15-25.

6:35-4:52

1225 C. H. Dodd, "The Sayings," in *Historical Tradition in the Fourth Gospel.* Cambridge: Cambridge University Press, 1963. Pp. 315-405.

6:35-44

1226 B. M. F. van Iersel, "Die wunderbare Speisung und das Abendmal in der synoptischen Tradition (Mk 6:35-44, 8:1-20)," *NovT* 7/3 (1964-1965): 167-94.

1227 Eugene A. LaVerdiere, "In Hundreds and Fifties," *Emmanuel* 91 (1985): 425-29.

1228 Otto Betz, "Jesu Tischsegen: Psalm 104 in Lehre und Wirken Jesu," in *Jesus: Der Messias Israels.* Tübingen: Mohr, 1987. Pp. 202-31.

6:35

1229 Marius Reiser, "Der Alexanderroman und das Markusevangelium," in Hubert Cancik, ed., *Markus-Philologie.* Tübingen: Mohr, 1984. Pp. 131-63.

6:37

1230 Joseph A. Grassi, " 'You Yourselves Give Them to Eat': An Easily Forgotten Command of Jesus," *BibTo* 97 (1978): 1704-1709.

6:38

1231 George H. Boobyer, "The Eucharistic Interpretation of the Miracles of the Loaves in St. Mark's Gospel," *JTS* 3 (1952): 161-71.

1232 George H. Boobyer, "The Miracles of the Loaves and the Gentiles in St. Mark's Gospel," *SJT* 6 (1953): 77-87.

1233 Enzo Bianchi, "'Chi dite che io sia?' Per una nuova conoscenza di Gesù di Nazareth," *Servitium* 6 (1972): 53-68, 205-18.

1234 Eero Repo, "Fünf Brote und zwei Fische," *SNTU-A* 3 (1978): 99-113.

6:42-52

1235 R. H. Lightfoot, "A Consideration of Three Passages in St. Mark's Gospel," in Werner Schmauch, ed., *In Memoriam Ernst Lohmeyer*. Stuttgart: Evangelisches Verlagswerk, 1951. Pp. 110-15.

6:43

1236 J. Duncan M. Derrett, "Crumbs in Mark," *DR* 102 (1984): 12-21.

6:45-8:26

1237 Vincent K. Pollard, "The 'Lukan Omission' of Mk 6:45-8:26," *BibTo* 29 (1967): 2032-34.

6:45-56

1238 Eugene A. LaVerdiere, "Resisting the Mission to the Nations," *Emmanuel* 96 (1990): 22-28.

6:45-52

1239 Eric F. F. Bishop, "Jesus and the Lake," *CBQ* 13 (1951): 398-414.

1240 A.-M. Denis, "La marche de Jésus sur les eaux: Contribution à l'histoire de la péricope dans la tradition évangélique," in Ignace de la Potterie, ed., *De Jesus aux Evangiles: Tradition et rédaction dans les Évangiles synoptiques*. BETL #25. Paris: Lethielleux, 1967. Pp. 233-47.

1241 Thierry Snoy, "La rédaction marcienne de la marche sur les eaux," *ETL* 44 (1968): 205-41, 433-81.

1242 Jacob Kremer, "Jesu Wandel auf dem See nach Mk 6,45-52. Auslegung und Meditation," *BibL* 10 (1969): 221-32.

1243 Léopold Sabourin, "The Miracles of Jesus (III): Healings, Resuscitations, Nature Miracles," *BTB* 5 (1975): 146-200.

1244 Hubert Ritt, "Der 'Seewandel Jesu' (Mk 6,45-52 Par)," *BZ* 23/1 (1979): 71-84.

1245 Christian Hartlich, "Ist die historisch-kritische Methode überholt?" *Conci* 16 (1980): 534-38.

1246 René Kieffer, "Deux types d'exégèse à base linguistique," *Conci* 15 (1980): 19-28.

1247 John P. Heil, *Jesus Walking on the Sea: Meaning and Gospel Functions of Matt 14:22-23, Mark 6:45-52, and John 6:15b-21*. Analecta Biblica 87. Rome: Biblical Institute Press, 1981.

1248 Grant R. Osborne, "Round Four: The Redaction Debate Continues," *JETS* 28 (1985): 399-410.

6:45-51

1249 C. H. Dodd, "The Appearances of the Risen Christ: An Essay in Form-Criticism of the Gospels," in D. E. Nineham, ed., *Studies in the Gospels* (festschrift for R. H. Lightfoot). Oxford: Blackwell, 1955. Pp. 9-35.

6:45

1250 John O'Hara, "Two Bethsaidas or One?" *Scr* 15 (1963): 24-27.

1251 Wilhelm Wildens, "Die Auslassung von Mark. 6,45 bei Lukas im Lichte der Komposition Luk. 9,1-50," *TZ* 32/4 (1976): 193-200.

6:46

1252 Benny R. Crockett, "The Function of Mathetological Prayer in Mark," *IBS* 10 (1988): 123-39.

6:48

1253 Thierry Snoy, "Marc 6,48: 'et il voulait les dépasser': Proposition pour la solution d'une énigme," in M. Sabbe, ed., *L'évangile selon Marc: Tradition et rédaction*. BETL #34. Louvain: Louvain University Press, 1968. Pp. 347-63.

1254 Maurice Baillet, "Les manuscrits de la Grotte 7 de Qumrân et le Nouveau Testament," *Bib* 54 (1973): 340-50.

1255 Pierre Benoit, "Nouvelle Note sur les Fragments Grecs de la Grotte 7 de Qumrân," *RB* 80/1 (1973): 5-12.

1256 Harry T. Fleddermann, " 'And He Wanted to Pass by Them' (Mark 6:48c)," *CBQ* 45/3 (1983): 389-95.

6:49

1257 David Hill, "The Walking on the Water: A Geographical or Linguistic Answer?" *ET* 99 (1987-1988): 267-69.

6:50

1258 Johannes Brinktrine, "Die Selbstaussage Jesu ἐγώ εἰμί," *TGl* 47 (1957): 34-36.

1259 William Manson, "The Ego Eimi of the Messianic Presence in the New Testament," in T. W. Manson, *Jesus and the Christian*. Grand Rapids: Eerdmans, 1967. Pp. 174-83.

6:51-52

1260 J. Renié, "Une antilogie évangelique (Mc 6,51-52; Mt 14,32-33)," *Bib* 36 (1955): 223-26.

6:52-53

1261 E. J. Vardaman, "The Earliest Fragments of the New Testament," *ET* 83 (1971-1972): 374-76.

1262 Maurice Baillet, "Les manuscrits de la Grotte 7 de Qumrân et le Nouveau Testament," *Bib* 53 (1972): 508-16.

1263 Eugene Fisher, "New Testament Documents among the Dead Sea Scrolls?" *BibTo* 61 (1972): 835-41.

1264 Joseph A. Fitzmyer, "A Qumran Fragment of Mark?" *America* 126 (1972): 647-50.

1265 Lucien Legrand, "The New Testsment at Qumran?" *IndES* 11 (1972): 157-66.

1266 José O'Callaghan, "Notas sobre 7Q tomadas en el 'Rockefeller Museum' de Jerusalén," *Bib* 53 (1972): 517-33.

1267 C. H. Roberts, "On Some Presumed Papyrus Fragments of the New Testament from Qumran," *JTS* 23 (1972): 446-47.

1268 Léopold Sabourin, "A Fragment of Mark at Qumran?" *BTB* 2 (1972): 308-12.

1269 Ernst Vogt, "Entdeckung neutestamentlicher Texte beim Toten Meer?" *Orient* 36 (1972): 138-40.

1270 Gordon D. Fee, "Some Dissenting Notes on 7Q5 = Mark 6:52-53," *JBL* 92 (1973): 109-12.

1271 Colin J. Hemer, "A Note on 7Q5," *ZNW* 65 (1974): 155-57.

1272 Camille Focant, "Un fragment du second évangile à Qumrân: 7Q5 = Mc 6,52-53?" *RTL* 16 (1985): 447-54.

1273 Hans-Udo Rosenbaum, "Cave 7Q5! Gegen die erneute inanspruchnahme des Qumran-Fragments 7Q5 als bruchstueck der aeltesten Evangelien-Handschrift," *BZ* 31/2 (1987): 189-205.

1274 Ferdinand Rohrhirsch, "Das Qumranfragment 7Q5," *NovT* 30 (1988): 97-99.

1275 José O'Callaghan, "Sobre el papiro de Marcos en Qumrán," *FilN* 5 (1992): 191-97.

<u>6:52</u>

1276 Quentin Quesnell, *The Mind of Mark: Interpretation and Method through the Exegesis of Mark 6:52*. Analecta Biblica 38. Rome: Pontifical Biblical Institute, 1969.

<u>6:53-56</u>

1277 Jozef Verheyden, "Mark 1:32-34 and 6:53-56: Tradition or Redaction?" *ETL* 64/4 (1988): 415-28.

<u>6:53</u>

1278 Pierre Benoit, "Note sur les fragments grecs de la grotte 7 de Qumrân," *RB* 79 (1972): 321-24.

1279 G. Rinaldi, "Traversata del lago e sbarco a Genezaret in 'Marco' 6,53," *BibO* 17 (1975): 43-46.

<u>6:55</u>

1280 Harald Sahlin, "Emendationsvorschläge zum griechischen Text des Neuen Testaments I," *NovT* 24 (1982): 160-79.

<u>7:1-8:26</u>

1281 Lennart Persson, "The Gentile Mission in the Markan Interpolation," *BTF* 12 (1980): 44-49.

7:1-23

1282 Josef Schmid, "Markus und der aramäische Matthaus," in Josef Schmid and Anton Vögtle, eds., *Synoptische Studien* (festschrift for Alfred Wikenhauser). Münich: Zink, 1953. Pp. 75-118.

1283 H.-J. Schoeps, "Jesus et la Loi juive," *RHPR* 33 (1953): 1-20.

1284 A. W. Argyle, " 'Outward' and 'Inward' in Biblical Thought," *ET* 68 (1956-1957): 196-99.

1285 John P. Brown, "Synoptic Parallels in the Epistles and Form-History," *NTS* 10 (1963-1964): 27-48.

1286 Y. Baer, "Concerning the Image of Judaism in the Synoptic Gospels," *Zion* 31 (1966): 117-52.

1287 Cyril S. Rodd, "Are the Ethics of Jesus Situation Ethics?" *ET* 79 (1967-1968): 167-70.

1288 Frederick R. Kellogg, "Tradition and Redaction in Mark 7:1-23 and Related Dialogues," doctoral dissertation, Yale University, New Haven CT, 1972.

1289 N. J. McEleney, "Authenticating Criteria and Mark 7:1-23," *CBQ* 34/4 (1972): 431-60.

1290 Hans Hübner, "Mark VII.1-23 und das 'Jüdisch-Hellenistische' Gesetzesverständnis," *NTS* 22/3 (1975-1976): 319-45.

1291 Jan Lambrecht, "Jesus and the Law. An Investigation of Mark 7:1-23," *ETL* 53 (1977): 24-82.

1292 Yochanan Ronen, "Mark 7:1-23: 'Traditions of the Elders'," *Immanuel* 12 (1981): 44-54.

1293 Phillip Sigal, "Matthean Priority in the Light of Mark 7," *EGLMBS* 3 (1983): 76-95.

1294 Andreas Pangritz, "Jesus und das 'System der Unreinheit': oder Fernando Belo die Leviten gelesen," *TexteK* 24 (1984): 28-46.

1295 Daniel R. Schwartz, "Viewing the Holy Utensils (P. Ox. V,840)," *NTS* 32 (1986): 153-59.

1296 Michael FitzPatrick, "From Ritual Observance to Ethics: The Argument of Mark 7:1-23," *ABR* 35 (1987): 22-27.

1297 Gregory Murray, "What Defiles a Man?" *DR* 106 (1988): 297-98.

1298 Eugene A. LaVerdiere, "Jesus and the Tradition of the Elders," *Emmanuel* 96 (1990): 278-85.

1299 Eugene A. LaVerdiere, "Tradition, Traditions, and the Word of God," *Emmanuel* 96 (1990): 206-209, 212-16.

1300 Meinrad Limbeck, "Hindernisse fürs Christein: Zur Verkündigung des Markusevangeliums," *BL* 64 (1991): 164-68.

1301 Elian Cuviller, "Tradition et rédaction en Marc 7:1-23," *NovT* 34/2 (1992): 169-92.

<u>7:1-13</u>

1302 Frederico Dattler, "A mixná no Nôvo Testamento," in J. Salvador, ed., *Alualidades Bíblicas* (festschrift for F. J. J. Pedreira de Castro. Petrópolis: Vozes, 1971. Pp. 395-402.

<u>7:1-8</u>

1303 Rudolf Pesch, "Pur et impur: Précepte humain et commandement divin, Mc 7,1-8, 14-15, 21-23," *AsSeign* 53 (1970): 50-59.

1304 Richard C. Brand, "Clean and Unclean," *ET* 98/1 (1986-1987): 16-17.

<u>7:1-2</u>

1305 James D. G. Dunn, "The Gospels as Oral Tradition," in *The Living Word*. London: SCM, 1987. Pp. 25-43.

<u>7:2</u>

1306 W. Storch, "Zur Perikope von der Syrophonizierin. Mk 7,2 und Ri 1,7," *BZ* 14/2 (1970): 256-57.

1307 J. H. van Halsema, "Het raadsel als literaire vorm in Marcus en Johannes," *GTT* 83/1 (1983): 1-17.

7:3

1308 P. R. Weis, "A Note on πυγμῇ," *NTS* 3 (1956-1957): 233-36.

1309 S. M. Reynolds, "Πυγμῇ (Mark 7:3) as 'Cupped Hand'," *JBL* 85 (1966): 87-88.

1310 Martin Hengel, "Mc 7:3 πυγμῇ: Die Geschichte einer exegetischen Aporie und der Versuch ihrer Lösung," *ZNW* 60 (1969): 182-98.

1311 S. M. Reynolds, "A Note on Dr. Hengel's Interpretation of *pygmē* in Mark 7:3," *ZNW* 62 (1971): 295-96.

1312 W. D. McHardy, "Mark 7:3: A Reference to the Old Testament?" *ET* 87 (1975-1976): 119.

1313 J. M. Ross, " 'With the Fist'," *ET* 87 (1975-1976): 374-75.

1314 Malcolm Lowe, "Who Were the Ἰουδαῖοι?" *NovT* 18 (1976): 101-30.

1315 T. C. Skeat, "A Note on πυγμῇ in Mark 7:3," *JTS* 41 (1990): 525-27.

7:4

1316 Eric F. F. Bishop, "Ἀπ' ἀγορᾶς: Mark vii.4," *ET* 61 (1949-1950): 219.

7:6-7

1317 Jon B. Daniels, "The Egerton Gospel: Its Place in Early Christianity," doctoral dissertation, Claremont Graduate School, Claremont CA, 1990.

7:6

1318 Pierre Grelot, "Miche 7,6 dans les evangiles et dans la littrature rabbinique," *Bib* 67/3 (1986): 363-77.

7:8-9

1319 J. A. Smit, "Mark 7:8-9 in Counter-Determining Context," *Neo* 25 (1991): 17-28.

7:9-13

1320 J. Duncan M. Derrett, ''Κορβᾶν, ὅ ἐστιν, Δῶρον,'' *NTS* 16/4 (1969-1970): 364-68.

1321 Raymond F. Collins, ''The Fourth Commandment: For Children or for Adults?'' *LivL* 14 (1977): 219-33.

7:10-13

1322 Michael Slusser, ''The Corban Passages in Patristic Exegesis,'' in Thomas Halton and Jospeh P. Williman, eds., *Diakonia* (festschrift for Robert T. Meyer). Washington DC: Catholic University Press, 1986. Pp. 101-107.

7:11

1323 Joseph A. Fitzmyer, ''The Aramaic Qorbān Inscription from Jebel Hallet el-Ṭûri and Mark 7:11/Matt 15:5,'' *JBL* 78 (1959): 60-65.

1324 George W. Buchanan, ''Some Vow and Oath Formulas in the New Testament,'' *HTR* 58 (1965): 319-26.

1325 Albert I. Baumgarten, ''Korban and the Pharisaic Paradosis,'' *JNES* 85 (1984): 521.

7:14-30

1326 J. I. Hasler, ''The Incident of the Syrophoenician Woman (Matt 15:21-28, Mark 7:14-30),'' *ET* 45 (1933-1934): 459-61.

7:14-23

1327 Diego A. Losada, ''Las parábolas de crecimiento en el evangelio de Marcos,'' *RevB* 38 (1976): 113-25.

1328 Eugene E. Lemcio, ''External Evidence for the Structure and Function of Mark IV.1-20, VII.14-23, and VIII.14-21,'' *JTS* 29/2 (1978): 323-38.

1329 Richard C. Brand, ''Clean and Unclean,'' *ET* 98/1 (1986-1987): 16-17.

7:14-15

1330 Rudolf Pesch, ''Pur et impur: Précepte humain et commandement divin, Mc 7,1-8, 14-15, 21-23,'' *AsSeign* 53 (1970): 50-59.

7:14

1331 John Thorley, "Aktionsart in New Testament Greek: Infinitive and Imperative," *NovT* 31 (1989): 290-315.

7:15-23

1332 J. Duncan M. Derrett, "Marco VII,15-23: il vero significato di 'purificare'," *ConRel* 2 (1975): 125-30.

7:15-19

1333 Gerhard Dautzenberg, "Gesetzeskritik und Gesetzesgehorsam in der Jesustradition," in Karl Kertelge, ed., *Das Gesetz im Neuen Testament*. Freiburg: Herder, 1986. Pp. 46-70.

7:15

1334 Harvey K. McArthur, "The Dependence of the Gospel of Thomas on the Synoptics," *ET* 71 (1959-1960): 286-87.

1335 Helmut Merkel, "Markus 7,15—das Jesuswort über die innere Verunreinigung," *ZRGG* 20 (1968): 340-63.

1336 Charles E. Carlston, "The Things that Defile (Mark 7:15) and the Law in Matthew and Mark," *NTS* 15/1 (1968-1969): 75-96.

1337 Jean Domon, "Du texte au sermon: Mc 7,15," *ÉTR* 45 (1970): 349-54.

1338 George D. Kilpatrick, "Jesus, His Family and His Disciples," *JSNT* 15 (1982): 3-19.

1339 Heikki Räisänen, "Jesus and the Food Laws: Reflectings on Mark 7.15," *JSNT* 16 (1982): 79-100.

1340 Heikki Räisänen, "Zur Herkunft von Markus 7,15," in Joël Delobel, ed., *Logia: Les Paroles de Jésus*. BETL #59. Louvain: Peeters Press, 1982. Pp. 477-84.

1341 James D. G. Dunn, "Jesus and Ritual Purity: A Study of the Tradition History of Mk 7,15," in Françios Refoulé, ed., *À cause de l'Evangile: Études sur les synoptiques et les Actes* (festschrift for Jacques Dupont). Paris: Cerf, 1985. Pp. 37-58.

1342 Barnabas Lindars, ''All Foods Clean: Thoughts on Jesus and the Law,'' in Barnabas Lindars, ed., *Law and Religion: Essays on the Place of Law in Israel and Early Christianity*. Cambridge: J. Clarke, 1988. Pp. 61-71.

7:18-19

1343 Harald Sahlin, ''Zum Verständnis der christologischen Anschauung des Markusevangeliums,'' *StTheol* 31 (1977): 1-19.

7:19

1344 Joseph Bonsirven, ''Sur une incise difficultueuse de Marc (7,19),'' in *Mélanges E. Podechard: Études de sciences religieuses*. Lyon: Facultés catholiques, 1945. Pp. 11-15.

1345 Dieter Lührmann, '' '. . . womit er alle Speisen für rein erklärte' (Mk 7,19),'' *WD* 16 (1981): 71-92.

7:21-23

1346 Rudolf Pesch, ''Pur et impur: Précepte humain et commandement divin, Mc 7,1-8, 14-15, 21-23,'' *AsSeign* 53 (1970): 50-59.

1347 Harald Sahlin, ''Emendationsvorschläge zum griechischen Text des Neuen Testaments I,'' *NovT* 24 (1982): 160-79.

7:22-26

1348 Donato Baldi, ''Il problema del sito di Bethsaida e delle moltiplicazioni dei pani,'' *SBFLA* 10 (1959-1960): 120-46.

7:24-37

1349 Eugene A. LaVerdiere, ''Jesus among the Gentiles,'' *Emmanuel* 96 (1990): 338-45.

7:24-31

1350 T. A. Burkill, ''The Syrophoenician Woman: The Congruence of Mark 7:24-31,'' *ZNW* 57 (1966): 23-37.

1351 T. A. Burkill, ''The Syrophoenician Woman: The Context of Mark 7:24-31,'' in L. Wallach, ed., *The Classical Tradition: Literary and Historical Studies* (festschrift for Harry Caplan). Ithaca NY: Cornell University Press, 1966. Pp. 329-44.

1352 T. A. Burkill, "The Historical Development of the Story of the Syrophoenician Woman," *NovT* 9 (1967): 161-77.

1353 T. A. Burkill, "The Syrophoenician Woman: Mark 7:24-31," *StudE* 4 (1968): 166-70.

1354 Jean-Paul Michaud and P. T. David, "Jésus au-delà des frontières de Tyr . . . Analyse de Marc 7,24-31," in A. Chené, et al., eds., *De Jésus et des femmes: Lectures sémiotiques* (festschrift for A. J. Greimas). Paris: Cerf, 1987. Pp. 35-57.

7:24-30

1355 Elmer A. McNamara, "The Syro-Phoenician Woman," *AmER* 127 (1952): 360-69.

1356 José Alonso Díaz, "Cuestión sinóptica y universalidad del mensaje cristiano en el pasaje evangélico de la mujer cananea," *CuBí* 20 (1963): 274-79.

1357 Roy A. Harrisville, "The Woman of Canaan: A Chapter in the History of Exegesis," *Int* 20 (1966): 274-87.

1358 P. E. Scherer, "A Gauntlet with a Gift in It: From Text to Sermon on Matthew 15:21-28 and Mark 7:24-30," *Int* 20 (1966): 387-99.

1359 Barnabas Flammer, "Die Syrophoenizerin. Mk 7,24-30," *TQ* 148 (1968): 463-78. (See the English translation, "The Syro-Phoenician Woman (Mk 7:24-30)," *TD* 18 (1970): 19-24.

1360 Léopold Sabourin, "The Miracles of Jesus (II). Jesus and the Evil Powers," *BTB* 4 (1974): 115-75.

1361 Alice Dermience, "Tradition et rédaction dans la péricope de la Syrophénicienne: Marc 7,24-30," *RTL* 8 (1977): 15-29.

1362 Balembo Buetubela, "La Syrophénicienne: Mc 7,24-30. Étude littéraire et exégétique," *RAfT* 2 (1978): 245-56.

1363 Georges Casalis, "Jesús, el exorcista," *BibFe* 6 (1980): 28-40.

1364 Pierre Guillemette, "La Forme des Recits d'Exorcisme de Bultmann: Un Dogme a Reconsiderer," *EgT* 11/2 (1980): 177-93.

1365 E. A. Russell, "The Canaanite Woman and the Gospels," *StudB* 2 (1980): 263-300.

1366 Josef Blank, "Frauen in den Jesusüberlieferungen," in Gerhard Dautzenberg, et al., eds., *Die Frau im Urchristentum*. Freiburg: Herder, 1983. Pp. 9-91.

1367 Gerd Theissen, "Lokal- und Sozialkolorit in der Geschichte von der Syrophönischen Frau (Mk 7:24-30)," *ZNW* 75/3-4 (1984): 202-25.

1368 Giuseppe Barbaglio, "Gesù e i non ebrei: la sirofenicia," *ParSpirV* 16 (1987): 101-14.

1369 Peter Pimentel, "The 'Unclean Spirits' of St. Mark's Gospel," *ET* 99 (1987-1988): 173-75.

1370 Mary Ann Beavis, "Women as Models of Faith in Mark," *BTB* 18 (1988): 3-9.

1371 Francis Dufton, "The Syrophoenician Woman and Her Dogs," *ET* 100 (1988-1989): 417.

7:26

1372 A. W. Argyle, "Did Jesus Speak Greek?" *ET* 67 (1955-1956): 92-93.

1373 Günther Schwarz, "Συροφοινίκισσα–Χαναναία (Markus 7:26; Matthäus 15:22)," *NTS* 30/4 (1984): 626-28.

1374 R. S. Sugirtharajah, "The Syrophoenician Woman," *ET* 98/1 (1986-1987): 13-15.

1375 J. K. Elliott, "Ἐρωτᾶν and ἐπερωτᾶν in the New Testament," *FilN* 2 (1989): 205-206.

7:27-9:1

1376 Ernst Haenchen, "Die Komposition von Mk VII,27-IX,1 und Par.," *NovT* 6 (1963): 81-109.

7:30

1377 P.-E. Bonnard, "La méthode historico-critique appliquée à Marc 6,30 à 7,30," *FV* 77 (1978): 6-18.

7:31-37

1378 Gerhard Schneider, "Mk 7,31-37," *DWort* 1 (1966): 133-38.

1379 Jean Delorme, "Guérison d'un sourd-bègue: Mc 7,31-37," *AsSeign* 2/54 (1972): 33-44.

1380 I. Paci, "Simbologia o storia? A proposito d'un testo di S. Mc 7,31-37," *PalCl* 55 (1976): 1204-1206.

1381 Ulrich Ruegg, H. Stotzer-Klos, and M. Voser, "Zur Kommunikation befreit. Jesus heilt einen Taubstummen (Markus 7,31-37). Ein Heilungswunder," in Anton Steiner, ed., *Wunder Jesu.* Bibelarbeit in der Gemeinde 2. Basel/Zürich: Reinhardt/Benziger, 1978. Pp. 59-76.

1382 Kristlieb Adloff, "Vernunft und alle Sinne. Predigtmeditalion als ganzheitliche Wahrnehmung des biblischen Textes. Am Beispiel von Markus 7,31-37," in R. Albertz, et al., eds., *Werden und Wirken des Alten Testaments* (festschrift for Claus Westermann). Göttingen: Vandenhoeck & Ruprecht, 1980. Pp. 394-411.

1383 Rudolf Frieling, "Heilungen," in *Christologische Aufsätze.* Stuttgart: Urachhaus, 1982. Pp. 189-246.

1384 R. F. Collins, "Jesus' Ministry to the Deaf and Dumb," *MeliT* 35/1 (1984): 12-36.

1385 Mary Ann Beavis, "The Trial before the Sanhedrin (Mark 14:53-65): Reader Response and Greco-Roman Readers," *CBQ* 49 (1987): 581-96.

1386 Scott Cunningham, "The Healing of the Deaf and Dumb Man (Mark 7:31-37), with Application to the African Context," *AJET* 9/2 (1990): 13-26.

7:31

1387 S. Thomas Parker, "The Decapolis Reviewed," *JBL* 94 (1975): 437-41.

1388 F. G. Lang, " 'Über Sidon mitten ins Gebiet der Dekapolis,' Geographie und Theologie in Markus 7,31," *ZDPV* 94 (1978): 145-60.

7:32-8:35

1389 Bonifatius Fischer, *Die lafeinischen Evangelien bis zum 10. Jahrhundert*. 11. *Varianten zu Markus*. Freiburg: Herder, 1989.

7:34-37

1390 Ulrich B. Müller, "Zur Rezeption Gesetzes-Kritischer Jesusuberlieferung im Fruhen Christentum," *NTS* 27/2 (1980-1981): 158-85.

7:34

1391 Isaac Rabinowitz, " 'Be Opened' = ephphatha (Mark 7:34): Did Jesus Speak Hebrew?" *ZNW* 53 (1962): 229-38.

1392 Louis Leloir, "Ephphatha," *AsSeign* 65 (1963): 31-41.

1393 Matthew Black, "Ephphatha (Mk 7:34) [ta] pascha (Mt 26:18W), [ta] sabbata (passim), [ta] didrachma (Mt 17:24 bis)," in Albert Descamps and André de Halleux, eds., *Mélanges bibliques en hommage au R. P. Béda Rigaux*. Gembloux: Duculot, 1970. Pp. 57-62.

1394 Isaac Rabinowitz, "Εφφαθα (Mark vii.34): Certainly Hebrew, Not Aramaic," *JSS* 16/2 (1971): 151-56.

1395 S. Morag, "Εφφαθα (Mark vii.34) Certainly Hebrew, Not Aramaic?" *JSS* 17/2 (1972): 198-202.

1396 Fred L. Horton, "Nochmals Εφφαθα in MK 7:34," *ZNW* 77/1 (1986): 101-108.

7:35

1397 Tom Baird, "Translating Orthō's at Mark 7:35," *ET* 92 (1980-1981): 337-38.

7:36

1398 James W. Leitch, "The Injunctions of Silence in Mark's Gospel," *ET* 66 (1954-1955): 178-82.

8:1-26

1399 L. H. Jenkins, "A Marcan Doublet: Mark 6.31-7.37, and 8.1-26," in Ernest A. Payne, ed., *Studies in History and Religion* (festschrift for H. Wheeler Robinson). London: Lutterworth, 1942. Pp. 87-111.

8:1-20

1400 B. M. F. van Iersel, "Die wunderbare Speisung und das Abendmal in der synoptischen Tradition (Mk 6:35-44, 8:1-20)," *NovT* 7/3 (1964-1965): 167-94.

8:1-10

1401 Alan Shaw, "The Marcan Feeding Narratives," *CQR* 162 (1961): 268-78.

1402 Joseph Knackstedt, "De duplici miraculo multiplicationis panum," *VD* 41 (1963): 39-51, 140-53.

1403 Giovanni Giavini, "Le due moltiplicazioni di pane nel vangelo di S. Marco," in *Miscellanea Carlo Figini*. Milano: La scuola cattolica, 1964. Pp. 31-46.

1404 G. Ory, "Des pains, des poissons et des hommes," *CCER* 18 (1971): 21-28.

1405 Jean-Marie van Cangh, "Le thème des poissons dans les récits évangéliques de la multiplication des pains," *RB* 78 (1971): 71-83.

1406 T. M. Suriano, "Eucharist Reveals Jesus: The Multiplication of the Loaves," *BibTo* 58 (1972): 642-51.

1407 Rámon Trevijano Etcheverría, "La multiplicación de los panes (Mc 6,30-46; 8,1-10 y par.)," *Bur* 15 (1974): 435-65.

1408 Jean-Marie van Cangh, "La multiplication des pains dans l'évangile de Marc: Essai d'exégèse globale," in M. Sabbe, ed., *L'évangile selon Marc: Tradition et rédaction*. BETL #34. Louvain: Louvain University Press, 1974. Pp. 309-46.

1409 Ignace de la Potterie, "Le sens primitif de la multiplication des pains," in J. Dupont, ed., *Jésus aux origines de la christologie*. BETL #40. Louvain: Louvain University Press, 1975. Pp. 303-29.

1410 Rámon Trevijano Etcheverría, "Historia de milagro y cristolo gía en la multiplicacion de los panes," *Bur* 17 (1976): 9-38.

1411 Léopold Sabourin, *The Divine Miracles Discussed and Defended.* Rome: Catholic Book Agency, 1977.

1412 Karl P. Donfried, "The Feeding Narratives and the Marcan Community: Mark 6,30-45 and 8,1-10," in Dieter Lührmann and Georg Strecker, eds., *Kirche* (festschrift for Günther Bornkamm). Tübingen: Mohr, 1980. Pp. 95-103

1413 Sarrae Masuda, "The Good News of the Miracle of the Bread: The Tradition and Its Markan Redaction," *NTS* 28 (1982): 191-219.

1414 Donald P. Senior, "The Eucharist in Mark: Mission, Reconciliation, Hope," *BTB* 12 (1982): 67-72.

1415 Eugene A. LaVerdiere, "The Evening of the Third Day," *Emmanuel* 91 (1985): 502-507.

1416 Francis J. Moloney, "Reading the Eucharist Texts in Mark," *PIBA* 14 (1991): 7-24.

<u>8:1-9</u>

1417 Austin M. Farrer, "Loaves and Thousands," *JTS* 4 (1953): 1-14.

1418 Henri Clavier, "La multiplication des pains dans le ministère de Jesus," *StudE* 1 (1959): 441-57.

1419 Gerhard Friedrich, "Die beiden Erzählungen von der Speisung in Mark 6,31-44; 8,1-9," *TZ* 20 (1964): 10-22.

1420 Alkuin Heising, "Exegese und Theologie der alt- und neutestamentlichen Speisewunder," *ZKT* 86 (1964): 80-96.

1421 E. Schuyler English, "A Neglected Miracle," *BSac* 126 (1969): 300-305.

1422 Robert M. Fowler, *Loaves and Fishes: The Function of the Feeding Stories in the Gospel of Mark.* Chico CA: Scholars Press, 1981.

1423 Ignace de la Potterie, "The Multiplication of the Loaves in the Life of Jesus," *Communio* 16 (1989): 499-516.

8:1-8

1424 C. H. Dodd, "The Sayings," in *Historical Tradition in the Fourth Gospel.* Cambridge: Cambridge University Press, 1963. Pp. 315-405.

8:3

1425 Frederick W. Danker, "Mark 8:3," *JBL* 82 (1963): 215-16.

8:4-6

1426 Lars Lode, "Narrative Paragraphs in the Gospels and Acts," *BT* 34/3 (1983): 322-35.

8:6

1427 Brian A. Mastin, " 'Jesus Said Grace'," *SJT* 24 (1971): 449-56.

8:7

1428 Lino Cignelli, "La grecità biblica," *SBFLA* 35 (1985): 203-48.

8:8

1429 J. Duncan M. Derrett, "Crumbs in Mark," *DR* 102 (1984): 12-21.

8:10-13

1430 Robert Schlarb, "Die Suche nach dem Messias: ζητέω als Terminus technicus der markinischen Messianologie," *ZNW* 81 (1990): 155-70.

8:10

1431 F. Pili, "Dalmanutha (Mc 8,10)," *BibO* 13 (1971): 227-30.

1432 Wilhelm Bruners, "'Und fuhr in das Gebiet von Dalmanutha' (Mk 8,10): Begegnung mit einer biblischen Landschaft - ein Tagebuch," *BL* 57 (1984): 200-207.

8:11-26

1433 Eugene A. LaVerdiere, "Who Do You Say That I Am?" *Emmanuel* 96 (1990): 506-509.

8:11-13

1434 Thierry Snoy, ''Les miracles dans l'évangile de Marc. Examen de quelques études récentes,'' *RTL* 3 (1972): 449-66; 4 (1973): 58-101.

1435 Jeffrey B. Gibson, ''Jesus' Refusal to Produce a 'Sign' (Mark 8:11-13),'' *JSNT* 38 (1990): 37-66.

8:11-12

1436 Olof Linton, ''The Demand for a Sign from Heaven (Mk 8,11-12 and Parallels),'' *StTheol* 19 (1965): 112-29.

1437 James Swetnam, ''No Sign of Jonah,'' *Bib* 66/1 (1985): 126-30.

1438 Gregory Murray, ''The Sign of Jonah,'' *DR* 107 (1989): 224-25.

8:12-38

1439 Max Meinertz, '' 'Dieses Geschlecht' im Neuen Testament,'' *BZ* 1 (1957): 283-89.

8:12

1440 Gustav Stählin, ''Zum Gebrauch von Beteuerungsformeln im Neuen Testament,'' *NovT* 5 (1962): 115-43.

1441 George W. Buchanan, ''Some Vow and Oath Formulas in the New Testament,'' *HTR* 58 (1965): 319-26.

1442 Dino Merli, ''Il segno di Giona,'' *BibO* 14 (1972): 61-77.

1443 Jeffrey B. Gibson, ''Mark 8:12a: Why Does Jesus 'Sigh Deeply'?'' *BT* 38/1 (1987): 122-25.

8:14-21

1444 Josef Schmid, ''Markus und der aramäische Matthaus,'' in Josef Schmid and Anton Vögtle, eds., *Synoptische Studien* (festschrift for Alfred Wikenhauser). Münich: Zink, 1953. Pp. 75-118.

1445 Otto Kuss, ''Zum Sinngehalt des Doppelgleichnisses vom Senfkorn und Sauerteig,'' *Bib* 40 (1959): 641-53.

1446 Charles Masson, "Des pains oubliés au levain des Pharisiens," in Charles Masson, *Vers les sources d'eau vive: Études d'exégèse et de théologie du Nouveau Testament.* Lausanne: Payot, 1961. Pp. 70-86.

1447 Jindrich Mánek, "Mark viii,14-21," *NovT* 7 (1964-1965): 10-14.

1448 Eugene E. Lemcio, "External Evidence for the Structure and Function of Mark IV.1-20, VII.14-23, and VIII.14-21," *JTS* 29/2 (1978): 323-38.

1449 Norman A. Beck, "Reclaiming a Biblical Text: The Mark 8:14-21 Discussion about Bread in the Boat," *CBQ* 43/1 (1981): 49-56.

1450 Robert M. Fowler, "Thoughts on the History of Reading Mark's Gospel," *EGLMBS* 4 (1984): 120-30.

1451 L. W. Countryman, "How Many Baskets Full? Mark 8:14-21," *CBQ* 47/4 (1985): 643-55.

1452 Jeffrey B. Gibson, "The Rebuke of the Disciples in Mark 8:14-21," *JSNT* 27 (1986): 31-47.

1453 W. Braun, "Were the New Testament Herodians Essenes? A Critique of an Hypothesis," *RevQ* 14 (1989): 75-88.

<u>8:15-19</u>

1454 C. H. Dodd, "The Sayings," in *Historical Tradition in the Fourth Gospel.* Cambridge: Cambridge University Press, 1963. Pp. 315-405.

<u>8:15</u>

1455 Georg Ziener, "Das Bildwort vom Sauerteig Mk 8,15," *TTZ* 67 (1958): 247-48.

1456 Jakob Jervell, "Herodes Antipas og hans plass i evangelieoverleveringen," *NTT* 61 (1960): 28-40.

1457 Athanase Negõitã and C. Daniel, "L'énigme du levain. Ad Mc. viii,15; Mt. xvi,6; et Lc. xii,1," *NovT* 9 (1967): 306-14.

1458 C. Leslie Mitton, ''Leaven,'' *ET* 84 (1972-1973): 339-43.

1459 Ethelbert Stauffer, ''Realistische Jesusworte,'' in William C. Weinrich, ed., *The New Testament Age* (festschrift for Bo Reicke). 2 vols. Macon GA: Mercer University Press, 1984. 2:503-10.

1460 K.-S. Krieger, ''Die Herodianer im Markusevangelium: Ein Versuch ihrer Identifizierung,'' *BibN* 59 (1991): 49-56.

8:19-20

1461 J. Duncan M. Derrett, ''Crumbs in Mark,'' *DR* 102 (1984): 12-21.

8:21

1462 Eugene A. LaVerdiere, '' 'Do You Stil] Not Understand?' Mark 8:21,'' *Emmanuel* 96 (1990): 382-89, 454-63.

8:22-10:52

1463 Ernest Best, ''Discipleship in Mark: Mark 8:22-10:52,'' *SJT* 23/3 (1970): 323-37.

1464 Ched Myers, ''Embracing the Way of Jesus: A Catechism of the Cross,'' *Soj* 16 (1987): 27-30.

8:22-30

1465 Eugene A. LaVerdiere, ''Jesus Christ, the Son of God,'' *Emmanuel* 96 (1990): 524-26.

8:22-26

1466 R. Beauvery, ''La guérison d'un aveugle à Bethsaïde (Mc. 8:22-26),'' *NRT* 90/10 (1968): 1083-91.

1467 Earl S. Johnson, ''Mark 8:22-26: The Blind Man from Bethsaida,'' *NTS* 25/3 (1978-1979): 370-83.

1468 W. J. P. Boyd, ''Is a Basis of Fact Discernible in the Miracle Story of the Healing of the Blind Man at Bethsaida (Mk viii.22-26)?,'' *StudE* 7 (1982): 83-85.

1469 J. K. Howard, ''Men as Trees, Walking: Mark 8.22-26,'' *SJT* 37 (1984): 163-70.

1470 Augustine Stock, ''Hinge Transitions in Mark's Gospel,'' *BTB* 15 (1985): 27-31.

1471 J.-F. Collange, "La déroute de L'aveugle (Mc 8,22-26): Écriture et pratique chrétienne," *RHPR* 66/1 (1986): 21-28.

1472 Paolo Neri, "Per guarire il cieco di Betsaida (Mc 8,22-26)," *BibO* 30 (1988): 138.

8:22

1473 John O'Hara, "Two Bethsaidas or One?" *Scr* 15 (1963): 24-27.

8:23

1474 John Ellington, "Mark 8:23," *BT* 34 (1983): 443-44.

8:24-9:12

1475 Gonzalo Aranda Pérez, "La versión fayúmica del Monasterio Blanco (Mc 8,24-9,12)," *RivSO* 53 (1979): 71-93.

8:24

1476 Herman Ljungvik, "Översättningsförslag och språkliga förklingar till skilde ställen i Nya Testamentet," *SEÅ* 30 (1965): 102-20.

1477 G. M. Lee, "Mark viii.24," *NovT* 20/1 (1978): 74.

1478 Juan Mateos, "Algunas notas sobre el Evangelio de Marcos (part 3)," *FilN* 4 (1991): 193-203.

8:26

1479 J. I. Miller, "Was Tischendorf Really Wrong? Mark 8:26b Revisited," *NovT* 28/2 (1986): 97-103.

1480 J. M. Ross, "Another Look at Mark 8:26," *NovT* 29/2 (1987): 97-99.

8:27-16:20

1481 R. C. Stedman, *The Servant Who Serves*. Waco TX: Word Books, 1976.

8:27-10:52

1482 Hejne Simonsen, "Mark 8,27-10,52 i Markusevangeliets komposition," *DTT* 27 (1956): 83-99.

1483 H.-J. Venetz, "Widerspruch und Nachfolge. Zur Frage des Glaubens an Jesus nach Mk 8,27-10,52," *FZPT* 19 (1972): 111-19.

1484 Dennis C. Duling, "Interpreting the Markan 'Hodology': Biblical Criticism in Preaching and Teaching," *Nexus* 17 (1974): 2-11.

1485 Matthew Vellanickal, "Suffering in the Life and Teaching of Jesus," *Je* 4 (1974): 144-61.

1486 Ernest Best, *Following Jesus. Discipleship in the Gospel of Mark*. Sheffield: JSOT Press, 1981.

<u>8:27-9:32</u>

1487 Oscar H. Hirt, "Interpretation in the Gospels: An Examination of the Use of Redaction Criticism in Mark 8:27-9:32," doctoral dissertation, Dallas Theological Seminary, Dallas TX, 1985.

<u>8:27-9:13</u>

1488 René Lafontaine and Pierre Mourlon Beernaert, "Essai sur la structure de Marc, 8,27-9,13," *RechSR* 57 (1969): 543-61.

1489 Maria Horstmann, *Studien zurn markinischen Christologie: Mk 8:27-9:13 als Zugang zum Christus bild des zweiten Evangeliums*. 2nd ed. Neutestamentliche Abhandlungen, N.F. Band 6. Münster: Aschendorff, 1973.

<u>8:27-9:9</u>

1490 Thomas F. Glasson, "The Uniqueness of Christ: The New Testament Witness," *EQ* 43 (1971): 25-35.

<u>8:27-9:1</u>

1491 Dietrich-Alex Koch, "Zum Verhältnis von Christologie und Eschatologie im Markusevangelium: Beobachtungen auf Grund von 8,27-9,1," in George Strecker, ed., *Jesus Christus in Historie und Theologie: Neutestamentliche Festschrift für Hans Conzelmann zum 60. Geburtstag*. Tübingen: Mohr, 1975. Pp. 395-408.

1492 James L. Mays, "An Exposition of Mark 8:27-9:1," *Int* 30/2 (1976): 174-78.

1493 Norman Perrin, "Redaction Criticism at Work: A Sample," in V. Tollers and J. R. Maier, eds., *The Bible in Its Literary Milieu*. Grand Rapids: Eerdmans, 1979. Pp. 344-61.

1494 Ruth Dannemann, "Geschichtlichkeit und Wunder im Markusevangelium: Eine Studie zu Mk 8:27-9:1," doctoral dissertation, Claremont Graduate School, Claremont CA, 1980.

1495 Paul S. Pudussery, *Discipleship: A Call to Suffering and Glory: An Exegetico-Theological Study of Mk 8,27-9,1; 13,9-13 and 13,24-27*. Rome: Libreria, 1987.

8:27-35

1496 Adelbert Denaux, "La confession de Pierre et la première annonce de la Passion. Mc 8,27-35," *AsSeign* 55 (1974): 31-39.

1497 Elisabeth Moltmann-Wendel and Jürgen Moltmann, "Who Do You Say That I Am? (Mark 8:27-35)," *RW* 40/8 (1989): 179-94.

8:27-33

1498 Josef Schmid, "Markus und der aramäische Matthaus," in Josef Schmid and Anton Vögtle, eds., *Synoptische Studien* (festschrift for Alfred Wikenhauser). Münich: Zink, 1953. Pp. 75-118.

1499 B. Willaert, "La connexion litteraire entre la premiere prediction de la passion et la confession de Pierre chez les synoptiques," *ETL* 32 (1956): 24-45.

1500 T. A. Burkill, "A Meaning that is Not Understood," in *Mysterious Revelation: An Examination of the Philosophy of St. Mark's Gospel*. Ithaca NY: Cornell University Press, 1963. Pp. 168-87.

1501 Carlo M. Martini, "La confessione messianica di Pietro a Caesarea e l'inizio del nuovo popolo di Dio secondo il Vangelo di S. Marco (8,27-33)," *CivCatt* 118 (1967): 544-51.

1502 Ignace de la Potterie, "La confessione messianica di Pietro in Marco 8,27-33," in Giovanni Canfora, ed., *San Pietro*. Brescia: Paideia, 1967. Pp. 59-77.

1503 Adelbert Denaux, "Petrusbelijdenis en eerste lijdensvoorspelling. Een exegese van Mc. 8,27-33 par. Lc. 9,18-22," *CBG* 15 (1969): 188-220.

1504 Josef Ernst, "Petrusbekenntnis—Leidensankündigung—Satanswort (Mk 8,27-33). Tradition und Redaktion," *Cath* 32 (1978): 46-73.

1505 Ulrich Luz, "The Secrecy Motif and Marcan Christology," in C. M. Tuckett, ed., *The Messianic Secret*. Philadelphia: Fortress Press, 1983. Pp. 75-96.

1506 Hendrikus Boers, "Reflections on the Gospel of Mark: A Structural Investigation," *SBLSP* 26 (1987): 255-67.

1507 Hans Klein, "Das Bekenntnis des Petrus und die Anfänge des Christusglaubens im Urchristentum," *EvT* 47 (1987): 176-92.

8:27-30

1508 A. G. Barkey Wolf, *De evangelisten en hun geschriften*. Kampen: Kok. 1950.

1509 Raymond E. Brown, "Incidents That Are Units in the Synoptic Gospels but Dispersed in St. John," *CBQ* 23 (1961): 143-60.

1510 A.-S. Di Marco, "Peter's Confession and the 'Satan' Saying: The Problem of Jesus' Messiahship," in J. M. Robinson, ed., *The Future of Our Religious Past* (festschrift for Rudolf Bultmann). C. E. Carlston and R. P. Scharlemann, trans. London: SCM, 1971. Pp. 169-202.

1511 Rudolf Pesch, "Das Messiasbekenntnis des Petrus (Mk 8,27-30). Neuverhandlung einer alten Frage," *BZ* 17 (1973): 178-95; 18 (1974): 20-31.

1512 Harald Sahlin, "Zum Verständnis der christologischen Anschauung des Markusevangeliums," *StTheol* 31 (1977): 1-19.

1513 Hubert Ordon, "Literacko-teologiczne przygotowanie perykopy o wyznaniu Piotra," *RoczTK* 29 (1982): 97-109.

1514 Léopold Sabourin, "About Jesus' Self-Understanding," *RSB* 3/3 (1983): 129-34.

1515 David R. Catchpole, "The 'Triumphal' Entry [Mk 8:27-30; 11:1-11]," in Ernst Bammel and C. F. D. Moule, eds., *Jesus and the Politics of His Day*. Cambridge: Cambridge University Press, 1984. Pp. 319-34.

1516 Lyle D. vander Broek, "Literary Context in the Gospels," *RR* 39/2 (1986): 113-17.

8:27-29

1517 Kurt Schubert, "Die Juden und die Römer," *BL* 36 (1962): 235-42.

8:27

1518 Gottfried Schille, "Prolegomena zur Jesusfrage," *TLZ* 93 (1968): 481-88.

1519 Enzo Bianchi, " 'Chi dite che io sia?' Per una nuova conoscenza di Gesù di Nazareth," *Servitium* 6 (1972): 53-68, 205-18.

1520 T. Bailey, "Saint Mark viii.27 Again," *StudE* 7 (1982): 17-20.

1521 Harald Sahlin, "Emendationsvorschläge zum griechischen Text des Neuen Testaments I," *NovT* 24 (1982): 160-79.

1522 Marvin W. Meyer, *Who Do People Say I Am? The Interpretation of Jesus in the New Testament Gospels*. Grand Rspids: Eerdmans, 1983.

8:28

1523 Carl H. Kraeling, "Was Jesus Accused of Necromancy?" (Mk 8:28) *JBL* 59 (1940): 147-57.

1524 Athol Gill, "Women Ministers in the Gospel of Mark," *ABR* 35 (1987): 14-21.

1525 S. J. Nortje, "John the Baptist and the Resurrection Traditions in the Gospels," *Neo* 23 (1989): 349-58.

8:29-9:1

1526 H. P. Hamann, "A Plea for Commonsense in Exegesis," *CTQ* 42 (1978): 115-29.

8:29

1527 Johannes Althausen, "Wer sagt denn ihr, dass ich sei? (Mk 8,29)," *LR* 27 (1977): 89-100.

1528 Harry T. Fleddermann, "The Central Question of Mark's Gospel: A Study of Mark 8:29," doctoral dissertation, Graduate Theological Union, Berkeley CA, 1978.

1529 Hubert Frankemölle, "Judische Messiaserwartung und christlicher Messiasglaube: Hermeneutische Anmerkungen im Kontext des Petrusbekenntnisses Mk 8,29," *K* 20 (1978): 97-109.

1530 Alfred Krass, "Christ in Our History: Not Just a Savior for Individual Sins," *OSide* 22/2 (1986): 61-63.

1531 Gérard Claudel, *La confession de Pierre: Trajectoire d'une péricope évangélique*. Paris: Gabalda, 1988.

8:30

1532 James W. Leitch, "The Injunctions of Silence in Mark's Gospel," *ET* 66 (1954-1955): 178-82.

8:31-11:10

1533 C. J. Reedy, "Mark 8:31-11:10 and the Gospel Ending," *CBQ* 34/2 (1972): 188-97.

8:31-39

1534 A. H. Snyman, "Style and Meaning in Romans 8:31-39," *Neo* 18 (1984): 94-103.

8:31-38

1535 Rudolf Schnackenburg, "Zur formgeschichtlichen Methode in der Evangelienforschung," *ZKT* 85 (1963): 16-32.

1536 José B. Metz, "Messianische Geschichte als Leidensgeschichte: Meditation zu Mk 8,31-38," in Joachim

Gnilka, ed., *Neues Testament und Kirche* (festschrift for Rudolf Schnackenburg). Freiburg: Herder, 1974. Pp. 63-70.

1537 José B. Metz and Jürgen Moltmann, *Leidensgeschichte: Zwei Meditationen zu Markus 8,31-38*. Freiburg: Herder, 1974.

8:31-37

1538 C. Milo Connick, "Auslegung von Markus 4,35-41 par; Markus 8,31-37 par; Römer 1,3f.," *EvErz* 20 (1968): 249-60.

8:31-36

1539 Nigel Turner, "The Minor Verbal Agreements of Mt. and Lk. against Mk.," *StudE* 1 (1959): 223-34.

8:31-34

1540 Robert J. Maddox, "The Function of the Son of Man according to the Synoptic Gospels," *NTS* 15 (1968-1969): 45-74.

8:31-33

1541 Eugene A. LaVerdiere, "First Prophetic Announcement of the Passion," *Emmanuel* 96 (1990): 574-79.

8:31

1542 Johannes B. Bauer, "Drei Tage," *Bib* 39 (1958): 354-58.

1543 Jacques Dupont, "Ressuscité 'le troisième jour'," *Bib* 40 (1959): 742-61.

1544 Georg Strecker, "Die Leidens- und Auferstehungsvoraussagen im Markusevangelium (Mk 8,31; 9,31; 10,32-34)," *ZTK* 64 (1964): 16-39.

1545 I. Howard Marshall, "The Synoptic Son of Man Sayings in Recent Discussion," *NTS* 12 (1965-1966): 327-51.

1546 Richard T. France, "The Servant of the Lord in the Teaching of Jesus," *TynB* 19 (1968): 26-52.

1547 Joachim Jeremias, "Gesù predice la sua passione: Morte e resurrezione (Mc 8,31 par etc.)," *PV* 15 (1970): 81-93.

1548 Carsten Colpe, "Traditionsüberschreitende Argumentationen zu Aussagen Jesu über sich selbst," in Gert Jeremias, et al., eds., *Tradition und Glaube: das frühe Christentum in seiner Umwelt* (festschrift for Karl Georg Kuhn). Göttingen: Vandenhoeck & Ruprecht, 1971. Pp. 230-45.

1549 Otto Michel, "Der Umbruch: Messianität = Menschensohn: Fragen zu Markus 8,31," in Gert Jeremias, et al., eds., *Tradition und Glaube: Das frühe Christentuminseiner Umwelt* (festschrift for Karl Georg Kuhn). Göttingen: Vandenhoeck & Ruprecht, 1971. Pp. 310-16.

1550 Paul Hoffmann, "Mk 8,31. Zur Herkunft und markinischen Rezeption einer alten Überlieferung," in Paul Hoffmann, ed., *Orientierung an Jesus: Zur Theologie der Synoptiker* (festschrift for Josef Schmid). Freiburg: Herder, 1973. Pp. 170-204.

1551 W. J. Bennett, "The Son of Man," *NovT* 17/2 (1975): 113-29.

1552 Marcel Bassin, "L'annonce de la passion et les critères de l'historicíte," *RevSR* 50 (1976): 289-329; 51 (1977): 187-213.

1553 Bruce A. Stevens, " 'Why Must the Son of Man Suffer?' The Divine Warrior in the Gospel of Mark," *BZ* 31 (1987): 101-10.

1554 Juan Mateos, "Algunas notas sobre el Evangelio de Marcos (part 2)," *FilN* 3 (1990): 159-66.

<u>8:32</u>

1555 Elian Cuviller, "Il proclamait ouvertement la parole: notule sur la traduction de Marc 8:32a," *TR* 63/3 (1988): 427-28.

<u>8:33</u>

1556 Frederiek Bussby, "Mark viii.33: A Mistranslation from the Aramaic?" *ET* 61 (1949-1950): 159.

1557 Tomas Arvedson, "Lärjungaskapets 'demoni'. Några reflexioner till Mk 8,33 par.," *SEÅ* 28/29 (1963): 54-63.

1558 Carl Kazmierski, "Mk 8,33—Eine Ermahnung andie Kirche?" in Helmut Merklein and Joachim Lange, eds., *Biblische Randbemerkungen: Schülerfestschrift für Rudolf Schnackenburg zum 60. Geburtstag*. Würzburg: Echter-Verlag, 1974. Pp. 103-12.

8:34-9:1

1559 John P. Brown, "Synoptic Parallels in the Epistles and Form-History," *NTS* 10 (1963-1964): 27-48.

1560 B. M. F. van Iersel and T. van den Ende, "Zelf-verloochening een taal-ontsporing," *Schrift* 63 (1979): 84-90.

1561 Jan Lambrecht, "Q-Influence on Mark 8,34-9,1," in Joël Delobel, ed., *Logia: Les Paroles de Jésus*. BETL #59. Louvain: Peeters Press, 1982. Pp. 277-304.

1562 Willem S. Vorster, "On Early Christian Communities and Theological Perspectives," *JTSA* 59 (1987): 26-34.

8:34-38

1563 J. J. A. Kahmann, "Het volgen van Christus door zelfverloochening en kruisdragen volgens Mark 8,34-38 par.," *TijT* 1 (1961): 205-26.

8:34-35

1564 J. G. Griffiths, "The Disciple's Cross," *NTS* 16 (1969-1970): 358-64.

1565 Robert C. Tannehill, "Reading It Whole: The Function of Mark 8:34-35 in Mark's Story," *QR* 2 (1982): 67-78.

8:34

1566 Günther Schwarz, " 'ἀπαρνησάσθω ἑαυτὸν . . . ?' (Markus VIII,34 parr)," *NovT* 17/2 (1975): 109-12.

1567 J. Duncan M. Derrett, "Taking Up the Cross and Turning the Cheek," in A. E. Harvey, ed., *Alternative Approaches to New Testament Study*. London: Latimer, 1985. Pp. 61-78.

1568 David P. Secco, "Take up Your Cross," in Peter T. O'Brien and David G. Patterson, eds., *God Who Is Rich in*

Mercy (festschrift for D. B. Knox). Grand Rapids: Baker, 1986. Pp. 139-51.

1569 Günther Schwarz, "Der Nachfolgespruch Markus 8:34b,c parr: Emendation und Rückübersetzung," *NTS* 33/2 (1987): 255-65.

1570 John Thorley, "Aktionsart in New Testament Greek: Infinitive and Imperative," *NovT* 31 (1989): 290-315.

8:35-38

1571 Klaus Berger, "Zu den sogenannten Sätzen heiligen Rechts," *NTS* 17 (1970-1971): 10-40.

1572 Ernest Best, "An Early Sayings Collection," *NovT* 18/1 (1976): 1-16.

1573 Joachim Schüling, *Studien zum Verhältnis von Logienquelle und Markusevangelium.* Würzburg: Echter, 1991.

8:35

1574 Wilhelm Pesch, *Der Lohngedanke in der Lehre Jesu: verplichen mit der religiösen Lohnlehre des Spätjudentums.* Münchener theologische Studien #I/7. Münich: Zink, 1955.

1575 C. H. Dodd, "Some Johannine 'Herrenworte' with Parallels in the Synoptic Gospels," *NTS* 2 (1955-1956): 75-86.

1576 Johannes B. Bauer, " 'Wer sein Leben retten will . . .' (Mk 8,35 Parr.)," in J. Blinzler, O. Duss, and F. Mussner, eds., *Neutestamentliche Aufsätze-Festschrift für Prof. Josef Schmid zum 70. Geburtstag.* Regensburg: Friedrich Pustet, 1963. Pp. 7-10.

1577 C. H. Dodd, "The Sayings," in *Historical Tradition in the Fourth Gospel.* Cambridge: Cambridge University Press, 1963. Pp. 315-405.

1578 J. Sudbrack, " 'Wer sein Leben um meinetwillen verliert . . .' (Mk 8,35). Biblische Uberlegungen zur Grundlegung christlicher Existenz," *GeistL* 40 (1967): 161-70.

1579 W. A. Beardslee, "Saving One's Life by Losing It," *JAAR* 47 (1979): 57-72.

1580 Grant Loewen, "The Loss Leader," *Crux* 20/2 (1984): 9-11.

1581 Walter Rebell, " 'Sein Leben verlieren' (Mark 8.35 parr.) als Strukturmoment vor- und nachosterlichen Glaubens," *NTS* 35/2 (1989): 202-18.

8:36

1582 George Howard, "Harmonistic Readings in the Old Syriac Gospels," *HTR* 73 (1980): 473-91.

1583 José O'Callaghan, "Nota crítica a Mc 8,36," *Bib* 64/1 (1983): 116-17.

8:37

1584 M. H. Marco, " '¿Que dará el hombre a cambio de su alma?' (Mc 8,37)," *CuBí* 31 (1974): 23-26.

1585 B. Janowski, "Auslösung des vervirkten Lebens: Zur Geschichte und Struktur der biblischen Lösegeldvorstellung," *ZTK* 79 (1982): 25-59.

8:38

1586 Ernst Käsemann, "Sätze heiligen Rechtes im Neuen Testament," *NTS* 1 (1954-1955): 248-60.

1587 H. P. Owen, "The Parousia of Christ in the Synoptic Gospels," *SJT* 12 (1959): 171-92.

1588 C. K. Barrett, "I Am Not Ashamed of the Gospel," *AnBib* 42 (1970): 19-41.

1589 J. F. Seitz, "The Future Coming of the Son of Man: Three Midrashic Formulations in the Gospel of Mark," *StudE* 6 (1973): 478-94.

1590 Howard Clark Kee, "The Linguistic Background of 'Shame' in the New Testament," in Matthew Black and W. A. Smalley, eds., *On Language, Culture and Religion* (festschrift for Eugene A. Nida). Paris: Mouton, 1974. Pp. 133-47.

1591 W. G. Kümmel, "Das Verhalten Jesus gegenüber und das Verhalten des Menschensohns. Markus 8,38 par. und Lukas

12,8f. par. und Matthäus 10,32f.,'' in Rudolf Pesch and Rudolf Schnackenburg, eds., with Odilo Kaiser, *Jesus und den Menschensohn* (festschrift for Anton Vögtle). Freiburg: Herder, 1975. Pp. 210-24.

1592 Rudolf Pesch, ''Über die Autorität Jesu: Eine Rückfrage anhand des Bekenner- und Verleugnerspruchs Lk 12,8f par,'' in Rudolf Schnackenburg, et al., eds., *Die Kirche des Anfangs* (festschrift for Heinz Schürmann). Leipzig: St. Benno, 1977. Pp. 25-56.

1593 George R. Beasley-Murray, ''The Parousia in Mark,'' *RevExp* 75/4 (1978): 565-81.

1594 Barnabas Lindars, ''Jesus as Advocate: A Contribution to the Christology Debate,'' *BJRL* 62/2 (1979-1980): 476-97.

1595 Alexandro Díez-Macho, ''La cristología del Hijo del Hombre y el uso de la tercera persona en vez de la primera,'' *ScripT* 14 (1982): 189-201.

1596 Ragnar Leivestad, ''Wer ist der Vater des Menschensohns? Einige Reflexionen über den Ausdruck 'in der Herrlichkeit seines Vaters' in Mk 8,38,'' in Jarmo Kiilunen, et al., eds., *Glaube und Gerechtigkeit* (festschrift for Rafael Gyllenberg). Helsinki: Finnish Exegetical Society, 1983. Pp. 95-108.

1597 J. M. Ross, ''Some Unnoticed Points in the Text of the New Testament,'' *NovT* 25 (1983): 59-72.

1598 E. A. Obeng, ''The 'Son of Man' Motif and the Intercession of Jesus,'' *AfTJ* 19 (1990): 155-67.

9:1-10

1599 Louis Soubigou, ''A Transfiguração de Cristo Segundo São Marcos (9,1-10),'' *RCB* 12 (1975): 59-72.

9:1

1600 Günther Bornkamm, ''Die Verzogerung der Parusie: Exegetische Bemerkungen zu zwei synoptischen Texten,'' in Werner Schmauch, ed., *In Memoriam Ernst Lohmeyer*. Stuttgart: Evangelisches Verlagswerk, 1951. Pp. 116-26.

1601 Ernst Fuchs, "Verheissung und Erfüllung," in *Zur Frage nach dem historischen Jesus*. Tübingen: Mohr, 1960. Pp. 66-78.

1602 T. A. Burkill, "The Exegesis of Mark 9:1," in *Mysterious Revelation: An Examination of the Philosophy of St. Mark's Gospel*. Ithaca NY: Cornell University Press, 1963. Pp. 165-67.

1603 Stephen S. Smalley, "The Delay of the Parousia," *JBL* 83 (1964): 41-54.

1604 Étienne Trocmé, "Mc 9:1: prédiction ou réprimande?" *StudE* 2 (1964): 259-65.

1605 Norman Perrin, "The Composition of Mark ix,1," *NovT* 11 (1969): 67-70.

1606 Charles L. Holman, "The Idea of an Imminent Parousia in the Synoptic Gospels," *SBT* 3 (1973): 15-31.

1607 I. A. Moir, "The Reading of Codex Bezae (D-05) at Mark 9:1," *NTS* 20 (1973-1974): 105.

1608 Juan Dobládez, "La apocaliptica como origen del género literario evangelio," *EstFr* 76 (1975): 131-57.

1609 Heinrich Greeven, "Nochmals Mk IX.1 in Codex Bezae," *NTS* 23/3 (1976-1977): 305-308.

1610 Martin Künzi, *Das Naherwartungslogion Markus 9,1 par: Geschichte seiner Auslegung, mit einem Nachwort zur Auslegungsgeschichte von Markus 13,30 par*. Beiträge zur Geschichte der biblischen Exegese 21. Tübingen: Mohr, 1977.

1611 Bruce D. Chilton, "An Evangelical and Critical Approach to the Sayings of Jesus," *Themelios* 3/3 (1978): 78-85.

1612 Kent E. Brower, "Mark 9:1: Seeing the Kingdom in Power," *JSNT* 6 (1980): 17-41.

1613 Bruce D. Chilton, " 'Not to Taste Death': A Jewish, Christian and Gnostic Usage," *StudE* 2 (1980): 29-36.

1614 Enrique Nardoni, "A Redactional Interpretation of Mark 9:1," *CBQ* 43/3 (1981): 365-84.

1615 M. Eugene Boring, *Sayings of the Risen Jesus: Christian Prophecy in the Synoptic Tradition.* SNTSMS #46. Cambridge: Cambridge University Press, 1982.

1616 Barry S. Crawford, "Near Expectation in the Sayings of Jesus," *JBL* 101/2 (1982): 225-44.

1617 Dietfried Gewalt, "1 Thess 4,15-17; 1 Kor 15,51 und Mk 9,1: Zur Abgrenzung Eines 'Herrenwortes'," *LB* 51 (1982): 105-13.

1618 John J. Kilgallen, "Mark 9:1: The Conclusion of a Pericope," *Bib* 63/1 (1982): 81-83.

1619 Heinz Giesen, "Mk 9,1—ein Wort Jesu über die nahe Parusie?" *TTZ* 92 (1983): 134-48.

1620 Domingo Muñoz León, "¿Logion de la parusía o logion de cumplimiento mesiánico?" in A. Vargas-Machuca and G. Ruiz, eds., *Palabra y Vida* (festschrift for José Díaz). Madrid: Universidad Pontificia Comillas, 1983. Pp. 135-52.

1621 Robert Smith, "Wounded Lion: Mark 9:1 and Other Missing Pieces," *CThM* 11/6 (1984): 333-49.

1622 David R. Jackson, "The Priority of the Son of Man Sayings," *WTJ* 47 (1985): 83-96.

1623 Joachim Schüling, *Studien zum Verhältnis von Logienquelle und Markusevangelium.* Würzburg: Echter, 1991.

9:2-13

1624 Charles Masson, "La transfiguration de Jesus (Marc 9:2-13)," *RTP* 97 (1964): 1-14.

1625 Sigfred Pedersen, "Die Proklamation Jesu als des eschatologischen Offenbarungstragers," *NovT* 17 (1975): 241-64.

1626 Felix H. Daniel, "The Transfiguration (Mark 9:2-13 and Parallels): A Redaction Critical and Traditio-historical

Study," doctoral dissertation, Vanderbilt University, Nashville TN, 1976.

1627 Morna D. Hooker, "What Doest Thou Here, Elijah: A Look at St. Mark's Account of the Transfiguration," in L. D. Hurst and N. T. Wright, eds., *The Glory of Christ in the New Testament*. Oxford: Clarendon Press, 1987. Pp. 59-70.

1628 Barbara E. Reid, "The Transfiguration: An Exegetical Study of Luke 9:28-36," doctoral dissertation, Catholic University of America, Washington DC, 1988.

9:2-10

1629 T. A. Burkill, "A Meaning that is Not Understood," in *Mysterious Revelation: An Examination of the Philosophy of St. Mark's Gospel*. Ithaca NY: Cornell University Press, 1963. Pp. 168-87.

1630 Rafael Silva Costoya, "El relato de la transfiguración. Problemas de crítica literaria y motivos teológicos en Mc 9,2-10; Mt 17,1-9; Lc 9,28-37," *Comp* 10 (1965): 5-26.

1631 Michel Coune, "Radieuse Transfiguration. Mt 17,1-9; Mc 9,2-10; Lc 9,28-36," *AsSeign* 15 (1973): 44-84.

1632 Stuart G. Hall, "Synoptic Transfigurations: Mark 9:2-10 and Partners," *KingsTR* 10 (1987): 41-44.

1633 Elizabeth Laursen, *Messiashemmeligheden i Markusevangeliet med udgangspunkft i Markus Kup. 9,2-10*. Arken-tryk #87. Copenhagen: Arken, 1989.

9:2-9

1634 Ernst L. Schnellbächer, "Sachgemässe Schriftauslegung," *NovT* 30 (1988): 114-31.

9:2-8

1635 C. H. Dodd, "The Appearances of the Risen Christ: An Essay in Form-Criticism of the Gospels," in D. E. Nineham, ed., *Studies in the Gospels* (festschrift for R. H. Lightfoot). Oxford: Blackwell, 1955. Pp. 9-35.

1636 George B. Caird, "The Transfiguration," *ET* 67 (1955-1956): 291-94.

1637 Anthony Kenny, "The Transfiguration and the Agony in the Garden," *CBQ* 19 (1957): 444-52.

1638 André Feuillet, "Les perspectives propres à chaque évangéliste dans les récits de la transfiguration," *Bib* 39 (1958): 281-301.

1639 T. A. Burkill, "The Confession and the Transfiguration," in *Mysterious Revelation: An Examination of the Philosophy of St. Mark's Gospel*. Ithaca NY: Cornell University Press, 1963. Pp. 145-64.

1640 S. Lewis Johnson, "The Transfiguration of Christ," *BSac* 124 (1967): 133-43.

1641 Robert H. Stein, "Is the Transfiguration a Misplaced Resurrection Account?" *JBL* 95/1 (1976): 79-96.

1642 Albert Fuchs, "Die Verklärungserzahlung des Mk-Ev in der Sicht moderner Exegese," *TPQ* 125 (1977): 29-37.

1643 Bruce D. Chilton, "The Transfiguration: Dominical Assurance and Apostolic Vision," *NTS* 27/1 (1980-1981): 115-24.

1644 James M. Robinson, "Jesus: From Easter to Valentinus (or the Apostles' Creed)," *JBL* 101 (1982): 5-37.

1645 Walter Wink, "Mark 9:2-8," *Int* 36/1 (1982): 63-67.

1646 Gerald O'Collins, "Luminous Appearances of the Risen Christ," *CBQ* 46 (1984): 247-54.

1647 Judith Brocklehurst, "Most Blessed, Holy and Glorious," *Touch* 3/1 (1985): 44-48.

1648 Jean Galot, "Révélation du Christ et liturgie juive," *EV* 98 (1988): 145-52.

1649 Jürgen Seim, "Offenbarung: Predigt über Markus 9.2-8," *EvT* 50 (1990): 275-78.

9:2-3

1650 L. F. Rivera, "El misterio del Hijo del Hombre en la transfiguración (Mr 9,2-3)," *RevB* 28 (1966): 19-34, 79-89.

9:2

1651 Jan W. Doeve, "Le rôle de la tradition orale dans la composition des Évangiles synoptiques," in J. Heuschen, ed., *La formation des évangiles: Problème synoptique et Formgeschichte*. Paris: Desclée, 1957. Pp. 70-84.

1652 Wolfgang Gerber, "Die Metamorphose Jesu, Mark. 9,2f. par.," *TZ* 23 (1967): 385-95.

1653 Foster R. McCurley, " 'And After Six Days' (Mark 9:2): A Semitic Literary Device," *JBL* 93/1 (1974): 67-81.

1654 Ernst L. Schnellbächer, "**Καὶ μετὰ ἡμέρας ἓξ** (Markus 9:2)," *ZNW* 71/3 (1980): 252-57.

1655 Jean Galot, "La prima professione di fede cristiana," *CC* 132 (1981): 27-40.

9:4-13

1656 A. Ragot, "Le retour d'Élie," *CCER* 15 (1967): 15-16.

9:4

1657 D. Baly, "The Transfiguration Story," *ET* 82 (1970-1971): 82-83.

1658 Jeremy Moiser, "Moses and Elijah," *ET* 96 (1984-1985): 216-17.

9:5-7

1659 J. Duncan M. Derrett, "Peter and the Tabernacles," *DR* 108 (1990): 37-48.

9:5

1660 Paul Ellingworth, "How Is Your Handbook Wearing?" *BT* 30 (1979): 236-41.

1661 José O'Callaghan, "Discussio Critica en Mt 17,4," *Bib* 65/1 (1984): 91-93.

1662 Benedict T. Viviano, "Rabbouni and Mark 9:5," *RB* 97 (1990): 207-18.

9:7

1663 W. Dekker, "De 'geliefde Zoon' in de synoptische evangeliën," *NTT* 16 (1961-1962): 94-106.

1664 P. G. Bretscher, "Exodus 4:22-23 and the Voice from Heaven," *JBL* 87 (1968): 301-11.

1665 Michael D. Goulder, "On Putting Q to the Test," *NTS* 24 (1977-1978): 218-34.

1666 Alfredo Scattolon, "L'ἀγαπητός sinottico nella luce della tradizione giudaica," *RBib* 26 (1978): 3-32.

1667 Christopher M. Tuckett, "On the Relationship between Matthew and Luke," *NTS* 30 (1984): 130-42.

9:8

1668 Nigel M. Watson, "Willi Marxsen's Approach to Christology," *ET* 97 (1985-1986): 36-42.

9:9-13

1669 Josef Schmid, "Markus und der aramäische Matthaus," in Josef Schmid and Anton Vögtle, eds., *Synoptische Studien* (festschrift for Alfred Wikenhauser). Münich: Zink, 1953. Pp. 75-118.

1670 Klaus Berger, *Die Auferstehung des Propheten und die Erhöhung des Menschensohnes: Traditionsgeschichtliche Untersuchungen zur Deutung des Geschickes Jesu in frühchristlichen Texte*. SUNT #13. Göttingen: Vandenhoeck & Ruprecht, 1976.

1671 Matthew Black, "The Theological Appropriation of the Old Testament by the New Testament," *SJT* 39/1 (1986): 1-17.

9:9-12

1672 Robert J. Maddox, "The Function of the Son of Man according to the Synoptic Gospels," *NTS* 15 (1968-1969): 45-74.

9:9

1673 James W. Leitch, "The Injunctions of Silence in Mark's Gospel," *ET* 66 (1954-1955): 178-82.

9:11-13

1674 Percy J. Heawood, "Mark ix.11-13," *ET* 64 (1952-1953): 239.

1675 C. Clare Oke, "The Rearrangement and Transmission of Mark ix.11-13," *ET* 64 (1952-1953): 187-88.

1676 Johannes M. Nützel, "Zu Schicksal der eschatologischen Propheten," *BZ* 20 (1976): 59-94.

1677 Joseph A. Fitzmyer, "More about Elijah Coming First," *JBL* 104 (1985): 295-96.

1678 Joel Marcus, "Mark 9:11-13: 'As It Has Been Written'," *ZNW* 80/1 (1989): 42-63.

1679 J. Taylor, "The Coming of Elijah, Mt 17,10-13 and Mk 9,11-13: The Development of the Texts," *RB* 98 (1991): 107-19.

9:11

1680 Dale C. Allison, "Elijah Must Come First," *JBL* 103 (1984): 256-58.

9:12-13

1681 J. Duncan M. Derrett, "Herod's Oath and the Baptist's Head (With an Appendix on Mk IX.12-13, Mal III.24, Micah VII.6)," *BZ* 9 (1965): 49-59, 233-46.

9:12

1682 J. Neville Birdsall, "The Withering of the Fig Tree," *ET* 73 (1961-1962): 191.

1683 Richard T. France, "The Servant of the Lord in the Teaching of Jesus," *TynB* 19 (1968): 26-52.

1684 Carsten Colpe, "Traditionsüberschreitende Argumentationen zu Aussagen Jesu über sich selbst," in Gert Jeremias, Heinz-Wolfgang Kung, and Hartmut Stegemann, eds., *Tradition und Glaube: das frühe Christentum in seiner*

Umwelt. Festgabe für Karl Georg Kuhn zum 65. Geburtstag. Göttingen: Vandenhoeck & Ruprecht, 1971. Pp. 230-45.

1685 W. J. Bennett, "The Son of Man," *NovT* 17/2 (1975): 113-29.

1686 Walter C. Kaiser, "The Promise of the Arrival of Elijah in Malachi and the Gospels," *GTJ* 3/2 (1982): 221-33.

1687 John A. T. Robinson, "Did Jesus Have a Distinctive Use of Scripture?" in *Twelve More New Testament Studies*. London: SCM, 1984. Pp. 35-43.

9:13-32

1688 Wilfrid J. Harrington, *A Key to the Parables*. New York: Paulist Press, 1964.

9:13

1689 Ethelbert Stauffer, "Realistische Jesusworte," in William C. Weinrich, ed., *The New Testament Age* (festschrift for Bo Reicke). 2 vols. Macon GA: Mercer University Press, 1984. 2:503-10.

1690 S. J. Nortje, "John the Baptist and the Resurrection Traditions in the Gospels," *Neo* 23 (1989): 349-58.

9:14-29

1691 Jean Levie, "L'évangile araméen de S. Matthieu est-il la source de l'évangile de S. Marc?" *NRT* 76 (1954): 689-715, 812-43.

1692 Harald Riesenfeld, "De fientlige andarna (Mk 9:14-29)," *SEÅ* 22/23 (1957): 64-74.

1693 Günther Bornkamm, "Πνεῦμα ἄλαλον: Eine Studie zum Markusevangelium," in Konrad Gaiser, ed., *Das Altertum und jedes neue Gute. Für Wolfgang Schadewadt zum 15 März 1970*. Stuttgart/Berlin/Köln/Mainz: Kohlhammer, 1970. Pp. 369-85.

1694 Wolfgang Schenk, "Tradition und Redaktion in der Epileptikerperikope, Mk 9:14-29," *ZNW* 63 (1972): 76-94.

1695 Paul J. Achtemeier, ''Miracles and the Historical Jesus: A Study of Mark 9:14-29,'' *CBQ* 37/4 (1975): 471-91.

1696 Gerhard Barth, ''Glaube und Zweifel in den synoptischen Evangelien,'' *ZTK* 72 (1975): 269-92.

1697 Walter Schmithals, ''Die Heilung des Epileptischen (Mk 9,14-29): Ein Beitrag zur notwendigen Revision der Formgeschichte,'' *TVia* 13 (1975): 211-33.

1698 Gerd Petzke, ''Der historische Frage nach den Wundertaten Jesu: Dargestellt am Beispiel des Exorzismus Mark. ix. 14-29 par,'' *NTS* 22 (1975-1976): 180-204.

1699 F. G. Lang, ''Sola Gratia im Markusevangelium: Die Soteriologie des Markus nach 9,14-29 und 10,17-31,'' in Johannes Friedrich, Wolfgang Pöhlmann, and Peter Stuhlmacher, eds., *Rechtfertigung* (festschrift for Ernst Käsemann). Tübingen Mohr, 1976. Pp. 321-37.

1700 J. González-Faus, ''Jesus y los demonios: Intróducción cristológica a la lucha por la justicia,'' *EE* 52 (1977): 487-519.

1701 Hermann Aichinger, ''Zur Traditionsgeschichte der Epileptiker-Perikope Mk 9,14-29 par Mt 17,14-21 par Lk 9,37-43a,'' *SNTU-A* 3 (1978): 114-43.

1702 Hans Dieter Betz, ''The Early Christian Miracle Story: Some Observations on the Form Critical Problem,'' *Semeia* 11 (1978): 69-81.

1703 Volker Weymann and H. Busslinger, ''Zum Standhalten befreit. Jesus heilt einen besessenen Knaben (Markus 9,14-29). Eine Dämonenaustreibung,'' in Anton Steiner, ed., *Wunder Jesu.* Bibelarbeit in der Gemeinde 2. Basel/Zürich: Reinhardt/Benziger, 1978. Pp. 89-112.

1704 Georges Casalis, ''Jesús, el exorcista,'' *BibFe* 6 (1980): 28-40.

1705 R. F. Collins, ''Jesus' Ministry to the Deaf and Dumb,'' *MeliT* 35/1 (1984): 12-36.

1706 Wolfgang Lipp, "Der rettende Glaube: Eine Untersuchung zu Wundergeschichten im Markusevangelium," doctoral dissertation, University of Marburg, Marburg, 1984.

1707 Peter Pimentel, "The 'Unclean Spirits' of St. Mark's Gospel," *ET* 99 (1987-1988): 173-75.

1708 Sumuel Chu, "The Healing of the Epileptic Boy in Mark 9:14-29: Its Rhetorical Structure and Theological Implications," doctoral dissertation, Vanderbilt University, Nashville TN, 1988.

1709 Gail R. O'Day, "Hope beyond Brokenness. A Markan Reflection on the Gift of Life," *CThM* 15 (1988): 244-51.

1710 Meinrad Limbeck, "Hindernisse fürs Christein: Zur Verkündigung des Markusevangeliums," *BL* 64 (1991): 164-68.

<u>9:14-27</u>

1711 C. H. Dodd, "The Sayings," in *Historical Tradition in the Fourth Gospel*. Cambridge: Cambridge University Press, 1963. Pp. 315-405.

1712 Ernst Fuchs, *Jesus: Wort und Tat*. Tübingen: Mohr, 1971.

1713 Philippe Rolland, "La guérison de l'enfant épileptique," *BLOS* 5 (1990): 3-7.

<u>9:14-19</u>

1714 Dominique Stein, "Une lecture psychanalytique de la Bible," *RSPT* 72 (1988): 95-108.

<u>9:14-17</u>

1715 Pierre Guillemette, "La Forme des Recits d'Exorcisme de Bultmann: Un Dogme a Reconsiderer," *EgT* 11/2 (1980): 177-93.

<u>9:17-27</u>

1716 Paul Ellingworth, "How Is Your Handbook Wearing?" *BT* 30 (1979): 236-41.

9:23

1717 Jean Carmignac, "Ah, Si tu peux—Tout est possible en faveur de celui qui croit (Marc 9:23)," in William C. Weinrich, ed., *The New Testament Age* (festschrift for Bo Reicke). 2 vols. Macon GA: Mercer University Press, 1984. 1:83-86.

9:24

1718 Rolf J. Erler, "Eine kleine Beobachtung an Karl Barths Lebensweg mit den Menschen 'ganz unten': 'Ich glaube, lieber Herr, hilf meinem Unglauben' (Mk 9:24)," *EvT* 47 (1987): 166-70.

9:26

1719 Martin J. Higgins, "New Testament Result Clauses with Infinitive," *CBQ* 23 (1961): 233-41.

9:28-29

1720 Benny R. Crockett, "The Function of Mathetological Prayer in Mark," *IBS* 10 (1988): 123-39.

9:28

1721 Cilliers Breytenbach, "Das Markusevangelium als episodische Erzählung: Mit Uberlegungen zum 'Aufbau' des zweiten Evangeliums," in Ferdinand Hahn, ed., *Der Erzähler des Evangeliums: Methodische Neuansätze in der Markusforschung*. Stuttgart: Verlag Katholisches Bibelwerk, 1985. Pp. 137-69.

9:30-37

1722 Jean Brière, "Le Fils de l'homme livré aux hommes. Mc 9,30-37," *AsSeign* 56 (1974): 42-52.

1723 Paul J. Achtemeier, "An Exposition of Mark 9:30-37," *Int* 30/2 (1976): 178-83.

9:30-32

1724 Carsten Colpe, "Traditionsüberschreitende Argumentationen zu Aussagen Jesu über sich selbst," in Gert Jeremias, Heinz-Wolfgang Kung, and Hartmut Stegemann, eds., *Tradition und Glaube: das frühe Christentum in seiner Umwelt. Festgabe für Karl Georg Kuhn zum 65. Geburtstag*. Göttingen: Vandenhoeck & Ruprecht, 1971. Pp. 230-45.

1725 Dominique Hermant, "La deuxième annonce de la Passion (Histoire du texte)," *BLOS* 1 (1989): 14-18.

9:30

1726 Jean-Marie van Cangh, "La Galilée dans l'évangile de Marc: un lieu théologique?" *RB* 79 (1972): 59-75.

9:31

1727 Jacques Dupont, "Ressuscité 'le troisième jour'," *Bib* 40 (1959): 742-61.

1728 Georg Strecker, "Die Leidens- und Auferstehungs-voraussagen im Markusevangelium (Mk 8,31; 9,31; 10,32-34)," *ZTK* 64 (1964): 16-39.

1729 Richard T. France, "The Servant of the Lord in the Teaching of Jesus," *TynB* 19 (1968): 26-52.

1730 Matthew Black, "The 'Son of Man' Passion Sayings in the Gospel Tradition," *ZNW* 60 (1969): 1-8.

1731 Marcel Bassin, "L'annonce de la passion et les critères de l'historicíte," *RevSR* 50 (1976): 289-329; 51 (1977): 187-213.

9:33-50

1732 Rudolf Schnackenburg, "Markus 9,33-50," in Josef Schmid and Anton Vögtle, eds., *Synoptische Studien* (festschrift for Alfred Wikenhauser). Münich: Zink, 1953. Pp. 184-206.

1733 Léon Vaganay, "Le schématisme du discours communautaire à la lumière de la critique des sources," *RB* 60 (1953): 203-44.

1734 Jean Levie, "L'évangile araméen de S. Matthieu est-il la source de l'évangile de S. Marc?" *NRT* 76 (1954): 689-715, 812-43.

1735 B. C. Butler, "M. Vagarnay and the 'Community Discourse'," *NTS* 1 (1954-1955): 283-90.

1736 Albert L. Descamps, "Du discours de Marc: ix,33-50 aux paroles de Jésus," in J. Heuschen, *La formation des évangiles: Problème synoptique et Formgeschichte*. Paris: Desclée, 1957. Pp. 152-77.

1737 Frans Neirynck, "The Tradition of the Sayings of Jesus: Mark 9,33-50," in Pierre Benoit and Roland E. Murphy, eds., *The Dynamism of the Biblical Tradition.* Theodore L. Westow, trans. Concilium #20. New York: Paulist Press, 1966. Pp. 62-74.

1738 J. I. H. McDonald, "Mark 9:33-50: Catechetics in Mark's Gospel," *StudB* 2 (1980): 171-77.

1739 Harry T. Fleddermann, "The Discipleship Discourse (Mark 9:33-50)," *CBQ* 43/1 (1981): 57-75.

1740 Dale C. Allison, "The Pauline Epistles and the Synoptic Gospels: The Pattern of the Parallels," *NTS* 28/1 (1982): 1-32.

1741 Christopher M. Tuckett, "Paul and the Synoptic Mission Discourse?" *ETL* 60 (1984): 376-81.

1742 Urban C. von Wahlde, "Mark 9:33-50: Discipleship: The Authority That Serves," *BZ* 29/1 (1985): 49-67.

9:33-42

1743 David Wenham, "A Note on Mark 9:33-42/Matt. 18:1-6/Luke 9:46-50," *JSNT* 14 (1982): 113-18.

9:33-41

1744 David R. Catchpole, "The Poor on Earth and the Son of Man in Heaven: A Reappraisal of Matthew 25:31-46," *BJRL* 61/2 (1978-1979): 355-97.

1745 M. S. Hostetler, "The Development of Meaning," *Theology* 82 (1979): 251-59.

9:33-37

1746 Gustav Kafka, "Bild und Wort in den Evangelien," *MTZ* 2 (1951): 263-87.

1747 Heinrich Helmbold, "Das 'Lukasprinzip' im Markusevangelium," in *Vorsynoptische Evangelien.* Stuttgart: Klotz, 1953. Pp. 19-32.

1748 Simon Légasse, "L'exercice de l'autorité dans l'Église d'après les évangiles synoptiques," *NRT* 85 (1963): 1009-22.

1749 Rudolf Schnackenburg, "Zur formgeschichtlichen Methode in der Evangelienforschung," *ZKT* 85 (1963): 16-32.

1750 Andrea Strus, "Mc. 9,33-37. Problema dell'autenticità e dell' interpretazione," *RBib* Supp. 20 (1972): 589-619.

1751 J. G. Inrig, "Called to Serve: Toward a Philosophy of Ministry," *BSac* 140 (1983): 335-49.

1752 Vernon K. Robbins, "Pronouncement Stories and Jesus' Blessing of Children: A Rhetorical Approach," *Semeia* 29 (1983): 43-74.

1753 Dominique Hermant, "La première scene d'enfants (Mt 18,1-5; Mc 9,33-37; Lc 9,46-48)," *BLOS* 3 (1990): 7-11.

9:33-34

1754 George D. Kilpatrick, "**Διαλέγεσθαι** and **διαλογίζεσθαι** in the New Testament," *JTS* 11 (1960): 338-40.

1755 Tjitze J. Baarda, "To the Roots of the Syriac Diatessaron Tradition," *NovT* 28 (1986): 1-25.

9:33

1756 Angelo Lancellotti, "La Casa Pietro a Cafarnao nel Vangeli Sinottici: Redazione e Tradizione," *Ant* 58/1 (1983): 48-69.

9:35-50

1757 Ernest Best, "Mark's Preservation of the Tradition," in M. Sabbe, ed., *L'évangile selon Marc: Tradition et rédaction.* BETL #34. Gembloux/Louvain: Duculot/Louvain University Press, 1974. Pp. 21-34.

9:35

1758 Ernest Best, "Mark's Use of the Twelve," *ZNW* 69/1-2 (1978): 11-35.

1759 Vernon K. Robbins, "Picking Up the Fragments: From Crossan's Analysis to Rhetorical Analysis," *Forum* 1 (1985): 31-64.

9:36

1760 Philippe Rolland, "Préliminaires à la premiere multiplication des pains," *BLOS* 3 (1990): 12-18.

9:37-42

1761 Ernest Best, "An Early Sayings Collection," *NovT* 18/1 (1976): 1-16.

9:37-41

1762 John P. Brown, "Synoptic Parallels in the Epistles and Form-History," *NTS* 10 (1963-1964): 27-48.

9:37-39

1763 Hans Kosmala, " 'In My Name'," *ASTI* 5 (1967): 87-109.

1764 A. Calmet, "Pour nous Contre nous? Marc 9,37-39," *BVC* 79 (1968): 52-53.

9:37

1765 C. H. Dodd, "Some Johannine 'Herrenworte' with Parallels in the Synoptic Gospels," *NTS* 2 (1955-1956): 75-86.

1766 C. H. Dodd, "The Sayings," in *Historical Tradition in the Fourth Gospel*. Cambridge: Cambridge University Press, 1963. Pp. 315-405.

1767 Eugene E. Lemcio, "The Unifying Kerygma of the New Testament," *JSNT* 33 (1988): 3-17.

9:38-48

1768 Jean Delorme, "Jésus enseigne ses disciples: Mc 9,38-48," *AsSeign* 2/57 (1971): 53-62.

9:38-41

1769 Thomas R. W. Longstaff, *Evidence of Conflation in Mark? A Study in the Synoptic Problem*. Society of Biblical Literature Dissertation Series 28. Missoula MT: Scholars Press, 1977.

1770 Roberta Finkelstein, ''Mark 9:38-41: An Unknown Exorcist,'' *UUC* 44/3-4 (1989): 78-87.

9:38-40

1771 E. A. Russell, ''A Plea for Tolerance (Mk 9.38-40),'' *IBS* 8 (1986): 154-60.

9:38-39

1772 Jacques Schlosser, ''L'exorciste étranger,'' *RevSR* 56 (1982): 229-39.

9:38

1773 William G. Morrice, ''Translating the Greek Imperative,'' *BT* 24 (1973): 129-34.

1774 J. M. Ross, ''Some Unnoticed Points in the Text of the New Testament,'' *NovT* 25 (1983): 59-72.

9:40

1775 Salvatore Garofalo, ''Mark 9,40 'apertura ecumenica'?'' *ED* 9 (1956): 343-49.

1776 Tibor Horvath, ''Is ἡμῶν in Mk 9,40 Authentic?'' *JES* 8 (1971): 385-86.

1777 E. M. Sidebottom, ''The So-Called Divine Passive in the Gospel Tradition,'' *ET* 87 (1975-1976): 200-204.

1778 Heinrich Baltensweiler, '''Wer nicht gegen uns (euch) ist, ist für uns (euch)!' Bemerkungen zu Mk 9,40 und Lk 9,50,'' *TZ* 40 (1984): 130-36.

1779 Vernon K. Robbins, ''Picking Up the Fragments: From Crossan's Analysis to Rhetorical Analysis,'' *Forum* 1 (1985): 31-64.

9:41

1780 James H. Smylie, ''Uncle Tom's Cabin Revisited: The Bible, the Romantic Imagination and the Sympathies of Christ,'' *Int* 27/1 (1973): 67-85.

9:42-10:12

1781 Will Deming, "Mark 9:42-10:12, Matthew 5:27-32, and b. Nid, 13b: A First Century Discussion of Male Sexuality," *NTS* 36/1 (1990): 130-41.

9:42-50

1782 Gustav Kafka, "Bild und Wort in den Evangelien," *MTZ* 2 (1951): 263-87.

1783 J. Duncan M. Derrett, "Salted with Fire," *Theology* 76 (1973): 364-68.

9:42

1784 J. Duncan M. Derrett, "Law in the New Testament: *Si scandalizaverit te manus tua, abscinde eam* (Mk 9,42) and Comparative Legal History," *RIDA* 20 (1973): 11-36.

1785 Helmut L. Egelkraut, "The Triple Tradition and Its Variants in the Travel Narrative," in *Jesus' Mission to Jerusalem: A Redaction-Critical Study of the Travel Narrative in the Gospel of Luke*. Bern: Lang, 1976. Pp. 62-133.

1786 George Howard, "Harmonistic Readings in the Old Syriac Gospels," *HTR* 73 (1980): 473-91.

1787 Lars Lode, "The Presentation of New Information," *BT* 35 (1984): 101-108.

1788 J. Duncan M. Derrett, "μύλος ὀνικὸς (Mk 9,42 Par)," *ZNW* 76/3 (1985): 284.

1789 J. Duncan M. Derrett, "Two Harsh Sayings of Christ Explained," *DR* 103 (1985): 218-29.

9:43-50

1790 Joseph Molitor, "Chanmetifragmente: Ein Beitrag zur Textgeschichte der altgeorgischen Bibelubersetzung. 2. Die Markustexte der Chanmetifragmente," *OrChr* 43 (1959): 17-24.

9:43-48

1791 B. M. F. van Iersel, "Mark 9,43-48 in a Martyrological Perspective," in A. A. R. Bastiaensen, et al., eds., *Fructus* *centesimus* (festschrift for Gerard J. M. Bartelink). Dordrecht: Kluwer, 1989. Pp. 333-41.

9:43-47

1792 C. Leslie Mitton, "Threefoldness in the Teaching of Jesus," *ET* 75 (1963-1964): 228-30.

1793 Helmut Koester, "Mark 9:43-47 and Quintilian 8.3.75," *HTR* 71 (1978): 151-53.

9:43

1794 Hildebrecht Hommel, "Herrenworte im Lichte sokratischer Überlieferung," *ZNW* 57 (1966): 1-23.

9:44-46

1795 J. M. Ross, "Some Unnoticed Points in the Text of the New Testament," *NovT* 25 (1983): 59-72.

9:49-50

1796 Wolfgang Nauck, "Salt as a Metaphor in Instructions for Discipleship," *StTheol* 6 (1952): 165-78.

1797 Helmut L. Egelkraut, "The Triple Tradition and Its Variants in the Travel Narrative," in *Jesus' Mission to Jerusalem: A Redaction-Critical Study of the Travel Narrative in the Gospel of Luke*. Bern: Lang, 1976. Pp. 62-133.

9:49

1798 Léon Vaganay, " 'Car chacun doit être salé au feu' (Marc 9,49)," in *Mémorial J. Chaine. Bibliothèque de la faculté catholique de théologie de Lyon*. Lyon: Facultés catholiques, 1950. Pp. 367-72.

1799 Oscar Cullmann, "Que signifie le sel dans la parabole de Jésus (Mc 9,49s par.)," *RHPR* 37 (1957): 36-43.

1800 Tjitze J. Baarda, "Mark 9:49," *NTS* 5 (1958-1959): 318-21.

1801 Heinrich Zimmermann, " 'Mit Feuer gesalzen werden': Eine Studie zu Mk 9:49," *TQ* 139 (1959): 28-39.

1802 Günther Schwarz, "πᾶς πυρὶ ἁλισθήσεται," *BibN* 11 (1980): 45.

1803 Weston W. Fields, " 'Everyone Will Be Salted With Fire' (Mark 9:49)," *GTJ* 6/2 (1985): 299-304.

9:50

1804 A. van Veldhurzen, "Ad Novum Testamentum observationes duae," in *Sertum Nabericum collectum a philologis Batavis ad celebrandum diem festum XVI mensis Julii anni MCMVIII*. Leiden: Brill, 1908. Pp. 415-18.

1805 Johannes B. Bauer, "Quod si sal infatuatum fuerit," *VD* 29 (1951): 228-30.

1806 Günther Schwarz, "Καλὸν τὸ ἅλας," *BibN* 7 (1978): 32-35.

1807 Michael Lattke, "Salz der Freundschaft in Mk 9,50c," *ZNW* 75/1 (1984): 44-59.

1808 Sigvard Hellestam, "Mysteriet med saltet," *SEÅ* 55 (1990): 59-63.

10:1-16:8

1809 Lionel A. Whiston, *Through Suffering to Victory: Relational Studies in Mark*. Waco TX: Word Books, 1976.

10:1-45

1810 Louis T. Brodie, "Mark 10:1-45 as a Creative Rewriting of 1 Peter 2:18-3:17," *PIBA* 4 (1980): 98.

1811 Paul A. Dominic, "The Threefold Call," *RevRel* 40 (1981): 283-96.

10:1-26

1812 J. K. Elliott, "The Relevance of Textual Criticism to the Synoptic Problem," in David L. Dungan, ed., *The Interrelations of the Gospels*. Louvain: Peeters Press, 1990. Pp. 348-59.

10:1-16

1813 Paul T. Eckel, "Mark 10:1-16," *Int* 42/3 (1988): 285-91.

10:1-12

1814 Rainer Riesner, "Wie sicher ist die Zwei-Quellen-Theorie?" *TBe* 8 (1977): 49-73.

1815 Albert L. Descamps, "Les textes évangéliques sur le mariage," *RTL* 9 (1978): 259-86.

1816 James R. Mueller, "The Temple Scroll and the Gospel Divorce Texts," *RevQ* 10 (1980): 247-56.

1817 Robert W. Herron, "Mark's Jesus on Divorce: Mark 10:1-12 Reconsidered," *JETS* 25/3 (1982): 273-81.

1818 Eugene A. LaVerdiere, "The Question of Divorce. Part 1: Is It Lawful?" *Emmanuel* 97 (1991): 454-60.

1819 Eugene A. LaVerdiere, "The Question of Divorce. Part 2: Cardiosclerosis," *Emmanuel* 97 (1991): 514-20.

10:1-11

1820 Paul Ellingworth, "How Is Your Handbook Wearing?" *BT* 30 (1979): 236-41.

10:1-7

1821 Rykle Borger, "NA[26] und die neutestamentliche Textkritik," *TR* 52 (1987): 1-58.

10:1

1822 Helmut L. Egelkraut, "The Triple Tradition and Its Variants in the Travel Narrative," in *Jesus' Mission to Jerusalem: A Redaction-Critical Study of the Travel Narrative in the Gospel of Luke*. Bern: Lang, 1976. Pp. 62-133.

10:2-16

1823 Jean Delorme, "Le mariage, les enfants et les disciples de Jésus. Mc 10,2-16," *AsSeign* 58 (1974): 42-51.

10:2-12

1824 Josef Schmid, "Markus und der aramäische Matthaus," in Josef Schmid and Anton Vögtle, eds., *Synoptische Studien* (festschrift for Alfred Wikenhauser). Münich: Zink, 1953. Pp. 75-118.

1825 H.-J. Schoeps, "Jesus et la Loi juive," *RHPR* 33 (1953): 1-20.

1826 Wilfrid J. Harrington, "Jesus' Attitude towards Divorce," *ITQ* 37 (1970): 199-209.

1827 David L. Dungan, "The Account of Jesus' Debate with the Pharisees Regarding Divorce (Matt. 19.3-9//Mark 10.2-12)," in *The Sayings of Jesus in the Churches of Paul*. Oxford: Blackwell, 1971. Pp. 102-31.

1828 David R. Catchpole, "The Synoptic Divorce Material as a Traditio-Historical Problem," *BJRL* 57/1 (1974-1975): 92-127.

1829 Rámon Trevijano Etcheverría, "Matrimonio y divorcio en Mc 10,2-12 y par.," *Bur* 18 (1977): 113-51.

1830 John J. Pilch, "Marriage in the Lord," *BibTo* 102 (1979): 2010-13.

1831 Robert H. Stein, " 'Is It Lawful for a Man to Divorce His Wife'?" *JETS* 22 (1979): 115-21.

1832 Antonio Vargas-Machuca, "Divorcio e indisolubilidad del matrimonio en la Sagrada Escritura," *EB* 39 (1981): 19-61.

10:2-9

1833 Richard N. Soulen, "Marriage and Divorce: A Problem in New Testament Interpretation," *Int* 23/4 (1969): 439-50.

1834 Gerhard Schneider, "Jesu Wort über die Ehescheidung in der Überlieferung des Neuen Testaments," *TTZ* 80 (1971): 65-87.

1835 C. Benton Kline, "Marriage Today: A Theological Carpet Bag," *JPC* 33/1 (1979): 24-37.

1836 James D. G. Dunn, "The Gospels as Oral Tradition," in *The Living Word*. London: SCM, 1987. Pp. 25-43.

10:2

1837 George Howard, "Stylistic Inversion and the Synoptic Tradition," *JBL* 97 (1978): 375-89.

1838 Augustine Stock, "Matthean Divorce Texts," *BTB* 8/1 (1978): 24-33.

1839 Paul Ellingworth, "Text and Context in Mark 10:2, 10," *JSNT* 5 (1979): 63-66.

10:5

1840 Klaus Berger, "Hartherzigkeit und Gottes Gesetz: Die Vorgeschichte des Antijudischen Vorwurfs in Mc 10:5," *ZNW* 61/1 (1970): 1-47.

10:6-8

1841 Bruce N. Kaye, " 'One Flesh' and Marriage," *CANZTR* 22 (1990): 46-57.

10:6

1842 Francesco Vattioni, "A propos de Marc 10,6," *ScE* 20 (1968): 433-36.

10:7-22

1843 Reginald H. Fuller, "The Decalogue in the NT," *Int* 43/3 (1989): 243-55.

10:8

1844 T. A. Burkill, "Two into One: The Notion of Carnal Union in Mark 10:8; 1 Cor 6:16; Eph 5:31," *ZNW* 62 (1971): 115-20.

10:10-12

1845 Charles C. Ryrie, "Biblical Teaching on Divorce and Remarriage," *GTJ* 3/2 (1982): 177-92.

1846 B. N. Wambacq, "Matthieu 5,31-32: Possibilite de Divorce ou Obligation de Rompre une Union Illigitime," *NRT* 104/1 (1982): 34-49.

1847 Eugene A. LaVerdiere, "The Question of Divorce. Part 3: In the Roman World," *Emmanuel* 97 (1991): 566-69, 582-84.

10:10

1848 Paul Ellingworth, "Text and Context in Mark 10:2, 10," *JSNT* 5 (1979): 63-66.

1849 Angelo Lancellotti, ''La Casa Pietro a Cafarnao nel Vangeli Sinottici. Redazione e Tradizione,'' *Ant* 58/1 (1983): 48-69.

<u>10:11-12</u>

1850 H. G. Coiner, ''Those 'Divorce and Remarriage' Passages (Matt. 5:32; 19:9; 1 Cor. 7:10-16), with Brief Reference to the Mark and Luke Passages,'' *CTM* 39 (1958): 367-84.

1851 Klaus Berger, ''Zu den sogenannten Sätzen heiligen Rechts,'' *NTS* 17 (1970-1971): 10-40.

1852 Helmut L. Egelkraut, ''The Triple Tradition and Its Variants in the Travel Narrative,'' in *Jesus' Mission to Jerusalem: A Redaction-Critical Study of the Travel Narrative in the Gospel of Luke*. Bern: Lang, 1976. Pp. 62-133.

1853 Bernadette J. Brooten, ''Konnten Frauen im alten Judentum die Scheidung betreiben? Überlegungen zu Mk 10,11-12 und 1 Kor 7,10-11,'' *EvT* 42 (1982): 65-80.

1854 Bernadette J. Brooten, ''Zur Debatte über das Scheidungsrecht der jüdischen Frau,'' *EvT* 43 (1983): 466-78.

1855 John S. Kloppenborg, ''Alms, Debt and Divorce: Jesus' Ethics in Their Mediterranean Context,'' *TJT* 6 (1990): 182-200.

<u>10:11</u>

1856 Gerhard Delling, ''Das Logion Mark x.11 [und seine abwandlungen] im Neuen Testament,'' *NovT* 1 (1956): 263-74.

1857 Peter Katz, ''Mark 10:11 Once Again,'' *BT* 11 (1960): 152.

1858 Ernst Bammel, ''Markus 10:11f. und das Judische Eherecht,'' *ZNW* 61/1 (1970): 95-101.

1859 Berndt Schaller, '' 'Commits Adultery with Her', Not 'Against Her', Mark 10:11,'' *ET* 83 (1971-1972): 107-108.

1860 Ernest Best, "An Early Sayings Collection," *NovT* 18/1 (1976): 1-16.

1861 Werner Stenger, "Zur Rekonstruktion eines Jesusworts anhand der synoptischen Ehescheidungslogien," *K* 26 (1984): 194-205.

10:12

1862 J. M. Casciaro Ramírez, "Un aspecto de la igualdad radical de los cónyuges en el matrimonio: Mc 10,12," in Domingo Muñoz León, ed., *Salvación en la palabra: Targum - Derash - Berith* (festschrift for Alejandro Díez Macho). Madrid: Cristiandad, 1986. Pp. 623-31.

10:13-52

1863 Helmut L. Egelkraut, "The Triple Tradition and Its Variants in the Travel Narrative," in *Jesus' Mission to Jerusalem: A Redaction-Critical Study of the Travel Narrative in the Gospel of Luke*. Bern: Lang, 1976. Pp. 62-133.

10:13-17

1864 Heinrich Helmbold, "Das 'Lukasprinzip' im Markusevangelium," in *Vorsynoptische Evangelien*. Stuttgart: Klotz, 1953. Pp. 19-32.

10:13-16

1865 Howard Clark Kee, " 'Becoming a Child' in the Gospel of Thomas," *JBL* 82 (1963): 307-14.

1866 Günter Klein, "Jesus und die Kinder: Bibelarbeit über Markus 10,13-16," in *Ärgernisse: Konfrontationen mit dem Neuen Testament*. Münich: Kaiser, 1970. Pp. 58-81.

1867 Charles Perrot, "La lecture d'un texte évangelique. Essai méthodologique à partir de Marc X,13-16," in H. Bouillard, et al., eds., *Le Point Théologique*. Paris: Beauchesne, 1972. Pp. 51-130.

1868 Günter Klein, "Bibelarbeit über Markus 10,13-16," in Gerhard Krause, ed., *Die Kinder im Evangelium*. Stuttgart: Klotz, 1973. Pp. 12-30.

1869 Giovanni Leonardi, "Mc 10,13-16 par," *StPa* 21 (1974): 538-40.

1870 Ernest Best, "Mark 10:13-16: The Child as Model Recipient," in Johnston R. McKay and James F. Miller, eds., *Biblical Studies* (festschrift for William Barclay). London: Collins, 1976. Pp. 119-34.

1871 Bartholomeus Vrijdaghs, "Werden wie Kinder . . . Die Seligpreisung der Kinder durch Jesus," *EvErz* 32 (1980): 170-81.

1872 Gerhard Barth, *Die Taufe in frühchristlicher Zeit.* Neukirchen-Vluyn: Neukirchener, 1981.

1873 Jürgen Sauer, "Der ursprünglichen 'Sitz im Leben' von Mk 10,13-16," *ZNW* 72/1 (1981): 27-50.

1874 John Dominic Crossan, "Kingdom and Children: A Study in the Aphoristic Tradition," *Semeia* 29 (1983): 75-95.

1875 J. Duncan M. Derrett, "Why Jesus Blessed the Children," *NovT* 25/1 (1983): 1-18.

1876 Andreas Lindemann, "Die Kinder und die Gottesherrschaft: Markus 10,13-16 und die Stellung der Kinder in der späthellenistischen Gesellschaft und im Urchristentum," *WD* 17 (1983): 77-104.

1877 Daniel Patte, "Jesus' Pronouncement about Entering the Kingdom Like a Child: A Structural Exegesis," *Semeia* 29 (1983): 3-42.

1878 Vernon K. Robbins, "Pronouncement Stories and Jesus' Blessing of Children: A Rhetorical Approach," *Semeia* 29 (1983): 43-74.

1879 Guy Bedouelle, "Reflection on the Place of the Child in the Church: 'Suffer the Little Children to Come unto Me'," *CICR* 12 (1985): 349-67.

1880 Gottfried Hoffmann, "The Baptism and Faith of Children," in Kurt E. Marquart, et al., eds., *A Lively Legacy*. Fort

Wayne IN: Concordia Theological Seminary, 1985. Pp. 79-95.

1881 Anthony O. Nkwoka, "Mark 10:13-16: Jesus' Attitude to Children and Its Modern Challenges," *AfTJ* 14 (1985): 100-10.

1882 Vernon K. Robbins, "Picking Up the Fragments: From Crossan's Analysis to Rhetorical Analysis," *Forum* 1 (1985): 31-64.

1883 John Dominic Crossan, "Jesus and Gospel," in J. J. Collins and John D. Crossan, eds., *The Biblical Heritage in Modern Catholic Scholarship*. Wilmington DE: Glazier, 1986. Pp. 106-30.

1884 Paul de Maat, " 'Als een erfgenaam?' Een hypothese voor de uitleg van Mc 10,13-16," W. Weren and N. Poulseen, eds., *Bij de put van Jakob: Exegetische opstellen*. Tilburg: University Press, 1986. Pp. 98-108.

1885 Camille Focant, "Les méthodes dans la lecture biblique: Un exemple: Mc 10,13-16," *FT* 16 (1986): 119-39.

1886 Gerhard Ringshausen, "Die Kinder der Weisheit. Zur Auslegung von Mk 10:13-16 par," *ZNW* 77/1 (1986): 34-63.

10:13

1887 James H. Smylie, "Uncle Tom's Cabin Revisited: The Bible, the Romantic Imagination and the Sympathies of Christ," *Int* 27/1 (1973): 67-85.

10:14

1888 Josef Blinzler, "Kind und Königreich Gottes (Mk 10,14f.)," in J. Blinzler, ed., *Ausder Welt und Umwelt des Neuen Testaments. Gesammelte Aufsätzel*. Stuttgarter Biblische Beiträge. Stuttgart: Katholisches Bibelwerk, 1969. Pp. 41-53.

1889 Jack P. Lewis, "Mark 10:14, Koluein, and Baptizein," *RQ* 21/3 (1978): 129-34.

10:15

1890 Wilhelm Pesch, *Der Lohngedanke in der Lehre Jesu: verplichen mit der religiösen Lohnlehre des Spätjudentums*. Münchener Theologische Studien #I/7. Münich: Zink, 1955.

1891 F. A. Schilling, "What Means the Saying about Receiving the Kingdom of God as a Little Child (τὴν βασιλείαν τοῦ θεοῦ ὡς παιδίον)? Mark 10:15; Luke 18:17," *ET* 77 (1965-1966): 56-58.

1892 J. I. H. McDonald, "Receiving and Entering the Kingdom: A Study of Mark 10:15," *StudE* 6 (1973): 328-32.

10:17-52

1893 Bonifatius Fischer, *Die lafeinischen Evangelien bis zum 10. Jahrhundert. 11. Varianten zu Markus*. Freiburg: Herder, 1989.

10:17-31

1894 Herbert Braun, " 'Umkehr' in spatjudisch-häretischer und in frühchristlicher Sicht," *ZTK* 50 (1953): 243-58.

1895 Walther Zimmerli, "Die Frage des Reichen nach dem Ewigen Leben (Mc 10,17-31 par.)," *EvT* 19 (1959): 90-97.

1896 Nikolaus Walter, "Zur Analyse von Mc 10:17-31," *ZNW* 53 (1962): 206-18.

1897 A. F. J. Klijn, "The Question of the Rich Young Man in a Jewish-Christian Gospel," *NovT* 8 (1966): 149-55.

1898 Simon Légasse, *L'appel du riche (Mc 10,17-31 et parallèles). Contribution à l'étude des fondements scripturaires de l'état religieux*. Verbum Salutis, collection annexe 1. Paris: Beauchesne, 1966.

1899 Benito Celada Abad, "Problemas acerca de la riqueza y seguimiento de Jesús en Mc 10:17-31," *CuBí* 26 (1969): 218-22.

1900 Albert L. Descamps, "Aux origines du ministère: La pensée de Jesus," *RTL* 2 (1971): 3-45; 3 (1972): 121-59.

1901 E. P. Sanders, "Mark 10:17-31 and Parallels," *SBLSP* 1/1 (1971): 257-70.

1902 Karl M. Fischer, "Asketische Radikalisierung der Nachfolge Jesu," *TheoV* 4 (1972): 11-25.

1903 F. G. Lang, "Sola Gratia im Markusevangelium: Die Soteriologie des Markus nach 9,14-29 und 10,17-31," in Johannes Friedrich, Wolfgang Pöhlmann, and Peter Stuhlmacher, eds., *Rechtfertigung* (festschrift for Ernst Käsemann). Tübingen: Mohr, 1976. Pp. 321-37.

1904 Simon Légasse, "The Call of the Rich Man," in Michael D. Quinan, ed. and trans., *Gospel Poverty: Essays in Biblical Theology*. Chicago: Franciscan Herald Press, 1977. Pp. 53-80.

1905 Wilhelm Egger, *Nachfolge als Weg zum Leben: Chancen neuer exegetischer Methoden dargelegt an Mk 10,17-31*. Österreichische Biblische Studien 1. Klosterneuburg: Österreichisches Katholisches Bibelwerk, 1979.

1906 Ottmar Fuchs, "Funktion und Prozedur herkömmlicher und neuerer Methoden in der Textauslegung," *BibN* 10 (1979): 48-69.

1907 Wilhelm Egger, "Nachfolge Jesu und Versicht auf Besitz. Mk 10,17-31 aus der Sicht der neuesten exegetischen Methoden," *TPQ* 128 (1980): 127-36.

1908 Istvun B. Barsi, "La péricope du jeune homme riche dans la littérature paléochrétienne," doctoral dissertation, University of Strasbourg, Strassbourg, France, 1982.

1909 Georges Casalis, "For Human Beings, Impossible!" *Conci* 187 (1986): 36-47.

<u>10:17-30</u>

1910 Simon Légasse, "Tout quitter pour suivre le Christ. Mc 10,17-30," *AsSeign* 59 (1974): 43-54.

1911 Rudolf Pesch, "Verkaule alles, was du hast," *TW* 14 (1974): 57-63.

<u>10:17-27</u>

1912 Ephren Florival, "Vends tes biens et suis-moi," *BVC* 37 (1961): 16-33.

1913 Wolfgang Harnisch, "Die Berufung des Reichen. Zur Analyse von Markus 10,17-27," in Gerhard Ebeling, Eberhard Jüngel, and Gerd Schunack, eds., *Festschrift für Ernst Fuchs*. Tübingen: Mohr/Siebeck, 1973. Pp. 161-76.

1914 Bernard Jay, "Le jeune homme riche. Notes homilétiqes sur Marc 10:17-27," *ÉTR* 53 (1978): 252-58.

1915 William J. Carl, "Mark 10:17-27 (28-31)," *Int* 33/3 (1979): 283-88.

<u>10:17-23</u>

1916 Richard W. Haskin, "The Call to Sell All: The History of the Interpretation of Mark 10:17-23 and Parallels," doctoral dissertation, Columbia University, New York, 1968.

<u>10:17-22</u>

1917 Henry Chadwick, "The Shorter Text of Luke 12:15-20," *HTR* 50 (1957): 249-58.

1918 Henri Troadec, "La vocation de l'homme riche," *VS* 120 (1969): 138-48.

1919 Ernst Fuchs, *Jesus: Wort und Tat*. Tübingen: Mohr, 1971.

1920 P. J. Riga, "Poverty as Counsel and as Precept," *BibTo* 65 (1973): 1123-28.

1921 I. C. M. Fairweather, "Two Different Pedagogical Methods in the Period of Oral Transmission," *StudE* 6 (1973): 100-108.

1922 Jean-Marie van Cangh, "Fondement Angelique de la Vie Religieuse," *NRT* 95/6 (1973): 635-47.

1923 J. J. Degenhardt, "Was muß ich tun, um das ewige Leben zu gewinnen? Zu Mk 10,17-22," in Helmut Merklein and Joachim Lange, eds., *Biblische Randbemerkungen* (festschrift for Rudolf Schnackenburg). Würzburg: Echter-Verlag, 1974. Pp. 159-68.

1924 Raymond F. Collins, "The Fourth Commandment: For Children or for Adults?" *LivL* 14 (1977): 219-33.

1925 M. L. O'Hara, "Jesus' Reflections on a Psalm," *BibTo* 90 (1977): 1237-40.

1926 Morris M. Faierstein, "Why Do the Scribes Say That Elijah Must Come First?" *JBL* 100 (1981): 75-86.

1927 H.-J. Venetz, "Theologische Grundstrukturen in der Verkundigung Jesu? Ein Vergleich von Mk 10,17-22; Lk 10,25-37 und Mt 5,21-48," in Pierre Casetti, et al., eds., *Mélanges Dominique Barthélemy*. Göttingen: Vandenhoeck & Ruprecht, 1981.

1928 Gareth L. Cockerill, "Jesus and the Geatest Commandment in Mark 10:17-22: A Test Case for John Wesley's 'Theology of Love'," *AsSem* 40/1 (1985): 13-21.

1929 Gregory Murray, "The Rich Young Man," *DR* 103 (1985): 144-46.

1930 Eberhard Jüngel, "Predigt zu Markus 10,17-22," in Thomas Franke, et al., eds., *Creatio ex amore: Beiträge zu einer Theologie* (festschrift for Alexandre Ganoczy). Würzburg: Echter, 1989. Pp. 125-33.

10:17-18

1931 Theodor Lorenzmeier, "Wider das Dogma von der Sündlosigkeit Jesu," *EvT* 31 (1971): 452-71.

10:18

1932 J. Alfaro del Valle, "Interpretación origeniana a Mc 10,18 a la luz de la tradicion eclesiástica," *AnaCal* 13 (1965): 5-59.

1933 G. M. Lee, "Studies in Texts: Mark 10:18," *Theology* 70 (1967): 167-68.

1934 Benito Celada Abad, " 'Nadie es bueno sino sólo Dios' (Mc 10:18)," *CuBí* 26 (1969): 106-108.

10:19

1935 Kenneth J. Thomas, ''Liturgical Citations in the Synoptics,'' *NTS* (1975-1976): 205-14.

10:20

1936 Lino Cignelli, ''La grecità biblica,'' *SBFLA* 35 (1985): 203-48.

1937 David A. Black, ''Some Dissenting Notes on R. Stein's *The Synoptic Problem* and Markan 'Errors','' *FilN* 1 (1988): 95-101.

10:21

1938 Giuseppe Segalla, ''La predicazione dell'amore nella tradizione presinottica,'' *RBib* 20 (1972): 481-528.

1939 Jean Galot, ''Le fondement évangélique du voeu religieux de pauvreté,'' *Greg* 56 (1975): 441-67.

10:23-31

1940 David Malone, ''Riches and Discipleship: Mark 10:23-31,'' *BTB* 9/2 (1979): 78-88.

10:23-27

1941 Simon Légasse, ''Jesus a-t-il Announce le Conversion Finale d'Israel? (a propos de Marc x.23-7),'' *NTS* 10/4 (1963-1964): 480-87.

1942 Miguel de Burgos Nuñez, ''La salvacion como 'Gratia Dei': Una interpretación eclesiológica de Marcos 10,23-27,'' *CiTom* 104 (1977): 513-56.

1943 Walter Wagner, ''Lubricating the Camel: Clement of Alexandria on Wealth and the Wealthy,'' in Walter Freitag, ed., *Festschrift: A Tribute to Dr. William Hordern.* Saskatoon: University of Saskatchewan Press, 1985. Pp. 64-77.

10:24-25

1944 José O'Callaghan, ''Examen critico de Mt 19,24,'' *Bib* 69/3 (1988): 401-405.

10:25

1945 William A. Beardslee, "Uses of the Proverb in the Synoptic Gospels," *Int* 24 (1970): 61-73.

1946 Ernest Best, "Uncomfortable Words: VII. The Camel and the Needle's Eye (Mark 10:25)," *ET* 82/3 (1970-1971): 83-89.

1947 R. Köbert, "Kamel und Schiffstau: Zu Markus 10,25 (Par.) und Koran 7,40/38," *Bib* 53 (1972): 229-33.

1948 Allan Boesak, "The Eye of the Needle," *IRM* 72 (1983): 7-10.

1949 Eduard Lohse, "Jesu Bußruf an die Reichen: Markus 10,25 Par," in Erich Grässer and O. Merk, eds., *Glaube und Eschatologie* (festschrift for W. G. Kümmel). Tübingen: Mohr, 1985. Pp. 159-63.

1950 J. Duncan M. Derrett, "A Camel through the Eye of a Needle," *NTS* 32/3 (1986): 465-70.

10:28-31

1951 William J. Carl, "Mark 10:17-27 (28-31)," *Int* 33/3 (1979): 283-88.

10:28-30

1952 Wilhelm Pesch, *Der Lohngedanke in der Lehre Jesu: verplichen mit der religiösen Lohnlehre des Spätjudentums*. Münchener Theologische Studien #I/7. Münich: Zink, 1955.

1953 Wolfgang Stegemann, "Wanderradikalismus im Urchristentum: historische und theologische Auseinandersetzung mit einer interessanten These," in Willy Schottroff and Wolfgang Stegemann, eds., *Der Gott der kleinen Leute*. Münich: Kaiser, 1979. Pp. 94-120.

10:28

1954 Ernest Best, "Mark's Preservation of the Tradition," in M. Sabbe, ed., *L'évangile selon Marc: Tradition et rédaction*. BETL #34. Gembloux/Louvain: Duculot/Louvain University, 1974. Pp. 21-34.

1955 Gerd Theissen, " 'Wir Haben Alles Verlassen' (Mc X,28). Nachfolge und Soziale Entwurzelung in der Jüdisch-Palästinischen Gesellschaft des I. Jahr-Hunderts N. Ch.," *NovT* 19/3 (1977): 161-96.

10:29-30

1956 Henri Clavier, "L'ironie dans l'enseignement de Jésus," *NovT* 1 (1956): 3-20.

1957 J. Garcia Burillo, "El ciento por uno (Mc 10,29-30 par). Historia de las interpretaciones y exégesis," *EB* 36 (1977): 173-203; 37 (1978): 29-55.

10:29-31

1958 David M. May, "Leaving and Receiving: A Social-Scientific Exegesis of Mark 10:29-31," *PRS* 17 (1990): 141-54.

10:29

1959 Hildebrecht Hommel, "Herrenworte im Lichte sokratischer Überlieferung," *ZNW* 57 (1966): 1-23.

1960 H. Fürst, "Verlust der Familie—Gewinn einer neuen Familie (Mk 10,29f parr.)," in Isaac Vazquez, ed., *Studia Historico-Ecclesiastica: Festgabe für Luchesius G. Spätling*. Rome: Pontificium Athenaeum Antonianum, 1977. Pp. 17-48.

1961 George E. Rice, "Is Bezae a Homogeneous Codex [variants to Codex B]," *PRS* 11 (1984): 39-54.

10:30-32

1962 Harald Sahlin, "Emendationsvorschläge zum griechischen Text des Neuen Testaments I," *NovT* 24 (1982): 160-79.

10:30

1963 George E. Rice, "Is Bezae a Homogeneous Codex [variants to Codex B]," *PRS* 11 (1984): 39-54.

10:31-33

1964 J. H. van Halsema, "Het raadsel als literaire vorm in Marcus en Johannes," *GTT* 83/1 (1983): 1-17.

10:31

1965 José O'Callaghan, "Nota crítica sobre Mt 19,30," *EB* 48 (1990): 271-73.

10:32-52

1966 Dan O. Via, "Mark 10:32-52—A Structural, Literary and Theological Interpretation," *SBLSP* 9/2 (1979): 187-203.

10:32-41

1967 Ernest Best, "Mark's Use of the Twelve," *ZNW* 69/1-2 (1978): 11-35.

10:32-34

1968 Georg Strecker, "Die Leidens- und Auferstehungs-voraussagen im Markusevangelium (Mk 8,31; 9,31; 10,32-34)," *ZTK* 64 (1964): 16-39.

1969 Richard T. France, "The Servant of the Lord in the Teaching of Jesus," *TynB* 19 (1968): 26-52.

1970 Carsten Colpe, "Traditionsüberschreitende Argumentationen zu Aussagen Jesu über sich selbst," in Gert Jeremias, Heinz-Wolfgang Kung, and Hartmut Stegemann, eds., *Tradition und Glaube: das frühe Christentum in seiner Umwelt* (festschrift for Karl Georg Kuhn) Göttingen: Vandenhoeck & Ruprecht, 1971. Pp. 230-45.

1971 Ray McKinnis, "An Analysis of Mark 10:32-34," *NovT* 18/2 (1976): 81-100.

10:32

1972 Anselm Schulz, *Nachfolgen und Nachahmen: Studien über das Verhältnis der neutestamentlichen Jüngerschaft zur urchristlichen Vorbildethik*. Münich: Kösel, 1962.

1973 Marla J. Selvidge, " 'And Those Who Followed Feared' (Mark 10:32)," *CBQ* 45/3 (1983): 396-400.

10:33-34

1974 Marcel Bassin, "L'annonce de la passion et les critères de l'historicíte," *RevSR* 50 (1976): 289-329; 51 (1977): 187-213.

10:34

1975 Johannes B. Bauer, "Drei Tage," *Bib* 39 (1958): 354-58.

1976 Jacques Dupont, "Ressuscité 'le troisième jour'," *Bib* 40 (1959): 742-61.

10:35-52

1977 Richard H. Hiers, *The Historical Jesus and the Kingdom of God: Present and Future in the Message and Ministry of Jesus*. University of Florida Humanities Monograph #38. Gainesville FL: University of Florida Press, 1973.

10:35-45

1978 Augustin George, "Le Service du Royaume (Marc 10,35-45)," *BVC* 25 (1959): 15-19.

1979 H. Urner, "Der Dienst Jesu Christi. Markus 10,35-45," *CVia* 2 (1959): 287-90.

1980 Anselm Schulz, *Nachfolgen und Nachahmen: Studien über das Verhältnis der neutestamentlichen Jüngerschaft zur urchristlichen Vorbildethik*. Münich: Kösel, 1962.

1981 Anselm Schulz, *Unter dem Anspruch Gottes: Das neutestamentliche Zeugnis von der Nachahmung*. Münich: Kösel, 1967.

1982 Jean Radermakers, "Revendiquer ou servir? Mk 10,35-45," *AsSeign* 60 (1975): 28-39.

1983 Harald Riesenfeld, "La tradition évangelique et la règle de foi dans l'église primitive," in *Unité et diversité dans le Nouveau Testament*. Paris: Cerf, 1979. Pp. 99-112.

1984 James D. Smart, "Mark 10:35-45," *Int* 33/3 (1979): 288-93.

1985 Jürgen Denker, "Identidad y mundo vivencial (Lebenswelt): en torno a Marcos 10:35-45 y Timoteo 2:5s," *RevB* 46/1-2 (1984): 159-69.

1986 P. Debergé, "Réflexion biblique et théologique sur le pouvoir à partir de Marc 10,35-45," doctoral dissertation, Pontifical University Greg., Rome, 1986.

1987 Robin W. Lovin, "Leadership: Mark 10:35-45," *Crit* 25/2 (1986): 18-21.

1988 Lyle D. vander Broek, "Literary Context in the Gospels," *RR* 39/2 (1986): 113-17.

1989 Patrick H. Reardon, "The Cross, Sacraments and Martyrdom: An Investigation of Mark 10:35-45," *SVTQ* 36/1-2 (1992): 103-15.

10:35-40

1990 Wilhelm Pesch, *Der Lohngedanke in der Lehre Jesu: verplichen mit der religiösen Lohnlehre des Spätjudentums*. Münchener Theologische Studien #I/7. Münich: Zink, 1955.

1991 André Feuillet, "La coupe et le baptême de la Passion (Mc x,35-40; cf. Mt xx,20-23; Lc xii,50)," *RB* 74 (1967): 356-91.

1992 Simon Légasse, "Approche de l'épisode préévangélique des fils de Zébédée," *NTS* 20/2 (1973-1974): 161-77.

1993 John B. Muddiman, "The Glory of Jesus: Mark 10:37," in L. D. Hurst and N. T. Wright, eds., *The Glory of Christ in the New Testament*. Oxford: Clarendon Press, 1987. Pp. 51-58.

10:35

1994 Günther Zuntz, "Wann wurde das Evangelium Marci geschrieben [Acts 12:2]," in Hubert Cancik, ed., *Markus-Philologie*. Tübingen: Mohr, 1984. Pp. 47-71.

10:37

1995 John B. Muddiman, "The Glory of Jesus: Mark 10:37," in L. D. Hurst and N. T. Wright, eds., *The Glory of Christ in the New Testament: Studies in Christology* (festschrift for George B. Caird). New York: Clarendon Press, 1987. Pp. 51-58.

1996 José O'Callaghan, "Fluctuación textual en Mt 20,21.26,27," *Bib* 71/4 (1990): 553-58.

10:38-42

1997 William Klassen, ''Musonius Rufus, Jesus, and Paul: Three First-Century Feminists,'' in Peter Richardson and John C. Hurd, eds., *From Jesus to Paul* (festschrift for F. W. Beare). Waterloo: Wilfrid Laurier University Press, 1984. Pp. 185-206.

10:38-40

1998 J. Duncan M. Derrett, ''Christ's Second Baptism (Lk 12:50; Mk 10:38-40),'' *ET* 100 (1988-1989): 294-95.

10:38-39

1999 Otto Kuss, ''Zur Frage einer vorpaulinischen Todestaufe,'' *MTZ* 4 (1953): 1-17.

2000 Gerhard Delling, ''**Βάπτισμα βαπτισθῆναι**,'' *NovT* 2 (1957-1958): 92-115.

2001 W. Ernest Moore, ''One Baptism,'' *NTS* 10 (1963-1964): 504-16.

2002 Eugene A. LaVerdiere, ''Can You Drink the Cup?'' *Emmanuel* 89 (1983): 490-95.

10:38

2003 Georg Braumann, ''Leidenskelch und Todestaufe (Mc 10:38f.),'' *ZNW* 56 (1965): 178-83.

2004 François Martin, ''Le baptême dans l'Esprit: Tradition du Nouveau Testament et vie de l'Église,'' *NRT* 106 (1984): 23-58.

10:41-45

2005 Simon Légasse, ''L'exercice de l'autorité dans l'Église d'après les évangiles synoptiques,'' *NRT* 85 (1963): 1009-22.

10:42

2006 Ulrich Hedinger, ''Jesus und die Volksmenge: Kritik der Qualifizierung der óchloi in der Evangelienauslegung,'' *TZ* 32 (1976): 201-206.

2007 Ethelbert Stauffer, ''Realistische Jesusworte,'' in William C. Weinrich, ed., *The New Testament Age* (festschrift for Bo Reicke). 2 vols. Macon GA: Mercer University Press, 1984. 2:503-10.

10:43-44

2008 William A. Beardslee, ''Uses of the Proverb in the Synoptic Gospels,'' *Int* 24 (1970): 61-73.

2009 Ernest Best, ''An Early Sayings Collection,'' *NovT* 18/1 (1976): 1-16.

2010 José O'Callaghan, ''Fluctuación textual en Mt 20,21.26,27,'' *Bib* 71/4 (1990): 553-58.

10:43

2011 Anton Fridrichsen, ''Exegetisches zum Neuen Testament,'' in *Sam Eitrem septuagenaric amicitiae munusculum*. Uppsala: Seminarium neotestamenticum upsaliense, 1942. Pp. 4-8.

10:45

2012 Paul E. Davies, ''Did Jesus Die as a Martyr-Prophet?'' *BR* 2 (1957): 19-30.

2013 C. K. Barrett, ''The Background of Mark 10:45,'' in A. J. B. Higgins, ed., *New Testament Essays: Studies in Memory of Thomas Walter Manson, 1893-1958*. Manchester: Manchester University Press, 1959. Pp. 1-18.

2014 J. A. Emerton, ''The Aramaic Background of Mark 10:45,'' *JTS* 11 (1960): 334-35.

2015 J. A. Emerton, ''Some New Testament Notes,'' *JTS* 11 (1960): 329-36.

2016 John P. Brown, ''Synoptic Parallels in the Epistles and Form-History,'' *NTS* 10 (1963-1964): 27-48.

2017 Joachim Jeremias, ''Das Lösegeld für Viele (Mk 10,45),'' in J. Jeremias, ed., *Abba: Studien zur neutestamentlichen Theologie und Zeitgeschichte*. Göttingen: Vandenhoeck & Ruprecht, 1966. Pp. 216-29.

2018 André Feuillet, ''Le logion sur la rançon,'' *RSPT* 51 (1967): 365-402.

2019 G. de Ru, ''Het losgeld voor velen (Marcus 10:45),'' *KerkT* 18 (1967): 107-28.

2020 H. J. B. Combrink, *Die diens van Jesus. 'n Eksegetiese beskouing oor Markus 10:45.* Groningen: V.R.B.—Offsetdrukkerij, 1968.

2021 Richard T. France, ''The Servant of the Lord in the Teaching of Jesus,'' *TynB* 19 (1968): 26-52.

2022 Augustin George, ''Comment Jésus a-t-il perçu sa propre mort?'' *LVie* 101 (1971): 34-59.

2023 Werner Grimm, ''Weil ich dich lieb habe, gebe ich einem Menschen als Lösegeld an deiner Statt,'' in *Das Institutum Iudaicum der Universität Tübingen, 1968-70*. Tübingen: Tübingen Institutum Iudaicum, 1971. Pp. 28-37.

2024 Louis Simon, ''De la situation de l'Eglise au sermon: Marc 10:45,'' *ÉTR* 46 (1971): 3-11.

2025 C. K. Barrett, ''Mark 10,45: A Ransom for Many,'' in C. K. Barrett, ed., *New Testament Essays*. London: SPCK, 1972. Pp. 20-26.

2026 Jürgen Roloff, ''Anfänge der Soteriologischen Deutung des Todes Jesu (MK. X.45 und XII.27),'' *NTS* 19/1 (1972-1973): 38-64.

2027 Paul E. Davies, ''Did Jesus Die as a Martyr-Prophet?'' *BR* 19 (1974): 37-47.

2028 Karl Kertelge, ''Der dienende Menschensohn (Mk 10,45),'' in Rudolf Pesch and Rudolf Schnackenburg, eds., *Jesus und der Menschensohn: Für Anton Vögtle*, in collaboration with Odilo Kaiser. Freiburg/Basel/Vienna: Herder, 1975. Pp. 225-39.

2029 Xavier Léon-Dufour, ''Jésus devant sa mort à la lumière des textes de l'Institution eucharistique et des discours d'adieu,'' in Jacques Dupont, ed., *Jésus aux origines de la christologie*. BETL #40. Louvain: Peeters Press, 1975. Pp. 141-68.

2030 P. Maurice Casey, "The Son of Man Problem," *ZNW* 67/3 (1976): 147-54.

2031 W. J. Moulder, "The Old Testament Background and the Interpretation of Mark 10:45," *NTS* 24/1 (1977-1978): 120-27.

2032 Marco Adinolfi, "Il servo di JHWH nel logion del servizio e del riscatto (Mc. 10,45)," *BibO* 21 (1979): 43-61.

2033 N. Hoffmann, " 'Stellvertretung': Grundgestalt und Mitte des Mysteriums. Ein Versuch trinitätstheologischer Begründung christlicher Sühne," *MTZ* 30 (1979): 161-91.

2034 Claudino del Mago, "O conceito teologico del serviço segundo Mc 10,45," doctoral dissertation, Studium Biblicum Franciscan, Jerusalem, 1979.

2035 S. H. T. Page, "The Authenticity of the Ransom Logion (Mark 10:45b)," in R. T. France and David Wenham, eds., *Gospel Perspectives: Studies of History and Tradition in the Four Gospels*. Sheffield: JSOT Press, 1980. 1:137-61.

2036 Barnabas Lindars, "Salvation Proclaimed. VII. Mark 10,45: A Ransom for Many," *ET* 93 (1981-1982): 292-95.

2037 B. Janowski, "Auslösung des vervirkten Lebens: Zur Geschichte und Struktur der biblischen Lösegeldvorstellung," *ZTK* 79 (1982): 25-59.

2038 Adrian Schenker, "Substitution du châtiment ou prix de la paix? Le don de la vie du Fils de l'homme en Mc 10,45 et par. à la lumière de l'Ancien Testament," in M. Benzerath, et al., eds., *La Pâque du Christ* (festschrift for F.-X. Durwell). Paris: Cerf, 1982. Pp. 75-90.

2039 A.-S. Di Marco, "Ipsissima verba Jesu: Mc 10,45: Risvolli linguistici ed ermeneutici," *Laur* 25 (1984): 165-286.

2040 David J. Lull, "Interpreting Mark's Story of Jesus' Death: Toward a Theology of Suffering," *SBLSP* 24 (1985): 1-12.

2041 Uwe Wegner, "Deu Jesus um sentido salvífico para sua morte: consideraçoes sobre Mc. 14:24 e 10:45," *EstT* 26/3 (1986): 209-46.

2042 David Seeley, "Was Jesus Like a Philosopher? The Evidence of Martyrological and Wisdom Motifs in Q, Pre-Pauline Traditions, and Mark," *SBLSP* 28 (1989): 540-49.

2043 Jürgen Becker, "Die neutestamentliche Rede vom Suhnetod Jesu," *ZTK* 8 (1990): 29-49.

10:46-13:37

2044 Cornelis J. den Heyer, *Exegetische methoden in discussie. Een analyrse van Markus 10,46-13,37*. Kampen: Kok, 1978.

10:46-12:40

2045 P. J. Farla, *Jezus' oordeel over Israel. Een form- en redaktionsgeschichtliche analyse van Mc 10,46-12.40*. Kampen: Kok, 1978.

10:46-52

2046 H. Ramsauer and M. Schmietenkoff, "Jesus von Nazareth - der Davidssohn: Analyse von Mk 10,46-52," *EvErz* 21 (1969): 487-94.

2047 André Paul, "Guérison de Bartimee. Mc 10,46-52," *AsSeign* 61 (1972): 44-52.

2048 Vernon K. Robbins, "The Healing of Blind Bartimaeus (10:46-52) in the Marcan Theology," *JBL* 92 (1973): 224-43.

2049 Dennis C. Duling, "Solomon, Exorcism, and the Son of David," *HTR* 68 (1975): 235-52.

2050 Ernest Lee Stoffel, "An Exposition of Mark 10:46-52," *Int* 30/3 (1976): 288-92.

2051 Paul J. Achtemeier, " 'And He Followed Him': Miracles and Discipleship in Mark 10:46-52," *Semeia* 11 (1978): 115-45.

2052 Hans Dieter Betz, "The Early Christian Miracle Story: Some Observations on the Form-Critical Problem," *Semeia* 11 (1978): 69-81.

2053 Earl S. Johnson, "Mark 10:46-52: Blind Bartimaeus," *CBQ* 40/2 (1978): 191-204.

2054 M. J. J. Menken, "Marcus 10,46-52: de 'genezing van de blinde Bartimeus' als roepingsverhaal," in A. J. M. Blijlevens, et al., eds., *Ambt en bediening in meervoud: Veelvormigheid van dienstverlening in de geloofsgemeenschap* (festschrift for H. Manders). Hilversum: Gooi en Sticht, 1978. Pp. 67-79, 288-91.

2055 Helge K. Nielsen, "Ein Beitrag zur Beurteilung der Tradition über die Heilungstätigkeit," *SNTU-A* 4 (1979): 5-26.

2056 Claude Chapalain, "Marc 10,46-52: Plan de travail," *SémBib* 20 (1980): 12-16.

2057 Joseph A. Mirro, "Bartimaeus: The Miraculous Cure," *BibTo* 20 (1982): 221-25.

2058 Jacques Dupont, "L'aveugle de Jéricho recouvre la vue et suit Jésus," *RAfT* 8 (1984): 165-81.

2059 Sylvester Lamberigts, "De genezing van de blinde Bartimeus," in *Wie is Hij toch? De Bijbel leren lezen om Jezus te kennen*. Tielt-Weesp: Lannoo, 1984. Pp. 132-40.

2060 Augustine Stock, "Hinge Transitions in Mark's Gospel," *BTB* 15 (1985): 27-31.

2061 Walter Brueggemann, "Theological Education: Healing the Blind Beggar," *CC* 103/5 (1986): 114-16.

2062 Jacques Dupont, "Blind Bartimaeus (Mark 10:46-52)," *TD* 33/2 (1986): 223-28.

2063 Michael G. Steinhauser, "The Form of the Bartimaeus Narrative (Mark 10.46-52)," *NTS* 32/4 (1986): 583-95.

2064 Stephen H. Smith, "The Literary Structure of Mark 11:1-12:40," *NovT* 31/2 (1989): 104-24.

2065 John N. Suggit, "Exegesis and Proclamation: Bartimaeus and Christian Discipleship (Mark 10:46-52)," *JTSA* 74 (1991): 57-63.

10:46

2066 Angel Ródenas, "La entrada de Jesús en Jericó (Mc 10,46)," *NatGrac* 22 (1975): 225-64.

10:47-48

2067 Evald Lövestam, "Die Davidssohnsfrage," *SEÅ* 27/28 (1962): 72-82.

10:50

2068 R. Alan Culpepper, "Mark 10:50: Why Mention the Garment?" *JBL* 101 (1982): 131-32.

2069 Michael G. Steinhauser, "Part of a 'Call Story'?" *ET* 94 (1982-1983): 204-206.

10:51

2070 William G. Morrice, "The Imperatival ἱνα," *BT* 23 (1972): 326-30.

10:52

2071 Georg Braumann, "Die Schuldner und die Sunderin Luk. VII.36-50," *NTS* 10/4 (1963-1964): 487-93.

11:1-13:37

2072 T. A. Burkill, "Strain on the Secret: An Examination of Mark 11:1-13:37," *ZNW* 51 (1960): 31-46.

2073 Ched Myers, "The Lesson of the Fig Tree: Mark 11:1-13:37—Jesus' Second Campaign of Nonviolent Direct Action," *Soj* 16 (1987): 30-33.

11:1-13:2

2074 Kaj Bollmann, "Die Rolle des Tempels im Neuen Testament (Mk 11,1-13,2): Beitrag zur Diskussion uber 'Die Einheit der Bibel'," *TexteK* 7 (1980): 19-31.

11:1-12:40

2075 Stephen H. Smith, "The Literary Structure of Mark 11:1-12:40," *NovT* 31/2 (1989): 104-24.

11:1-12:12

2076 Jan W. Doeve, "Purification du Temple et dessèchement du figuier: Sur la structurc du 21ème chapitre de Matthieu et parallèles," *NTS* 1 (1954-1955): 297-308.

11:1-25

2077 Paul B. Duff, "The March of the Divine Warrior and the Advent of the Greco-Roman King: Mark's Account of Jesus' Entry into Jerusalem," *JBL* 111 (1992): 55-71.

11:1-20

2078 Richard T. France, "Chronological Aspects of 'Gospel Harmony'," *VoxE* 16 (1986): 33-59.

11:1-19

2079 Helmut L. Egelkraut, "The Triple Tradition and Its Variants in the Travel Narrative," in *Jesus' Mission to Jerusalem: A Redaction-Critical Study of the Travel Narrative in the Gospel of Luke*. Bern: Lang, 1976. Pp. 62-133.

11:1-17

2080 Richard H. Hiers, *The Historical Jesus and the Kingdom of God: Present and Future in the Message and Ministry of Jesus*. University of Florida Humanities Monograph #38. Gainesville FL: University of Florida Press, 1973.

11:1-14

2081 A. B. Kolenkow, "Two Changing Patterns: Conflicts and the Necessity of Death—John 2 and 12 and Markan Parallels," *SBLSP* 9/1 (1979): 123-26.

11:1-13

2082 J. H. van Halsema, "Het raadsel als literaire vorm in Marcus en Johannes," *GTT* 83/1 (1983): 1-17.

11:1-11

2083 Brian A. Mastin, "The Date of the Triumphal Entry," *NTS* 16 (1969-1970): 76-82.

2084 R. Bartnicki, "Mesjański charakter perykopy Marka o wjeździe Jezusa do Jerozolimy (Mk 11,1-11)," *RoczTK* 20 (1973): 5-16.

2085 V. Mariadasan, *Le triomphe messianiaue de Jésus et son entrée à Jérusalem. Étude critico-littéraire des traditions évangéliques.* Tindivanam, India: Catechetical Centre, 1978.

2086 David R. Catchpole, "The 'Triumphal' Entry [Mk 8:27-30; 11:1-11]," in Ernst Bammel and C. F. D. Moule, eds., *Jesus and the Politics of His Day* . Cambridge: Cambridge University Press, 1984. Pp. 319-34.

11:1-10

2087 J. Duncan M. Derrett, "Law in the New Testament: The Palm Sunday Colt," *NovT* 13 (1971): 241-58.

2088 André Paul, "L'entrée de Jésus à Jérusalem," *AsSeign* 19 (1971): 4-26.

2089 R. Bartnicki, "Il carattere messianico delle pericopi di Marco e Matteo sull'ingresso di Gesù in Gerusalemme (Mc. 11,1-10; Mt. 21,1-9)," *RBib* 25 (1977): 5-27.

2090 R. Bartnicki, "Teologia ewangelistów w perykopach o wjeździe Jezusa do Jerozolimy," *SThV* 15 (1977): 55-76.

2091 Willem A. Visser 't Hooft, "Triumphalism in the Gospels," *SJT* 38 (1985): 491-504.

11:1-7

2092 F. C. Synge, "A Matter of Tenses—Fingerprints of an Annotator in Mark," *ET* 88 (1976-1977): 168-71.

11:1-4

2093 Guy Wagner, "Le figuier stérile et la destruction du temple: Marc 11:1-4 et 20-26," *ÉTR* 62/3 (1987): 335-42.

11:1

2094 Werner Schauch, "Der Ölberg: Exegese zu einer Ortsangabe besonders bei Matthaus und Markus," *TLZ* 77 (1952): 391-96.

2095 Charles F. Nesbitt, "The Bethany Traditions in the Gospel Narratives," *JBR* 29 (1961): 119-24.

11:2-7

2096 Walter Bauer, "The Colt on Palm Sunday," *JBL* 72 (1953): 220-29.

11:3

2097 Robert G. Bratcher, "A Note on Mark xi.3 Ὁ κύριος αὐτοῦ χρείν ἔχει," *ET* 64 (1952-1953): 93.

2098 Henry Osborn, "A Quadruple Quote in the Triumphal Entry Account in Warao," *BT* 18/1 (1967): 30-32.

2099 J. M. Ross, "Names of God: A Comment on Mark 11.3 and Parallels," *BT* 35 (1984): 443.

11:6-11

2100 Gerald M. Browne, "An Old Nubian Version of Mark 11,6-11," *ZPE* 44 (1981): 155-66.

11:9-10

2101 John Dominic Crossan, "Redaction and Citation in Mark 11:9-10 and 11:17," *BR* 17 (1972): 33-50.

2102 John Dominic Crossan, "Redaction and Citation in Mark 11:9-10, 17 and 14:27," *SBLSP* 2 (1972): 17-60.

2103 Joseph A. Fitzmyer, "Aramaic evidence affecting the interpretation of hosanna in the New Testament," in Gerald F. Hawthorne and Otto Betz, eds., *Tradition & Interpretation in the New Testament* (festschrift for E. Earle Ellis). Grand Rapids: Eerdmans, 1987. Pp. 110-18.

11:9

2104 José L. Sicre, "El uso del Salmo 118 en la Cristología Neotestamentaria," *EE* 52 (1977): 73-90.

11:11-25

2105 Thomas G. Long, "Shaping Sermons by Plotting the Text's Claim upon Us," in Don Wardlaw, ed., *Preaching Biblically*. Philadelphia: Westminster, 1983. Pp. 84-100.

11:11-23

2106 Ernest C. Colwell, "Method in the Study of the Gospel Lectionaries," in Ernest C. Colwell, *Studies in Methodology in Textual Criticism of the New Testament.* Leiden: Brill, 1969. Pp. 84-95.

11:11-14

2107 Michal Wojciechowski, "Marc 11.14 et Targum Gen. 3.22: les fruits de la loi enlevés à Israël," *NTS* 33/2 (1987): 287-89.

11:11-12

2108 Charles F. Nesbitt, "The Bethany Traditions in the Gospel Narratives," *JBR* 29 (1961): 119-24.

11:11

2109 Ernest Best, "Mark's Use of the Twelve," *ZNW* 69/1-2 (1978): 11-35.

11:12-25

2110 José L. Mesa, "Oseas y la higuera y el templo de Marcos," in A. Vargas-Machuca and G. Ruiz, eds., *Palabra y Vida* (festschrift for José Díaz). Madrid: Universidad Pontificia Comillas, 1983. Pp. 153-58.

11:12-21

2111 James R. Edwards, "Markan Sandwiches: The Significance of Interpolations in Markan Narratives," *NovT* 31 (1989): 193-216.

11:12-14

2112 V. Anzalone, "Il fico maledetto (Mc. XI,12-14 e 20-25)," *PalCl* 37 (1958): 257-64.

2113 Gerhard Mündelein, "Die 19 Verfluchung des Fegenbaumes (Mk. XI. 12-14)," *NTS* 10 (1963): 88-104.

2114 Constantin Daniel, "Esséniens, Zélotes el Sicaires et leur mention par paronymie dans le N.T.," *Numen* 13 (1966): 88-115.

2115 Enric Cortés, "El secamiento de la higuera a la luz de los profetas de AT y de sus targumim (Mc 11,12-14.20-21)," *EstFr* 69 (1968): 41-68; 70 (1969): 5-23.

2116 Hugues Cousin, "Le figuier désséche. Un exemple de l'actualisation de la geste évangélique: Mc 11,12-14, 20-25; Mt 21,18-22," *FV* 70 (1971): 82-93.

2117 Constantin Daniel, "Enigma smochinului si zelotii sf. Evanghelii," *StudE* 24 (1972): 45-58.

2118 J. Duncan M. Derrett, "Figtrees in the New Testament," *HeyJ* 14 (1973): 249-65.

2119 Kazimierz Romaniuk, " 'Car ce n'était pas la saison des figues . . .' (Mk 11:12-14 parr)," *ZNW* 66 (1975): 275-78.

2120 Heinz Giesen, "Der Verdorrte Feigenbaum—Eine Symbolische Aussage? zu Mk 11,12-14.20f.," *BZ* 20 (1976): 95-111.

2121 L. A. Loslie, "The Cursing of the Fig Tree: Tradition Criticism of a Marcan Pericope (Mark 11:12-14, 20-25)," *SBT* 7 (1977): 3-18.

2122 William R. Telford, *The Barren Temple and the Withered Tree. A Redaction-Critical Analysis of the Cursing of the Fig Tree Pericope in Mark's Gospel and Its Relation to the Cleansing of the Temple Tradition.* JSNT Supp. 1. Sheffield: JSOT Press, 1980.

2123 Craig L. Blomberg, "The Miracles as Parables," in David Wenham and Craig L. Blomberg, eds., *Gospel Perspectives*. Sheffield: JSOT Press, 1986. 6:327-59.

2124 Lyle D. vander Broek, "Literary Context in the Gospels," *RR* 39/2 (1986): 113-17.

2125 Bettina von Kienle, "Mk 11:12-14.20-25: der verdorrte Feigenbaum," *BibN* 57 (1991): 17-25.

2126 Günther Schwarz, "Jesus und der Feigenbaum am Wege (Mk 11:12-14, 20-25/Mt 21:18-22)," *BibN* 61 (1992): 36-37.

<u>11:13</u>

2127 C. W. F. Smith, "Fishers of Men: Footnotes on a Gospel Figure," *HTR* 52 (1959): 187-203.

2128 Cornelis J. den Heyer, " 'Want Het was de tijd niet voor vijgen'," *GTT* 76/3 (1976): 129-40.

2129 Günther Schwarz, "Ἀπὸ μακρόθεν / ἐπὶ τῆς ὁδοῦ," *BibN* 20 (1983): 56-57.

2130 Wendy J. Cotter, "For It Was Not the Season for Figs," *CBQ* 48/1 (1986): 62-66.

<u>11:15-19</u>

2131 T. W. Manson, "The Cleansing of the Temple," *BJRL* 33 (1950-1951): 271-82.

2132 F. A. Cooke, "The Cleansing of the Temple," *ET* 63 (1951-1952): 321-22.

2133 George W. Buchanan, "Mark 11:15-19: Brigands in the Temple," *HUCA* 30 (1959): 169-77.

2134 George W. Buchanan, "An Additional Note to 'Mark 11:15-19: Brigands in the Temple'," *HUCA* 31 (1960): 103-105.

2135 S. Jérôme, "La violence de Jésus," *BVC* 41 (1961): 13-17.

2136 Neill Q. Hamilton, "Temple Cleansing and Temple Bank," *JBL* 83 (1964): 365-72.

2137 Robert E. Dowda, "The Cleansing of the Temple in the Synoptic Gospels," doctoral dissertation, Duke University, Durham NC, 1972.

2138 J. Duncan M. Derrett, "The Zeal of the House and the Cleansing of the Temple," *DR* 95 (1977): 79-94.

2139 Thomas R. W. Longstaff, *Evidence of Conflation in Mark? A Study in the Synoptic Problem*. Society of Biblical Literature Dissertation Series #28. Missoula MT: Scholars Press, 1977.

2140 A. B. Kolenkow, "Two Changing Patterns: Conflicts and the Necessity of Death—John 2 and 12 and Markan Parallels," *SBLSP* 9/1 (1979): 123-26.

2141 R. Alan Culpepper, "Mark 11:15-19," *Int* 34/2 (1980): 176-81.

2142 Victor P. Furnish, "War and Peace in the New Testament," *Int* 38 (1984): 363-79.

2143 Egon Spiegel, "War Jesus gewalttatig? Bemerkungen zur Tempelreinigung," *TGl* 75 (1985): 239-47.

2144 Douglas Cunningham, "God's Order Versus the Jewish/Roman Social Order: An Exegesis of Mark 11:15-19," *Tugn* 8/3 (1988): 312-24.

2145 Jacob Neusner, "Penningväxlarna i templet (Mark 11:15-19): Mishnas förklaring [M. Sheqalim 1:3]," *SEÅ* 53 (1988): 63-68.

2146 Jacob Neusner, "Money-Changers in the Temple: The Mishnah's Explanation," *NTS* 35/2 (1989): 287-90.

2147 George W. Buchanan, "Symbolic Money-Changers in the Temple?" *NTS* 37 (1991): 280-90.

11:15-18

2148 J. Duncan M. Derrett, "No Stone upon Another: Leprosy and the Temple," *JSNT* 30 (1987): 3-20.

11:15-17

2149 Joachim Jeremias, "Zwei Miszellen: 1. Antik-Judische Munzdeutungen. 2. Zur Geschichtlichkeit der Tempelreinigung," *NTS* 23/2 (1976-1977): 177-79.

2150 Paul Ellingworth, "Translating Parallel Passages in the Gospels," *BT* 34 (1983): 401-407.

2151 Richard J. Bauckham, "Jesus' Demonstration in the Temple," in Barnabas Lindars, ed., *Law and Religion: Essays on the Place of Law in Israel and Early Christianity*. Cambridge: J. Clarke, 1988. Pp. 72-89.

2152 Robert J. Miller, "The (A)Historicity of Jesus' Temple Demonstration: A Test Case in Methodology," *SBLSP* 30 (1991): 235-52.

11:15

2153 Étienne Trocmé, "L'expulsion des marchands du Temple," *NTS* 15 (1968-1969): 1-22.

11:16

2154 J. M. Ford, "Money 'Bags' in the Temple (Mark 11:16)," *Bib* 57 (1976): 249-53.

11:17

2155 Jean Mouson, " 'Non veni vocare justos, sed peccatores'," *CollM* 43 (1958): 134-39.

2156 R. B. Montgomery, "The House of Prayer: Mark 11:17," *CollBQ* 36 (1959): 21-27.

2157 John Dominic Crossan, "Redaction and Citation in Mark 11:9-10 and 11:17," *BR* 17 (1972): 33-50.

2158 John Dominic Crossan, "Redaction and Citation in Mark 11:9-10, 17 and 14:27," *SBLSP* 2 (1972): 17-60.

2159 C. K. Barrett, "The House of Prayer and the Den of Thieves," in E. Earle Ellis and Erich Grässer, eds., *Jesus und Paulus: Festschrift für Werner Georg Kümmel zum 70. Geburtstag*. Göttingen: Vandenhoeck & Ruprecht, 1975. Pp. 13-20.

2160 Craig A. Evans, "Jesus' Action in the Temple: Cleansing or Portent of Destruction?" *CBQ* 51 (1989): 237-70.

11:18-19

2161 Robert Schlarb, "Die Suche nach dem Messias: ζητέω als Terminus technicus der markinischen Messianologie," *ZNW* 81 (1990): 155-70.

11:20-26

2162 Guy Wagner, "Le figuier stérile et la destruction du temple: Marc 11:1-4 et 20-26," *ÉTR* 62/3 (1987): 335-42.

11:20-25

2163 Josef Schmid, "Markus und der aramäische Matthaus," in Josef Schmid and Anton Vögtle, eds., *Synoptische Studien* (festschrift for Alfred Wikenhauser). Münich: Zink, 1953. Pp. 75-118.

2164 John Coutts, "The Authority of Jesus and of the Twelve in St. Mark's Gospel," *JTS* 8 (1957): 111-18.

2165 V. Anzalone, "Il fico maledetto (Mc. XI,12-14 e 20-25)," *PalCl* 37 (1958): 257-64.

2166 Hugues Cousin, "Le figuier désséche. Un exemple de l'actualisation de la geste évangélique: Mc 11,12-14, 20-25; Mt 21,18-22," *FV* 70 (1971): 82-93.

2167 Malacby Marrion, "Petitionary Prayer in Mark and in the Q Material," doctoral dissertation, Catholic University of America, Washington DC, 1974.

2168 L. A. Loslie, "The Cursing of the Fig Tree: Tradition Criticism of a Marcan Pericope (Mark 11:12-14, 20-25)," *SBT* 7 (1977): 3-18.

2169 Jacques Schlosser, "Mc 11:25: tradition et rédaction," in Françios Refoulé, ed., *À cause de l'Évangile: Études sur les synoptiques et les Actes* (festschrift for Jacques Dupont). Paris: Cerf, 1985. Pp. 277-301.

2170 Bettina von Kienle, "Mk 11:12-14.20-25: der verdorrte Feigenbaum," *BibN* 57 (1991): 17-25.

2171 Günther Schwarz, "Jesus und der Feigenbaum am Wege (Mk 11:12-14, 20-25/Mt 21:18-22)," *BibN* 61 (1992): 36-37.

11:20-24

2172 J. G. Kahn, "La parabole du figuier stérile et les arbres récalcitrants de la Genèse," *NovT* 13 (1971): 38-45.

11:20-21

2173 Enric Cortés, "El secamiento de la higuera a la luz de los profetas de AT y de sus targumim (Mc 11,12-14.20-21)," *EstFr* 69 (1968): 41-68; 70 (1969): 5-23.

11:20

2174 Heinz Giesen, "Der Verdorrte Feigenbaum—Eine Symbolische Aussage? zu Mk 11,12-14.20f.," *BZ* 20 (1976): 95-111.

11:22-25

2175 Ernest Best, ''Mark's Preservation of the Tradition,'' in M. Sabbe, ed., *L'évangile selon Marc: Tradition et rédaction*. BETL #34. Gembloux/Louvain: Duculot/Louvain University Press, 1974. Pp. 21-34.

2176 Edwin K. Broadhead, ''Which Mountain Is 'This Mountain'? A Critical Note on Mark 11:22-25,'' *Paradigms* 2/1 (1986): 33-38.

2177 Sharyn E. Dowd, *Prayer, Power, and the Problem of Suffering: Mark 11:22-25 in the Context of Markan Theology*. Atlanta: Scholars Press, 1988.

11:22-23

2178 Gerhard Barth, ''Glaube und Zweifel in den synoptischen Evangelien,'' *ZTK* 72 (1975): 269-92.

2179 Helmut L. Egelkraut, ''The Triple Tradition and Its Variants in the Travel Narrative,'' in *Jesus' Mission to Jerusalem: A Redaction-Critical Study of the Travel Narrative in the Gospel of Luke*. Bern: Lang, 1976. Pp. 62-133.

11:22

2180 H.-W. Bartsch, ''Ein neuer Textus Receptus für das griechische Neue Testament?'' *NTS* 27 (1980-1981): 585-92.

2181 J. Duncan M. Derrett, ''Moving Mountains and Uprooting Trees,'' *BibO* 30 (1988): 231-44.

11:23-25

2182 Giancarlo Biguzzi, ''Mc. 11,23-25 e il Pater,'' *RBib* 27 (1979): 57-68.

11:23

2183 Ernest Best, ''An Early Sayings Collection,'' *NovT* 18/1 (1976): 1-16.

2184 Günther Schwarz, ''Πίστιν ὡς κόκκον σινάπεως,'' *BibN* 25 (1984): 27-35.

11:24-25

2185 Benny R. Crockett, "The Function of Mathetological Prayer in Mark," *IBS* 10 (1988): 123-39.

11:24

2186 John Dominic Crossan, "Aphorism in Discourse and Narrative," *Semeia* 43 (1988): 121-40.

11:25

2187 C. A. Wanamaker, "Mark 11:25 and the Gospel of Matthew," *StudB* 2 (1980): 339-50.

2188 Jacques Schlosser, "Mc 11,25: tradition et rédaction," in Françios Refoulé, ed., *À cause de l'Evangile: Études sur les synoptiques et les Actes* (festschrift for Jacques Dupont). Paris: Cerf, 1985. Pp. 277-301.

2189 Giuseppe Segalla, "Perdono 'cristiano' e correzione fraterna nella communità di 'Matteo' (Mt 18,15-17.21-35)," *StPa* 38 (1991): 499-518.

11:27-12:12

2190 Young-Heon Lee, "Jesus und die Jüdische Autorität: eine exegetische Untersuchung zu Mk 11,27-12,12," *ZKT* 106/4 (1984): 505-506.

11:27-33

2191 Heinrich Helmbold, "Das 'Lukasprinzip' im Markusevangelium," in *Vorsynoptische Evangelien*. Stuttgart: Klotz, 1953. Pp. 19-32.

2192 Jacob Kremer, "Jesu Antwort auf die Frage nach seiner Vollmacht. Eine Auslegung von Mk 11,27-33," *BibL* 9 (1968): 128-36.

2193 Rudolf Schnackenburg, "Die Vollmacht Jesu. Zu Mk 11,27-33," *KathGed* 27 (1971): 105-109.

2194 G. S. Shae, "The Question on the Authority of Jesus," *NovT* 16 (1974): 1-29.

2195 V. N. Makrides, "Considerations on Mark 11:27-33 par.," *DBM* 14 (1985): 43-55.

2196 Corrado Marucci, "Die implizite Christologie in der sogenannten Vollmachtsfrage," *ZKT* 108 (1986): 292-300.

2197 Knut Backhaus, *Die 'Jungerkreise' des Täufers Johannes: Eine Studie zu den religionsgeschichtlichen Ursprungen des Christentums*. Paderborn: Schoningh, 1991.

11:27

2198 Eric F. F. Bishop, "Jesus Walking or Teaching in the Temple," *ET* 63 (1951-1952): 226-27.

2199 Heinrich Greeven, "Erwägungen zur synoptischen Textkritik," *NTS* 6 (1959-1960): 282-96.

11:28

2200 Roland Minnerath, *Jésus et le pouvoir*. Le point theologique #46. Paris: Beauchesne, 1987.

11:34

2201 Marcel Didier, "La parabole des talents et des mines," in Ignace de la Potterie, ed., *De Jesus aux Evangiles: Tradition et rédaction dans les Évangiles synoptiques*. BETL #25. Paris: Lethielleux, 1967. Pp. 308-36.

12:1-37

2202 David Daube, "The Earliest Structure of the Gospels," *NTS* 5 (1958-1959): 174-87.

12:1-17

2203 George R. Edwards, "Biblical and Contemporary Aspects of War Tax Resistance," in Ronald H. Stone and Dana W. Wilbanks, eds., *The Peacemaking Struggle: Militarism and Resistance*. Lanham MD: University Press of America, 1985. Pp. 111-22.

12:1-12

2204 Ernst Lohmeyer, "Das Gleichnis von den Bösen Weingärtnern," in *Urchristliche Mystik: Neutestamentliche Studien*. 2nd ed. Darmstadt: Gentner, 1958. Pp. 159-81.

2205 John J. Vincent, "The Parables of Jesus as Self-Revelation," *StudE* 1 (1959): 79-99.

2206 Harvey K. McArthur, "The Dependence of the Gospel of Thomas on the Synoptics," *ET* 71 (1959-1960): 286-87.

2207 Johannes Herz, "Die Gleichnisse der Evangelien Matthaus, Markus und Lukas in ihrer geschichtlichen Überlieferung und ihrem religiös-sittlichen Inhalt," in E.-H. Amberg and U. Kühn, eds., *Bekenntnis zur Kirche* (festschrift for Ernst Sommerlath). Berlin: Evangelische Verlagsanstalt, 1960. Pp. 52-93.

2208 C. H. Dodd, *The Parables of the Kingdom*. Rev. ed. London: Nisbet, 1961.

2209 J. Duncan M. Derrett, "Fresh Light on the Wicked Vinedressers," *RIDA* 10 (1963): 11-41.

2210 Wilfrid J. Harrington, *A Key to the Parables*. New York: Paulist Press, 1964.

2211 Hans Dombois, "Juristische Bemerkungen zum Gleichnis von den bösen Weingärtnem (Mk 12,1-12)," *NZSTR* 8 (1966): 360-73.

2212 Martin Hengel, "Das Gleichnis von den Weingärtnern Mc 12:1-12 im Lichte der Zenonpapyri und der rabbinischen Gleichnisse," *ZNW* 59 (1968): 1-39.

2213 Hans-Josef Klauck, "Das Gleichnis vom Mord im Weinberg (Mk 12,1-12; Mt 21,33-46; Lk 20,9-19)," *BibL* 11 (1970): 118-45.

2214 John Dominic Crossan, "The Parable of the Wicked Husbandmen," *JBL* 90/4 (1971): 451-65.

2215 Augustin George, "Comment Jésus a-t-il perçu sa propre mort?" *LVie* 101 (1971): 34-59.

2216 John Drury, "The Sower, the Vineyard, and the Place of Allegory in the Interpretation of Mark's Parables," *JTS* 24/2 (1973): 367-79.

2217 Erhardt Güttgemanns, "Narrative Analyse Synoptischer Texte," *LB* 25/26 (1973): 50-73.

2218 Dino Merli, "La parabola dei vignaioliinfedeli (Mc. 12,1-12)," *BibO* 15 (1973): 97-108.

2219 Josef Blank, "Die Sendung des Sohnes: Zur christologischen Bedeutung des Gleichnisses von den bösen Winzern Mk 12,1-12," in Joachim Gnilka, ed., *Neues Testament und Kirche: Für Rudolf Schnackenburg*. Freiburg: Herder, 1974. Pp. 11-41.

2220 B. Dehandschutter, "La parabole des vignerons homicides (Mc. XII,1-12) et l'évangile selon Thomas," in M. Sabbe, ed., *L'évangile selon Marc: Tradition et rédaction*. BETL #34. Louvain: Louvain University Press, 1974. Pp. 203-19.

2221 Klyne R. Snodgrass, "The Parable of the Wicked Husbandmen: Is the Gospel of Thomas Version the Original?" *NTS* 21 (1974-1975): 142-44.

2222 Andrea Strus, "Funkcja obrazu w przekazie biblijnym: obraz winnicy w Iz 5,1-7 i w Ewangelii," *SThV* 15 (1977): 25-54.

2223 Sjef van Tilborg, "De materialistische exegese als keuze," *TijT* 18/2 (1978): 109-30.

2224 Rudolf Frieling, "Gleichnisse," in *Christologische Aufsätze*. Stuttgart: Urachhaus, 1982. Pp. 249-322.

2225 Helmut Koester, "Three Thomas Parables," in A. H. B. Logan and A. J. M. Wedderburn, eds., *The New Testament and Gnosis* (festschrift for Robert McL. Wilson). Edinburgh: T. & T. Clark, 1983. Pp. 195-203.

2226 Craig A. Evans, "On the Vineyard Parables of Isaiah 5 and Mark 12," *BZ* 28 (1984): 82-86.

2227 A. Cornette, "Notes sur la parabole des vignerons," *FV* 84/1-2 (1985): 42-48.

2228 Klaus Berger, *Einführung in die Formgeschichte*. UTB #1444. Tübingen: Francke, 1987.

2229 Edna Brocke and Gerhard Bauer, "Dialog-Bibelarbeit zu Markus 12,1-12," *KIsr* 2 (1987): 69-79.

2230 Corina Combet-Galland, ''La vigne et l'écriture, histoire de reconnaissances: Marc 12:1-12,'' *ÉTR* 62/4 (1987): 489-502.

2231 John R. Donahue, ''The Parables in Mark,'' in *The Gospel in Parable: Metaphor, Narrative, and Theology in the Synoptic Gospels*. Philadelphia: Fortress Press, 1988. Pp. 28-62.

2232 Xavier Alegre, ''La paràbola dels vinyatares homicides segons la versió de Marc (12,1-12),'' *RCT* 14 (1989): 163-74.

2233 Jean P. Duplantier, ''Les vignerons meurtriers: le travail d'une parabole,'' in Jean Delorme, ed., *Les paraboles évangéliques: perspectives nouvelles*. Paris: Cerf, 1989. Pp. 259-70.

2234 Aaron A. Milavec, ''A Fresh Analysis of the Parable of the Wicked Husbandmen in the Light of Jewish-Christian Dialogue,'' in Clemens Thoma, et al, eds., *Parable and Story in Judaism and Christianity*. New York: Paulist Press, 1989. Pp. 81-117.

2235 Bernard B. Scott, *Hear Then the Parable: A Commentary on the Parables of Jesus*. Minneapolis: Fortress Press, 1989.

2236 David Stern, ''Jesus' Parables from the Perspective of Rabbinic Literature: The Example of the Wicked Husbandmen,'' in Clemens Thoma, et al., eds., *Parable and Story in Judaism and Christianity*. New York: Paulist Press, 1989. Pp. 42-80.

2237 Michel Trimaille, ''La parabole des vignerons meurtriers (Mc 12,1-12),'' in Jean Delorme, ed., *Les paraboles évangéliques: perspectives nouvelles*. Paris: Cerf, 1989. Pp. 247-58.

2238 E. van Eck and A. G. van Aarde, ''A Narratological Analysis of Mark 12:1-12: The Plot of the Gospel of Mark in a Nutshell,'' *HTS* 45/4 (1989): 778-800.

2239 Aaron A. Milavec, ''The Identity of 'the Son' and 'the Others': Mark's Parable of the Wicked Husbandmen Reconsidered,'' *BTB* 20 (1990): 30-37.

2240 J. G. du Plessis, ''Speech Act Theory and New Testament Interpretation with Special Reference to G. N. Leech's Pragmatic Principles [Mk 12:1-12],'' in Patrick J. Hartin and J. H. Petzer, eds., *Text and Interpretation: New Approaches in the Criticism of the New Testament*. Leiden: Brill, 1991. Pp. 129-42.

12:1-11

2241 Madeleine I. Boucher, *The Parables*. Wilmington DE: Glazier, 1981.

2242 Louis Panier, ''Analyse sémiotique: 'Pour commencer','' *SémBib* 38 (1985): 1-31.

2243 Aaron A. Milavec, ''Mark's Parable of the Wicked Husbandmen as Reaffirming God's Predilection for Israel,'' *JES* 26 (1989): 289-312.

12:1-9

2244 W. G. Kümmel, ''Das Gleichnis von den bösen Weingärtnern (Mark 12,1-9),'' in *Aux sources de la tradition chrétienne*. Paris: Delachaux & Niestlé, 1950. Pp. 120-31.

2245 Wilhelm Pesch, *Der Lohngedanke in der Lehre Jesu: verplichen mit der religiösen Lohnlehre des Spätjudentums*. Münchener theologische Studien #I/7. Münich: Zink, 1955.

2246 W. Bammel, ''Das Gleichnis von den bösen Winzern und das jüdische Erbrecht,'' *RIDA* 6 (1959): 11-17.

2247 W. G. Kümmel, ''Das Gleichnis von den bösen Weingärtnern (Mk 12,1-9),'' *MThSt* 3 (1965): 207-17.

12:1-8

2248 M. H. Marco, ''Las espigas arrancadas en sabado (Mt 12,1-8 par.): Tradición y elaboración literaria,'' *EB* 28 (1969): 313-48.

2249 John Dominic Crossan, "The Servant Parables of Jesus," *Semeia* 1 (1974): 17-62.

2250 William G. Morrice, "Murder Amongst the Vines," *ET* 97/5 (1985-1986): 145-47.

12:1

2251 Gerhard Sellin, "Gleichnisstrukturen," *LB* 31 (1974): 89-115.

12:6

2252 W. Dekker, "De 'geliefde Zoon' in de synoptische evangeliën," *NTT* 16 (1961-1962): 94-106.

2253 Alfredo Scattolon, "L'ἀγαπητός sinottico nella luce della tradizione giudaica," *RBib* 26 (1978): 3-32.

12:9-11

2254 William G. Morrice, "Translating the Greek Imperative," *BT* 24 (1973): 129-34.

12:10-26

2255 John A. T. Robinson, "Did Jesus Have a Distinctive Use of Scripture?" in *Twelve More New Testament Studies*. London: SCM, 1984. Pp. 35-43.

12:10-11

2256 L. W. Barnard, "The Testimonium Concerning the Stone in the New Testament and in the Epistle of Barnabas," *StudE* 3 (1964): 306-13.

2257 J. Duncan M. Derrett, " 'The Stone that the Builders Rejected'," *StudE* 4 (1968): 180-86.

12:10

2258 F. F. Bruce, "The Corner Stone," *ET* 84 (1972-1973): 231-35.

12:12-17

2259 Arthur Ogle, "What Is Left for Caesar," *TT* 35/3 (1978): 254-64.

12:12

2260 Robert Schlarb, "Die Suche nach dem Messias: ζητέω als Terminus technicus der markinischen Messianologie," *ZNW* 81 (1990): 155-70.

12:13-17

2261 J. Duncan M. Derrett, "'Render to Caesar. . .'," in J. Duncan M. Derrett, *Law in the New Testament*. London: Darton, Longman & Todd, 1970. Pp. 313-38.

2262 Augustin George, "Jésus devant le problème politique," *LV* 105 (1971): 5-17.

2263 Kenzo Tagawa, "Jésus critiquant l'idéologie théocratique. Une étude de Mc 12,13-17," *FV* 70 (1971): 117-25.

2264 Reinhard Breymayer, "Zur Pragmatik des Bildes. Semiotische Beobachtungen zum Streitgespräch Mk 12,13-17 ('Der Zinsgroschen') unter Berücksichtigung der Spieltheorie," *LB* 13/14 (1972): 19-51.

2265 Gerd Petzke, "Der historische Jesus in der sozialethischen Diskussion: Mk 12.13-17 par," in Georg Strecker, ed., *Jesus Christus in Historie und Theologie* (festschrift for Hans Conzelmann). Tübingen: Mohr, 1975. Pp. 223-36.

2266 E. A. Russell, "Church and State in the New Testament," *ITQ* 44 (1977): 192-207.

2267 Sjef van Tilborg, "Het strukturalisme binnen de exegese: een variant van het burgerlijke denken," *Bij* 40 (1979): 364-79.

2268 John R. Donahue, "A Neglected Factor in the Theology of Mark," *JBL* 101 (1982): 563-94.

2269 Hans G. Klemm, "De Cencu Caesaris. Beobachtungen zu J. Duncan M. Derrett's Interpretation der Perikope Mk. 12:13-17 Par," *NovT* 24/3 (1982): 234-54.

2270 John Dominic Crossan, "Mark 12:13-17," *Int* 37/4 (1983): 397-401.

2271 H. St. J. Hart, "The Coin of 'Render unto Caesar. . .': A Note on Some Aspects of Mark 12:13-17; Matt. 22:15-22;

Luke 20:20-26,'' in Ernst Bammel and C. F. D. Moule, eds., *Jesus and the Politics of His Day*. Cambridge: Cambridge University Press, 1984. Pp. 241-48.

2272 Ethelbert Stauffer, ''Realistische Jesusworte,'' in William C. Weinrich, ed., *The New Testament Age* (festschrift for Bo Reicke). 2 vols. Macon GA: Mercer University Press, 1984. 2:503-10.

2273 Klaus Haacker, ''Kaisertribut und Gottesdienst,'' *TBe* 17 (1986): 285-92.

2274 Otto Betz, ''Jesus und die Zeloten (Zur Perikope von der Kaisersteuer Mark. 12,13-17,'' in P. Beyerhaus and W. Künneth, eds., *Gewalt in Jesu Namen?* Bielefeld: Missionsverlag, 1987. Pp. 30-45.

2275 Christopher Rowland, ''Render to God What Belongs to God,'' *NBlack* 70 (1989): 365-71.

2276 Uwe Wegner, ''O que fazem os denários de César na Palestina?'' *EstT* 29/1 (1989): 87-105.

2277 Jon B. Daniels, ''The Egerton Gospel: Its Place in Early Christianity,'' doctoral dissertation, Claremont Graduate School, Claremont CA, 1990.

<u>12:13</u>

2278 Constantin Daniel, ''Les 'Herodiens' du Nouveau Testament sont-ils des Esseniens?'' *RevQ* 6 (1967): 31-53.

2279 W. J. Bennett, ''The Herodians of Mark's Gospel,'' *NovT* 17/1 (1975): 9-14.

2280 Augustine Stock, ''Jesus, Hypocrites, and Herodians,'' *BTB* 16/1 (1986): 3-7.

<u>12:14</u>

2281 G. Wormser, '' 'Rendez à César' (Mc 12,14 par.),'' *NC* 3 (1967): 43-53.

<u>12:15</u>

2282 Philippe Rolland, ''Jésus connaissait leurs pensées,'' *ETL* 62 (1986): 118-21.

2283 John Thorley, "Aktionsart in New Testament Greek: Infinitive and Imperative," *NovT* 31 (1989): 290-315.

12:16-18

2284 Georg Baudler, "Das Gleichnis vom Mord im Weinberg," *EvErz* 41 (1989): 466-70.

12:16-17

2285 Benedikt Schwank, "Ein griechisches Jesuslogion: Uberlegungen zu Antwort Jesu auf die Steuerfrage (Mk 12,16-17 parr)," in Norbert Brox, et al., eds., *Anfänge der Theologie*. Louvain: Louvain University Press, 1987. Pp. 61-63.

12:16

2286 L. Y. Rahmani, " 'Whose Likeness and Inscription is This?' (Mark 12:16)," *BA* 49/1 (1986): 60-61.

12:17

2287 J. Spencer Kennard, *Render to God! A Study of the Tribute Passage*. New York: Oxford University Press, 1950.

2288 Leonhard Goppelt, "Die Freiheit zur Kaisersteuer. Zu Mk. 12,17 und Röm. 13,1-7," in Georg Kretschmar and Bernhard Lohse, eds., *Ecclesia und res publica. Kurt Dietrich Schmidt zum 65. Geburtstag*. Göttingen: Vandenhoeck & Ruprecht, 1961. Pp. 40-50.

2289 Jan N. Sevenster, " 'Geeft den keizer wat des keizers is, en Gode wat Gods is,' " *NedTT* 17 (1961): 21-31.

2290 Leonhard Goppelt, "The Freedom to Pay the Imperial Tax (Mk 12,17)," *StudE* 2 (1964): 183-94.

2291 Charles H. Giblin, " 'The Things of God' in the Question Concerning Tribute to Caesar," *CBQ* 33/4 (1971): 510-27.

2292 Maurice Baillet, "Les manuscrits de la Grotte 7 de Qumrân et le Nouveau Testament," *Bib* 54 (1973): 340-50.

2293 Pierre Benoit, "Nouvelle Note sur les Fragments Grecs de la Grotte 7 de Qumrân," *RB* 80/1 (1973): 5-12.

2294 Heda Jason, ''Der Zinsgroschen: Analyse der Erzählstruktur,'' *LB* 41/42 (1977): 49-87.

2295 Victor P. Furnish, ''War and Peace in the New Testament,'' *Int* 38 (1984): 363-79.

2296 James I. Packer, ''How to Recognize a Christian Citizen,'' *CT* 29/7 (1985): 4-8.

2297 Benedict T. Viviano, ''Render unto Caesar,'' *BibTo* 26 (1988): 272-76.

12:18-27

2298 Gilles Carton, ''Comme des anges dans le ciel (Marc 12,18-27),'' *BVC* 28 (1959): 46-52.

2299 Sebastián Bartina, ''Jesús y los saduceos: 'El Dios qe Abraham, de Isaac y de Jacob' es 'El que hace existir','' *EB* 21 (1962): 151-60.

2300 Franz Mussner, ''Jesu Lehre über das kommende Leben nach den Synoptikern,'' *Conci* 6 (1970): 692-95.

2301 Antonio Ammassari, ''Gesù ha veramente insegnato la risurrezione!'' *BibO* 15 (1973): 65-73.

2302 Miguel de Burgos Nuñez, ''Hemos sido creados para la vida y na para la muerte: La enseñanza de Jesús sobre la resurrección, según Marcos 12,18-27,'' *CiTom* 105 (1978): 529-60.

2303 François Vouga, ''Controverse sur la résurrection des morts,'' *LV* 179 (1986): 49-61.

2304 Marius Reiser, ''Das Leben nach dem Tod in der Verkündigung Jesu,'' *ErAu* 66 (1990): 381-90.

12:20-23

2305 J. Duncan M. Derrett, ''Marcan Priority and Marcan Skill,'' *BibO* 29 (1987): 135-40.

12:23-31

2306 Walter Simonis, ''Gottesliebe - Nächstenliebe: Uberlegungen zum sogenannten Doppelgebot im Lichte des biblischen Schöpfungs- und Bundesglaubens,'' in Thomas Franke, et al., eds., *Creatio ex amore: Beiträge zu einer Theologie* (festschrift for Alexandre Ganoczy). Würzburg: Echter, 1989. Pp. 60-83.

12:24-32

2307 M. Collin and P. Lenhardt, *Évangile et tradition d'Israël.* Paris: Éditions du Cerf, 1990.

12:24-27

2308 D. H. van Daalen, ''Some Observations on Mark 12,24-27,'' *StudE* 4 (1968): 241-45.

2309 F. Gerald Downing, ''The Resurrection of the Dead: Jesus and Philo,'' *JSNT* 15 (1982): 42-50.

12:26-27

2310 F.-P. Dreyfus, ''L'argument scripturaire de Jésus en faveur de la résurrection des morta (Marc XII,26-27),'' *RB* 66 (1959): 213-25.

2311 Dan M. Cohn-Sherbok, ''Jesus' Defence of the Resurrection of the Dead,'' *JSNT* 11 (1981): 64-73.

2312 Hans C. Cavallin, ''Jesus gör de döda levande,'' *SEÅ* 50/51 (1985): 40-49.

12:26

2313 J. Gerald Janzen, ''Resurrection and Hermeneutics: On Exodus 3:6 in Mark 12:26,'' *JSNT* 23 (1985): 43-58.

12:28-40

2314 Étienne Trocmé, ''Jésus et les lettrés d'après Marc 12:28-40,'' *FV* 84/1-2 (1985): 33-41.

12:28-34

2315 Jay B. Stern, ''Jesus' Citation of Dt 6,5 and Lv 19,18 in the Light of Jewish Tradition,'' *CBQ* 28 (1966): 312-16.

2316 Josef Ernst, ''Die Einheit von Gottes- und Nächstenliebe in der Verkündigung Jesu,'' *TGl* 60 (1970): 3-14.

2317 Giuseppe Segalla, ''La predicazione dell'amore nella tradizione presinottica,'' *RBib* 20 (1972): 481-528.

2318 I. C. M. Fairweather, "Two Different Pedagogical Methods in the Period of Oral Transmission," *StudE* 6 (1973): 100-108.

2319 Ludwig Berg, "Das neutestamentliche Liebesgebot. Prinzip der Sittlichkeit," *TTZ* 83 (1974): 129-45.

2320 Arland J. Hultgren, "The Double Commandment of Love in Mt 22:34-40: Its Sources and Composition," *CBQ* 36 (1974): 373-78.

2321 Helmut L. Egelkraut, "The Triple Tradition and Its Variants in the Travel Narrative," in *Jesus' Mission to Jerusalem: A Redaction-Critical Study of the Travel Narrative in the Gospel of Luke*. Bern: Lang, 1976. Pp. 62-133.

2322 Ferdinand Hahn, "Neutestamentliche Grundlagen einer christlichen Ethik," *TTZ* 86 (1977): 31-41.

2323 Simon Légasse, "L'étendue de l'amour interhumain d'après le Nouveau Testament: limites et promesses," *RTL* 8 (1977): 137-59, 293-304.

2324 Walter Diezinger, "Zum Liebesgebot Mk XII,28-34 und Parr," *NovT* 20/2 (1978): 81-83.

2325 George W. Hoyer, "Mark 12:28-34," *Int* 33/3 (1979): 293-98.

2326 Franz Prast, "Ein Appell zur Besinnung auf das Juden wie Christen gemeinsam verpflichtende Erbe im Munde Jesu: Das Anliegen einer alten vormarkinischen Tradition (Mk 12,28-34)," in Horst Goldstein, ed., *Gottesverächter und Menschenfeinde*. Düsseldorf: Patmos-Verlag, 1979. Pp. 79-98.

2327 Morris M. Faierstein, "Why Do the Scribes Say That Elijah Must Come First?" *JBL* 100 (1981): 75-86.

2328 Ferdinand Hahn, "Neutestamentliche Ethik als Kriterium menschlicher Rechtsordnung," in E. L. Behrendt, ed., *Rechtstaat und Christentum*. Münich: Behrendt, 1982. Pp. 377-79.

2329 Gregory Murray, "The Questioning of Jesus," *DR* 101 (1984): 271-75.

2330 Giuseppe Ghiberti, "Il primo di tutti i comandamenti (Mc 12,28-34)," *ParSpirV* 11 (1985): 97-110.

2331 Karl Kertelge, "Das Doppelgebot der Liebe im Markusevangelium," in Françios Refoulé, ed., *À cause l'Evangile: Études sur les synoptiques et les Actes* (festschrift for Jacques Dupont). Paris: Cerf, 1985. Pp. Pp. 303-22.

2332 J. Hamilton, "The First Commandment: A Theological Reflection," *NBlack* 69 (1988): 174-81.

2333 Jarmo Killunen, *Das Doppelgebot der Liebe in synoptischer Sicht: Ein redaktionskritischer Versuch über Mk 12,28-34 und die Parallelen.* Annales Academiae Scientiarum Fennicae #B/250. Helsinki: Suomalainen Tiedeakatemia, 1989.

2334 Simon Légasse, *"Et qui est mon prochain?" Étude sur l'objet de l'agapè dans le Nouveau Testament.* Lectio Divina #136. Paris: Cerf, 1989.

12:28-31

2335 Willem K. Grossouw, "Wat leert het Nieuwe Testament over de liefde tol God?" *TijT* 3 (1963): 230-51.

2336 Manuel Miguéns, "Amour, alpha et omega de l'existence, Mc 12,28-31," *AsSeign* 62 (1970): 53-62.

2337 M. W. Patrick, *The Love Commandment: How to Find Its Meaning for Today.* St. Louis MO: CBP Press, 1984.

12:28

2338 N. Lohfink, "Das Hauptgebot im Alten Testament," *GeistL* 36 (1963): 271-81.

2339 N. Lohfink, "Il 'comandamento primo' nell'Antico Testamento," *BibO* 7 (1965): 49-60.

2340 Lino Cignelli, "La grecità biblica," *SBFLA* 35 (1985): 203-48.

12:29-30

2341 Kenneth J. Thomas, "Liturgical Citations in the Synoptics," *NTS* (1975-1976): 205-14.

12:29

2342 Frederico Dattler, "A mixná no Nôvo Testamento," in J. Salvador, ed., *Alualidades Bíblicas* (festschrift for F. J. J. Pedreira de Castro). Petrópolis: Vozes, 1971. Pp. 395-402.

12:30-31

2343 George M. Soares-Prabhu, "The Synoptic Love-Commandment: The Dimensions of Love in the Teaching of Jesus," *Je* 13 (1983): 85-103.

2344 Karl Kertelge, "Das Doppelgebot der Liebe im Markusevangelium," in Françios Refoulé, ed., *À cause de l'Evangile: Études sur les synoptiques et les Actes* (festschrift for Jacques Dupont). Paris: Cerf, 1985. Pp. 303-22.

12:31

2345 Hugh W. Montefiore, "Thou Shalt Love Thy Neighbour as Thyself," *NovT* 5 (1962): 157-70.

12:33

2346 James Van Vurst, "The Scribe's Insight," *BibTo* 25 (1987): 37-41.

12:34

2347 Bonaventura Rinaldi, "Νουνεχῶς," *BibO* 20 (1978): 26.

2348 John Thorley, "Aktionsart in New Testament Greek: Infinitive and Imperative," *NovT* 31 (1989): 290-315.

12:35-37

2349 Robert P. Gagg, "Jesus und die Davidssohnfrage: Zur Exegese von Markus 12,35-37," *TZ* 7 (1951): 18-30.

2350 Otto Betz, "Donnersöhne, Menschenfischer und der Davidische Messias," *RevQ* 3 (1961): 41-70.

2351 Evald Lövestam, "Die Davidssohnsfrage," *SEÅ* 27/28 (1962): 72-82.

2352 Joseph A. Fitzmyer, "The Son of David Tradition and Mt 22:41-46 and Parallels," *Conci* 10/2 (1966): 40-46.

2353 Gerhard Schneider, "Die Davidssohnfrage (Mk 12,35-37)," *Bib* 53 (1972): 65-90.

2354 Fritz Neugebauer, "Die Davidssohnfrage (Mark XII,35-37 Parr.) und der Menschensohn," *NTS* 21/1 (1974-1975): 81-108.

2355 Dennis C. Duling, "Solomon, Exorcism, and the Son of David," *HTR* 68 (1975): 235-52.

2356 Bruno Moriconi, "Chi è Gesà? Mc 12,35-37 momento culminante di rivelazione," *ECarm* 30 (1979): 23-51.

2357 Bruce D. Chilton, "Jesus *ben David:* Reflections on the *Davidssohnfrage,*" *JSNT* 14 (1982): 88-112.

2358 Marinus de Jonge, "Jesus, Son of David and Son of God," in Spike Draisma," ed., *Intertextuality in Biblical Writings* (festschrift for Bastiaan M. F. van Iersel). Kampen: J. H. Kok, 1989. Pp. 95-104.

<u>12:35-36</u>

2359 W. R. G. Loader, "Christ at the Right Hand - Ps. cx. 1 in the New Testament," *NTS* 24 (1977-1978): 199-217.

<u>12:35</u>

2360 Gerhard Schneider, "Zur Vorgeschichte des christologischen Prädikats 'Sohn Davids'," *TTZ* 80 (1971): 247-53.

<u>12:36</u>

2361 Andreas Baumeister, " 'Setze dich zu meiner Rechten': Die Bibelauslegung Jesu," *Ent* 40/4 (1985): 28-29.

2362 J. K. Elliott, "The Relevance of Textual Criticism to the Synoptic Problem," in David L. Dungan, ed., *The Interrelations of the Gospels*. Louvain: Peeters Press, 1990. Pp. 348-59.

12:37-40

2363 Harry T. Fleddermann, "A Warning About the Scribes (Mark 12:37b-40)," *CBQ* 44/1 (1982): 52-67.

12:38-44

2364 Paul Ternant, "La dévotion contrefaite et l'authentique générosité," *AsSeign* 63 (1971): 53-63.

12:38

2365 Karl H. Rengstorf, "Die *stolai* der Schriftgelehrten. Eine Erläuterung zu Mark. 12,38," in Otto Betz, Martin Hengel, and Peter Schmidt, eds., *Abraham unser Vater: Juden und Christen in Gespräch über die Bibel: Festschrift für Otto Michel zum 60. Geburtstag*. Leiden/Köln: Brill, 1963. Pp. 383-404.

12:40

2366 J. Duncan M. Derrett, " 'Eating Up the Houses of Widows': Jesus' Comment on Lawyers?" *NovT* 14/1 (1972): 1-9.

12:41-44

2367 Louis Simon, "Le sou de la veuve. Marc 12/41-4," *ÉTR* 44 (1969): 115-26.

2368 Joachim Jeremias, "Zwei Miszellen: 1. Antik-Judische Munzdeutungen. 2. Zur Geschichtlichkeit der Tempelreinigung," *NTS* 23/2 (1976-1977): 177-79.

2369 Eugene A. LaVerdiere, "The Widow's Mite," *Emmanuel* 92 (1986): 341.

2370 Gregory Murray, "Did Luke Use Mark?" *DR* 104 (1986): 268-71.

2371 Mary Ann Beavis, "Women as Models of Faith in Mark," *BTB* 18 (1988): 3-9.

2372 Elizabeth Struthers Malbon, "The Poor Widow in Mark and Her Poor Rich Readers," *CBQ* 53 (1991): 589-604.

2373 R. S. Sugirtharajah, "The Widow's Mites Revalued," *ET* 103/2 (1992-1993): 42-43.

12:42

2374 Daniel Sperber, "Mark 12:42 and its Metrological Background. A Study in Ancient Syriac Versions," *NovT* 9 (1967): 178-90.

12:44

2375 Harald Sahlin, "Emendationsvorschläge zum griechischen Text des Neuen Testaments I," *NovT* 24 (1982): 160-79.

13:1-37

2376 Charles Perrot, "Essai sur le Discours eschatologique (Mc. XIII,1-37; Mt. XXIV,1-36; Lc. XXI,5-36)," *RechSR* 47 (1959): 481-514.

2377 Ingo Hermann, "Die Gefährdung der Welt und ihre Erneuerung: Auslegung von Mk 13.1-37," *BibL* 7 (1966): 305-309.

2378 Hugo Lattanzi, "Eschatologici sermonis Domini logica interpretatio," *Div* 11 (1967): 71-92.

2379 John Kallikuzhuppil, "The Glorification of the Suffering Church," *BB* 9 (1983): 247-57.

13:1-2

2380 Richard H. Hiers, *The Historical Jesus and the Kingdom of God: Present and Future in the Message and Ministry of Jesus*. University of Florida Humanities Monograph #38. Gainesville FL: University of Florida Press, 1973.

2381 Stephen H. Smith, "The Literary Structure of Mark 11:1-12:40," *NovT* 31/2 (1989): 104-24.

13:2

2382 Jacques Dupont, "Il n'en sera pas laissé pierre sur pierre (Marc 13,2; Luc 19,44)," *Bib* 52 (1971): 301-20.

2383 Jacques Schlosser, "Mc 11:25: tradition et rédaction," in Françios Refoulé, ed., *À cause de l'Evangile: Études sur les synoptiques et les Actes* (festschrift for Jacques Dupont). Paris: Cerf, 1985. Pp. 277-301.

2384 Jacques Schlosser, "La parole de Jésus sur la fin du temple," *NTS* 36 (1990): 398-414.

13:3-37

2385 Ton Veerkamp, "Am Ende nur die Hoffnung," *TexteK* 28 (1985): 4-31.

13:3

2386 Werner Schauch, "Der Ölberg: Exegese zu einer Ortsangabe besonders bei Matthaus und Markus," *TLZ* 77 (1952): 391-96.

13:5-37

2387 Willem S. Vorster, "Literary Reflections on Mark 13:5-37: A Narrated Speech of Jesus," *Neo* 21 (1987): 203-24.

13:5-31

2388 M. Eugene Boring, *Sayings of the Risen Jesus: Christian Prophecy in the Synoptic Tradition*. SNTSMS #46. Cambridge: Cambridge University Press, 1982.

13:5-27

2389 Geert Hallbäck, "Der Anonyme Plan: Analyse von Mark 13,5-27 im Hinblick auf die Relevanz der Apokalyptischen Rede für die Problematik der Aussage," *LB* 49 (1981): 38-53.

13:5-23

2390 Gert Lüderitz, "Rhetorik, Poetik, Kompositionstechnik im Markusevangelium," in Hubert Cancik, ed., *Markus-Philologie*. Tübingen: Mohr, 1984. Pp. 165-203.

13:6

2391 Hans Kosmala, " 'In My Name'," *ASTI* 5 (1967): 87-109.

2392 William Manson, "The 'Ego Eimi' of the Messianic Presence in the New Testament," in T. W. Manson, *Jesus and the Christian*. Grand Rapids: Eerdmans, 1967. Pp. 174-83.

13:9-13

2393 C. H. Dodd, "The Sayings," in *Historical Tradition in the Fourth Gospel*. Cambridge: Cambridge University Press, 1963. Pp. 315-405.

2394 Joachim Gnilka, "Martyriumsparänese und Sühnetod in synoptischen und jüdischen Traditionen," in Rudolf

Schnackenburg, et al., eds., *Die Kirche des Anfangs* (festschrift for H. Schürmann). Leipzig: St. Benno-Verlag, 1977. Pp. 223-46.

2395 Bo Reicke, "A Test of Synoptic Relationships: Matthew 10:17-23 and 24:9-14 with Parallels," in William R. Farmer, ed., *New Synoptic Studies*. Macon GA: Mercer University Press, 1983. Pp. 209-29.

2396 Helen R. Graham, "A Markan Theme: Endurance in Time of Persecution," *BibTo* 23 (1985): 297-304.

2397 Helen R. Graham, "A Passion Prediction for Mark's Community: Mark 13:9-13," *BTB* 16/1 (1986): 18-22.

2398 Paul S. Pudussery, *Discipleship: A Call to Suffering and Glory: An Exegetico-Theological Study of Mk 8,27-9,1; 13,9-13 and 13,24-27*. Rome: Libreria, 1987.

2399 John R. Levison, "Did the Spirit Inspire Rhetoric? An Exploration of George Kennedy's Definition of Early Christian Rhetoric," in Duane F. Watson, ed., *Persuasive Artistry: Studies in New Testament Rhetoric* (festschrift for George A. Kennedy). Sheffield: JSOT Press, 1991. Pp. 25-40.

<u>13:9-11</u>

2400 George D. Kilpatrick, "The Gentile Missions in Mark and Mark 13:9-11," in D. E. Nineham, ed., *Studies in the Gospels* (festschrift for R. H. Lightfoot). Oxford: Blackwell, 1955. Pp. 145-58.

2401 Jacques Dupont, "La persécution comme situation missionaire (Marc 13,9-11)," in Rudolf Schnackenburg, et al., eds., *Die Kirche des Anfangs* (festschrift for Heinz Schürmann). Leipzig: St. Benno, 1977; Freiburg/Basel: Herder, 1978. Pp. 97-114.

<u>13:9-10</u>

2402 George D. Kilpatrick, "Mark 13:9-10," *JTS* 9 (1958): 81-86.

13:9

2403 Frederick W. Danker, "Double-Entendre in Mark 13:9," *NovT* 10/2 (1968): 162-63.

2404 Frederico Dattler, "A mixná no Nôvo Testamento," in J. Salvador, ed., *Alualidades Bíblicas* (festschrift for F. J. J. Pedreira de Castro). Petrópolis: Vozes, 1971. Pp. 395-402.

13:10

2405 Austin M. Farrer, "An Examination of Mark 13:10," *JTS* 7 (1956): 75-79.

2406 David Bosch, *Die Heidenmission in der Zukunftsschau Jesu. Eine Untersuchung zur Eschatologie der synoptischen Evangelien.* Zürich: Zwingli, 1959.

2407 James W. Thompson, "The Gentile Mission as an Eschatological Necessity," *RQ* 14/1 (1971): 18-27.

2408 Charles L. Holman, "The Idea of an Imminent Parousia in the Synoptic Gospels," *SBT* 3 (1973): 15-31.

2409 Gergard Dautzenberg, "Das Wort von der weltweiten Verkündigung des Evangeliums (Mk 13,10) und seine Vorgeschichte," in Karl Kertelge, ed., *Christus bezeugen* (festschrift for Wolfgang Trilling). Leipzig: St. Benno-Verlag, 1989. Pp. 150-65.

2410 Philippe Rolland, "Luc, témoin de la forme primitive du Discours eschatologique," *BLOS* 2 (1989): 9-11.

13:11

2411 Matthew Mahoney, "Luke 21:14-15: Editorial Rewriting or Authenticity?" *ITQ* 47/3 (1980): 220-38.

13:12-14:3

2412 J. Harold Greenlee, *Nine Uncial Palimpsests of the Greek New Testament.* Salt Lake City: University of Utah, 1968.

13:12

2413 Roy A. Harrisville, "Jesus and the Family," *Int* 23/4 (1969): 425-38.

2414 Pierre Grelot, ''Miche 7,6 dans les evangiles et dans la littrature rabbinique,'' *Bib* 67/3 (1986): 363-77.

13:14-20

2415 Sidney G. Sowers, ''The Circumstances and Recollection of the Pella Flight,'' *TZ* 26 (1970): 305-20.

2416 John J. Gunther, ''The Fate of the Jerusalem Church: The Flight to Pella,'' *TZ* 29 (1973): 81-94.

13:14-18

2417 Gordon D. Fee, ''A Text-Critical Look at the Synoptic Problem,'' *NovT* 22/1 (1980): 12-28.

13:14

2418 Harold A. Guy, ''Mark xiii.14: **ὁ ἀναγινώσκων νοείτω**,'' *ET* 65 (1953-1954): 30.

2419 Béda Rigaux, ''**Βδέλυγμα τῆς ἐρημώσεως** (Mc 13,14; Mt 4,15),'' *Bib* 40 (1959): 675-83.

2420 G. C. Aalders, ''De 'gruwel der verwoesting,'' *GTT* 60 (1960): 1-5.

2421 R. H. Shaw, ''A Conjecture on the Signs of the End,'' *ATR* 47 (1965): 96-102.

2422 C. H. Dodd, ''The Fall of Jerusalem and the 'Abomination of Desolation',''[1947] in *More New Testament Studies*. Manchester: University Press, 1968. Pp. 69-83.

2423 Desmond Ford, *The Abomination of Desolation in Biblical Eschatology*. Washington DC: University Press of America, 1979.

2424 Günther Zuntz, ''Wann wurde das Evangelium Marci geschrieben [Acts 12:2],'' in Hubert Cancik, ed., *Markus-Philologie*. Tübingen: Mohr, 1984. Pp. 47-71.

2425 Ernest Best, ''The Gospel of Mark: Who Was the Reader?'' *IBS* 11 (1989): 124-32.

2426 Ronald E. Clements, ''Apocalyptic, Literacy and the Canonical Tradition,'' in W. Huelitt Gloer, ed., *Eschatology* *and the New Testament* (festschrift for G. R. Beasley-Murray). Peabody MA: Hendrickson, 1989. Pp. 15-27.

13:17-18

2427 Paul Glaube, "Einige Stellen, die Bedeutung des Codex D charakterisieren," *NovT* 2 (1957-1958): 310-15.

13:18-27

2428 John R. Donahue, "A Neglected Factor in the Theology of Mark," *JBL* 101 (1982): 563-94.

13:18

2429 Graham N. Stanton, " 'Pray That Your Flight May Not Be in Winter or on a Sabbath' (Matthew 24:20)," *JSNT* 37 (1989): 17-30.

13:20

2430 H. P. Owen, "The Parousia of Christ in the Synoptic Gospels," *SJT* 12 (1959): 171-92.

2431 Rainer Stuhlmann, *Das eschatologische Maß im Neuen Testament.* Göttingen: Vandenhoeck & Ruprecht, 1983.

2432 Philippe Rolland, "Luc, témoin de la forme primitive du Discours eschatologique," *BLOS* 2 (1989): 9-11.

13:21-23

2433 Thierry Snoy, "Les miracles dans l'évangile de Marc. Examen de quelques études récentes," *RTL* 3 (1972): 449-66; 4 (1973): 58-101.

2434 Marinus de Jonge, "The Earliest Christian Use of Christos: Some Suggestions," *NTS* 32 (1986): 321-43.

13:22-27

2435 Philippe Rolland, "Luc, témoin de la forme primitive du Discours eschatologique," *BLOS* 2 (1989): 9-11.

13:22

2436 John Thorley, "Aktionsart in New Testament Greek: Infinitive and Imperative," *NovT* 31 (1989): 290-315.

13:24-27

2437 Franz Mussner, "Die Wiederkunft des Menschensohnes nach Markus 13,24-27 und 14,61-62," *BK* 16 (1961): 105-107.

2438 John S. Kloppenborg, "Didache 16:6-8 and Special Matthaean Tradition," *ZNW* 70/1 (1979): 54-67.

2439 Paul S. Minear, "Some Archetypal Origins of Apocalyptic Predictions," *HBT* 1 (1979): 105-35.

2440 Peter Maser, "Sonne und Mond: exegetische Erwägungen zum Fortleben der Spätantik-jüdischen in der frühchristlichen Kunst," *K* 25/1-2 (1983): 41-67.

2441 Paul S. Pudussery, *Discipleship: A Call to Suffering and Glory: An Exegetico-Theological Study of Mk 8,27-9,1; 13,9-13 and 13,24-27*. Rome: Libreria, 1987.

13:24-32

2442 Rudolf Pesch, "Der Menschensohn wird kommen," *TW* 144 (1974): 55-61.

2443 W. Sibley Towner, "An Exposition of Mark 13:24-32," *Int* 30/3 (1976): 292-96.

13:26-27

2444 J. F. Seitz, "The Future Coming of the Son of Man: Three Midrashic Formulations in the Gospel of Mark," *StudE* 6 (1973): 478-94.

13:26

2445 George R. Beasley-Murray, "The Parousia in Mark," *RevExp* 75/4 (1978): 565-81.

13:27

2446 Paul T. Coke, "Angels of the Son of Man," *SNTU-A* 3 (1978): 91-98.

2447 Harald Sahlin, "Emendationsvorschläge zum griechischen Text des Neuen Testaments I," *NovT* 24 (1982): 160-79.

13:28-37

2448 Wilfrid J. Harrington, *A Key to the Parables*. New York: Paulist Press, 1964.

13:28-36

2449 Bernard B. Scott, *Hear Then the Parable: A Commentary on the Parables of Jesus*. Minneapolis: Fortress Press, 1989.

13:28-34

2450 John R. Donahue, ''A Neglected Factor in the Theology of Mark,'' *JBL* 101 (1982): 563-94.

13:28-32

2451 Allan McNicol, ''The Lesson of the Fig Tree in Mark 13:28-32: A Comparison between Two Exegetical Methodologies,'' *RQ* 27/4 (1984): 193-207.

13:28-31

2452 J. Duncan M. Derrett, ''Figtrees in the New Testament,'' *HeyJ* 14 (1973): 249-65.

13:28-29

2453 Johannes Herz, ''Die Gleichnisse der Evangelien Matthaus, Markus und Lukas in ihrer geschichtlichen Überlieferung und ihrem religiös-sittlichen Inhalt,'' in E.-H. Amberg and U. Kühn, eds., *Bekenntnis zur Kirche* (festschrift for Ernst Sommerlath). Berlin: Evangelische Verlagsanstalt, 1960. Pp. 52-93.

2454 Jacques Dupont, ''La parabole du figuier qui bourgeonne (Mc xiii,28-29 et par.),'' *RB* 75 (1968): 526-48.

2455 John R. Donahue, ''The Parables in Mark,'' in *The Gospel in Parable: Metaphor, Narrative, and Theology in the Synoptic Gospels*. Philadelphia PA: Fortress, 1988. Pp. 28-62.

13:28

2456 Bernard B. Scott, *Jesus, Symbol-Maker for the Kingdom*. Philadelphia: Fortress Press, 1981.

13:30-32

2457 Brian M. Nolan, ''Some Observations on the Parousia and New Testament Eschatology,'' *ITQ* 36 (1969): 283-314.

13:30

2458 Ernst Fuchs, "Verheissung und Erfüllung," in *Zur Frage nach dem historischen Jesus*. Tübingen: Mohr, 1960. Pp. 66-78.

2459 Evald Lövestam, "En problematisk eskatologisk utsaga: Mark. 13:30 par.," *SEÅ* 28/29 (1963): 64-80.

2460 Martin Künzi, *Das Naherwartungslogion Markus 9,1 par: Geschichte seiner Auslegung, mit einem Nachwort zur Auslegungsgeschichte von Markus 13,30 par*. Beiträge zur Geschichte der biblischen Exegese 21. Tübingen: Mohr, 1977.

2461 Evald Lövestam, "The ἡ γενεὰ αὕτη: Eschatology in Mk 13,30 parr," in Jan Lambrecht, ed., *L'Apocalypse johannique et l'Apocalyptique dans le Nouveau Testament*. BETL #53. Louvain: Peeters Press, 1980. Pp. 403-13.

2462 Barry S. Crawford, "Near Expectation in the Sayings of Jesus," *JBL* 101/2 (1982): 225-44.

2463 Heinz Giesen, "Christliche Existenz in der Well und der Menschensohn: Versuch einer Neuinterpretation des Terminwortes Mk 13,30," *SNTU-A* 8 (1983): 18-69.

2464 Franz Mussner, "Wer ist 'dieses Geschlecht' in Mk 13,30 parr.?" *K* 29 (1987): 23-28.

2465 J. K. Elliott, "The Relevance of Textual Criticism to the Synoptic Problem," in David L. Dungan, ed., *The Interrelations of the Gospels*. Louvain: Peeters Press, 1990. Pp. 348-59.

13:32-37

2466 John B. Trotti, "Mark 13:32-37," *Int* 32/4 (1978): 410-15.

13:32

2467 Max Meinertz, " 'Dieses Geschlecht' im Neuen Testament," *BZ* 1 (1957): 283-89.

2468 Sosio Pezzella, "Marco 13,32 e la scienza di Cristo," *RBib* 7 (1959): 147-52.

2469 Erich Fascher, " 'Von dem Tage aber und von der Stunde weiss niemand . . .' Der Anstoss in Mark 13,32 (Matth. 24,36). Eine exegetische Skizze zum Verhältnis von historisch-kritischer und christologischer Interpretation," in *Ruf und Antwort* (festschrift for Emil Fuchs). Leipzig: Koehler and Amelang, 1964. Pp. 475-83.

2470 R. Beguer, "Estudio critico-exégetico de Mc 13,32. Significación escatológica," *ASV* 5 (1965): 131-53.

2471 Giuseppe Segalla, "Il figlio non conosce il giorno della parusia," *PV* 10 (1965): 250-54.

2472 Erich Fascher, "Probleme der Zukunfterwartung nach Mk 13,32 und Mt 24,36," in E. Fascher, ed., *Frage und Antwort: Studien zur Theologie und Religionsgeschichte*. Berlin-Ost: Evangelische Verlagsanstalt, 1968. Pp. 68-84.

2473 Jacques Winandy, "Le logion de l'ignorance (Mc, XIII,32; Mt., XXIV,36)," *RB* 75 (1968): 63-79.

13:33-37

2474 C. H. Dodd, *The Parables of the Kingdom*. Rev. ed. London: Nisbet, 1961.

2475 Evald Lövestam, "Le portier qui veille la nuit, Mc 13,33-37," *AsSeign* 2 (1969): 44-53.

2476 Richard Eckstein, "Vom rechten Warten. Markus 13.33-37," in C. Bourbeck, ed., *Gleichnisse aus Altem und Neuem Testament*. Stuttgart: Klotz, 1971. Pp. 145-48.

2477 Richard J. Bauckham, "Synoptic Parousia Parables and the Apocalypse," *NTS* 23 (1976-1977): 162-76; 29 (1983): 129-34.

2478 John R. Donahue, "The Parables in Mark," in *The Gospel in Parable: Metaphor, Narrative, and Theology in the Synoptic Gospels*. Philadelphia PA: Fortress, 1988. Pp. 28-62.

13:34-14:30

2479 J. Harold Greenlee, *Nine Uncial Palimpsests of the Greek New Testament*. Salt Lake City: University of Utah, 1968.

13:34-37

2480 John Dominic Crossan, "The Servant Parables of Jesus," *Semeia* 1 (1974): 17-62.

13:34-36

2481 Jacques Dupont, "La parabole du maître qui rentre dans la nuit (Mc 13,34-36)," in Albert Descamps and André de Halleux, eds., *Mélanges bibliques en hommage au R. P. Béda Rigaux*. Gembloux: Duculot, 1970. Pp. 89-116.

14:1-16:8

2482 Ched Myers, "The Last Days of Jesus, Mark 14:1-16:8: Collapse and Restoration of Discipleship," *Soj* 16 (1987): 32-36.

14:1-15:47

2483 Matthew Vellanickal, "The Passion Narrative in the Gospel of Mark," *BB* 9 (1983): 258-78.

14:1-52

2484 John P. Heil, "Mark 14:1-52: Narrative Structure and Reader Response," *Bib* 71/3 (1990): 305-32.

14:1-41

2485 Arnold A. van Ruler, *Marcus 14: Vs. 1-41*. Kampen: Kok, 1971.

14:1-25

2486 Frederick W. Danker, "The Literary Unity of Mark 14:1-25," *JBL* 85/4 (1966): 467-72.

2487 Cornelis J. den Heyer, "Jesus, de lijdende rechtvaardige en de knecht des Heren," in H. H. Grosheide, et al., eds., *De knechtsgestalte van Christus* (festschrift for H. N. Ridderbos). Kampen: Kok, 1978. Pp. 54-64.

2488 Sylvester Lamberigts, "Lezing erl uitleg van Mc. 14,1-25," in *Wie is Hij toch? De Bijbel leren lezen om Jezus te kennen*. Tielt-Weesp: Lannoo, 1984. Pp. 183-92.

14:1-12

2489 Ludger Schenke, *Studien zur Passionsgeschichte des Markus. Tradition und Redaktion in Markus 14.1-12*. Forschung zur Bibel 4. Würzburg/Stuttgart: Echter-Verlag/Katholisches Bibelwerk, 1971.

14:1-11

2490 Fritzleo Lentzen-Deis, "Passionsbericht als Handlungsmodell: Uberlegungen zu Anstössen aus der 'pragmatischen' Sprachwissenschaft für die exegetischen Methoden," in Josef Blank and Karl Kertelge, eds., *Der Prozess gegen Jesus: historische Rückfrage und theologische*. Freiburg: Herder, 1988. Pp. 191-232.

2491 James R. Edwards, "Markan Sandwiches: The Significance of Interpolations in Markan Narratives," *NovT* 31 (1989): 193-216.

14:1-9

2492 Edwin K. Broadhead, "Mark 14:1-9: A Gospel within a Gospel," *Paradigms* 1/1 (1985): 32-41.

14:1-2

2493 Robert Schlarb, "Die Suche nach dem Messias: ζητέω als Terminus technicus der markinischen Messianologie," *ZNW* 81 (1990): 155-70.

14:2

2494 Christoph Burchard, "Fussnoten zum neutestamentlichen Griechisch," *ZNW* 61 (1970): 157-71.

2495 Ulrich Hedinger, "Jesus und die Volksmenge: Kritik der Qualifizierung der óchloi in der Evangelienauslegung," *TZ* 32 (1976): 201-206.

14:3-9

2496 André Legault, "An Application of the Form-Critique Method to the Anointings in Galilee (Lk 7,36-50) and Bethany (Mt 26,6-13; Mk 14,3-9; Lk 12,1-8)," *CBQ* 16 (1954): 131-45.

2497 A. Meli, " 'Sempre i poveri avete con voi, ma non sempre avete me' (Mc 14,3.9 par)," *Hum* 14 (1959): 338-43.

2498 C. H. Dodd, "The Sayings," in *Historical Tradition in the Fourth Gospel.* Cambridge: Cambridge University Press, 1963. Pp. 315-405.

2499 J. Duncan M. Derrett, "The Anointing at Bethany," *StudE* 2 (1964): 174-82.

2500 Joachim Jeremias, "Die Salbungsgeschichte Mk 14,3-9," in J. Jeremias, ed., *Abba: Studien zur neutestamentlichen Theologie und Zeitgeschichte.* Göttingen: Vandenhoeck & Ruprecht, 1966. Pp. 107-15.

2501 Richard H. Hiers, *The Historical Jesus and the Kingdom of God: Present and Future in the Message and Ministry of Jesus.* University of Florida Humanities Monograph #38. Gainesville FL: University of Florida Press, 1973.

2502 Rudolf Pesch, "Die Salbung Jesu in Bethanien (Mk 14,3-9): Eine Studie zur Passionsgeschichte," in Paul Hoffmann, ed., *Orientierung an Jesus: Zur Theologie der Synoptiker: Für Josef Schmid*, in collaboration with Norbert Bröx and Wilhelm Pesch. Freiburg/Basel/Vienna: Herder, 1973. Pp. 267-85.

2503 Harald Sahlin, "Zum Verständnis der christologischen Anschauung des Markusevangeliums," *StTheol* 31 (1977): 1-19.

2504 Winsome Munro, "The Anointing in Mark 14:3-9 and John 12:1-8," *SBLSP* 9/1 (1979): 127-30.

2505 Nelson H. Brickham, "The Dependence of the Fourth Gospel on the Gospel of Mark: A Redaction-Critical Approach," doctoral dissertation, American University, Washington DC, 1982.

2506 Franz Schnider, "Christusverkündigung und Jesuserzählungen: Exegetische Überlegungen zu Mk 14,3-9," *K* 24 (1982): 171-80.

2507 John N. Suggit, "An Incident from Mark's Gospel," *JTSA* 50 (1985): 25-55.

2508 Richard C. Brand, "Grace Is Everywhere," *ET* 97/9 (1985-1986): 277-78.

2509 Mary Ann Beavis, "Women as Models of Faith in Mark," *BTB* 18 (1988): 3-9.

2510 J. F. Coakley, "The Anointing at Bethany and the Priority of John," *JBL* 107/2 (1988): 241-56.

2511 Stephen C. Barton, "Mark as Narrative: The Story of the Anointing Woman (Mark 14:3-9)," *ET* 102 (1990-1991): 230-34.

2512 Cilliers Breytenbach, "**MNHMONEΨEIN**: Das 'Sich-Erinnern' in der urchristlichen Überlieferung. Die Bethanienepisode (Mk 14,3-9/Jn 12,1-8) als Beispiel," in Adelbert Denaux, ed., *John and the Synoptics*. BETL #101. Louvain: Peeters Press, 1992. Pp. 548-57.

14:3-8

2513 Luise Schottroff, " 'Was sie tun konnte, hat sie getan': Die Salbung in Bethanien," in Luise Schottroff and D. Sölle, *Hannas Aufbruch*. Gütersloh: Gütersloher Verlagsanstalt, 1990. Pp. 142-54.

14:3

2514 Charles F. Nesbitt, "The Bethany Traditions in the Gospel Narratives," *IBR* 29 (1961): 119-24.

2515 Friedrich Wulf, " 'Der Geist ist willig, das Fleisch schwach' (Mk 14,3b)," *GeistL* 37 (1964): 241-43.

14:4

2516 Johannes B. Bauer, "Ut Quid Perditio Ista?—zu Mk 14,4f. und Parr.," *NovT* 3 (1959): 54-56.

2517 R. Deichgräber, "Die Gemeinderegel (1QS) X4," *RevQ* 2 (1960): 277-80.

2518 Rainer Storch, " 'Was soll diese Verschwendung?' Bemerkungen zur Auslegungsgeschichte von Mk 14,4f.," in Eduard Lohse, ed., *Der Ruf Jesu und die Antwort der Gemeinde: Exegetische Untersuchungen. Joachim Jeremias zum 70. Geburtstag gewidmet von seinen Schülern*, in collaboration with Christoph Burchard and Berndt Schaller. Göttingen: Vandenhoeck & Ruprecht, 1970. Pp. 247-58.

14:5

2519 George D. Kilpatrick, ''Ἐπάνω: Mark xiv.5,'' in *The Principles and Practice on New Testament Textual Criticism*. BETL #96. Louvain: Peeters Press, 1990. Pp. 305-306.

14:7

2520 Ethelbert Stauffer, ''Realistische Jesusworte,'' in William C. Weinrich, ed., *The New Testament Age* (festschrift for Bo Reicke). 2 vols. Macon GA: Mercer University Press, 1984. 2:503-10.

2521 R. S. Sugirtharajah, '' 'For You Always Have the Poor with You': An Example of Hermeneutics of Suspicion,'' *AsiaJT* 4 (1990): 102-107.

14:8

2522 Robert Holst, ''The One Anointing of Jesus: Another Application of the Form-Critical Method,'' *JBL* 95 (1976): 435-46.

14:9

2523 J. Harold Greenlee, ''Εἰς μνημόσυνον αὐτῆς: 'For Her Memorial': Mt xxvi.13, Mk xiv.9,'' *ET* 71 (1959-1960): 245.

2524 Joachim Jeremias, ''Mark 14:9,'' in J. Jeremias, ed., *Abba: Studien zur neutestamentlichen Theologie und Zeitgeschichte*. Göttingen: Vandenhoeck & Ruprecht, 1966. Pp. 115-20.

2525 C. J. Maunder, ''A *Sitz im Leben* for Mark 14:9,'' *ET* 99/3 (1987-1988): 78-80.

14:10

2526 J.-A. Morin, ''Les deux derniers des Douze: Simon le Zelote et Judas Iskariôth,'' *RB* 80 (1973): 332-58.

2527 Yoël Arbeitman, ''The Suffix of Iscariot,'' *JBL* 99 (1980): 122-23.

14:11

2528 Tjitze J. Baarda, "Markus 14:11: ἐπηγγείλαντο: 'Bron' or 'Redaktie'?" *GTT* 73 (1973): 65-75.

14:12-15:41

2529 Frans Lefevre, "Met Marcus van Getsemane naar Golgota: Hoofdlijnen van het passieverhaal," *CBG* 11 (1981): 22-49.

14:12-31

2530 C. H. Dodd, "The Sayings," in *Historical Tradition in the Fourth Gospel.* Cambridge: Cambridge University Press, 1963. Pp. 315-405.

2531 Donald P. Senior, "The Eucharist in Mark: Mission, Reconciliation, Hope," *BTB* 12 (1982): 67-72.

14:12-26

2532 Rudolf Pesch, "Das Evangelium in Jerusalem: Mk 14,12-26 als ältestes Überlieferungsgut der Urgemeinde," in Peter Stuhlmacher, ed., *Das Evangelium und die Evangelien.* Tübingen: Mohr, 1983. Pp. 113-55.

2533 Rudolf Pesch, "The Gospel in Jerusalem: Mark 14:12-26 as the Oldest Tradition of the Early Church," in Peter Stuhlmacher, ed., *The Gospel and the Gospels.* J. Vriend, trans. Grand Rapids: Eerdmans, 1991. Pp. 106-48.

14:12-25

2534 Vernon K. Robbins, "Last Meal: Preparation, Betrayal and Absence (Mk 14:12-25)," in Werner H. Kelber, ed., *The Passion in Mark: Studies on Mark 14-16.* Philadelphia: Fortress, 1976. Pp. 21-40.

14:12-21

2535 Thomas R. W. Longstaff, *Evidence of Conflation in Mark? A Study in the Synoptic Problem.* Society of Biblical Literature Dissertation Series 28. Missoula MT: Scholars Press, 1977.

14:12-17

2536 F. C. Synge, "A Matter of Tenses—Fingerprints of an Annotator in Mark," *ET* 88 (1976-1977): 168-71.

14:12-16

2537 Jean Delorme, "La Cène et la Pâque dans le Nouveau Testament," *LV* 31 (1957): 9-48.

2538 Philippe Rolland, "La préparation du repas pascal," *BLOS* 2 (1989): 3-8.

14:12

2539 Arthur G. Arnott, " 'The First Day of Unleavened . . .' Mt 26.17, Mk 14.12, Lk 22.7," *BT* 35 (1984): 235-38.

14:14-15:20

2540 J. Duncan M. Derrett, "The Upper Room and the Dish," *HeyJ* 26 (1985): 373-82.

14:16

2541 Wolfgang Feneberg, "Das Neue Testament: Sprache der Liebe—Zum Problem des Antijudaismus," *ZKT* 107 (1985): 333-40.

14:17-52

2542 Pierre Mourlon Beernaert, "Structure littéraire et lecture théologique de Marc 14,17-52," in M. Sabbe, ed., *L'évangile selon Marc: Tradition et rédaction.* BETL #34. Louvain: Louvain University Press, 1974. Pp. 241-67.

14:17-31

2543 Francis J. Moloney, "The Eucharist as Jesus' Presence to the Broken," *Pacifica* 2 (1989): 151-74.

14:17-26

2544 Stanislas Dockx, "Le récit du repas pascal. Marc 14,17-26," *Bib* 46 (1965): 445-53.

14:18-25

2545 F. C. Synge, "Mark 14:18-25: Supper and Rite," *JTSA* 4 (1973): 38-43.

14:20-22

2546 J. Neville Birdsall, "The Withering of the Fig Tree," *ET* 73 (1961-1962): 191.

2547 Madeleine I. Boucher, *The Parables.* Wilmington DE: Glazier, 1981.

14:21

2548 Jens Christensen, "Menneskesønnen gaar bort, som der staar skrevet om ham," *DTT* 19 (1956): 83-92.

2549 I. Howard Marshall, "The Synoptic Son of Man Sayings in Recent Discussion," *NTS* 12 (1965-1966): 327-51.

2550 P. Maurice Casey, "The Son of Man Problem," *ZNW* 67/3 (1976): 147-54.

14:22-62

2551 Bonifatius Fischer, *Die lafeinischen Evangelien bis zum 10. Jahrhundert. 11. Varianten zu Markus*. Freiburg: Herder, 1989.

14:22-25

2552 Manuel de Tuya, "La doctrina eucarística de los Sínopticos," *CiTom* 84 (1957): 217-81.

2553 David Bosch, *Die Heidenmission in der Zukunftsschau Jesu. Eine Untersuchung zur Eschatologie der synoptischen Evangelien*. Zürich: Zwingli, 1959.

2554 J.-B. du Roy, "Le dernier repas de Jésus," *BVC* 26 (1959): 44-52.

2555 J. Steinbeck, "Das Abendmahl Jesu unter Berucksichtigung moderner Forschung," *NovT* 3 (1959): 70-79.

2556 Heinz Schürmann, "Die Symbolhandlungen Jesu als eschatologische Erfüllungszeichen: Eine Rückfrage nach dem historischen Jesus," *BibL* 11 (1970): 29-41, 73-78.

2557 Enrique Nardoni, "Por una communidad libre. La última cena segun Mc 14,22-25 y el éxodo," *RevB* 33 (1971): 27-42.

2558 Giuseppe Barbaglio, "L'istituzione dell'eucaristia (Mc 14,22-25; 1 Cor 11,23-24 e par.)," *ParSpirV* 7 (1983): 125-41.

2559 William J. Carl, "Mark 14:22-25," *Int* 39/3 (1985): 296-301.

2560 Peder Borgen, "John and the Synoptics: Can Paul Offer Help?" in Gerald F. Hawthorne and Otto Betz, eds., *Tradition & Interpretation in the New Testament* (festschrift for E. Earle Ellis). Grand Rapids: Eerdmans, 1987. Pp. 80-94.

2561 Jürgen Becker, "Die neutestamentliche Rede vom Suhnetod Jesu," *ZTK* 8 (1990): 29-49.

14:22-24

2562 Heinz Schürmann, "Die Semitismen im Einsetzungsbericht bei Markus und bei Lukas," *ZKT* 73 (1951): 72-77.

2563 José Alonso Díaz, "Los elementos de la tradición eucarística en relación con Jesucristo," *RET* 23 (1963): 47-60.

2564 Carter Lindberg, "The Conception of the Eucharist according to Erasmus and Karlstadt," in Mark Lienhard and André Séguenny, eds., *Les dissidents du 16ue siècle*. Baden Baden: V. Koerner, 1983. Pp. 79-94.

14:22-23

2565 Brian A. Mastin, " 'Jesus Said Grace'," *SJT* 24 (1971): 449-56.

14:22

2566 Paul E. Davies, "Did Jesus Die as a Martyr-Prophet?" *BR* 2 (1957): 19-30.

2567 B. E. Thiering, " 'Breaking of Bread' and 'Harvest' in Mark's Gospel," *NovT* 12 (1970): 1-12.

2568 Joachim Jeremias, " 'This is My Body'," *ET* 83 (1971-1972): 196-203.

2569 Paolo Ricca, "Lutero e Zwingli: la Cena," in Giuseppe Alberigo, et al., eds., *Lutero nel suo e nel nostro tempo*. Torino: Claudiana, 1983. Pp. 227-45.

14:24-25

2570 Willem A. Saayman, "The Eucharist in Mission Perspective," *ThEv* 18/2 (1985): 18-24.

2571 J. M. Casciaro Ramírez, "The Original Aramaic Form of Jesus' Interpretation of the Cup," *JTS* 41 (1990): 1-12.

14:24

2572 J. A. Emerton, "The Aramaic Underlying τὸ αἷμά μου τῆς διαθήκης," *JTS* 6 (1955): 238-40.

2573 J. A. Emerton, "τὸ αἷμά μου τῆς διαθήκης: The Evidence of the Syriac Versions," *JTS* 13 (1962): 111-17.

2574 J. A. Emerton, "Mark 14:24 and the Targum to the Psalter," *JTS* 15 (1964): 58-59.

2575 Richard T. France, "The Servant of the Lord in the Teaching of Jesus," *TynB* 19 (1968): 26-52.

2576 Wilfried Pigulla, "Das für viele vergossene Blut," *MTZ* 23 (1972): 72-82.

2577 N. Hoffmann, " 'Stellvertretung': Grundgestalt und Mitte des Mysteriums. Ein Versuch trinitätstheologischer Begründung christlicher Sühne," *MTZ* 30 (1979): 161-91.

2578 Jean Galot, "La conscience de la mission rédemptrice," *Did* 14 (1984): 139-55.

2579 Klara Myhre, " 'Paktens blod' i vinordet: En undersøkelse av henspillingen på Ex 24,8 i Mark 14,24/Matt 26,28," *TTK* 55 (1984): 271-86.

2580 Uwe Wegner, "Deu Jesus um sentido salvífico para sua morte: consideraçoes sobre Mc. 14:24 e 10:45," *EstT* 26/3 (1986): 209-46.

2581 P. Maurice Casey, "The Original Aramaic Form of Jesus' Interpretation of the Cup," *JTS* 41 (1990): 1-12.

14:25

2582 Heinrich Vogels, "Mk 14,25 und Parallelen," in N. Adler, ed., *Vom Wort des Lebens* (festschrift for Max Meinertz). Münster: Aschendorff, 1951. Pp. 93-104.

2583 Jean Delorme, "La Cène et la Pâque dans le Nouveau Testament," *LV* 31 (1957): 9-48.

2584 Augustin George, ''Le bonheur promis par Jésus d'après le Nouveau Testament,'' *LVie* 52 (1961): 37-58.

2585 D. W. Palmer, ''Defining a Vow of Abstinence,'' *CANZTR* 5 (1973): 38-41.

2586 Xavier Léon-Dufour, ''Jésus devant sa mort à la lumière des textes de l'Institution eucharistique et des discours d'adieu,'' in Jacques Dupont, ed., *Jésus aux origines de la christologie*. BETL #40. Louvain: Peeters Press, 1975. Pp. 141-68.

2587 Josef Blank, ''Der 'eschatologische Ausblick' Mk 14,25 und seine Bedeutung,'' in P. G. Müller and W. Stenger, eds., *Kontinuität und Einheit* (festschrift for Franz Mußner). Freiburg: Herder, 1981. Pp. 508-18.

2588 Barry S. Crawford, ''Near Expectation in the Sayings of Jesus,'' *JBL* 101/2 (1982): 225-44.

2589 Balembo Buetubela, ''Le produit de la vigne et le vin nouveau: Analyse exégétique de Mc 14.25,'' *RAfT* 8 (1984): 5-16.

2590 Michal Wojciechowski, ''Le Nazireat et la Passion (Mc 14,25a; 15,23),'' *Bib* 65/1 (1984): 94-96.

2591 Ray Carlton Jones, ''The Lord's Supper and the Concept of Anamnesis,'' *WW* 6/4 (1986): 434-45.

14:26-53

2592 Max Küchler, ''Die 'Füsse des Herrn' (Eus, DE 6,18): Spurensicherung des abwesenden Kyrios an Texten und Steinen als eine Aufgabe der historischkritischen Exegese,'' in Max Küchler and Christoph Uehlinger, eds., *Jerusalem*. Freiburg: Universitätsverlag, 1987. Pp. 11-35.

14:26-52

2593 Walter S. Lawrence, ''Reader-Response Criticism for Markan Narrative with a Commentary on Mark 14:26-52,'' doctoral dissertation, St. Louis University, St. Louis MO, 1990.

14:26-42

2594 R. H. Lightfoot, "A Consideration of Three Passages in St. Mark's Gospel," in Werner Schmauch, ed., *In Memoriam Ernst Lohmeyer*. Stuttgart: Evangelisches Verlagswerk, 1951. Pp. 110-15.

14:26-31

2595 Max Wilcox, "The Denial Sequence in Mark xiv.26-31, 66-72," *NTS* 17 (1970-1971): 426-36.

2596 Rudolf Pesch, "Die Verleugnung des Petrus: Eine Studie zu Mk 14,54.66-72 (und Mk 14,26-31)," in Joachim Gnilka, ed., *Neues Testament und Kirche: Für Rudolf Schnackenburg*. Freiburg/Basel/Vienna: Herder, 1974. Pp. 42-62.

2597 Jerome H. Neyrey, "The Absence of Jesus' Emotions—The Lucan Redaction of Lk 22,39-49," *Bib* 61/2 (1980): 153-71.

14:26

2598 Werner Schauch, "Der Ölberg: Exegese zu einer Ortsangabe besonders bei Matthaus und Markus," *TLZ* 77 (1952): 391-96.

2599 John Ellington, "The Translation of ὑμνέω, 'Sing a Hymn' in Mark 14:26 and Matthew 26:30," *BT* 30 (1979): 445-46.

14:27-28

2600 Wilfred Tooley, "The Shepherd and Sheep Image in the Teaching of Jesus," *NovT* 7 (1964-1965): 15-25.

2601 Thorwald Lorenzen, "Ist der Auferstandene in Galiläa erschienen? Bemerkungen zu einem Aufsatz von B. Steinseifer," *ZNW* 64 (1973): 209-21.

14:27

2602 John Dominic Crossan, "Redaction and Citation in Mark 11:9-10, 17 and 14:27," *SBLSP* 2 (1972): 17-60.

2603 R. P. Schroeder, "The 'Worthless' Shepherd. A Study of Mark 14:27," *CThM* 2 (1975): 342-44.

14:28

2604 P. Cornelius Odenkirchen, " 'Praecedam vos in Galilaeam'," *VD* 46 (1968): 193-223.

2605 Jean-Marie van Cangh, "La Galilée dans l'évangile de Marc: un lieu théologique?" *RB* 79 (1972): 59-75.

2606 Robert H. Stein, "A Short Note on Mark 14:28 and 16:7," *NTS* 20 (1973-1974): 445-52.

2607 Paul Ternant, "La Galilée dans le message des Evangiles et l'origine de l'église en Galilée," *POC* 30 (1980): 75-131.

2608 Bas M. F. van Iersel, " 'To Galilee' or 'in Galilee' in Mark 14:28 and 16:7?" *ETL* 58 (1982): 365-70.

2609 Domingo Muñoz León, " 'Iré delante de vosotros a Galilea' (Mt 26,32 y par). Sentido mesiánico y posible sustrato arameo del logion," *EB* 48 (1990): 215-41.

14:30

2610 Louis Saltet, "Rétablissement du texte de saint Marc 14,30 et de l'unité primitive de la tradition correspondante sur les reniements de saint Pierre," in *Mélanges offerts au R. P. Ferdinand Cavallera doyen de la faculté de Théologie de Toukouse*. Toulouse: Bibliothèque de l'Institut Catholique, 1948. Pp. 31-45.

2611 Cuthbert Lattey, "A Note on Cockcrow," *Scr* 6 (1953-1954): 53-55.

14:32-15:47

2612 Raymond E. Brown, "The Passion according to Mark," *Worship* 59 (1985): 116-26.

14:32-42

2613 Manuel de Tuya, "La 'agonia' de Jesucristo en el Gethsemani," *CiTom* 82 (1955): 519-67.

2614 J. A. Colunga, "La agonía de Jésus en Getsemaní," *CuBí* 16 (1959): 13-17.

2615 Raymond E. Brown, "Incidents That Are Units in the Synoptic Gospels but Dispersed in St. John," *CBQ* 23 (1961): 143-60.

2616 Jean Héring, "Zwei exegetische Problemein der Periope von Jesus in Gethsemane," in *Neotestamentica et Patristica* (festschrift for Oscar Cullmann). Novum Testamentum Supplement 6. Leiden: Brill, 1962. Pp. 64-69.

2617 R. S. Barbour, "Uncomfortable Words: VIII. Status and Titles," *ET* 82/5 (1970-1971): 137-42.

2618 Mario Galizzi, *Gesù nel Getsemani (Mc 14:32-42; Mt 26:36-46; Lc 22:39-46)*. Biblioteca di Scienze Religiose. Zürich: PAS-Verlag, 1972.

2619 Werner H. Kelber, "Mark 14:32-42: Gethsemane. Passion Christology and Discipleship Failure," *ZNW* 63 (1972): 166-87.

2620 Sjef van Tilborg, "A Form-Criticism of the Lord's Prayer," *NovT* 14/2 (1972): 94-105.

2621 Werner Mohn, "Gethsemane (Mk 14:32-42)," *ZNW* 64/3 (1973): 195-208.

2622 Rinaldo Fabris, "La preghiera del Getsemani," *PV* 19 (1974): 258-67.

2623 Werner H. Kelber, "The Hour of the Son of Man and the Temptation of the Disciples (Mark 14:32-42)," in Werner H. Kelber, ed., *The Passion in Mark: Studies on Mark 14-16*. Philadelphia: Fortress, 1976. Pp. 41-60.

2624 Gene Szarek, "A Critique of Kelber's 'The Hour of the Son of Man and the Temptation of the Disciples: Mark 14:32-42'," *SBLSP* 6 (1976): 111-18.

2625 Jean Giblet, "La prière de Jésus," in H. Limet and J. Ries, eds., *L'expérience de la prière dans les grandes religions*. Louvain-la-Neuve: Centre d'histoire des religions, 1980. Pp. 261-73.

2626 Joseph Thomas, ''La scène du jardin selon Marc 14:32-42,'' *Chr* 28 (1981): 350-60.

2627 Michel Gourgues, *Le défi de la fidélité: L'expérience de Jésus*. Paris: Cerf, 1985.

2628 Thomas Söding, ''Gebet und Gebetsmahnung Jesu in Getsemani: eine redaktionskritische Auslegung von Mk 14:32-42,'' *BZ* 31/1 (1987): 76-100.

2629 Benny R. Crockett, ''The Function of Mathetological Prayer in Mark,'' *IBS* 10 (1988): 123-39.

2630 Sharyn E. Dowd, *Prayer, Power, and the Problem of Suffering: Mark 11:22-25 in the Context of Markan Theology*. Atlanta: Scholars Press, 1988.

2631 Reinhard Feldmeier, ''Die Krisis des Gottessohnes: die markinische Gethsemaneperikope als Markuspassion,'' *TLZ* 113 (1988): 234-36.

2632 Karen E. Smith, ''Mark 14:32-42,'' *RevExp* 88 (1991): 433-37.

14:32-40

2633 Richard H. Hiers, *The Historical Jesus and the Kingdom of God: Present and Future in the Message and Ministry of Jesus*. University of Florida Humanities Monograph #38. Gainesville FL: University of Florida Press, 1973.

14:35-51

2634 John Bligh, ''Christ's Death Cry (Mark 14:35-51),'' *HeyJ* 1 (1960): 142-46.

14:35-39

2635 David Daube, ''A Prayer Pattern in Judaism,'' in K. Aland, et al., eds., *Studia Evangelica 1: Paper Presented to the International Congress on ''The Four Gospels in 1957'' held at Christ Church, Oxford, 1957*. Texte und Untersuchungen zur Geschichte der altchristlichen Literatur 73. Berlin: Akademie-Verlag, 1959. Pp. 539-45.

14:35

2636 Benoît Standaert, "Crying 'Abba' and Saying 'Our Father': An Intertextual Approach of the Dominical Prayer," in Spike Draisma, *Intertextuality in Biblical Writings* (festschrift for Bastiaan M. F. van Iersel). Kampen: J. H. Kok, 1989. Pp. 141-58.

14:36

2637 Joachim Jeremias, "Kennzeichen der ipsissima vox Jesu," in Josef Schmid and Anton Vögtle, eds., *Synoptische Studien* (festschrift for Alfred Wikenhauser). Münich: Zink, 1953. Pp. 86-93.

2638 S. Vernon McCasland. " 'Abba, Father'," *JBL* 72 (1953): 79-91.

2639 Thor Boman, "Der Gebetskampf Jesu," *NTS* 10 (1963-1964): 261-73.

2640 W. C. van Unnik, " 'Alles ist dir möglich' (Mk 14,36)," in Otto Böcher and Naus Haacker, eds., *Verborum veritas. Festschrift für Gustav Stählin zum 70. Geburtstag.* Wuppertal: Theologischer Verlag Rolf Brockhaus, 1970. Pp. 27-36.

2641 Maria L. Amerio, "Il nesso Αββα ὁ πατήρ in Clemente Alessandrino," *AugR* 16 (1976): 291-316.

2642 Wilhelm Vischer, "Abba," *ÉTR* 54 (1979): 683-86.

2643 Joseph A. Grassi, "Abba, Father (Mark 14:36): Another Approach," *JAAR* 50/3 (1982): 449-58.

2644 Pierre Grelot, "Une mention inaperçue de 'Abba' dans le Testament araméen de Lévi," *Semitica* 33 (1983): 101-108.

2645 Mark Riley, " 'Lord Save My Life' (Ps 116:4) as a Generative Text for Jesus' Gethsemane Prayer (Mark 14:36a)," *CBQ* 48/4 (1986): 655-59.

2646 E. A. Obeng, "Abba, Father: The Prayer of the Sons of God," *ET* 99 (1987-1988): 363-66.

14:37

2647 Jan W. Doeve, ''Le rôle de la tradition orale dans la composition des Évangiles synoptiques,'' in J. Heuschen, ed., *La formation des évangiles: Problème synoptique et Formgeschichte*. Paris: Desclée, 1957. Pp. 70-84.

14:41

2648 George H. Boobyer, ''**Ἀπέχει** in Mark 14:41,'' *NTS* 2 (1955-1956): 44-48.

2649 Patrick P. Saydon, ''Some Biblico-Liturgical Passages Reconsidered,'' *MeliT* 18/1 (1966): 10-17.

2650 P.-R. Berger, ''Zum Aramäischen der Evangelien und der Apostelgeschichte,'' *TheoR* 82 (1986): 1-17.

2651 Klaus W. Müller, ''Apechei (Mk 14:41): absurda lectio,'' *ZNW* 77/1-2 (1986): 83-100.

2652 Robert G. Bratcher, ''Unusual Sinners,'' *BT* 39 (1988): 335-37.

14:42-47

2653 W. Boyd Barrick, ''The Rich Man from Arimathea (Matt 27:57-60) and 1QIsa[a],'' *JBL* 96 (1977): 235-39.

14:43-16:8

2654 Mark F. S. C. McVann, ''The Passion in Mark: Transformation Ritual,'' *BTB* 18 (1988): 96-101.

14:43-52

2655 Gerhard Schneider, ''Die Verhaftung Jesu: Traditionsgeschichte von Mk 14:43-52,'' *ZNW* 63/3 (1972): 188-209.

14:43-51

2656 Jean Cantinat, ''Jesus devant le Sanhedrin,'' *NRT* 75 (1953): 300-308.

14:43

2657 Donald P. Senior, '' 'With Swords and Clubs . . .': The Setting of Mark's Community and His Critique of Abusive Power,'' *BTB* 17 (1987): 10-20.

14:44

2658 Carlo Buzzetti, "Parallels in the Synoptic Gospels: A Case Study," *BT* 34 (1984): 425-31.

14:45

2659 F. W. Belcher, "A Comment on Mark xiv.45," *ET* (1952-1953): 240.

14:47

2660 Mark F. S. C. McVann, "Conjectures about a Guilty Bystander: The Sword Slashing in Mark 14:47," *List* 21 (1986): 123-37.

2661 Benedict T. Viviano, "The High Priest's Servant's Ear: Mark 14:47," *RB* 96 (1989): 71-80.

14:49

2662 A. W. Argyle, "The Meaning of καθ' ἡμέραν in Mark xiv.49," *ET* 63 (1951-1952): 354.

2663 William G. Morrice, "The Imperatival ἵνα," *BT* 23 (1972): 326-30.

14:50

2664 Thorwald Lorenzen, "Ist der Auferstandene in Galiläa erschienen? Bemerkungen zu einem Aufsatz von B. Steinseifer," *ZNW* 64 (1973): 209-21.

2665 L. Paul Trudinger, "Davidic Links with the Betrayal of Jesus: Some Further Observations," *ET* 86 (1974-1975): 278-79.

14:51-52

2666 John Knox, "A Note on Mark 14:51-52," in S. E. Johnson, ed., *The Joy of Study: Papers on New Testament and Related Subjects* (festschrift for F. C. Grant). New York: Macmillan, 1951. Pp. 27-30.

2667 Albert Vanhoye, "La fuite du jeune homme nu (Mc 14,51-52)," *Bib* 52 (1971): 401-406.

2668 Robin Scroggs and Kent I. Groff, "Baptism in Mark: Dying and Rising with Christ," *JBL* 92 (1973): 531-48.

2669 Harry T. Fleddermann, "The Flight of a Naked Young Man (Mark 14:51-52)," *CBQ* 41/3 (1979): 412-18.

2670 J. Duncan M. Derrett, *The Anastasis: The Resurrection of Jesus as an Historical Event*. Shipston-on-Stour: Drinkwater, 1982.

2671 Michael R. Cosby, "Mark 14:51-52 and the Problem of Gospel Narrative," *PRS* 11/3 (1984): 219-31.

2672 Hans M. Schenke, "The Mystery of the Gospel of Mark," *SecCent* 2 (1984): 65-82.

2673 A. Krijger, "De neaniskos-teksten in Marcus," *KerkT* 36 (1985): 99-116.

2674 Marvin W. Meyer, "The Youth in the Secret Gospel of Mark," *Semeia* 49 (1990): 129-53.

14:53-15:47

2675 Marinus de Jonge, "The Use of ὁ Χριστός in the Passion Narratives," in Jacques Dupont, ed., *Jésus aux origines de la christologie*. BETL #40. Louvain: Peeters Press, 1975. Pp. 169-92.

2676 Olivette Genest, *Le Christ de la passion: Perspective structurale: Analgse de Marc 14,53-15,47 des parallèles bibliques et extra-bibliques*. Recherches Théologie #21. Tournai: Desclée, 1978.

14:53-15:15

2677 Joachim Gnilka, "Der Prozess Jesu nach den Berichten des Markus und Matthäus mit einer Rekonstruktion des historischen Verlaufs," in Josef Blank and Karl Kertelge, eds., *Der Prozess gegen Jesus: historische Rückfrage und theologische*. Freiburg: Herder, 1988. Pp. 11-40.

14:53-15:1

2678 Gerhard Schneider, "Gab es Eine Vorsynoptische Szene 'Jesus vor dem Synedrium'?" *NovT* 12/1 (1970): 22-39.

2679 Gerhard Schneider, "Jesus vor dem Synedrium," *BibL* 11 (1970): 1-15.

14:53-67

2680 Paul Lamarche, "Procès et outrages (14,53-67)," in P. Lamarche, ed., *Révélation de Dieu chez Marc.* Le Point Théologique 20. Paris: Beauchesne, 1976. Pp. 105-18.

14:53-65

2681 Kurt Schubert, "Die Juden und die Römer," *BL* 36 (1962): 235-42.

2682 Otto Betz, *What Do We Know About Jesus?* M. Kohl, trans. London: SCM, 1968.

2683 Donald H. Juel, "The Messiah and the Temple: A Study of Jesus' Trial before the Sanhedrin in the Gospel of Mark," doctoral dissertation, Yale University, New Haven CT, 1973.

2684 W. C. van Unnik, "Jesu Verhöhnung vor dem Synedrium," in W. C. van Unnik, ed., *Sparsa Collecta: The Collected Essays of W. C. van Unnik. Part One: Evangelia—Paulina—Acta.* Novum Testamentum Supplement 29. Leiden: Brill, 1973. Pp. 3-5.

2685 Donald H. Juel, "The Function of the Trial of Jesus in Mark's Gospel," *SBLSP* 5 (1975): 83-104.

2686 August Strobel, *Die Stunde der Wahrheit: Untersuchungen zum Strafverfahren gegen Jesus.* Tübingen: Mohr, 1980.

2687 Nelson H. Brickham, "The Dependence of the Fourth Gospel on the Gospel of Mark: A Redaction-Critical Approach," doctoral dissertation, American University, Washington DC, 1982.

2688 Renatus Kempthorne, "Anti-Christian Tendency in Pre-Marcan Traditions of the Sanhedrin Trial," *StudE* 7 (1982): 283-85.

2689 Mary Ann Beavis, "The Trial before the Sanhedrin (Mark 14:53-65): Reader Response and Greco-Roman Readers," *CBQ* 49 (1987): 581-96.

14:53-54

2690 K. E. Dewey, "Peter's Curse and Cursed Peter (Mark 14:53-54, 66-72)," in Werner H. Kelber, ed., *The Passion in Mark: Studies on Mark 14-16*. Philadelphia: Fortress, 1976. Pp. 96-114.

14:53

2691 Paul Winter, "Markus 14:53b., 55-56: Ein Geblide des Evangelisten," *ZNW* 53 (1962): 260-63.

14:54

2692 George W. Buchanan, "Mark 14:54," *ET* 54 (1956): 27.

2693 Rudolf Pesch, "Die Verleugnung des Petrus: Eine Studie zu Mk 14,54.66-72 (und Mk 14,26-31)," in Joachim Gnilka, ed., *Neues Testament und Kirche: Für Rudolf Schnackenburg*. Freiburg/Basel/Vienna: Herder, 1974. Pp. 42-62.

2694 Josef Ernst, "Noch einmal: Die Verleugnung Jesu durch Petrus (Mk 14,54.66-72)," *Cath* 30 (1976): 207-26.

2695 George Howard, "Stylistic Inversion and the Synoptic Tradition," *JBL* 97 (1978): 375-89.

2696 Robert W. Herron, "Mark's Account of Peter's Denial of Jesus: A Representative History of Interpretation of Mark 14:54, 66-72," doctoral dissertation, Rice University, Houston TX, 1989.

14:55-65

2697 Raymond E. Brown, "Incidents That Are Units in the Synoptic Gospels but Dispersed in St. John," *CBQ* 23 (1961): 143-60.

14:55-64

2698 Jean Cantinat, "Jesus devant le Sanhedrin," *NRT* 75 (1953): 300-308.

2699 Georg Braumann, "Markus 15:2-5 und Markus 14:55-64," *ZNW* 52 (1961): 273-78.

2700 Dieter Lührmann, "Markus 14:55-64: Christologie und Zerstörung des Tempels im Markusevangelium," *NTS* 27 (1980-1981): 457-74.

2701 Kurt Schubert, "Biblical Criticism Criticised: With Reference to the Markan Report of Jesus's Examination before the Sanhedrin [Mk 14:55-64; 15:2-5; Lk 22:66-71]," in Ernst Bammel and C. F. D. Moule, eds., *Jesus and the Politics of His Day*. Cambridge: Cambridge University Press, 1984. Pp. 385-402.

14:55-56

2702 Paul Winter, "Markus 14:53b., 55-56: Ein Geblide des Evangelisten," *ZNW* 53 (1962): 260-63.

14:57-58

2703 Frank Connolly-Weinert, "Assessing Omissions as Redaction: Luke's Handling of the Charge Against Jesus as Detractor of the Temple," in Maurya P. Horgan and Paul J. Kobelski, eds., *To Touch the Text: Biblical and Related Studies in Honor of Joseph A. Fitzmyer*. New York: Crossroad, 1989. Pp. 358-68.

14:58

2704 Gerd Theissen, "Die Tempelweissagung Jesu. Prophetie im Spannungsfeld von Stadt und Land," *TZ* 32 (1976): 144-58.

2705 Giancarlo Biguzzi, "Mc. 14,58: un tempio ἀχειροποίητον," *RBib* 26 (1978): 225-40.

2706 Anton Vögtle, "Das markinische Verständnis der Tempelworte," in Ulrich Luz and Hans Weder, eds., *Die Mitte des Neuen Testaments: Einheit and vielfalt neutestamentlicher theologie* (festschrift for Eduard Schweizer). Göttingen: Vandenhoeck & Ruprecht, 1983. Pp. 362-83.

2707 Benedetto Prete, "Formazione e storicità del detto di Gesù sul tempio secondo Mc. 14,58," *BibO* 27 (1985): 3-16.

2708 P.-R. Berger, "Zum Aramäischen der Evangelien und der Apostelgeschichte," *TheoR* 82 (1986): 1-17.

14:61-64

2709 Jacob Kremer, " 'Sohn Gottes': Zur Klärung des biblischen Hoheitstitels Jesu," *BL* 46 (1973): 3-21.

2710 Klaus Berger, "Die koniglichen Messiastraditionen des Neuen Testaments," *NTS* 20 (1973-1974): 1-44.

2711 Craig A. Evans, "In What Sense Blasphemy? Jesus before Caiaphas in Mark 14:61-64," *SBLSP* 30 (1991): 215-34.

14:61-62

2712 Franz Mussner, "Die Wiederkunft des Menschensohnes nach Markus 13,24-27 und 14,61-62," *BK* 16 (1961): 105-107.

2713 Norman Perrin, "The High Priest's Question and Jesus' Answer (Mark 14:61-62)," in Werner H. Kelber, ed., *The Passion in Mark: Studies on Mark 14-16*. Philadelphia: Fortress, 1976. Pp. 80-95.

2714 W. R. G. Loader, "Christ at the Right Hand—Ps. cx. 1 in the New Testament," *NTS* 24 (1977-1978): 199-217.

2715 Léopold Sabourin, *The Bible and Christ: The Unity of the Two Testaments*. New York: Alba, 1980.

14:61

2716 Evald Lövestam, "Die Frage des Hohenpriesters (Mark 14,61 par. Matth. 26,63)," *SEÅ* 26/27 (1961): 93-107.

2717 J. C. O'Neill, "The Silence of Jesus," *NTS* 15/2 (1968-1969): 153-69.

2718 Johannes Schreiber, "Das Schweigen Jesu," in Klaus Wegenast, ed., *Theologie und Unterricht: über die Repräsentanz des Christlichen in der Schule* (festschrift for Hans Stock). Gütersloh: Mohr, 1969. Pp. 79-87.

2719 Joel Marcus, "Mark 14:61: 'Are You the Messiah-Son-of-God?' " *NovT* 31 (1989): 125-41.

14:62-15:46

2720 J. N. Birdsall, "MS. 894: A Collation and an Analysis," in J. N. Birdsall and R. W. Thompson, eds., *Biblical and*

Patristic Studies (festschrift for Robert Pierce Casey). Freiburg: Herder, 1963. Pp. 20-24.

14:62

2721 E. J. Tinsley, "The Sign of the Son of Man (Mk 14,62)," *SJT* 8 (1955): 297-306.

2722 J. A. T. Robinson, "The Second Coming: Mark 14:62," *ET* 67 (1955-1956): 336-40.

2723 Harvey K. McArthur, "Mark xiv.62," *NTS* 4 (1957-1958): 156-58.

2724 H. P. Owen, "The Parousia of Christ in the Synoptic Gospels," *SJT* 12 (1959): 171-92.

2725 Thomas F. Glasson, "The Reply to Caiaphas (Mark 14:62)," *NTS* 7 (1960-1961): 88-93.

2726 André Feuillet, "Le triomphe du Fils de l'homme d'après la déclaration du Christ aux Sanhédrites," in Édouard Massaux, ed., *La venue du Messie: Messianisme et eschatologie*. Burgee: Desclée, 1962. Pp. 149-71.

2727 A. M. Goldberg, "Sitzend zur Rechten der Kraft. Zur Gottesbezeichnung Gebura in der frühen rabbinischen Literatur," *BZ* 8 (1964): 284-93.

2728 I. Howard Marshall, "The Synoptic Son of Man Sayings in Recent Discussion," *NTS* 12 (1965-1966): 327-51.

2729 Norman Perrin, "Mark XIV.62: The End Product of a Christian Pesher Tradition?" *NTS* 12 (1965-1966): 150-55.

2730 F. H. Borsch, "Mark 14:62 and I Enoch 62:5," *NTS* 14 (1967-1968): 565-67.

2731 J. F. Seitz, "The Future Coming of the Son of Man: Three Midrashic Formulations in the Gospel of Mark," *StudE* 6 (1973): 478-94.

2732 Renatus Kempthorne, "The Marcan Text of Jesus' Answer to the High Priest (Mark 14:62)," *NovT* 19/3 (1977): 197-208.

2733 George R. Beasley-Murray, "The Parousia in Mark," *RevExp* 75/4 (1978): 565-81.

2734 Antonio Vargas-Machuca, "¿Por qué condenaron a muerte a Jesús de Nazaret?" *EE* 54 (1979): 441-70.

2735 George R. Beasley-Murray, "Jesus and Apocalyptic: With Special Reference to Mark 14,62," in Jan Lambrecht, ed., *L'Apocalypse johannique et l'apocalyptique dans le Nouveau Testament*. Gembloux: J. Duculot, 1980. Pp. 415-29.

2736 Dennis C. Duling, "Insights from Sociology for New Testament Christology: A Test Case," *SBLSP* 24 (1985): 351-68.

2737 Matthew Black, "The Theological Appropriation of the Old Testament by the New Testament," *SJT* 39/1 (1986): 1-17.

2738 Pieter J. Maartens, "The Son of Man as a Composite Metaphor in Mk 14:62," in J. H. Petzer and P. J. Hartin, eds., *A South African Perspective on the New Testament* (festschrift for Bruce M. Metzger). Leiden: Brill, 1986. Pp. 76-98.

2739 Jane Schaberg, "Mark 14:62: Early Christian Merkabah Imagery?" in Joel Marcus and Marion L. Soards, eds., *Apocalyptic and the New Testament* (festschrift for J. Louis Martyn). Sheffield: JSOT Press, 1989. Pp. 69-94.

14:64

2740 Paul Lamarche, "Le 'blasphème' de Jésus devant le Sanhédrin," *RechSR* 50 (1962): 74-85.

2741 David R. Catchpole, "You Have Heard His Blasphemy," *TynB* 16 (1965): 10-18.

2742 J. C. O'Neill, "The Charge of Blasphemy at Jesus' Trial before the Sanhedrin," in Ernst Bammel, ed., *The Trial of Jesus* (festschrift for C. F. D. Moule). Naperville IL: Allenson, 1970. Pp. 272-77.

14:65-72

2743 Michael D. Goulder, "On Putting Q to the Test," *NTS* 24 (1977-1978): 218-34.

2744 Christopher M. Tuckett, "On the Relationship between Matthew and Luke," *NTS* 30 (1984): 130-42.

14:65

2745 Paul Glaube, "Einige Stellen, die Bedeutung des Codex D charakterisieren," *NovT* 2 (1957-1958): 310-15.

2746 Robert H. Gundry, "1Q Isaiah 50,6 and Mark 14,65," *RevQ* 2 (1960): 559-67.

2747 Pierre Benoit, "Les outrages à Jésus Prophète (Mc 14,65 par)," in *Neotestamentica et Patristica* (festschrift for Oscar Cullmann). Novum Testamentum Supplement 6. Leiden: Brill, 1962. Pp. 92-110.

2748 David Flusser, " 'Who Is It that Struck You?'," *Immanuel* 20 (1986): 27-32.

2749 Frans Neirynck, "**ΤΙΣ ΕΣΤΙΝ Ο ΠΑΙΣΑΣ ΣΕ**: Mt 26,68/Lk 22,64 (diff. Mk 14,65)," *ETL* 63/1 (1987): 5-47.

14:66-72

2750 Jean Cantinat, "Jesus devant le Sanhedrin," *NRT* 75 (1953): 300-308.

2751 Max Wilcox, "The Denial Sequence in Mark xiv.26-31, 66-72," *NTS* 17 (1970-1971): 426-36.

2752 Rudolf Pesch, "Die Verleugnung des Petrus: Eine Studie zu Mk 14,54.66-72 (und Mk 14,26-31)," in Joachim Gnilka, ed., *Neues Testament und Kirche: Für Rudolf Schnackenburg*. Freiburg/Basel/Vienna: Herder, 1974. Pp. 42-62.

2753 K. E. Dewey, "Peter's Curse and Cursed Peter (Mark 14:53-54, 66-72)," in Werner H. Kelber, ed., *The Passion in Mark: Studies on Mark 14-16*. Philadelphia: Fortress, 1976. Pp. 96-114.

2754 Josef Ernst, "Noch einmal: Die Verleugnung Jesu durch Petrus (Mk 14,54.66-72)," *Cath* 30 (1976): 207-26.

2755 Dietfried Gewalt, "Die Verleugnung des Petrus," *LB* 43 (1978): 113-44.

2756 Kim E. Dewey, "Peter's Denial Reexamined: John's Knowledge of Mark's Gospel," *SBLSP* 9/1 (1979): 109-12.

2757 Rudolf Frieling, "Der Weg des Christus," in *Christologische Aufsätze*. Stuttgart: Urachhaus, 1982. Pp. 1-186.

2758 Robert W. Herron, "Mark's Account of Peter's Denial of Jesus: A Representative History of Interpretation of Mark 14:54, 66-72," doctoral dissertation, Rice University, Houston TX, 1989.

2759 N. J. McEleney, "Peter's Denials—How Many? To Whom?" *CBQ* 52 (1990): 467-72.

<u>14:68-72</u>

2760 J. Duncan M. Derrett, "The Reason for the Cock-Crowings," *NTS* 29 (1983): 142-44.

<u>14:68-71</u>

2761 Robert W. Herron, *Mark's Account of Peter's Denial of Jesus*. Lanham MD: University Press America, 1991.

<u>14:68</u>

2762 W. J. P. Boyd, "Peter's Denials—Mark 14:68, Luke 22:57," *ET* 67 (1955-1956): 341.

<u>14:71</u>

2763 J. F. Seitz, "Peter's 'Profanity': Mark 14:71 in the Light of Matthew 16:22," *StudE* 1 (1959): 516-19.

<u>14:72</u>

2764 G. M. Lee, "Mark, xiv.72: ἐπιβαλὼν ἔκλαιεν," *ET* 61 (1949-1950): 160.

2765 J. Neville Birdsall, "Τὸ ῥῆμα ὡς εἶπεν αὐτῷ ὁ Ιησοῦς: Mark 14:72," *NovT* 2 (1957-1958): 272-75.

2766 Hans Kosmala, "The Time of the Cock-Crow," *ASTI* 2 (1963): 118-20.

2767 Hans Kosmala, "The Time of the Cock-Crow, II," *ASTI* 6 (1968): 132-34.

2768 G. M. Lee, "Mark 14,72: *epibalōn eklaien*," *Bib* 53 (1972): 411-12.

2769 Eugene A. LaVerdiere, "Peter Broke Down and Began to Cry," *Emmanuel* 92 (1986): 70-73.

15:1-46

2770 Christopher M. Tuckett, "On the Relationship between Matthew and Luke," *NTS* 30 (1984): 130-42.

15:1-26

2771 Marinus de Jonge, "The Earliest Christian Use of Christos: Some Suggestions," *NTS* 32 (1986): 321-43.

15:1-20

2772 C. H. Dodd, "The Sayings," in *Historical Tradition in the Fourth Gospel*. Cambridge: Cambridge University Press, 1963. Pp. 315-405.

15:1-15

2773 Donald H. Juel, "The Function of the Trial of Jesus in Mark's Gospel," *SBLSP* 5 (1975): 83-104.

2774 Ernst Bammel, "The Trial before Pilate," in Ernst Bammel and C. F. D. Moule, eds., *Jesus and the Politics of His Day*. Cambridge: University Press, 1984. Pp. 415-51.

2775 Gerhard Schneider, "The Political Charge against Jesus," in Ernst Bammel and C. F. D. Moule, eds., *Jesus and the Politics of His Day*. Cambridge: University Press, 1984. Pp. 403-14.

2776 Daphne C. Wiggins, "The Road of Least Resistance," *AMEZQR* 97/1 (1985): 43-46.

15:1

2777 Michael D. Goulder, "On Putting Q to the Test," *NTS* 24 (1977-1978): 218-34.

15:2-21

2778 Klaus Berger, "Die koniglichen Messiastraditionen des Neuen Testaments," *NTS* 20 (1973-1974): 1-44.

15:2-5

2779 Georg Braumann, "Markus 15:2-5 und Markus 14:55-64," *ZNW* 52 (1961): 273-78.

2780 August Strobel, *Die Stunde der Wahrheit: Untersuchungen zum Strafverfahren gegen Jesus*. Tübingen: Mohr, 1980.

15:2-3

2781 Gerhard Schneider, "The Political Charge against Jesus," in Ernst Bammel and C. F. D. Moule, eds., *Jesus and the Politics of His Day*. Cambridge: Cambridge University Press, 1984. Pp. 403-14.

15:2

2782 Klaus Haacker, "Einige Fälle von 'erlebter Rede' im Neuen Testament," *NovT* 12 (1970): 70-77.

2783 Klaus Berger, "Zum Problem der Messianität Jesu," *ZTK* 71 (1974): 1-30.

15:3

2784 Martin J. Higgins, "New Testament Result Clauses with Infinitive," *CBQ* 23 (1961): 233-41.

2785 Marinus de Jonge, "The Earliest Christian Use of Christos: Some Suggestions," *NTS* 32 (1986): 321-43.

15:5

2786 Johannes Schreiber, "Das Schweigen Jesu," in Klaus Wegenast, ed., *Theologie und Unterricht: über die Repräsentanz des Christlichen in der Schule* (festschrift for Hans Stock). Gütersloh: Mohr, 1969. Pp. 79-87.

15:7-15

2787 Hyam Z. Maccoby, "Jesus and Barabbas," *NTS* 16 (1969-1970): 55-60.

2788 Robert L. Merritt, "Jesus Barabbas and the Paschal Pardon," *JBL* 104 (1985): 57-68.

15:7

2789 Alois Bajsić, "Pilatus, Jesus und Barabbas," *Bib* 48 (1967): 7-28.

2790 Günter Scholz, " 'Joseph von Arimathaa' und 'Barabbas'," *LB* 57 (1985): 81-94.

15:8

2791 G. M. Lee, "Mark xv.8," *NovT* 20 (1978): 74.

15:9-14

2792 C.-I. Foulon-Piganiol, "Le rôle du peuple dans le procès de Jesus: Une hypothèse juridique et théologique," *NRT* 98 (1976): 627-37.

15:9

2793 Klaus Haacker, "Einige Fälle von 'erlebter Rede' im Neuen Testament," *NovT* 12 (1970): 70-77.

15:13

2794 Ulrich Hedinger, "Jesus und die Volksmenge: Kritik der Qualifizierung der óchloi in der Evangelienauslegung," *TZ* 32 (1976): 201-206.

2795 John Thorley, "Aktionsart in New Testament Greek: Infinitive and Imperative," *NovT* 31 (1989): 290-315.

15:16-32

2796 Ernest C. Colwell, "Method in the Study of the Gospel Lectionaries," in Ernest C. Colwell, *Studies in Methodology in Textual Criticism of the New Testament*. Leiden: Brill, 1969. Pp. 84-95.

15:16-27

2797 F. C. Synge, "A Matter of Tenses—Fingerprints of an Annotator in Mark," *ET* 88 (1976-1977): 168-71.

15:18

2798 Klaus Berger, "Zum Problem der Messianität Jesu," *ZTK* 71 (1974): 1-30.

15:20-47

2799 C. H. Dodd, "The Sayings," in *Historical Tradition in the Fourth Gospel*. Cambridge: Cambridge University Press, 1963. Pp. 315-405.

15:20-41

2800 Theodore J. Weeden, "The Cross as Power in Weakness (Mark 15:20b-41)," in Werner H. Kelber, ed., *The Passion in Mark: Studies on Mark 14-16*. Philadelphia: Fortress, 1976. Pp. 115-34.

2801 Martin Friedrich, "Tabellen zur markinischen Vorzugsvokabeln," in Johannes Schreiber, ed., *Der Kreuzigungsbericht des Markusevangeliums: Mk 15,20b-41*. New York: de Gruyter, 1986. Pp. 395-433.

2802 Johannes Schreiber, *Der Kreuzigungsbericht des Markusevangeliums: Mk 15,20b-41. Eine traditionsgeschichtliche und methodenkritische Untersuchung nach William Wrede (1859-1906)*. BZNW #48. New York: de Gruyter, 1986.

15:20-39

2803 Kenneth E. Bailey, "The Fall of Jerusalem and Mark's Account of the Cross," *ET* 102 (1991-1992): 102-105.

15:21-41

2804 José R. Scheifler, "El Salmo 22 y la Crucifixión del Señor," *EB* 24 (1965): 5-83.

2805 Daniel Guichard, "La reprise du psaume 22 dans le récit de la mort de Jésus," *FV* 87/5 (1988): 59-64.

15:21

2806 G. M. Lee, "Mark 15:21: 'The Father of Alexander and Rufus'," *NovT* 17/4 (1975): 303.

2807 Marion L. Soards, "Tradition, Composition, and Theology in Jesus' Speech to the 'Daughters of Jerusalem' (Luke 23,26-32)," *Bib* 68/2 (1987): 221-44.

15:22-32

2808 Philippe Rolland, "Jésus est mis en croix," *BLOS* 6 (1990): 11-17.

15:22-29

2809 Miguel de Burgos Nuñez, "La communión de Dios con el crucificado. Cristología de Marcos 15,22-39," *EB* 37 (1978): 243-66.

15:23

2810 Michal Wojciechowski, ''Le Nazireat et la Passion (Mc 14,25a; 15,23),'' *Bib* 65/1 (1984): 94-96.

15:24

2811 Joseph A. Fitzmyer, ''Crucifixion in Ancient Palestine, Qumran Literature, and the New Testament,'' *CBQ* 40/4 (1978): 493-513.

15:25

2812 Sebastián Bartina, ''Ignolum *episēmon* gabex,'' *VD* 36 (1958): 16-37.

2813 Matthew Mahoney, ''A New Look at 'The Third Hour' of Mark 15:25,'' *CBQ* 28 (1966): 292-99.

2814 Bonaventura Rinaldi, ''Ora terza, sesta, nona, le ore della Passione di Cristo,'' *BibO* 23 (1981): 86.

2815 Johannes D. Karavidopoulos, ''L'heure de la crucifixion de Jésus selon Jean et les Synoptiques. Mc 15,25 par rapport à Jn 19,14-16,'' in Adelbert Denaux, ed., *John and the Synoptics*. BETL #101. Louvain: Peeters Press, 1992. Pp. 608-13.

15:26

2816 Günther Baumbach, ''Die Stellung Jesu im Judentum seiner Zeit,'' *FZPT* 20 (1973): 285-305.

2817 Klaus Berger, ''Zum Problem der Messianität Jesu,'' *ZTK* 71 (1974): 1-30.

2818 Ernst Bammel, ''The *titulus*,'' in Ernst Bammel and C. F. D. Moule, eds., *Jesus and the Politics of His Day*. Cambridge: Cambridge University Press, 1984. Pp. 353-64.

15:28

2819 P. Rodgers, ''Mark 15:28,'' *EQ* 69/1 (1989): 81-84.

2820 George D. Kilpatrick, ''Mark xv.28,'' in *The Principles and Practice on New Testament Textual Criticism*. BETL #96. Louvain: Peeters Press, 1990. Pp. 307-11.

15:29

2821 Klaus Haacker, "Einige Fälle von 'erlebter Rede' im Neuen Testament," *NovT* 12 (1970): 70-77.

2822 Jacques Schlosser, "Mc 11:25: tradition et rédaction," in Françios Refoulé, ed., *À cause de l'Evangile: Études sur les synoptiques et les Actes* (festscrift for Jacques Dupont). Paris: Cerf, 1985. Pp. 277-301.

15:32

2823 Harald Sahlin, "Emendationsvorschläge zum griechischen Text des Neuen Testaments I," *NovT* 24 (1982): 160-79.

15:33-16:8

2824 Ton Veerkamp, "Vom ersten Tag nach jenem Sabbat: Der Epilog des Markusevangeliums: 15:33-16:8," *TexteK* 13 (1982): 5-34.

15:33-39

2825 J. Bruckmoser, "Zur Deutung des Todes Jesu nach Mk 15,33-39," doctoral dissertation, University of Salzburg, Salzburg, Austria, 1978.

2826 M. Josuttis, "Die permanente Passion. Predigt über Markus 15,33-39," *EvT* 38 (1978): 160-63.

2827 Gerhard Schneider, "Die theologische Sicht des Todes Jesu in den Kreuzigungsberichten der Evangelien," *TPQ* 126 (1978): 14-22.

2828 Frank J. Matera, "The Death of Jesus according to Luke: A Question of Sources," *CBQ* 47 (1985): 469-85.

2829 G. Pella, "'Porquoi m'as-tu abandonné?' Marc 15,33-39," *Hokhmah* 39 (1988): 3-24.

15:33-37

2830 Ermenegildo Manicardi, "Gesù e la sua morte secondo Marco 15,33-37," in G. Danieli, ed., *Gesù e la sua morte*. Brescia: Paideia, 1984. Pp. 9-28.

15:33-34

2831 Bonaventura Rinaldi, "Ora terza, sesta, nona, le ore della Passione di Cristo," *BibO* 23 (1981): 86.

15:33

2832 R. M. Grández, "Las tinieblas en la muerte de Jésus: Historia de la exégesis de Lc 23,44-45a," *EB* 47 (1989): 177-223.

15:34-39

2833 Paul Glaube, "Einige Stellen, die Bedeutung des Codex D charakterisieren," *NovT* 2 (1957-1958): 310-15.

2834 Hartmut Gese, "Psalm 22 und das Neue Testament," *ZTK* 65/1 (1968): 1-22.

15:34-37

2835 Heribert Schützeichel, "Der Todesschrei Jesu: Bemerkungen zu einer Theologie des Kreuzes," *TTZ* 83 (1974): 1-16.

2836 Lorraine Caza, "Le relief que Marc a donné au cri de la croix," *ScE* 39 (1987): 171-91.

15:34

2837 Julius R. Mantey, "The Causal Use of εἰς in the New Testament," *JBL* 70 (1951): 45-48.

2838 David H. C. Read, "The Cry of Dereliction," *ET* 68 (1956-1957): 260-62.

2839 Martin Rehm, "Eli, Eli lamma sahachthani," *BZ* 2 (1958): 275-78.

2840 Joachim Gnilka, " 'Mein Gott, mein Gott, warum hastdu mich verlassen?' (Mk 15,34 Par.)," *BZ* 3 (1959): 294-97.

2841 John Wilkinson, "Seven Words from the Cross," *SJT* 17 (1964): 69-82.

2842 Frederick W. Danker, "The Demonic Secret in Mark: A Reexamination of the Cry of Dereliction (15:34)," *ZNW* 61 (1970): 48-69.

2843 Georg Braumann, "Wozu? (Mark 15,34)," *Theok* 2 (1973): 155-65.

2844 John H. Reumann, "Psalm 22 at the Cross: Lament and Thanksgiving for Jesus Christ," *Int* 28/1 (1974): 39-58.

2845 L. Paul Trudinger, " 'Eli, Eli, Lama Sabachthani?' A Cry of Derelicition? or Victory?" *JETS* 17 (1974): 235-38.

2846 S. J. Kistemaker, "The Seven Words from the Cross," *WTJ* 38 (1976): 182-91.

2847 Harald Sahlin, "Zum Verständnis der christologischen Anschauung des Markusevangeliums," *StTheol* 31 (1977): 1-19.

2848 Ryszard Rubinkiewicz, "Mk 15,34 i Hbr 1,8-9 w świetle tradycji targumicznej," *RoczTK* 25 (1978): 59-67.

2849 Haim H. Cohn, "Jesus' Cry on the Cross: An Alternative View," *ET* 93 (1981-1982): 215-17.

2850 Christoph Burchard, "Markus 15,34," *ZNW* 74/1 (1983): 1-11.

2851 Jean-Claude Sagne, "The Cry of Jesus on the Cross," *Conci* 169 (1983): 52-58.

2852 David Atkinson, "A Cry of Faith," *ET* 96 (1984-1985): 146-47.

2853 P.-R. Berger, "Zum Aramäischen der Evangelien und der Apostelgeschichte," *TheoR* 82 (1986): 1-17.

2854 Aldo Ceresa-Gastaldo, " 'Dio mio, Dio mio, perche mi hai abbandonato?' (Matteo 27,46 e Marco 15,34)," *Renovatio* 23 (1988): 101-106.

15:35-39

2855 Kent E. Brower, "Elijah in the Markan Passion Narrative," *JSNT* 18 (1983): 85-101.

15:36

2856 G. M. Lee, "Two Notes on St. Mark," *NovT* 18/1 (1976): 36.

15:37-39

2857 Harry L. Chronis, "The Torn Veil: Cultus and Christology in Mark 15:37-39," *JBL* 101/1 (1982): 97-114.

2858 Howard M. Jackson, "The Death of Jesus in Mark and the Miracle from the Cross," *NTS* 33/1 (1987): 16-37.

15:37-30

2859 Marius Reiser, "Der Alexanderroman und das Markusevangelium," in Hubert Cancik, ed., *Markus-Philologie*. Tübingen: Mohr, 1984. Pp. 131-63.

15:38

2860 Gösta Lindeskog, "The Veil of the Temple," in *Coniectanea neotestamenties, XI, in honorem Antonii Fridrichsen sexagenarii*. Lund: Gleerup, 1947. Pp. 132-37.

2861 André Pelletier, "La tradition synoptique du 'voile déchire' a la lumière des réalités archéologiques," *RechSR* 46 (1958): 161-80.

2862 Marinus de Jonge, "De berichten over het scheuren van het voorhangsel bij Jezus' dood in de synoptische evangeliën," *NTT* 21 (1966-1967): 90-114.

2863 Paul Lamarche, "La mort du Christ et le voile du temple selon Marc," *NRT* 96 (1974): 583-99.

2864 Simon Légasse, "Les voiles du Temple de Jérusalem," *RB* 87 (1980): 560-89.

2865 Marinus de Jonge, "Two Interesting Interpretations of the Rending of the Temple-Veil in the Testaments of the Twelve Patriarchs," *Bij* 46 (1985): 350-62.

2866 S. Motyer, "The Rending of the Veil: A Markan Pentecost?" *NTS* 33/1 (1987): 155-57.

2867 David Ulansey, "The Heavenly Veil Torn: Mark's Cosmic Inclusio [linking 1:10 and 15:38]" *JBL* 110 (1991):123-25.

15:39

2868 Robert G. Bratcher, "A Note on υἱὸς θεοῦ," *ET* 68 (1956-1957): 27-28.

2869 J. R. Michaels, "The Centurion's Confession and the Spear Thrust," *CBQ* 29 (1967): 102-109.

2870 P. H. Bligh, "A Note on υἱὸς θεοῦ in Mark 15:39," *ET* 80 (1968-1969): 51-53.

2871 Thomas F. Glasson, "Mark 15:39: The Son of God," *ET* 80 (1968-1969): 286.

2872 Harold A. Guy, "Son of God in Mark 15:39," *ET* 81 (1969-1970): 151.

2873 John Pobee, "The Cry of the Centurion: A Cry of Defeat." in Ernst Bammel, ed., *The Trial of Jesus* (festschrift for C. F. D. Moule). Naperville IL: Allenson, 1970. Pp. 91-102.

2874 Philip B. Harner, "Qualitative Anarthrous Predicate Nouns: Mark 15:39 and John 1:1," *JBL* 92 (1973): 75-87.

2875 Klemens Stock, "Das Bekenntnis des Centurio. Mk 15,39 im Rahmen des Markusevangeliums," *ZKT* 100 (1978): 289-301.

2876 Gerhard Schneider, "Christologische Aussagen des 'Credo' im Lichte des Neuen Testaments," *TTZ* 89 (1980): 282-92.

2877 Chris U. Manus, "The Centurion's Confession of Faith (Mc 15:39): Reflections on Mark's Christology and Its Significance in the Life of African Christians," *BTAf* 7 (1985): 261-78.

2878 Earl S. Johnson, "Is Mark 15:39 the Key to Mark's Christology?" *JSNT* 31 (1987): 3-22.

2879 Ernst L. Schnellbächer, "Sachgemässe Schriftauslegung," *NovT* 30 (1988): 114-31.

2880 Gerhard Dautzenberg, "Zwei unterschiedliche 'Kompendien' markinischer Christologie? Überlegungen zum Verhältnis von Mk 15,39 zu Mk 14,61," in B. Jendorff and G. Schmalenberg, eds., *Evangelium Jesu Christi heute verkündigen* (festschrift for C. Mayer). Gießen: Selbstverlag des Fachbereichs, 1989. Pp. 17-32.

15:40-16:8

2881 Édouard Dhanis, "L'ensevelissement de Jésus et la visite au tombeau dans l'évangile de saint Marc (Mc. XV,40-XVI,8)," *Greg* 39 (1958): 367-410.

15:40-47

2882 John Dominic Crossan, "Mark and the Relatives of Jesus," *NovT* 15 (1973): 81-113.

2883 Lorenz Oberliner, *Historische Überlieferung und christologische Aussage. Zur Frage der "Bruder Jesu" in der Synopse*. Stuttgart: Katholisches Bibelwerk, 1975.

2884 Luise Schottroff, "Maria Magdalena und die Frauen am Grabe Jesu," *EvT* 42 (1982): 3-25.

15:40-41

2885 Anselm Schulz, *Nachfolgen und Nachahmen: Studien über das Verhältnis der neutestamentlichen Jüngerschaft zur urchristlichen Vorbildethik*. Münich: Kösel, 1962.

2886 William Klassen, "Musonius Rufus, Jesus, and Paul: Three First-Century Feminists," in Peter Richardson and John C. Hurd, eds., *From Jesus to Paul* (festschrift for F. W. Beare). Waterloo: Wilfrid Laurier University Press, 1984. Pp. 185-206.

2887 Augustine Stock, "Hinge Transitions in Mark's Gospel," *BTB* 15 (1985): 27-31.

15:40

2888 J. Mehlmann, "Da Origem e do Significado do Nome 'Salomé' (Mc 15,40; 16,1)," *RCB* 7 (1963): 93-107.

2889 Josef Blinzler, "Die Brüder Jesu," *TGeg* 10 (1967): 8-15.

15:42-16:8

2890 Gottfried Schille, *Osterglaube*. Arbeiten zur Theologie #51. Stuttgart: Calwer, 1973.

2891 A. Cordoba, "Relatos de la tumba vacía," *May* 3 (1977): 297-328.

15:42-47

2892 J. Spencer Kennard, "The Burial of Jesus," *JBL* 74 (1955): 227-38.

2893 Charles Masson, "L'ensevelissement de Jésus," in Charles Masson, *Vers les sources d'eau vive: Études d'exégèse et de théologie du Nouveau Testament*. Lausanne: Payot, 1961. Pp. 102-113.

2894 Josef Blinzler, "Die Grablegung Jesu in historischer Sicht," in Édouard Dhanis, ed., *Resurrexit*. Città del Vaticano: Liberia Editrice Vaticana, 1974. Pp. 56-107.

2895 Raymond E. Brown, "The Burial of Jesus," *CBQ* 50 (1988): 233-45.

15:43

2896 Günter Scholz, " 'Joseph von Arimathäa' und 'Barabbas'," *LB* 57 (1985): 81-94.

15:46

2897 Michael D. Goulder, "On Putting Q to the Test," *NTS* 24 (1977-1978): 218-34.

2898 D. Moody Smith, "Mark 15:46: The Shroud of Turin as a Problem of History and Faith," *BA* 46/4 (1983): 251-54.

16:1-20

2899 Gerald O'Collins, "Mary Magdalene as Major Witness to Jesus' Resurrection," *TS* 48 (1987): 631-46.

16:1-13

2900 Albert L. Descamps, "La structure des récits évangéliques de la résurrection," *Bib* 40 (1959): 726-41.

16:1-8

2901 T. W. Manson, *The Servant-Messiah: A Study of the Public Ministry of Jesus*. Cambridge: Cambridge University Press, 1953.

2902 Gabriel Hebert, "The Resurrection Narrative in St. Mark's Gospel," *ABR* 7 (1959): 58-65.

2903 Josef A. Sint, "Die Auferstehung Jesu in der Verkündigung der Urgemeinde," *ZKT* 84 (1962): 129-51.

2904 C. H. Dodd, "The Sayings," in *Historical Tradition in the Fourth Gospel*. Cambridge: Cambridge University Press, 1963. Pp. 315-405.

2905 Enrico Galbiati, "È risorto, non è qui (Marco 16,1-8)," *BibO* 5 (1963): 67-72.

2906 Christian Dietzfelbinger, "Mk 16,1-8," in Hugo Schnell, ed., *Kranzbacher Gespräch: der Lutherischen Bischofskonferenz zur Auseinandersetzung um die Bibel*. Berlin/Hamburg: Lutherisches Verlagshaus, 1967. Pp. 9-22.

2907 Ludger Schenke, *Auferstehung und leeres Grab. Eine traditionsgeschichtliche Untersuchung von Mk 16,1-8*. Stuttgarter Bibelstudien 33. Stuttgart: Katholisches Bibelwerk, 1968.

2908 Jean Delorme, "Les femmes au tombeau, Mc 16,1-8," *AsSeign* 2 (1969): 58-67.

2909 Edward L. Bode, *The First Easter Morning: The Gospel Accounts of the Women's Visit to the Tomb of Jesus*. Analecta Biblica 45. Rome: Biblical Institute Press, 1970.

2910 Jean Delorme, "The Resurrection and Jesus' Tomb: Mark 16:1-8 in the Gospel Tradition," in P. de Surgy, et al., eds., *Resurrection and Modern Biblical Thought*. C. U. Quinn, trans. New York: Corpus, 1970. Pp. 87-101.

2911 Heinrich Schlier, "Die Osterbotschaft aus dem Grab (Markus 16,1-8)," *KathGed* 27 (1971): 1-6.

2912 Erhardt Güttgemanns, "Linguistische Analyse von Mk 16,1-8," *LB* 11/12 (1972): 13-53.

2913 Robert Smith, "New and Old in Mark 16:1-8," *CTM* 43/8 (1972): 518-27.

2914 Giovanni Giavini, "La risurrezione di Gesù come problema esegetico," *ScC* 101 (1973): 217-37.

2915 Tibor Horvath, "The Early Markan Tradition on the Resurrection (Mk 16,1-8)," *RUO* 43 (1973): 445-48.

2916 Peter Stuhlmacher, " 'Kritischer müssten mir die Historisch-Kritischen sein!'," *TQ* 3 (1973): 244-51.

2917 Antonio Ammassari, "Il racconto degli awenimenti della mattina di Pasqua secondo Marco 16,1-8," *BibO* 16 (1974): 49-64.

2918 H.-W. Bartsch, "Der ursprüngliche Schluß der Leidensgeschichte: Überlieferungsgeschichtliche Studien zum Markus-Schluß," in M. Sabbe, ed., *L'évangile selon Marc: Tradition et rédaction*. BETL #34. Louvain: Louvain University Press, 1974. Pp. 411-33.

2919 F. C. Synge, "Mark 16.1-8," *JTSA* 11 (1975): 71-73.

2920 Klaus Berger, *Die Auferstehung des Propheten und die Erhöhung des Menschensohnes: Traditionsgeschichtliche Untersuchungen zur Deutung des Geschickes Jesu in frühchristlichen Texte*. SUNT #13. Göttingen: Vandenhoeck & Ruprecht, 1976.

2921 John Dominic Crossan, "Empty Tomb and Absent Lord," in Werner H. Kelber, ed., *The Passion in Mark: Studies on Mark 14-16*. Philadelphia: Fortress, 1976. Pp. 135-52.

2922 Harald Sahlin, "Zum Verständnis der christologischen Anschauung des Markusevangeliums," *StTheol* 31 (1977): 1-19.

2923 Robert H. Stein, "Was the Tomb Really Empty?" *JETS* 20 (1977): 23-29.

2924 John Dominic Crossan, "A Form for Absence: The Markan Creation of Gospel," *Semeia* 12 (1978): 41-55.

2925 Craig A. Evans, "Mark's Use of the Empty Tomb Tradition," *SBT* 8 (1978): 50-55.

2926 Heinz-Wolfgang Kuhn, "Predigt über Markus 16,1-8," *EvT* 38 (1978): 155-60.

2927 F.-J. Niemann, "Die Erzählung vom leeren Grab bei Markus," *ZKT* 101 (1979): 188-99.

2928 Andreas Lindemann, "Die Osterbotschaf, des Markus. Zur Theologischen Interpretation von Mark 16.1-8," *NTS* 26/3 (1979-1980): 298-17.

2929 Frans Neirynck, "Marc 16,1-8. Tradition et rédaction," *ETL* 56 (1980): 56-88.

2930 Henning Paulsen, "Mark 16:1-8," *NovT* 22/2 (1980): 138-75.

2931 Michel Clevenot, "Auferstehung - Aufstand. Lektüre von Mk. 16,1-8 und Apg. 17,1-10," D. Schirmer, ed., *Die Bibel als politisches Buch: Beiträge zu einer befreienden Christologie*. Stuttgart: Kohlhammer, 1982. Pp. 57-64.

2932 Luise Schottroff, "Maria Magdalena und die Frauen am Grabe Jesu," *EvT* 42 (1982): 3-25.

2933 Hubert Ritt, "Die Frauen und die Osterbotschaft: Synopse der Grabesgeschichten," in G. Dautzenberg, et al., eds, *Die Frau im Urchristentum*. Frieburg: Herder, 1983. Pp. 117-33.

2934 Juan A. Ruiz de Gopegui, "Para uma volta à catequese narrativa: Fé pascal e 'historia de Jesus' em Mc 16,1-8," *PerT* 16 (1984): 313-31.

2935 Ingo Broer, " 'Der Herr ist wahrhaft auferstanden' (Lk 24,34): Auferstehung Jesu und historischkritische Methode. Erwägungen zur Entstehung des Osterglaubens," in Lorenz Oberlinner, ed., *Auferstehung Jesu—Auferstehung der Christen: Deutungen des Osterglaubens*. Freiburg: Herder, 1986. Pp. 39-62.

2936 Heinz Giesen, "Der Auferstandene und seine Gemeinde: Zum Inhalt und zur Funktion des ursprünglichen Markusschlusses (16,1-8)," *SNTU-A* 12 (1987): 99-139.

2937 Zane C. Hodges, "The Women and the Empty Tomb," *BSac* 123 (1966): 301-309.

2938 Philippe Rolland, "La découverte du tombeau vide," *BLOS* 6 (1990): 3-10.

2939 J. M. Strijdom and A. G. van Aarde, "Markus 16:1-8 in die konteks van 'n konstruksie van die Markaanse gemeente," *HTS* 46 (1990): 153-89.

2940 Raymond E. Brown, *A Risen Christ in Eastertime: Essays on the Gospel Narratives of the Resurrection.* Collegeville MN: Liturgical Press, 1991.

16:1

2941 J. Mehlmann, "Da Origem e do Significado do Nome 'Salomé' (Mc 15,40; 16,1)," *RCB* 7 (1963): 93-107.

2942 D. Barag, "Two Roman Glass Bottles with Remnants of Oil," *IEJ* 22 (1972): 24-26.

2943 Lorenz Oberliner, *Historische Überlieferung und christologische Aussage. Zur Frage der "Bruder Jesu" in der Synopse.* Forschung zur Bibei 19. Stuttgart: Katholisches Bibelwerk, 1975.

2944 Michael D. Goulder, "On Putting Q to the Test," *NTS* 24 (1977-1978): 218-34.

2945 Christopher M. Tuckett, "On the Relationship between Matthew and Luke," *NTS* 30 (1984): 130-42.

16:2-8

2946 Joseph Molitor, "Chanmetifragmente: Ein Beitrag zur Textgeschichte der altgeorgischen Bibelubersetzung. 2. Die Markustexte der Chanmetifragmente," *OrChr* 43 (1959): 17-24.

16:2

2947 Felice Montagninni, " '. . . Valde mane una sabbatorum veniunt ad monumentum . . .' (Mc 16,2). Contributo ad una pagina di armonia evangelica," *ScC* 85 (1957): 111-20.

2948 Frans Neirynck, "ἀνατείλαντος τοῦ ἡλίου (Mc 16,2)," *ETL* 54 (1978): 70-103.

16:4

2949 D. W. Palmer, "The Origin, Form, and Purpose of Mark XVI.4 in Codex Bobbiensis," *JTS* 27/1 (1976): 113-22.

16:5-7

2950 J. H. McIndoe, "The Young Man at the Tomb," *ET* 80 (1968-1969): 125.

2951 A. Krijger, "De neaniskos-teksten in Marcus," *KerkT* 36 (1985): 99-116.

16:5

2952 Robin Scroggs and Kent I. Groff, "Baptism in Mark: Dying and Rising with Christ," *JBL* 92 (1973): 531-48.

2953 Michel Gourgues, "À propos du symbolisme christologique et baptismal de Marc 16:5," *NTS* 27 (1980-1981): 672-78.

2954 Allan K. Jenkins, "Young Man or Angel?" *ET* 94/8 (1982-1983): 237-40.

2955 Eugene A. LaVerdiere, "Robed in Radiant White," *Emmanuel* 90 (1984): 138-42.

16:6

2956 William Lillie, "The Empty Tomb and the Resurrection," in D. E. Nineham, et al., eds., *Historicity and Chronology in the New Testament*. London: SPCK, 1965. Pp. 117-34.

2957 Aldo Locatelli, " 'È risorto, non è qui' (Mc. 16,6): La risurrezione di Crislo è anche motivo di credibilità," *ScC* 101 (1973): 251-80.

2958 J. J. A. Kahmann, " 'Il est ressuscité, le Crucifie'. Marc 16,6a et sa place dans l'évangile de Marc," in M. Benzertah, et al., eds., *La Pâque du Christ* (festschrift for F.-X. Durrwell). Paris: Cerf, 1982. Pp. 121-30.

2959 Robert Schlarb, "Die Suche nach dem Messias: ζητέω als Terminus technicus der markinischen Messianologie," *ZNW* 81 (1990): 155-70.

16:7-8

2960 Ralf Oppermann, ''Eine Beobachtung in bezug auf das Problem des Markusschlusses,'' *BibN* 40 (1987): 24-29.

2961 Andrew T. Lincoln, ''The Promise and the Failure: Mark 16:7-8,'' *JBL* 108/2 (1989): 283-300.

16:7

2962 Hans Kosmala, '' 'In My Name','' *ASTI* 5 (1967): 87-109.

2963 P. Cornelius Odenkirchen, '' 'Praecedam vos in Galilaeam','' *VD* 46 (1968): 193-223.

2964 Bernd Steinseifer, ''Der Ort der Erscheinungen des Auferstandenen,'' *ZNW* 62/3 (1971): 232-65.

2965 Jean-Marie van Cangh, ''La Galilée dans l'évangile de Marc: un lieu théologique?'' *RB* 79 (1972): 59-75.

2966 Thorwald Lorenzen, ''Ist der Auferstandene in Galiläa erschienen? Bemerkungen zu einem Aufsatz von B. Steinseifer,'' *ZNW* 64 (1973): 209-21.

2967 Robert H. Stein, ''A Short Note on Mark 14:28 and 16:7,'' *NTS* 20 (1973-1974): 445-52.

2968 B. M. F. van Iersel, '' 'To Galilee' or 'in Galilee' in Mark 14:28 and 16:7?'' *ETL* 58 (1982): 365-70.

2969 Eugene A. LaVerdiere, ''The End, a Beginning,'' *Emmanuel* 90 (1984): 484-91.

2970 George E. Rice, ''Is Bezae a Homogeneous Codex [variants to codex B],'' *PRS* 11 (1984): 39-54.

2971 Knut Backhaus, '' 'Dort werdet ihr Ihn sehen' (Mk 16,7): Die redaktionelle Schlußnotiz des zweiten Evangeliums als dessen christologische Summe,'' *TGl* 76 (1986): 277-94.

2972 Domingo Muñoz León, '' 'Iré delante de vosotros a Galilea' (Mt 26,32 y par). Sentido mesiánico y posible sustrato arameo del logion,'' *EB* 48 (1990): 215-41.

16:8

2973 C. F. D. Moule, "St. Mark xvi.8 Once More," *NTS* 2 (1955-1956): 58-59.

2974 Jesús Luzarraga, "Retraducción semítica de φοβέομαι en Mc 16,8," *Bib* 50 (1969): 497-510.

2975 Robert P. Meye, "Mark 16:8: The Ending of Mark's Gospel," *BR* 15 (1969): 33-43.

2976 Jeanine Depasse-Livet, "Le problème de la finale de Marc: Mc 16,8. État de la question," doctoral dissertation, University of Louvain, Louvain, Belgium, 1970.

2977 P. W. van der Horst, "Can a Book End with γάρ? A Note On Mark 16:8," *JTS* 23 (1972): 121-24.

2978 Thomas E. Boomershine, "Mark 16:8 and the Apostolic Commission," *JBL* 100/2 (1981): 225-39.

2979 Thomas E. Boomershine and Gilbert L. Bartholomew, "The Narrative Technique of Mark 16:8," *JBL* 100/2 (1981): 213-23.

2980 Roger A. Bush, "Mark's Call to Action: A Rhetorical Analysis of Mark 16:8," in John H. Morgan, ed., *Church Divinity*. Notre Dame IN: Privately published, 1985. Pp. 22-30.

2981 Gerald O'Collins, "The Fearful Silence of Three Women (Mark 16:8c)," *Greg* 69/3 (1988): 489-503.

2982 Roberto Vignolo, "Una finale reticente: interpretazione narrativa di Mc 16:8," *RBib* 38 (1990): 129-89.

16:9-20

2983 Ernest C. Colwell, "Mark 16:9-20 in the Armenian Version," *JBL* 56 (1937): 369-86.

2984 M. van der Valk, *Observations on Mark 16,9-20 in Relation to St. Mark's Gospel*. Coimbra: Faculdade de Letras da Universidade de Coimbra, 1958.

2985 Eugen Helzle, ''Der Schluß des Markusevangeliums (Mk 16,9-20) und das Freer-Logion (Mk 16,14 W), ihre Tendenzen und ihre gegenseitiges Verhältnis: Eine wortexegetische Untersuchung,'' doctoral dissertation, University of Tübingen, Tübingen, 1959.

2986 Kenneth W. Clark, ''The Theological Relevance of Textual Variation in Current Criticism of the Greek New Testament,'' *JBL* 85 (1966): 1-16.

2987 F. R. Colino, ''Autenticidad crítico-histórica de la conclusión canónica Mc. 16,9-20,'' *StudL* 7 (1966): 177-224.

2988 Frans Wagenaars, ''Structura Litteraria et Momentum Theologicum Pericopae Mc 16:9-20,'' *VD* 45/1 (1967): 19-22.

2989 G. W. Trompf, ''The First Resurrection Appearance and the Ending of Mark's Gospel,'' *NTS* 18 (1971-1972): 308-30.

2990 G. W. Trompf, ''The *Markusschluß* in Recent Research,'' *ABR* 21 (1973): 15-26.

2991 William R. Farmer, *The Last Twelve Verses of Mark.* SNTSMS #25. Cambridge: University Press, 1974.

2992 D. R. Moore, ''The Continuation of Mark,'' doctoral dissertation, Duke University, Durham NC, 1974.

2993 Klaus Berger, *Die Auferstehung des Propheten und die Erhöhung des Menschensohnes: Traditionsgeschichtliche Untersuchungen zur Deutung des Geschickes Jesu in frühchristlichen Texte.* SUNT #13. Göttingen: Vandenhoeck & Ruprecht, 1976.

2994 Joseph Hug, *La finale de l'évangile de Marc (Mc 16,9-20).* Études Bibliques. Paris: J. Gabalda, 1978.

2995 Barclay M. Newman, '' 'Verses Marked with Brackets. . .','' *BT* 30 (1979): 233-36.

2996 John C. Thomas, ''A Reconsideration of the Ending of Mark,'' *JETS* 26 (1983): 407-19.

2997 Ton Veerkamp, "Das Hinauswerfen der Dämonen: Ein echter Markusschluss," *TexteK* 17 (1983): 26-43.

2998 Paul A. Mirecki, "Mark 16:9-20: Composition, Tradition and Redaction," doctoral dissertation, Harvard University, Cambridge MA, 1986.

2999 Raymond E. Brown, *A Risen Christ in Eastertime: Essays on the Gospel Narratives of the Resurrection.* Collegeville MN: Liturgical Press, 1991.

16:9

3000 Tjitze J. Baarda, *The Gospel Quotations of Aphrahat the Persian Sage. 1. Aphrahat's Text of the Fourth Gospel.* Amsterdam: Krips Repro, 1975.

16:13-23

3001 Anton Vögtle, "Messiasbekenntnis und Petrusverheissung: Zur Komposition Mt 16:13-23 par.," *BZ* 1 (1957): 252-72.

16:14-20

3002 Félix Asensio, "Trasfondo profético-evangélico πᾶσα ἐξουσία de la 'Gran Mision'," *EB* 27 (1968): 27-48.

3003 Gerhard Barth, *Die Taufe in frühchristlicher Zeit.* Neukirchen-Vluyn: Neukirchener, 1981.

3004 Gerhard Schneider, "Die Missionsauftrag Jesu in der Darstellung der Evangelien," in Karl Kertelge, ed., *Mission im Neuen Testament.* Freiburg: Herder, 1982. Pp. 71-92.

16:14-18

3005 E. N. Testa, "I 'Discorsi di Missione' di Gesù," *SBFLA* 29 (1979): 7-41. a

3006 Dale C. Allison, "Paul and the Missionary Discourse," *ETL* 61 (1985): 369-75.

16:14-15

3007 C. H. Dodd, "The Appearances of the Risen Christ: An Essay in Form-Criticism of the Gospels," in D. E. Nineham, ed., *Studies in the Gospels* (festschrift for R. H. Lightfoot). Oxford: Blackwell, 1955. Pp. 9-35.

16:14

3008 Rainer Stuhlmann, *Das eschatologische Maß im Neuen Testament*. Göttingen: Vandenhoeck & Ruprecht, 1983.

16:15-20

3009 Paul Ternant, "La prédication universelle de l'Évangile du Signeur, Mc 16,15-20," *AsSeign* 2 (1969): 38-48.

3010 Gilles Becquet, "La mission universelle de l'Église par la foi et ses signes (Mc 16,15-20)," *EV* 80 (1970): 297-300.

16:16

3011 C. H. Dodd, "The Sayings," in *Historical Tradition in the Fourth Gospel*. Cambridge: Cambridge University Press, 1963. Pp. 315-405.

3012 Andrzej F. Dziuba, " 'He Who Believes and Is Baptized' (Mk 16,16)," *RuchB* 37 (1984): 493-500.

3013 Paul A. Mirecki, "The Antithetic Saying in Mark 16:16: Formal and Redactional Features," in Birger Pearson, ed., et al., *eds., The Future of Early Christianity* (festschrift for Helmut Koester). Minneapolis: Fortress, 1991. Pp. 229-41.

16:17-18

3014 Frank Stagg, "Explain the Ending of the Gospel of Mark: Mark 16:17-18," in C. Frazier, ed., *What Did the Bible Mean?* Nashville: Broadman Press, 1971. Pp. 122-25.

16:19-20

3015 Brian K. Donne, "The Significance of the Ascension of Jesus Christ in the New Testament," *SJT* 30 (1977): 555-68.

16:19

3016 W. R. G. Loader, "Christ at the Right Hand—Ps. cx. 1 in the New Testament," *NTS* 24 (1977-1978): 199-217.

3017 Elmer L. Towns, "The Ascension of Jesus Christ," *FundJ* 3/6 (1984): 12-14.

16:21-22

3018 James C. G. Greig, "Eukairos," *ET* 65 (1953-1954): 158-59.

16:30-44

3019 Eugene A. LaVerdiere, "The Breaking of the Bread," *Emmanuel* 95 (1989): 554-60, 577.

16:41

3020 Eugene A. LaVerdiere, "It Was a Huge Stone," *Emmanuel* 92 (1986): 394-400.

16:66-72

3021 Gregory Murray, "Saint Peter's Denials," *DR* 103 (1985): 296-98.

PART TWO

Citations by Subjects

Abiathar

3022 C. S. Morgan, " 'When Abiathar Was High Priest,' (Mark 2:26)," *JBL* 98 (1979): 409-10.

3023 Craig A. Evans, "Patristic Interpretation of Mark 2:26: 'When Abiathar was High Priest'," *VC* 40/2 (1986): 183-86.

anti-Semitism

3024 T. A. Burkill, "Anti-Semitism in St. Mark's Gospel," *NovT* 3 (1959): 34-53.

3025 Heinrich Baarlink, *Anti-Judaïsme in het oudste Evangelie?* Kampen: Kok, 1979.

3026 Heinrich Baarlink, "Zur Frage nach dem Antijudaismus im Markusevangelium," *ZNW* 70 (1979): 166-93.

apocalyptic

3027 William J. Crowder, "Jesus' Use of Apocalyptic Language in the Synoptic Gospels," doctoral dissertation, Southern Baptist Theological Seminary, Louisville KY, 1937.

3028 H.-J. Schoeps, "Ebionitische Apokalyptik in Neuen Testament," *ZNW* 51 (1960): 101-11.

3029 Nikolaus Walter, "Tempelzerstörung und synoptische Apokalypse," *ZNW* 57 (1966): 38-49.

3030 Josef Blinzler, "Jesusverkundigung im Markusevangelium," in Wilhelm Pesch, ed., *Jesus in den Evangelien.* Stuttgart: Katholisches Bibelwerk, 1970. Pp. 71-104.

3031 Bonaventura Mariani, "Il Vangelo di Marco posteriore alla distruione di Gerusalemme del 70?" in *La distruzione di Gerusalemme del 70 nei suoi riflessi storico-letterari. Atti del V Convegno biblico francescano, Roma 22-27 settembre 1969.* Assisi: Studio teologico Porziuncola, 1971. Pp. 167-80.

3032 Alexander Sand, "Zur Frage nach dem 'Sitz im Leben' der Apokalyptischen Texte des Neuen Testaments," *NTS* 18/2 (1971-1972): 167-77.

3033 Roger Lapointe, ''Actualité de l'apocalyptique,'' *EgT* 4 (1973): 197-211.

3034 Morton S. Enslin, ''A New Apocalyptic,'' *RL* 44 (1975): 105-10.

3035 Sophie Laws, ''Can Apocalyptic be Relevant?'' in Morna Hooker and Colin Hick-Ling, eds., *What About the New Testament? Essays in Honour of Christopher Evans*. London: SCM Press, 1975. Pp. 89-102.

3036 Per Bilde, ''Afspejler Mark 13 et jødisk apokalyptisk forlaeg for kriseaaret 40?'' in Sigfred Pedersen, ed., *Nytestamentlige Studier*. Aarhus: Forlaget Aros, 1976. Pp. 105-34.

3037 Diego A. Losada, ''Jesús camina sobre las aguas. Un relato apocalíptico,'' *RevB* 38 (1976): 311-19.

3038 Priscilla C. Patten, ''Parable and Secret in the Gospel of Mark in Light of Select Apocalyptic Literature,'' doctoral dissertation, Drew University, Madison NJ, 1976.

3039 Paul J. Achtemeier, ''An Apocalyptic Shift in Early Christian Tradition: Reflections on Some Canonical Evidence,'' *CBQ* 45 (1983): 231-48.

3040 John A. McGuckin, ''The Vine and the Elm Tree: The Patristic Interpretation of Jesus' Teachings on Wealth,'' in W. J. Sheils and Diana Wood, eds., *The Church and Wealth*. New York: Blackwell, 1986. Pp. 1-14.

3041 Timothy Radcliffe, ''The Coming of the Son of Man: Mark's Gospel and the Subversion of 'the Apocalyptic Imagination','' in *Language, Meaning, and God* (festschrift for Herbert McCabe). London: G. Chapman, 1987. Pp. 176-89.

3042 Ronald E. Clements, ''Apocalyptic, Literacy and the Canonical Tradition,'' in W. Huelitt Gloer, ed., *Eschatology and the New Testament* (festschrift for G. R. Beasley-Murray). Peabody MA: Hendrickson, 1989. Pp. 15-27.

apologetics

3043 David M. Stanley, "Mark and Modern Apologetics," *BibTo* 1 (1962): 58-64.

3044 S. G. F. Brandon, "The Apologetical Factor in the Markan Gospel," *StudE* 2 (1964): 34-46.

3045 D. F. Brezine, "The Marcan Apologetic," *BibTo* 11 (1964): 918-22.

audience criticism

3046 Paul S. Minear, "Audience Criticism and Markan Ecclesiology," in Heinrich Baltensweiler and Bo Reicke, eds., *Neues Testament und Geschichte: Historisches Geschehen und Deutung im Neuen Testament: Oscar Cullmann zum 70. Geburtstag*. Zürich: Theologischer Verlag/Tübingen: Mohr, 1972. Pp. 79-89.

authorities

3047 Dieter Lührmann, "Die Pharisäer und die Schriftgelehrten im Markusevangelium," *ZNW* 78 (1987): 169-85.

3048 Anthony J. Saldarini, "The Social Class of the Pharisees in Mark," in Jacob Neusner, ed., *The Social World of Formative Christianity and Judaism: Essays in Tribute to Howard Clark Kee*. Philadelphia: N.p., 1988. Pp. 69-77.

3049 Elizabeth Struthers Malbon, "The Jewish Leaders in the Gospel of Mark: A Literary Study of the Marcan Characterization," *JBL* 108 (1989): 259-81.

3050 Jack D. Kingsbury, "The Religious Authorities in the Gospel of Mark," *NTS* 36 (1990): 42-65.

authorship

3051 Kurt Niederwimmer, "Johannes Markus und die Frage nach dem Verfasser des zweiten Evangeliums," *ZNW* 58 (1967): 172-88.

3052 Pierson Parker, "The Authorship of the Second Gospel," *PRS* 5 (1978): 4-9.

baptism

3053 F. E. Lownds, "The Baptism of Our Lord," *ET* 62 (1950-1951): 274-75.

3054 J. E. Yates, "The Form of Mark 1:8b: 'I Baptized You with Water; He Will Baptize You with the Holy Spirit'," *NTS* 4 (1957-1958): 334-38.

3055 C. A. Poirier, "The Sacrament of Baptism and the Word," *CJT* 9 (1963): 75-81.

3056 Anton Weber, "Die Taufe Jesu im Jordan als Anfang nach Eusebius von Casarea," *TheoP* 41 (1966): 20-29.

3057 Michel Coune, "Baptême, Transfiguration, et Passion," *NRT* 92 (1970): 165-79.

3058 James D. G. Dunn, "Spirit-and-Fire Baptism," *NovT* 14 (1972): 81-92.

3059 Daniel A. Bertrand, *Le baptême cie Jésus*. Tübingen: Mohr, 1973.

3060 Lars Hartman, "Baptism 'Into the Name of Jesus' and Early Christology: Some Tentative Considerations," *StTheol* 28 (1974): 21-48.

3061 J. K. Elliott, "Ho baptizōn and Mark i.4," *TZ* 31 (1975): 14-15.

3062 D. J. Murray, "Mark's Theology of Baptism," *JPC* 8 (1976): 92-97.

3063 André Feuillet, "Vocation et mission des prophètes, Baptême et mission de Jésus. Étude de christologie biblique," *NovVet* 54 (1979): 22-40.

3064 Frederick A. Niedner, "Markan Baptismal Theology: Renaming the Markan Secret," *CThM* 9 (1982): 93-106.

3065 Eugen Ruckstuhl, "Jesus als Gottessohn im Spiegel des markinischen Taufberichts [Mk 1:9-11]," in Ulrich Luz and Hans Weder, eds., *Die Mitte des Neuen Testaments: Einheit and vielfalt neutestamentlicher theologie* (festschrift for Eduard Schweizer). Göttingen: Vandenhoeck & Ruprecht, 1983. Pp. 193-220.

3066 Gerhard Sellin, "Das Leben des Gottessohnes: Taufe und Verklärung Jesu als Bestandteile eines vormarkinischen 'Evangeliums'," *K* 25/3-4 (1983): 237-53.

3067 John Drury, "Mark 1:1-15: An Interpretation," in A. E. Harvey, ed., *Alternative Approaches to New Testament Study*. London: Latimer, 1985. Pp. 25-36.

3068 Gottfried Hoffmann, "The Baptism and Faith of Children," in Kurt E. Marquart, et al., eds., *A Lively Legacy*. Fort Wayne IN: Concordia Theological Seminary, 1985. Pp. 79-95.

3069 Bas M. F. van Iersel, "He Will Baptize You with the Holy Spirit (Mark 1,8)," in Tjitze Baarda, ed., *Text and Testimony: Essays on New Testament and Apocryphal Literature* (festschrift for A. F. J. Klijn). Kampen: Kok, 1988. Pp. 132-41.

3070 Joel Marcus, "The Time Has Been Fulfilled (Mark 1:15)," in Joel Marcus and Marion L. Soards, eds., *Apocalyptic and the New Testament* (festschrift for J. Louis Martyn). Sheffield: JSOT Press, 1989. Pp. 49-68.

3071 Mark F. S. C. McVann, "Baptism, Miracles, and Boundary Jumping in Mark," *BTB* 21 (1991): 151-57.

Bartimaeus

3072 Vernon K. Robbins, "The Healing of Blind Bartimaeus (10:46-52) in the Marcan Theology," *JBL* 92 (1973): 224-43.

3073 Earl S. Johnson, "Mark 10:46-52: Blind Bartimaeus," *CBQ* 40/2 (1978): 191-204.

3074 Michael G. Steinhauser, "The Form of the Bartimaeus Narrative (Mark 10.46-52)," *NTS* 32/4 (1986): 583-95.

3075 Scott G. Sinclair, "The Healing of Bartimaeus and the Gaps in Mark's Messianic Secret," *SLJT* 33 (1990): 249-57.

bibliography

3076 James E. Lackey, "A Critique of Twentieth Century Markan Studies," doctoral dissertation, Iliff School of Theology, Denver CO, 1968.

3077 L. F. Rivera, "Bibliografía sobre el evangelio de Marcos: [1962-1910]," *RevB* 32 (1970): 351-54.

3078 P.-É. Langevin, *Bibliographie biblique*. I. 1930-1970. Québec: Les Presses de l'Université Laval, 1972; II. 1930-1975, 1978; III. 1930-1983, 1985.

3079 Gerard S. Sloyan, "Recent Literature on the Trial Narratives of the Four Gospels," in T. J. Ryan, ed., *Critical History and Biblical Faith: New Testament Perspectives*. Philadelphia: Fortress Press, 1973. Pp. 136-76.

3080 J. A. Brooks, "An Annotated Bibliography on Mark," *SouJT* 21 (1978): 75-82.

3081 William L. Lane, "The Gospel of Mark in Current Study," *SouJT* 21 (1978): 7-21.

3082 Hugh M. Humphrey, *A Bibliography for the Gospel of Mark 1954-1980*. Lewiston NY: Edwin Mellen Press, 1981.

3083 Günter Wagner, *An Exegetical Bibliography on the Gospels of Matthew and Mark*. Macon GA: Mercer University Press, 1984.

3084 Daniel J. Harrington, "A Map of Books on Mark (1975-1984)," *BTB* 15 (1985): 12-16.

3085 William R. Telford, "Select Bibliography," in William R. Telford, ed., *The Interpretation of Mark*. Issues in Religion and Theology #7. Philadelphia: Fortress Press, 1985. Pp. 167-74.

3086 Larry W. Hurtado, "The Gospel of Mark in Recent Study," *Themelios* 14 (1988-1989): 47-52.

3087 David E. Garland, *One Hundred Years of Study on the Passion Narrative*. NABPR Bibliographic Series #3. Macon GA: Mercer University Press, 1989.

3088 Joanna Dewey, "Recent Studies on Mark," *RSR* 17 (1991): 12, 14-16.

3089 Vernon K. Robbins, "Text and Context in Recent Studies of the Gospel of Mark," *RSR* 17 (1991): 16-22.

blasphemy

3090 Eugene W. Daily, "A Study of Blasphemy in the Gospels," doctoral dissertation, Southern Baptist Theological Seminary, Louisville KY, 1947.

3091 Yves Congar, "Blasphemy Against the Holy Spirit," *Conci* 10/9-10 (1974): 47-57.

3092 T. A. Burkill, "Blasphemy: St. Mark's Gospel as Damnation History," in Jacob Neusner, ed., *Christianity, Judaism and Other Greco-Roman Cults: Studies for Morton Smith at Sixty*. Studies in Judaism in Late Antiquity 12. Leiden: Brill, 1975. 1:51-74.

Caesar

3093 G. Wormser, " 'Rendez à César' (Mc 12,14 par.)," *NC* 3 (1967): 43-53.

3094 Charles H. Giblin, " 'The Things of God' in the Question Concerning Tribute to Caesar," *CBQ* 33/4 (1971): 510-27.

3095 Arthur Ogle, "What Is Left for Caesar," *TT* 35/3 (1978): 254-64.

christology

3096 Günther Dehn, *Der Gottessohn: Eine Einführung in das Evangelium des Markus*. Hamburg: Furche, 1953.

3097 Christian Maurer, "Knecht Gottes und Sohn Gottes im Passionsbericht des Markusevangeliums," *ZTK* 50 (1953): 1-38.

3098 G. D. Coover, "The Deity of Christ according to Mark," doctoral dissertation, Dallas Theological Seminary, Dallas TX, 1954.

3099 Harold St. John, *An Analysis of the Gospel of Mark: The Son of God as Mark Portrayed Him.* London: Pickering and Inglis, 1956.

3100 Paul W. Meyer, ''The Problem of the Messianic Self-Consciousness of Jesus,'' *NovT* 4 (1960): 122-38.

3101 Johannes Schreiber, ''Die Christologie des Markusevangeliums. Beobachtungen zur Theologie und Komposition des zweiten Evangeliums,'' *ZTK* 58 (1961): 154-83.

3102 Christian P. Ceroke, ''The Divinity of Christ in the Gospels,'' *CBQ* 24 (1962): 125-39.

3103 José Alonso Díaz, ''Jesús 'Hijo de Dios' en el Evangelio de Marcos,'' *CuBí* 21 (1964): 131-36.

3104 Philip Vielhauer, ''Erwägungen zur Christologie des Markusevangeliums,'' in Erich Dinkler, ed., *Zeit und Geschichte. Dankesgabe an Rudolf Bultmann zum 80. Geburtstag*, in collaboration with Hartwig Thyen. Tübingen: Mohr/Siebeck, 1964. Pp. 155-69.

3105 Leander E. Keck, ''Mark 3:7-12 and Mark's Christology,'' *JBL* 84/4 (1965): 341-58.

3106 N. W. Hutchinson, ''The Deity or Jesus in the Gospel of St. Mark,'' doctoral dissertation, Trinity College, Dublin, 1966.

3107 Johannes Schreiber, *Theologische Erkenntnis und unterrichtlicher Vollzug: Dargestellt am Markusevangelium.* Hamburg: Furche-Verlag, 1966.

3108 Lone Fatum, ''Jesu 'selvbevidstked' og kristologien,'' *DTT* 30 (1967): 147-82.

3109 I. Howard Marshall, ''The Divine Sonship of Jesus,'' *Int* 21 (1967): 87-103.

3110 K. Weinholt Petersen, ''Messiashemmelighed og lignelsesforkyndelse i Markusevangeliet,'' *DTT* 30 (1967): 1-25.

3111 F. Poeppig, *Das Markus-Evangelium. Die Sprache des kosmischen Christus im Markus-Evangelium.* Freiburg: Verlag Die Kommenden, 1967.

3112 Étienne Trocmé, "Pour un Jésus public: les évangélistes Marc et Jean aux prises avec l'intimisme de la tradition," in Felix Christ, ed., *Oikonomia: Heilsgeschichte als Thema der Theologie. O. Cullmann zum 65. Geburtstag gewidmet.* Hamburg-Bergstedt: Reich, 1967. Pp. 42-50.

3113 Felix Christ, *Jesus Sophia. Die Sophia-Christologie bei den Synoptikem.* Zürich: Zwingli, 1970.

3114 Eduard Lohse, "Apokalyptik und Christologie," *ZNW* 62 (1971): 48-67.

3115 Norman Perrin, "The Christology of Mark: A Study in Methodology," *JR* 51 (1971): 173-87.

3116 Otto Betz, "The Concept of the So-called 'Divine Man' in Mark's Christology," in David Edward Aune, ed., *Studies in New Testament and Early Christian Literature: Essays in Honor of Allen P. Wikgren.* Novum Testamentum Supplement 33. Leiden: Brill, 1972. Pp. 229-40.

3117 Werner H. Kelber, "Mark 14:32-42: Gethsemane. Passion Christology and Discipleship Failure," *ZNW* 63 (1972): 166-87.

3118 J. A. Kirk, "The Messianic Role of Jesus and the Temptation Narrative: A Contemporary Perspective," *EQ* 44 (1972): 11-29.

3119 Franz J. Schierse, "Das Christusbild im Markusevangelium: Neuere Untersuchungen zur markinischen Christologie," *BK* 27 (1972): 114-16.

3120 J. S. Setzer, "A Fresh Look at Jesus' Eschatology and Christology in Mark's Petrine Stratum," *LQ* 24 (1972): 240-53.

3121 Harald Weinacht, *Die Menschwerdung des Sohnes Gottes im Markusevangelium. Studien zur Christologie des*

Markusevangeliums. Hermeneutische Untersuchungen für Theologie 13. Tübingen: Mohr, 1972.

3122 Jens Christensen and W. Christensen, *God in Action: Mark's View of Jesus*. Wheaton IL: Tyndale, 1973.

3123 Jan Lambrecht, ''The Christology of Mark,'' *BTB* 3 (1973): 256-73.

3124 Ulrich B. Müller, ''Die christologische Absicht des Markusevangeliums und die Verklärungsgeschichte,'' *ZNW* 64 (1973): 159-93.

3125 Lionel Swain, ''The Divine Face of Man: Mark's Christology,'' *ClerR* 58 (1973): 696-708.

3126 Étienne Trocmé, ''Is there a Markan Christology?'' in Barnabas Lindars and Stephen S. Smalley, eds., *Christ and Spirit in the New Testament: In Honour of Charles Francis Digby Moule*. Cambridge/New York: Cambridge University Press, 1973. Pp. 3-13.

3127 Edward J. Cuba, *Who Do You Say I Am? An Adult Inquiry into the First Three Gospels*. Staten Island NY: Alba House, 1974.

3128 Lars Hartman, ''Baptism 'Into the Name of Jesus' and Early Christology: Some Tentative Considerations,'' *StTheol* 28 (1974): 21-48.

3129 William L. Lane, ''*Theios anēr* Christology and the Gospel of Mark,'' in Richard N. Longenecker and Merrill C. Tenney, eds., *New Dimensions in New Testament Study*. Grand Rapids: Zondervan, 1974. Pp. 144-61.

3130 Ernest R. Martinez, ''The Identity of Jesus in Mark,'' *CICR* 1 (1974): 323-42.

3131 Dietrich-Alex Koch, ''Zum Verhältnis von Christologie und Eschatologie im Markusevangelium: Beobachtungen auf Grund von 8,27-9,1,'' in Georg Strecker, ed., *Jesus Christus in Historie und Theologie: Neutestamentliche Festschrift für Hans Conzelmann zum 60. Geburtstag*. Tübingen: Mohr, 1975. Pp. 395-408.

3132 Dietrich-Alex Koch, *Die Bedeutung der Wundererzählungen für die Christologie des Markus-Evangeliums*. Beiheft zur *ZNW* 42. New York: de Gruyter, 1975.

3133 Hugolinus Langkammer, "Chrystologia ewangelii Marka," *RoczTK* 22 (1975): 49-63.

3134 George Mangatt, "The Christological Kerygma of the Gospel of Mark," *BB* 1 (1975): 19-36.

3135 Robert P. Rousseau, "John the Baptist: Jesus' Forerunner in Mark's Christology," *BibTo* 77 (1975): 316-22.

3136 Peter von der Osten-Saeken, "Streitgespräch und Parabel als Formen markinischer Christologie," in Georg Strecker, ed., *Jesus Christus in Historie und Theologie: neutestamentliche Festschrift für Hans Conzelmann zum 60. Geburtstag*. Tübingen: Mohr, 1975. Pp. 375-94.

3137 Miguel de Burgos Nuñez, "El Evangelio de San Marcos como 'Theologia Crucis.' La teología de la Cruz como instancia crítica de la cristología y la eclesiología según el Evangelio de San Marcos," *Communio* 10 (1977): 207-455.

3138 Hans Lubsczyk, "Kyrios Jesus: Beobachtungen und Gedanken zum Schluß des Markusevangeliums," in Rudolf Schnackenburg, Josef Ernest, and Joachim Wanke, eds., *Die Kirche des Anfangs: Festschrift für Heinz Schürmann zum 65. Geburtstag*. Erfurter Theologische Studien 38. Leipzig: St. Benno, 1977; Freiburg/Basel: Herder, 1978. Pp. 133-74.

3139 Eduard Schweizer, "Towards a Christology of Mark?" in Jacob Jervell and Wayne A. Meeks, eds., *God's Christ and His People: Studies in Honor of Nils Alstrup Dahl*. Oslo: Universitetsforlaget, 1977. Pp. 29-42.

3140 James Blevins, "The Christology of Mark," *RevExp* 75/4 (1978): 505-17.

3141 John R. Donahue, "Jesus as the Parable of God in the Gospel of Mark," *Int* 32 (1978): 369-86.

3142 Harry T. Fleddermann, "The Central Question of Mark's Gospel: A Study of Mark 8:29," doctoral dissertation, Graduate Theological Union, Berkeley CA, 1978.

3143 Allan H. Howe, "The Teaching-Jesus Figure in the Gospel of Mark: A Redaction-Critical Study in Markan Christology," doctoral dissertation, Garrett-Northwestern Seminary, Evanston IL, 1978.

3144 Philip G. Davis, " 'Truly This Man was the Son of God': The Christological Focus of the Markan Redaction," doctoral dissertation, McMaster University, Hamilton, Ontario, 1979.

3145 Robert C. Tannehill, "The Gospel of Mark as Narrative Christology," *Semeia* 16 (1979): 57-95.

3146 Barnabas Lindars, "Jesus as Advocate: A Contribution to the Christology Debate," *BJRL* 62/2 (1979-1980): 476-97.

3147 Paul J. Achtemeier, " 'He Taught Them Many Things': Reflections on Marcan Christology," *CBQ* 42 (1980): 465-81.

3148 Bertrand Buby, "A Christology of Relationship in Mark," *BTB* 10/4 (1980): 149-54.

3149 Hubert Frankemölle, "Jewish and Christian Messianism," *TD* 28/3 (1980): 233-36.

3150 Heinz J. Held, "Der Christusweg und die Nachfolge der Gemeinde: Christologie und Ekklesiologie im Markusevangelium," in Dieter Lührmann and Georg Strecker, eds., *Kirche* (festschrift for Günther Bornkamm). Tübingen: Mohr, 1980. Pp. 79-93.

3151 Thomas R. W. Longstaff, "Crisis and Christology: The Theology of the Gospel of Mark," *PJ* 33 (1980): 28-40.

3152 Jack D. Kingsbury, "The 'Divine Man' as the Key to Mark's Christology: The End of an Era?" *Int* 35 (1981): 243-57.

3153 Harry L. Chronis, "The Torn Veil: Cultus and Christology in Mark 15:37-39," *JBL* 101/1 (1982): 97-114.

3154 Robert D. Rowe, "Is Daniel's 'Son of Man' Messianic?" in H. H. Rowdon, ed., *Christ the Lord: Studies in Christology* (festschrift for Donald Guthrie). Leicester UK: InterVarsity Press, 1982. Pp. 71-96.

3155 Jack D. Kingsbury, *The Christology of Mark's Gospel.* Philadelphia: Fortress Press, 1983.

3156 M. Eugene Boring, "The Christology of Mark: Hermeneutical Issues for Systematic Theology," *Semeia* 30 (1984): 125-53.

3157 M. Eugene Boring, *Truly Human / Truly Divine: Christological Language and the Gospel Form.* St. Louis: CBP Press, 1984.

3158 Wilfrid J. Harrington, "Story and Christology: Two Marcan Studies," *MillSt* 16 (1985): 57-64.

3159 Sharon H. Ringe, *Jesus, Liberation, and the Biblical Jubilee: Images for Ethics and Christology.* Overtures to Biblical Theology #19. Philadelphia PA: Fortress Press, 1985.

3160 Earl S. Johnson, "Is Mark 15:39 the Key to Mark's Christology?" *JSNT* 31 (1987): 3-22.

3161 Howard Clark Kee, "Christology in Mark's Gospel," in Jacon Neusner, et al., eds., *Judaisms and Their Messiahs at the Turn of the Christian Era.* Cambridge: Cambridge University Press, 1987. Pp. 187-208.

3162 Ole Davidsen, "Narrativité et existence: Sur une détermination du Jésus narratif dans l'évangile de Marc," *SémBib* 48 (1988): 18-41

3163 Michael Theobald, "Gottessohn und Menschensohn: Zur polaren Struktur der Christologie im Markusevangelium," *SNTU-A* 13 (1988): 37-79.

3164 Aloysius M. Ambrozic, "Jesus as the Ultimate Reality in St. Mark's Gospel," *URM* 12 (1989): 169-76.

3165 Philip G. Davis, "Mark's Christological Paradox," *JSNT* 35 (1989): 3-18.

3166 M. Apparicio, "El Espíritu de Jesús Mesías y la novedad de la historia: Perfil de cristología sinóptica del Espíritu," *May* 16 (1990): 325-481.

3167 James R. Edwards, "The Baptism of Jesus According to the Gospel of Mark [1:9-11]," *JETS* 34 (1991): 43-57.

3168 Edwin K. Broadhead, "Christology as Polemic and Apologetic: The Priestly Portrait of Jesus in the Gospel of Mark," *JSNT* 47 (1992): 21-34.

composition

3169 D. E. Nineham, "St. Mark's Gospel," *Theology* 60 (1957): 267-72.

3170 Gerard S. Sloyan, "The Gospel according to St. Mark," *Worship* 32 (1958): 547-57.

3171 David M. Stanley, "Mark and Modern Apologetics," *BibTo* 1 (1962): 58-64.

3172 Samuel Sandmel, "Prolegomena to a Commentary on Mark," *JBL* 31 (1963): 294-300.

3173 N. Q. Hamilton, "Resurrection Tradition and the Composition of Mark," *JBL* 34 (1965): 415-21.

3174 Norman Perrin, "The Composition of Mark ix,1," *NovT* 11 (1969): 67-70.

3175 Cesae Angelini, "Portrait de saint Marc," *ÉtudF* 20 (1970): 217-20.

3176 Adelbert Denaux, "Kleine inleiding op het Marcusevangelie," *CBG* 16 (1970): 309-41.

3177 J. W. Michaux, "L'evangile selon Marc," *BVC* 93 (1970): 37-41.

3178 James M. Robinson, "On the *Gattung* of Mark (and John)," *Persp* 11 (1970): 99-129.

3179 Robert Butterworth, "The Composition of Mark 1-12," *HeyJ* 13/1 (1972): 5-26.

3180 Friedrich Janssen, "Die synoptischen Passionsberichte. Ihre theologische Konzeption und literarische Komposition," *BibL* 14 (1973): 40-57.

3181 W. W. Isenberg, "A Short Catechism of the Gospel of Mark," *CThM* 2 (1975): 316-25.

3182 F. G. Lang, "Kompositionsanalyse des Markusevangeliums," *ZTK* 74 (1977): 1-24.

3183 Gerd Theissen, "Die aretalogische Evangelienkomposition des Markus," in R. Pesch, ed., *Das Markus-Evangelium.* Wege der Forschung 411. Darmstadt: Wissenschaftliche Buchgesellschaft, 1979. Pp. 377-89.

3184 Willem S. Vorster, "Mark: Collector, Redactor, Author, Narrator?" *JTSA* 31 (1980): 46-61.

3185 Marion Smith, "The Composition of Mark 11-16," *HeyJ* 22/4 (1981): 363-77.

3186 Paul A. Mirecki, "Mark 16:9-20: Composition, Tradition and Redaction," doctoral dissertation, Harvard University, Cambridge MA, 1986.

<u>conflict</u>

3187 Arland J. Hultgren, *Jesus and His Adversaries: The Form and Function of the Conflict Stories in the Synoptic Tradition.* Minneapolis: Augsburg, 1979.

3188 Jack D. Kingsbury, *Conflict in Mark: Jesus, Authorities, Disciples.* Philadelphia: Fortress Press, 1989.

<u>deconstruction</u>

3189 Patrick J. Hartin, "Disseminating the Word: A Deconstructive Reading of Mark 4:1-9 and Mark 4:13-20," in Patrick J. Hartin and J. H. Petzer, eds., *Text and*

Interpretation: New Approaches in the Criticism of the New Testament. Leiden: Brill, 1991. Pp. 187-200.

demonology

3190 H. A. Kelly, "The Devil in the Desert," *CBQ* 26 (1964): 190-220.

3191 Alfred T. Hennelly, "The Gerasene Perikope (Mk 5:1-20): A Study in Redaction-Criticism," doctoral dissertation, Marquette University, Milwaukee WI, 1968.

3192 M. de Mello, "The Gerasene Demoniac: The Power of Jesus Confronts the Power of Satan," *EcumRev* 23 (1971): 409-18.

3193 J. P. Comiskey, "Begone, Satan!" *TBT* 58 (1972): 620-26.

3194 B. A. E. Osborne, "Peter, Stumbling-Block and Satan," *NovT* 15/3 (1973): 187-90.

3195 Richard H. Hiers, "Satan, Demons, and the Kingdom of God," *SJT* 27 (1974): 35-47.

3196 Meinrad Limbeck, "Jesus und die Dämonen: Der exegetische Befund," *BK* 30 (1975): 7-11.

3197 Franz Annen, "Die Damonenaustreibungen Jesu in den synoptischen Evangelien," *TB* 5 (1976): 107-46.

3198 E. C. B. MacLaurin, "Beelzeboul," *NovT* 20/2 (1978): 156-60.

3199 William M. Alexander, *Demonic Possession in the New Testament: Its Historical, Medical, and Theological Aspects*. Grand Rapids: Baker, 1980.

3200 Paul W. Hollenbach, "Jesus, Demoniacs, and Public Authorities: A Socio-Historical Study," *JAAR* 49 (1981): 567-88.

3201 Alfred Suhl, "Überlegungen zur Hermeneutik an Hand von Mk 1:21-28," *K* 26/1-2 (1984): 28-38.

3202 Peter Pimentel, "The 'Unclean Spirits' of St. Mark's Gospel," *ET* 99 (1987-1988): 173-75.

3203 Ken Frieden, "The Language of Demonic Possession: A Key-Word Analysis," in Robert Detweiler and W. G. Doty, eds., *The Daemonic Imagination: Biblical Text and Secular Story*. Atlanta: Scholars Press, 1990. Pp. 41-52.

disciples

3204 Clarence B. Burke, "The Attitude of the Synoptic Writers Towards the Twelve," master's thesis, Southern Baptist Theological Seminary, Louisville KY, 1955.

3205 John Coutts, "The Authority of Jesus and of the Twelve in St. Mark's Gospel," *JTS* 8 (1957): 111-18.

3206 Heinrich Kahlefeld, "Jünger des Herrn," *GeistL* 30 (1957): 1-6.

3207 Wim Burgers, "De instelling van de Twaalf in het Evangelie van Marcus," *ETL* 36 (1960): 625-54.

3208 Joseph B. Tyson, "The Blindness of the Disciples in Mark," *JBL* 80 (1961): 261-68.

3209 Oscar Cullmann, "Le douzième apôtre," *RHPR* 42 (1962): 133-40.

3210 F. Agnew, "Vocatio primorum discipulorum in traditione synoptica," *VD* 46 (1968): 129-47.

3211 Sean Freyne, *The Twelve: Disciples and Apostles: A Study in the Theology of the First Three Gospels*. London: Sheed & Ward, 1968.

3212 Robert P. Meye, *Jesus and the Twelve. Discipleship and Revelation in Mark's Gospel*. Grand Rapids: Eerdmans, 1968.

3213 Karl Kertelge, "Die Funktion der 'Zwölf' im Markusevangelium," *TTZ* 78 (1969): 193-206.

3214 Francis W. Beare, "The Mission of the Disciples and the Mission Charge: Matthew 10 and Parallels," *JBL* 89/1 (1970): 1-13.

3215 Günther Schmahl, "Die Berufung der Zwölf im Markusevangelium," *TTZ* 81 (1972): 203-13.

3216 Walter Schmithals, "Der Markusschluß, die Verklärungsgeschichte und die Aussendung der Zwölf," *ZTK* 69 (1972): 379-411.

3217 Günther Schmahl, *Die Zwölf im Markusevangelium: eine redaktionsgeschichtliche Untersuchung*. Trierer Theologische Studien 30. Trier: Paulinus-Verlag, 1974.

3218 Klemens Stock, *Boten aus dem Mit-Ihm-Sein. Das Verhältnis zwischen Jesus und den Zwölf nach Markus*. Analecta Biblica 70. Rome: Biblical Institute Press, 1975.

3219 Werner H. Kelber, "The Hour of the Son of Man and the Temptation of the Disciples (Mark 14:32-42)," in Werner H. Kelber, ed., *The Passion in Mark: Studies on Mark 14-16*. Philadelphia: Fortress, 1976. Pp. 41-60.

3220 Gene Szarek, "A Critique of Kelber's 'The Hour of the Son of Man and the Temptation of the Disciples: Mark 14:32-42'," *SBLSP* 6 (1976): 111-18.

3221 Ernest Best, "The Role of the Disciples in Mark," *NTS* 23 (1976-1977): 377-401.

3222 Robert C. Tannehill, "The Disciples in Mark: The Function of a Narrative Role," *JR* 57 (1977): 386-405.

3223 Ernest Best, "Mark's Use of the Twelve," *ZNW* 69/1-2 (1978): 11-35.

3224 M. F. Kirby, "Mark's Prerequisite for Being an Apostle," *BibTo* 18 (1980): 77-81.

3225 Edward L. Taylor, "The Disciples of Jesus in the Gospel of Mark," doctoral dissertation, Southern Baptist Theological Seminary, Louisville KY, 1980.

3226 A.-M. Denis, "L'intégration des Douze à l'évangile de Marc," *StudE* 7 (1982): 161-64.

3227 Joanna Dewey, "Point of View and the Disciples in Mark," *SBLSP* 21 (1982): 97-106.

3228 Edwin D. Freed, "The Disciples in Mark and the *maskilim* in Daniel: A Comparison," *JSNT* 16 (1982): 7-23.

3229 Edwin D. Freed, "At Cross Purposes: Jesus and the Disciples in Mark," in R. Drury, ed., *The New Testament as Personal Reading*. Springfield IL: Templegate Publishers, 1983. Pp. 54-68.

3230 Robert E. Morosco, "Matthew's Formation of a Commissioning Type Scene Out of the Story of Jesus' Commissioning of the Twelve," *JBL* 103/4 (1984): 539-56.

3231 J. M. Kapolyo, "Mark's Understanding of the Call: Appointment and Training of the Twelve," doctoral dissertation, Aberdeen University, Aberdeen, 1985.

3232 David P. Secco, "Take up Your Cross," in Peter T. O'Brien and David G. Patterson, eds., *God Who Is Rich in Mercy* (festschrift for D. B. Knox). Grand Rapids: Baker, 1986. Pp. 139-51.

3233 James R. Butts, "The Voyage of Discipleship: Narrative, Chreia, and Call Story," in Craig A. Evans and William F. Stinespring, eds., *Early Jewish and Christian Exegesis* (festscrift for William H. Brownlee). Atlanta: Scholars Press, 1987. Pp. 199-219.

3234 John B. Muddiman, "The Glory of Jesus: Mark 10:37," in L. D. Hurst and N. T. Wright, eds., *The Glory of Christ in the New Testament*. Oxford: Clarendon Press, 1987. Pp. 51-58.

3235 Pieter J. J. Botha, "Die dissipels in die Markusevangelie," doctoral dissertation, University of South Africa, Pretoria, 1989.

3236 Elisabeth Schüssler Fiorenza, "Les Douze dans la communauté des disciples égaux: contradiction ou malentendu?" *FV* 88/5 (1989): 13-24.

discipleship

3237 William T. Smith, "Cross-Bearing in the Synoptic Gospels," doctoral dissertation, Southern Baptist Theological Seminary, Louisville KY, 1953.

3238 D. R. Fletcher, "Condemned to Die. The Logion on Crossbearing: What Does It Mean?" *Int* 18 (1964): 156-64.

3239 Theo Aerts, "Suivre Jésus. Évolution d'un thème biblique dans les Évangiles synoptiques," *ETL* 42 (1966): 476-512.

3240 Jeremiah Crosby, "The Call to Discipleship in Mark 1:17-18," *BibTo* 27 (1966): 1919-22.

3241 Ernest Best, "Discipleship in Mark: Mark 8:22-10:52," *SJT* 23/3 (1970): 323-37.

3242 C. M. Murphy, "Discipleship in Mark as Movement with Christ," *BibTo* 53 (1971): 305-308.

3243 Wilkie Au, "Discipleship in Mark," *TBT* 67 (1973): 1249-51.

3244 David R. Catchpole, "Discipleship, the Law and Jesus of Nazareth," *Crux* 11 (1973): 8-16.

3245 James Donaldson, " 'Called to Follow': A Twofold Experience of Discipleship in Mark," *BTB* 5 (1975): 67-77.

3246 B. V. Manno, "The Identity of Jesus and Christian Discipleship in the Gospel of Mark," *REd* 70 (1975): 619-28.

3247 Werner Bracht, "Jüngerschaft und Nachfolge: Zur Gemeindesituation im Markusevangelium," in Josef Hainz, ed., *Kirche im Werden: Studien zum Thema Amt und Gemeinde im Neuen Testament,* in collaboration with the Collegium Biblicum München. Münich/Paderborn/Vienna: Verlag Ferdinand Schönigh, 1976. Pp. 143-65.

3248 Joanna Dewey, *Disciples of the Way: Mark on Discipleship*. Cincinnati: United Methodist Church, 1976.

3249 Francisco de la Calle, "La experiencia cristiana de Jésus, según el evangelio de Marcos," in A. Vargas-Machuca, ed., *Jesucristo en la historia y en la fe*. Semana Internacional de Teología. Madrid/Salamanca: Fundacion Juan March/Ediciones Sigueme, 1977. Pp. 125-32.

3250 Robert C. Tannehill, *A Mirror for Disciples. Following Jesus through Mark*. Nashville: Discipleship Resources, 1977.

3251 H. F. Peacock, "Discipleship in the Gospel of Mark," *RevExp* 75 (1978): 555-64.

3252 Eduard Schweizer, "The Portrayal of the Life of Faith in the Gospel of Mark," *Int* 32 (1978): 387-99.

3253 B. L. Emslie, "Jesus' Command in the Synoptic Gospels to Take Up the Cross: An Exegetical Study," doctoral dissertation, University of South Africa, Pretoria, 1980.

3254 Paul S. Pudussery, "The Meaning of Discipleship in the Gospel of Mark," *Je* 10 (1980): 93-110.

3255 Harry T. Fleddermann, "The Discipleship Discourse (Mark 9:33-50)," *CBQ* 43/1 (1981): 57-75.

3256 David M. Stanley, *The Call to Discipleship: The Spiritual Exercices with the Gospel of St. Mark*. Osterley, UK: The Way, 1982.

3257 Augustine Stock, *Call to Discipleship: A Literary Study of Mark's Gospel*. Wilmington DE: Glazier, 1982.

3258 John R. Donahue, *The Theology and Setting of Discipleship in the Gospel of Mark*. Milwaukee WI: Marquette University Press, 1983.

3259 Elizabeth Struthers Malbon, "Fallible Followers: Women and Men in the Gospel of Mark," *Semeia* 28 (1983): 29-48.

3260 William G. Thompson, *The Gospels for Your Whole Life: Mark and John in Prayer and Study*. Minneapolis: Winston Press, 1983.

3261 Gregory L. Waybright, ''Discipleship and Possessions in the Gospel of Mark: A Narrative Study,'' doctoral dissertation, Marquette University, Milwaukee WI, 1984.

3262 Thomas Söding, ''Die Nachfolgeforderung Jesu im Markusevangelium,'' *TTZ* 94 (1985): 292-310.

3263 Demetrios Trakatellis, ''*Akolouthei moi*—Follow Me (Mk 2:14): Discipleship and Priesthood,'' *GOTR* 30 (1985): 271-85.

3264 Urban C. von Wahlde, ''Mark 9:33-50: Discipleship: The Authority That Serves,'' *BZ* 29/1 (1985): 49-67.

3265 Ernest Best, *Disciples and Discipleship: Studies in the Gospel according to Mark*. Edinburgh: T. & T. Clark, 1986.

3266 Joong S. Suh, ''Discipleship and Community in the Gospel of Mark,'' doctoral dissertation, Boston University, Boston MA, 1986.

3267 John J. Vincent, *Radical Jesus*. London: Marshall Pickering, 1986.

3268 Ched Myers, ''The Last Days of Jesus, Mark 14:1-16:8: Collapse and Restoration of Discipleship,'' *Soj* 16 (1987): 32-36.

3269 Dennis M. Sweetland, *Our Journey with Jesus: Discipleship according to Mark*. Good News Studies #22. Wilmington DE: Glazier, 1987.

3270 William G. Thompson, ''Mark's Gospel and Faith Development,'' *CS* 26 (1987): 139-54.

3271 Ivan Habener, ''Taking up One's Cross: Mark's Gospel of Discipleship,'' *BibTo* 26 (1988): 41-47.

3272 Paul S. Pudussery, ''Discipleship and Suffering in the Gospel of Mark,'' *Je* 18 (1988): 121-39.

3273 John C. Thomas, ''Discipleship in Mark's Gospel,'' in Paul Elbert, ed., *Faces of Renewal* (festschrift for Stanley M. Horton). Peabody MA: Hendrickson, 1988. Pp. 64-80.

3274 Michael S. Curry, ''The Cause of Discipleship,'' *Soj* 18 (1989): 30-31.

3275 Douglas J. W. Milne, ''Mark—the Gospel of Servant Discipleship,'' *RTR* 49 (1990): 20-29.

3276 Graham Twelftree, ''Discipleship in Mark's Gospel,'' *SMR* 141 (1990): 5-11.

3277 John N. Suggit, ''Exegesis and Proclamation: Bartimaeus and Christian Discipleship (Mark 10:46-52),'' *JTSA* 74 (1991): 57-63.

ecclesiology

3278 H. H. Graham, ''The Reflection of the Church in Mark, Matthew, Paul's Letters and Acts,'' doctoral dissertation, Union Theological Seminary, New York, 1959.

3279 Bernhard Schultze, ''Die ekklesioklogische Bedeutung des Gleichnisses vom Senfkorn,'' *OCP* 27 (1961): 362-86.

3280 J. M. Casciaro Ramírez, ''Iglesia y pueblo de Dios en el Evangelio de S. Marcos,'' in *Concepto de la Iglesia en el Nuevo Testamento (y) otros estudios*. Semaña Bíblica Española #19. Madrid: Consejo Superior de Investigaciones Científicas, Instituto Francisco Suárez, 1962. Pp. 19-99.

3281 F. M. Uricchio, ''Presenza della Chiesa primitiva nel Vangelo di S. Marco,'' *MiscFranc* 66 (1966): 29-87.

3282 John H. Elliott, ''Ministry and Church Order in the NT: A Traditio-Historical Analysis,'' *CBQ* 32/3 (1970): 367-91.

3283 Paul S. Minear, ''Audience Criticism and Markan Ecclesiology,'' in Heinrich Baltensweiler and Bo Reicke, eds., *Neues Testament und Geschichte: Historisches Geschehen und Deutung im Neuen Testament: Oscar Cullmann zum 70. Geburtstag*. Zürich: Theologischer Verlag/Tübingen: Mohr, 1972. Pp. 79-89.

3284 James N. Lewis, "The Church in the Synoptic Tradition," doctoral dissertation, Southern Baptist Theological Seminary, Louisville KY, 1973.

3285 Patrick H. Reardon, "Kenotic Ecclesiology in Mark," *BibTo* 70 (1974): 1476-82.

3286 Eugene C. Szarek, "Markan Ecclesiology and Anthropology: A Structural Analysis of Mark 3:7-12," doctoral dissertation, Marquette University, Milwaukee WI, 1975.

3287 Miguel de Burgos Nuñez, "El Evangelio de San Marcos como 'Theologia Crucis.' La teología de la Cruz como instancia crítica de la cristología y la eclesiología según el Evangelio de San Marcos," *Communio* 10 (1977): 207-455.

3288 Heinz J. Held, "Der Christusweg und die Nachfolge der Gemeinde: Christologie und Ekklesiologie im Markusevangelium," in Dieter Lührmann and Georg Strecker, eds., *Kirche* (festschrift for Günther Bornkamm). Tübingen: Mohr, 1980. Pp. 79-93.

3289 John Kallikuzhuppil, "The Church and the Kingdom of God in the Synoptic Gospels: A Comparative and Synthetic Study," *Je* 15 (1985): 85-93.

3290 Mark F. S. C. McVann, "Markan Ecclesiology: An Anthropological Experiment," *List* 23/2 (1988): 95-105.

3291 Antonio Rodríguez Carmona, "La Iglesia en Marcos," *EE* 63 (1988): 129-63.

ending

3292 J. K. Elliott, "The Text and Language of the Endings to Mark's Gospel," *TZ* 27 (1971): 255-62.

3293 Bruce Metzger, "The Ending of the Gospel According to Mark in the Ethiopic Manuscripts," in John Reumann, ed., *Understanding the Sacred Text: Essays in Honor of Morton S. Enslin on the Hebrew Bible and Christian Beginnings*. Valley Forge PA: Judson Press, 1972. Pp. 165-80.

3294 Norman R. Petersen, "When Is the End Not the End? Literary Reflections on the Ending of Mark's Narrative," *Int* 34 (1980): 151-66.

<u>eschatology</u>

3295 Alexander Jones, "The Eschatology of the Synoptic Gospels," *Scr* 4 (1949-1951): 222-31.

3296 George R. Beasley-Murray, "A Century of Eschatological Discussion," *ET* 64 (1952-1953): 312-16.

3297 George R. Beasley-Murray, *Jesus and the Future: An Examination of the Criticism of the Eschatological Discourse. Mark 13, with Special Reference to the Little Apocalypse Theory*. New York: Macmillan, 1954.

3298 J. G. Bellshaw, "The Eschatology of the Gospel of Mark," doctoral dissertation, Dallas Theological Seminary, Dallas TX, 1954.

3299 J. A. T. Robinson, "The Second Coming: Mark 14:62," *ET* 67 (1955-1956): 336-40.

3300 Delbert G. Fann, "A Critical Evaluation of Realized Eschatology," master's thesis, Golden Gate Baptist Theological Seminary, Mill Valley CA, 1959.

3301 H. P. Owen, "The Parousia of Christ in the Synoptic Gospels," *SJT* 12 (1959): 171-92.

3302 Otto Michel, "Eine philologische Frage zur Einzugsgeschichte," *NTS* 6 (1959-1960): 81-82.

3303 George R. Beasley-Murray, "The Eschatological Discourse of Jesus," *RevExp* 57 (1960): 153-66.

3304 John Bligh, "Eschatology and Social Doctrine," *HeyJ* 3 (1962): 262-67.

3305 Edwin A. Schick, "History, Eschatology, and Time in Modern Biblical Studies with Special Reference to Redemptive Time in the Gospel of Mark," doctoral dissertation, Princeton Theological Seminary, Princeton NJ, 1962.

3306 Georg Braumann, " 'An Jenem Tag' Mk 2:20," *NovT* 6 (1963): 264-67.

3307 Ernst Bammel, "Erwagungen zur Eschatologie Jesu," *StudE* 3 (1964): 3-32.

3308 George Eldon Ladd, *Jesus and the Kingdom: The Eschatology of Biblical Realism*. New York: Harper & Row, 1964.

3309 Franz Mussner, *Christ and the End of the World. A Biblical Study in Eschatology*. Maria von Eroes, trans. Contemporary Catechetics Series #2. Notre Dame: University of Notre Dame Press, 1965.

3310 R. H. Shaw, "A Conjecture on the Signs of the End," *ATR* 47 (1965): 96-102.

3311 J. K. Howard, "Our Lord's Teaching Concerning His Parousia: A Study in the Gospel of Mark," *EQ* 38 (1966): 52-58, 68-75, 150-57.

3312 A. L. Moore, *The Parousia in the New Testament*. Leiden: Brill, 1966.

3313 Günther Bornkamm, "Die Verzögerung der Parusie: Exegetische Bemerkungen zu zwei synoptischen Texten," in Günther Bornkamm, ed., *Geshichte und Glaube*. Beiträge zur evangelischen Theologie 48. München: C. Kaiser, 1968. Pp. 46-55.

3314 Eduard Schweizer, "Eschatology in Mark's Gospel," in E. Earle Ellis and Max Wilcox, eds., *Neotestamentica et Semitica: Studies in Honour of Matthew Black*. Edinburgh: T. & T. Clark, 1969. Pp. 114-18.

3315 Jacques Dupont, "La parabole du maître qui rentre dans la nuit (Mc 13,34-36)," in Albert Descamps and André de Halleux, eds., *Mélanges bibliques en hommage au R. P. Béda Rigaux*. Gembloux: Duculot, 1970. Pp. 89-116.

3316 Werner H. Kelber, "Kingdom and Parousia in the Gospel of Mark," doctoral dissertation, University of Chicago, Chicago IL, 1970.

3317 Alfons Weiser, "Von der Predigt Jesu zur Erwartung der Parusie. Uberlieferungsgeschichtliches zum Gleichnis vom Türhüter," *BibL* 12 (1971): 25-31.

3318 C. C. Marcheselli, "La ricerca di Dio nei segni dei tempi: la struttura tematico-letteraria di Mc 1,21-3,6 parr," in François Bovon, et al., eds., *Analyse structurale et exégèse biblique: Essais d'interprétation*. Neuchâtel: Delachaux et Niestlé, 1972. Pp. 289-313.

3319 J. S. Setzer, "A Fresh Look at Jesus' Eschatology and Christology in Mark's Petrine Stratum," *LQ* 24 (1972): 240-53.

3320 Samuel T. O. Akande, "The Concept of Eschatological Suddenness in the Synoptic Tradition," doctoral disseration, Southern Baptist Theological Seminary, Louisville KY, 1973.

3321 Charles L. Holman, "The Idea of an Imminent Parousia in the Synoptic Gospels," *SBT* 3 (1973): 15-31.

3322 O. G. White, "The Resurrection and the Second Coming of Jesus in Mark," *StudE* 6 (1973): 615-18.

3323 Hugolinus Langkammer, "Paruzja syna czlowieczego (Mk 13)," *RoczTK* 21 (1974): 61-74.

3324 George R. Beasley-Murray, "New Testament Apocalyptic: A Christological Eschatology," *RevExp* 72 (1975): 317-30.

3325 Johannes M. Nützel, "Hoffnung und Treue: Zur Eschatologie des Markusevangeliums," in Peter Fiedler and Dieter Zeller, eds., *Gegenwart und kommendes Reich: Schülergabe Anton Vögtle zum 65. Geburtstag*. Stuttgarter Biblische Monographien. Stuttgart: Verlag Katholisches Bibelwerk, 1975. Pp. 79-90.

3326 G. Henry Waterman, "The Sources of Paul's Teaching on the Second Coming of Christ in 1 and 2 Thessalonians," *JETS* 18/2 (1975): 105-13.

3327 Adalberto Bonora, *La speranza del cristiano nel Vangelo di Marco*. Cognoscere il Vangelo 8. Padua: Messaggero, 1976.

3328 George R. Beasley-Murray, ''Eschatology in the Gospel of Mark,'' *SouJT* 21 (1978): 37-53.

3329 George R. Beasley-Murray, ''The Parousia in Mark,'' *RevExp* 75/4 (1978): 565-81.

3330 Desmond Ford, *The Abomination of Desolation in Biblical Eschatology*. Washington DC: University Press of America, 1979.

3331 Evald Lövestam, ''The ἡ γενεὰ αὕτη: Eschatology in Mk 13,30 parr,'' in Jan Lambrecht, ed., *L'Apocalypse johannique et l'Apocalyptique dans le Nouveau Testament*. BETL #53. Louvain: Peeters Press, 1980. Pp. 403-13.

3332 Frans Neirynck, ''Marc 13: examen critique de l'interprétation de R. Pesch,'' in Jan Lambrecht, ed., *L'Apocalypse johannique et l'apocalyptique dans le Nouveau Testament*. Gembloux: J. Duculot, 1980. Pp. 369-401.

3333 Johannes Nissen, ''Prophetische Apokalyptik und Ethos der frühen Christen,'' in Dieter Birnbaum, ed., *Hermeneutik eschatologischer biblischer Texte*. Greifswald: Ernst-Moritz-Arndt-Universität, 1982. Pp. 49-78.

3334 Welton O. Seal, ''The Parousia in Mark: A Debate with Norman Perrin and His 'School','' doctoral dissertation, Union Theological Seminary, New York NY, 1982.

3335 G. K. Beale, ''The Use of Daniel in the Synoptic Eschatological Discourse and in the Book of Revelation,'' in David Wenham and Craig Blomberg, eds., *Gospel Perspectives. 6. The Miracles of Jesus*. Sheffield: JSOT Press, 1985. Pp. 129-53.

3336 Erich Grässer, ''Καὶ ἦν μετὰ τῶν θηρίων (Mk 1,13b): Ansätze einer theologischen Tierschutzethik,'' in Wolfgang Schrage, ed., *Studien zum Text und zur Ethik des Neuen Testaments* (festschrift for Heinrich Greeven). Berlin: de Gruyter, 1986. Pp. 144-57.

3337 Pieter J. Maartens, "The Son of Man as Compound Metaphor in Mk 14:62," in J. H. Petzer and P. J. Hartin, eds., *A South African Perspective on the New Testament*. Leiden: Brill, 1986. Pp. 76-98.

3338 Ulrich B. Müller, "Apokalyptische Strömungen," in Jürgen Becker, et al., eds., *Die Anfänge des Christentums*. Stuttgart: Kohlhammer, 1987. Pp. 217-54.

3339 Ched Myers, "The Last Days of Jesus, Mark 14:1-16:8: Collapse and Restoration of Discipleship," *Soj* 16 (1987): 32-36.

3340 Timothy J. Geddert, *Watchwords: Mark 13 in Markan Eschatology*. Sheffield: JSOT Press, 1989.

3341 Joachim Gnilka, "Apokalyptik und Ethik: die Kategorie der Zukunft als Anweisung für sittliches Handeln," in Helmut Merklein, ed., *Neues Testament und Ethik* (festschrift for Rudolf Schnackenburg). Freiburg: Herder, 1989. Pp. 464-81.

3342 C. Clifton Black, "An Oration at Olivet: Some Rhetorical Dimensions of Mark 13," in Duane F. Watson, *Persuasive Artistry: Studies in New Testament Rhetoric* (festschrift for George A. Kennedy). Sheffield: JSOT Press, 1991. Pp. 66-92.

3343 Chris L. Mearns, "Parables, Secrecy and Eschatology in Mark's Gospel," *SJT* 44 (1991): 423-42.

3344 Marinus de Jonge, "The Radical Eschatology of the Fourth Gospel and the Eschatology of the Synoptics. Some Suggestions," in Adelbert Denaux, ed., *John and the Synoptics*. BETL #101. Louvain: Peeters Press, 1992. Pp. 481-87.

ethics

3345 Dale W. Brown, "Some Possibilities for a Biblical Case for Tax Refusal," *BLT* 19/2 (1974): 101-12.

3346 Sharon H. Ringe, *Jesus, Liberation, and the Biblical Jubilee: Images for Ethics and Christology*. Overtures to Biblical Theology #19. Philadelphia: Fortress Press, 1985.

3347 Dan O. Via, *The Ethics of Mark's Gospel: In the Middle of Time*. Philadelphia: Fortress Press, 1985.

3348 Bruce D. Chilton and J. I. H. McDonald, *Jesus and the Ethics of the Kingdom*. London: SPCK, 1987.

3349 Joachim Gnilka, ''Apokalyptik und Ethik: die Kategorie der Zukunft als Anweisung für sittliches Handeln,'' in Helmut Merklein, ed., *Neues Testament und Ethik* (festschrift for Rudolf Schnackenburg). Freiburg: Herder, 1989. Pp. 464-81.

3350 John S. Kloppenborg, ''Alms, Debt and Divorce: Jesus' Ethics in Their Mediterranean Context,'' *TJT* 6 (1990): 182-200.

3351 Augustine Stock, '' 'Render to Caesar','' *BibTo* 62 (n.d.): 929-34.

exorcism

3352 William V. Roosa, ''The Significance of Exorcism in the Gospel of Mark,'' doctoral dissertation, University of Chicago, Chicago IL, 1934.

3353 Billy C. Jett, ''Exorcism as the Representative Messianic Miracle in Mark,'' master's thesis, Southern Baptist Theological Seminary, Louisville KY, 1957.

3354 James H. Johnson, ''The Use of the Name 'Jesus' in New Testament Exorcism,'' master's thesis, Southeastern Baptist Theological Seminary, Wake Forest NC, 1962.

3355 C. H. Cave, ''The Obedience of Unclean Spirits,'' *NTS* 11/1 (1964-1965): 93-97.

3356 Howard Clark Kee, ''The Terminology of Mark's Exorcism Stories,'' *NTS* 14 (1967-1968): 232-46.

3357 David L. Bartlett, ''Exorcism Stories in the Gospel of Mark,'' doctoral dissertation, Yale University, New Haven CT, 1972.

3358 Kenneth Grayston, ''Exorcism in the New Testament,'' *EpRev* 2 (1975): 90-94.

3359 Gerd Petzke, "Die historische Frage nach den Wundertaten Jesu. Dargestellt am Beispiel des Exorzismus Mark ix.14-29 par," *NTS* 22 (1975-1976): 180-204.

3360 Ernest Best, "Exorcism in the New Testament and Today," *BibTh* 27 (1977): 1-9.

3361 Pierre Guillemette, "La Forme des Recits d'Exorcisme de Bultmann, un Dogme a Reconsiderer," *EgT* 11/2 (1980): 177-93.

3362 J. K. Howard, "New Testament Exorcism and Its Significance Today," *ET* 96/4 (1984-1985): 105-109.

3363 Roberta Finkelstein, "Mark 9:38-41: An Unknown Exorcist," *UUC* 44/3-4 (1989): 78-87.

3364 Carol S. LaHurd, "Biblical Exorcism and Reader Response to Ritual in Narrative," in Robert Detweiler and William Doty, eds., *The Daemonic Imagination: Biblical Text and Secular Story*. Atlanta: Scholars Press, 1990. Pp. 53-63.

<u>faith</u>

3365 Paul Althaus, *Fact and Faith in the Kerygma of Today*. D. Cairns, trans. Philadelphia: Muhlenberg, 1960.

3366 Eric F. F. Bishop, " 'Faith has Still its Olivet and Love its Galilee'," *EQ* 44/1 (1972): 3-10.

3367 Daniel C. Arichea, " 'Faith' in the Gospels of Matthew, Mark, and Luke," *BT* 29 (1978): 420-24.

3368 Paul Cho Yonggi, "Active Faith," *SEAJT* 23/2 (1982): 121-25.

3369 Lee Oo Chung, "One Woman's Confession of Faith," *IRM* 74 (1985): 212-16.

3370 Mary Ann Beavis, "Mark's Teaching on Faith," *BTB* 16 (1986): 139-42.

3371 Christopher Burdon, *Stumbling on God: Faith and Vision in Mark's Gospel*. Grand Rapids: Eerdmans, 1990.

fall of Jerusalem

3372 S. G. F. Brandon, *The Fall of Jerusalem and the Christian Church: A Study of the Effects of the Jewish Overthrow of A.D. 70 on Christianity*. London: SPCK, 1951.

3373 S. G. F. Brandon, "Jesus and the Zealots," *StudE* 4 (1968): 8-20.

fasting

3374 Alistair Kee, "The Question about Fasting," *NovT* 11 (1969): 161-73.

3375 Joseph Keller, "Jesus and the Critics: A Logico-Critical Analysis of the Marcan Confrontation," *Int* 40/1 (1986): 29-38.

feeding the four- five-thousand

3376 Georg Ziener, "Die Brotwunder im Markusevangelium," *BZ* 4/2 (1960): 282-85.

3377 Ivor Buse, "The Gospel Accounts of the Feeding of the Multitudes," *ET* 74 (1962-1963): 167-70.

3378 T. M. Suriano, "Eucharist Reveals Jesus: The Multiplication of the Loaves," *BibTo* 58 (1972): 642-51.

3379 Konrad Raiser, "Bibelarbeit über Markus 6,32-44," in Hansgeorg Kraft and Hans Mayr, eds., *Botschafter von der Versöhnung* (festschrift for Walter Arnold). N.p., 1979. Pp. 115-21.

3380 Karl P. Donfried, "The Feeding Narratives and the Marcan Community: Mark 6,30-45 and 8,1-10," in Dieter Lührmann and Georg Strecker, eds., *Kirche* (festschrift for Günther Bornkamm). Tübingen: Mohr, 1980. Pp. 95-103.

3381 Ernst Bammel, "The Feeding of the Multitude," in Ernst Bammel and C. F. D. Moule, eds., *Jesus and the Politics of His Day*. Cambridge: Cambridge University Press, 1984. Pp. 211-40.

3382 Stephen C. Barton, "The Miraculous Feedings in Mark," *ET* 97/4 (1985-1986): 112-13.

3383 Jouette M. Bassler, "The Parable of the Loaves," *JR* 66/2 (1986): 157-72.

3384 Fritz Neugebauer, "Die wunderbare Speisung (Mk 6:30-44 parr) und Jesu Identität," *KD* 32/4 (1986): 254-77.

3385 Ched Myers, "The Miracle of One Loaf [Mk 4:35-8:21; pt 3 on Gospel of Mark]," *Soj* 16 (1987): 31-34.

3386 Paul Beauchamp, "Paraboles de Jésus, vie de Jésus: l'encadrement évangélique et scripturaire des paraboles (Mc 4,1-34)," in Jean Delorme, ed., *Les paraboles évangéliques: perspectives nouvelles*. Paris: Cerf, 1989. Pp. 151-70.

3387 Gerhard Lohfink, "Wie werden im Reich Gottes die Hungernden satt? zur Erzählintention von Mk 6,30-44," in Johannes J. Degenhardt, *Die Freude an Gott: Unsere Kraft* (festschrift for Otto B. Knoch). Stuttgart: Verlag Katholisches Bibelwerk, 1991. Pp. 135-44.

fig tree

3388 C. W. F. Smith, "No Time for Figs," *JBL* 79 (1960): 315-27.

3389 J. Neville Birdsall, "The Withering of the Fig Tree," *ET* 73 (1961-1962): 191.

3390 A. de Q. Robin, "The Cursing of the Fig Tree in Mark XI. A Hypothesis," *NTS* 8 (1961-1962): 276-81.

3391 R. Hull, "The Cursing of the Fig Tree: A Study in Social Change and the Theology of Hope," *CC* 84 (1967): 1429-31.

3392 Richard H. Hiers, " 'Not the Season for Figs'," *JBL* 87/4 (1968): 394-400.

3393 L. A. Loslie, "The Cursing of the Fig Tree: Tradition Criticism of a Marcan Pericope (Mark 11:12-14, 20-25)," *SBT* 7 (1977): 3-18.

3394 Allan McNicol, "The Lesson of the Fig Tree in Mark 13:28-32: A Comparison between Two Exegetical Methodologies," *RQ* 27/4 (1984): 193-207.

3395 Jacques Schlosser, "Mc 11:25: tradition et rédaction," in Françios Refoulé, ed., *À cause de l'Evangile: Études sur les synoptiques et les Actes* (festscrift for Jacques Dupont). Paris: Cerf, 1985. Pp. 277-301.

3396 Wendy J. Cotter, "For It Was Not the Season for Figs," *CBQ* 48/1 (1986): 62-66.

3397 Stephen Hre Kio, "A Prayer Framework in Mark 11," *BT* 37/3 (1986): 323-28.

3398 Ched Myers, "The Lesson of the Fig Tree: Mark 11:1-13:37—Jesus' Second Campaign of Nonviolent Direct Action," *Soj* 16 (1987): 30-33.

3399 Guy Wagner, "Le figuier stérile et la destruction du temple: Marc 11:1-4 et 20-26," *ÉTR* 62/3 (1987): 335-42.

3400 Michal Wojciechowski, "Marc 11.14 et Targum Gen. 3.22: les fruits de la loi enlevés à Israël," *NTS* 33/2 (1987): 287-89.

3401 Bettina von Kienle, "Mk 11:12-14.20-25: der verdorrte Feigenbaum," *BibN* 57 (1991): 17-25.

<u>form criticism</u>

3402 V. E. Gideon, "Mark's Gospel in Source and Form Criticism," *SouJT* 1 (1958): 63-73.

3403 Zane C. Hodges, "Form Criticism and the Resurrection Accounts," *BSac* 124 (1967): 339-48.

3404 Josef Kürzinger, "Formgeschichte im 1. Jahrhundert. Das Papiaszeugnis in neuer Interpretation," *TGeg* 10 (1967): 157-64.

3405 Robert L. Mowery, "The Jewish Religious Leaders in the Gospel of Mark: A Study in *Formgeschichte*," doctoral dissertation, Northwestern University, Evanston IL, 1967.

3406 A. T. Hanson, "The Great Form Critic," *SJT* 22/3 (1969): 296-304.

3407 J. C. Meagher, "Die Form- und Redaktionsungeschickliche Methoden: The Principle of Clumsiness and the Gospel of Mark," *JAAR* 43 (1975): 459-72.

3408 George B. Caird, "The Study of the Gospels. II. Form Criticism," *ET* 87/4 (1976): 137-41.

3409 Hans Dieter Betz, "The Early Christian Miracle Story: Some Observations on the Form Critical Problem," *Semeia* 11 (1978): 69-81.

3410 B. M. F. van Iersel and A. J. M. Linmans, "The Storm on the Lake, Mk iv,35-41 and Mt viii,18-27 in the Light of Form Criticism, '*Redaktionsgeschichte*' and Structural Analysis," in T. Baarda, A. F. J. Klihn, and W. C. van Unnik, eds., *Miscellanea Neotestamentica.* Novum Testamentum Supplement #48. Leiden: Brill, 1978. 2:17-48.

3411 J. C. Meagher, *Clumsy Construction in Mark's Gospel. A Critique of Form- and Redaktionsgeschichte*. Toronto Studies in Theology 3. New York/Toronto: Edwin Mellen Press, 1980.

3412 C. J. Maunder, "A *Sitz im Leben* for Mark 14:9," *ET* 99/3 (1987-1988): 78-80.

genre

3413 Gottfried Schille, "Bemerkungen zur Formgeschichte des Evangeliums. Rahmen und Aufbau des Markus-Evangeliums," *NTS* 4 (1957-1958): 1-24.

3414 R. J. Dillon, "Mark and the New Meaning of 'Gospel'," *DunR* 7 (1967): 131-61.

3415 David L. Barr, "Toward a Definition of the Gospel Genre: A Generic Analysis and Comparison or the Synoptic Gospels and the Socratic Dialogues by Means of Aristotle's Theory of Tragedy," doctoral dissertation, Florida State University, Tallahassee FL, 1974.

3416 Gerhard Dautzenberg, "Zur Stellung des Markusevangeliums in der Geschichte der urchristlichen Theologie," *K* 18 (1976): 282-91.

3417 Benoît Standaert, *L'évangile selon Marc. Composition et genre littéraire.* Zevenkerken/Brugge: Sint-Andriesabdij, 1978.

3418 John F. O'Grady, "The Origins of the Gospels: Mark," *BTB* 9 (1979): 154-64.

3419 Vernon K. Robbins, "Mark as Genre," *SBLSP* 19 (1980): 371-99.

3420 Robert A. Guelich, "The Gospel Genre," in Peter Stuhlmacher, ed., *Das Evangelium und die Evangelien.* Tübingen: Mohr, 1983. Pp. 183-219.

3421 Adela Y. Collins, *Is Mark's Gospel a Life of Jesus? The Question of Genre.* Milwaukee WI: Marquette University Press, 1989.

gentiles

3422 George H. Boobyer, "The Miracles of the Loaves and the Gentiles in St. Mark's Gospel," *SJT* 6 (1953): 77-87.

3423 George D. Kilpatrick, "The Gentile Missions in Mark and Mark 13:9-11," in D. E. Nineham, ed., *Studies in the Gospels* (festschrift for R. H. Lightfoot). Oxford: B. Blackwell, 1955. Pp. 145-58.

3424 Joseph Anthonysamy, "The Gentile Mission in the Gospel of Mark: A Redaction Critical Study of Passages with a Gentile Tendency," doctoral dissertation, Pontifical University, Rome, 1982.

Gerasene demoniac

3425 Harald Sahlin, "Die Perikope vom gerasenischen Besessenen und der Plan des Markusevangeliums," *StTheol* 18 (1964): 159-72.

3426 John Craghan, "The Gerasene Demoniac," *CBQ* 30/4 (1968): 522-36.

3427 John Bligh, "The Gerasene Demoniac and the Resurrection of Christ," *CBQ* 31 (1969): 383-90.

3428 M. de Mello, "The Gerasene Demoniac: The Power of Jesus Confronts the Power of Satan," *EcumRev* 23 (1971): 409-18.

3429 Rudolf Pesch, "The Markan Version of the Healing of the Gerasene Demoniac," *EcumRev* 23 (1971): 349-76.

3430 Franz J. Leenhardt, "Essai exégétique: Marc 5:1-20," in François Bovon, et al., eds., *Analyse structurale et exégèse biblique: Essais d'interprétation.* Neuchâtel: Delachaux et Niestlé, 1972. Pp. 95-121.

3431 Rudolf Pesch, *Der Besessene von Gerasa. Entstehung und Überlieferung einer Wundergeschichte.* Stuttgarter Bibelstudien 56. Stuttgart: Katholisches Bibelwerk, 1972.

3432 Jean Starobinski, "Le démoniaque de Gérasa: analyse littéraire de Marc 5:1-20," in François Bovon, et al., eds., *Analyse structurale et exégèse biblique: Essais d'interprétation.* Neuchâtel: Delachaux et Niestlé, 1972. Pp. 63-94.

3433 Miguel de Burgos Nuñez, "El poseso de Gerasa (Mc 5,1-20): Jesús portador de una existencia liberadora," *Communio* 6 (1973): 103-18.

3434 Franz Annen, *Heil für die Heiden: Zur Bedeutung und Geschichte der Tradition vom Besessenen Gerasener (Mk 5.1-20 parr.).* Frankfurter Theologische Studien 20. Frankfurt: Knecht, 1976.

3435 Helmut Harsch, "Psychologische Interpretation biblischer Texte. Ein Versuch zu Mk 5,1-20: Die Heilung des Besessenen von Gerasa," *UnSa* 32 (1977): 39-45.

3436 J. Duncan M. Derrett, "Contributions to the Study of the Gerasene Demoniac," *JSNT* 3 (1979): 2-17.

3437 A. J. R. Uleyn, "The Possessed Man of Gerasa: A Psychoanalytic Interpretation of Reader Reactions," in J. A. van Belzen and J. M. van der Lars, eds., *Current Issues in Psychology of Religion.* Amsterdam: Rodopi, 1986. Pp. 90-96.

3438 J. Duncan M. Derrett, "Legend and Event: The Gerasene Demoniac: An Inquest into History and Liturgical Projection," *StudB* 2 (1980): 63-73.

3439 Ken Frieden, "The Language of Demonic Possession: A Key-Word Analysis," in Robert Detweiler and W. G. Doty, eds., *The Daemonic Imagination: Biblical Text and Secular Story*. Atlanta: Scholars Press, 1990. Pp. 41-52.

3440 David Jasper, "Siding with the Swine: A Moral Problem for Narrative." in Robert Detweiler and W. G. Doty, eds., *The Daemonic Imagination: Biblical Text and Secular Story*. Atlanta: Scholars Press, 1990. Pp. 65-75.

3441 Carol S. LaHurd, "Reader Response to Ritual Elements in Mark 5:1-20," *BTB* 20 (1990): 154-60.

Gethsemane

3442 Jean Héring, "Zwei exegetische Problemein der Periope von Jesus in Gethsemane," in *Neotestamentica et Patristica* (festschrift for Oscar Cullmann). Novum Testamentum Supplement 6. Leiden: Brill, 1962. Pp. 64-69.

3443 Theodor Lescow, "Jesus in Gethsemane," *EvT* 26 (1966): 141-59.

3444 R. S. Barbour, "Gethsemane in the Tradition of the Passion," *NTS* 16 (1969-1970): 231-51.

3445 Werner H. Kelber, "Mark 14:32-42: Gethsemane. Passion Christology and Discipleship Failure," *ZNW* 63 (1972): 166-87.

3446 Werner Mohn, "Gethsemane (Mk 14:32-42)," *ZNW* 64/3 (1973): 195-208.

3447 Mark Riley, " 'Lord Save My Life' (Ps 116:4) as a Generative Text for Jesus' Gethsemane Prayer (Mark 14:36a)," *CBQ* 48/4 (1986): 655-59.

3448 Reinhard Feldmeier, "Die Krisis des Gottessohnes: die markinische Gethsemaneperikope als Markuspassion," *TLZ* 113 (1988): 234-36.

3449 Barbara Saunderson, "Gethsemane: The Missing Witness," *Bib* 70/2 (1989): 224-33.

grammatical studies

3450 Cecil S. Emden, "St. Mark's Use of the Imperfect Tense," *ET* (1953-1954): 146-49.

3451 J. C. Hindley, "Our Lord's Aramaic: A Speculation," *ET* 72 (1960-1961): 180-81.

3452 Robert E. Baker, "An Exegetical Inquiry into Mark's Use of the Imperfect Tense," doctoral dissertation, Southwestern Baptist Theological Seminary, Fort Worth TX, 1961.

3453 John C. Doudna, *The Greek of the Gospel of Mark*. JBLMS #12. Philadelphia: Society of Biblical Literature and Exegesis, 1961.

3454 George D. Kilpatrick, "The Order of Some Noun and Adjective Phrases in the New Testament," *NovT* 5 (1962): 111-14.

3455 George D. Kilpatrick, "Ἰδού and ἴδε in the Gospels," *JTS* 18 (1967): 425-26.

3456 Stephen M. Reynolds, "The Zero Tense in Greek: A Critical Note," *WTJ* 32 (1969): 68-72.

3457 Takumitsu Muraoka, "On the Syriac Particle *it*," *BibOr* 34 (1977): 21-22.

3458 Carroll D. Osburn, "The Historical Present in Mark as a Text-Critical Criterion," *Bib* 64 (1983): 486-500.

3459 Hans P. Rüger, "Die lexikalischen Aramaismen im Markusevangelium," in Hubert Cancik, ed., *Markus-Philologie: Historische, literergeschichtliche und stilistische Untersuchungen zum zweiten Evangelium*. Tübingen: Mohr, 1984. Pp. 73-84.

3460 Elliott C. Maloney, "The Historical Present in the Gospel of Mark," in M. P. Horgan and P. J. Kobelski, eds., *To Touch the Text* (festschrift for Joseph A. Fitzmyer). New York: Crossraod, 1989. Pp. 67-78.

3461 H. Harwood Hess, "Dynamics of the Greek Noun Phrase in Mark," *OPTAT* 4/4 (1990): 353-70.

3462 George D. Kilpatrick, "The Possessive Pronouns in the New Testament," in *The Principles and Practice on New Testament Textual Criticism.* BETL #96. Louvain: Peeters Press, 1990. Pp. 161-62.

Herodians

3463 W. A. A. Wilson, "Who Married Herodias? (And Other Questions from the Gospel of Mark)," *BT* 21/3 (1970): 138-40.

3464 W. J. Bennett, "The Herodians of Mark's Gospel," *NovT* 17/1 (1975): 9-14.

history of interpretation

3465 Johan A. Allan, "The Gospel of the Son of God: Recent Study in the Gospel according to Mark," *Int* 9 (1955): 131-43.

3466 R. S. Barbour, "Recent Study of the Gospel According to St. Mark," *ET* 79 (1968-1969): 324-29.

3467 Bruno Corsani, "Vangelo secondo Marco: Recenti studi sulla interpretazione e esegesi," *Protest* 25 (1970): 136-54.

3468 N. Thien An Vo, "Interpretation of Mark's Gospel in the Last Two Decades," *SBT* 2 (1972): 37-62.

3469 J. Garcia Burillo, "El ciento por uno (Mc 10,29-30 par). Historia de las interpretaciones y exégesis," *EB* 36 (1977): 173-203; 37 (1978): 29-55.

3470 Howard Clark Kee, "Mark's Gospel in Recent Research," *Int* 32/4 (1978): 353-68.

3471 William L. Lane, "From Historian to Theologian: Milestones in Markan Scholarship," *RevExp* 75 (1978): 601-17.

3472 Jack D. Kingsbury, "The Gospel of Mark in Current Research," *RSR* 5 (1979): 101-107.

3473 Seán P. Kealy, *Mark's Gospel: A History of Its Interpretation from the Beginning until 1979*. New York: Paulist Press, 1982.

3474 Elizabeth Struthers Malbon, "Galilee and Jerusalem: History and Literature in Marcan Interpretation," *CBQ* 44 (1982): 242-55.

historical criticism

3475 Janusz Czerski, "Die Passion Christi in den synoptischen Evangelien im Lichte der historisch-literarischen Kritik," *CollT* 46 (1976): 81-96.

3476 Detlev Dormeyer, *Der Sinn des Leidens Jesu. Historisch-kritische und textpragmatische Analysen zur Markuspassion*. Stuttgarter Bibelstudien 96. Stuttgart: Katholisches Bibelwerk, 1979.

historical Jesus

3477 Peter Biehl, "Zur Frage nach dem historischen Jesus," *TR* 24 (1956-1957): 54-76.

3478 Günther Bornkamm, *Jesus of Nazareth*. I. McLuskey, et. al., trans. London: Hodder & Stoughton, 1960.

3479 Norbert Brox, "Das messianische Selbslverständnis des historischen Jesus," in Kurt Schubert, ed., *Vom Messias zum Christus: Die Fülle der Zeit in religionsgeschichtlicher und theologischer Sicht*. Freiburg: Herder, 1964. Pp. 165-201.

3480 Günther Bornkamm, "Jesus of Nazareth," in Harvey K. McArthur, ed., *In Search of the Historical Jesus*. New York: Scribner, 1969. Pp. 164-73.

history in Mark's gospel

3481 James M. Robinson, *The Problem of History in Mark*. Studies in Biblical Theology 21. London: SCM, 1957.

3482 James M. Robinson, "The Problem of History in Mark, Reconsidered," *USQR* 20 (1965): 131-47.

3483 Jürgen Roloff, "Das Markusevangelium als Geschichtsdarstellung," *EvT* 29 (1969): 73-93.

holy spirit

3484 Lucien Cerfaux, " 'L'aveuglement d'esprit' dans l'évangile de saint Marc," in *Mélanges L. Th. Lefort*. Louvain: Peeters Press, 1946. Pp. 267-79.

3485 I. W. Batdorf, "The Spirit of God in the Synoptic Gospels: An Historical Comparison and Re-Appraisal," doctoral dissertation, Princeton Theological Seminary, Princeton NJ, 1955.

3486 Eugen Ruckstuhl, "Jesus als Gottessohn im Spiegel des markinischen Taufberichts [Mk 1:9-11]," in Ulrich Luz and Hans Weder, eds., *Die Mitte des Neuen Testaments: Einheit and vielfalt neutestamentlicher theologie* (festschrift for Eduard Schweizer). Göttingen: Vandenhoeck & Ruprecht, 1983. Pp. 193-220.

3487 Robert L. Mowery, "The Articular References to the Holy Spirit in the Synoptic Gospels and Acts," *BR* 31 (1986): 26-45.

3488 S. Motyer, "The Rending of the Veil: A Markan Pentecost?" *NTS* 33/1 (1987): 155-57.

3489 E. A. Obeng, "Abba, Father: The Prayer of the Sons of God," *ET* 99 (1987-1988): 363-66.

3490 B. M. F. van Iersel, "He Will Baptize You with the Holy Spirit (Mark 1,8)," in Tjitze Baarda, ed., *Text and Testimony: Essays on New Testament and Apocryphal Literature* (festschrift for A. F. J. Klijn). Kampen: Kok, 1988. Pp. 132-41.

interpretation

3491 H. G. Leder, "Sundenfallerzahlung und Versuchungsgeschichte. Zur Interpretation von Mc 1,12f.," *ZNW* 54 (1963): 188-216.

3492 Edward C. Hobbs, "Norman Perrin on Methodology in the Interpretation of Mark," in Hans Dieter Betz, ed., *Christology and a Modern Pilgrimage: A Discussion with Norman Perrin*. Claremont CA: New Testament Colloquium, 1971. Pp. 79-91.

3493 Norman Perrin, "Towards an Interpretation of the Gospel of Mark," in Hans Dieter Betz, ed., *Christology and a Modern Pilgrimage: A Discussion with Norman Perrin*. Claremont CA: New Testament Colloquium, 1971. Pp. 1-78.

3494 N. Thien An Vo, "Interpretation of Mark's Gospel in the Last Two Decades," *SBT* 2 (1972): 37-62.

3495 Norman Perrin, "The Interpretation of the Gospel of Mark," *Int* 30 (1976): 115-24.

3496 Andreas Lindemann, "Die Osterbotschaf, des Markus. Zur Theologischen Interpretation von Mark 16.1-8," *NTS* 26/3 (1979-1980): 298-17.

3497 Helmut Koester, "Using Quintilian to Interpret Mark," *BAR* 6/3 (1980): 44-45.

3498 David Jasper, "St. Mark's Gospel and the Interpretive Community," *RIL* 6 (1989): 173-81.

introduction

3499 A. E. Breen, *A Harmonized Exposition of the Four Gospels*. 4 vols. Rochester NY: Smith, 1908.

3500 C. J. Callan, *The Four Gospels*. New York: Wagner, 1917.

3501 B. W. Bacon, *Is Mark a Roman Gospel?* New York: Kraus, 1969. First published in 1919.

3502 P.-L. Couchoud, "Notes de Critique verbale sur St. Marc et St. Matthieu," *JTS* 34 (1933): 113-38.

3503 J. Chapman, *Matthew, Mark and Luke*. London: Longmans & Green, 1937.

3504 Walter E. Bundy, "Dogma and Drama in the Gospel of Mark," in Edwin P. Booth, ed., *New Testament Studies: Critical Essays in New Testament Interpretation with Special Reference to the Meaning and Worth of Jesus*. New York: Abingdon, 1942. Pp. 70-94.

3505 M. W. Jones, "The Function of the Gospel of Mark," doctoral dissertation, University of Chicago, Chicago IL, 1945.

3506 H. H. Lightenstern, "Markus und sein Evangelium," *BL* 17 (1950-1951): 267-71.

3507 Eric F. F. Bishop, "Some Notes on the Version of St. Mark in the Spoken Language of Palestine," *BT* 2 (1951): 124-28.

3508 Austin M. Farrer, *A Study in St. Mark.* Westminster: Dacre, 1951.

3509 Léon Vaganay, "L'absence du Sermon sur la montagne chez Marc," *RB* 58 (1951): 5-46.

3510 Philip Carrington, *The Primitive Christian Calendar: A Study in the Making of the Markan Gospel.* Cambridge: Cambridge University Press, 1952.

3511 Robert P. Casey, "St. Mark's Gospel," *Theology* 55 (1952): 362-70.

3512 Anton Fridrichsen, *Markusevangeliet.* Stockholm: Diakonistyrelse, 1952.

3513 J.-G. Gourbillon, "L'Évangile selon saint Marc, ou la bonne nouvelle annoncée par saint Pierre aux Romains," *ÉCB* 6 (1952): 23-36.

3514 Esko Haapa, *Markuksen evankeliumi.* Helsinki: Joensuu, 1952.

3515 Thomas Henshaw, "The Gospel according to Mark," in *New Testament Literature in the Light of Modern Scholarship.* London: Allen & Unwin, 1952. Pp. 92-110.

3516 Vincent Taylor, "Mark's Use of Gospel Tradition," *NTS* 3 (1952): 29-39.

3517 George H. Boobyer, "Galilee and Galileans in St. Mark's Gospel," *BJRL* 35 (1952-1953): 334-48.

3518 Cecil S. Emden, "The Gospel of Mark Made More Vivid," *ET* 64 (1952-1953): 334-36.

3519 Philip Carrington, "St. Mark and His Calendar," *CQR* 154 (1953): 211-18.

3520 C. H. Dodd, "The Framework of the Gospel Narrative," [1932] *New Testament Studies*. Manchester: University Press, 1953. Pp. 1-11.

3521 F. C. Grant, *The Earliest Gospel: Studies of the Evangelic Tradition at Its Point of Crystallization in Writing*. Nashville: Abingdon, 1953.

3522 A. J. van der Voort, "The Origin of St Mark's Gospel: A New Theory," *Scr* 6 (1953-1954): 100-107.

3523 William H. Crouch, "Jesus and the Teaching of the Elders in the Synoptic Gospels," master's thesis, Southern Baptist Theological Seminary, Louisville KY, 1954.

3524 Harold A. Guy, *The Origin of the Gospel of Mark*. New York: Harper Brothers, 1954.

3525 Kenneth L. Carroll, "The Creation of the Fourfold Gospel," *BJRL* 37 (1954-1955): 58-77.

3526 Robert E. Burks, "Some Primitive Elements in the Gospels—Chronology and Folklore," master's thesis, Southern Baptist Theological Seminary, Louisville KY, 1955.

3527 Samuel A. Cartledge, "The Gospel of Mark," *Int* 9 (1955): 186-99.

3528 Philip Carrington, "The Calendrical Hypothesis of the Origin of Mark," *ET* 67 (1955-1956): 100-103.

3529 William D. Davies, "Reflections on Archbishop Carrington's 'The Primitive Christian Calendar'," in W. D. Davies and D. Daube, eds., *The Background of the New Testament and Its Eschatology, in Honour of Charles Harold Dodd*. Cambridge: University Press, 1956. Pp. 124-52.

3530 C. E. Faw, "The Heart of the Gospel of Mark," *JBR* 24 (1956): 77-82.

3531 H. S. John, *An Analysis of the Gospel of Mark*. London: Pickering and Inglis, 1956.

3532 H. A. Rigg, "Papias on Mark," *NovT* 1 (1956): 161-83.

3533 James M. Robinson, "Mark's Understanding of History," *SJT* 9 (1956): 393-409.

3534 Norman K. Bakken, "Avenues of Thought in Mark's Gospel," *LQ* 9 (1957): 222-33.

3535 Curtis Beach, "Form, Structure, and Purpose in the Gospel of Mark," doctoral dissertation, University of Southern California, Los Angeles CA, 1957.

3536 Nils A. Dahl, "Markusevangeliets sikte," *SEÅ* 22/23 (1957): 32-46.

3537 C. E. Faw, "The Outline of Mark," *JBR* 25 (1957): 19-23.

3538 Gottfried Schille, "Die Topographie des Markusevangeliums, ihre Hintergrunde und ihre Einordnung," *ZDPV* 73 (1957): 133-66.

3539 Vincent Taylor, *The Formation of the Gospel Tradition*. 4th ed. London: Macmillan, 1957.

3540 Robert G. Bratcher, "Introduction to the Gospel of Mark," *RevExp* 55 (1958): 351-66.

3541 R. C. Briggs, "Exposition of the Gospel of Mark," *RevExp* 55 (1958): 367-92.

3542 George D. Kilpatrick, *Mark: A Greek-English Diglot for the Use of Translators*. London: British and Foreign Bible Society, 1958.

3543 Alfred Kuby, "Zur Konzeption des Markus-Evangeliums," *ZNW* 49 (1958): 52-64.

3544 A. T. Robertson, *Studies in Mark's Gospel.* Rev. and ed. H. F. Peacock. Nashville: Broadman Presss, 1958.

3545 Paul Althaus, *The So-Called Kerygma and the Historical Jesus*. Edinburgh: Oliver and Boyd, 1959.

3546 Gilbert G. Bilezikian, "The Gospel of Mark and Greek Tragedy," *GR* 5 (1959): 79-86.

3547 J. P. Brown, "An Early Revision of the Gospel of Mark," *JBL* 78 (1959): 215-27.

3548 S. G. F. Brandon, "The Date of the Markan Gospel," *NTS* 7 (1960-1961): 126-41.

3549 J. C. Hindley, "Our Lord's Aramaic: A Speculation," *ET* 72 (1960-1961): 180-81.

3550 Robert G. Bratcher and Eugene A. Nida, *A Translator's Handbook on the Gospel of Mark.* Help for Translators #2. Leiden: Brill (for the UBS), 1961.

3551 Josef Blinzler, "Markus, Evangelist," *LTK* 7 (1962): 12-13.

3552 C. H. Dodd, *The Apostolic Preaching and Its Developments: Three Lectures, with an Appendix on Eschatology and History.* [1936] 9th ed. New York: Harper, 1962.

3553 Patrick Fannon, "The Four Gospels: I. St. Mark's Message," *ClerR* 47 (1962): 404-14.

3554 W. J. Harrington, *The Gospel According to St. Mark.* Doctrine and Life Series. Dublin: Dominican Publications, 1962.

3555 William Barclay, *Many Witnesses, One Lord.* London: SCM, 1963.

3556 T. A. Burkill, "St. Mark's Preface," in *Mysterious Revelation: An Examination of the Philosophy of St. Mark's Gospel.* Ithaca NY: Cornell University Press, 1963. Pp. 9-23.

3557 T. A. Burkill, ''Introduction,'' in *Mysterious Revelation: An Examination of the Philosophy of St. Mark's Gospel*. Ithaca NY: Cornell University Press, 1963. Pp. 1-6.

3558 W. C. van Unnik, ''Zur Papias-Notiz über Markus (Eusebius *H. E.* III 39,15,'' *ZNW* 54 (1963): 276-77.

3559 José Alonso Díaz, ''Evangelio de San Marcos,'' in *La Sagrada Escritura: Texto y comentario por profesores de la Compañía de Jesús. Nuevo Testamento*. 1. *Evangelios*. 2nd ed. Madrid: Católica, 1964. Pp. 317-487.

3560 L. W. Barnard, ''St. Mark and Alexandria,'' *HTR* 57 (1964): 145-50.

3561 K. L. Brooks, *Mark: The Gospel of God's Servant*. Chicago: Moody, 1964.

3562 W. H. Harter, ''The Historical Method of Mark,'' *USQR* 20 (1964): 21-38.

3563 Arnold Schabert, *Das Markus-Evangelium: Eine Auslegung für die Gemeinde*. Münich: Claudius, 1964.

3564 A. J. Stackpole, ''A Note on the Dating of St. Mark's Gospel,'' *Scr* 16 (1964): 106-10.

3565 K. Bäschlin, *Aus dem Markusevangelium*. Bern: Troxler, 1965.

3566 Edward M. Blaiklock, *The Young Man Mark: Studies in Some Aspects of Mark and His Gospel*. Exeter: Paternoster, 1965.

3567 James W. Leitch, *The King Comes: An Exposition of Mark 1-7*. London: SCM, 1965.

3568 Robert G. Newman, ''Tradition and Interpretation in Mark,'' doctoral dissertation, Drew University, Madison NJ, 1965.

3569 Ignace de la Potterie, ''De compositione evangelii Marci,'' *VD* 44 (1966): 135-41.

3570 J. Dooley, *Gospel of Mark*. London: Stockwell, 1966.

3571 Patrick Fannon, *The Four Gospels: A Short Introduction to Their Making and Message*. Notre Dame IN: Fides, 1966.

3572 François Halkin, ''Une notice de l'évangéliste Marc,'' *AnBoll* 84 (1966): 127-28.

3573 Clive F. Jacks, ''The Epiphany Narratives in Mark and Matthew: A Study in Cultic and Literary Tradition,'' doctoral dissertation, Union Theological Seminary, New York, 1966.

3574 A. J. Jewell, ''Did St. Mark 'Remember'?'' *LQHR* 35 (1966): 117-20.

3575 O. M. Rao, ''The Problem of History in St. Mark's Gospel,'' *IJT* 15 (1966): 60-66.

3576 Béda Rigaux, *The Testimony of St. Mark*. Malachy Carroll, trans. Herald Scriptural Library. Chicago: Franciscan Herald Press, 1966.

3577 Kenzo Tagawa, *Miracles et Évangile. La pensée personnel le de l'évangéliste Marc*. Études d'histoire et de philosophie religieuses 62. Paris: Presses universitaires de France, 1966.

3578 François Halkin, ''Actes inédits de Saint Marc,'' *AnBoll* 87 (1969): 343-71.

3579 William Barclay, *The First Three Gospels*. London: SCM, 1967.

3580 Edward M. Blaiklock, *Mark: The Man and His Message*. Chicago: Moody, 1967.

3581 Roy A. Harrisville, *The Miracle of Mark: A Study in the Gospel*. Minneapolis: Augsburg, 1967.

3582 Jean G. H. Hoffmann, ''Saint Marc ou l'Évangile de Jesus, le Fils de Dieu: Résumé de l'Introduction à l'Évangile de Marc de Rudolf Grob,'' *RevRef* 18 (1967): 1-64.

3583 George G. Parker, "The Argument of the Gospel of Mark," doctoral dissertation, Dallas Theological Seminary, Dallas TX, 1967.

3584 Siegfried Vierzig, *Das Markus-Evangelium im Unterricht: Einführung in das historisch-kritische Bibelverständnis*. Kassel: Evangelischer Presseverband Kurhessen-Waldeck, 1967.

3585 Olof Linton, "Evidences of a Second-Century Revised Edition of St. Mark's Gospel," *NTS* 14 (1967-1968): 321-55.

3586 Christopher F. Evans, *The Beginning of the Gospel. Four Lectures on St. Mark's Gospel*. London: SPCK, 1968.

3587 Helmut Flender, "Das Verständnis der Welt bei Paulus, Markus und Lukas," *KD* 14 (1968): 1-27.

3588 A. A. K. Graham, "Mark and Hebrews," *StudE* 4 (1968): 411-16.

3589 Ernst Haenchen, "Historie und Verkündigung bei Markus und Lukas," in E. Haenchen, ed., *Die Bibel und Wir. Gesammelte Aufsätze. Zweiter Band*. Tübingen: Mohr, 1968. Pp. 156-81.

3590 H.-D. Knigge, "The Meaning of Mark. The Exegesis of the Second Gospel," *Int* 22 (1968): 53-70.

3591 Charles Masson, *L'Évangile de Marc et l'Église de Rome*. Bibliothèque Théologique. Neuchâtel/Paris: Delachaux & Niestlé, 1968.

3592 Theodore J. Weeden, "The Heresy that Necessitated Mark's Gospel," *ZNW* 59 (1968): 145-58.

3593 Ralph P. Martin, "A Gospel in Search of a Life-Setting," *ET* 80 (1968-1969): 361-64.

3594 Kurt Aland, "Bemerkungen zum Schluß des Markusevangeliums," in E. Earle Ellis and Max Wilcox, eds., *Neotestamentica et Semitica: Studies in Honour of*

Matthew Black. Edinburgh: T. & T. Clark, 1969. Pp. 157-80.

3595 H. A. Blair, "Fact and Gospel," in Elizabeth A. Livingstone, ed., *StudE* 5 (1969): 14-19.

3596 M. Eugene Boring, "Christian Prophets and the Gospel of Mark," doctoral dissertation, Vanderbilt University, Nashville TN, 1969.

3597 D. B. J. Campbell, *The Synoptic Gospels*. New York: Seabury, 1969.

3598 William L. Lane, "Mark—A New Literary Form," in G. W. Barker, et al., *The New Testament Speaks*. New York: Harper & Row, 1969. Pp. 248-59.

3599 Robert L. Lindsey, *A Hebrew Translation of the Gospel of Mark: Greek-Hebrew Diglot with English Introduction*. Jerusalem: Dugith, 1969.

3600 Eta Linnemann, "Der (wiedergefundene) Markusschluß," *ZTK* 66 (1969): 255-87.

3601 Jan M. Lockman, "Gospel for Atheists," *TT* 26/3 (1969): 299-311.

3602 Henry E. Turlington, "Mark," in C. J. Allen, et al., eds., *The Broadman Bible Commentary: General Articles. Matthew-Mark*. Nashville: Broadman, 1969. 8:254-402.

3603 Pierson Parker, "Mark, Acts and Galilean Christianity," *NTS* 16 (1969-1970): 295-304.

3604 G. Dambricourt, *L'initiation chrétienne selon saint Marc*. Paris: Apostolat des Éditions, 1970.

3605 Børge K. Diderichsen, *Markusevangeliet: De aeldste kendte fortaellinger om Jesus fra Nazaret*. København: Gyldendal, 1970.

3606 David L. Dungan, "Mark: The Abridgement of Matthew and Luke," in D. G. Buttrick, ed., *Jesus and Man's Hope*.

Pittsburgh: Pittsburgh Theological Seminary, 1970. Pp. 51-97.

3607 Richard A. Edwards, "A New Approach to the Gospel of Mark," *LQ* 22/3 (1970): 330-35.

3608 Karl Gutbrod, *Wir lesen das Evangelium nach Markus: Einblicke in Gestalt, Aufbau und Zielsetzung*. Stuttgart: Calwer, 1970.

3609 M. H. Marco, "El Jordán y el mar de Galilea en el marco geográfico de los Evangelios," *EB* 29 (1970): 327-52.

3610 Harald Riesenfeld, "On the Composition of the Gospel of Mark," in *The Gospel Tradition: Essays*. E. M. Rowley and R. A. Kraft, trans. Philadelphia: Fortress Press, 1970. Pp. 51-74.

3611 H. C. Snape, "Christian Origins in Rome with Special Reference to Mark's Gospel," *MC* 13 (1970): 230-44.

3612 R. S. Barbour, "Uncomfortable Words: VIII. Status and Titles," *ET* 82/5 (1970-1971): 137-42.

3613 David Blatherwick, "The Markan Silhouette?" *NTS* 17 (1970-1971): 184-92.

3614 H.-W. Bartsch, "Der Schluß der Markus-Evangeliums. Ein überlieferungsgeschichtliches Problem," *TZ* 27 (1971): 241-54.

3615 Martin Dibelius, *From Tradition to Gospel*. B. L. Woolf, trans. Greenwood SC: Attic Press, 1971.

3616 Richard Kugelman, "With Today's Biblical Books, with Today's Mark and John," *BTB* 9 (1971): 316-21.

3617 Heinz-Wolfgang Kuhn, *Ältere Sammlungen im Markusevangelium*. Studien zur Umwelt des Neuen Testaments 8. Göttingen: Vandenhoeck & Ruprecht, 1971.

3618 L. F. Rivera, "¿Escribió Marcos para nuestro tiempo?" *RevB* 33 (1971): 195-224.

3619 Theodore J. Weeden, *Mark—Traditions in Conflict*. Philadelphia: Fortress, 1971.

3620 T. A. Burkill, *New Light on the Earliest Gospel: Seven Markan Studies*. Ithaca NY: Cornell University Press, 1972.

3621 T. A. Burkill, ''Theological Antinomies: Ben Sira and St. Mark,'' in T. A. Burkill, ed., *New Light on the Earliest Gospel: Seven Markan Studies*. Ithaca NY: Cornell University Press, 1972. Pp. 121-79.

3622 Jean Delorme, *Lecture de l'Évangile selon saint Marc*. Paris: Cerf, 1972.

3623 I. L. Jensen, *Mark: A Self-Study Guide*. Chicago: Moody, 1972.

3624 Karl-Georg Reploh, ''Das unbekannte Evangelium. Das Markus-Evangelium in der Theologiegeschichte,'' *BK* 27 (1972): 108-10.

3625 Georg Strecker, ''Literarkirtische Überlegungen zum εὐαγγέλιον-Begriff im Markusevangelium,'' in Heinrich Baltensweiler and Bo Reicke, eds., *Neues Testament und Geschichte: Historisches Geschehen und Deutung im Neuen Testament* (festschrift for Oscar Cullmann). Zürich: Theologischer Verlag/Tübingen: Mohr, 1972. Pp. 91-104.

3626 Henry Hogarth, ''A New Look at Mark's Gospel,'' *ET* 84 (1972-1973): 88-90.

3627 J. Blanchard, *Read, Mark, Learn: 45 Studies in the Gospel of Mark*. Wheaton IL: Tyndale, 1973.

3628 David R. Cartlidge and David L. Dungan, *Sourcebook of Texts for the Comparative Study of the Gospels: Literature of the Hellenistic and Roman Period Illuminating the Milieu and Character of the Gospels*. 3rd ed. Missoula MT: Society of Biblical Literature, 1973.

3629 Bruno de Solages, *Comment sont nés les évangiles: Marc-Luc-Matthieu*. Toulouse: Privat, 1973.

3630 E. P. Groenewald, *Die Evangelie van Markus*. Cape Town: N.G. Kerk-Uitgewers, 1973.

3631 John J. McHugh, "The Origins and Growth of the Gospel Traditions," *ClerR* 58 (1973): 2-9, 83-95, 162-75.

3632 Ralph P. Martin, *Mark: Evangelist and Theologian*. Grand Rapids: Zondervan Publishing House, 1973.

3633 Rudolf Schnackenburg, " 'Das Evangelium' im Verständnis des ältesten Evangelisten," in Paul Hoffmann, ed., *Orientierung an Jesus: Zur Theologie der Synoptiker: Für Josef Schmid*, in collaboration with Norbert Brox and Wilhelm Pesch. Freiburg/Basel/Vienna: Herder, 1973. Pp. 309-24.

3634 Morton Smith, *Clement of Alexandria and a Secret Gospel of Mark*. Cambridge MA: Harvard University Press, 1973.

3635 Morton Smith, *The Secret Gospel. The Discovery and Interpretation of the Secret Gospel According to Mark*. New York: Harper & Row, 1973.

3636 Rámon Trevijano Etcheverría, "El plan del Evangelio de San Marcos," *Bur* 14 (1973): 9-40.

3637 F. F. Bruce, *The "Secret" Gospel of Mark*. London: Athlone, 1974.

3638 Jean Delorme, "L'évangile selon Marc," in Jean Delorme, ed., *Le ministère et les ministères selon le Nouveau Testament: Dossier exégétique et réflexion théologique*. Parole de Dieu 10. Paris: Éditions du Seuil, 1974. Pp. 155-81.

3639 Kenneth R. R. Gros-Louis, "The Gospel of Mark," in J. S. Ackerman and T. S. Warshaw, eds., *Literary Interpretations of Biblical Narratives*. Nashville TN: Abingdon. 1974. Pp. 296-329.

3640 Eugene E. Lemcio, "Some New Proposals for Interpreting the Gospel according to Mark," doctoral dissertation, Cambridge University, Cambridge, 1974.

3641 Dale Miller, *The Adult Son: A Study of the Gospel of Mark*. Des Moines IA: Miller Books, 1974.

3642 André Paul, ''Le récit (biblique) comme surface. Éléments théoriques pour une sémantique narrative,'' *RSPT* 58 (1974): 584-98.

3643 Étienne Trocmé, ''Trois critiques au miroir de l'Évangile selon Marc,'' *RHPR* 55 (1974): 289-95.

3644 William Barclay, *Introduction to the First Three Gospels*. Philadelphia: Westminster, 1975.

3645 Francisco de la Calle, *Situación al servicio del Keri (Cuadro geográfico del Evangelio de Marcos)*. Colección de Estudios del Instituto Superior de Pastoral 9. Salamanca/Madrid: Instituto Superior de Pastoral de la Universidad Pontificia de Salamanca, 1975.

3646 W. J. Harrington, ''The Gospel of Mark: A Tract for Our Times,'' *DocLife* 25 (1975): 482-99.

3647 E. R. Kalin, ''Early Traditions about Mark's Gospel: Canonical Status Emerges, the Story Grows,'' *CThM* 2 (1975): 332-41.

3648 Theresa Moser, ''Mark's Gospel: A Drama?'' *BibTo* 80 (1975): 528-33.

3649 Leonard Ramaroson, ''Le plan du second Evangile,'' *ScE* 27 (1975): 219-33.

3650 Louis Soubigou, ''O Plano do Evangelho segundo Sao Marcos,'' *RCB* 12 (1975): 84-96.

3651 Étienne Trocmé, *The Formation of the Gospel according to Mark*. Pamela Gaughan, trans. Philadelphia: Westminster, 1975.

3652 C. Leslie Mitton, ''Some Further Studies in St. Mark's Gospel,'' *ET* 87 (1975-1976): 297-301.

3653 Michel Bouttier, ''Commencement, force et fin de l'evangile,'' *ÉTR* 51 (1976): 465-93.

3654 I. F. Church, *A Study of the Marcan Gospel*. New York: Vantage Press, 1976.

3655 Wilhelm Egger, *Frohbotschaft und Lehre: Die Sammelberichte des Wirkens Jesu im Markusevangelium*. Frankfurter Theologische Studien 19. Frankfurt: Knecht, 1976.

3656 H. H. Graham, "The Gospel According to St. Mark: Mystery and Ambiguity," *ATR* Supplement 7 (1976): 43-55.

3657 T. Y. Mullins, "Papias and Clement and Mark's Two Gospels," *VC* 30 (1976): 189-92.

3658 Norman Perrin, "Mark," in *The Interpreter's Dictionary of the Bible Supplementary Volume*. Nashville: Abingdon Press, 1976. Pp. 571-73.

3659 Rámon Trevijano Etcheverría, "Lecturas materialistas del Evangelio de San Marcos," *Bur* 17 (1976): 477-503.

3660 Gilbert G. Bilezikian, *The Liberated Gospel: A Comparison of the Gospel of Mark and Greek Tragedy*. Grand Rapids: Baker Book House, 1977.

3661 M. Eugene Boring, "The Paucity of Sayings in Mark: A Hypothesis," *SBLSP* 7 (1977): 371-77.

3662 E. F. Glusman, "The Shape of Mark and John: A Primitive Gospel Outline," doctoral dissertation, Duke University, Durham NC, 1977.

3663 Ben Hemelsoet, *Marcus*. Kampen: Kok, 1977.

3664 Herman Hendrickx, "Theological and Pastoral Perspectives: Mark," in *The Passion Narratives of the Synoptic Gospels*. Manila: East Asian Pastoral Institute, 1977. Pp. 138-41.

3665 Howard Clark Kee, *Community of the New Age: Studies in Mark's Gospel*. London: SCM, 1977.

3666 Josef Kürzinger, "Die Aussage des Papias von Hierapolis zur literarischen Form des Markusevangeliums," *BZ* 21 (1977): 245-64.

3667 Elizabeth Struthers Malbon, "Elements of an Exegesis of the Gospel of Mark according to Levi-Strauss' Methodology," *SBLSP* 7 (1977): 155-70.

3668 Morton R. Mulholland, "The Markan Opponents of Jesus," doctoral dissertation, Harvard University, Cambridge MA, 1977.

3669 Petr Pokorný, " 'Anfang des Evangeliums': Zum Problem des Anfangs und des Schlusses des Markusevangeliums," in Rudolf Schnackenburg, Josef Ernest, and Joachim Wanke, eds., *Die Kirche des Anfangs* (festschrift for Heinz Schürmann). Erfurter Theologische Studien #38. Leipzig: Freiburg: Herder, 1977. Pp. 115-32.

3670 Kenzo Tagawa, " 'Galilée et Jérusalem': l'attention portée par l'évangéliste Marc a l'histoire de son temps," *RHPR* 57 (1977): 439-70.

3671 A. J. R. Uleyn, "A Psychoanalytic Approach to Mark's Gospel," *LV* 32 (1977): 479-93.

3672 R. Alan Culpepper, "An Outline of the Gospel according to Mark," *RevExp* 75 (1978): 619-22.

3673 Wilhelm Egger, *Glaube und Nachfolge. Ein Arbeitsheft zum Markusevangelium*. Gespräche zur Bibel 5. Nosterneuburg: Österreichisches Katholisches Bibelwerk, 1978.

3674 Heinz Giesen, "Markus und seine Traditionen: Zu einem neuen Markuskommentar," *TGeg* 21 (1978): 179-83.

3675 E. F. Glusman, "Criteria for a Study of the Outlines of Mark and John," *SBLSP* 8/2 (1978): 239-50.

3676 G. L. Munn, "The Teaching Outline of the Gospel of Mark," *SouJT* 21 (1978): 71-73.

3677 Norman R. Petersen, " 'Point of View' in Mark's Narrative," *Semeia* 12 (1978): 97-121.

3678 Édouard Pousset, et al., *Une présentation de l'Évangile selon saint Marc*. Paris: Desclée, 1978.

3679 Antonio Rodríguez Carmona, "Visión panorámica de los estudios sobre el evangelio de Marcos," *CuBí* 35 (1978): 21-38.

3680 Ernest Best, "Mark: Some Problems," *IBS* 1 (1979): 77-98.

3681 Hermann Binder, "Von Markus zu den Grossevangelien," *TZ* 35 (1979): 283-89.

3682 Jean Delorme, "Rhétorique et sémiotique devant l'évangile de Marc," *SémBib* 16 (1979): 36-44.

3683 J. Hamilton, "The Divisions of the Gospel of Mark: A Redactional Examination of Its Structure," doctoral dissertation, Aberdeen, 1979.

3684 Frank Kermode, *The Genesis of Secrecy: On the Interpretation of Narrative*. Cambridge MA: Harvard University Press, 1979.

3685 Frans Neirynck, *L'Évangile de Marc. À propos du commentaire de R. Pesch.* Analecta Lovaniensia Biblica et Orientalia V,42. Louvain: Peeters Press, 1979.

3686 Vincent Parkin, *Reading St. Mark*. Belfast: Christian Journals, 1979.

3687 Donald P. Senior, "The Gospel of Mark," *BibTo* 103 (1979): 2096-104.

3688 Theodore J. Weeden, "Metaphysical Implications of Kelber's Approach to Orality and Textuality: A Response to Werner Kelber's 'Mark and the Oral Tradition'," *SBLSP* 9/2 (1979): 153-66.

3689 David R. Cartlidge and David L. Dungan, *Documents for the Study of the Gospels*. Cleveland OH: Collins, 1980.

3690 A. E. Harvey, "The Use of Mystery Language in the Bible," *JTS* 31/2 (1980): 320-36.

3691 B. Hurault, *Sinopsis Pastoral de Mateo-Marcos-Lucas-(Juan) con notas exegéticas y pastorales*. Madrid: Paulinas, 1980.

3692 Eric Johns and David Major, *Witness in a Pagan World: A Study of Mark's Gospel*. London: Lutterworth Press, 1980.

3693 Jan Lambrecht, "A Man to Follow: The Message of Mark," *RAfT* 4 (1980): 37-53.

3694 William L. Lane, "A Pamphlet for Hard Times: The Gospel of Mark," in William L. Lane, *Highlights of the Bible*. Ventura CA: Regal Books, 1980. Pp. 1-15.

3695 Albert C. Outler, "The Gospel According to St. Mark," *PJ* 33 (1980): 3-9.

3696 B. M. F. van Iersel, "The Gospel according to St. Mark—Written for a Persecuted Community?" *NedTT* 34 (1980): 15-36.

3697 Adrien Delclaux, "Deux témoignages de Papias sur la composition de Marc?" *NTS* 27 (1980-1981): 401-11.

3698 Joseph Auneau, "Évangile de Marc," in Joseph Auneau, et al., *Évangiles synoptiques et Actes des apôtres*. Paris: Desclée, 1981. Pp. 55-129.

3699 John N. Blackwell, "Myth, Meaning and Hermeneutic: The Method of Claude Lévi-Strauss Applied to Narrative in Mark," doctoral dissertation, Claremont School of Theology, Claremont CA, 1981.

3700 Hendrikus Boers, "The Unity of the Gospel of Mark," *ScrSA* 4 (1981): 1-7.

3701 Robert G. Bratcher, *A Translator's Guide to the Gospel of Mark*. New York: United Bible Societies, 1981.

3702 Hubert Cancik, "Die Gattung Evangelium: Das Evangelium des Markus im Rahmen der antiken Historiographie," in E. Olshausen, ed., *Das Christentum in der anhken Welt*. Humanistische Bildung #4. Stuttgart: Historisches Institut, 1981. Pp. 63-101.

3703 John F. O'Grady, *Mark: The Sorrowful Gospel. An Introduction to the Second Gospel*. New York: Ramsey, 1981.

3704 Brian G. Powley, "Revisiting Mark," *ScrB* 12 (1981): 40-45.

3705 Vernon K. Robbins, "Summons and Outline in Mark: The Three 25-Step Progression," *NovT* 23 (1981): 97-114.

3706 D. Moody Smith, "B. W. Bacon on John and Mark," *PRS* 8 (1981): 201-18.

3707 Ernest Best, "The Purpose of Mark," *PIBA* 6 (1982): 19-35.

3708 T. A. Burkill, "Mark's Gospel as Damnation History," *StudE* 7 (1982): 87-89.

3709 Jean Carmignac, ed., *Évangiles de Matthieu et de Marc traduits en hébreu en 1668 par Ciovanni Battista lona retouchés en 1805 par Thomas Yeates*. Turnhout: Brepols, 1982.

3710 John J. Gunther, "The Association of Mark and Barnabas with Egyptian Christianity," *EQ* 54 (1982): 219-33; 55 (1983): 21-29.

3711 Stephen J. Hartdegen, ed., *The Gospel of Mark: Pathway to Glory through the Cross*. Washington, DC: United States Catholic Conference, 1982.

3712 Seán P. Kealy, "Mark: Hope for Our Tragic Times," *BTB* 12 (1982): 128-30.

3713 Seán P. Kealy, "Reflections on the History of Mark's Gospel," *EGLMBS* 2 (1982): 46-62.

3714 Patrick R. Keifert, "Meaning and Reference: The Interpretation of Verisimilitude in 'The Gospel according to St. Mark'," doctoral dissertation, Divinity School, University of Chicago, Chicago IL, 1982.

3715 Dieter Lührmann, ''Zur Datierung des Markusevangeliums,'' in R. Wegner, ed., *Die Datierung der Evangelien*. Paderborn: Deutsches Institut für Bildung und Wissen, 1982. Pp. 314-20.

3716 Hugh McGinlay, ed., *The Year of Mark*. Northcote, Australia: Desbooks, 1982.

3717 Frank J. Matera, *The Kingship of Jesus: Composition and Theology in Mark 15*. Chico CA: Scholars Press, 1982.

3718 Klemens Stock, ''Theologie der Mission bei Markus,'' in Karl Kertelge, ed., *Mission im Neuen Testament*. Freiburg: Herder, 1982. Pp. 130-44.

3719 Raymond E. Brown, ''Possible Supplements to Our Knowledge of Early Roman Christianity: Mark,'' in Raymond E. Brown and John P. Meier, *Antioch & Rome: New Testament Cradles of Catholic Christianity*. London: Chapman, 1983. Pp. 191-201.

3720 Jean Carmignac, ''La datation des évangiles: État actuel de la recherche,'' *RevRef* 34 (1983): 111-21.

3721 Charles T. Davis, ''Mark: The Petrine Gospel,'' in William R. Farmer, ed., *New Synoptic Studies*. Macon GA: Mercer University Press, 1983. Pp. 441-66.

3722 John H. Elliott, ''The Roman Provenance of 1 Peter and the Gospel of Mark: A Response to David Dungan,'' in Bruce Corley, ed., *Colloquy on New Testament Studies*. Macon GA: Mercer University Press, 1983. Pp. 181-94.

3723 G. R. Evans, ''Crumbs, Gleanings and Fragments. An Exegetical Topos,'' *RTAM* 50 (1983): 242-45.

3724 Daniel J. Harrington, *The Gospel according to Mark: An Access Guide for Scripture Study*. New York: Sadlier, 1983.

3725 Thomas P. Haverly, ''Oral Traditional Literature and the Composition of Mark's Gospel,'' doctoral dissertation, Faculty of Divinity, University of Edinburgh, Edinburgh, 1983.

3726 Paul R. Hinlicky, ''The Gospel and the Knowledge of God: St. Mark's Theologia Crucis,'' doctoral dissertation, Union Theological Seminary, New York, 1983.

3727 Dietrich-Alex Koch, ''Inhaltliche Gliederung und geographischer Aufriss im Markusevangelium,'' *NTS* 29 (1983): 145-66.

3728 Helmut Koester, ''History and Development of Mark's Gospel: From Mark to Secret Mark and 'Canonical' Mark,'' in Bruce Corley, ed., *Colloquy on New Testament Studies*. Macon GA: Mercer University Press, 1983. Pp. 35-57.

3729 George Mangatt, ''The Gospel of Mark: An Exegetical Survey,'' *BB* 9 (1983): 229-40.

3730 Gregory Murray, ''Order in St. Mark's Gospel,'' *DR* 101 (1983): 182-86.

3731 Albert C. Outler, ''Canon Criticism and the Gospel of Mark,'' in William R. Farmer, ed., *New Synoptic Studies*. Macon GA: Mercer University Press, 1983. Pp. 233-43.

3732 Philippe Rolland, ''Marc, première harmonie évangélique?'' *RB* 90 (1983): 23-79.

3733 B. M. F. van Iersel, ''Locality, Structure, and Meaning in Mark,'' *LB* 53 (1983): 45-54.

3734 François Bassin, *L'Évangile de Marc*. Vaux-sur-Seine: Edifac, 1984.

3735 Cilliers Breytenbach, *Nachfolge und Zukunftserwartung nach Markus: Eine methodenkritische Studie*. ATANT #71. Zürich: Theologischer Verlag, 1984.

3736 F. F. Bruce, ''The Date and Character of Mark,'' in Ernst Bammel and C. F. D. Moule, eds., *Jesus and the Politics of His Day*. Cambridge: Cambridge University Press, 1984. Pp. 69-89.

3737 Hubert Cancik, ed., *Markus-Philologie: Historische, literargeschichtliche und stilistische Untersuchungen zum zweifen Evangelium*. WUNT #33. Tübingen: Mohr, 1984.

3738 David Cranmer, "Translating for Paragraph Cohesion," *BT* 35/4 (1984): 432-36.

3739 Stanislas Dockx, "Chronologie de la vie de Jésus," in *Chronologies néotestamentaires et vie de l'Église primitive: Recherches exégétiques*. 2nd ed. Louvain: Peeters Press, 1984. Pp. 3-29.

3740 Stanislas Dockx, "Essai de chronologie de la vie de Saint Marc," in *Chronologies néotestamentaires et vie de l'Église primitive: Recherches exégétiques*. 2nd ed. Louvain: Peeters Press, 1984. Pp. 179-98.

3741 Charles W. Hedrick, "The Role of 'Summary Statements' in the Composition of the Gospel of Mark: A Dialog with Karl Schmidt and Norman Perrin," *NovT* 26 (1984): 289-311.

3742 Howard Clark Kee, "The Social Setting of Mark: An Apocalyptic Community," *SBLSP* 23 (1984): 245-55.

3743 Gert Lüderitz, "Rhetorik, Poetik, Kompositionstechnik im Markusevanglium," in Hubert Cancik, ed., *Markus-Philologie: Historische, literergeschichtliche und stilistische Untersuchungen zum zweiten Evangelium*. Tübingen: Mohr, 1984. Pp. 165-203.

3744 Gregory Murray, "Mark the Conflator," *DR* 102 (1984): 157-62.

3745 S. Rabacchi, "Il vangelo secondo Marco," *SacD* 29 (1984): 482-502.

3746 Léopold Sabourin, "Is Mark the Earliest Gospel?" *RSB* 4 (1984): 61-72.

3747 Adolf Schlatter, *Markus: Der Evangelist für die Griechen*, ed. K. H. Rengstorf. 2nd ed. Stuttgart: Calwer, 1984.

3748 James L. Bailey, "Perspectives on the Gospel of Mark," *CThM* 12 (1985): 15-25.

3749 John G. Cook, "A Text Linguistic Approach to the Gospel of Mark," doctoral dissertation, Emory University, Atlanta, 1985.

3750 Joseph Dahmus, *The Puzzling Gospels: Suggested Explanations of Puzzling Passages in Matthew, Mark, Luke and John.* Chicago IL: Thomas More Press, 1985.

3751 Cornelis J. den Heyer, *Marcus I-II. Een praktische bijbelverklaring.* 2 vols. Kampen: Kok, 1985.

3752 J. Duncan M. Derrett, *The Making of Mark: The Scriptural Bases of the Earliest Gospel.* 2 vols. Shipston-on-Stour: Drinkwater, 1985.

3753 Robert M. Fowler, "The Rhetoric of Indirection in the Gospel of Mark," *EGLMBS* 5 (1985): 47-56.

3754 Martin Hengel, "The Gospel of Mark: Time of Origin and Situation," in *Studies in the Gospel of Mark.* J. Bowden, trans. Philadelphia: Fortress Press, 1985. Pp.1-30.

3755 Martin Hengel, "Literary, Theological and Historical Problems in the Gospel of Mark," in *Studies in the Gospel of Mark.* J. Bowden, trans. Philadelphia: Fortress Press, 1985. Pp. 31-58.

3756 Diarmuid McGann, *The Journeying Self: The Gospel of Mark through a Jungian Perspective.* New York: Paulist Press, 1985.

3757 Pierre Mourlon Beernaert, *Saint Marc.* Le temps de lire #2. Brussells: Lumen Vitae, 1985.

3758 Ivor Powell, *Mark's Superb Gospel.* Grand Rapids: Kregel, 1985.

3759 E. A. Russell, "The Gospel of Mark: Pastoral Response to a Life or Death Situation? Some Reflections," *IBS* 7 (1985): 206-23.

3760 Wolfgang Schenk, "Wird Markus auf der Couch materialistisch? Oder: Wie idealistisch ist die 'materialistische Exegese'?" *LB* 57 (1985): 95-106.

3761 Walter Schmithals, *Einleitung in die drei ersten Evangelien.* New York: de Gruyter, 1985.

3762 William R. Telford, "Introduction: The Gospel of Mark," in William R. Telford, ed., *The Interpretation of Mark.* Issues in Religion and Theology #7. Philadelphia: Fortress Press, 1985. Pp. 1-41.

3763 George A. Wright, "Markan Intercalations: A Study in the Plot of the Gospel," doctoral dissertation, Southern Baptist Theological Seminary, Louisville KY, 1985.

3764 José Cárdenas-Pallares, *A Poor Man Called Jesus: Reflections on the Gospel of Mark.* R. R. Barr, trans. Maryknoll NY: Orbis, 1986.

3765 Luigi Cirillo, "Un recente volume su Papia," *CrNSt* 7/3 (1986): 553-63.

3766 Elizabeth Struthers Malbon, "Mark: Myth and Parable," *BTB* 16 (1986): 8-17.

3767 Hermann Mentz, *Das Markus-Evangelium neu erzählt.* Göttingen: Vandenhoeck & Ruprecht, 1986.

3768 Jacob Neusner, "Death-Scenes and Farewell Stories: An Aspect of the Master-Disciple Relationship in Mark and in Some Talmudic Tales," *HTR* 79 (1986): 187-97.

3769 Adolf Pohl, *Das Evangelium des Markus.* Wuppertal: Brockhaus, 1986.

3770 J. C. de Klerk and C. W. Schnell, *A New Look at Jesus: Literary and Sociological-Historical Interpretations of Mark and John.* Pretoria: van Schaik, 1987.

3771 John Drury, "Mark," in R. Alter and F. Kermode, eds., *The Literary Guide to the Bible.* Cambridge MA: Harvard University Press, 1987. Pp. 402-17.

3772 F. Lambiasi, *Vangelo di Marco.* La Bibbia: gli scritti di Dio. Casale Monferrato: Piemme, 1987.

3773 Frank J. Matera, *What Are They Saying about Mark?* New York: Paulist Press, 1987.

3774 Gregory Murray, "Saint Mark's Extra Material," *DR* 105 (1987): 239-42.

3775 Walter J. Ong, "Text as Interpretation: Mark and After," *Semeia* 39 (1987): 7-26.

3776 David B. Peabody, *Mark as Composer*. New Gospel Studies #1. Macon GA: Mercer University Press, 1987.

3777 C. Clifton Black, "The Quest of Mark the Redactor: Why Has It Been Pursued, and What Has It Taught Us?" *JSNT* 33 (1988): 19-39.

3778 Mark E. Glasswell, "St. Mark's Attitude to the Relationship between History and the Gospel," *StudB* 2 (1980): 115-27.

3779 Steven M. Larocco, "Mark's Sowing: The Effacement and Encrypting of Jesus," doctoral dissertation, Rice University, Houston TX, 1988.

3780 François Martin, "Literary Theory, Philosophy of History and Exegesis," *Thomist* 52/4 (1988): 575-604.

3781 John Sergeant, *Lion Let Loose: The Structure and Meaning of St. Mark's Gospel*. Exeter: Paternoster, 1988.

3782 George Aichele, "Literary Fantasy and the Composition of the Gospels," *Forum* 5/3 (1989): 42-60.

3783 Heinrich Baarlink, "Het evangelie naar Marcus," in Heinrich Baarlink, ed., *Inleiding tot het Nieuwe Testament*. Kampen: Kok, 1989. Pp. 114-28.

3784 Temma F. Berg, "Reading in/to Mark," *Semeia* 48 (1989): 187-206.

3785 Matthew Black, "The Use of Rhetorical Terminology in Papias on Mark and Matthew," *JSNT* 37 (1989): 31-41.

3786 Thomas E. Boomershine, "Epistemology at the Turn of the Ages in Paul, Jesus, and Mark: Rhetoric and Dialectic in

Apocalyptic and the New Testament,'' in Joel Marcus and Marion Soards, eds., *Apocalyptic and the New Testament* (festschrift for J. Louis Martyn). Sheffield: JSOT Press, 1989. Pp. 147-67.

3787 Robert M. Fowler, ''The Rhetoric of Direction and Indirection in the Gospel of Mark,'' *Semeia* 48 (1989): 115-34.

3788 Howard Clark Kee, ''Mark,'' in Bernard W. Anderson, ed., *The Books of the Bible. 2. The Apocrypha and the New Testament.* New York: Scribner, 1989. Pp. 149-69.

3789 Helmut Koester, ''From the Kerygma-Gospel to Written Gospels,'' *NTS* 35 (1989): 361-81.

3790 Dieter Lührmann, ''Das Markusevangelium als Erzählung,'' *EvErz* 41 (1989): 212-22.

3791 Robert L. Mowery, ''Pharisees and Scribes, Galilee and Jerusalem,'' *ZNW* 80/3-4 (1989): 266-68.

3792 Harold Riley, *The Making of Mark: An Exploration.* Macon GA: Mercer University Press, 1989.

3793 Philip H. Sellew, ''Composition of Didactic Scenes in Mark's Gospel,'' *JBL* 108 (1989): 613-34.

3794 J. Darù, *Principio del Vangelo di Gesù Cristo secondo Marco.* Bologna: Dehoniane, 1990.

3795 W. Dicharry, *Human Authors of the New Testament*: 1. *Mark, Matthew, and Luke.* Collegeville: Liturgical Press, 1990.

3796 Detlev Dormeyer, ''O evangelho de Marcos: Uma biografia querigmática e historiográfica,'' *RevBB* 7 (1990): 98-125.

3797 David J. Hawkin, ''The Markan Horizon of Meaning,'' in David J. Hawkin and Thomas Robinson, eds., *Self-Definition and Self-Discovery in Early Christianity.* Lewiston, NY: Edwin Mellen Press, 1990. Pp. 1-30.

3798 Dominique Hermant, "À propos des 'expressions doubles' de Marc," *BLOS* 3 (1990): 19.

3799 Larry W. Hurtado, "The Gospel of Mark: Evolutionary or Revolutionary Document?" *JSNT* 40 (1990): 15-32.

3800 Helmut Koester, *Ancient Christian Gospels: Their History and Development*. Philadelphia: Trinity Press International, 1990.

3801 Nadia M. Lahutsky, "Paris and Jerusalem: Alfred Loisy and Pere Lagrange on the Gospel of Mark," *CBQ* 52 (1990): 444-66.

3802 William L. Lane, "The Present State of Markan Studies," in William L. Lane and M. J. Robertson, eds., *The Gospels Today: A Guide to Some Recent Developments*. Philadelphia: Skilton House Publishers, 1990. Pp. 51-81.

3803 Edouard Massaux, *The Influence of the Gospel of Saint Matthew on Christian Literature before Saint Irenaeus*. 1. *The First Ecclesiastical Writers*. N. J. Belval and S. Hechl, trans. Macon GA: Mercer University Press, 1990.

3804 Dale Miller and Patricia Miller, *The Gospel of Mark as Midrash on Earlier Jewish and New Testament Literature*. Lewiston NY: Edwin Mellen Press, 1990.

3805 R. Nicholls and P. Vaughan, *The Gospel of Mark Illuminated*. Sutherland NSW: Albatross, 1990.

3806 Gerald O'Mahony, *Praying St. Mark's Gospel*. London: Chapman, 1990.

3807 Barbara E. Reid, "Recent Work on the Gospel of Mark," *NTheoR* 3 (1990): 98-103.

3808 S. Johnson Samuel, "Mark as Composer," *BTF* 22 (1990): 45-63.

3809 Albrecht Dihle, "The Gospels and Greek Biography," in Peter Stuhlmacher, ed., *The Gospel and the Gospels*. J. Vriend, trans. Grand Rapids: Eerdmans, 1991. Pp. 361-86.

3810 B. D. Ehrman, "The Text of Mark in the Hands of the Orthodox," *LQ* 5 (1991): 143-56.

3811 Folkert Fendler, *Studien zum Markusevangelium: Zur Gattung, Chronologie, Messiasgeheimnistheorie und Überlieferung des zweiten Evangeliums*. Göttingen: Vandenhoeck & Ruprecht, 1991.

3812 B. B. Taylor, "Following Jesus Through Mark," *QR* 11 (1991): 87-106.

3813 C. K. Barrett, "The Place of John and the Synoptics within the Early History of Christian Thought," in Adelbert Denaux, ed., *John and the Synoptics*. BETL #101. Louvain: Peeters Press, 1992. Pp. 63-80.

3814 R. Bieringer, "Traditionsgeschichtlicher Ursprung und theologische Bedeutung der ὑπέρ-Aussagen im Neuen Testament," in F. Van Segbroeck, et al., eds., *The Four Gospels 1992* (festschrift for Frans Neirynck). BETL #100. 3 vols. Louvain: Peeters Press, 1992. 1:219-48.

3815 J. K. Elliott, *The Language and Style of the Gospel of Mark*. Leiden: Brill, 1993.

<u>irony</u>

3816 Bruce Hollenbach, "Lest They Should Turn and Be Forgiven: Irony," *BT* 34/3 (1983): 312-21.

3817 Jerry A. Camery-Hoggatt, "Word Plays: Evidence of Dramatic Irony in the Gospel of Mark," doctoral dissertation, Boston University, Boston MA, 1985.

<u>Jesus and spirit</u>

3818 Robert E. Burks, "Jesus and the Spirit in the Synoptic Gospels," doctoral dissertation, Southern Baptist Theological Seminary, Louisville KY, 1961.

<u>Jesus as teacher</u>

3819 A. F. Graudin, "Jesus as Teacher in Mark," *CJ* 3 (1977): 32-35.

3820 James T. Dillon, "The Effectiveness of Jesus as a Teacher," *LV* 36 (1981): 135-62.

3821 David Seeley, "Was Jesus Like a Philosopher? The Evidence of Martyrological and Wisdom Motifs in Q, Pre-Pauline Traditions, and Mark," *SBLSP* 28 (1989): 540-49.

Jesus in Gospel of Mark

3822 T. C. Hall, *The Message of Jesus according to the Synoptists*. The Messages of the Bible 9. New York: Scribner, 1901.

3823 Lemuel Hall, "The Growing Apprehension of Jesus in the Synoptics," doctoral dissertation, Southern Baptist Theological Seminary, Louisville KY, 1928.

3824 Eric Werner, " 'Hosanna' in the Gospels," *JBL* 65 (1946): 97-122.

3825 J. Spencer Kennard, " 'Hosanna' and the Purpose of Jesus," *JBL* 67 (1948): 171-76.

3826 Joseph Klausner, *Jesus von Nazareth: Seine Zeit, sein Leben und seine Lehre*. 3rd ed. Jerusalem: Jewish Publishing House, 1952.

3827 Paul E. Davies, "Mark's Witness to Jesus," *JBL* 73 (1954): 197-202.

3828 Walter E. Bundy, *Jesus and the First Three Gospels*. Cambridge: Harvard University Press, 1955.

3829 John J. Vincent, "The Evangelium of Jesus," *JBR* 23 (1955): 266-71.

3830 John L. Riach, "St. Mark's Portrait of Christ," *ET* 67 (1955-1956): 215-16.

3831 Joachim Jeremias, "The Present Position in the Controversy Concerning the Problem of the Historical Jesus," *ET* 69 (1957-1958): 333-39.

3832 Ned B. Stonehouse, *The Witness of Matthew and Mark to Christ*. Grand Rapids: Eerdmans, 1958.

3833 Heinz-Wolfgang Kuhn, "Das Reittier Jesu in der Einzugsgeschichte des Markusevangeliums," *ZNW* 50 (1959): 82-91.

3834 T. H. Robinson, *St. Mark's Life of Jesus*. London: Epworth, 1962.

3835 L. O. Bristol, "Jesus in the Gospel of Mark," *RL* 32 (1963): 429-37.

3836 Martin Kähler, *The So-Called Historical Jesus and the Historic Biblical Christ*, ed. and trans. C.E. Braaten. Philadelphia: Fortress Press, 1964.

3837 Ernst Käsemann, "The Problem of the Historical Jesus," in *Essays on New Testament Themes*. W. J. Montague, trans. Studies in Biblical Theology #41. London: SCM, 1964. Pp. 15-47.

3838 Erich Fascher, "Jesus und die Tiere," *TLZ* 90 (1965): 561-70.

3839 William Manson, "The Early Ministry of Jesus according to St. Mark: A Theological Approach," in T. W. Manson, *Jesus and the Christian*. Grand Rapids: Eerdmans, 1967. Pp. 32-49.

3840 Dorothy M. Slusser and Gerald H. Slusser, *The Jesus of Mark's Gospel*. Philadelphia: Westminster Press, 1967.

3841 J.-L. Choroat, *Jésus devant sa mort dans l'évangile de Marc*. Lire la Bible #21. Paris: Éditions du Cerf, 1970.

3842 Martin Hengel, *Was Jesus a Revolutionist?* W. Klassen, trans. Philadelphia: Fortress Press, 1971.

3843 David Hill, "The Rejection of Jesus at Nazareth: Luke 4:16-30," *NovT* 13/3 (1971): 161-80.

3844 Ulrich Luz, "Das Jesusbild der vormarkinischen Tradition," in Georg Strecker, ed., *Jesus Christus in Historie und Theologie: Neutestamentliche Festschrift für Hans Conzelmann zum 60. Geburtstag*. Tübingen: Mohr, 1975. Pp. 347-74.

3845 B. V. Manno, "The Identity of Jesus and Christian Discipleship in the Gospel of Mark," *REd* 70 (1975): 619-28.

3846 Seán P. Kealy, *Who Is Jesus of Nazareth? The Challenge of Mark's Gospel for Contemporary Man.* Denville NJ: Dimension Books, 1977.

3847 Phillip van Linden, *Knowing Christ Through Mark's Gospel.* Herald Biblical Booklets. Chicago: Franciscan Herald Press, 1977.

3848 Evald Lövestam, "De synoptiska Jesus-orden om skilsmássa och omgifte: referensramar och implikationer," *SEÅ* 43/44 (1978): 65-73.

3849 James M. Reese, *Jesus, His Word and Work: The Gospels of Matthew, Mark and Luke*. God's Work Today #5. A New Study Guide to the Bible. New York: Pueblo, 1978.

3850 William D. Carroll, "The Jesus of Mark's Gospel," *BibTo* 103 (1979): 2105-12.

3851 J. A. Estrada Díaz, "Las relaciones Jesús-pueblo-discípulos en el evangelio de Marcos," *EE* 54 (1979): 151-70.

3852 Werner H. Kelber, *Mark's Story of Jesus*. Philadelphia: Fortress Press, 1979.

3853 Thomas H. Olbricht, *The Power to Be: The Life-Style of Jesus from Mark's Gospel.* Austin TX: Sweet Publication Co., 1979.

3854 Pierre Guillemette, "Un enseignement nouveau, plein d'autorite," *NovT* 22 (1980): 222-47.

3855 Desmond O'Donnell, *Meet Jesus in Mark*. Notre Dame IN: Ave Maria Press, 1980.

3856 Elizabeth Struthers Malbon, "The Jesus of Mark and the Sea of Galilee," *JBL* 103 (1984): 363-77.

3857 Vernon K. Robbins, *Jesus the Teacher: A Socio-Rhetorical Interpretation of Mark*. Philadelphia: Fortress Press, 1984.

3858 Pieter J. Maartens, "Jesus as Jewish Rebel: A Theoretically-Founded Evaluation," doctoral dissertation, University of Pretoria, Pretoria, South Africa, 1985.

3859 M. Guttler, "Mark," in W. R. Domeris, *Portraits of Jesus: A Contextual Approach to Bible Study—Matthew, Mark, Luke, John*. London: Collins, 1987.

3860 Donald E. Cook, "A Marcan Portrait of Jesus," *FM* 5 (1988): 58-63.

3861 R. Knopp, *Finding Jesus in the Gospels: A Companion to Mark, Matthew, Luke and John*. Notre Dame IN: Ave Maria Press, 1989.

3862 William L. Osborne, "The Markan Theme of 'Who Is Jesus'," *AsiaJT* 3 (1989): 302-14.

3863 Pamela Thimmes, "Fear as a Reaction to Jesus in the Markan Gospel," *EGLMBS* 9 (1989): 138-47.

3864 Frank J. Matera, "Jesus in the Gospel according to Mark: The Crucified Messiah," *P&P* 4 (1990): 87-90.

3865 Bruno Maggioni, "Il Gesù di Marco," *PV* 27 (1982): 164-73.

Jesus tradition

3866 W. J. Bennett, "The Gospel of Mark and Traditions about Jesus," *Enc* 38 (1977): 1-11.

3867 Paul J. Achtemeier, "Mark as Interpreter of the Jesus Traditions," *Int* 32 (1978): 339-52.

3868 Gerhard Dautzenberg, "Gesetzeskritik und Gesetzesgehorsam in der Jesustradition," in Karl Kertelge, ed., *Das Gesetz im Neuen Testament* . Freiburg: Herder, 1986. Pp. 46-70.

3869 John F. O'Grady, *The Four Gospels and the Jesus Tradition*. New York: Paulist Press, 1989.

Jesus, anointing of

3870 J. K. Elliott, "The Anointing of Jesus," *ET* 85 (1973-1974): 105-107.

3871 William W. Roe, "The Anointing of Jesus in Mark and John," doctoral dissertation, Southern Baptist Theological Seminary, Louisville KY, 1985.

Jesus, authority of

3872 John Coutts, "The Authority of Jesus and of the Twelve in St. Mark's Gospel," *JTS* 8 (1957): 111-18.

3873 G. S. Shae, "The Question on the Authority of Jesus," *NovT* 16 (1974): 1-29.

3874 Robert Faricy, "The Power of Jesus over Sea and Serpent," *BibTo* 21 (1983): 260-67.

Jesus, baptism of

3875 C. E. B. Cranfield, "The Baptism of Our Lord: A Study of St. Mark 1:9-11," *SJT* 8 (1955): 53-63.

3876 Ivor Buse, "The Markan Account of the Baptism of Jesus and Isaiah LXIII," *JTS* 7 (1956): 74-75.

3877 André Legault, "Le Baptême de Jésus et la doctrine du Serviteur souffrant," *SE* 13 (1961): 147-66.

3878 André Feuillet, "Le Baptême de Jésus," RB 71 (1964): 321-52. See *TD* 14 (1966): 213-22.

3879 L. F. Rivera, "El Bautismo de Jesus en San Marcos," *RevB* 27 (1965): 140-52.

3880 Antonio Vargas-Machuca, "La narración del bautismo de Jesus (Mc 1,9-11) y la exégesis reciente. ¿Visión real o 'género didáctico'?" *CuBí* 30 (1973): 131-41.

3881 J. Riquelme, "Significación del Bautismo de Jésus," *TyV* 15 (1974): 115-39.

3882 Stephen Gero, "The Spirit as a Dove at the Baptism of Jesus," *NovT* 18 (1976): 17-35.

3883 Simon Légasse, ''Le Baptême de J'aaesus et le Baptême chrétien,'' *SBFLA* 27 (1977): 51-68.

3884 James R. Edwards, ''The Baptism of Jesus According to the Gospel of Mark [1:9-11],'' *JETS* 34 (1991): 43-57.

3885 Donald H. Juel, ''The Baptism of Jesus,'' *WW* Supplement 1 (1992): 119-26.

Jesus, death of

3886 Haim H. Cohn, *The Trial and Death of Jesus*. New York: KTAV, 1977.

3887 Virgil Howard, ''Did Jesus Speak About His Own Death?'' *CBQ* 39/4 (1977): 515-27.

3888 Rudolf Pesch, ''The Last Supper and Jesus' Understanding of His Death,'' *BB* 3 (1977): 58-75.

3889 David J. Lull, ''Interpreting Mark's Story of Jesus' Death: Toward a Theology of Suffering,'' *SBLSP* 24 (1985): 1-12.

3890 Frank J. Matera, ''The Death of Jesus according to Luke: A Question of Sources,'' *CBQ* 47 (1985): 469-85.

3891 Terence B. Ellis, ''The Death of Jesus Theme in the Plot of the Gospel of Mark,'' doctoral dissertation, New Orleans Baptist Theological Seminary, New Orleans LA, 1987.

3892 Howard M. Jackson, ''The Death of Jesus in Mark and the Miracle from the Cross,'' *NTS* 33/1 (1987): 16-37.

Jesus, life of

3893 W. F. Beck, *The Christ of the Gospels: The Life and Work of Jesus as Told by Matthew, Mark, Luke, and John*. St. Louis MO: Concordia Publishing House, 1959.

3894 C. H. Dodd, ''The Portrait of Jesus in John and in the Synoptics,'' in William R. Farmer, et al., eds., *Christian History and Interpretation* (festschrift for John Knox). Cambridge: Cambridge University Press, 1967. Pp. 183-98.

3895 Leonard Doohan, ''Mark's Portrait of Jesus,'' *MillSt* 21 (1988): 62-86.

Jesus, ministry of

3896 Norman D. Price, "The Place of Galilee in the Ministry of Christ," doctoral dissertation, Southern Baptist Theological Seminary, Louisville KY, 1941.

3897 R. F. Collins, "Jesus' Ministry to the Deaf and Dumb," *MeliT* 35/1 (1984): 12-36.

3898 Scaria Kuthirakkattel, *The Beginning of Jesus' Ministry according to Mark's Gospel*. Analecta Biblica #123. Rome: Biblical Institute Press, 1990.

Jesus, mission of

3899 Fred B. Moseley, "The Use of the Term 'Son of Man' in Mark: A Study in the Mission of Jesus," doctoral dissertation, New Orleans Baptist Theological Seminary, New Orleans LA, 1946.

Jesus, opponents of

3900 J. C. Weber, "Jesus' Opponents in the Gospel of Mark," *JBR* 34 (1966): 214-22.

Jesus, relatives of

3901 John Dominic Crossan, "Mark and the Relatives of Jesus," *NovT* 15 (1973): 81-113.

3902 Jan Lambrecht, "The Relatives of Jesus in Mark," *NovT* 16 (1974): 241-58.

3903 R. Garafalo, "The Family of Jesus in Mark's Gospel," *ITQ* 57 (1991): 265-76.

Jesus, sayings of

3904 Robert R. Darby, "A Study of the Variations of the Gethsemane Sayings of Jesus Common to the Synoptics," doctoral dissertation, New Orleans Baptist Theological Seminary, New Orleans LA, 1953.

3905 Christian P. Ceroke, "Is Mark 2:10 a Saying of Jesus?" *CBQ* 22 (1960): 369-90.

3906 David L. Dungan, "The Account of Jesus' Debate with the Pharisees Regarding Divorce (Matt. 19.3-9//Mark

10.2-12)," in *The Sayings of Jesus in the Churches of Paul.* Oxford: Blackwell, 1971. Pp. 102-31.

3907 Norman Hook, "The Dominical Cup Saying," *Theology* 77 (1974): 624-30.

3908 Bruce D. Chilton, "An Evangelical and Critical Approach to the Sayings of Jesus," *Themelios* 3/3 (1978): 78-85.

3909 M. J. Down, "The Sayings of Jesus about Marriage and Divorce," *ET* 95/11 (1983-1984): 332-34.

3910 J. Duncan M. Derrett, "Two Harsh Sayings of Christ Explained," *DR* 103 (1985): 218-29.

3911 Philip H. Sellew, "Early Collections of Jesus' Words: The Development of Dominical Discourses," doctoral dissertation, Harvard University, Cambridge MA, 1986.

Jesus, teaching of

3912 William H. Crouch, "Jesus and the Teaching of the Elders in the Synoptic Gospels," master's thesis, Southern Baptist Theological Seminary, Louisville KY, 1954.

3913 Robert H. Taylor, "Jesus' Conception of Man in the Synoptics," doctoral dissertation, Southwestern Baptist Theological Seminary, Fort Worth TX, 1961.

3914 Richard T. France, "The Servant of the Lord in the Teaching of Jesus," *TynB* 19 (1968): 26-52.

3915 Morton Smith, "Forms, Motives, and Omissions in Mark's Account of the Teaching of Jesus," in John Reumann, ed., *Understanding the Sacred Text: Essays in Honor of Morton S. Enslin on the Hebrew Bible and Christian Beginnings.* Valley Forge PA: Judson Press, 1972. Pp. 153-64.

3916 R. L. Pavelsky, "The Commandment of Love and the Christian Clinical Psychologist," *SBT* 3 (1973): 57-65.

3917 Richard T. France, "Mark and the Teaching of Jesus," in R. T. France and David Wenham, eds., *Gospel*

Perspectives: Studies of History and Tradition in the Four Gospels. Sheffield: JSOT Press, 1980. 1:101-36.

Jesus, temptation of

3918 R. F. Collins, ''The Temptation of Jesus,'' *MeliT* 26 (1974): 32-45.

3919 Klaus-Peter Koppen, ''The Interpretation of Jesus' Temptations (Mt. 4,1-11; Mk. 1,12f; Lk. 4,1-3) by the Early Church Fathers,'' *PatByzR* 8/1 (1989): 41-43.

Jesus, tomb of

3920 J. H. McIndoe, ''The Young Man at the Tomb,'' *ET* 80 (1968-1969): 125.

3921 Jean Delorme, ''Résurrection et tombeau de Jésus: Mc 16,1-8 dans la tradition évangélique,'' in E. de Surgy et al., eds., *La Résurrection du Christ et l'exégèse modern*. Lectio Divina 50. Paris: Éditions du Cerf, 1969. Pp. 105-51.

3922 Jean Delorme, ''Les femmes au tombeau, Mc 16,1-8,'' *AsSeign* 2 (1969): 58-67.

3923 Edward L. Bode, *The First Easter Morning: The Gospel Accounts of the Women's Visit to the Tomb of Jesus*. Analecta Biblica 45. Rome: Biblical Institute Press, 1970.

3924 John Dominic Crossan, ''Empty Tomb and Absent Lord,'' in Werner H. Kelber, ed., *The Passion in Mark: Studies on Mark 14-16*. Philadelphia: Fortress, 1976. Pp. 135-52.

3925 David R. Catchpole, ''The Fearful Silence of the Women at the Tomb: A Study in Markan Theology,'' *JTSA* 18 (1977): 3-10.

3926 George Mangatt, ''At the Tomb of Jesus,'' *BB* 3 (1977): 91-96.

3927 Pieter J. J. Botha, ''**Οὐκ ἔστιν ὧδε** . . . : Mark's Stories of Jesus' Tomb and History,'' *Neo* 23/2 (1989): 195-218.

Jesus, trial of

3928 T. A. Burkill, ''The Trial of Jesus,'' *VC* 12 (1958): 1-18.

3929 Olof Linton, "The Trial of Jesus and the Interpretation of Psalm cx," *NTS* 7 (1960-1961): 258-62.

3930 John R. Donahue, *Are You the Christ? The Trial Narrative in the Gospel of Mark*. SBLDS #10. Missoula MT: Society of Biblical Literature, 1973.

3931 John R. Donahue, "Temple, Trial, and Royal Christology (Mark 14:53-65)," in Werner H. Kelber, ed., *The Passion in Mark: Studies on Mark 14-16*. Philadelphia: Fortress, 1973. Pp. 61-79.

3932 Haim Cohn, *The Trial and Death of Jesus*. New York: KTAV, 1977.

3933 Donald H. Juel, *Messiah and Temple. The Trial of Jesus in the Gospel of Mark*. SBLDS #31. Missoula MT: Scholars Press, 1977.

<u>John the Baptist</u>

3934 Francis L. Andersen, "The Diet of John the Baptist (Mc 1,7)," *AbrN* 3 (1961-1962): 60-74.

3935 Ernst Bammel, "The Baptist in Early Christian Tradition," *NTS* 18 (1971-1972): 95-128.

3936 Samuel T. Lachs, "John the Baptist and His Audience," *GCAJS* 4 (1975): 28-32.

3937 Robert P. Rousseau, "John the Baptist: Jesus' Forerunner in Mark's Christology," *BibTo* 76 (1975): 316-22.

3938 Ronald A. Kittel, "John the Baptist in the Gospel according to Mark," doctoral dissertation, Graduate Theological Union, Berkeley CA, 1977.

3939 Balembo Buetubela, "Jean Baptiste dans l'évangile de Marc: Analyse littéraire et interprétation christologique," doctoral dissertation, Ponticial Biblical Institue, Rome, 1983.

3940 Wolfgang Schenk, "Gefangenschaft und Tod des Taufers. Erwagungen zur Chronologie und Ihren Konsequenzen," *NTS* 29/4 (1983): 453-83.

3941 John Drury, "Mark 1:1-15: An Interpretation," in A. E. Harvey, ed., *Alternative Approaches to New Testament Study*. London: Latimer, 1985. Pp. 25-36.

3942 Klauspeter Blaser, "Der Stärkere: biblische Besinnung zu Mk 1:1-15 par," *ZMiss* 17/1 (1991): 3-7.

3943 Jan Lambrecht, "John the Baptist and Jesus in Mark 1:1-15: Markan Redaction of Q?" *NTS* 38 (1992): 357-84.

kingdom of God

3944 Leon Bell Patterson, "A Comparative Study of the Johannine Concept of Eternal Life and the Synoptic Concept of the Kingdom," master's thesis, Southwestern Baptist Theological Seminary, Fort Worth TX, 1958.

3945 Sverre Aalen, " 'Reign' and 'House' in the Kingdom of God in the Gospels," *NTS* 8 (1961-1962): 215-40.

3946 Richard H. Hiers, *The Kingdom of God in the Synoptic Tradition*. University of Florida Humanities Monograph #33. Gainesville FL: University of Florida Press, 1970.

3947 Werner H. Kelber, "Kingdom and Parousia in the Gospel of Mark," doctoral dissertation, University of Chicago, Chicago IL, 1970.

3948 James D. G. Dunn, "Spirit and Kingdom," *ET* 82/2 (1970-1971): 36-40.

3949 Richard H. Hiers, "Purification of the Temple: Preparation for the Kingdom of God," *JBL* 90 (1971): 82-90.

3950 Werner H. Kelber, "The History of the Kingdom in Mark—Aspects of Markan Eschatology," *SBLSP* 2 (1972): 63-95.

3951 C. C. Marcheselli, "La ricerca di Dio nei segni dei tempi: la struttura tematico-letteraria di Mc 1,21-3,6 parr," in François Bovon, et al., eds., *Analyse structurale et exégèse biblique: Essais d'interprétation*. Neuchâtel: Delachaux et Niestlé, 1972. Pp. 289-313.

3952 Schuyler Brown, "The Secret of the Kingdom of God," *JBL* 92/1 (1973): 60-74.

3953 Theodore J. Weeden, "The Conflict Between Mark and His Opponents Over Kingdom Theology," *SBLSP* 3/2 (1973): 203-41.

3954 Richard H. Hiers, "Satan, Demons, and the Kingdom of God," *SJT* 27 (1974): 35-47.

3955 Werner H. Kelber, *The Kingdom in Mark: A New Place and a New Time*. Philadelphia: Fortress Press, 1974.

3956 Earl Breech, "Kingdom of God and the Parables of Jesus," *Semeia* 12 (1978): 15-40.

3957 Aage Pilgaard, "Gudsrigebegrebet i Markusevangeliet," *DTT* 43 (1980): 20-35.

3958 David Hill, "Towards an Understanding of the 'Kingdom of God'," *IBS* 3 (1981): 62-76.

3959 Mauro Orsatti, "Il 'regno di Dio' al centro del Messaggio di Gesù in Marco," *PV* 26 (1981): 429-37.

3960 J. Arthur Baird, *Rediscovering the Power of the Gospels: Jesus' Theology of the Kingdom.* Wooster OH: Iona Press, 1982.

3961 Heinz Giesen, "Jésus et l'imminence du règne de Dieu selon Marc," in M. Benzerath, ed., *La Pâque du Christ* (festschrift for F.-X. Durrwell). Paris: Cerf, 1982. Pp. 91-119.

3962 Perry V. Kea, "Perceiving the Mystery: Encountering the Reticence of Mark's Gospel," *EGLMBS* 4 (1984): 181-94.

3963 John Kallikuzhuppil, "The Church and the Kingdom of God in the Synoptic Gospels: A Comparative and Synthetic Study," *Je* 15 (1985): 85-93.

3964 Gerhard Lohfink, "Die Korrelation von Reich Gottes und Volk Gottes bei Jesus," *TQ* 165 (1985): 173-83.

3965 Andreas Lindemann, "Erwägungen zum Problem einer 'Theologie der synoptischen Evangelien'," *ZNW* 77/1-2 (1986): 1-33.

3966 John M. McDermott, "Gegenwärtiges und kommendes Reich Gottes," *IKaZ* 15/2 (1986): 142-44.

3967 Joel Marcus, *The Mystery of the Kingdom of God.* Atlanta: Scholars Press, 1986.

3968 George R. Beasley-Murray, "Jesus and the Kingdom of God," *BQ* 32 (1987): 141-46.

3969 M. Eugene Boring, "The Kingdom of God in Mark," in W. Willis, ed., *The Kingdom of God in 20th Century Interpretation.* Peabody MA: Hendrickson Publishers, 1987. Pp. 131-45.

3970 Bruce D. Chilton, *God in Strength: Jesus' Announcement of the Kingdom.* Sheffield, JSOT Press, 1987.

3971 Bruce D. Chilton and J. I. H. McDonald, *Jesus and the Ethics of the Kingdom.* London: SPCK, 1987.

3972 Burton L. Mack, "The Kingdom Sayings in Mark," *Forum* 3/1 (1987): 3-47.

3973 Paul Beauchamp, "Paraboles de Jésus, vie de Jésus: l'encadrement évangélique et scripturaire des paraboles (Mc 4,1-34)," in Jean Delorme, ed., *Les paraboles évangéliques: perspectives nouvelles.* Paris: Cerf, 1989. Pp. 151-70.

3974 Chrys C. Caragounis, "Kingdom of God, Son of Man and Jesus' Self-Understanding," *TynB* 40 (1989): 3-23; 223-38.

3975 Vittorio Fusco, "Mc 4,1-34: la section des paraboles," in Jean Delorme, ed., *Les paraboles évangéliques: perspectives nouvelles.* Paris: Cerf, 1989. Pp. 219-34.

3976 Jean-Claude Giroud, "La parabole ou l'opacité incontournable: a propos de Mc 4,1-34," in Jean Delorme, ed., *Les paraboles évangéliques: perspectives nouvelles.* Paris: Cerf, 1989. Pp. 235-46.

3977 Gerhard Dautzenberg, "Mk 4:1-34 als Belehrung über das Reich Gottes: Beobachtungen zum Gleichniskapitel," *BZ* 34/1 (1990): 38-62.

3978 D. B. Kraybill, *The Upside-Down Kingdom.* Scottdale PA: Herald, 1990.

3979 Gerhard Lohfink, "Wie werden im Reich Gottes die Hungernden satt? zur Erzählintention von Mk 6,30-44," in Johannes J. Degenhardt, ed., *Die Freude an Gott: Unsere Kraft* (festschrift for Otto B. Knoch). Stuttgart: Verlag Katholisches Bibelwerk, 1991. Pp. 135-44.

3980 Chrys C. Caragounis, "The Kingdom of God in John and the Synoptics: Realized or Potential Eschatology?" in Adelbert Denaux, ed., *John and the Synoptics*. BETL #101. Louvain: Peeters Press, 1992. Pp. 473-80.

korban

3981 Solomon Zeitlin, "Korban," *JQR* 53 (1962): 160-63.

3982 Solomon Zeitlin, "Korban: A Gift," *JQR* 59 (1968): 133-35.

3983 Albert I. Baumgarten, "Korban and the Pharisaic Paradosis," *JNES* 85 (1984): 521.

law

3984 Charles E. Carlston, "The Things that Defile (Mark 7:14) and the Law in Matthew and Mark," *NTS* 15/1 (1968-1969): 75-96.

3985 J. Duncan M. Derrett, "Law in the New Testament: The Palm Sunday Colt," *NovT* 13 (1971): 241-58.

3986 David R. Catchpole, "Discipleship, the Law and Jesus of Nazareth, " *Crux* 11 (1973): 8-16.

3987 J. Duncan M. Derrett, "Law in the New Testament: Si scandalizaverit te manus tua, abscinde eam (Mk 9,42) and Comparative Legal History," *RIDA* 20 (1973): 11-36.

3988 J. Duncan M. Derrett, "Law in the New Testament: The Syrophoenician Woman and the Centurion of Capernaum," *NovT* 15/3 (1973): 161-86.

3989 Jan Lambrecht, "Jesus and the Law. An Investigation of Mark 7:1-23," *ETL* 53 (1977): 24-82.

3990 James D. G. Dunn, "Mark 2:1-3:6: A Bridge Between Jesus and Paul on the Question of the Law," *NTS* 30/3 (1984): 395-415.

3991 James D. G. Dunn, *Jesus, Paul and the Law: Studies in Mark and Galatians*. Louisville KY: Westminster/John Knox Press, 1990.

<u>literary character of the Gospel of Mark</u>

3992 Henry B. Carré, "The Literary Structure of the Gospel of Mark," in Shirley Jackson Case, ed., *Studies in Early Christianity*. Cambridge MA: Harvard University Press, 1928. Pp. 105-26.

3993 George D. Kilpatrick, "Some Notes on Marcan Usage," *BT* 7 (1956): 51-56.

3994 A. W. Mosley, "Jesus' Audiences in the Gospels of St. Mark and St. Luke," *NTS* 10 (1963-1964): 139-49.

3995 Frans Neirynck, "Duality in Mark," *ETL* 47 (1971): 394-463.

3996 Frans Neirynck, "Mark in Greek," *ETL* 47 (1971): 144-91.

3997 Frans Neirynck, "Duplicate Expressions in the Gospel of Mark," *ETL* 48 (1972): 150-209.

3998 J. Duncan M. Derrett, "Allegory and the Wicked Vinedressers," *JTS* 25 (1974): 426-32.

3999 C. Castro Tello, "Estructura literaria y teológica del Evangelo de S. Marcos," *RevTL* 10 (1976): 31-47.

4000 Janusz Czerski, "Die Passion Christi in den synoptischen Evangelien im Lichte der historisch-literarischen Kritik," *CollT* 46 (1976): 81-96.

4001 Jean Delorme, "L'intégration des petites unités littéraires dans l'Évangile de Marc du point de vue de la sémiotique structurale," *NTS* 25 (1978-1979): 469-91.

4002 Augustine Stock, "Literary Criticism and Mark's Mystery Play," *BibTo* 100 (1979): 1909-15.

4003 Arnold E. Sternheim, "Time and Narrative Construction," doctoral dissertation, Columbia University, New York NY, 1980.

4004 M. Philip Scott, "Chiastic Structure: A Key to the Interpretation of Mark's Gospel," *BTB* 15 (1985): 17-26.

4005 Joanna Dewey, "Oral Methods of Structuring Narrative in Mark," *Int* 43 (1989): 32-44.

4006 Stephen D. Moore, *Literary Criticism and the Gospels*. New Haven CT: Yale University Press, 1989.

4007 Brigid C. Frein, "Fundamentalism and Narrative Approaches to the Gospels," *BTB* 22/1 (1992): 13-18.

Lord's Supper

4008 A. J. B. Higgins, *The Lord's Supper in the New Testament*. Studies in Biblical Theology #6. London: SCM, 1952.

4009 Willi Marxsen, "Der Ursprung des Abendmahls," *EvT* 12 (1952-1953): 293-303.

4010 Nigel Turner, "The Style of St. Mark's Eucharistic Words," *JTS* 8 (1957): 108-11.

4011 John A. O'Flynn, "The Date of the Last Supper," *ITQ* 25 (1958): 58-63.

4012 Bernard Cooke, "Synoptic Presentation of the Eucharist as Covenant Sacrifice," *TS* 21 (1960): 1-44.

4013 B. M. Ahern, "Gathering the Fragments: The Lord's Supper," *Worship* 35 (1961): 424-29.

4014 A. Gilmore, "The Date and Significance of the Last Supper," *SJT* 14 (1961): 256-69.

4015 José Alonso Díaz, "Los elementos de la tradición eucarística en relación con Jesucristo," *RET* 23 (1963): 47-60.

4016 W. E. Lynch, "The Eucharist: A Covenant Meal," *BibTo* 1 (1963): 319-23.

4017 Raymond E. Brown, "The Date of the Last Supper," *BibTo* 11 (1964): 727-33.

4018 William Barclay, *The Lord's Supper*. London: SCM, 1967.

4019 Jacques Dupont, " 'This Is My Body'—'This Is My Blood'," in R. A. Tartre, ed., *The Eucharist Today: Essays on the Theology and Worship of the Real Presence*. New York: P. J. Kennedy and Sons, 1967, Pp. 13-28.

4020 Heinz Schürmann, "Jesus' Words in the Light of His Actions at the Last Supper," *Conci* 40 (1969): 119-31.

4021 Frank Stagg, "The Lord's Supper in the New Testament," *RevExp* 66/1 (1969): 5-14.

4022 Norman A. Beck, "The Last Supper as an Efficacious Symbolic Act," *JBL* 89 (1970): 192-98.

4023 Kenneth Hein, "Judas Iscariot: Key to the Last Supper Narratives?" *NTS* 17/2 (1970-1971): 227-32.

4024 Karl Kertelge, "Die soteriologischen Aussagen in der urchristlichen Abendmahlsüberlieferung und ihre Beziehung zum geschichtlichen Jesus," *TTZ* 81 (1972): 193-202.

4025 David Flusser, "The Last Supper and the Essenes," *Immanuel* 2 (1973): 23-27.

4026 E. J. Kilmartin, "The Eucharistic Prayer: Content and Function of Some Early Eucharistic Prayers," in Richard J. Clifford and George W. MacRae, eds., *The Word in the World* (festschrift for Frederick L. Moriarty, S.J.). Cambridge MA: Weston College Press, 1973. Pp. 117-34.

4027 F. C. Synge, "Mark 14:18-25: Supper and Rite," *JTSA* 4 (1973): 38-43.

4028 Joseph A. Grassi, "The Eucharist in the Gospel of Mark," *AmER* 168 (1974): 595-608.

4029 Jean-Marie van Cangh, *La multiplication des pains et l'Eucharistie*. Lectio Divina 86. Paris: Éditions du Cerf, 1975.

4030 Richard H. Hiers and C. A. Kennedy, "The Bread and Fish Eucharist in the Gospels and Early Christian Art," *PRS* 3 (1976): 20-47.

4031 A. R. Winnett, "The Breaking of the Bread: Does it Symbolize the Passion?" *ET* 88 (1976-1977): 181-82.

4032 Joachim Jeremias, *The Eucharistic Words of Jesus*. Norman Perrin, trans. Philadelphia: Fortress Press, 1977.

4033 Helmut Merklein, "Erwägungen zur Überlieferungsgeschichte der Neutestamentlichen Abendmahlstraditionen," *BZ* 21/1 (1977): 88-101, 235-44.

4034 Rudolf Pesch, "The Last Supper and Jesus' Understanding of His Death," *BB* 3 (1977): 58-75.

4035 Adrian Schenker, *Das Abendmahl Jesu als Brennpunkt des Alten Testaments. Begegnung zwischen den beiden Testamenten—eine bibeltheologische Studie*. Biblische Beiträge 13. Geneva: Schweizerisches Katholisches Bibelwerk, 1977.

4036 Anthony Edanad, "Institution of the Eucharist according to the Synoptic Gospels," *BB* 4 (1978): 322-32.

4037 Leonard F. Badia, *The Dead Sea People's Sacred Meal and Jesus' Last Supper*. Lanham MD: University Press of America, 1979.

4038 Karl Kertelge, "Das Abendmahl Jesu im Markusevangelium," in Josef Zmifewski and Ernst Nellessen, eds., *Begegnung mit dem Wort: Festschrift für Heinrich Zimmermann*. Bonner biblische Beiträge 53. Bonn: Peter Hanstein, 1980. Pp. 67-80.

4039 Robert J. Daly, "The Eucharist and Redemption: The Last Supper and Jesus' Understanding of His Death," *BTB* 11/1 (1981): 21-27.

4040 I. Howard Marshall, *Last Supper and Lord's Supper*. Grand Rapids: Eerdmans, 1981.

4041 Carter Lindberg, "The Conception of the Eucharist according to Erasmus and Karlstadt," in Mark Lienhard and André Séguenny, eds., *Les dissidents du 16ue siècle*. Baden Baden: V. Koerner, 1983. Pp. 79-94.

4042 Rudolf Pesch, "Das Evangelium in Jerusalem: Mk 14,12-26 als ältestes Uberlieferungsgut der Urgemeinde," in Peter Stuhlmacher, ed., *Das Evangelium und die Evangelien*. Tübingen: Mohr, 1983. Pp. 113-55.

4043 Paolo Ricca, "Lutero e Zwingli: la Cena," in Giuseppe Alberigo, et al., eds., *Lutero nel suo e nel nostro tempo*. Torino: Claudiana, 1983. Pp. 227-45.

4044 Michael Pettem, "Le premier récit de la multiplication des pains et le problème synoptique," *SR* 14/1 (1985): 73-83.

4045 Willem A. Saayman, "The Eucharist in Mission Perspective," *ThEv* 18/2 (1985): 18-24.

4046 Ray C. Jones, "The Lord's Supper and the Concept of Anamnesis," *WW* 6/4 (1986): 434-45.

4047 Uwe Wegner, "Deu Jesus um sentido salvífico para sua morte: consideraçoes sobre Mc. 14:24 e 10:45," *EstT* 26/3 (1986): 209-46.

4048 Christoph Burchard, "The Importance of Joseph and Aseneth for the Study of the New Testament: A General Survey and a Fresh Look at the Lord's Supper," *NTS* 33/1 (1987): 102-34.

4049 Ben F. Meyer, "The Expiation Motif in the Eucharistic Words: A Key to the History of Jesus?" *Greg* 69 (1988): 461-87.

4050 John Navone, "The Last Day and the Last Supper in Mark's Gospel," *Theology* 9 (1988): 38-43.

4051 Francis J. Moloney, "The Eucharist as Jesus' Presence to the Broken," *Pacifica* 2 (1989): 151-74.

<u>marriage/divorce</u>

4052 Jacques Dupont, *Mariage et divorce dans l'Évangile: Matthieu 19,3-12 et parallèles*. Brugge: Desclée, 1959.

4053 Richard N. Soulen, "Marriage and Divorce: A Problem in New Testament Interpretation," *Int* 23/4 (1969): 439-50.

4054 J. Duncan M. Derrett, "The Teaching of Jesus on Marriage and Divorce," in J. Duncan M. Derrett, *Law in the New Testament*. London: Darton, Longman & Todd, 1970. Pp. 363-88.

4055 Wilfrid J. Harrington, "Jesus' Attitude towards Divorce," *ITQ* 37 (1970): 199-209.

4056 Berndt Schaller, "Die Sprüche über Ehescheidung und Wiederheirat in der synoptischen Überlieferung," in Eduard Lohse, ed., *Der Ruf Jesu und die Antwort der Gemeinde: Exegetische Untersuchungen* (festschrift for Joachim Jeremias). Göttingen: Vandenhoeck & Ruprecht, 1970. Pp. 226-46.

4057 T. A. Burkill, "Two into One: The Notion of Carnal Union in Mark 10:8; 1 Cor 6:16; Eph 5:31," *ZNW* 62 (1971): 115-20.

4058 David L. Dungan, "The Account of Jesus' Debate with the Pharisees Regarding Divorce (Matt. 19.3-9//Mark 10.2-12)," in *The Sayings of Jesus in the Churches of Paul*. Oxford: Blackwell, 1971. Pp. 102-31.

4059 Alousius M. Ambrozic, "Indissolubility of Marriage in the New Testament: Law or Ideal?" *StCan* 6 (1972): 269-88.

4060 J. D. McCaughey, "Marriage and Divorce: Some Reflections on the Relevant Passages in the New Testament," *CANZTR* 4 (1972): 24-39.

4061 George W. MacRae, "New Testament Perspectives on Marriage and Divorce," in L. G. Wrenn, ed., *Divorce and Remarriage in the Catholic Church.* New York: Paulist Press, 1973. Pp. 1-15.

4062 D. O'Callaghan, "How Far Is Christian Marriage Indissoluble?" *ITQ* 40/2 (1973): 162-73.

4063 D. W. Palmer, "Defining a Vow of Abstinence," *CANZTR* 5 (1973): 38-41.

4064 David R. Catchpole, "The Synoptic Divorce Material as a Traditio-Historical Problem," *BJRL* 57/1 (1974-1975): 92-127.

4065 José Alonso Díaz, "La indisolubilidad del matrimonio o el divorcio hoy visto por escriturislas y teólogos," *StOvet* 3 (1975): 203-26.

4066 Evald Lövestam, "Die funktionale Bedeutung der synoptischen Jesusworte über Ehescheidung und Wiederheirat," in Albert Fuchs, ed., *Theologie aus dem Norden.* Studien zum Neuen Testament und seiner Umwelt A,2. Linz: SNTU, 1977. Pp. 19-28.

4067 Rámon Trevijano Etcheverría, "Matrimonio y divorcio en Mc 10,2-12 y par.," *Bur* 18 (1977): 113-51.

4068 Albert L. Descamps, "Les textes évangéliques sur le mariage," *RTL* 9 (1978): 259-86.

4069 Ben Hemelsoet, "Créé à l'image de Dieu: la question du divorce dans Marc X," in T. Baarda, A. F. J. Klihn, and W. C. van Unnik, eds., *Miscellanea Neotestamentica.* Novum Testamentum Supplement 48. Leiden: Brill, 1978. 2:49-57.

4070 Augustine Stock, "Matthean Divorce Texts," *BTB* 8/1 (1978): 24-33.

4071 C. Benton Kline, "Marriage Today: A Theological Carpet Bag," *JPC* 33/1 (1979): 24-37.

4072 John J. Pilch, "Marriage in the Lord," *BibTo* 102 (1979): 2010-13.

4073 Robert H. Stein, " 'Is It Lawful for a Man to Divorce His Wife'?" *JETS* 22 (1979): 115-21.

4074 Kevin Condon, "Apropos of the Divorce Sayings," *IBS* 2 (1980): 40-51.

4075 Antonio Vargas-Machuca, "Divorcio e indisolubilidad del matrimonio en la Sagrada Escritura," *EB* 39 (1981): 19-61.

4076 Robert W. Herron, "Mark's Jesus on Divorce: Mark 10:1-12 Reconsidered," *JETS* 25/3 (1982): 273-81.

4077 Charles C. Ryrie, "Biblical Teaching on Divorce and Remarriage," *GTJ* 3/2 (1982): 177-92.

4078 B. N. Wambacq, "Matthieu 5,31-32. Possibilite de Divorce ou Obligation de Rompre une Union illigitime," *NRT* 104/1 (1982): 34-49.

4079 M. J. Down, "The Sayings of Jesus about Marriage and Divorce," *ET* 95/11 (1983-1984): 332-34.

4080 W. F. Luck, *Divorce and Remarriage: Recovering the Biblical View*. San Francisco: Harper & Row, 1987.

4081 Will Deming, "Mark 9:42-10:12, Matthew 5:27-32, and b. Nid, 13b: A First Century Discussion of Male Sexuality," *NTS* 36/1 (1990): 130-41.

4082 Barbara Green, "Jesus' Teaching on Divorce in the Gospel of Mark," *JSNT* 38 (1990): 67-75.

4083 John S. Kloppenborg, "Alms, Debt and Divorce: Jesus' Ethics in Their Mediterranean Context," *TJT* 6 (1990): 182-200.

Mary

4084 Harvey K. McArthur, " 'Son of Mary'," *NovT* 15 (1973): 38-58.

4085 Karl P. Donfried, "Mary in the Gospel of Mark," in Raymond E. Brown, et al., eds., *Mary in the New Testament: A Collaborative Assessment by Protestant and Roman Catholic Scholars*. Philadelphia: Fortress Press, 1978. Pp. 51-72.

4086 John C. Fenton, "The Mother of Jesus in Mark's Gospel and Its Revisions," *Theology* 86 (1983): 433-37.

Mary Magdalene

4087 Gerald O'Collins, "Mary Magdalene as Major Witness to Jesus' Resurrection," *TS* 48 (1987): 631-46.

Mary of Bethany

4088 E. E. Platt, "The Ministry of Mary of Bethany," *TT* 34 (1977): 29-39.

messianic secret

4089 Vincent Taylor, "W. Wrede's *The Messianic Secret in the Gospels*," *ET* 65 (1953-1954): 246-50.

4090 T. W. Manson, "Realized Eschatology and the Messianic Secret," in D. E. Nineham, ed., *Studies in the Gospels* (festschrift for R. H. Lightfoot). Oxford: Blackwell, 1955. Pp. 209-22.

4091 T. A. Burkill, "The Injunctions to Silence in St. Mark's Gospel," *TZ* 12 (1956): 585-604.

4092 T. A. Burkill, "Concerning St. Mark's Conception of Secrecy," *HJ* 55 (1956-1957): 150-58.

4093 Vincent Taylor, "The Messianic Secret in Mark: A Rejoinder to the Rev. Dr. T. A. Burkill," *HJ* 55 (1956-1957): 241-48.

4094 Félix Gils, "Le secret messianique dans les Évangiles: Examen de la théorie de E. Sjoberg," in J. Coppens, et al., eds., *Sacra Pagina: Miscellanea Biblica Congressus Internationalis Catholici de Re Biblica*. BETL #12-13. 2 vols. Paris: Gabalda, 1959. 2:101-20.

4095 George H. Boobyer, "The Secrecy Motif in St. Mark's Gospel," *NTS* 6 (1959-1960): 225-35.

4096 T. A. Burkill, "Strain on the Secret: An Examination of Mark 11:1-13:37," *ZNW* 51 (1960): 31-46.

4097 Otto Betz, "Die Frage nach dem messianischen Bewußtsein Jesu," *NovT* 6 (1963): 20-48.

4098 Reginald H. Fuller, "The Messianic Secret in Mark," in *Interpreting the Miracles*. Philadelphia: Westminster, 1963. Pp. 75-77.

4099 Georg Strecker, "Zur Messiasgeheimnistheorie im Markusevangelium," *StudE* 3 (1964): 86-104.

4100 Édouard Dhanis, "The Messianic Secret," *TD* 13 (1965): 127-28.

4101 Eduard Schweizer, "Zur Frage des Messiasgeheimnisses bei Markus," *ZNW* 56 (1965): 1-8.

4102 Eduardo Guerra, "The Secrecy Data in the Gospel of Mark: A Traditio-Historical Study of W. Wrede's Views," doctoral dissertation, Union Theological Seminary, New York NY, 1967.

4103 L. S. Hay, "Mark's Use of the Messianic Secret," *JAAR* 35 (1967): 16-27.

4104 Robert P. Meye, "Messianic Secret and Messianic Didache in Mark's Gospel," in Felix Christ, ed., *Oikonomia: Heilsgeschichte als Thema der Theologie* (festschrift for Oscar Cullmann). Geburtstag gewidmet. Hamburg-Bergstedt: Reich, 1967. Pp. 57-68.

4105 H. H. Straton, "The Son-of-Man and the Messianic Secret," *JRT* 24 (1967): 31-49.

4106 Christian Maurer, "Das Messiasgeheimnis des Markusevangeliums," *NTS* 14 (1967-1968): 515-26.

4107 Gaëtan Minette de Tillesse, *Le secret messianique dans l'évangile de Marc*. Lectio Divina 47. Paris: Éditions du Cerf, 1968.

4108 Brian G. Powley, "The Purpose of the Messianic Secret: A Brief Survey," *ET* 80 (1968-1969): 308-10.

4109 David E. Aune, "The Problem of the Messianic Secret," *NovT* 11 (1969): 1-31.

4110 R. N. Longenecker, "The Messianic Secret in the Light of Recent Discoveries," *EQ* 41 (1969): 207-15.

4111 Léopold Sabourin, "Secretum messianicum in Marco," *VD* 47 (1969): 303-306.

4112 James D. G. Dunn, "The Messianic Secret in Mark," *TynB* 21 (1970): 92-117.

4113 André Myre, "Un ouvrage récent sur le secret messianique dans l'Évangile de Marc," *SE* 22 (1970): 241-47.

4114 Hejne Simonsen, "Messiashemmeligheden og Markusevangeliets struktur," *SEÅ* 37/38 (1972): 107-24.

4115 William Wrede, *The Messianic Secret*. J. C. G. Greig, trans. The Library of Theological Translations. Greenwood SC: Attic, 1972.

4116 W. C. Robinson, "The Quest for Wrede's Secret Messiah," *Int* 27 (1973): 10-30.

4117 James L. Blevins, "Seventy-two Years of the Messianic Secret," *PRS* 1 (1974): 187-94.

4118 J. Delgado, "El silencio, lenguaje revelador del misterio de Cristo en el Evangelio de Marcos. Un estudio exégetico-teologico," *EX* 24 (1974): 133-211.

4119 Morna D. Hooker, "The Johannine Prologue and the Messianic Secret," *NTS* 21 (1974-1975): 40-58.

4120 C. F. D. Moule, "On Defining the Messianic Secret in Mark," in E. Earle Ellis and Erich Grässer, eds., *Jesus und Paulus: Festschrift für Werner Georg Kümmel zum 70. Geburtstag*. Göttingen: Vandenhoeck & Ruprecht, 1975. Pp. 239-52.

4121 Heikki Räisänen, *Das "Messiasgeheimnis" im Markusevangelium. Ein redaktionskritischer Versuch.* Schriften der Finnischen Exegetischen Gesellschaft 28. Helsinki: Finnish Exegetical Society, 1976. English translation, Edinburgh: T. & T. Clark, 1993

4122 John J. Kilgallen, "The Messianic Secret and Mark's Purpose," *BTB* 7 (1977): 60-65.

4123 F. J. Steinmetz, "Das Rätsel der Schweige-Gebote im Markus-Evangelium," *GeistL* 50 (1977): 92-102.

4124 Ronald J. Kernaghan, "The Messianic Secret in Mark's Gospel," doctoral dissertation, Fuller Theological Seminary, Pasadena CA, 1979.

4125 Pieter W. van der Horst, "Het 'Geheime Markusevangelie': Over een nieuwe vondst," *NTT* 33 (1979): 27-51.

4126 Brian G. Powley, "Vincent Taylor and the Messianic Secret in Mark's Gospel," *StudB* 2 (1980): 243-46.

4127 James L. Blevins *The Messianic Secret in Markan Research, 1901-1976.* Washington DC: University Press of America, 1981.

4128 Robert M. Fowler, "Irony and the Messianic Secret in the Gospel of Mark," *EGLMBS* 1 (1981): 26-36.

4129 Michael FitzPatrick, "Marcan Theology and the Messianic Secret," *ACR* 59 (1982): 404-16.

4130 Brian G. Powley, "Understanding the 'Messianic Secret' in Mark's Gospel," *EpRev* 9 (1982): 54-59.

4131 Christopher M. Tuckett, ed., *The Messianic Secret.* Issues in Religion and Theology #1. Philadelphia: Fortress Press, 1983.

4132 Perry V. Kea, "Perceiving the Mystery: Encountering the Reticence of Mark's Gospel," *EGLMBS* 4 (1984): 181-94.

4133 Raymond A. Martin, "The Messianic Secret in Mark," *CThM* 11 (1984): 350-52.

4134 Elias J. Bickerman, "Das Messiasgeheimnis und die Komposition des Markusevangeliums," in *Studies in Jewish and Christian History. Part Three*. Leiden: Brill, 1986. Pp. 34-52.

4135 J. Engelbrecht, "William Wrede en die Messiasgeheim," *ThEv* 19 (1986): 14-21.

4136 Hendrikus Boers, "Reflections on the Gospel of Mark: A Structural Investigation," *SBLSP* 26 (1987): 255-67.

4137 Gerhard Sellin, "Einige symbolische und esoterische Züge im Markus-Evangelium," in Dietrich-Alex Koch, et al., eds., *Jesu Rede von Gott und ihre Nachgeschichte im frühen Christentum* (festschrift for Willi Marxsen). Gütersloh: Güterloher Verlag, 1989. Pp. 74-90.

4138 Heikki Räisänen, *The "Messianic Secret" in Mark's Gospel*. C. M. Tuckett, trans. Edinburgh: T. & T. Clark, 1990.

4139 Scott G. Sinclair, "The Healing of Bartimaeus and the Gaps in Mark's Messianic Secret," *SLJT* 33 (1990): 249-57.

<u>miracle/miracles</u>

4140 George H. Boobyer, "The Eucharistic Interpretation of the Miracles of the Loaves in St. Mark's Gospel," *JTS* 3 (1952): 161-71.

4141 George H. Boobyer, "The Miracles of the Loaves and the Gentiles in St. Mark's Gospel," *SJT* 6 (1953): 77-87.

4142 George H. Boobyer, "Mark 2:10a and the Interpretations of the Healing of the Paralytic," *HTR* 47 (1954): 115-20.

4143 T. A. Burkill, "The Notion of Miracle with Special Reference to St. Mark's Gospel," *ZNW* 50 (1959): 33-48.

4144 R. T. Mead, "The Healing of the Paralytic—a Unit?" *JBL* 80 (1961): 348-54.

4145 Alan Shaw, "The Marcan Feeding Narratives," *CQR* 162 (1961): 268-78.

4146 Raymond E. Brown, "The Gospel Miracles," in John L. McKenzie, ed., *The Bible in Current Catholic Thought* (festschrift for M. J. Gruenthaner). New York: Herder & Herder, 1963. Pp. 184-201.

4147 Reginald H. Fuller, "Five Groups of Miracles in Mark," in *Interpreting the Miracles*. Philadelphia: Westminster, 1963. Pp. 69-75.

4148 Reginald H. Fuller, "The Marcan Material," in *Interpreting the Miracles*. Philadelphia PA: Westminster, 1963. Pp. 48-63.

4149 Gerhard F. Erlangen, "Die beiden Erzählungen von der Speisung in Mark 6:31-44; 8:1-9," *TZ* 20 (1964): 10-22.

4150 Mark E. Glasswell, "The Use of Miracles in the Markan Gospel," in C. F. D. Moule, ed., *Miracles: Cambridge Studies in their Philosophy and History*. London: A. R. Mowbray & Co., 1965. Pp. 149-62.

4151 John Wilkinson, "The Case of the Epileptic Boy," *ET* 79/3 (1967-1968): 39-42.

4152 E. Schuyler English, "A Neglected Miracle," *BSac* 126 (1969): 300-305.

4153 Robert H. Thouless, "Miracles and Physical Research," *Theology* 72 (1969): 253-58.

4154 Dino Merli, "Lo scopo dei miracoli nell'Evangelo di Marco," *BibO* 12 (1970): 184-98.

4155 Dorothy M. Slusser, "The Healing Narratives in Mark," *CC* 87 (1970): 597-99.

4156 J. K. Elliott, "The Conclusion of the Pericope of the Healing of the Leper and Mark i.45," *JTS* 22 (1971): 153-57.

4157 Paul J. Achtemeier, "Gospel Miracle Tradition and the Divine Man," *Int* 26 (1972): 174-97.

4158 Myles M. Bourke, "The Miracle Stories of the Gospels," *DunR* 12 (1972): 21-34.

4159 Jean-Marie van Cangh, "Les sources de l'Évangile: les collections pré-marciennes de miracles," *RTL* 3 (1972): 76-85.

4160 Vernon K. Robbins, "The Healing of Blind Bartimaeus (10:46-52) in the Marcan Theology," *JBL* 92 (1973): 224-43.

4161 J. P. M. Sweet, "A Saying, a Parable, a Miracle," *Theology* 76 (1973): 125-33.

4162 Léopold Sabourin, "The Miracles of Jesus (II). Jesus and the Evil Powers," *BTB* 4 (1974): 115-75.

4163 Ludger Schenke, *Die Wundererzählungen des Markusevangeliums*. Stuttgarter Biblische Beiträge 5. Stuttgart: Katholisches Bibelwerk, 1974.

4164 Paul J. Achtemeier, "Miracles and the Historical Jesus: A Study of Mark 9:14-29," *CBQ* 37/4 (1975): 471-91.

4165 Léopold Sabourin, "The Miracles of Jesus (III): Healings, Resuscitations, Nature Miracles," *BTB* 5 (1975): 146-200.

4166 Geoffrey Walker, "The Blind Recover Their Sight," *ET* 87 (1975-1976): 23.

4167 A. B. Kolenkow, "Healing Controversy as a Tie between Miracle and Passion Material for a Proto-Gospel," *JBL* 95/4 (1976): 623-38.

4168 Jean-Noël Aletti, "Une lecture en questions," in Xavier Léon-Dufour, ed., *Les miracles de Jésus selon le Nouveau Testament*. Paris: Éditions du Seuil, 1977. Pp. 189-208.

4169 Louis Beirnaert, "Approche psychanalytique," in Xavier Léon-Dufour, ed., *Les miracles de Jésus selon le Nouveau Testament*. Paris: Éditions du Seuil, 1977. Pp. 183-88.

4170 Paul Lamarche, "Les miracles de Jésus selon Marc," in Xavier Léon-Dufour, ed., *Les miracles de Jésus selon le*

Nouveau Testament. Paris: Éditions du Seuil, 1977. Pp. 213-26.

4171 R. L. Sturch, "The Markan Miracles and the Other Synoptists," *ET* 89 (1977-1978): 375-76.

4172 Paul J. Achtemeier, " 'And He Followed Him': Miracles and Discipleship in Mark 10:46-52," *Semeia* 11 (1978): 115-45.

4173 Ernest Best, "The Miracles in Mark," *RevExp* 75 (1978): 539-54.

4174 Hans Dieter Betz, "The Early Christian Miracle Story: Some Observations on the Form Critical Problem," *Semeia* 11 (1978): 69-81.

4175 J. K. Elliott, "The Healing of the Leper in the Synoptic Parallels," *TZ* 34 (1978): 175-76.

4176 M. J. J. Menken, "Mc 10,46-52: de 'genezing van de blinde Bartimeü' als roepingsverhaal," in A. J. M. Blijlevens, et al., eds., *Ambt en bediening in meervoud: Veelvormigheid van dienstverlening in de geloofsgemeenschap* (festschrift for H. Manders). Hilversum: Gooi en Sticht, 1978. Pp. 67-79.

4177 Robert P. Meye, "Psalm 107 as 'Horizon' for Interpreting the Miracle Stories of Mark 4:35-8:26," in Robert A. Guelich, ed., *Unity and Diversity in New Testament Theology: Essays in Honor of George E. Ladd*. Grand Rapids: Eerdmans, 1978. Pp. 1-13.

4178 C. H. Cave, "The Leper: Mark 1:40-45," *NTS* 25 (1978-1979): 245-50.

4179 Earl S. Johnson, "Mark 8:22-26: The Blind Man from Bethsaida," *NTS* 25/3 (1978-1979): 370-83.

4180 Robert M. Fowler, "The Feeding of the Five Thousand: A Markan Composition," *SBLSP* 9/1 (1979): 101-104.

4181 Karl P. Donfried, "The Feeding Narratives and the Marcan Community: Mark 6,30-45 and 8,1-10," in Dieter

Lührmann and Georg Strecker, eds., *Kirche* (festschrift for Günther Bornkamm). Tübingen: Mohr, 1980. Pp. 95-103

4182 Jan Lach, "Funkcja cudów w ewangelii Markowej," *SThV* 18 (1980): 5-27.

4183 J. Duncan M. Derrett, "Why and How Jesus Walked on the Sea," *NovT* 23/4 (1981): 330-48.

4184 K. M. Fisher and W. C. von Wahlde, "The Miracles of Mark 4:35-5:43: Their Meaning and Function in the Gospel Framework," *BTB* 11/1 (1981): 13-16.

4185 John P. Heil, *Jesus Walking on the Sea: Meaning and Gospel Functions of Matt 14:22-23, Mark 6:45-52, and John 6:15b-21*. Analecta Biblica 87. Rome: Biblical Institute Press, 1981.

4186 J. Engelbrecht, "The Function of the Miracle Narratives in Mark," doctoral dissertation, University of South Africa, Pretoria, South Africa, 1983.

4187 Aage Pilgaard, *Jesus som undergører i Markusevangeliet: undertraditionens betydning for Markusevangeliets kristologi*. Cophagen: Gad, 1983.

4188 Jean Carmignac, "Ah, Si tu peux—Tout est possible en faveur de celui qui croit (Marc 9:23)," in William C. Weinrich, ed., *The New Testament Age* (festschrift for Bo Reicke). 2 vols. Macon GA: Mercer University Press, 1984. 1:83-86.

4189 Frans Neirynck, "Papyrus Egerton 2 and the Healing of the Leper," *ETL* 61/1 (1985): 153-60.

4190 John J. Pilch, "Healing in Mark: A Social Science Analysis," *BTB* 15 (1985): 142-50.

4191 Stephen C. Barton, "The Miraculous Feedings in Mark," *ET* 97/4 (1985-1986): 112-13.

4192 Kent E. Brower, "Synoptic Miracle Stories: A Jewish Religious and Social Setting," *Forum* 2/4 (1986): 55-76.

4193 Walter Brueggemann, "Theological Education: Healing the Blind Beggar," *CC* 103/5 (1986): 114-16.

4194 Fred L. Horton, "Nochmals Εφφαθα in Mk 7:34," *ZNW* 77/1 (1986): 101-108.

4195 Ched Myers, "The Miracle of One Loaf [Mk 4:35-8:21; pt. 3 on Gospel of Mark]," *Soj* 16 (1987): 31-34.

4196 John F. O'Grady, "A Question of Miracles," *BibTo* 25 (1987): 367-73.

4197 Ivor Bailey, "The Cripple's Story," *ET* 99 (1987-1988): 110-12.

4198 P.-G. Klumbies, "Die Sabbatheilungen Jesu nach Markus und Lukas," in Dietrich-Alex Koch, et al., eds., *Jesu Rede von Gott und ihre Nachgeschichte im frühen Christentum* (festschrift for Willi Marxsen). Gütersloh: Güterloher Verlag, 1989. Pp. 165-78.

4199 Michal Wojciechowski, "The Touching of the Leper (Mark 1:40-45) as a Historical and Symbolic Act of Jesus," *BZ* 33/1 (1989): 114-19.

4200 Ulrich Busse, "Metaphorik in neutestamentlichen Wundergeschichten? Mk 1,21-28; Joh 9,1-41," in Karl Kertelge, ed., *Metaphorik und Mythos im Neuen Testament*. Freiburg: Herder, 1990. Pp. 110-34.

4201 Scott Cunningham, "The Healing of the Deaf and Dumb Man (Mark 7:31-37), with Application to the African Context," *AJET* 9/2 (1990): 13-26.

4202 Jeffrey B. Gibson, "Jesus' Refusal to Produce a 'Sign' (Mark 8:11-13)," *JSNT* 38 (1990): 37-66.

4203 John E. Phelan, "The Function of Mark's Miracles," *CQ* 48 (1990): 3-14.

4204 Joseph A. Grassi, *Loaves and Fishes: The Gospel Feeding Narratives*. Collegeville MN: Liturgical Press, 1991.

4205 Mark F. S. C. McVann, "Baptism, Miracles, and Boundary Jumping in Mark," *BTB* 21 (1991): 151-57.

4206 Carl Kazmierski, "Evangelist and Leper: A Socio-Cultural Study of Mark 1:40-45," *NTS* 38 (1992): 37-50.

4207 Isabelle Parlier, "L'autorité qui révèle la foi et l'incrédulite: Marc 2/1-12," *ÉTR* 67/2 (1992): 243-47.

mission

4208 Edgar S. Mizell, "The Missionary Idea in the Synoptic Gospels," doctoral dissertation, Midwestern Baptist Theological Seminary, Kansas City KS, 1946.

4209 Francis W. Beare, "The Mission of the Disciples and the Mission Charge: Matthew 10 and Parallels," *JBL* 89/1 (1970): 1-13.

4210 Paul T. Coke, "The Mission of Jesus in the Gospel of Mark," doctoral dissertation, General Theological Seminary, New York, 1971.

4211 Joseph Anthonysamy, "The Gospel of Mark and the Universal Mission," *BB* 6 (1980): 81-96.

4212 Joseph Anthonysamy, "The Gentile Mission in the Gospel of Mark: A Redaction-Critical Study of Passages with a Gentile Tendency," doctoral dissertation, Pontifical University, Rome, 1982.

4213 Anthony Gittins, "Call and Response: Missionary Considerations," *LouvS* 10/3 (1985): 264-85.

4214 Lucien Legrand, "The Missionary Command of the Risen Christ: I. Mission and Resurrection," *ITS* 23 (1986): 290-309.

motif/motifs

4215 T. A. Burkill, "St. Mark's Philosophy of History," *NTS* 3 (1956-1957): 142-48.

4216 Gottfried Schille, "Die Topographie des Markusevangeliums, ihre Hintergrunde und ihre Einordnung," *ZDPV* 73 (1957): 133-66.

4217 Charles L. Smith, "Tabernacles in the Fourth Gospel and Mark," *NTS* 9 (1962-1963): 130-46.

4218 T. A. Burkill, *Mysterious Revelation: An Examination of the Philosophy of St. Mark's Gospel*. Ithaca NY: Cornell University Press, 1963.

4219 Ulrich W. Mauser, *Christ in the Wilderness: The Wilderness Theme in the Second Gospel and Its Basis in the Biblical Tradition*. Studies in Biblical Theology #39. Naperville IL: Allenson, 1963.

4220 Frederick W. Danker, "Mark 1:45 and the Secrecy Motif," *CTM* 37 (1966): 492-99.

4221 Gottfried Schille, "Der Beitrag des Evangelisten Markus zum kirchenbildenden (ökumenischen) Gesprach seiner Tage," *KD* 12 (1966): 135-53.

4222 Frederick W. Danker, "Postscript to the Markan Secrecy Motif," *CTM* 38 (1967): 24-27.

4223 Richard C. Nevius, *The Divine Names in the Gospels*. Studies and Documents #30. Salt Lake City UT: University of Utah Press, 1967.

4224 Ludger Schenke, *Glory and the Way of the Cross. The Gospel of Mark*. Robin Scroggs, trans. Herald Biblical Booklets. Chicago: Franciscan Herald Press, 1972.

4225 Gerhard Krause, ed., *Die Kinder im Evangelium*. Praktische Schriftauslegung 10. Stuttgart/Göttingen: Klotz, 1973.

4226 Alois Stöger, "Das Kerygma des Markusevangeliums," *BL* 46 (1973): 22-29.

4227 Emery A. Lekai, "The Theology of the People of God in Ernst Lohmeyer's *Commentaries on the Gospels of Mark and Matthew*," doctoral dissertation, Catholic University of America, Washington DC, 1974.

4228 Paul Lamarche, *Révélation de Dieu chez Marc*. Le point théologique #20. Paris: Beauchesne, 1976.

4229 Philip Van Linden, *Gospel of St. Mark.* Read and Pray #4. Chicago: Franciscan Herald Press, 1976.

4230 Paul Lamarche, "L'humiliation du Christ," *Chr* 26 (1979): 461-70.

4231 Marian Madore, "Wilderness and Marketplace: Prayer and Action in Mark's Gospel," *RevRel* 38 (1979): 197-201.

4232 Robert W. Stacy, " 'Fear' in the Gospel of Mark," doctoral dissertation, Southern Baptist Theological Seminary, Louisville KY, 1979.

4233 Leslie F. Weber, "Consolation in the Gospel of Mark," doctoral dissertation, Christ Seminary-Seminex, Chicago IL, 1979.

4234 Frank J. Matera, *The Kingship of Jesus: Composition and Theology in Mark 15*. Chico CA: Scholars Press, 1982.

4235 John Navone, "The Story Told by Mark: God's Word of Love," *ClerR* 67 (1982): 199-203.

4236 Ronald E. Bracewell, "Shepherd Imagery in the Synoptic Gospels," doctoral dissertation, Southern Baptist Theological Seminary, Louisville KY, 1983.

4237 George B. Caird, "The One and the Many in Mark and John," in H. Davies, ed. *Studies of the Church in History* (festschrift for Robert S. Paul). Pittsburgh Theological Seminary Monograph Series #5. Allison Park PA: Pickwick Press, 1983. Pp. 39-54.

4238 Donna Runnalls, "The King as Temple Builder: A Messianic Typology," in Edward J. Furcha, ed., *Spirit within Structure* (festschrift for George Johnston). Allison Park PA: Pickwick Press, 1983. Pp. 15-37.

4239 Ernst L. Schnellbächer, "The Temple as Focus of Mark's Theology," *HBT* 5 (1983): 95-112.

4240 Wolfgang Schenk, "The Mystery of the Gospel of Mark," *SecCent* 4 (1984): 65-82.

4241 Jerome H. Neyrey, ''The Idea of Purity in Mark's Gospel,'' *Semeia* 35 (1986): 91-128.

4242 W. Ernest Moore, '' 'Outside' and 'Inside' a Markan Motif,'' *ET* 98/2 (1986-1987): 39-43.

4243 Edwin K. Broadhead, ''The Role of *Wundergeschichten* in the Characterization of Jesus in the Gospel of Mark,'' doctoral dissertation, Southern Baptist Theological Seminary, Louisville KY, 1987.

4244 W. J. Ireland, '' 'By What Authority?': Toward the Construction of a Symbolic World in Mark,'' doctoral dissertation, Southern Baptist Theological Seminary, Louisville KY, 1987.

4245 Dorothy A. Lee-Pollard, ''Powerlessness as Power: A Key Emphasis in the Gospel of Mark,'' *SJT* 40 (1987): 173-88.

4246 Mecklin R. Mansfield, *''Spirit and Gospel'' in Mark*. Peabody MA: Hendrickson Publishers, 1987.

4247 David M. May, ''The Role of House and Household Language in the Markan Social World,'' doctoral dissertation, Southern Baptist Theological Seminary, Louisville KY, 1987.

4248 Paul R. Hinlicky, ''Conformity to Christ in the Gospel of Mark,'' *CThM* 15 (1988): 364-68.

4249 Ben F. Meyer, ''The Expiation Motif in the Eucharistic Words: A Key to the History of Jesus?'' *Greg* 69 (1988): 461-87.

4250 Gail R. O'Day, ''Hope beyond Brokenness: A Markan Reflection on the Gift of Life,'' *CThM* 15 (1988): 244-51.

4251 Dan O. Via, ''Irony as Hope in Mark's Gospel: A Reply to Werner Kelber,'' *Semeia* 43 (1988): 21-27.

4252 Hugh M. Humphrey, ''Jesus as Wisdom in Mark,'' *BTB* 19/2 (1989): 48-53.

4253 Christopher D. Marshall, *Faith as a Theme in Mark's Narrative*. SNTSMS #64. Cambridge: Cambridge University Press, 1989.

4254 Stephen H. Smith, "The Role of Jesus' Opponents in the Markan Drama," *NTS* 35 (1989): 161-82.

4255 Richard G. Walsh, "Tragic Dimensions in Mark," *BTB* 19 (1989): 94-99.

4256 T. R. Dwyer, "The Motif of Wonder in the Gospel of Mark," doctoral dissertation, University of Aberdeen, Aberdeen, 1990.

names in

4257 Richard C. Nevius, *The Divine Names in St. Mark*. Studies and Documents 25. Salt Lake City: University of Utah Press, 1964.

4258 Richard C. Nevius, "The Use of Proper Names in St. Mark," *StudE* 2 (1964): 225-28.

narrative criticism

4259 Detlev Dormeyer, " 'Narrative Analyse' von Mk 2,1-12," *LB* 31 (1974): 68-88.

4260 Hans-Josef Klauck, "Die erzählerische Rolle der Jünger im Markusevangelium: Eine narrative Analyse," *NovT* 24 (1982): 1-26.

4261 David Rhoads, "Narrative Criticism and the Gospel of Mark," *JAAR* 50 (1982): 411-34.

4262 David Rhoads and D. Michie, *Mark as Story: An Introduction to the Narrative of a Gospel*. Philadelphia: Fortress Press, 1982.

4263 William A. Beardslee, "Narrative and History in the Post-Modern World: The Case of the Gospel of Mark," in S. Putzell-Korab and Robert Detweiler, eds., *The Crisis in the Humanities: Interdisciplinary Responses*. Madrid: José Porrúa Turanzas, 1983. Pp. 47-60.

4264 Lars Lode, "Narrative Paragraphs in the Gospels and Acts," *BT* 34/3 (1983): 322-35.

4265 Michael R. Cosby, ''Mark 14:51-52 and the Problem of Gospel Narrative,'' *PRS* 11/3 (1984): 219-31.

4266 Cilliers Breytenbach, ''Das Markusevangelium als episodische Erzählung: Mit Uberlegungen zum 'Aufbau' des zweiten Evangeliums,'' in Ferdinand Hahn, ed., *Der Erzähler des Evangeliums: Methodische Neuansätze in der Markusforschung*. Stuttgart: Verlag Katholisches Bibelwerk, 1985. Pp. 137-69.

4267 John N. Blackwell, *The Passion as Story: The Plot of Mark*. Philadelphia: Fortress, 1986.

4268 Benoît Standaert, ''La rhétorique ancienne dans saint Paul,'' in Albert Vanhoye, ed., *L'Apôtre Paul: personnalité, style et conception du ministère*. Louvain: Louvain University Press, 1986. Pp. 78-92.

4269 Charles W. Hedrick, ''Narrator and Story in the Gospel of Mark: *Hermeneia* and *Paradosis*,'' *PRS* 14 (1987): 239-58.

4270 Ernest Best, *Mark: The Gospel as Story*. 2nd ed. Edinburgh: T. & T. Clark, 1988.

4271 John Dominic Crossan, ''Aphorism in Discourse and Narrative,'' *Semeia* 43 (1988): 121-40.

4272 Werner H. Kelber, ''Narrative and Disclosure: Mechanisms of Concealing, Revealing, and Reveiling,'' *Semeia* 43 (1988): 1-20.

4273 Timothy J. Kevil, ''At Once in All Its Parts: Narrative Unity in the Gospel of Mark,'' doctoral dissertation, North Texas State University, Denton TX, 1988.

4274 Ernest Best, ''Mark's Narrative Technique,'' *JSNT* 37 (1989): 43-58.

4275 James R. Edwards, ''Markan Sandwiches: The Significance of Interpolations in Markan Narratives,'' *NovT* 31 (1989): 193-216.

4276 Jean-Claude Giroud, ''La parabole ou l'opacité incontournable: a propos de Mc 4,1-34,'' in Jean Delorme, ed., *Les paraboles évangéliques: perspectives nouvelles*. Paris: Cerf, 1989. Pp. 235-46.

4277 Vicente Balaguer, *Testimonio y tradición en San Marcos: Narratología del segundo evangelio*. Pamplona: Ed. Univ. de Navarra, 1990.

4278 Corina Combet-Galland, "Qui roulera la peur? Finales d'évangile et figures de lecteur (a partir du chapitre 16 de l'Evangile de Marc)," *TR* 65/2 (1990): 171-89.

4279 William G. Doty, "Afterword: Sacred Pigs and Secular Cookies: Mark and Atwood Go Postmodern," in Robert Detweiler and W. G. Doty, eds., *The Daemonic Imagination: Biblical Text and Secular Story*. Atlanta: Scholars Press, 1990. Pp. 191-207.

4280 A.-J. Morey, "The Old In/Out," in Robert Detweiler and W. G. Doty, eds., *The Daemonic Imagination: Biblical Text and Secular Story*. Atlanta: Scholars Press, 1990. Pp. 169-79.

4281 Paul Ricoeur, "Interpretative Narrative," in Regina M. Schwartz, ed., *The Book and the Text: The Bible and Literary Theory*. Cambridge MA: Blackwell, 1990. Pp. 237-57.

4282 Pieter J. J. Botha, "Mark's Story as Oral Traditional Literature: Rethinking the Transmission of Some Traditions about Jesus," *HTS* 47 (1991): 304-31.

4283 Paul L. Danove, *The End of Mark's Story: A Methodological Story*. Leiden: Brill, 1993.

parables

4284 A. Herranz, "Las parábolas: Un problema y una solución," *CuBí* 12 (1955): 128-37.

4285 T. A. Burkill, "The Cryptology of Parables in St. Mark's Gospel," *NovT* 1 (1956): 246-62.

4286 Oscar Cullmann, "Que signifie le sel dans la parabole de Jésus (Mc 9,49s par.)," *RHPR* 37 (1957): 36-43.

4287 Franz Mussner, "1QHodajoth und das Gleichnis vom Senfkorn (Mk 4:30-32 Par)," *BZ* 4/1 (1960): 128-30.

4288 Harold S. Songer, "A Study of the Background of the Concepts of Parable in the Synoptic Gospels," doctoral dissertation, Southern Baptist Theological Seminary, Louisville KY, 1962.

4289 Elizabeth A. Bogert, "The Parable and the Greenhouse: Mark 4:1-20," *HartQ* 4 (1964): 61-64.

4290 Wilfrid J. Harrington, *A Key to the Parables*. New York: Paulist Press, 1964.

4291 G. V. Jones, *The Art and Truth of the Parables: A Study in their Literary Form and Modern Interpretation*. London: SPCK, 1964.

4292 K. D. White, "The Parable of the Sower," *JTS* 15 (1964): 300-307.

4293 Wilhelm Wilkens, "Die Redaktion des Gleichniskapitels Mark 4 durch Matth," *TZ* 20 (1964): 305-27.

4294 Eugen Biser, *Die Gleichnisse Jesu: Versuch einer Deulung*. Münich: Kösel, 1965.

4295 William Neil, "Expounding the Parables: II. The Sower (Mark 4:3-8)," *ET* 77 (1965-1966): 74-77.

4296 F. D. Howard, *Interpreting the Lord's Parables*. Nashville: Broadman Press, 1966.

4297 Aloysius M. Ambrozic, "Mark's Concept of the Parable," *CBQ* 29 (1967): 220-27.

4298 D. H. S. Armstrong, "The Parables of the Synoptic Gospels, with Special Reference to Modern Interpretation," doctoral dissertation, Trinity College, Dublin, 1967.

4299 Edward A. Armstrong, *The Gospel Parables*. London: Hodder & Stoughton, 1967.

4300 Jan Lambrecht, "De Vijf Parabels van Mc. 4: Structuur en Theologie van de Parabeelrede," *Bij* 29/1 (1968): 25-53.

4301 E. Cyril Blackman, "New Methods of Parable Interpretation," *CJT* 15 (1969): 3-13.

4302 William Barclay, *And Jesus Said: A Handbook on the Parables of Jesus*. Philadelphia: Westminster, 1970.

4303 Jacques Dupont, "La parabole du maître qui rentre dans la nuit (Mc 13,34-36)," in Albert Descamps and André de Halleux, eds., *Mélanges bibliques en hommage au R. P. Béda Rigaux*. Gembloux: Duculot, 1970. Pp. 89-116.

4304 Alistair Kee, "The Old Coat and the New Wine. A Parable of Repentance," *NovT* 12 (1970): 13-21.

4305 J. Ajuria, *Marcos, Mateo, Lucas y Juan. palabras basicas del evangelio*. Madrid: EPESA, 1971.

4306 John Dominic Crossan, "The Parable of the Wicked Husbandmen," *JBL* 90/4 (1971): 451-65.

4307 William G. Doty, "An Interpretation: Parable of the Weeds and Wheat," *Int* 25 (1971): 185-93.

4308 Harvey K. McArthur, "The Parable of the Mustard Seed," *CBQ* 33/2 (1971): 198-210.

4309 Michel Morlet, "Le chapitre des paraboles dans l'Évangile de Marc," *EV* 81 (1971): 513-20.

4310 J. W. Pryor, "Markan Parable Theology: An Inquiry into Mark's Principles of Redaction," *ET* 83/4 (1971-1972): 242-45.

4311 J. E. Newell and R. R. Newell. "The Parable of the Wicked Tenants," *NovT* 14 (1972): 226-37.

4312 Norman Perrin, "Historical Criticism, Literary Criticism, and Hermeneutics: The Interpretation of the Parables of Jesus and the Gospel of Mark Today," *JR* 52 (1972): 361-75.

4313 Michel Bouttier, "Les paraboles du maître dans la tradition synoptique," *ÉTR* 48 (1973): 175-95.

4314 John Dominic Crossan, "Parable as Religious and Poetic Experience," *JR* 53/3 (1973): 330-58.

4315 John Drury, "The Sower, the Vineyard, and the Place of Allegory in the Interpretation of Mark's Parables," *JTS* 24/2 (1973): 367-79.

4316 W. G. Kümmel, "Noch einmal: Das Gleichnis von der selbstwachsende Saat. Bemerkungen zur neutestamentlichen Diskussion um die Auslegung der Gleichnisse Jesu," in Paul Hoffmann, ed., with Norbert Brox and Wilhelm Pesch, *Orientierung an Jesu. Zur Theologie der Synoptiker. Für Josef Schmid.* Freiburg: Herder, 1973. Pp. 220-37.

4317 Heikki Räisänen, *Die Parabeltheorie im Markusevangelium.* Schriften der Finnischen Exegetischen Gesellschaft 26. Helsinki/Leiden: Finnish Exegetical Society/Brill, 1973.

4318 J. P. M. Sweet, "A Saying, a Parable, a Miracle," *Theology* 76 (1973): 125-33.

4319 David Wenham, "The Interpretation of the Parable of the Sower," *NTS* 20 (1973-1974): 299-319.

4320 John W. Bowker, "Mystery and Parable: Mark 4:1-20," *JTS* 25/2 (1974): 301-17.

4321 B. Dehandschutter, "La parabole des vignerons homicides (Mc. XII,1-12) et l'évangile selon Thomas," in M. Sabbe, ed., *L'évangile selon Marc: Tradition et rédaction.* BETL #34. Louvain: Louvain University Press, 1974. Pp. 203-19.

4322 B. Englezakis, "Markan Parable: More than Word Modality, a Revelation of Contents," *DBM* 2 (1974): 349-57.

4323 Michel Hubaut, "Le 'mystère' révélé dans les paraboles (Mc 4,11-12)," *RTL* 5 (1974): 454-61.

4324 A. N. Wilder, "The Parable of the Sower: Naivete and Method in Interpretation," *Semeia* 2 (1974): 134-51.

4325 J. A. T. Robinson, "The Parable of the Wicked Husbandmen: A Test of Synoptic Relationships," *NTS* 21/4 (1974-1975): 443-61.

4326 Charles E. Carlston, *The Parables of the Triple Tradition.* Philadelphia: Fortress, 1975.

4327 Jan Lambrecht, "Parabels in Mc. 4," *TijT* 15 (1975): 26-43.

4328 Jean Alexandre, "Note sur l'esprit des paraboles, en réponse a P. Ricceur," *ÉTR* 51 (1976): 367-72.

4329 Félix Casá, "Parabolas y catequesis," *RevB* 38 (1976): 97-111.

4330 Michel Hubaut, *La parabole des vignerons homicides.* Cahiers de la Revue Biblique 16. Paris: Gabalda, 1976.

4331 Léopold Sabourin, "The Parables of the Kingdom," *BTB* 6 (1976): 115-60.

4332 Étienne Trocmé, "Why Parables? A Study of Mark IV," *BJRL* 59/2 (1976-1977): 458-71.

4333 Tullio Aurelio, *Disclosures in den Gleichnissen Jesu.* Frankfurt: Lang, 1977.

4334 Madeleine I. Boucher, *The Mysterious Parable. A Literary Study.* CBQMS #6. Washington DC: Catholic Biblical Association, 1977.

4335 J. R. Kirkland, "The Earliest Understanding of Jesus' Use of Parables: Mark 4:10-12 in Context," *NovT* 19/1 (1977): 1-21.

4336 Earl Breech, "Kingdom of God and the Parables of Jesus," *Semeia* 12 (1978): 15-40.

4337 John R. Donahue, "Jesus as the Parable of God in the Gospel of Mark," *Int* 32 (1978): 369-86.

4338 Peter R. Jones, "The Seed Parables of Mark," *RevExp* 75 (1978): 519-38.

4339 Gerald O'Mahony, "Mark's Gospel and the Parable of the Sower," *BibTo* 98 (1978): 1764-68.

4340 P. B. Payne, "The Order of Sowing and Ploughing in the Parable of the Sower," *NTS* 25 (1978-1979): 123-29.

4341 Theodore J. Weeden, "Recovering the Parabolic Intent in the Parable of the Sower," *JAAR* 47 (1979): 97-120.

4342 P. B. Payne, "The Seeming Inconsistency of the Interpretation of the Parable of the Sower," *NTS* 26/4 (1979-1980): 564-68.

4343 J. Duncan M. Derrett, "ἦσαν γὰρ ἁλιεῖς (Mk. 1,16): Jesus' Fishermen and the Parable of the Net," *NovT* 22 (1980): 108-37.

4344 Peter R. Jones, "The Modern Study of Parables," *SouJT* 22 (1980): 7-22.

4345 P. B. Payne, "The Authenticity of the Parable of the Sower and Its Interpretation," in R. T. France and David Wenham, eds., *Gospel Perspectives: Studies of History and Tradition in the Four Gospels*. Sheffield: JSOT Press, 1980. 1:163-207.

4346 John A. Sproule, "The Problem of the Mustard Seed," *GTJ* 1/1 (1980): 37-42.

4347 Edmund Arens, "Gleichnisse als kommunikative Handlungen Jesu: Überlegungen zu einer pragmatischen Gleichnistheorie," *TheoP* 56 (1981): 47-69.

4348 John Drury, "Origins of Mark's Parables," in M. Wadsworth, ed., *Ways of Reading the Bible*. Totowa NJ: Barnes & Noble Books, 1981. Pp. 171-89.

4349 Peter Rhea Jones, *The Teaching of the Parables*. Nashville TN: Broadman Press, 1982.

4350 José Cárdenas-Pallares, "El misterio del reinado de Dios; las parabolas segun San Marcos," *Servitum* 20 (1984): 215-45.

4351 Joel Marcus, ''Mark 4:10-12 and Markan Epistemology,'' *JBL* 103/4 (1984): 557-74.

4352 Craig A. Evans, ''On the Isaianic Background of the Parable of the Sower,'' *CBQ* 47/3 (1985): 464-68.

4353 I. H. Jones, ''Recent Work on the Parables,'' *EpRev* 12 (1985): 89-96.

4354 Jonathan Bishop, ''Parabole and Parrhesia in Mark,'' *Int* 40/1 (1986): 39-52.

4355 Richard Bauckham, ''The Parable of the Vine: Rediscovering a Lost Parable of Jesus,'' *NTS* 33/1 (1987): 84-101.

4356 Corina Combet-Galland, ''La vigne et l'écriture, histoire de reconnaissances: Marc 12:1-12,'' *ÉTR* 62/4 (1987): 489-502.

4357 Claude N. Pavur, ''The Grain is Ripe: Parabolic Meaning in Mark 4:26-29,'' *BTB* 17/1 (1987): 21-23.

4358 Christopher M. Tuckett, ''Mark's Concerns in the Parables Chapter (Mark 4,1-34),'' *Bib* 69/1 (1988): 1-26.

4359 Jean P. Duplantier, ''Les vignerons meurtriers: le travail d'une parabole,'' in Jean Delorme, ed., *Les paraboles évangéliques: perspectives nouvelles*. Paris: Cerf, 1989. Pp. 259-70.

4360 Vittorio Fusco, ''Mc 4,1-34: la section des paraboles,'' in Jean Delorme, ed., *Les paraboles évangéliques: perspectives nouvelles*. Paris: Cerf, 1989. Pp. 219-34.

4361 Aaron A. Milavec, ''A Fresh Analysis of the Parable of the Wicked Husbandmen in the Light of Jewish-Christian Dialogue,'' in Clemens Thoma, et al., eds., *Parable and Story in Judaism and Christianity*. New York: Paulist Press, 1989. Pp. 81-117.

4362 Aaron A. Milavec, ''Mark's Parable of the Wicked Husbandmen as Reaffirming God's Predilection for Israel,'' *JES* 26 (1989): 289-312.

4363 Maurice Nicoll, "The Grain of the Mustard Seed," *ParaM* 14/3 (1989): 79.

4364 David Stern, "Jesus' Parables from the Perspective of Rabbinic Literature: The Example of the Wicked Husbandmen," in Clemens Thoma, et al., eds., *Parable and Story in Judaism and Christianity*. New York: Paulist Press, 1989. Pp. 42-80.

4365 Michel Trimaille, "La parabole des vignerons meurtriers (Mc 12,1-12)," in Jean Delorme, ed., *Les paraboles évangéliques: perspectives nouvelles*. Paris: Cerf, 1989. Pp. 247-58.

4366 George Aichele, "The Fantastic in the Parabolic Language of Jesus," *Neo* 24 (1990): 93-105.

4367 Gerhard Dautzenberg, "Mk 4:1-34 als Belehrung über das Reich Gottes: Beobachtungen zum Gleichniskapitel," *BZ* 34/1 (1990): 38-62.

4368 Aaron A. Milavec, "The Identity of 'the Son' and 'the Others': Mark's Parable of the Wicked Husbandmen Reconsidered," *BTB* 20 (1990): 30-37.

4369 Michael Stahl, "Vom Verstehen des Neuen Testaments in der einen Welt," *ZMiss* 16/4 (1990): 224-35.

4370 Patrick J. Hartin, "Disseminating the Word: A Deconstructive Reading of Mark 4:1-9 and Mark 4:13-20," in Patrick J. Hartin and J. H. Petzer, eds., *Text and Interpretation: New Approaches in the Criticism of the New Testament*. Leiden: Brill, 1991. Pp. 187-200.

4371 Fritzleo Lentzen-Deis, "Handlungsorientierte Exegese der 'Wachstums-Gleichnisse' in Mk 4,1-34: pragmalinguistische Aspekte bei der Auslegung fiktionaler Texte," in Johannes J. Degenhardt, *Die Freude an Gott: Unsere Kraft* (festschrift for Otto B. Knoch). Stuttgart: Verlag Katholisches Bibelwerk, 1991. Pp. 117-34.

4372 John P. Heil, "Reader-Response and the Narrative Context of the Parables about Growing Seed in Mark 4:1-34," *CBQ* 54 (1992): 271-86.

4373 Marie Sabin, "Reading Mark 4 as Midrash," *JSNT* 45 (1992): 3-26.

passion

4374 Harold Reed, "The Narrative of Christ's Passion in Mark and Luke," doctoral dissertation, Southern Baptist Theological Seminary, Louisville KY, 1929.

4375 A. Barr, "The Use and Disposal of the Marcan Source in Luke's Passion Narrative," *ET* 55 (1943-1944): 227-31.

4376 Eric F. F. Bishop, "With Jesus on the Road from Galilee to Calvary: Palestinian Glimpses into the Days Around the Passion," *CBQ* 11 (1949): 428-44.

4377 C. Hope, "The Story of the Passion and Resurrection in the English Primer," *JTS* 2 (1951): 68-82.

4378 Kenneth Grayston, "The Darkness of the Cosmic Sea: A Study of Symbolism in Mark's Narrative of the Crucifixion," *Theology* 55 (1952): 122-27.

4379 Karl G. Kuhn, "Jesus in Gethsemane," *EvT* 12 (1952-1953): 260-85.

4380 Christian Maurer, "Knecht Gottes und Sohn Gottes im Passionsbericht des Markusevangeliums," *ZTK* 50 (1953): 1-38.

4381 Josef Blinzler, "Der Entscheid des Pilatus: Exekutionsbefehl oder Todesurteil?" *MTZ* 5 (1954): 171-84.

4382 Josef Schmid, "Die Darstellung der Passion Jesu in den Evangelien," *GeistL* 27 (1954): 6-15.

4383 Vincent Taylor, "The Origin of the Marcan Passion Sayings," *NTS* 1 (1954-1955): 159-67.

4384 O. A. Piper, "God's Good News. The Passion Story according to Mark," *Int* 9 (1955): 165-82.

4385 Franz J. Leenhardt, "Reflexions sur la mort de Jesus-Christ," *RHPR* 37 (1957): 18-23.

4386 T. A. Burkill, "St. Mark's Philosophy of the Passion," *NovT* 2 (1957-1958): 245-71.

4387 Ivor Buse, "St. John and the Marcan Passion Narrative," *NTS* 4 (1957-1958): 215-19.

4388 T. A. Burkill, "The Trial of Jesus," *VC* 12 (1958): 1-18.

4389 John C. Fenton, *Preaching the Cross: The Passion and Resurrection according to St. Mark with an Introduction and Notes*. London: SPCK, 1958.

4390 Peder Borgen, "John and the Synoptics in the Passion Narrative," *NTS* 5 (1958-1959): 246-59.

4391 Jan W. Doeve, "Die Gefangennahme Jesu in Gethsemane: Eine traditionsgeschichtliche Untersuchung," *StudE* 1 (1959): 458-80.

4392 Xavier Léon-Dufour, "Mt et Mc dans le récit de las Passion," *Bib* 40 (1959): 684-96.

4393 Xavier Léon-Dufour, "Autour des recits de la Passion," *RechSR* 48 (1960): 489-507.

4394 F. F. Bruce, "The Book of Zechariah and the Passion Narrative," *BJRL* 43 (1960-1961): 336-53.

4395 William Barclay, *Crucified and Crowned*. London: SCM, 1961.

4396 Francis Dewar, "Chapter 13 and the Passion Narrative in St. Mark," *Theology* 64 (1961): 99-107.

4397 H.-W. Bartsch, "Historische Erwägungen zur Leidensgeschichte," *EvT* 22 (1962): 449-59.

4398 A. M. Ramsey, *The Narratives of the Passion*. Contemporary Studies in Theology #2. London: Mowbrays, 1962.

4399 Paul Winter, "The Marcan Account of Jesus' Trial by the Sanhedrin," *JTS* 14 (1963): 94-102.

4400 C. J. Armbruster, "The Messianic Significance of the Agony in the Garden," *Scr* 16 (1964): 111-19.

4401 H.-W. Bartsch, "Die Bedeutung des Sterbens Jesu nach den Synoptikern," *TZ* 20 (1964): 87-102.

4402 J. McRuer, *The Trial of Jesus*. Toronto: Clarke, Irwin & Co., 1964.

4403 John Wilkinson, "Seven Words from the Cross," *SJT* 17 (1964): 69-82.

4404 Ernest Best, *The Temptation and the Passion: The Markan Soteriology*. SNTSMS #2. Cambridge/New York: Cambridge University Press, 1965.

4405 W. Koch, *Der Prozess Jesu: Versuch eines Tatsachenberichts*. Koln: Kiepenheuer & Witsch, 1966.

4406 Wolfgang Trilling, "Die Passionsgeschichte in den synoptischen Evangelien," *LZ* 1 (1966): 28-46.

4407 André Feuillet, "Les trois grandes prophéties de la Passion et de la Résurrection des évangiles synoptiques," *RT* 67 (1967): 533-60; 68 (1968): 41-74.

4408 F. H. Milling, "History and Prophecy in the Marcan Passion Narrative," *IJT* 16 (1967): 42-53.

4409 W. J. Bennett, "The Role of δεῖ in the Marcan Understanding of the Passion," doctoral dissertation, Drew University, Madison NJ, 1968.

4410 G. M. Lee, "The Inscription on the Cross," *PEQ* 100 (1968): 144.

4411 Matthew Black, "The Son of Man's Passion Sayings in the Gospel Tradition," *ZNW* 60 (1969): 58-65.

4412 Jacob Kremer, *Das Ärgernis des Kreuzes. Eine Hinführung zum Verstehen der Leidensgeschichte nach Markus*. Stuttgart: Katholisches Bibelwerk, 1969.

4413 Johannes Schreiber, *Die Markuspassion. Wege zur Erforschung der Leidensgeschichte Jesu.* Hamburg: Furche-Verlag, 1969.

4414 August Strobel, "Die Deutung des Todes Jesu im ältesten Evangelium," in P. Rieger, ed., *Das Kreuz Jesu: theologische Überlegnugen. Beiträge von Georg Strobel.* Forum 12. Göttingen: Vandenhoeck & Ruprecht, 1969. Pp. 32-64.

4415 R. S. Barbour, "Gethsemane in the Tradition of the Passion," *NTS* 16 (1969-1970): 231-51.

4416 J. E. Allen, "Why Pilate?" in E. Bammel, ed., *The Trial of Jesus* (festschrift for C. F. D. Moule). London: SCM, 1970. Pp. 78-83.

4417 Hans Conzelmann, "History and Theology in the Passion Narratives of the Synoptic Gospels," *Int* 24 (1970): 178-97.

4418 Michel Coune, "Baptême, Transfiguration, et Passion," *NRT* 92 (1970): 165-79.

4419 Frederick W. Danker, "The Demonic Secret in Mark: A Reexamination of the Cry of Dereliction (15:34)," *ZNW* 61 (1970): 48-69.

4420 Eta Linnemann, *Studien zur Passionsgeschichte.* Forschungen zur Religion und Literatur des Alten und Neuen Testaments 102. Göttingen: Vandenhoeck & Ruprecht, 1970.

4421 David R. Catchpole, "The Answer of Jesus to Caiaphas (Matthew 26:64)," *NTS* 17/2 (1970-1971): 213-26.

4422 M. Bednarz, "Les éléments parénétiques dans la description de la Passion chez les synoptiques," doctoral dissertation, Pontifical University of St. Thomas, Rome, 1971.

4423 S. G. F. Brandon, "The Trial of Jesus," *Judaism* 20 (1971): 43-48.

4424 J. Duncan M. Derrett, "Law in the New Testament: The Palm Sunday Colt," *NovT* 13 (1971): 241-58.

4425 David Flusser, "A Literary Approach to the Trial of Jesus," *Judaism* 20 (1971): 32-36.

4426 Werner H. Kelber, et al., "Reflections on the Question: Was there a Pre-Markan Passion Narrative?" *SBLSP* 1/2 (1971): 503-85.

4427 M. H. Marco, "Un problema de crítica histórica en el relato de la Pasión: la liberación de Barrabás," *EB* 30 (1971): 137-60.

4428 Hermann Patsch, "Der Einzug Jesu in Jerusalem. Ein historischer Versuch," *ZTK* 63 (1971): 1-26.

4429 Ludger Schenke, *Studien zur Passionsgeschichte des Markus. Tradition und Redaktion in Markus 14.1-12.* Forschung zur Bibel 4. Würzburg/Stuttgart: Echter-Verlag/Katholisches Bibelwerk, 1971.

4430 Gerard S. Sloyan, "The Last Days of Jesus," *Judaism* 20 (1971): 56-68.

4431 Albert Vanhoye, "Les récits de la passion dans les évangiles synoptiques," *AsSeign* 19 (1971): 38-67.

4432 Siegfried Vierzig, *Passionsgeschichten.* Gütersloh: Mohr, 1971.

4433 Gerhard Schneider, "Das Problem Einer Vorkanonischen Passionserzahlung," *BZ* 16/2 (1972): 222-44.

4434 Robert O. Byrd, "The Jewish and the Roman Proceedings against Jesus in Recent Research," doctoral dissertation, Southern Baptist Theological Seminary, Louisville KY, 1973.

4435 John R. Donahue, "Temple, Trial, and Royal Christology (Mark 14:53-65)," in Werner H. Kelber, ed., *The Passion in Mark: Studies on Mark 14-16.* Philadelphia: Fortress Press, 1973. Pp. 61-79.

4436 George W. Knight, "The Theological Significance of Kerygmatic Diversity in the Marcan Interpretation of the

Death of Jesus,'' doctoral dissertation, Southern Baptist Theological Seminary, Louisville KY, 1973.

4437 Robert Smith, ''Darkness at Noon: Mark's Passion Narrative,'' *CTM* 44 (1973): 325-38.

4438 Thomas E. Boomershine, ''Mark the Storyteller: A Rhetorical-Critical Investigation of Mark's Passion and Resurrection Narrative,'' doctoral dissertation, Union Theological Seminary, New York, 1974.

4439 Adelbert Denaux, ''La confession de Pierre et la première annonce de la Passion. Mc 8,27-35,'' *AsSeign* 55 (1974): 31-39.

4440 Detlev Dormeyer, *Die Passion Jesu als Verhaltensmodell: literarische und theologische Analyse der Traditions- und Redaktionsgeschichte der Markuspassion.* Neutestamentliche Abhandlungen, Neue Folge, 11. Münster: Verlag Aschendorff, 1974.

4441 Jacques Guillet, ''Les récits de la Passion,'' *LV* 23 (1974): 6-17.

4442 Wolfgang Schenk, ''Die gnostisierende Deutung des Todes Jesu und ihre kritische Interpretation durch den Evangelisten Markus,'' in Karl-Wolfgang Tröger, ed., *Gnosis und Neues Testament: Studien aus Religionswissenschaft und Theologie.* Gütersloh: Gütersloher Verlagshaus Gerd Mohn, 1974. Pp. 231-43.

4443 Wolfgang Schenk, *Der Passionsbericht nach Markus. Untersuchungen zur Überlieferungsgeschichte der Passionstraditionen.* Gütersloh: Mohn, 1974.

4444 Ludger Schenke, *Der gekreuzigte Christus. Versuch einer literarkritischen und traditionsgeschichtlichen Bestimmung der vormarkinischen Passionsgeschichte.* Stuttgarter Bibelstudien 69. Stuttgart: Katholisches Bibelwerk, 1974.

4445 Heinrich Schlier, *Die Markuspassion.* Kriterien 32. Einsiedeln: Johannes-Verlag, 1974.

4446 P. H. Schüngel, "Die Erzählung des Markus über den Tod Jesu," *Orient* 38 (1974): 62-65.

4447 Rudolf Pesch, "Die Passion des Menschensohnes: Eine Studie zu den Menschensohnworten der vormarkinischen Passionsgeschichte," in Rudolf Pesch and Rudolf Schnackenburg, eds., *Jesus und der Menschensohn: Für Anton Vögtle*, with Odilo Kaiser. Freiburg/Basel/Vienna: Herder, 1975. Pp. 166-95.

4448 J. M. Ford, " 'Crucify Him, Crucify Him' and the Temple Scroll," *ET* 87 (1975-1976): 275-78.

4449 Marcel Bastin, *Jésus devant sa passion*. Paris: Cerf, 1976.

4450 Janusz Czerski, "Die Passion Christi in den synoptischen Evangelien im Lichte der historisch-literarischen Kritik," *CollT* 46 (1976): 81-96.

4451 K. E. Dewey, "Peter's Curse and Cursed Peter (Mark 14:53-54, 66-72)," in Werner H. Kelber, ed., *The Passion in Mark: Studies on Mark 14-16*. Philadelphia: Fortress Press, 1976. Pp. 96-114.

4452 John R. Donahue, "Introduction: From Passion Traditions to Passion Narrative," in Werner H. Kelber, ed., *The Passion in Mark: Studies on Mark 14-16*. Philadelphia: Fortress Press, 1976. Pp. 1-20.

4453 André Feuillet, "Il significato fondamentale dell'agonia del Getsèmani," in *La sapienza della croce oggi*. 1. *Atti del Congresso internazionale: Roma 13-18 ottobre 1975*. Torino Leumann: Elle Di Ci, 1976. Pp. 69-85.

4454 Werner H. Kelber, "Conclusion: From Passion Narrative to Gospel," in Werner H. Kelber, ed., *The Passion in Mark: Studies on Mark 14-16*. Philadelphia: Fortress, 1976. Pp. 153-80.

4455 Werner H. Kelber, "The Hour of the Son of Man and the Temptation of the Disciples (Mark 14:32-42)," in Werner H. Kelber, ed., *The Passion in Mark: Studies on Mark 14-16*. Philadelphia: Fortress Press, 1976. Pp. 41-60.

4456 Werner H. Kelber, ed., *The Passion in Mark. Studies on Mark 14-16*. Philadelphia: Fortress Press, 1976.

4457 A. B. Kolenkow, "Healing Controversy as a Tie between Miracle and Passion Material for a Proto-Gospel," *JBL* 95/4 (1976): 623-38.

4458 Gerald O'Collins, "The Crucifixion," *DocLife* 26 (1976): 247-63.

4459 Angel Pérez Gordo, "Gli annunci della passione," in *La Sapienza della Croce oggi. Atti del Coneresso internazionale: Roma, 13-18 ottobre 1975. Vol. 1: La sapienza della Croce nella rivelazione e nell'ecumenismo*. Torino Leumann: Elle Di Ci, 1976. 1:106-25.

4460 Angel Pérez Gordo, "Notas sobre los anuncios de la Pasión," *Bur* 17 (1976): 251-70.

4461 Norman Perrin, "The High Priest's Question and Jesus' Answer (Mark 14:61-62)," in Werner H. Kelber, ed., *The Passion in Mark: Studies on Mark 14-16*. Philadelphia: Fortress Press, 1976. Pp. 80-95.

4462 Theodore J. Weeden, "The Cross as Power in Weakness (Mark 15:20b-41)," in Werner H. Kelber, ed., *The Passion in Mark: Studies on Mark 14-16*. Philadelphia: Fortress, 1976. Pp. 115-34.

4463 A. R. Winnett, "The Breaking of the Bread: Does it Symbolize the Passion?" *ET* 88 (1976-1977): 181-82.

4464 W. Boyd Barrick, "The Rich Man from Arimathea (Matt 27:57-60) and 1QIsa[a]," *JBL* 96 (1977): 235-39.

4465 André Feuillet, *L'Agonie de Gethsémani: enquête exegetique et théologique suivi d'une étude du "Mystere de Jésus" de Pascal*. Paris: Éditions Gabalda, 1977.

4466 Leander E. Keck, "Mark and the Passion," *Int* 31 (1977): 432-34.

4467 Kent E. Brower, "The Old Testament in the Markan Passion Narrative," doctoral dissertation, University of Manchester, Manchester, UK, 1978.

4468 R. Alan Culpepper, "The Passion and Resurrection in Mark," *RevExp* 75 (1978): 583-600.

4469 Miguel de Burgos Nuñez, "La communión de Dios con el crucificado. Cristología de Marcos 15,22-39," *EB* 37 (1978): 243-66.

4470 Joseph A. Fitzmyer, "Crucifixion in Ancient Palestine, Qumran Literature, and the New Testament," *CBQ* 40/4 (1978): 493-513.

4471 R. L. Overstreet, "Roman Law and the Trial of Christ," *BSac* 135 (1978): 323-32.

4472 Xavier Léon-Dufour, "Jésus à Gethsémani: Essai de lecture synchronique," *SE* 31 (1979): 251-68.

4473 Dortee Lorenzen, "Jesu lidelsesudsagn i Markusevangeliet," *DTT* 42 (1979): 217-54.

4474 Julius Oswald, "Die Beziehungen zwischen Psalm 22 und dem vormarkinischen Passionsbericht," *ZKT* 101 (1979): 53-66.

4475 Dieter Zeller, "Die Handlungsstruktur der Markuspassion. Der Frtrag strukturalistischer Literaturwissenschaft für die Exegese," *TQ* 59 (1979): 213-27.

4476 Josef Ernst, "Die passionserzahlung des Markus und die Aporien der Forschung," *TGl* 70 (1980): 160-80.

4477 David Flusser, *Last Days in Jerusalem: A Current Study of the Easter Week*. Tel Aviv: Sadan, 1980.

4478 Louis Marin, *The Semiotics of the Passion Narrative: Topics and Figures*. A. M. Johnson, trans. Pittsburg PA: Pickwick Press, 1980.

4479 George W. E. Nickelsburg, "The Genre and Function of the Markan Passion Narrative," *HTR* 73 (1980): 153-84.

4480 John F. O'Grady, "The Passion in Mark," *BTB* 10 (1980): 83-87.

4481 Samuel O. Abogunrin, "The Language and Nature of the Resurrection of Jesus Christ in the New Testament," *JETS* 24 (1981): 55-65.

4482 D. Carr, "Jesus, the King of Zion: A Traditio-Historical Inquiry into the So-Called 'Triumphal Entry' of Jesus," doctoral dissertation, King's College, London, 1981.

4483 Jay Cassel, "The Reader in Mark: The Crucifixion Narrative," doctoral dissertation, Iowa University, Iowa City IA, 1981.

4484 Robert M. Fowler, "Irony and the Messianic Secret in the Gospel of Mark," *EGLMBS* 1 (1981): 26-36.

4485 Johannes Schreiber, "Die Bestattung Jesu," *ZNW* 72/3 (1981): 141-77.

4486 Mario Galizzi, "La passione di Gesù in Marco," *PV* 27 (1982): 46-58.

4487 Giuseppe Tosatto, "La passione di Gesù in Marco," *PV* 27 (1982): 24-32.

4488 Günter Bader, "Jesu Tod als Opfer," *ZTK* 80 (1983): 411-31.

4489 Kent E. Brower, "Elijah in the Markan Passion Narrative," *JSNT* 18 (1983): 85-101.

4490 Johnny V. Miller, "The Time of the Crucifixion," *JETS* 26/2 (1983): 157-66.

4491 Rudolf Pesch, "Das Evangelium in Jerusalem: Mk 14,12-26 als ältestes Uberlieferungsgut der Urgemeinde," in Peter Stuhlmacher, ed., *Das Evangelium und die Evangelien.* Tübingen: Mohr, 1983. Pp. 113-55.

4492 L. I. J. Stadelmann, "The Passion Narrative in the Synoptics as Structured on Ps 22 (21)," *PerT* 15 (1983): 193-221.

4493 Étienne Trocmé, *The Passion as Liturgy: A Study in the Origin of the Passion Narratives in the Four Gospels*. London: SCM, 1983.

4494 Matthew Vellanickal, "The Passion Narrative in the Gospel of Mark," *BB* 9 (1983): 258-78.

4495 Ernst Bammel, "The *titulus*," in Ernst Bammel and C. F. D. Moule, eds., *Jesus and the Politics of His Day*. Cambridge: University Press, 1984. Pp. 353-64.

4496 Ernst Bammel, "The Trial before Pilate," in Ernst Bammel and C. F. D. Moule, eds., *Jesus and the Politics of His Day*. Cambridge: University Press, 1984. Pp. 415-51.

4497 David R. Catchpole, "The 'Triumphal' Entry [Mk 8:27-30; 11:1-11]," in Ernst Bammel and C. F. D. Moule, eds., *Jesus and the Politics of His Day*. Cambridge: University Press, 1984. Pp. 319-34.

4498 John Navone, "Mark's Story of the Death of Jesus," *NBlack* 65 (1984): 123-35.

4499 Gerhard Schneider, "The Political Charge against Jesus (Lk 23:2) [Mk 15:1-5; Lk 23:1-5]," in Ernst Bammel and C. F. D. Moule, eds., *Jesus and the Politics of His Day*. Cambridge: University Press, 1984. Pp. 403-14.

4500 Donald P. Senior, *The Passion of Jesus in the Gospel of Mark*. Wilmington DE: Glazier, 1984.

4501 Jean-Noël Aletti, "Mort de Jésus en los evangelios," *RechSR* 73 (1985): 147-60.

4502 Dale C. Allison, *The End of the Ages Has Come: An Early Interpretation of the Passion and Resurrection of Jesus*. Philadelphia: Fortress, 1985.

4503 Raymond E. Brown, "The Passion according to Mark," *Worship* 59 (1985): 116-26.

4504 Jean Delorme, "Sémiotique du récit et récit de la passion," *RechSR* 73 (1985): 85-109.

4505 Frank J. Matera, "The Death of Jesus according to Luke: A Question of Sources," *CBQ* 47 (1985): 469-85.

4506 Marion L. Soards, "The Question of a Pre-Markan Passion Narrative," *BB* 11 (1985): 144-69.

4507 Charles P. Anderson, "The Trial of Jesus as Jewish-Christian Polarization: Blasphemy and Polemic in Mark's Gospel," in P. Richardson and D. Granskou, eds., *Anti-Judaism in Early Christianity. 1. Paul and the Gospels.* Waterloo, Ont.: Wilfrid Laurier University Press, 1986. Pp. 107-25.

4508 John N. Blackwell, *The Passion as Story: The Plot of Mark.* Philadelphia: Fortress, 1986.

4509 John C. Fenton, "The Passion Narrative in St Mark's Gospel," in J. Butterworth, ed., *The Reality of God.* London: Severn House Publishers, 1986.

4510 Helen R. Graham, "A Passion Prediction for Mark's Community: Mark 13:9-13," *BTB* 16/1 (1986): 18-22.

4511 Verner Hoefelmann, "O caminho da paixao de Jesus na perspectiva do evangelista Marcos," *EstT* 26/2 (1986): 99-119.

4512 David P. Secco, "Take up Your Cross," in Peter T. O'Brien and David G. Patterson, eds., *God Who Is Rich in Mercy* (festschrift for D. B. Knox). Grand Rapids: Baker Book House, 1986. Pp. 139-51.

4513 Uwe Wegner, "Deu Jesus um sentido salvífico para sua morte: consideraçoes sobre Mc. 14:24 e 10:45," *EstT* 26/3 (1986): 209-46.

4514 Mary Ann Beavis, "The Trial before the Sanhedrin (Mark 14:53-65): Reader Response and Greco-Roman Readers," *CBQ* 49 (1987): 581-96.

4515 Thomas E. Boomershine, "Peter's Denial as Polemic or Confession: The Implications of Media Criticism for Biblical Hermeneutics," *Semeia* 39 (1987): 47-68.

4516 Robert T. Fortna, "Sayings of the Suffering and Risen Christ: The Quadruple Tradition," *Forum* 3/3 (1987): 63-69.

4517 M. S. Hostetler, *Backward into Light: The Passion and Resurrection of Jesus according to Matthew and Mark*. London: SCM, 1987.

4518 Howard M. Jackson, "The Death of Jesus in Mark and the Miracle from the Cross," *NTS* 33/1 (1987): 16-37.

4519 Earl S. Johnson, "Is Mark 15:39 the Key to Mark's Christology?" *JSNT* 31 (1987): 3-22.

4520 Maria Ruhland, *Die Markuspassion aus der Sicht der Verleugnung*. Eilsbrunn: Koamar, 1987.

4521 J. L. White, "The Way of the Cross: Was There a Pre-Markan Passion Narrative?" *Forum* 3 (1987): 35-49.

4522 B. Beck, "Gethsemane in the Four Gospels," *EpRev* 15 (1988): 57-65.

4523 Raymond E. Brown, "The Burial of Jesus," *CBQ* 50 (1988): 233-45.

4524 Reinhard Feldmeier, "Die Krisis des Gottessohnes: die markinische Gethsemaneperikope als Markuspassion," *TLZ* 113 (1988): 234-36.

4525 Robert W. Funk, "The Markan Passion Narrative," in *The Poetics of Biblical Narrative*. Sonoma CA: Polebridge, 1988. Pp. 245-62.

4526 Mark F. S. C. McVann, "The Passion in Mark: Transformation Ritual," *BTB* 18 (1988): 96-101.

4527 S. J. Binz, *The Passion and Resurrection Narratives of Jesus: A Commentary*. Collegeville MN: Liturgical Press, 1989.

4528 Frank Connolly-Weinert, "Assessing Omissions as Redaction: Luke's Handling of the Charge Against Jesus as Detractor of the Temple," in Maurya P. Horgan and Paul J.

Kobelski, eds., *To Touch the Text: Biblical and Related Studies in Honor of Joseph A. Fitzmyer*. New York: Crossroad, 1989. Pp. 358-68.

4529 Leonard Doohan, "Mark's Portrait of the Suffering Christ," *Emmanuel* 95 (1989): 190-97.

4530 David E. Garland, *One Hundred Years of Study on the Passion Narrarive*. NABPR Bibliographic Series #3. Macon GA: Mercer University Press, 1989.

4531 Joachim Gnilka, "Der Prozeß Jesu nach den Berichten des Markus und Matthäus mit einer Rekonstruktion des historischen Verlaufs," in Karl Kertelge, ed., *Der Prozeß gegen Jesus: Historische Rückfrage und theologische Deutung*. 2nd ed. Freiburg: Herder, 1989. Pp. 11-40.

4532 David Seeley, "Was Jesus Like a Philosopher? The Evidence of Martyrological and Wisdom Motifs in Q, Pre-Pauline Traditions, and Mark," *SBLSP* 28 (1989): 540-49.

4533 Paul Ricoeur, "Interpretative Narrative," in Regina M. Schwartz, ed., *The Book and the Text: The Bible and Literary Theory*. Cambridge MA: Blackwell, 1990. Pp. 237-57.

4534 Craig A. Evans, "In What Sense Blasphemy? Jesus before Caiaphas in Mark 14:61-64." *SBLSP* 30 (1991): 215-34.

4535 Patrick H. Reardon, "The Cross, Sacraments and Martyrdom: An Investigation of Mark 10:35-45," *SVTQ* 36/1-2 (1992): 103-15.

<u>Peter</u>

4536 Cecil S. Emden, "St. Mark's Debt to St. Peter," *CQR* 154 (1953): 61-71.

4537 W. J. P. Boyd, "Peter's Denials—Mark 14:68, Luke 22:57," *ET* 67 (1955-1956): 341.

4538 H. E. W. Turner, "The Tradition of Mark's Dependence upon Peter," *ET* 71 (1959-1960): 260-63.

4539 Günter Klein, "Die Verleugnung des Petrus. Eine traditionsgeschichtliche Untersuchung," *ZTK* 58 (1961): 285-328.

4540 Félix Gils, "Pierre et la Foi au Christ Ressuscite," *ETL* 38 (1962): 5-43.

4541 Teruo Kobayashi, "The Role of Peter according to the Theological Understanding of Paul, Mark and Luke-Acts," doctoral dissertation, Drew University, Madison NJ, 1963.

4542 Paul Lamarche, "La guérison de la belle-mère de Pierre," *NRT* 87 (1965): 515-26.

4543 Eta Linnemann, "Die Verleugnung des Petrus," *ZTK* 63 (1966): 1-32.

4544 Giovanni Canfora, ed., *San Pietro*. Brescia: Paideia, 1967.

4545 Günter Klein, "Die Berufung des Petrus," *ZNW* 58 (1967): 1-44.

4546 Efrem Ravarotto, "La 'casa' del Vangelo di Marco è la casa di Simone-Pietro?" *Ant* 42 (1967): 399-419.

4547 Ernest Best, "1 Peter and the Gospel Tradition," *NTS* 16 (1969-1970): 95-113.

4548 G. W. H. Lampe, "St. Peter's Denial," *BJRL* 55 (1972-1973): 346-68.

4549 Josef Blank, "Neotestamentliche Petrus-Typologie und Petrusamt," *Concilium* 9 (1973): 173-79.

4550 Raymond E. Brown, et al., eds., *Peter in the New Testament: A Collaborative Assessment by Protestant and Roman Catholic Scholars*. New York: Paulist Press, 1973.

4551 Adelbert Denaux, "La confession de Pierre et la première annonce de la Passion. Mc 8,27-35," *AsSeign* 55 (1974): 31-39.

4552 Béda Rigaux, "Pietro e il Vangelo di Marco," *MiscFranc* 74 (1974): 294-317.

4553 Kim E. Dewey, "Peter's Curse and Cursed Peter (Mark 14:53-54, 66-72)," in Werner H. Kelber, ed., *The Passion in Mark: Studies on Mark 14-16*. Philadelphia: Fortress Press, 1976. Pp. 96-114.

4554 Robert T. Fortna, "Jesus and Peter at the High Priest's House: A Test Case for the Question of the Relation Between Mark's and John's Gospels," *NTS* 24 (1977-1978): 371-83.

4555 Ernest Best, "Peter in the Gospel According to Mark," *CBQ* 40/4 (1978): 547-58.

4556 Dietfried Gewalt, "Die Verlegnung des Petrus," *LB* 43 (1978): 113-44.

4557 Giancarlo Biguzzi, "Mc. 11,23-25 e il Pater," *RBib* 27 (1979): 57-68.

4558 David Brady, "The Alarm to Peter in Mark's Gospel," *JSNT* 4 (1979): 42-57.

4559 Kim E. Dewey, "Peter's Denial Reexamined: John's Knowledge of Mark's Gospel," *SBLSP* 9/1 (1979): 109-12.

4560 John H. Elliott, "Peter, Silvanus and Mark in 1 Peter and Acts: Sociological-Exegetical Perspectives on a Petrine Group in Rome," in Wilfrid Haubeck and W. Bachmann, eds., *Wort in der Zeit: Neutestamentliche Studien* (festschrift for K. H. Rengstorf). Leiden: Brill, 1980. Pp. 250-67.

4561 Josef Ernst, "Die Petrustradition im Markusevangelium—ein altes Problem neu angegangen," in Josef Zmifewski and Ernst Nellessen, eds., *Begegnung mit dem Wort: Festschrift für Heinrich Zimmerman*. Bonner Biblische Beiträge 53. Bonn: Peter Hanstein, 1980. Pp. 35-65.

4562 Ulrich H. J. Körtner, "Markus der Mitarbeiter des Petrus," *ZNW* 71 (1980): 160-73.

4563 Josef Ernst, "Simon-Kephas-Petrus: Historische und typologische Perspektiven im Markusevangelium," *TGl* 71 (1981): 438-56.

4564 Craig A. Evans, " 'Peter Warming Himself': The Problem of an Editorial 'Seam'," *JBL* 101/2 (1982): 245-49.

4565 Samuel O. Abogunrin, "The Three Variant Accounts of Peter's Call: A Critical and Theological Examination of the Texts," *NTS* 31 (1985): 587-602.

4566 Claude Coulot, "Les figures du maître et de ses disciples dans les premières communautés chrétiennes," *RevSR* 59/1: (1985): 1-11.

4567 Rinaldo Fabris, "San Pietro apostolo nella prima chiesa," *SM* 35 (1986): 41-70.

4568 Ekkehard W. Stegemann, "Zur Rolle von Petrus, Jakobus und Johannes im Markusevangelium," *TZ* 42 (1986): 366-74.

4569 Ruth Fox, "Peter's Denial in Mark's Gospel," *BibTo* 25 (1987): 298-303.

4570 Hans Klein, "Das Bekenntnis des Petrus und die Anfänge des Christusglaubens im Urchristentum," *EvT* 47 (1987): 176-92.

4571 Gerald O'Collins, "Mary Magdalene as Major Witness to Jesus' Resurrection," *TS* 48 (1987): 631-46.

4572 Willem S. Vorster, "Characterization of Peter in the Gospel of Mark," *Neo* 21 (1987): 57-76.

4573 Thomas P. Waverly, "Conversion Narratives: Wesley's Aldersgate Narrative and the Portrait of Peter in the Gospel of Mark," *WesTJ* 24 (1989): 54-73.

4574 J. Duncan M. Derrett, "Peter and the Tabernacles," *DR* 108 (1990): 37-48.

possessions/wealth

4575 Walter R. Edwards, "The Doctrine of Stewardship in the Synoptic Gospels," doctoral dissertation, Midwestern Baptist Theological Seminary, Kansas City KS, 1945.

4576 G. M. Lee, "The Story of the Widow's Mite," *ET* 82 (1970-1971): 314.

4577 Adolf M. Ritter, "Christentum und Eigentum bei Klemens von Alexandrien auf dem Hintergrund der frühchristlichen 'Armenfrömmigkeit' und der Ethik der kaiserlichen Stoa," *ZKG* 86/1 (1975): 1-25.

4578 Simon Légasse, "The Call of the Rich Man," in Michael D. Quinan, ed. and trans., *Gospel Poverty: Essays in Biblical Theology*. Chicago: Franciscan Herald Press, 1977. Pp. 53-80.

4579 J. M. R. Tillard, "Le propos de pauvreté et l'exigence évangélique," *NRT* 100 (1978): 207-32.

4580 Ernst Bammel, "The Poor and the Zealots," in Ernst Bammel and C. F. D. Moule, eds., *Jesus and the Politics of His Day*. Cambridge: Cambridge University Press, 1984. Pp. 109-28.

4581 Elizabeth Struthers Malbon, "The Poor Widow in Mark and Her Poor Rich Readers," *CBQ* 53 (1991): 589-604.

prayer

4582 C. F. D. Moule, "An Unsolved Problem in the Temptation Clause in the Lord's Prayer," *RTR* 33/3 (1974): 65-75.

4583 James MacCaffrey, "Prayer: The Heart of the Gospels," *ClerR* 71 (1986): 24-26, 68-71.

4584 E. A. Obeng, "Abba, Father: The Prayer of the Sons of God," *ET* 99 (1987-1988): 363-66.

purpose

4585 Ralph L. West, "The Purpose of Mark's Gospel," master's thesis, New Orleans Baptist Theological Seminary, New Orleans LA, 1944.

4586 Peter H. Igarashi, "Motives in the Gospel of Mark," doctoral dissertation, Harvard University, Cambridge MA, 1950.

4587 Daniel E. Wonderly, "The Purpose and Distinctive Content of the Gospel According to Mark," master's thesis, Midwestern Baptist Theological Seminary, Kansas City KS, 1955.

4588 Curtis Beach, "Form, Structure, and Purpose in the Gospel of Mark," doctoral dissertation, University of Southern California, Los Angeles CA, 1957.

4589 James Kallas, "The Special Interest of Mark," in *Jesus and the Power of Satan*. Philadelphia PA: Westminster Press, 1968. Pp. 20-28.

4590 Heinrich Baarlink, *Anfängliches Evangelium. Ein Beitrag zur näheren Bestimmung der theologischen Motive im Markusevangelium*. Kampen: J. H. Kok, 1977.

4591 Eugene E. Lemcio, "The Intention of the Evangelist, Mark," *NTS* 32 (1986): 187-206.

Q

4592 B. H. Streeter, "The Original Extent of Q," in William Sanday, ed., *Studies in the Synoptic Problem by Members of the University of Oxford*. Oxford: Clarendon, 1911. Pp. 185-208.

4593 B. H. Streeter, "On the Original Order of Q," in William Sanday, ed., *Studies in the Synoptic Problem by Members of the University of Oxford*. Oxford: Clarendon, 1911. Pp. 141-64.

4594 B. H. Streeter, "St. Mark's Knowledge and Use of Q," in William Sanday, ed., *Studies in the Synoptic Problem by Members of the University of Oxford*. Oxford: Clarendon, 1911. Pp. 165-208.

4595 B. H. Streeter, "Synoptic Criticism and the Eschatological Problem," in William Sanday, ed., *Studies in the Synoptic Problem by Members of the University of Oxford*. Oxford: Clarendon, 1911. Pp. 425-36.

4596 T. E. Floyd Honey, "Did Mark Use Q?" *JBL* 62 (1943): 319-31.

4597 Burton H. Throckmorton, "Did Mark Know Q?" *JBL* 67 (1948): 319-29.

4598 C. F. D. Moule and A. M. G. Stephenson, "R. G. Heard on Q and Mark," *NTS* 2 (1955-1956): 114-18.

4599 J. P. Brown, "Mark as Witness to an Edited Form of Q," *JBL* 80 (1961): 29-44.

4600 Joseph A. Fitzmyer, "The Priority of Mark and the 'Q' Source in Luke," *Persp* 11 (1970): 131-70.

4601 Siegfried Schulz, *Q: Die Spruchquelle der Evangelisten*. Zürich: Theologischer Verlag, 1972.

4602 E. P. Sanders, "The Overlaps of Mark and Q and the Synoptic Problem," *NTS* 19 (1972-1973): 453-65.

4603 Michel Devisch, "La relation entre l'évangile de Marc et le document Q," in M. Sabbe, ed., *L'évangile selon Marc: Tradition et rédaction*. BETL #34. Louvain: Louvain University Press, 1974. Pp. 59-91.

4604 Petros Vassiliadis, "Prolegomena to a Discussion on the Relationship between Mark and the Q Document," *DBM* 3 (1975): 31-46.

4605 Wolfgang Schenk, "Der Einfluss der Logien-Quelle auf das Markusevangelium," *ZNW* 70/3 (1979): 141-65.

4606 Jan Lambrecht, "Q-Influence on Mark 8,34-9,1," in Joël Delobel, ed., *Logia: Les Paroles de Jésus*. BETL #59. Louvain: Peeters Press, 1982. Pp. 277-304.

4607 Frans Neirynck, "Réponse à P. Rolland," *ETL* 60/4 (1984): 363-66.

4608 Nigel M. Watson, "Willi Marxsen's Approach to Christology," *ET* 97 (1985-1986): 36-42.

4609 Gerhard Dautzenberg, ''Gesetzeskritik und Gesetzesgehorsam in der Jesustradition,'' in Karl Kertelge, ed., *Das Gesetz im Neuen Testament*. Freiburg: Herder, 1986. Pp. 46-70.

4610 Heinzpeter Hempelmann, ''Is Q but the Invention of Luke and Mark? Method and Argument in the Griesbach Hypothesis,'' *RSB* 8 (1988): 15-32.

4611 Dieter Lührmann, ''The Gospel of Mark and the Sayings Collection Q,'' *JBL* 108 (1989): 51-71.

4612 David Seeley, ''Was Jesus Like a Philosopher? The Evidence of Martyrological and Wisdom Motifs in Q, Pre-Pauline Traditions, and Mark,'' *SBLSP* 28 (1989): 540-49.

4613 John S. Kloppenborg, ''City and Wasteland: Narrative World and the Beginning of the Sayings Gospel (Q),'' *Semeia* 52 (1990): 145-60.

4614 D. Kosch, ''Q and Jesus,'' *BZ* 36/1 (1992): 30-38.

4615 Jan Lambrecht, ''John the Baptist and Jesus in Mark 1:1-15: Markan Redaction of Q?'' *NTS* 38 (1992): 357-84.

<u>Quintilian</u>

4616 Helmut Koester, ''Mark 9:43-47 and Quintilian 8.3.75,'' *HTR* 71 (1978): 151-53.

4617 Helmut Koester, ''Using Quintilian to Interpret Mark,'' *BAR* 6/3 (1980): 44-45.

<u>Qumran</u>

4618 Josef Blinzler, ''Qumran-Kalender und Passionschronologie,'' *ZNW* 49 (1958): 238-51.

4619 R. Deichgräber, ''Die Gemeinderegel (1QS) X4,'' *RevQ* 2 (1960): 277-80.

4620 Franz Mussner, ''1QHodajoth und das Gleichnis vom Senfkorn (Mk 4:30-32 Par),'' *BZ* 4/1 (1960): 128-30.

4621 E. Earle Ellis, "Jesus, the Sadducees and Qumran," *NTS* 10 (1963-1964): 274-79.

4622 Hans Kosmala, "The Three Nets of Belial: A Study in the Terminology of Qumran and the New Testament," *ASTI* 4 (1965): 91-113.

4623 Pierre Benoit, "Note sur les fragments grecs de la grotte 7 de Qumrân," *RB* 79 (1972): 321-24.

4624 Jean Bernardi, "L'évangile de Saint Marc et la grotte 7 de Qumrân," *ÉTR* 47 (1972): 453-56.

4625 Eugene Fisher, "New Testament Documents among the Dead Sea Scrolls?" *BibTo* 61 (1972): 835-41.

4626 Colin J. Hemer, "New Testament Fragments at Qumran?" *TynB* 23 (1972): 125-28.

4627 Pierson Parker, "7Q5: Enthält das Papyrusfragment 5 aus der Höhlec 7 von Qumran einen Markustext?" *ErAu* 48 (1972): 467-69.

4628 C. H. Roberts, "On Some Presumed Papyrus Fragments of the New Testament from Qumran," *JTS* 23 (1972): 446-47.

4629 Léopold Sabourin, "A Fragment of Mark at Qumran?" *BTB* 2 (1972): 308-12.

4630 Pierre Benoit, "Nouvelle Note sur les Fragments Grecs de la Grotte 7 de Qumrãn," *RB* 80/1 (1973): 5-12.

4631 David Flusser, "The Last Supper and the Essenes," *Immanuel* 2 (1973): 23-27.

4632 José O'Callaghan, "Les Papyrus de la Grotte 7 de Qumran," *NRT* 95/2 (1973): 188-95.

4633 E. J. Vardaman, "The Gospel of Mark and 'The Scrolls'," *CT* 17 (1973): 1284-87.

4634 Colin J. Hemer, "A Note on 7Q5," *ZNW* 65 (1974): 155-57.

4635 Joseph A. Fitzmyer, "Crucifixion in Ancient Palestine, Qumran Literature, and the New Testament," *CBQ* 40/4 (1978): 493-513.

4636 Leonard F. Badia, *The Dead Sea People's Sacred Meal and Jesus' Last Supper*. Lanham MD: University Press of America, 1979.

4637 Otto Betz, "Early Christian Cult in the Light of Qumran," *RSB* 2 (1982): 73-85.

4638 Carsten P. Thiede, "7Q-Eine Ruckkehr zu den Neutestamentlichen Papyrus-Fragmenten in der Siebten Hohle von Qumran," *Bib* 65/4 (1984): 538-59.

4639 Matthew Black, "The Theological Appropriation of the Old Testament by the New Testament," *SJT* 39/1 (1986): 1-17.

4640 William R. Domeris, "The Office of the Holy One," *JTSA* 54 (1986): 35-38.

4641 Hans-Udo Rosenbaum, "Cave 7Q5! Gegen die erneute inanspruchnahme des Qumran-Fragments 7Q5 als bruchstueck der aeltesten Evangelien-Handschrift," *BZ* 31/2 (1987): 189-205.

4642 Peter Pimentel, "The 'Unclean Spirits' of St. Mark's Gospel," *ET* 99 (1987-1988): 173-75.

4643 Ferdinand Rohrhirsch, "Das Qumranfragment 7Q5," *NovT* 30 (1988): 97-99.

4644 George J. Brooke, "The Temple Scroll and the New Testament," in George J. Brooke, ed., *Temple Scroll Studies*. Sheffield: JSOT Press, 1989. Pp. 181-99.

4645 S. R. Pickering and R. R. E. Cook, *Has a Fragrnent of the Gospel of Mark Been Found at Qumran?* Sydney: Macquarie University, 1989.

4646 Ferdinand Rohrhirsch, *Markus in Qumran? Eine Auseinandersetzung mit den Argumenten für und gegen das Fragment 7Q5 mit Hilfe des methodischen Fallibilismusprinzips*. Wuppertal: Brockhaus, 1990.

reader criticism

4647 Fernando Belo, *A Materialist Reading of the Gospel of Mark*. M. J. O'Connell, trans. Maryknoll NY: Orbis Books, 1980.

4648 Robert M. Fowler, "Who Is 'the Reader' of Mark's Gospel?" *SBLSP* 22 (1983): 31-53.

4649 Robert M. Fowler, "Thoughts on the History of Reading Mark's Gospel," *EGLMBS* 4 (1984): 120-30.

4650 Robert M. Fowler, "Reading Matthew Reading Mark: Observing the FirstSteps toward Meaning-as-Reference in the Synoptic Gospels," *SBLSP* 25 (1986): 1-16.

4651 Elizabeth Struthers Malbon, "Disciples/Crowds/Whoever: Markan Characters and Readers," *NovT* 28 (1986): 104-30.

4652 Mary Ann Beavis, "The Trial before the Sanhedrin (Mark 14:53-65): Reader Response and Greco-Roman Readers," *CBQ* 49 (1987): 581-96.

4653 B. M. F. van Iersel, "The Reader of Mark as Operator of a System of Connotations," *Semeia* 48 (1989): 83-114.

4654 B. M. F. van Iersel, *Reading Mark*. W. H. Bisscheroux, trans. Edinburgh: T. & T. Clark, 1989.

4655 Carol S. LaHurd, "Biblical Exorcism and Reader Response to Ritual in Narrative," in Robert Detweiler and W. G. Doty, eds., *The Daemonic Imagination: Biblical Text and Secular Story*. Atlanta: Scholars Press, 1990. Pp. 53-63. Cf. *BTB* 20 (1990): 154-60.

4656 Walter S. Lawrence, "Reader-Response Criticism for Markan Narrative with a Commentary on Mark 14:26-52," doctoral dissertation, St. Louis University, St. Louis MO, 1990.

4657 Joanna Dewey, "Mark as Interwoven Tapestry: Forecasts and Echoes for a Listening Audience," *CBQ* 53 (1991): 221-36.

4658 Robert M. Fowler, *Let the Reader Understand: Reader-Response Criticism and the Gospel of Mark.* Minneapolis: Fortress Press, 1991.

redaction

4659 Edgar J. Goodspeed, "The Marcan Redactor," in Lewis Gaston Leary, ed., *From the Pyramids to Paul: Studies in Theology, Archaeology and Related Subjects.* New York: Nelson, 1935. Pp. 57-66.

4660 Harald Riesenfeld, "Tradition und Redaktion im Markusevangelium," in W. Eltester, ed., *Neutestamentliche Studien* (festschrift for Rudolf Bultmann). Berlin: Alfred Töpelmann, 1954. Pp. 157-64.

4661 Willi Marxsen, "Redaktionsgeschichtliche Erklärung der sogenannte Parabeltheorie des Markus," *ZTK* 52 (1955): 255-71.

4662 Manfred Karnetzki, "Die galiläische Redaktion im Markusevangelium," *ZNW* 52 (1961): 238-72.

4663 Manfred Karnetzki, "Die letzte Redaktion des Markusevangeliums," in Ernst Wolf, ed., *Zwischenstation: Festschrift für Karl Kupisch zum 60. Geburtstag.* Münich: Chr. Kaiser Verlag, 1963. Pp. 161-74.

4664 Jan Lambrecht, "Redactio Sermonis Eschatologici," *VD* 43 (1965): 278-87.

4665 Jan Lambrecht, *Die Redaktion der Markus-Apokalypse: Literarische Analyse und Strukturuntersuchung.* Analecta Biblica 28. Rome: Pontifical Biblical Institute, 1967.

4666 Jan Lambrecht, "La structure de Mc. XIII," in I. de la Potterie, ed., *De Jésus aux Évangiles: Tradition et Rédaction dans les Évangiles synoptiques. Donum natalicum Iosepho Coppens septuagesimum annum complenti D.D.D. collegae et amici.* BETL #25. Gembloux/Paris: Duculot/Lethielleux, 1967. Pp. 141-64.

4667 L. F. Rivera, "Una estructura en la redacción de Marcos," *RevB* 29 (1967): 1-21.

4668 Johannes Schreiber, *Theologie des Vertrauens. Eine redaktionsgeschichtliche Untersuchung des Markusevangeliums*. Hamburg: Furche-Verlag, 1967.

4669 Frank J. Matera, "Interpreting Mark: Some Recent Theories of Redaction Criticism," *LouvS* 2 (1968): 113-31.

4670 William L. Lane, "Redaktionsgeschichte and the Dehistoricizing of the New Testament Gospel," *JETS* 11 (1968-1969): 21-33.

4671 Willi Marxsen, *Mark the Evangelist: Studies on the Redaction History of the Gospel*. James Boyce, Donald Juel, and Wm. Poehlmann, trans. Nashville: Abingdon, 1969.

4672 Karl-Georg Reploh, *Markus—Lehrer der Gemeinde. Eine redaktionsgeschichtliche Studie zu den Jüngerperikopen des Markus-Evangeliums*. Stuttgarter Biblische Monographien 9. Stuttgart: Katholische Bibelwerk, 1969.

4673 L. F. Rivera, "El relato de la Transfiguración en la redacción del evangelio de Marcos," *RevB* 31 (1969): 143-58, 229-43.

4674 Erich Grässer, "Jesus in Nazareth (Mark 6:1-6a): Notes on the Redaction and Theology of St. Mark," *NTS* 16 (1969-1970): 1-23.

4675 P. E. Dinter, "Redaction Criticism of the Gospel of Mark: A Survey," *DunR* 10 (1970): 178-97.

4676 Felix Flückiger, "Die Redaktion der Zukunftsrede in Mark 13," *TZ* 26/6 (1970): 395-409.

4677 Karl Kertelge, *Die Wunder Jesu im Markusevangelium. Eine redaktionsgeschichtliche Untersuchung*. Studien zum Alten und Neuen Testament 23. München: Kösel-Verlag, 1970.

4678 Benito Marconcini, "Il miracolo nella redazione di Marco: interpretazione storica e interpretazione esistenziale," *PV* 15/3 (1970): 179-90.

4679 Robert H. Stein, "The 'Redaktionsgeschichtlich' Investigation of a Markan Seam (Mc 1:21f.)," *ZNW* 61 (1970): 70-94.

4680 Howard Clark Kee, "Mark as Redactor and Theologian: A Survey of Some Recent Markan Studies," *JBL* 90 (1971): 333-36.

4681 Heinz-Wolfgang Kuhn, "Zum Problem des Verhältnisses der markinischen Redaktion zur Israelitisch-jüdischen Tradition," in Gert Jeremias, Heinz-Wolfgang Kuhn, and Hartmut Stegemann, eds., *Tradition und Glaube: Das frühe Christentum in seiner Umwelt: Festgabe für Karl Georg Kuhn zum 65. Geburtstag*. Göttingen: Vandenhoeck & Ruprecht, 1971. Pp. 299-309.

4682 Robert H. Stein, "The Proper Methodology for Ascertaining a Markan Redaction History," *NovT* 13 (1971): 181-98.

4683 J. W. Pryor, "Markan Parable Theology: An Inquiry into Mark's Principles of Redaction," *ET* 83/4 (1971-1972): 242-45.

4684 Aloysius M. Ambrozic, *The Hidden Kingdom: A Redaction-Critical Study of the References to the Kingdom of God in Mark's Gospel*. CBQMS #2. Washington DC: The Catholic Biblical Association of America, 1972.

4685 John Dominic Crossan, "Redaction and Citation in Mark 11:9-10 and 11:17," *BR* 17 (1972): 33-50.

4686 David J. Hawkin, "The Incomprehension of the Disciples in the Marcan Redaction," *JBL* 91 (1972): 491-500.

4687 Frans Neirynck, *Duality in Mark: Contributions to the Study of the Markan Redaction*. BETL #31. Louvain: Louvain University Press, 1972.

4688 Wolfgang Schenk, "Tradition und Redaktion in der Epileptikerperikope, Mk 9:14-29," *ZNW* 63 (1972): 76-94.

4689 Hejne Simonsen, "Zur Frage der grundlegenden Problematik in form- und redaktionsgeschichtlicher Evangelienforschung," *StTheol* 26 (1972): 1-23.

4690 Hugolinus Langkammer, "Tradycja i redakcja w prologu Ewangelii Marka (1,1-15)," *RoczTK* 20 (1973): 37-57.

4691 James C. Little, "Redaction Criticism and the Gospel of Mark with Special Reference to Mark 4:1-34," doctoral dissertation, Duke University, Durham NC, 1973.

4692 Kurt Aland, "Der Schluß des Markusevangeliums," in M. Sabbe, ed., *L'évangile selon Marc: Tradition et rédaction*. BETL #34. Louvain: Louvain University Press, 1974. Pp. 435-70.

4693 Pierre Mourlon Beernaert, "Structure littéraire et lecture théologique de Marc 14,17-52," in M. Sabbe, ed., *L'évangile selon Marc: Tradition et rédaction*. BETL #34. Louvain: Louvain University Press, 1974. Pp. 241-67.

4694 M.-É. Boismard, "Influences matthénnes sur l'ultime rédaction de l'évangile de Marc," in M. Sabbe, ed., *L'évangile selon Marc: Tradition et rédaction*. BETL #34. Louvain: Louvain University Press, 1974. Pp. 93-101.

4695 Joseph Coppens, "Les logia du Fils de l'homme dans l'évangile de Marc," in M. Sabbe, ed., *L'évangile selon Marc: Tradition et rédaction*. BETL #34. Louvain: Louvain University, 1974. Pp. 487-528.

4696 Albert L. Descamps, "Pour une histoire du titre 'Fils de Dieu': Les antécédents par rapport à Marc," in M. Sabbe, ed., *L'évangile selon Marc: Tradition et rédaction*. BETL #34. Gembloux/Louvain: Duculot/Louvain University Press, 1974. Pp. 529-71.

4697 Detlev Dormeyer, *Die Passion Jesu als Verhaltensmodell: literarische und theologische Analyse der Traditions- und Redaktionsgeschichte der Markuspassion*. Neutestamentliche Abhandlungen, Neue Folge, 11. Münster: Verlag Aschendorff, 1974.

4698 David L. Dungan, "Reactionary Trends in the Gospel Producing Activity of the Early Church: Marcion, Tatian, Mark," in M. Sabbe, ed., *L'évangile selon Marc: Tradition et rédaction*. BETL #34. Louvain: Louvain University Press, 1974. Pp. 179-202.

4699 W. M. A. Hendriks, "Zur Kollektionsgeschichte des Markusevangeliums," in M. Sabbe, ed., *L'évangile selon Marc: Tradition et rédaction.* BETL #34. Louvain: Louvain University Press, 1974. Pp. 35-57.

4700 Johan Konings, "The Pre-Markan Sequence in John 6: A Critical Re-examination," in M. Sabbe, ed., *L'évangile selon Marc: Tradition et rédaction.* BETL #34. Louvain: Louvain University Press, 1974. Pp. 147-77.

4701 Jan Lambrecht, "Redaction and Theology in Mk. IV," in M. Sabbe, ed., *L'évangile selon Marc: Tradition et rédaction.* BETL #34. Louvain: Louvain University Press, 1974. Pp. 269-307.

4702 James M. Robinson, "The Literary Composition of Mark," in M. Sabbe, ed., *L'évangile selon Marc: Tradition et rédaction.* BETL #34. Louvain: Louvain University Press, 1974. Pp. 11-19.

4703 Maurits Sabbe, ed., *L'évangile selon Marc: Tradition et rédaction.* BETL #34. Louvain: Louvain University Press, 1974.

4704 Gottfried Schille, *Offen für alle Menschen. Redaktionsgeschichtliche Beobachtungen zur Theologie des Markus-Evangeliums.* Arbeiten zur Theologie, Heft 55. Stuttgart: Calwer Verlag, 1974.

4705 Camille Focant, "L'incompréhension des disciples dans le deuxième évangile. Tradition et rédaction," *RB* 82 (1975): 161-85.

4706 J. C. Meagher, "Die Form- und Redaktionsungeschickliche Methoden: The Principle of Clumsiness and the Gospel of Mark," *JAAR* 43 (1975): 459-72.

4707 George B. Caird, "The Study of the Gospels. III. Redaction Criticism," *ET* 87/4 (1976): 168-72.

4708 Roger Mohrlang, "Redaction Criticism and the Gospel of Mark: An Evaluation of the Work of W. Marxsen," *SBT* 6 (1976): 18-33.

4709 Manfred Karnetzki, "Die Gegenwart des Freudenboten. Zur letzten Redaktion des Markus-Evangeliums," *NTS* 23 (1976-1977): 101-108.

4710 Alice Dermience, "Tradition et rédaction dans la péricope de la Syrophénicienne: Marc 7,24-30," *RTL* 8 (1977): 15-29.

4711 David J. Hawkin, "The Symbolism and Structure of the Marcan Redaction," *EQ* 49 (1977): 98-110.

4712 Josef Ernst, "Petrusbekenntnis-Leidensankündigung-Satanswort (Mk 8,27-33). Tradition und Redaktion," *Cath* 32 (1978): 46-73.

4713 E. J. Pryke, *Redactional Style in the Markan Gospel. A Study of Syntax and Vocabulary as Guides to Redaction in Mark*. SNTSMS #33. Cambridge: University Press, 1978.

4714 J. Hamilton, "The Divisions of the Gospel of Mark: A Redactional Examination of Its Structure," doctoral dissertation, University of Aberdeen, Aberdeen, Scotland, 1979.

4715 Carl Kazmierski, *Jesus, the Son of God: A Study of the Markan Tradition and its Redaction by the Evangelist*. Forschung zur Bibel 33. Würzburg: Echter Verlag, 1979.

4716 Ronald J. Kernaghan, "History and Redaction in the Controversy Stories in Mark 2:1-3:6," *SBT* 9 (1979): 23-47.

4717 Grant R. Osborne, "Redactional Trajectories in the Crucifixion Narrative," *EQ* 51 (1979): 80-96.

4718 J. C. Meagher, *Clumsy Construction in Mark's Gospel. A Critique of Form- and Redaktionsgeschichte*. Toronto Studies in Theology 3. New York/Toronto: Edwin Mellen Press, 1980.

4719 Frans Neirynck, "Marc 16,1-8. Tradition et rédaction," *ETL* 56 (1980): 56-88.

4720 William R. Telford, *The Barren Temple and the Withered Tree. A Redaction-Critical Analysis of the Cursing of the*

Fig Tree Pericope in Mark's Gospel and Its Relation to the Cleansing of the Temple Tradition. JSNT Supplement 1. Sheffield: JSOT Press, 1980.

4721 George Eldon Ladd, "A Redactional Study of Mark," *ET* 92 (1980-1981): 10-13.

4722 Enrique Nardoni, "A Redactional Interpretation of Mark 9:1," *CBQ* 43/3 (1981): 365-84.

4723 Nelson H. Brickham, "The Dependence of the Fourth Gospel on the Gospel of Mark: A Redaction-Critical Approach," doctoral dissertation, American University, Washington DC, 1982.

4724 Angelo Lancellotti, "La Casa Pietro a Cafarnao nel Vangeli Sinottici. Redazione e Tradizione," *Ant* 58/1 (1983): 48-69.

4725 Grant R. Osborne, *The Resurrection Narratives: A Redactional Study.* Grand Rapids: Baker Book House, 1984.

4726 Oscar H. Hirt, "Interpretation in the Gospels: An Examination of the Use of Redaction Criticism in Mark 8:27-9:32," doctoral dissertation, Dallas Theological Seminary, Dallas TX, 1985.

4727 David I. Procter, "A Redaction-Critical Study of Synoptic Tendencies with Special Reference to Bultmann's Law of Increasing Distinctness," doctoral dissertation, Baylor University, Waco TX, 1985.

4728 C. Clifton Black, "An Evaluation of the Investigative Method and Exegetical Results of Redaction Criticism of the Gospel of Mark: The Role of the Disciples as a Test-Case in Current Research," doctoral dissertation, Duke University, Durham NC, 1986.

4729 Paul A. Mirecki, "Mark 16:9-20: Composition, Tradition and Redaction," doctoral dissertation, Harvard University, Cambridge MA, 1986.

4730 Thomas Söding, "Gebet und Gebetsmahnung Jesu in Getsemani: eine redaktionskritische Auslegung von Mk 14:32-42," *BZ* 31/1 (1987): 76-100.

4731 Elian Cuviller, "Tradition et Redaction en Marc 7:1-23," *NovT* 34/2 (1992): 169-92.

4732 Jan Lambrecht, "John the Baptist and Jesus in Mark 1:1-15: Markan Redaction of Q?" *NTS* 38 (1992): 357-84.

relation to John

4733 Edwin D. Johnston, "A Re-Examination of the Relation of the Fourth Gospel to the Synoptics," doctoral dissertation, Southern Baptist Theological Seminary, Louisville KY, 1954.

4734 Ivor Buse, "John v.8 and Johannine-Marcan Relationships," *NTS* 1 (1954-1955): 134-36.

4735 E. K. Lee, "St. Mark and the Fourth Gospel," *NTS* 3 (1956-1957): 50-58.

4736 Pierson Parker, "John and John Mark," *JBL* 79 (1960): 97-110.

4737 Richard Kugelman, "Mark and John," *BibTo* 53 (1971): 316-21.

4738 C. K. Barrett, "John and the Synoptic Gospels," *ET* 85 (1973-1974): 228-33.

4739 Lloyd R. Kittlaus, "The Fourth Gospel and Mark: John's Use of Markan Redaction and Composition," doctoral dissertation, Divinity School, University of Chicago, Chicago IL, 1978.

4740 Lloyd R. Kittlaus, "John and Mark: A Methodological Evaluation of Norman Perrin's Suggestion," *SBLSP* 8/2 (1978): 269-80.

4741 Arthur H. Maynard, "Common Elements in the Outlines of Mark and John," *SBLSP* 8/2 (1978): 251-60.

4742 Lloyd R. Kittlaus, "Evidence from John 12 that the Author of John Knew the Gospel of Mark," *SBLSP* 9/1 (1979): 119-22.

4743 Mark E. Glasswell, "The Relationship between John and Mark," *JSNT* 23 (1985): 99-115.

4744 J. F. Coakley, "The Anointing at Bethany and the Priority of John," *JBL* 107/2 (1988): 241-56.

4745 René Kieffer, "Jean et Marc: convergences dans la structure et dans les détails," in Adelbert Denaux, ed., *John and the Synoptics*. BETL #101. Louvain: Peeters Press, 1992. Pp. 109-26.

4746 Frans Neirynck, "John and the Synoptics: 1975-1990," in Adelbert Denaux, ed., *John and the Synoptics*. BETL #101. Louvain: Peeters Press, 1992. Pp. 3-61.

relation to Judaism

4747 A. M. Goldberg, "Sitzend zur Rechten der Kraft. Zur Gottesbezeichnung Gebura in der frühen rabbinischen Literatur," *BZ* 8 (1964): 284-93.

4748 John W. Bowman, *The Gospel of Mark: The New Christian Jewish Passover Haggadah*. Studia Post-Biblica 8. Leiden: Brill, 1965.

4749 Yitshak Baer, "Some Aspects of Judaism as Presented in the Synoptic Gospels," *Zion* 31/3 (1966): 117-52.

4750 W. Ziffer, "Two Epithets for Jesus of Nazareth in Talmud and Midrash," *JBL* 85 (1966): 356-57.

4751 Robert L. Mowery, "The Jewish Religious Leaders in the Gospel of Mark: A Study in *Formgeschichte*," doctoral dissertation, Northwestern University, Evanston IL, 1967.

4752 Otto Michel, "Zur Methodik der Forschung," in O. Michel, S. Safrai, R. le Déut, et al., eds., *Studies on the Jewish Background of the New Testament*. Assen: Van Gorcum, 1969. Pp. 1-11.

4753 Thomas L. Budesheim, "Jesus and the Disciples in Conflict with Judaism," *ZNW* 62/3 (1971): 190-209.

4754 James Donaldson, "The Title Rabbi in the Gospels: Some Reflections on the Evidence of the Synoptics," *JQR* 63 (1972-1973): 287-91.

4755 J. Duncan M. Derrett, "Judaica in St. Mark," *JRAS* (1975): 2-15.

4756 Michael J. Cook, *Mark's Treatment of the Jewish Leaders*. Novum Testamentum Supplement 51. Leiden: Brill, 1978.

4757 H. L. Strack and Paul Billerbeck, *Das Evangelium nach Markus, Lukas und Johannes und die Apostelgeschichte erläutert aus Talmud und Midrasch.* Kommentar zum Neuen Testament aus Talmud und Midrasch, 2. 7th ed. Münich: Beck, 1978.

4758 Dan M. Cohn-Sherbok, "An Analysis of Jesus' Arguments concerning the Plucking of Grain on the Sabbath," *JSNT* 2 (1979): 31-41.

4759 Donald E. Cook, "A Gospel Portrait of the Pharisees," *RevExp* 84 (1987): 221-33.

4760 Anthony J. Saldarini, "Political and Social Roles of the Pharisees and Scribes in Galilee," *SBLSP* 19 (1988): 200-209.

4761 William A. Johnson, " 'The Jews' in Saint Mark's Gospel," *RIL* 6 (1989): 182-92.

4762 Frans Neirynck, "The Apocryphal Gospels and the Gospel of Mark," in J.-M. Servin, ed., *The New Testament in Early Christianity: La réception des écrits néotestamentaires dans le christianisme primitif.* BETL #86. Louvain: Peeters Press, 1989. Pp. 123-75.

4763 Marie Sabin, "Reading Mark 4 as Midrash," *JSNT* 45 (1992): 3-26.

relation to Luke

4764 A. E. Haefner, "The Bridge between Mark and Acts," *JBL* 77 (1958): 67-71.

relation to the Old Testament

4765 Edward C. Hobbs, "The Gospel of Mark and the Exodus," doctoral dissertation, University of Chicago, Chicago IL, 1958.

4766 F. F. Bruce, "The Book of Zechariah and the Passion Narrative," *BJRL* 43 (1960-1961): 336-53.

4767 George L. Balentine, "The Concept of the New Exodus in the Gospels," doctoral dissertation, Southern Baptist Theological Seminary, Louisville KY, 1961.

4768 Siegfried Schulz, "Markus und das Alte Testament," *ZTK* 58 (1961): 184-97.

4769 Karl H. Rengstorf, "Old and New Testament Traces of a Formula of the Judean Royal Ritual," *NovT* 5 (1962): 229-44.

4770 Simon Légasse, "Jesus a-t-il Announce le Conversion Finale d'Israel? (a propos de Marc x.23-7)," *NTS* 10/4 (1963-1964): 480-87.

4771 Alfred Suhl, *Die Funktion der alttestamentlichen Zitate und Anspielungen im Markusevangelium*. Gütersloh: Mohr, 1965.

4772 Hartmut Gese, "Psalm 22 und das Neue Testament," *ZTK* 65/1 (1968): 1-22.

4773 J. W. Deenick, "The Fourth Commandment and Its Fulfillment," *RTR* 28/2 (1969): 54-61.

4774 Margaret Thrall, "Elijah and Moses in Mark's Account of the Transfiguration," *NTS* 16/4 (1969-1970): 305-11.

4775 S. Hashimoto, "The Function of the Old Testament Quotations and Allusions in the Marcan Passion Narrative," doctoral dissertation, Princeton Theological Seminary, New York, 1970.

4776 Howard Clark Kee, ''Scripture Quotations and Allusions in Mark 11-16,'' *SBLSP* 1/2 (1971): 475-502.

4777 Matthew Black, ''The Christo-Logical Use of the Old Testament in the New Testament,'' *NTS* 18/1 (1971-1972): 1-14.

4778 Hugh Anderson, ''The Old Testament in Mark's Gospel,'' in James M. Effird, ed., *The Use of the Old Testament in the New and Other Essays: Studies in Honor of William Franklin Stinespring*. Durham NC: Duke University Press, 1972. Pp. 280-306.

4779 Klaus Berger, *Die Gesetzeeuslegung Jesu. Ihr historischer Hintergrund im Judentum und im Alten Testament. Teil I: Markus und Parallelen*. Wissenschaftliche Monographien zum Alten und Neuen Testament 40. Neukirchen-Vluyn: Neukirchener, 1972.

4780 James M. Efird, ''Note on Mark 5:43,'' in James M. Efird, ed., *The Use of the Old Testament in the New and Other Essays: Studies in Honor of William Franklin Stinespring*. Durham NC: Duke University, 1972. Pp. 307-309.

4781 Rudolf Schnackenburg, '' 'Das Evangelium' im Verständnis des ältesten Evangelisten,'' in P. Hoffmann, et al., eds., *Orientierung an Jesus: Zur Theologie der Synoptiker* (festschrift for Josef Schmid). Basel: Herder, 1973. Pp. 309-24.

4782 John H. Reumann, ''Psalm 22 at the Cross: Lament and Thanksgiving for Jesus Christ,'' *Int* 28/1 (1974): 39-58.

4783 Jean Calloud, G. Bombet, and J. Delorme, ''Essaie d'analyse sémiotique,'' in Xavier Léon-Dufour, ed., *Les miracles de Jésus selon le Nouveau Testament*. Parole de Dieu. Paris: Éditions du Seuil, 1977. Pp. 151-81.

4784 Yvan Almeida, *L'opérativité sémantique des récits-paraboles. Sémiotique narrative et textuelle. Herméneutique du discours religieux*. Bibliothèque des cahiers de l'Institut de Linguistique de Louvain 13. Paris/Louvain: Éditions Cerf/Peeters Press, 1978.

4785 Kent E. Brower, ''The Old Testament in the Markan Passion Narrative,'' doctoral dissertation, University of Manchester, Manchester, UK, 1978.

4786 F. F. Bruce, *The Time Is Fulfilled: Five Aspects of the Fulfilment of the Old Testament in the New*. Grand Rapids: Eerdmans, 1978.

4787 Julius Oswald, ''Die Beziehungen zwischen Psalm 22 und dem vormarkinischen Passionsbericht,'' *ZKT* 101 (1979): 53-66.

4788 Léopold Sabourin, *The Bible and Christ: The Unity of the Two Testaments*. New York: Alba, 1980.

4789 H. J. Steichele, *Der leidende Sohn Gottes. Eine Untersuchung einiger alttestamentlicher Motive in der Christologie des Markusevangeliums. Zugleich ein Beitrag zur Erhellung des überlieferungsgeschichtlichen Zusammenhangs zwischen Altem und Neuem Testament*. Biblische Untersuchungen 14. Münchener Universitäts-Schriften, Katholisch-Theologische Fakultät. Regensburg: F. Pustet, 1980.

4790 Francis J. Moloney, ''The Re-interpretation of Psalm VIII and the Son of Man Debate,'' *NTS* 27 (1980-1981): 656-72.

4791 Craig A. Evans, ''The Function of Isaiah 6:9-10 in Mark and John,'' doctoral dissertation, Claremont Graduate School, Berkeley CA, 1981.

4792 Craig A. Evans, ''A Note on the Function of Isaiah vi,9-10 in Mark iv,'' *RB* 88 (1981): 234-35.

4793 Michael W. Baird, ''Jesus' Use of the Decalogue in the Synoptics: An Exegetical Study,'' doctoral dissertation, Southwestern Baptist Theological Seminary, Louisville KY, 1982.

4794 Walter Brueggemann, '' 'Impossibility' and Epistemology in the Faith Tradition of Abraham and Sarah,'' *ZAW* 94/4 (1982): 615-34.

4795 Lynn M. Jordan, "Elijah Transfigured: A Study of the Narrative of the Transfiguration in the Gospel of Mark," doctoral dissertation, Duke University, Durham NC, 1982.

4796 Walter C. Kaiser, "The Promise of the Arrival of Elijah in Malachi and the Gospels," *GTJ* 3/2 (1982): 221-33.

4797 Kent E. Brower, "Elijah in the Markan Passion Narrative," *JSNT* 18 (1983): 85-101.

4798 Robert A. Guelich, "The Gospel Genre," in Peter Stuhlmacher, ed., *Das Evangelium und die Evangelien.* Tübingen: Mohr, 1983. Pp. 183-219.

4799 Anthony T. Hanson, "The Use of Scripture in Mark's Gospel," in *The Living Utterances of God: The New Testament Exegesis of the Old.* London: Darton, Longman & Todd. 1983. Pp. 63-70.

4800 Eugen Ruckstuhl, "Jesus als Gottessohn im Spiegel des markinischen Taufberichts [Mk 1:9-11]," in Ulrich Luz and Hans Weder, eds., *Die Mitte des Neuen Testaments: Einheit and vielfalt neutestamentlicher theologie* (festschrift for Eduard Schweizer). Göttingen: Vandenhoeck & Ruprecht, 1983. Pp. 193-220.

4801 Craig A. Evans, "On the Isaianic Background of the Parable of the Sower," *CBQ* 47/3 (1985): 464-68.

4802 Karl Kertelge, "Das Doppelgebot der Liebe im Markusevangelium," in Françios Refoulé, ed., *À cause l'Evangile: Études sur les synoptiques et les Actes* (festschrift for Jacques Dupont). Paris: Cerf, 1985. Pp. Pp. 303-22.

4803 Gerhard Dautzenberg, "Gesetzeskritik und Gesetzesgehorsam in der Jesustradition," in Karl Kertelge, ed., *Das Gesetz im Neuen Testament* . Freiburg: Herder, 1986. Pp. 46-70.

4804 Joseph A. Fitzmyer, "Aramaic Evidence Affecting the Interpretation of Hosanna in the New Testament," in Gerald F. Hawthorne and Otto Betz, eds., *Tradition &*

Interpretation in the New Testament (festschrift for E. Earle Ellis). Grand Rapids: Eerdmans, 1987. Pp. 110-18.

4805 Morna D. Hooker, " 'What Doest Thou Here, Elijah': A Look at St Mark's Account of the Transfiguration," in L. D. Hurst and N. T. Wright, eds., *The Glory of Christ in the New Testament*. Oxford: Clarendon Press, 1987. Pp. 59-70.

4806 John Wright, "Spirit and Wilderness: The Interplay of Two Motifs within the Hebrew Bible as a Background to Mark 1:2-13," in Edgar W. Conrad and Edward G. Newing, eds., *Perspectives on Language and Text* (festschrift for Francis Andersen). Winona Lake IN: Eisenbrauns, 1987. Pp. 269-98.

4807 Barnabas Lindars, "All Foods Clean: Thoughts on Jesus and the Law," in Barnabas Lindars, ed., *Law and Religion: Essays on the Place of Law in Israel and Early Christianity*. Cambridge: J. Clarke, 1988. Pp. 61-71.

4808 W.Roth, *Hebrew Gospel: Cracking the Code of Mark*. Oak Park IL: Meyer-Stone, 1988.

4809 Paul Beauchamp, "Paraboles de Jésus, vie de Jésus: l'encadrement évangélique et scripturaire des paraboles (Mc 4,1-34)," in Jean Delorme, ed., *Les paraboles évangéliques: perspectives nouvelles*. Paris: Cerf, 1989. Pp. 151-70.

4810 George J. Brooke, "The Temple Scroll and the New Testament," in George J. Brooke, ed., *Temple Scroll Studies*. Sheffield: JSOT Press, 1989. Pp. 181-99.

4811 Marinus de Jonge, "Jesus, Son of David and Son of God," in Spike Draisma, ed., *Intertextuality in Biblical Writings* (festschrift for Bastiaan M. F. van Iersel). Kampen: J. H. Kok, 1989. Pp. 95-104.

4812 Reginald H. Fuller, "The Decalogue in the NT," *Int* 43/3 (1989): 243-55.

4813 Ulrich Luck, "Was wiegt leichter? Zu Mk 2,9," in Hubert Frankemölle, ed., *Vom Urchristentum zu Jesus* (festschrift for Joachim Gnilka). Freiburg: Herder, 1989. Pp. 103-108.

4814 Jane Schaberg, ''Mark 14:62: Early Christian Merkabah Imagery?'' in Joel Marcus and Marion L. Soards, eds., *Apocalyptic and the New Testament* (festschrift for J. Louis Martyn). Sheffield: JSOT Press, 1989. Pp. 69-94.

4815 Walter Simonis, ''Gottesliebe - Nächstenliebe: Überlegungen zum sogenannten Doppelgebot im Lichte des biblischen Schöpfungs- und Bundesglaubens,'' in Thomas Franke, et al., eds., *Creatio ex amore: Beiträge zu einer Theologie* (festschrift for Alexandre Ganoczy). Würzburg: Echter Verlag, 1989. Pp. 60-83.

4816 M.-É. Boismard, ''Réponse aux deux autres hypothèses: 1. La théorie des deux sources: Mc 3:7:12 et parallèles; 2. La 'Two-Gospel Hypothesis','' in David L. Dungan, ed., *The Interrelations of the Gospels: A Symposium Led by M.-É. Boismard, W. R. Farmer, F. Neirynck, Jerusalem 1984*. Louvain: Peeters Press, 1990. BETL #95. Pp. 259-88.

4817 Willem S. Vorster, ''Bilingualism and the Greek of the New Testament: Semitic Interference in the Gospel of Mark,'' *Neo* 24 (1990): 215-28.

4818 C. Dahm, *Israel im Markusevanglium*. New York: Lang, 1991.

4819 J. Taylor, "The Coming of Elijah, Mt 17,10-13 and Mk 9,11-13: The Development of the Texts," *RB* 98 (1991): 107-19.

4820 Tal Ilan, "Man Born of Woman . . . (Job 14:1): The Phenomenon of Men Bearing Metronymes at the Time of Jesus,'' *NovT* 34 (1992): 23-45.

4821 W. Roth, ''Mark, John and Their Old Testament Codes,'' in Adelbert Denaux, ed., *John and the Synoptics*. BETL #101. Louvain: Peeters Press, 1992. Pp. 459-66.

<u>relation to Paul</u>

4822 J. W. Bailey, ''Light from Paul on Gospel Origins,'' *ATR* 28 (1946): 217-26.

4823 John C. Fenton, "Paul and Mark," in D. E. Nineham, ed., *Studies in the Gospels: Essays in Memory of R. H. Lightfoot.* Oxford: B. Blackwell, 1955. Pp. 89-112.

4824 G. M. M. Pelser, "Die Nagmaal by Markus en Paulus," *HTS* 30 (1974): 138-49.

4825 Kazimierz Romaniuk, "Le Problème des Paulinismes dans l'Évangile de Marc," *NTS* 23 (1976-1977): 266-74.

4826 Dale C. Allison, "The Pauline Epistles and the Synoptic Gospels: The Pattern of the Parallels," *NTS* 28/1 (1982): 1-32.

4827 David W. Johnson, "The Conciliatory Role for the Gospel of Mark in Relation to the Background of the Epistle to the Romans," doctoral dissertation, Southwestern Baptist Theological Seminary, Fort Worth TX, 1990.

<u>relation to Rome</u>

4828 Thomas L. Cashwell, "The Publicans in the Synoptic Gospels," doctoral dissertation, Southern Baptist Theological Seminary, Louisville KY, 1953.

4829 James E. Wood, "Christianity and the State," *JAAR* 35/3 (1967): 257-70.

4830 José Alonso Díaz, "El compromiso politico de Jesús," *BibFe* 4 (1978): 151-74.

4831 Ernst Bammel, "The Revolution Theory from Reimarus to Brandon," in Ernst Bammel and C. F. D. Moule, eds., *Jesus and the Politics of His Day.* Cambridge: Cambridge University Press, 1984. Pp. 11-68.

4832 Ernst Bammel and C. F. D. Moule, eds., *Jesus and the Politics of His Day.* Cambridge: Cambridge University Press, 1984.

4833 F. F. Bruce, "Render to Caesar," in Ernst Bammel and C. F. D. Moule, eds., *Jesus and the Politics of His Day.* Cambridge: University Press, 1984. Pp. 249-63.

4834 Carlos Bravo-Gallardo, *Jesús, hombre en conflicto: El relato de Marcos en America Latina.* Santander: Sal Terrae, 1986.

4835 Michael Bünker, " 'Gebt dem Kaiser, was des Kaisers ist!' - Aber: Was ist des Kaisers? Überlegungen zur Perikope von der Kaisersteuer," in Luise Schottroff and Willy Schottroff, eds., *Wer ist unser Gott? Beiträge zu einer Befreiungstheologie im Kont ext der "ersten" Welt.* Münich: Kaiser, 1986. Pp. 153-72.

4836 Paula Fredriksen, "Jesus and the Temple, Mark and the War," *SBLSP* 29 (1990): 293-310.

resurrection

4837 James L. Hall, "A Study of the Significance of the Appearances of Christ after the Resurrection," master's thesis, Southern Baptist Theological Seminary, Louisville KY, 1949.

4838 C. Hope, "The Story of the Passion and Resurrection in the English Primer," *JTS* 2 (1951): 68-82.

4839 John C. Fenton, *Preaching the Cross: The Passion and Resurrection according to St. Mark with an Introduction and Notes.* London: SPCK, 1958.

4840 J. L. Cheek, "The Historicity of the Markan Resurrection Narrative," *JBR* 27 (1959): 191-200.

4841 F.-P. Dreyfus, "L'argument scripturaire de Jésus en faveur de la résurrection des morta (Marc XII,26-27)," *RB* 66 (1959): 213-25.

4842 Gabriel Hebert, "The Resurrection Narrative in St. Mark's Gospel," *ABR* 7 (1959): 58-65.

4843 Françiois-Xavier Durrwell, *The Resurrection: A Biblical Study.* R. Sheed, trans. New York: Sheed & Ward, 1960.

4844 Charles E. Carlston, "Transfiguration and Resurrection," *JBL* 80 (1961): 233-40.

4845 Félix Gils, ''Pierre et la Foi au Christ Ressuscite,'' *ETL* 38 (1962): 5-43.

4846 Gabriel Hebert, ''The Resurrection Narrative in St. Mark's Gospel,'' *SJT* 15 (1962): 66-73.

4847 A. Rose, ''L'influence des psaumes sur les annonces et les récits de la Passion et de la Résurrection dans les Évangiles,'' *OrBibLov* 4 (1962): 297-356.

4848 D. J. Bowman, ''The Resurrection in Mark,'' *BibTo* 11 (1964): 709-13.

4849 N. Q. Hamilton, ''Resurrection Tradition and the Composition of Mark,'' *JBL* 34 (1965): 415-21.

4850 William Lillie, ''The Empty Tomb and the Resurrection,'' in D. E. Nineham, et al., eds., *Historicity and Chronology in the New Testament.* London: SPCK, 1965. Pp. 117-34.

4851 Max Brandle, ''Zum urchristlichen Verständnis der Auferstehung Jesu,'' *Orient* 31 (1967): 65-71.

4852 André Feuillet, ''Les trois grandes prophéties de la Passion et de la Résurrection des évangiles synoptiques,'' *RT* 67 (1967): 533-60; 68 (1968): 41-74.

4853 Zane C. Hodges, ''Form-Criticism and the Resurrection Accounts,'' *BSac* 124 (1967): 339-48.

4854 John Bligh, ''The Gerasene Demoniac and the Resurrection of Christ,'' *CBQ* 31 (1969): 383-90.

4855 Ingo Broer, ''Zur heutigen Diskussion der Grabesgeschichte,'' *BibL* 10 (1969): 40-52.

4856 Jean Delorme, ''Les femmes au tombeau, Mc 16,1-8,'' *AsSeign* 2 (1969): 58-67.

4857 Jean Delorme, ''Résurrection et tombeau de Jésus: Mc 16,1-8 dans la tradition évangélique,'' in E. de Surgy et al., eds., *La Résurrection du Christ et l'exégèse modern.* Lectio Divina 50. Paris: Éditions du Cerf, 1969. Pp. 105-51.

4858 André Legault, "Christophanies et angélophanies dans les récils évangeliques de la résurrection," *SE* 21 (1969): 443-57.

4859 Edward L. Bode, *The First Easter Morning: The Gospel Accounts of the Women's Visit to the Tomb of Jesus*. Analecta Biblica 45. Rome: Biblical Institute Press, 1970.

4860 Edward L. Bode, "A Liturgical *Sitz im Leben* for the Gospel Tradition of the Women's Easter Visit to the Tomb of Jesus?" *CBQ* 32 (1970): 237-42.

4861 Willi Marxsen, *The Resurrection of Jesus of Nazareth*. M. Kohl, trans. Philadelphia: Fortress Press, 1970.

4862 Robert P. Meye, "Mark's Special Easter Emphasis," *CT* 15/13 (1971): 584-86.

4863 G. W. Trompf, "The First Resurrection Appearance and the Ending of Mark's Gospel," *NTS* 18 (1971-1972): 308-30.

4864 Nikolaus Walter, "Eine Vormatthaische Schilderung der Auferstehung Jesus," *NTS* 19/4 (1972-1973): 415-29.

4865 Antonio Ammassari, "Gesu ha veramente insegnato la risurrezione!" *BibO* 15 (1973): 65-73.

4866 Jean Radermakers, "On Preaching the Risen Christ," *LV* 28/2 (1973): 267-80.

4867 O. G. White, "The Resurrection and the Second Coming of Jesus in Mark," *StudE* 6 (1973): 615-18.

4868 Thomas E. Boomershine, "Mark the Storyteller: A Rhetorical-Critical Investigation of Mark's Passion and Resurrection Narrative," doctoral dissertation, Union Theological Seminary, New York, 1974.

4869 John E. Alsup, *The Post-Resurrection Appearance Stories of the Gospel Tradition: A History-of-Tradition Analysis with Text-Synopsis*. Stuttgart: Calwer, 1975.

4870 John E. Alsup, "John Dominic Crossan, 'Empty Tomb and Absent Lord'—A Response," *SBLSP* 6 (1976): 263-67.

4871 Giuseppe Ghiberti, ''Discussione sulla risurrezione di Gesù,'' *RBib* 24 (1976): 57-93.

4872 Michael D. Goulder, ''The Empty Tomb,'' *Theology* 79 (1976): 206-14.

4873 Thomas R. W. Longstaff, ''Empty Tomb and Absent Lord: Mark's Interpretation of Tradition,'' *SBLSP* 6 (1976): 269-77.

4874 Robert H. Stein, ''Is the Transfiguration a Misplaced Resurrection Account?'' *JBL* 95/1 (1976): 79-96.

4875 Jean Cantinat, *Réflexions sur la resurrection de Jésus (d'après saint Paul et saint Marc)*. Paris: Gabalda, 1978.

4876 Jean Cantinat, ''La résurrection de Jésus dans les 15 premiers chapitres de Marc,'' in *Réflexions sur la resurrection de Jésus (d'après saint Paul et saint Marc)*. Paris: Gabalda, 1978. Pp. 94-105.

4877 Jean Cantinat, ''Saint Marc et la résurrection de Jésus,'' in *Réflexions sur la resurrection de Jésus (d'après saint Paul et saint Marc)*. Paris: Gabalda, 1978. Pp. 79-106.

4878 R. Alan Culpepper, ''The Passion and Resurrection in Mark,'' *RevExp* 75 (1978): 583-600.

4879 Herman Hendrickx, *The Resurrection Narratives of the Synoptic Gospels*. Manila: East Asian Pastoral Institute, 1978.

4880 Deuk J. Kim, ''Mark—A Theologian of Resurrection,'' doctoral dissertation, Drew University, Madison NJ, 1978.

4881 Gerald O'Mahony, ''The Empty Tomb,'' *ClerR* 63 (1978): 207-10.

4882 Eduard Schweizer, ''Resurrection—Fact or Illusion?'' *Horizons* 1 (1979): 137-59.

4883 Samuel O. Abogunrin, ''The Language and Nature of the Resurrection of Jesus Christ in the New Testament,'' *JETS* 24 (1981): 55-65.

4884 Dan M. Cohn-Sherbok, ''Jesus' Defence of the Resurrection of the Dead,'' *JSNT* 11 (1981): 64-73.

4885 Miguel de Burgos Nuñez, ''La resurrección de Jesús, revelación escatológica del poder de Dios sobre la muerte,'' *Communio* 15 (1982): 155-93.

4886 J. Duncan M. Derrett, *The Anastasis: The Resurrection of Jesus as an Historical Event.* Shipston-on-Stour: Drinkwater, 1982.

4887 F. Gerald Downing, ''The Resurrection of the Dead: Jesus and Philo,'' *JSNT* 15 (1982): 42-50.

4888 Giuseppe Ghiberti, *La risurrezione di Gesù.* Brescia: Paideia, 1982.

4889 M. H. Smith, *Easter Gospels: The Resurrection of Jesus according to the Four Evangelists.* Minneapolis MN: Augsburg, 1983.

4890 Grant R. Osborne, *The Resurrection Narratives: A Redactional Study.* Grand Rapids: Baker Book House, 1984.

4891 Dale C. Allison, *The End of the Ages Has Come: An Early Interpretation of the Passion and Resurrection of Jesus.* Philadelphia: Fortress Press, 1985.

4892 J. Gerald Janzen, ''Resurrection and Hermeneutics: On Exodus 3:6 in Mark 12:26,'' *JSNT* 23 (1985): 43-58.

4893 R. A. McKenzie, *The First Day of the Week: The Mystery and Message of the Empty Tomb of Jesus.* New York: Paulist Press, 1985.

4894 James Swetnam, ''No Sign of Jonah,'' *Bib* 66/1 (1985): 126-30.

4895 Nigel M. Watson, ''Willi Marxsen's Approach to Christology,'' *ET* 97 (1985-1986): 36-42.

4896 Hans F. Bayer, *Jesus' Predictions of Vindication and Resurrection: The Provenance, Meaning and Correlation of the Synoptic Predictions*. Tübingen: Mohr, 1986.

4897 Barry W. Henaut, "Empty Tomb or Empty Argument: A Failure of Nerve in Recent Studies of Mark 16," *SR* 15/2 (1986): 177-90.

4898 Lucien Legrand, "The Missionary Command of the Risen Christ: I. Mission and Resurrection," *ITS* 23 (1986): 290-309.

4899 Robert T. Fortna, "Sayings of the Suffering and Risen Christ: The Quadruple Tradition," *Forum* 3/3 (1987): 63-69.

4900 Heinz Giesen, "Der Auferstandene und seine Gemeinde: Zum Inhalt und zur Funktion des ursprünglichen Markusschlusses (16,1-8)," *SNTU-A* 12 (1987): 99-139.

4901 M. S. Hostetler, *Backward into Light: The Passion and Resurrection of Jesus according to Matthew and Mark*. London: SCM, 1987.

4902 Howard M. Jackson, "The Death of Jesus in Mark and the Miracle from the Cross," *NTS* 33/1 (1987): 16-37.

4903 Gerald O'Collins, "Mary Magdalene as Major Witness to Jesus' Resurrection," *TS* 48 (1987): 631-46.

4904 John P. Galvin, "The Origin of Faith in the Resurrection of Jesus: Two Recent Perspectives," *TS* 49 (1988): 25-44.

4905 S. J. Binz, *The Passion and Resurrection Narratives of Jesus: A Commentary*. Collegeville: Liturgical Press, 1989.

4906 J. I. H. McDonald, *The Resurrection: Narrative and Belief*. London: SPCK, 1989.

4907 Willem S. Vorster, "The Religio-Historical Context of the Resurrection of Jesus and Resurrection Faith in the New Testament," *Neo* 23 (1989): 159-75.

4908 Roberto Vignolo, "Una finale reticente: interpretazione narrativa di Mc 16:8," *RBib* 38 (1990): 129-89.

4909 Raymond E. Brown, *A Risen Christ in Eastertime: Essays on the Gospel Narratives of the Resurrection.* Collegeville MN: Liturgical Press, 1991.

<u>sabbath</u>

4910 Francis W. Beare, "The Sabbath Was Made for Man?" *JBL* 79 (1960): 130-36.

4911 James W. Leitch, "Lord Also of the Sabbath," *SJT* 19/4 (1966): 426-33.

4912 Christoph Hinz, "Jesus und der Sabbat," *KD* 19 (1973): 91-108.

4913 D. A. Carson, "Jesus and the Sabbath in the Four Gospels," in D. A. Carson, ed., *From Sabbath to Lord's Day: A Biblical, Historical, and Theological Investigation.* Grand Rapids: Zondervan, 1982. Pp. 57-97.

4914 Luise Schottroff and Wolfgang Stegemann, "The Sabbath Was Made for Man: The Interpretation of Mark 2:23-28," in Willy Schottroff and W. Stegemann, eds., *God of the Lowly: Socio-Historical Interpretation of the Bible.* Maryknoll NY: Orbis, 1984. Pp. 118-28.

<u>Samaritans</u>

4915 Walter D. Zorn, "Mark and the Samaritans," doctoral dissertation, Michigan State University, East Lansing MI, 1983.

<u>Sanhedrin</u>

4916 M. H. Marco, "El proceso ante el Sanhedrin y el Ministerio Público de Jesus," *EB* 34 (1974): 83-111; 35 (1975): 49-78, 187-222; 36 (1976): 35-55.

4917 Kurt Schubert, "Biblical Criticism Criticised: With Reference to the Markan Report of Jesus's Examination before the Sanhedrin [Mk 14:55-64; 15:2-5; Lk 22:66-71]," in Ernst Bammel and C. F. D. Moule, eds., *Jesus and the Politics of His Day.* Cambridge: University Press, 1984. Pp. 385-402.

4918 Mary Ann Beavis, "The Trial before the Sanhedrin (Mark 14:53-65): Reader Response and Greco-Roman Readers," *CBQ* 49 (1987): 581-96.

scribes

4919 Harry T. Fleddermann, "A Warning About the Scribes (Mark 12:37b-40)," *CBQ* 44/1 (1982): 52-67.

4920 Étienne Trocmé, "Jésus et les lettrés d'après Marc 12:28-40," *FV* 84/1-2 (1985): 33-41.

4921 Peter M. Head, "Observations on Early Papyri of the Synoptic Gospels, especially on the 'Scribal Habits'," *Bib* 71/2 (1990): 240-47.

shroud of Turin

4922 Dan M. Cohn-Sherbok, "The Jewish Shroud of Turin?" *ET* 92/1 (1980-1981): 13-16.

4923 D. Moody Smith, "Mark 15:46: The Shroud of Turin as a Problem of History and Faith," *BA* 46/4 (1983): 251-54.

sociology

4924 James Wilde, "A Social Description of the Community Reflected in the Gospel of Mark," doctoral dissertation, Drew University, Madison NJ, 1974.

4925 James Wilde, "The Social World of Mark's Gospel: A Word about Method," *SBLSP* 8/2 (1978): 47-70.

4926 Vernon K. Robbins, *Jesus the Teacher: A Socio-Rhetorical Interpretation of Mark*. Philadelphia PA: Fortress Press, 1984.

son of God

4927 Christian Maurer, "Knecht Gottes und Sohn Gottes im Passionsbericht des Markusevangeliums," *ZTK* 50 (1953): 1-38.

4928 John A. Phillips, *The Son of God. An Explanation of St. Mark's Gospel*. New York: Thomas Nelson, 1963.

4929 L. S. Hay, "The Son-of-God Christology in Mark," *JBR* 32 (1964): 106-14.

4930 I. Howard Marshall, "Son of God or Servant of Yahweh? A Reconsideration of Mark 1:11," *NTS* 15 (1968-1969): 326-36.

4931 Harold A. Guy, "Son of God in Mark 15:39," *ET* 81 (1969-1970): 151.

4932 John R. Richards, *Jesus, Son of God and Son of Man: A Markan Study*. Pantyfedwen Trust Lectures 1972. Penarth, Southeast Wales: Church in Wales Publications, 1973.

4933 Martin Hengel, *The Son of God: The Origins of Christology and the History of Jewish-Hellenstic Religion*. J. Bowden, trans. Philadelphia: Fortress Press, 1976.

4934 J. Slomp, "Are the Words 'Son of God' in Mark 1:1 Original?" *BT* 28 (1977): 143-50.

4935 Carl Kazmierski, *Jesus, the Son of God: A Study of the Markan Tradition and its Redaction by the Evangelist*. Forschung zur Bibel 33. Würzburg: Echter Verlag, 1979.

4936 Jack D. Kingsbury, "The Spirit and the Son of God in Mark's Gospel," in Daniel Durken, ed., *Sin, Salvation, and the Spirit: Commemorating the Fiftieth Year of the Liturgical Press*. Collegeville MN: Liturgical Press, 1979. Pp. 195-202.

4937 John M. McDermott, "Jesus and the Son of God Title," *Greg* 62 (1981): 277-318.

4938 Alexander Globe, "The Caesarean Omission of the Phrase 'Son of God' in Mark 1:1," *HTR* 75 (1982): 209-18.

4939 Eugen Ruckstuhl, "Jesus als Gottessohn im Spiegel des markinischen Taufberichts [Mk 1:9-11]," in Ulrich Luz and Hans Weder, eds., *Die Mitte des Neuen Testaments: Einheit and vielfalt neutestamentlicher theologie* (festschrift for Eduard Schweizer). Göttingen: Vandenhoeck & Ruprecht, 1983. Pp. 193-220.

4940 W. A. Brindle, ''A Definition of the Title 'Son of God' in the Synoptic Gospels,'' doctoral dissertation, Dallas Theological Seminary, Dallas TX, 1988.

4941 Marinus de Jonge, ''Jesus, Son of David and Son of God,'' in Spike Draisma, *Intertextuality in Biblical Writings* (festschrift for Bastiaan M. F. van Iersel). Kampen: J. H. Kok, 1989. Pp. 95-104.

4942 Joel Marcus, ''Mark 14:61: 'Are You the Messiah-Son-of-God?' '' *NovT* 31 (1989): 125-41.

son of man

4943 Pierson Parker, ''The Meaning of 'Son of Man',' *JBL* 60 (1941): 151-57.

4944 Fred B. Moseley, ''The Use of the Term 'Son of Man' in Mark: A Study in the Mission of Jesus,'' doctoral dissertation, New Orleans Baptist Theological Seminary, New Orleans LA, 1946.

4945 Cecil W. Jones, ''The Use of the Title 'Son of Man' in Mark,'' doctoral dissertation, Southern Baptist Theological Seminary, Louisville KY, 1948.

4946 E. J. Tinsley, ''The Sign of the Son of Man (Mk 14,62),'' *SJT* 8 (1955): 297-306.

4947 Jens Christensen, ''Le fils de l'homme s'en van, ainsi qu'il est écrit de lui,'' *StTheol* 10 (1956): 28-39.

4948 I. L. Sanders, ''The Origin and Significance of the Title 'The Son of Man' as Used in the Gospels,'' *Scr* 10 (1958): 49-56.

4949 Eric Ashby, ''The Coming of the Son of Man,'' *ET* 72 (1960-1961): 360-63.

4950 T. A. Burkill, ''The Hidden Son of Man in St. Mark's Gospel,'' *ZNW* 52 (1961): 189-213.

4951 Maria F. Sulzbach, ''Who Was Jesus? The Theology of the Son of Man,'' *RL* 30 (1961): 179-86.

4952 Eduard Schweizer, ''The Son of Man again,'' *NTS* 9 (1962-1963): 256-61.

4953 Frederick H. Borsch, ''The Son of Man,'' *ATR* 45 (1963): 174-90.

4954 Samuel Sandmel, '' 'Son of Man' in Mark,'' in Daniel J. Silver, ed., *In the Time of Harvest.* New York: Macmillan, 1963. Pp. 355-67.

4955 A. J. B. Higgins, *Jesus and the Son of Man.* Philadelphia: Fortress Press, 1965.

4956 I. Howard Marshall, ''The Synoptic Son of Man Sayings in Recent Discussion,'' *NTS* 12 (1965-1966): 327-51.

4957 Ransom Marlow, ''The Son of Man in Recent Journal Literature,'' *CBQ* 28 (1966): 20-30.

4958 Frederick H. Borsch, *The Son of Man in Myth and History.* London: SCM, 1967.

4959 Morna D. Hooker, *The Son of Man in Mark. A Study of the Background of the Term ''Son of Man'' and Its Use in St. Mark's Gospel.* London: SPCK, 1967.

4960 H. H. Straton, ''The Son-of-Man and the Messianic Secret,'' *JRT* 24 (1967): 31-49.

4961 J. M. Ford, '' 'The Son of Man'—A Euphemism?'' *JBL* 87 (1968): 257-66.

4962 Norman Perrin, ''The Creative Use of the Son of Man Traditions by Mark,'' *USQR* 23 (1968): 357-65.

4963 Norman Perrin, ''The Son of Man in the Synoptic Tradition,'' *BR* 13 (1968): 3-25.

4964 Robert J. Maddox, ''The Function of the Son of Man according to the Synoptic Gospels,'' *NTS* 15 (1968-1969): 45-74.

4965 Matthew Black, ''The Son of Man's Passion Sayings in the Gospel Tradition,'' *ZNW* 60 (1969): 58-65.

4966 J. Neville Birdsall, "Who is this Son of Man?" *EQ* 42/1 (1970): 7-17.

4967 Frederick H. Borsch, *The Christian and Gnostic Son of Man*. London: SCM, 1970.

4968 John H. Elliott, "Man and the Son of Man in the Gospel according to Mark," in T. Rendtorff and A. Rich, eds., *Humane Gesellschaft: Beitrage zu ihrer sozialen Gestaltung* (festschrift for Heinz-Dietrich Wendland). Zürich: Zwingli, 1970. Pp. 47-59.

4969 L. S. Hay, "The Son of Man in Mark 2:10 and 2:28," *JBL* 89 (1970): 69-75.

4970 I. Howard Marshall, "The Son of Man in Contemporary Debate," *EQ* 42 (1970): 67-87.

4971 Jean-Marie van Cangh, "Le Fils de l'homme dans la tradition synoptique," *RTL* 1 (1970): 411-19.

4972 R. G. Rank, "Who Is This Man? The Son of Man According to Mark," *BibTo* 63 (1972): 959-65.

4973 William O. Walker, "The Origin of the Son of Man Concept as Applied to Jesus," *JBL* 91/4 (1972): 482-90.

4974 Joseph Coppens, *De Mensenzoon-Logia in het Markus-Evangelie*. Mededelingen van de Koninklijke Academie voor Wetenschappen, Letteren en schone Kunsten van België, Klasse der Letteren, Jaargang XXXV, nr. 3. Brussels: Koninklijke Academie, 1973.

4975 John R. Richards, *Jesus, Son of God and Son of Man: A Markan Study*. Pantyfedwen Trust Lectures 1972. Penarth, Southeast Wales: Church in Wales Publications, 1973.

4976 W. J. Bennett, "The Son of Man," *NovT* 17/2 (1975): 113-29.

4977 Barnabas Lindars, "Re-Enter the Apocalyptic Son of Man," *NTS* 22 (1975-1976): 52-72.

4978 P. Maurice Casey, "The Son of Man Problem," *ZNW* 67/3 (1976): 147-54.

4979 Werner H. Kelber, "The Hour of the Son of Man and the Temptation of the Disciples (Mark 14:32-42)," in Werner H. Kelber, ed., *The Passion in Mark: Studies on Mark 14-16*. Philadelphia: Fortress Press, 1976. Pp. 41-60.

4980 Gene Szarek, "A Critique of Kelber's 'The Hour of the Son of Man and the Temptation of the Disciples: Mark 14:32-42'," *SBLSP* 6 (1976): 111-18.

4981 John W. Bowker, "The Son of Man," *JTS* 28 (1977): 19-48.

4982 John P. Brown, "The Son of Man: 'This Fellow'," *Bib* 58 (1977): 361-87.

4983 David R. Catchpole, "The Poor on Earth and the Son of Man in Heaven: A Reappraisal of Matthew 25:31-46," *BJRL* 61/2 (1978-1979): 355-97.

4984 Joseph A. Fitzmyer, "Another View of the 'Son of Man' Debate," *JSNT* 4 (1979): 58-68.

4985 George R. Beasley-Murray, "Jesus and Apocalyptic: With Special Reference to Mark 14,62," in Jan Lambrecht, ed., *L'Apocalypse johannique et l'apocalyptique dans le Nouveau Testament*. Gembloux: J. Duculot, 1980. Pp. 415-29.

4986 Barnabas Lindars, "The New Look on the Son of Man," *BJRL* 63 (1980-1981): 437-62.

4987 Francis J. Moloney, "The Re-interpretation of Psalm VIII and the Son of Man Debate," *NTS* 27 (1980-1981): 656-72.

4988 Carsten Colpe, "Neue Untersuchungen zum Menschensohn-Problem," *TheoR* 77 (1981): 353-71.

4989 F. F. Bruce, "The Background to the Son of Man Sayings," in Harold H. Rowdon, ed., *Christ the Lord: Studies in Christology* (festschrift for Donald Guthrie). Leicester: InterVarsity Press, 1982. Pp. 50-70.

4990 J. F. Seitz, "The Rejection of the Son of Man: Mark Compared with Q," *StudE* 7 (1982): 451-65.

4991 Darrell J. Doughty, "The Authority of the Son of Man," *ZNW* 74/3-4 (1983): 161-81.

4992 Jürgen Denker, "Identidad y mundo vivencial (Lebenswelt): en torno a Marcos 10:35-45 y Timoteo 2:5s," *RevB* 46/1-2 (1984): 159-69.

4993 Douglas R. A. Hare, "The Quest of the Son of Man: A Progress Report," *EGLMBS* 4 (1984): 166-80.

4994 Mogens Müller, "The Expression 'the Son of Man' as Used by Jesus," *StTheol* 38 (1984): 47-64.

4995 P. Maurice Casey, "Aramaic Idiom and Son of Man Sayings," *ET* 96 (1984-1985): 233-36.

4996 David R. Jackson, "The Priority of the Son of Man Sayings," *WTJ* 47 (1985): 83-96.

4997 Paul Ricoeur, "Le récit interprétatif: exégèse et théologie dans les récits de la passion," *RechSR* 73 (1985): 17-38.

4998 David R. Jackson, "A Survey of the 1967-1981 Study of the Son of Man," *RQ* 28 (1985-1986): 67-78.

4999 Chris L. Mearns, "The Son of Man Trajectory and Eschatological Development," *ET* 97/1 (1985-1986): 8-12.

5000 John R. Donahue, "Recent Studies on the Origin of 'Son of Man' in the Gospels," *CBQ* 48 (1986): 484-98.

5001 Pieter J. Maartens, "The Son of Man as a Composite Metaphor in Mk 14:62," in J. H. Petzer and P. J. Hartin, eds., *A South African Perspective on the New Testament* (festschrift for Bruce M. Metzger). Leiden: Brill, 1986. Pp. 76-98.

5002 J. M. Casciaro Ramírez, "General, Generic and Indefinite: The Use of the Term 'Son of Man' in Aramaic Sources and in the Teaching of Jesus," *JSNT* 29 (1987): 21-56.

5003 Adela Y. Collins, "The Origin of the Designation of Jesus as 'Son of Man'," *HTR* 80 (1987): 391-407.

5004 Bruce A. Stevens, " 'Why *Must* the Son of Man Suffer?' The Divine Warrior in the Gospel of Mark," *BZ* 31 (1987): 101-10.

5005 John P. Galvin, "The Origin of Faith in the Resurrection of Jesus: Two Recent Perspectives," *TS* 49 (1988): 25-44.

5006 Chrys C. Caragounis, "Kingdom of God, Son of Man and Jesus' Self-Understanding," *TynB* 40 (1989): 3-23.

5007 Jane Schaberg, "Mark 14:62: Early Christian Merkabah Imagery?" in Joel Marcus and Marion L. Soards, eds., *Apocalyptic and the New Testament* (festschrift for J. Louis Martyn). Sheffield: JSOT Press, 1989. Pp. 69-94.

5008 M.-É. Boismard, "Réponse aux deux autres hypothèses: 1.: La théorie des deux sources: Mc 3:7-12 et parallèles; 2. La 'Two-Gospel Hypothesis'," in David L. Dungan, ed., *The Interrelations of the Gospels: A Symposium Led by M.-É. Boismard, W. R. Farmer, F. Neirynck, Jerusalem 1984.* Louvain: Peeters Press, 1990. BETL #95. Pp. 259-88.

5009 Craig A. Evans, "In What Sense Blasphemy? Jesus before Caiaphas in Mark 14:61-64," *SBLSP* 30 (1991): 215-34.

5010 Bruce D. Chilton, "The Son of Man: Human and Heavenly," in F. Van Segbroeck, et al., eds., *The Four Gospels 1992* (festschrift for Frans Neirynck). BETL #100. 3 vols. Louvain: Peeters Press, 1992. 1:203-18.

5011 Morna D. Hooker, "The Son of Man and the Synoptic Problem," in F. Van Segbroeck, et al., eds., *The Four Gospels 1992* (festschrift for Frans Neirynck). BETL #100. 3 vols. Louvain: Peeters Press, 1992. 1:189-201.

soteriology

5012 John C. Fenton, "Destruction and Salvation in the Gospel according to St. Mark," *JTS* 3 (1952): 56-58.

5013 Ernest Best, *The Temptation and the Passion: The Markan Soteriology*. SNTSMS #2. Cambridge: University Press, 1965.

5014 J. A. Ziesler, "The Transfiguration Story and the Markan Soteriology," *ET* 81 (1969-1970): 263-68.

5015 F. McCombie, "Jesus and the Leaven of Salvation," *NBlack* 59 (1978): 450-62.

5016 Barnabas Lindars, "Christ and Salvation," *BJRL* 64/2 (1981-1982): 481-500.

5017 Jean Delorme, "Le salut dans l'évangile de Marc," *LTP* 41 (1985): 79-108.

5018 Walter Wagner, "Lubricating the Camel: Clement of Alexandria on Wealth and the Wealthy," in Walter Freitag, ed., *Festschrift: A Tribute to Dr. William Hordern*. Saskatoon: University of Saskatchewan Press, 1985. Pp. 64-77.

source criticism

5019 Norman Huffman, "The Source of Mark," in Robert P. Casey, et al., eds., *Quantulacumque* (festschrift for Kirsopp Lake). London: Christophers, 1937. Pp. 123-29.

5020 T. W. Manson, *The Beginning of the Gospel*. Oxford: University Press, 1950.

5021 B. C. Butler, *The Originality of St. Matthew: A Critique of the Two-Documents Hypothesis*. Cambridge: Cambridge University Press, 1951.

5022 Wilfred L. Knox, *The Sources of the Synoptic Gospels: 1. St. Mark,* ed. H. Chadwick. Cambridge: University Press, 1953.

5023 Pierson Parker, *The Gospel before Mark*. Chicago: University of Chicago Press, 1953.

5024 V. E. Gideon, "Mark's Gospel in Source and Form-Criticism," *SouJT* 1 (1958): 63-73.

5025 Gerhart J. Neumann, "A Newly Discovered Manuscript of Melchior Rinck," *MQR* 35 (1961): 197-204.

5026 Austin M. Farrer, *St. Matthew and St. Mark*. 2nd ed. Westminster: Dacre Press, 1966.

5027 Lamar Cope, "The Beelzebul Controversy, Mark 3:19-30 and Parallels: A Model Problem in Source Analysis," *SBLSP* 1/1 (1971): 251-56.

5028 Pierre Benoit and M.-É. Boismard, *Synopse des quatre Évangiles avec parallèles des apocryphes et des Pères*. Paris: Cerf, 1972.

5029 Petros Vassiliadis, "Behind Mark: Towards a Written Source," *NTS* 20 (1973-1974): 155-60.

5030 Helmut Merkel, "Auf den Spuren des Urmarkus? Ein neuer Fund und seine Beurteilung," *ZTK* 71 (1974): 123-44.

5031 Howard Clark Kee, *Aretalogies, Hellenistic "Lives," and the Sources of Mark. Protocol of the Twelfth Colloquy: 8 December 1974*. Protocol Series #12. Berkeley CA: Center for Hermeneutical Studies in Hellenistic and Modern Culture, 1975.

5032 George B. Caird, "The Study of the Gospels: 1. Source Criticism," *ET* 87/4 (1975-1976): 99-104.

5033 P. B. Lewis, "Indications of a Liturgical Source in the Gospel of Mark," *Enc* 39 (1978): 385-94.

5034 Pierson Parker, "A Second Look at *The Gospel before Mark*," *SBLSP* 9/1 (1979): 147-68.

5035 Frans Neirynck, "The Matthew-Luke Agreements in Matt 14:13-14 and Lk 9:10-11 (par Mk 6:30-34): The Two-Source Theory behind the Impasse," *ETL* 60/1 (1984): 25-44.

5036 Frank J. Matera, "The Death of Jesus according to Luke: A Question of Sources," *CBQ* 47 (1985): 469-85.

5037 Bo Reicke, *The Roots of the Synoptic Gospels*. Philadelphia: Fortress Press, 1986.

5038 William R. Farmer, ''Source Criticism: Some Comments on the Present Situation,'' *USQR* 42/1 (1988): 49-58.

5039 Frans Neirynck, ''Marc 6:14-16 et par.,'' *ETL* 65/1 (1989): 105-109.

5040 Philip H. Sellew, ''Oral and Written Sources in Mark 4:1-34,'' *NTS* 36 (1990): 234-67.

5041 D. Kosch, ''Q and Jesus,'' *BZ* 36/1 (1992): 30-38.

5042 Jan Lambrecht, ''John the Baptist and Jesus in Mark 1:1-15: Markan Redaction of Q?'' *NTS* 38 (1992): 357-84.

spirit baptism

5043 H. A. Blair, ''Spirit-Baptism in St. Mark 's Gospel,'' *CQR* 155 (1954): 369-77

5044 Leander E. Keck, ''The Spirit and the Dove,'' *NTS* 17 (1970-1971): 41-67.

spirituality

5045 Gary A. Phillips, ''Gethsemane: Spirit and Discipleship in Mark's Gospel,'' in A. W. Sadler, ed., *The Journey of Western Spirituality*. Chicago: Scholars Press, 1981. Pp. 49-63.

5046 J. E. McDermott, ''The Spirituality of the Gospel of Mark,'' doctoral dissertation, Southern Baptist Theological Seminary, Louisville KY, 1989.

structuralism

5047 B. M. F. van Iersel and A. J. M. Linmans, ''The Storm on the Lake, Mk iv,35-41 and Mt viii,18-27 in the Light of Form Criticism, '*Redaktionsgeschichte*' and Structural Analysis,'' in T. Baarda, A. F. J. Klihn, and W. C. van Unnik, eds., *Miscellanea Neotestamentica*. Novum Testamentum Supplement #48. Leiden: Brill, 1978. 2:17-48.

5048 Jean Calloud, ''Toward a Structural Analysis of the Gospel of Mark,'' *Semeia* 16 (1979): 133-65.

5049 Elizabeth Struthers Malbon, "Narrative Space and Mythic Meaning: A Structural Exegesis in the Gospel of Mark," doctoral dissertation, Florida State University, Tallahassee FL, 1980.

5050 Daniel Patte, "Entering the Kingdom Like Children: A Structural Analysis," *SBLSP* 21 (1982): 371-96.

5051 Daniel Patte, "Jesus' Pronouncement about Entering the Kingdom Like a Child: A Structural Exegesis," *Semeia* 29 (1983): 3-42.

5052 John Drury, "Mark 1:1-15: An Interpretation," in A. E. Harvey, ed., *Alternative Approaches to New Testament Study*. London: Latimer, 1985. Pp. 25-36.

5053 Michael A. Harris, "Structuralism, Hermeneutics, and the Gospel of Mark," *PRS* 15 (1988): 61-70.

5054 Stephen D. Moore, *Mark and Luke in Poststructuralist Perspectives*. New Haven: Yale University Press, 1992.

structure

5055 D. W. Riddle, "The Structural Units of the Gospel Tradition," *JBL* 55 (1936): 45-58.

5056 Harry Sawyerr, "The Marcan Framework," *SJT* 14 (1961): 279-94.

5057 David F. Noble, "An Examination of the Structure of St. Mark's Gospel," doctoral dissertation, University of Edinburgh, Edinburgh, 1972.

5058 Joanna Dewey, "The Literary Structure of the Controversy Stories in Mark 2:1-3:6," *JBL* 92/3 (1973): 394-401.

5059 Willard M. Swartley, "A Study in Markan Structure: The Influence of Israel's Holy History upon the Structure of the Gospel of Mark," doctoral dissertation, Princeton Theological Seminary, Princeton NJ, 1973.

5060 Jean Radermakers, "L'évangile de Marc: Structure et théologie," in M. Sabbe, ed., *L'évangile selon Marc:*

Tradition et rédaction. BETL #34. Louvain: Louvain University Press, 1974. Pp. 221-39.

5061 P. F. Ellis, "Patterns and Structures of Mark's Gospel," in Miriam Ward, ed., *Biblical Studies in Contemporary Thought*. Burlington VT: Trinity College Biblical Institute; Somerville MA: Greeno/Hadden, 1975. Pp. 88-103.

5062 David J. Hawkin, "The Symbolism and Structure of the Marcan Redaction," *EQ* 49 (1977): 98-110.

5063 Joanna Dewey, *Markan Public Debate: Literary Technique, Concentric Structure and Theology in Mark 2:1-3:6*. Chico CA: Scholars Press, 1978.

5064 Eugene E. Lemcio, "External Evidence for the Structure and Function of Mark IV.1-20, VII.14-23, and VIII.14-21," *JTS* 29/2 (1978): 323-38.

5065 Elizabeth Struthers Malbon, "Mythic Structure and Meaning in Mark: Elements of a Levi-Straussian Analysis," *Semeia* 16 (1979): 97-132.

5066 Krikor Haleblian, "Contextualization and French Structuralism: A Method to Delineate the Deep Structures of the Gospel," doctoral dissertation, Fuller Theological Seminary, Pasadena CA, 1982.

5067 Charles W. Hedrick, "What Is a Gospel? Geography, Time and Narrative Structure," *PRS* 10/3 (1983): 255-68.

5068 James L. Magness, "Sense and Absence: Structure and Suspension in the Ending of the Gospel of Mark," doctoral dissertation, Emory University, Atlanta, 1984.

5069 Augustine Stock, "The Structure of Mark," *BibTo* 23 (1985): 291-96.

5070 Greg Fay, "Introduction to Incomprehension: The Literary Structure of Mark 4:1-34," *CBQ* 51/1 (1989): 65-81.

5071 Stephen H. Smith, "The Literary Structure of Mark 11:1-12:40," *NovT* 31/2 (1989): 104-24.

5072 John P. Heil, "Mark 14:1-52: Narrative Structure and Reader Response," *Bib* 71/3 (1990): 305-32.

symbolism

5073 Kenneth Grayston, "The Darkness of the Cosmic Sea: A Study of Symbolism in Mark's Narrative of the Crucifixion," *Theology* 55 (1952): 122-27.

5074 I. Paci, "Simbologia o storia? A proposito d'un testo di S. Mc 7,31-37," *PalCl* 55 (1976): 1204-1206.

5075 David J. Hawkin, "The Symbolism and Structure of the Marcan Redaction," *EQ* 49 (1977): 98-110.

synopsis

5076 Neal M. Flanagan, *Mark, Matthew, and Luke: A Guide to the Gospel Parallels. A Companion for Individuals and Study Groups to the* Gospel Parallels *of Burton H. Throckmorton, Jr.* Collegeville MN: Liturgical Press, 1978.

5077 Christian Fahner, *Synopsis van de vier evangeliën: Mattheüs, Markus, Lukas, Johannes. Met een inleiding tot het synoptische probleem.* Utrecht: De Banier, 1981.

synoptic problem

5078 Henry L. Jackson, "The Present State of the Synoptic Problem," in Henry B. Sweet, ed., *Essays on Some Biblical Questions of the Day.* London: Macmillan, 1909. Pp. 421-60.

5079 W. E. Addis, "The Criticism of the Hexateuch Compared with that of the Synoptic Gospels," in William Sanday, ed., *Studies in the Synoptic Problem by Members of the University of Oxford.* Oxford: Clarendon, 1911. Pp. 367-88.

5080 W. C. Allen, "The Book of Sayings Used by the Editor of the First Gospel," in William Sanday, ed., *Studies in the Synoptic Problem by Members of the University of Oxford.* Oxford: Clarendon, 1911. Pp. 235-86.

5081 John C. Hawkins, "Probabilities as to the So-Called Double Tradition of St. Matthew and St. Luke," in William Sanday, ed., *Studies in the Synoptic Problem by Members of the University of Oxford*. Oxford: Clarendon, 1911. Pp. 95-140.

5082 John C. Hawkins, "Three Limitations to St. Luke's Use of St. Mark's Gospel," in William Sanday, ed., *Studies in the Synoptic Problem by Members of the University of Oxford*. Oxford: Clarendon, 1911. Pp. 29-94.

5083 William Sanday, "The Conditions Under Which the Gospels Were Written," in William Sanday, ed., *Studies in the Synoptic Problem by Members of the University of Oxford*. Oxford: Clarendon, 1911. Pp. 3-28.

5084 B. H. Streeter, "The Literary Evolution of the Gospels," in William Sanday, ed., *Studies in the Synoptic Problem by Members of the University of Oxford*. Oxford: Clarendon, 1911. Pp. 209-28.

5085 B. H. Streeter, "The Original Extent of Q," in William Sanday, ed., *Studies in the Synoptic Problem by Members of the University of Oxford*. Oxford: Clarendon, 1911. Pp. 185-208.

5086 B. H. Streeter, "On the Original Order of Q," in William Sanday, ed., *Studies in the Synoptic Problem by Members of the University of Oxford*. Oxford: Clarendon, 1911. Pp. 141-64.

5087 B. H. Streeter, "St. Mark's Knowledge and Use of Q," in William Sanday, ed., *Studies in the Synoptic Problem by Members of the University of Oxford*. Oxford: Clarendon, 1911. Pp. 165-208.

5088 B. H. Streeter, "Synoptic Criticism and the Eschatological Problem," in William Sanday, ed., *Studies in the Synoptic Problem by Members of the University of Oxford*. Oxford: Clarendon, 1911. Pp. 425-36.

5089 N. P. Williams, "A Recent Theory of the Origin of St. Mark's Gospel," in William Sanday, ed., *Studies in the Synoptic Problem by Members of the University of Oxford*. Oxford: Clarendon, 1911. Pp. 389-424.

5090 H. G. Wood, "Some Characteristics of the Synoptic Writers," in F. J. Foakes Jackson, ed., *The Parting of the Roads: Studies in the Development of Judaism and Early Christianity*. London: Edward Arnold, 1912. Pp. 133-71.

5091 Paul Fiebig, "Die Mündliche Überlieferung als Quelle der Syoptiker," in Hans Windisch, ed., *Neutestamentliche Studien Georg Heinrici zu seinem 70. Geburtstag*. Leipzig: Hinrichs'sche, 1914. Pp. 79-91.

5092 C. A. Bernoulli, "Queleques difficultés non résolues du problème synoptique et leur interprétation psychologique," in P.-L. Counchoud, ed., *Congrès d'historie du Christianisme: Jubilé Alfred Loisy*. Paris: Rieder, 1928. I:178-87.

5093 Donald W. Riddle, "The Aramaic Gospels and the Synoptic Problem," *JBL* 54 (1935): 127-38.

5094 B. C. Butler, "Notes on the Synoptic Problem," *JTS* 4 (1953): 24-27.

5095 Jean Levie, "L'évangile araméen de S. Matthieu est-il la source de l'évangile de S. Marc?" *NRT* 76 (1954): 689-715, 812-43.

5096 B. C. Butler, "The Synoptic Problem Again," *DR* 73 (1955): 24-46.

5097 Bruno de Solages, "Note sur l'utilisation de l'analyse combinatoire pour la solution du problème synoptique," in J. Heuschen, *La formation des évangiles: Problème synoptique et Formgeschichte*. Paris: Desclée, 1957. Pp. 213-14.

5098 Heinrich Baltensweiler, *Die Verklärung Jesu: Historisches Ereignis und synoptische Berichte*. Zürich: Zwingli, 1959.

5099 J. H. Ludlum, "Are We Sure of Mark's Priority?" *CT* 3/24 (1959): 11-14; 3/25 (1960): 9-10.

5100 José Alonso Díaz, "Cuestión sinóptica y universalidad del mensaje cristiano en el pasaje evangélico de la mujer cananea," *CuBí* 20 (1963): 274-79.

5101 Eduardo Martínez Dalmau, *A Study on the Synoptic Gospels: A New Solution to an Old Problem. The Dependence of the Greek Gospels of St. Matthew and St. Luke upon the Gospel of St. Mark.* New York: Speller, 1964.

5102 R. T. Simpson, ''The Major Agreements of Matthew and Luke against Mark,'' *NTS* 12 (1965-1966): 273-84.

5103 M.-É. Boismard, ''Évangile des Ébionites et problème synoptique (Mc. I,2-6 et par.),'' *RB* 73 (1966): 321-52.

5104 William R. Farmer, ''The Two-Document Hypothesis as a Methodological Criterion in Synoptic Research,'' *ATR* 48 (1966): 380-96.

5105 Joachim Jeremias, ''Zum Problem des Urmarkus,'' in J. Jeremias, ed., *Abba: Studien zur neutestamentlichen Theologie und Zeitgeschichte*. Göttingen: Vandenhoeck & Ruprecht, 1966. Pp. 87-90.

5106 Swithun McLoughlin, ''Les accords mineurs Mt-Lc contra Mc et le problème synoptique,'' *ETL* 43 (1967): 17-40.

5107 Francis E. Williams, ''Fourth Gospel and Synoptic Tradition,'' *JBL* 86/3 (1967): 311-19.

5108 A. M. Honoré, ''A Statistical Study of the Synoptic Problem,'' *NovT* 10 (1968): 95-147.

5109 Edward W. Burrows, ''A Study of the Agreements of Matthew and Luke against Mark,'' doctoral dissertation, Oxford, 1969.

5110 Antonio Gaboury, *La structure des évangiles synoptiques: La structure-type à l'origine des synoptiques*. Leiden: Brill, 1970.

5111 Marvin F. Cain, ''An Analysis of the Sources of Mark 1:1-3:35 and Parallels,'' doctoral dissertation, Duke University, Durham NC, 1971.

5112 William R. Farmer, ''The Gospel of Mark,'' in Donald G. Miller and D. Y. Hadidan, eds., *Jesus and Man's Hope*, #II.

Pittsburhg: Pittsburgh Theological Seminary, 1971. Pp. 343-44.

5113 H. P. Hamann, "*Sic et Non*: Are We So Sure of Matthean Dependence on Mark?" *CTM* 41 (1971): 462-69.

5114 A. W. H. Moule, "The Pattern of the Synoptists," *EQ* 43/3 (1971): 162-71.

5115 Tim Schramm, *Der Markus-Stoff bei Lukas: Eine literarkritische und redaktionsgeschichtliche Untersuchung*. Cambridge: Cambridge University Press, 1971.

5116 Jean-Noël Aletti, "Problème synoptique et théorie des permutations," *RechSR* 60 (1972): 575-94.

5117 Jean F. Bouhours, "Une étude de l'ordonnance de la triple tradition," *RechSR* 60 (1972): 595-614.

5118 David Wenham, "The Synoptic Problem Revisited: Some New Suggestions about the Composition of Mark 4:1-34," *TynB* 23 (1972): 3-38.

5119 E. P. Sanders, "The Overlaps of Mark and Q and the Synoptic Problem," *NTS* 19 (1972-1973): 453-65.

5120 Francis W. Beare, "On the Synoptic Problem: A New Documentary Theory," *ATR* Supp. #3 (1974): 15-28.

5121 Frans Neirynck, et al., *The Minor Agreements of Matthew and Luke against Mark with a Cumulative List*. BETL #37. Louvain: Louvain University Press, 1974.

5122 Frans Neirynck, "Urmarcus redivivus? Examen critique de l'hypothèse des insertions matthéennes dans Marc," in M. Sabbe, ed., *L'évangile selon Marc: Tradition et rédaction*. BETL #34. Louvain: Louvain University Press, 1974. Pp. 103-45.

5123 David R. Catchpole, "The Synoptic Divorce Material as a Traditio-Historical Problem," *BJRL* 57/1 (1974-1975): 92-127.

5124 Robert Banks, *Jesus and the Law in the Synoptic Tradition.* Cambridge: Cambridge University Press, 1975.

5125 Petros Vassiliadis, ''Prolegomena to a Discussion on the Relationship between Mark and the Q Document,'' *DBM* 3 (1975): 31-46.

5126 Edward W. Burrows, ''The Use of Textual Theories to Explain the Agreements of Matthew and Luke against Mark,'' in James K. Elliott, ed., *Studies in New Testament Language and Text* (festschrift for George D. Kilpatrick). Leiden: Brill, 1976. Pp. 87-99.

5127 John B. Orchard, *Matthew, Luke & Mark.* Griesbach Solution to the Synoptic Question #1. Manchester: Koinonia, 1976.

5128 R. L. Thomas, ''An Investigation of the Agreements between Matthew and Luke against Mark,'' *JETS* 19 (1976): 103-12.

5129 Sangbok D. Kim, ''A Critical Investigation of the Priority of Mark,'' doctoral dissertation, Grace Theological Seminary, Winona Lake IN, 1977.

5130 Thomas R. W. Longstaff, *Evidence of Conflation in Mark? A Study in the Synoptic Problem.* SBLDS #28. Missoula MT: Scholars Press, 1977.

5131 Gordon D. Fee, ''Modern Text Criticism and the Synoptic Problem,'' in Bernard Orchard and T. R. Longstaff, eds., *J. J. Griesbach: Synoptic and Text-Critical Studies 1776-1976*. Cambridge: Cambridge University Press, 1978. Pp. 154-70.

5132 David B. Peabody, ''A Pre-Markan Prophetic Sayings Tradition and the Synoptic Problem,'' *JBL* 97 (1978): 391-409.

5133 John M. Rist, *On the Independence of Matthew and Mark.* Society for New Testament Studies Monograph Series 32. Cambridge: University Press, 1978.

5134 Hans-Herbert Stoldt, "Geschichte und Kritik der Markus-hypothese," *SBLSP* 8/2 (1978): 145-58.

5135 Vinton A. Dearing, "The Synoptic Problem: Prolegomena to a New Solution," in W. D. O'Flaherty, ed., *The Critical Study of Sacred Texts*. Berkeley CA: Graduate Theological Union, 1979. Pp. 121-37.

5136 René Jacob, *Les péricopes de l'entrée à Jérusalem et de la préparation de la cène. Contribution a l'étude du problème synoptique*. Église nouvelle-Église ancienne, Études bibliques 2. Paris: Beauchesne, 1979.

5137 George F. Melick, *John Mark and the Origin of the Gospels: A Foundation Document Hypothesis*. Ardmore PA: Dorrance, 1979.

5138 M.-É. Boismard, "The Two-Source Theory at an Impasse," *NTS* 26/1 (1979-1980): 1-17.

5139 Rudolf Laufen, *Die Doppelüberlieferungen der Logienquelle und des Markusevangeliums*. Bonner biblische Beiträge #54. Bonn: Hanstein, 1980.

5140 Dale C. Allison, "The Pauline Epistles and the Synoptic Gospels: The Pattern of the Parallels," *NTS* 28/1 (1982): 1-32.

5141 Malcolm Lowe, "The Demise of Arguments from Order for Markan Priority," *NovT* 24 (1982): 27-36.

5142 Hans-Herbert Stoldt, *History and Criticism of the Markan Hypothesis*. Donald L. Niewyk, trans. Macon GA: Mercer University Press, 1982.

5143 G. M. Styler, "The Priority of Mark," in C. F. D. Moule, *The Birth of the New Testament*. 3rd ed. San Francisco: Harper & Row, 1982. Pp. 285-316.

5144 Richard B. Vinson, "A Study of Matthean Doublets with Marcan Parallels," *SBT* 12 (1982): 239-59.

5145 Lamar Cope, "The Argument Revolves: The Pivotal Evidence for Markan Priority Is Reversing Itself," in

William R. Farmer, ed., *New Synoptic Studies*. Macon GA: Mercer University Press, 1983. Pp. 143-59.

5146 David L. Dungan, "The Purpose and Provenance of the Gospel of Mark according to the 'Two-Gospel' Hypothesis," in William R. Farmer, ed., *New Synoptic Studies*. Macon GA: Mercer University Press, 1983. Pp. 411-40.

5147 Frans Neirynck, "Les expressions doubles chez Marc et le problème synoptique," *ETL* 59/4 (1983): 303-30.

5148 Pierson Parker, "The Posteriority of Mark," in William R. Farmer, ed., *New Synoptic Studies*. Macon GA: Mercer University Press, 1983. Pp. 67-142.

5149 David B. Peabody, "The Late Secondary Redaction of Mark's Gospel and the Griesbach Hypothesis: A Response to Helmut Koester," in Bruce Corley, ed., *Colloquy on New Testament Studies*. Macon GA: Mercer University Press, 1983. Pp. 87-132.

5150 Phillip Sigal, "Aspects of Mark Pointing to Matthean Priority," in William R. Farmer, ed., *New Synoptic Studies*. Macon GA: Mercer University Press, 1983. Pp. 185-208.

5151 Phillip Sigal, "Matthean Priority in the Light of Mark 7," *EGLMBS* 3 (1983): 76-95.

5152 David L. Dungan, "A Griesbachian Perspective on the Argument from Order," in Christopher M. Tuckett, ed., *Synoptic Studies: The Ampleforth Conferences of 1982 and 1983*. Sheffield: JSOT Press, 1984. Pp. 67-74.

5153 Robert M. Fowler, "Thoughts on the History of Reading Mark's Gospel," *EGLMBS* 4 (1984): 120-30.

5154 Timothy A. Friedrichsen, "The Minor Agreements of Matthew and Luke against Mark 1974-1984," doctoral dissertation, University of Louvain, Louvain, Belgium, 1984.

5155 I. Howard Marshall, "How to Solve the Synoptic Problem: Luke 11:43 and Parallels, " in William C. Weinrich, ed.,

The New Testament Age (festschrift for Bo Reicke). 2 vols. Macon GA: Mercer University Press, 1984. 2:313-25.

5156 Frans Neirynck, "Réponse à P. Rolland," *ETL* 60/4 (1984): 363-66.

5157 Richard B. Vinson, "The Significance of the Minor Agreements as an Argument Against the Two-Document Hypothesis," doctoral dissertation, Duke University, Durham NC, 1984.

5158 David L. Dungan, "Synopses of the Future," *Bib* 66/4 (1985): 457-92.

5159 W. G. Kümmel, "In Support of Markan Priority," in Arthur Bellinzoni, ed., *The Two-Source Hypothesis*. Macon GA: Mercer University Press, 1985. Pp. 53-62.

5160 E. P. Sanders, "Suggested Exceptions to the Priority of Mark," in Arthur Bellinzoni, ed., *The Two-Source Hypothesis*. Macon GA: Mercer University Press, 1985. Pp. 199-203.

5161 B. H. Streeter, "The Priority of Mark," in Arthur Bellinzoni, ed., *The Two-Source Hypothesis*. Macon GA: Mercer University Press, 1985. Pp. 23-36.

5162 Raymond E. Brown, "The Gospel of Peter and Canonical Gospel Priority," *NTS* 33 (1987): 321-43.

5163 J. Duncan M. Derrett, "Marcan Priority and Marcan Skill," *BibO* 29 (1987): 135-40.

5164 Joanna Dewey, "Order in the Synoptic Gospels: A Critique," *SecCent* 6 (1987-1988): 68-82.

5165 F. Gerald Downing, "Compositional Conventions and the Synoptic Problem," *JBL* 107 (1988): 69-85.

5166 Heinzpeter Hempelmann, "Is Q but the Invention of Luke and Mark? Method and Argument in the Griesbach Hypothesis," *RSB* 8 (1988): 15-32.

5167 Timothy A. Friedrichsen, "The Matthew-Luke Agreements against Mark—A Survey of Recent Studies: 1974-1989," in Frans Neirynck, ed., *L'Évangile de Luc - The Gospel of Luke*. BETL #32. Louvain: Louvain University Press, 1989. Pp. 335-92.

5168 Timothy A. Friedrichsen, "The Minor Agreements of Matthew and Luke against Mark: Critical Observations on R. B. Vinson's Statistical Analysis," *ETL* 65 (1989): 395-408.

5169 J. J. McDonnell, *Acts to Gospels: A New Testament Path*. Lanham MD: University Press of America, 1989.

5170 Harold Riley, *The Making of Mark: An Exploration*. Macon GA: Mercer University Press, 1989.

5171 E. P. Sanders and M. Davies, *Studying the Synoptic Gospels*. London: SCM, 1989.

5172 David Seeley, "Was Jesus Like a Philosopher? The Evidence of Martyrological and Wisdom Motifs in Q, Pre-Pauline Traditions, and Mark," *SBLSP* 28 (1989): 540-49.

5173 Samuel O. Abogunrin, "The Synoptic Gospel Debate: A Re-Examination in the African Context," *AJBS* 2 (1987): 25-51.

5174 David E. Aune, "Synoptic Gospels: Matthew, Mark and Luke," *BRev* 6 (1990): 42-43.

5175 M.-É. Boismard, "Réponse aux deux autres hypothèses: 1. La théorie des deux sources: Mc 3:7:12 et parallèles; 2. La 'two-Gospel hypothesis'," in David L. Dungan, ed., *The Interrelations of the Gospels*. Macon, GA: Mercer University Press, 1990. Pp. 259-88.

5176 Frans Neirynck, "The Two-Source Hypothesis: Introduction," in David L. Dungan, ed., *The Interrelations of the Gospels*. Macon, GA: Mercer University Press, 1990. Pp. 3-22.

5177 M. J. Paul, "De Marcushypothese," in G. van der Brink, et al., eds., *Verkenningen in de evangelië*. Kampen: Kok, 1990. Pp. 39-45.

5178 Philip H. Sellew, "Oral and Written Sources in Mark 4:1-34," *NTS* 36 (1990): 234-67.

5179 Frans Neirynck, "The Minor Agreements and Proto-Mark: A Response to H. Koester," *ETL* 67/1 (1991): 82-94.

5180 Tom Shepherd, "Intercalation in Mark and the Synoptic Problem," *SBLSP* 30 (1991): 687-97.

5181 John W. Wenham, *Redating Matthew, Mark and Luke: A Fresh Assault on the Synoptic Problem*. London: Hodder & Stoughton, 1991.

5182 F. Gerald Downing, "A Paradigm Perplex: Luke, Matthew and Mark," *NTS* 38/1 (1992): 15-36.

5183 J. K. Elliott, "Printed Editions of Greek Synopses and their Influence on the Synoptic Problem," in F. Van Segbroeck, et al., eds., *The Four Gospels 1992* (festschrift for Frans Neirynck). BETL #100. 3 vols. Louvain: Peeters Press, 1992. 1:337-57.

5184 Morna D. Hooker, "The Son of Man and the Synoptic Problem," in F. Van Segbroeck, et al., eds., *The Four Gospels 1992* (festschrift for Frans Neirynck). BETL #100. 3 vols. Louvain: Peeters Press, 1992. 1:189-201.

5185 John S. Kloppenborg, "The Theological Stakes in the Synoptic Problem," in F. Van Segbroeck, et al., eds., *The Four Gospels 1992* (festschrift for Frans Neirynck). BETL #100. 3 vols. Louvain: Peeters Press, 1992. 1:93-120.

5186 John W. Wenham, *Redating Matthew, Mark and Luke: A Fresh Assault on the Synoptic Problem*. Downers Grove IL: InterVarsity Press, 1992.

Syrophoenician woman

5187 J. I. Hasler, "The Incident of the Syrophoenician Woman (Matt 15:21-28; Mark 7:14-30)," *ET* 45 (1933-1934): 459-61.

5188 T. A. Burkill, "The Syrophoenician Woman," in L. Wallach, ed., *The Classical Tradition: Literary and Historical Studies in Honor of Harry Caplan.* Ithaca NY: Cornell University Press, 1966. Pp. 329-44.

5189 T. A. Burkill, "The Syrophoenician Woman: The Congruence of Mark 7:24-31," *ZNW* 57 (1966): 23-37.

5190 T. A. Burkill, "The Historical Development of the Story of the Syrophoenician Woman," *NovT* 9 (1967): 161-77.

5191 T. A. Burkill, "The Syrophoenician Woman: Mark 7:24-31," *StudE* 4 (1968): 166-70.

5192 Barnabas Flammer, "Die Syrophoenizerin. Mk 7,24-30," *TQ* 148 (1968): 463-78. (See the English translation, "The Syro-Phoenician Woman (Mk 7:24-30)," *TD* 18 (1970): 19-24.

5193 W. Storch, "Zur Perikope von der Syrophonizierin," *BZ* 14/2 (1970): 256-57.

5194 J. Duncan M. Derrett, "Law in the New Testament: The Syrophoenician Woman and the Centurion of Capernaum," *NovT* 15/3 (1973): 161-86.

5195 Alice Dermience, "Tradition et rédaction dans la péricope de la Syrophénicienne: Marc 7,24-30," *RTL* 8 (1977): 15-29.

5196 Günther Schwarz, "**Συροφοινίκισσα-χαναναία** (Markus 7:26; Matthäus 15:22)," *NTS* 30/4 (1984): 626-28.

5197 Gerd Theissen, "Lokal- und Sozialkolorit in der Geschichte von der Syrophonikischen Frau (Mk 7,24-30)," *ZNW* 75/3 (1984): 202-25.

5198 Francis Dufton, "The Syrophoenician Woman and Her Dogs," *ET* 100 (1988-1989): 417.

Temple

5199 George W. Buchanan, "Mark 11:15-19: Brigands in the Temple," *HUCA* 30 (1959): 169-77.

5200 George W. Buchanan, "An Additional Note to 'Mark 11:15-19: Brigands in the Temple'," *HUCA* 31 (1960): 103-105.

5201 J. M. Ford, "Money 'Bags' in the Temple (Mark 11:16)," *Bib* 57 (1976): 249-53.

5202 J. Duncan M. Derrett, "No Stone upon Another: Leprosy and the Temple," *JSNT* 30 (1987): 3-20.

5203 Jacob Neusner, "Penningväxlarna i templet (Mark 11:15-19): Mishnas förklaring [M. Sheqalim 1:3]," *SEÅ* 53 (1988): 63-68.

5204 Paula Fredriksen, "Jesus and the Temple, Mark and the War," *SBLSP* 29 (1990): 293-310.

5205 George W. Buchanan, "Symbolic Money-Changers in the Temple?" *NTS* 37 (1991): 280-90.

Temple, cleansing of

5206 Ivor Buse, "The Cleansing of the Temple in the Synoptics and in John," *ET* 70 (1958-1959): 22-24.

5207 Cecil Roth, "The Cleansing of the Temple and Zechariah 14:21," *NovT* 4 (1960-1961): 174-81.

5208 Victor Eppstein, "The Historicity of the Gospel Account of the Cleansing of the Temple (Mc 11, Mt 21, Lc 19)," *ZNW* 55 (1964): 42-58.

5209 C. J. Bjerkelund, "En tradisjons- og redaksjonshistorisk analyse av perikopene om tempelrenselsen," *NTT* 69 (1968): 206-18.

5210 Neal M. Flanagan, "Mark and the Temple Cleansing," *TBT* 63 (1972): 980-84.

5211 J. Duncan M. Derrett, "The Zeal of the House and the Cleansing of the Temple," *DR* 95 (1977): 79-94.

5212 William R. Telford, *The Barren Temple and the Withered Tree. A Redaction-Critical Analysis of the Cursing of the Fig Tree Pericope in Mark's Gospel and Its Relation to the*

Cleansing of the Temple Tradition. JSNT Supplement 1. Sheffield: JSOT Press, 1980.

5213 Richard T. France, "Chronological Aspects of 'Gospel Harmony'," *VoxE* 16 (1986): 33-59.

5214 Guy Wagner, "Le figuier stérile et la destruction du temple: Marc 11:1-4 et 20-26," *ÉTR* 62/3 (1987): 335-42.

5215 Richard J. Bauckham, "Jesus' Demonstration in the Temple," in Barnabas Lindars, ed., *Law and Religion: Essays on the Place of Law in Israel and Early Christianity.* Cambridge: J. Clarke, 1988. Pp. 72-89.

5216 Craig A. Evans, "Jesus' Action in the Temple: Cleansing or Portent of Destruction?" *CBQ* 51 (1989): 237-70.

<u>Temple, destruction of</u>

5217 Markus N. A. Bockmuehl, "Why Did Jesus Predict the Destruction of the Temple?" *Crux* 25/3 (1989): 11-18.

5218 Jacques Schlosser, "La parole de Jésus sur la fin du temple," *NTS* 36 (1990): 398-414.

<u>Temple, veil of</u>

5219 Gösta Lindeskog, "The Veil of the Temple," in *Coniectanea neotestamenties, XI, in honorem Antonii Fridrichsen sexagenarii.* Lund: Gleerup, 1947. Pp. 132-37.

<u>temptation</u>

5220 Ernest Best, *The Temptation and the Passion: The Markan Soteriology.* SNTSMS #2. Cambridge: University Press, 1965.

5221 J. A. Kirk, "The Messianic Role of Jesus and the Temptation Narrative: A Contemporary Perspective," *EQ* 44 (1972): 11-29.

<u>textual criticism</u>

5222 C. Rauch, "Bemerkungen zum Markustexte," *ZNW* 3 (1902): 300-314.

5223 John W. Bowman, "The Robertson Codex (Codex 2358-v, Dob): A Study in Textual Criticism with Special Reference to the Text of Mark,'' doctoral dissertation, Southern Baptist Theological Seminary, Louisville KY, 1930.

5224 Ernest C. Colwell, ''The Complex Character of the Late Byzantine Texts of the Gospels,'' *JBL* 54 (1935): 211-21.

5225 Silva T. Lake, ''Family Π and the Codex Alexandrinus in the Gospel of Mark,'' doctoral dissertation, Brown University, Providence RI, 1936.

5226 Norman Huffman, ''Suggestions from the Gospel of Mark for a New Textual Theory,'' *JBL* 56 (1937): 347-59.

5227 Hope B. Dows, ''The Peshitto as a Revision: Its Background in Syriac and Greek Texts of Mark,'' *JBL* 63 (1944): 141-59.

5228 H. W. Huston, ''Mark 6 and 11 in P^{45} and in the Caesarean Text,'' *JBL* 74 (1955): 262-71.

5229 Ernest C. Colwell, ''The Significance of Grouping New Testament Manuscripts,'' *NTS* 4 (1957-1958): 73-92.

5230 Henry B. Moeller, ''A Textual Lexicon of Mark with Vocabulary Statistics,'' doctoral dissertation, Midwestern Baptist Theological Seminary, Kansas City KS, 1958.

5231 Ernest C. Colwell, ''Method in Locating a Newly-Discovered Manuscript,'' *StudE* 1 (1959): 757-77.

5232 Kurt Treu, ''Zur vermeintlichen Kontraktion von *hierosolyma* in 0188, Berlin P. 13416,'' *ZNW* 52 (1961): 278-80.

5233 J. A. Emerton, ''Τὸ αἷμα μου τῆς διαθήκης: The Evidence of the Syriac Versions,'' *JTS* 13 (1962): 111-17.

5234 J. A. Emerton, ''Mark 14:24 and the Targum to the Psalter,'' *JTS* 15 (1964): 58-59.

5235 Thomas F. Glasson, ''Did Matthew and Luke Use a 'Western' Text of Mark?'' *ET* 77 (1965-1966): 120-21.

5236 Kenneth W. Clark, "The Theological Relevance of Textual Variation in Current Criticism of the Greek New Testament," *JBL* 85 (1966): 1-16.

5237 Thomas F. Glasson, "An Early Revision of the Gospel of Mark," *JBL* 85 (1966): 231-33.

5238 Daniel Sperber, "Mark 12:42 and its Metrological Background. A Study in Ancient Syriac Versions," *NovT* 9 (1967): 178-90.

5239 John C. Fenton, "The Greek Text behind the 'Revised Standard Version' of Mark," *StudE* 5 (1968): 182-87.

5240 Jacob Geerlings, *Family E and its Allies in Mark.* Salt Lake City: University of Utah, 1968.

5241 J. Neville Birdsall, "A Report of the Textual Complexion of the Gospel of Mark in Ms 2533," *NovT* 11 (1969): 233-39.

5242 Ernest C. Colwell, "Method in the Study of the Gospel Lectionaries," in Ernest C. Colwell, *Studies in Methodology in Textual Criticism of the New Testament.* Leiden: Brill, 1969. Pp. 84-95.

5243 Kurt Aland, "Der wiedergefundene Markusschluß? Eine methodologische Bemerkung zur textkritischen Arbeit," *ZTK* 67 (1970): 3-13.

5244 Larry W. Hurtado, "Text-Critical Methodology and the Caesarean Text," *SBLSP* 1/1 (1971): 139-63.

5245 Klaus Haacker, "Bemerkungen zum Freer-Logion," *ZNW* 63 (1972): 125-29.

5246 José O'Callaghan, "New Testament Papyri in Qumran Cave 7?" *JBL* Supplement 91/2 (1972): 1-20.

5247 Hans Quecke, "Eine neue koptische Bibelhandschrift (P. Palau Rib. Inv.-Nr. 182)," *Or* 41 (1972): 469-71.

5248 Hans Quecke, ed., *Das Markusevangelium saïdisch. Text der Handschrift Palau Rib. Inv.-Nr. 182 mit den Varianten* *der Handschrift M 569*. Papyrologica Castroctaviana 4. Barcelona: Papyrologica Castroctaviana, 1972.

5249 Kurt Aland, ''Neue neutestamentliche Papyri? Ein Nachwort zu den angeblichen Entdeckungen von Professor O'Callaghan,'' *BK* 28 (1973): 19-20.

5250 I. A. Moir, ''The Reading of Codex Bezae (D-05) at Mark 9:1,'' *NTS* 20 (1973-1974): 105.

5251 Gerald M. Browne, ''Notes on the Sahidic Gospel of Mark,'' *BASP* 12 (1975): 9-11.

5252 Roger L. Omanson, ''The Claremont Profile Method and the Grouping of Byzantine New Testament Manuscripts in the Gospel of Mark,'' doctoral dissertation, Southern Baptist Theological Seminary, Louisville KY, 1975.

5253 Morton Smith, ''Merkel on the Longer Text of Mark,'' *ZTK* 72/2 (1975): 133-50.

5254 Gerald M. Browne, ''The Gospel of Mark in Fayumic Coptic,'' *BASP* 13 (1976): 41-43.

5255 Reginald H. Fuller, *Longer Mark: Forgery, Interpolation, or Old Tradition?* Protocol of the Colloquy of the Center for Hermeneutical Studies in Hellenistic and Modern Culture 18. Berkeley CA: Center for Hermeneutical Studies in Hellenistic and Modern Culture, 1976. Pp. 1-11; responses, pp. 12-71.

5256 J. Harold Greenlee, ''Codex 0269, A Palimpsest Fragment of Mark,'' in J. K. elliott, ed., *Studies in New Testament and Text: Essays in Honour of George D. Kilpatrick on the Occasion of his Sixty-fifth Birthday*. Novum Testamentum Supplement #44. Leiden: Brill, 1976. Pp. 235-38.

5257 J. M. Plumley and C. H. Roberts, ''An Uncial Text of St. Mark in Greek from Nubia,'' *JTS* 27 (1976): 34-45.

5258 Heinrich Greeven, ''Nochmals Mk IX.1 in Codex Bezae,'' *NTS* 23/3 (1976-1977): 305-308.

5259 J. K. Elliott, "In Defence of Thorough-Going Eclecticism in New Testament Textual Criticism," *RQ* 21/2 (1978): 95-115.

5260 Gordon D. Fee, "Modern Text Criticism and the Synoptic Problem," in Bernard Orchard and T. R. Longstaff, eds., *J. J. Griesbach: Synoptic and Text-Critical Studies 1776-1976*. Cambridge: Cambridge University Press, 1978. Pp. 154-70.

5261 D. B. Gain, *Evidence for Supposing that Our Greek Text of the Gospel of St. Mark is Translated from Latin, that Most of this Latin Still Survives, and that by Following the Latin We Can Recover Words and Actions of Jesus Which Have Been Falsified in the Greek Translation*. Grahamstown, South Africa: Rhodes University, 1978.

5262 J. J. Griesbach, "Commentatio qua Marci Evangelium totum e Matthaei et Lucae commentariis decerptum esse monstratur," in Bernard Orchard and Thomas R. W. Longstaff, eds., *J. J. Griesbach: Synoptic and Text-Critical Studies 1776-1976*. SNTSMS #34. Cambridge/New York: Cambridge University Press, 1978. Pp. 68-135.

5263 Michael McCormick, "Two Leaves from the Lost Uncial Codex 0167: Mark 4:24-29 and 4:37-41," *ZNW* 70/3-4 (1979): 238-42.

5264 W. F. Macomber, "The Anaphora of Saint Mark according to the Kacmarcik Codex," *OCP* 45 (1979): 75-98.

5265 Günther Schwarz, "Zum Freer-Logion—ein Nachtrag," *ZNW* 70 (1979): 119.

5266 Gordon D. Fee, "The Text of John and Mark in the Writings of Chrysostom," *NTS* 26 (1979-1980): 525-47.

5267 Gordon D. Fee, "A Text-Critical Look at the Synoptic Problem," *NovT* 22/1 (1980): 12-28.

5268 Gerald M. Browne, "An Old Nubian Version of Mark 11,6-11," *ZPE* 44 (1981): 155-66.

5269 R. J. D. Clarence, "An Edition of the Versions in Bodleian MS. Hatton 38 of the West-Saxon Translations of St. Mark's Gospel, with a Parallel Text from British Library MS. Royal IA.XIV," doctoral dissertation, Oxford University, Oxford UK, 1981.

5270 Larry W. Hurtado, *Text-Critical Methodology and the Pre-Caesarean Text. Codex W in the Gospel of Mark.* Grand Rapids: Eerdmans, 1981.

5271 Carroll D. Osburn, "The Historical Present in Mark as a Text-Critical Criterion," *Bib* 64 (1983): 486-500.

5272 George E. Rice, "Is Bezae a Homogeneous Codex [Variants to Codex B]," *PRS* 11 (1984): 39-54.

5273 Rykle Borger, "NA^{26} und die neutestamentliche Textkritik," *TR* 52 (1987): 1-58.

5274 Gonzalo Aranda Pérez, *El Evangelio de San Marcos en copto sahídico.* Madrid: Consejo Superior de Investigaciones Científicas, 1988.

5275 Roy M. Liuzza, "The Yale Fragments of the West Saxon Gospels," in Peter Clemoes, et al., eds., *Anglo-Saxon England.* Cambridge: University Press, 1988. 7:67-82.

5276 Jon B. Daniels, "The Egerton Gospel: Its Place in Early Christianity," doctoral dissertation, Claremont Graduate School, Claremont CA, 1990.

5277 George D. Kilpatrick, "Western Text and Original Text in the Gospels and Acts," in *The Principles and Practice on New Testament Textual Criticism.* BETL #96. Louvain: Peeters Press, 1990. Pp. 113-27.

5278 Roger L. Omanson, "What Do Those Parentheses Mean?" *BT* 41 (1990): 205-14.

5279 Peter M. Head, "A Text-Critical Study of Mark 1:1: 'The Beginning of the Gospel of Jesus Christ'," *NTS* 37 (1991): 621-29.

theology

5280 Innozenz Daumoser, *Berufung und Erwählung bei den Synoptikern.* Stuttgart: KBW, 1954.

5281 H. F. Peacock, "The Theology of the Gospel of Mark," *RevExp* 55 (1958): 393-99.

5282 Eduard Schweizer, "Anmerkungen zur Theologie des Markus," in *Neotestamentica et Patristica* (festschrift for Oscar Cullmann). Novum Testamentum Supplement #6. Leiden: Brill, 1962. Pp. 35-46.

5283 Jean Delorme, "Aspects doctrinaux du second Évangile," *ETL* 43 (1967): 74-99.

5284 Dieter Zeller, "Jesus als Mittler des Glaubens nach dem Markusevangelium," *BibL* 9 (1968): 278-86.

5285 Friedrich Wulf, "Einssein und Uneinssein: Mit Gott und mit den Mitmenschen," *GeistL* 42/4 (1969): 311-15.

5286 B. M. F. van Iersel, "Theology and Detailed Exegesis," in Roland E. Murphy, ed., *Theology, Exegesis and Proclamation.* Concilium 70. New York: Herder and Herder, 1971. Pp. 80-89.

5287 W. R. Bouman, " 'Reflections on Mark from a Confessional Theologian'," *CThM* 2 (1975): 326-31.

5288 W. J. Harrington, "The Gospel of Mark: A *Theologia Crucis,*" *DocLife* 26 (1976): 24-33.

5289 Heinz Kruse, "Das Reich Satans," *Bib* 58/1 (1977): 29-61.

5290 Ralph P. Martin, "The Theology of Mark's Gospel," *SouJT* 21 (1978): 23-36.

5291 Douglas D. J. Riddle, "God with Us: A Curricular Resource on the Gospel of Mark," doctoral dissertation, School of Theology, Claremont CA, 1978.

5292 Robert J. Daly, "The Eucharist and Redemption: The Last Supper and Jesus' Understanding of His Death," *BTB* 11/1 (1981): 21-27.

5293 John Goldingay, "Divine Ideals, Human Stubbornness, and Scriptural Inerrancy," *Trans* 2/4 (1985): 1-4.

5294 Siegfried Schulz, "Mark's Significance for the Theology of Early Christianity" in William R. Telford, ed., *The Interpretation of Mark*. Philadelphia: Fortress Press, 1985. Pp. 158-66.

5295 Thomas G. Wilkens, "Liberation Theology: A Potpourri of Voices and Perspectives," *Dialog* 26/1 (1987): 35-39.

5296 Balembo Buetubela, "Le péché dans l'évangile de Marc," *RAfT* 12 (1988): 23-29.

5297 Werner H. Kelber, "Recit et revelation: voiler, devoiler et revoiler," *RHPR* 69 (1989): 389-410.

5298 Jacob Neusner, "Money-Changers in the Temple: The Mishnah's Explanation," *NTS* 35/2 (1989): 287-90.

tradition criticism

5299 Sharon H. Ringe, "The Jubilee Proclamation in the Ministry and Teaching of Jesus: A Tradition-Critical Study in the Synoptic Gospels and Acts," doctoral dissertation, Union Theological Seminary, New York NY, 1982.

5300 Paul A. Mirecki, "Mark 16:9-20: Composition, Tradition and Redaction," doctoral dissertation, Harvard University, Cambridge MA, 1986.

5301 Marion L. Soards, "Tradition, Composition, and Theology in Jesus' Speech to the 'Daughters of Jerusalem' (Luke 23,26-32)," *Bib* 68/2 (1987): 221-44.

tradition, oral

5302 Werner H. Kelber, "Mark and Oral Tradition," *Semeia* 16 (1979): 7-56.

tradition, primitive

5303 B. S. Easton, "A Primitive Tradition in Mark," in Shirley Jackson Case, ed., *Studies in Early Christianity*. Cambridge: Harvard University Press, 1928. Pp. 85-101.

transfiguration

5304 J. B. Bernardin, "The Transfiguration," *JBL* 52 (1933): 181-89.

5305 Morton S. Enslin, "The Artistry of Mark," *JBL* 66 (1947): 385-99.

5306 George B. Caird, "The Transfiguration," *ET* 67 (1955-1956): 291-94.

5307 A.-M. Denis, "Une théologie de la Rédemption. La Transfiguration chez saint Marc," *VS* 41 (1959): 136-49.

5308 H.-P. Müller, "Die Verklärung Jesu. Eine motivgeschichtliche Studie," *ZNW* 51 (1960): 56-64.

5309 Charles E. Carlston, "Transfiguration and Resurrection," *JBL* 80 (1961): 233-40.

5310 Gerald F. Dillon, "A Study of the Literary Form and Underlying Theology of the Transfiguration," doctoral dissertation, St. Michael's College, Toronto, Ont., 1963.

5311 Xavier Léon-Dufour, "La Transfiguration de Jesus," *AsSeign* 28 (1963): 27-44.

5312 Charles Masson, "La transfiguration de Jesus (Marc 9:2-13)," *RTP* 97 (1964): 1-14.

5313 Rafael Silva Costoya, "El relato de la transfiguración. Problemas de crítica literaria y motivos teológicos en Mc 9,2-10; Mt 17,1-9; Lc 9,28-37," *Comp* 10 (1965): 5-26.

5314 Wolfgang Gerber, "Die Metamorphose Jesu, Mark. 9,2f. par.," *TZ* 23 (1967): 385-95.

5315 L. F. Rivera, "El relato de la Transfiguración en la redacción del evangelio de Marcos," *RevB* 31 (1969): 143-58, 229-43.

5316 Margaret Thrall, "Elijah and Moses in Mark's Account of the Transfiguration," *NTS* 16/4 (1969-1970): 305-11.

5317 J. A. Ziesler, "The Transfiguration Story and the Markan Soteriology," *ET* 81 (1969-1970): 263-68.

5318 Michel Coune, "Baptême, Transfiguration, et Passion," *NRT* 92 (1970): 165-79.

5319 F. C. Synge, "The Transfiguration Story," *ET* 82 (1970-1971): 82-83.

5320 S. Gennarini, "Le principali interpretazioni postliberali della pericope della trasfigurazione di Gesù," *RSLR* 8 (1972): 80-132.

5321 Howard Clark Kee, "The Transfiguration in Mark: Epiphany or Apocalyptic Vision?" in John Reumann, ed., *Understanding the Sacred Text: Essays in Honor of Morton S. Enslin on the Hebrew Bible and Christian Beginnings*. Valley Forge PA: Judson Press, 1972. Pp. 135-52.

5322 Walter Schmithals, "Der Markusschluß, die Verklärungsgeschichte und die Aussendung der Zwölf," *ZTK* 69 (1972): 379-411.

5323 Michel Coune, "Radieuse Transfiguration. Mt 17,1-9; Mc 9,2-10; Lc 9,28-36," *AsSeign* 15 (1973): 44-84.

5324 Johannes M. Nützel, *Die Verklärungserzählung im Markusevangelium. Eine redaktionsgeschichtliche Untersuchun*. Forschung zur Bibel 6. Würzburg: Echter Verlag, 1973.

5325 Walter L. Liefeld, "Theological Motifs in the Transfiguration Narrative," in R. N. Longenecker and M. C. Tenney, eds., *New Dimensions in New Testament Study*. Grand Rapids: Zondervan, 1974. Pp. 162-79.

5326 Y.-B. Trémel, "Des récits apocalyptiques: Baptême et Transfiguration," *LV* 23 (1974): 70-83.

5327 Louis Soubigou, "A Transfiguração de Cristo Segundo São Marcos (9,1-10)," *RCB* 12 (1975): 59-72.

5328 Robert H. Stein, "Is the Transfiguration a Misplaced Resurrection Account?" *JBL* 95/1 (1976): 79-96.

5329 Enrique Nardoni, *La transfiguración de Jesús y el diálogo sobre Elías según el evangelio de San Marcos*. Buenos Aires: Editora Patria Grande, 1977.

5330 Allison A. Trites, "The Transfiguration of Jesus: The Gospel in Microcosm," *EQ* 51 (1979): 67-79.

5331 Morton Smith, "The Origin and History of the Transfiguration Story," *USQR* 36 (1980): 39-44.

5332 Bruce D. Chilton, "The Transfiguration: Dominical Assurance and Apostolic Vision," *NTS* 27/1 (1980-1981): 115-24.

5333 Thomas F. Best, The Transfiguration: A Select Bibliography," *JETS* 24 (1981): 157-61.

5334 Ernest Best, "The Markan Redaction of the Transfiguration," *StudE* 7 (1982): 41-53.

5335 Ronald Lynn Farmer, "The Significance of the Transfiguration for the Synoptic Accounts of the Ministry of Jesus," doctoral dissertation, Southwestern Baptist Theological Seminary, Fort Worth TX, 1982.

5336 Lynn M. Jordan, "Elijah Transfigured: A Study of the Narrative of the Transfiguration in the Gospel of Mark," doctoral dissertation, Duke University, Durham NC, 1982.

5337 Hans M. Schenke, "The Mystery of the Gospel of Mark," *SecCent* 2 (1984): 65-82.

5338 David R. Cartlidge, "Transfigurations of Metamorphosis Traditions in the Acts of John, Thomas, and Peter," *Semeia* 38 (1986): 53-66.

5339 Stuart G. Hall, "Synoptic Transfigurations: Mark 9:2-10 and Partners," *KingsTR* 10 (1987): 41-44.

5340 Morna D. Hooker, " 'What Doest Thou Here, Elijah?' A Look at St. Mark's Account of the Transfiguration," in L.

D. Hurst and N. T. Wright, eds., *The Glory of Christ in the New Testament* (festschrift for G. B. Caird). Oxford: Clarendon, 1987. Pp. 59-70.

5341 Jerome Murphy-O'Connor, ''What Really Happened at the Transfiguration?'' *BibRev* 3/3 (1987): 8-21.

5342 Barbara E. Reid, ''The Transfiguration: An Exegetical Study of Luke 9:28-36,'' doctoral dissertation, Catholic University of America, Washington DC, 1988.

translation

5343 Willard L. Bruce, ''An Investigation Preliminary to Translating the Gospel of Mark into the English Language,'' doctoral dissertation, Concordia Seminary, Fort Wayne IN, 1963.

5344 Robert L. Lindsey, *A Hebrew Translation of the Gospel of Mark. Greek-Hebrew Diglot with English Introduction.* Jerusalem: Dugith, 1969.

5345 J. K. Elliott, ''The Use of Brackets in the Text of the United Bible Societies' Greek New Testament,'' *Bib* 60/4 (1979): 575-77.

5346 Owen E. Evans, ''Three New Translations of the Bible: II. The New Testament,'' *ET* 91/4 (1979-1980): 101-105.

women in Mark

5347 Marla J. Selvidge, ''Women as Leaders in the Marcan Communities,'' *List* 15 (1980): 250-56.

5348 John J. Schmitt, ''Women in Mark's Gospel,'' *BibTo* 19 (1981): 228-33.

5349 Winsome Munro, ''Women Disciples in Mark?'' *CBQ* 44 (1982): 225-41.

5350 Elisabeth Schüssler Fiorenza, ''The Gospel of Mark,'' in *In Memory of Her: A Feminist Theological Reconstruction of Christian Origins*. New York: Crossroad, 1983. Pp. 316-23.

5351 William Klassen, ''Musonius Rufus, Jesus, and Paul: Three First-Century Feminists,'' in Peter Richardson and John C. Hurd, eds., *From Jesus to Paul* (festschrift for F. W. Beare). Waterloo: Wilfrid Laurier University Press, 1984. Pp. 185-206.

5352 Jane Kopas, ''Jesus and Women in Mark's Gospel,'' *RevRel* 44 (1985): 912-20.

5353 Athol Gill, ''Women Ministers in the Gospel of Mark,'' *ABR* 35 (1987): 14-21.

5354 Mary Ann Beavis, ''Women as Models of Faith in Mark,'' *BTB* 18 (1988): 3-9.

5355 Gerald O'Collins, ''The Fearful Silence of Three Women (Mark 16:8c),'' *Greg* 69/3 (1988): 489-503.

5356 Lone Fatum, ''En kvindehistorie om tro og køn,'' *DTT* 53 (1990): 278-99.

word studies

5357 Charles L. Smith, ''A Greek-Aramaic Glossary of the Vocabulary of Jesus in the Gospel of Mark,'' doctoral dissertation, Yale University, New Haven CT, 1947.

5358 Eric F. F. Bishop, ''Ἀπ' ἀγορᾶς: Mark vii.4,'' *ET* 61 (1949-1950): 219.

5359 F. J. Botha, ''Ἐβάπτισα in Mark i.8,'' *ET* 64 (1952-1953): 286.

5360 C. H. Bird, ''Some γάρ Clauses in St. Mark's Gospel,'' *JTS* 4 (1953): 171-87.

5361 J. A. Emerton, ''The Aramaic Underlying τὸ αἷμά μου τῆς διαθήκης,'' *JTS* 6 (1955): 238-40.

5362 C. C. Cowling, ''Mark's Use of ὥρα,'' *ABR* 5 (1956): 155-60.

5363 H. E. W. Turner, ''The Translation of μοιχᾶται in Mark 10:11,'' *BT* 7 (1956): 151-52.

5364 P. R. Weis, "A Note on *Pygmei,*" *NTS* 3 (1956-1957): 233-36.

5365 P. H. Boulton, "Διακονέω and Its Cognates in the Four Gospels," *StudE* 1 (1959): 415-22.

5366 Robert F. Berkey, "**ΕΓΓΙΖΕΙΝ, ΦΘΑΝΕΙΝ**, and Realized Eschatology," *JBL* 82 (1963): 177-87.

5367 Dieter Meyer, "**Πολλὰ παθεῖν**," *ZNW* 55 (1964): 132.

5368 J. J. O'Rourke, "A Note Concerning the Use of *eis* and *en* in Mark," *JBL* 85 (1966): 349-51.

5369 S. M. Reynolds, "Πυγμῇ (Mark 7:3) as 'Cupped Hand'," *JBL* 85 (1966): 87-88.

5370 Theo Aerts, *À la suite de Jésus: Le verbe* **ἀκολουθεῖν** ***dans la tradition synoptique. Gembloux: Duculot, 1967.***

5371 ***Félix Asensio, "Trasfondo profético-evangélico*** **πᾶσα ἐξουσία** de la 'Gran Mision'," *EB* 27 (1968): 27-48.

5372 Martin Hengel, "Mc 7:3 **πυγμῇ**: Die Geschichte einer exegetischen Aporie und der Versuch ihrer Lösung," *ZNW* 60 (1969): 182-98.

5373 Richard M. Mackowski, "What Mark Said: A Philological Analysis of the Special Vocabulary of the Gospel according to St. Mark," doctoral dissertation, University of Jerusalem, Jerusalem, 1971.

5374 S. M. Reynolds, "A Note on Dr. Hengel's Interpretation of *pygmē* in Mark 7:3," *ZNW* 62 (1971): 295-96.

5375 G. Blocher, "Menschenmeinung oder Gotteswort," *KRS* 128 (1972): 130-34, 146-49.

5376 Giuseppe Ferraro, "Il termine 'ora' nei vangeli sinottici," *RBib* 21 (1973): 383-400.

5377 George D. Kilpatrick, "Κύριος Again," in Paul Hoffmann, et al., eds., *Orientierung an Jesus: Zur theologie der*

Synoptiker (festschrift for Josef Schmid). Freiburg: Herder, 1973. Pp. 214-19.

5378 Vernon K. Robbins, "*Dynameis* and *Sēmeia* in Mark," *BR* 18 (1973): 5-20.

5379 William L. Lane, "*Theios anēr* Christology and the Gospel of Mark," in Richard N. Longenecker and Merrill C. Tenney, eds., *New Dimensions in New Testament Study*. Grand Rapids: Zondervan, 1974. Pp. 144-61.

5380 Eduardo Arens, *The* ΗΛΘΟΝ-*Sayings in the Synoptic Tradition: A Historico-Critical Investigation*. Göttingen: Vandenhoeck & Ruprecht, 1976.

5381 K. W. Clark, "The Meaning of *kata kyrieyein*," in J. K. Elliott, ed., *Studies in New Testament and Text: Essays in Honour of George D. Kilpatrick on the Occasion of his Sixty-fifth Birthday*. Novum Testamentum Supplement #44. Leiden: Brill, 1976. Pp. 100-105.

5382 J. K. Elliott, "Is *ho exelthōn* a Title for Jesus in Mark 1:45?" *JTS* 27 (1976): 402-405.

5383 Juan Mateos, "Εὐθύς y sinonimos en el evangelio de Marcos y demas escritos del Nuevo Testamento," in A. Urbán-Fernandez, et al., *Cuestiones de gramatica y lexico*. Madrid: Cristandad, 1977. Pp. 105-39.

5384 Paul Ellingworth, "How Soon is 'Immediately' in Mark?" *BT* 29 (1978): 414-19.

5385 John Ellington, "The Translation of ὑμνέω, 'Sing a Hymn' in Mark 14:26 and Matthew 26:30," *BT* 30 (1979): 445-46.

5386 Christian Bonnet, "Le désert. Sa signification dans l'Évangile de Marc," *Hokhmah* 13 (1980): 20-34.

5387 Ralph Earle, *Word Meanings in the New Testament:* 1. *Matthew, Mark and Luke*. 2 vols. Grand Rapids: Baker, 1980.

5388 Ernst L. Schnellbächer, "Das Rätsel des νεανίσκος bei Markus," *ZNW* 73/1 (1982): 127-35.

5389 Elizabeth Struthers Malbon, "τῇ οἰκίᾳ αὐτοῦ: Mark 2:15 in Context," *NTS* 31/2 (1985): 282-92.

5390 Frans Neirynck, "Words Characteristic of Mark: A New List," *ETL* 63/4 (1987): 367-74.

5391 D. C. Kanijirakompil, "Proclamation in Mark: An Exegetical Study of the Kerygmatic Terminology in the Second Gospel," doctoral dissertation, Pontifical Biblical Institute, Rome, 1988. 2 vols.

5392 George D. Kilpatrick, "Πορεύεσθαι and Its Compounds," in *The Principles and Practice on New Testament Textual Criticism*. BETL #96. Louvain: Peeters Press, 1990. Pp. 223-24.

5393 T. C. Skeat, "A Note on *Pygme* in Mark 7:3," *JTS* 41 (1990): 525-27.

<u>zealots</u>

1 S. G. F. Brandon, "Jesus and the Zealots," *StudE* 4 (1968): 8-20.

1 S. G. F. Brandon, "Jesus and the Zealots: Aftermath," *BJRL* 54 (1971-1972): 47-66.

2 Ernst Bammel, "The Poor and the Zealots," in Ernst Bammel and C. F. D. Moule, eds., *Jesus and the Politics of His Day*. Cambridge: Cambridge University Press, 1984. Pp. 109-28.

PART THREE

Commentaries

5397 Jean-Baptiste Rose, *Évangile selon S. Marc: Traduction et commentaire*. La pensée chrétienne. Paris: Bloud, 1904.

5398 J. M. S. Baljon, *Commentaar op het evangelie van Markus*. Utrecht: Van Boekhoven, 1906.

5399 Johannes Weiss, *Die drei älteren Evangelien*. Die Schriften des Neuen Testaments neu übersetzt und für die Gegenwart erklärt, 1. Göttingen: Vandenhoeck & Ruprecht, 1906.

5400 William H. Bennett, *The Life of Christ according to St. Mark*. London: Hodder and Stoughton. 1907.

5401 Claude G. Montefiore, *The Synoptic Gospels*. Edited with an Introduction and a Commentary. London: Macmillan, 1909.

5402 Gustav Wohlenberg, *Das Evangelium des Markus ausgelegt*. Kommentar zum Neuen Testament, 2. Leipzig: Deichert, 1910.

5403 M.-J. Lagrange, *Évangile selon saint Marc*. Études bibliques. Paris: Gabalda, 1911.

5404 Alfred Loisy, *L'évangile selon Marc*. Paris: Nourry, 1912.

5405 Adriaan van Veldhuizen, *Het evangelie van Markus*. Tekst en uitleg. Groningen: Wolters, 1914.

5406 Willougby C. Allen, *The Gospel according to Saint Mark*. The Oxford Church Biblical Commentary. London: Oxford, 1915.

5407 Petrus Dausch, *Die drei älteren Evangelien übersetzt und erklärt*. Die Heilige Schrift des Neuen Testaments, 2. Bonn: Hanstein, 1918. Pp. 352-98.

5408 B. W. Bacon, *The Beginnings of Gospel Story: A Historico-Critical Inquiry into the Sources and Structure of the Gospel according to Mark with Expository Notes upon the Text, for English Readers*. The Modern Commentary. New Haven, CT: Yale University Press, 1920.

5409 Arthur Drews, *Das Markus-Evangelium als Zeugnis gegen die Geschichtlichkeit Jesu*. Jena: Diederichs, 1920.

5410 James V. Bartlett, *St. Mark: Introduction, Revised Version, with Notes, Index and Map*. The Century Bible. 2nd ed. Edinburgh: Jack, 1922.

5411 A. E. J. Rawlinson, *St. Mark with Introduction: Commentary and Additional Notes*. Westminster Commentaries. London: Methuen, 1925.

5412 Oskar Holtzmann, *Das Neue Testament nach dem Stuttgarter griechischen Text übersetzt und erklärt*. Erster Band 1. Die Synoptischen Evangelien. Apostelgeschichte. Giessen: Topelmann, 1926. Pp. 1-77.

5413 Prosper Alfaric, *La plus ancienne vie de Jesus. L'évangile selon Marc. Traduction nouvelle avec introduction et notes*. Paris: Rieder, 1929.

5414 Paul Joüon, *L'évangile de Notre-Seigneur Jésus-Christ. Traduction et commentaire du text original grec compte tenu du substrat semitique*. Verbum Salutis #5. Paris, 1930.

5415 Frans C. Ceulemans, *Commentarius in evangelium secundum Marcum et in evangelium secundum Lucam*. Mechelen: Dessain, 1931.

5416 Fery voo Edelsheim, *Das Evangelion nach Markos psychologisch dargestellt mit einem Anhang Schallanalytische Auswertung des Marcus-Evangelium von E. Sievers*. Leipzig: Pfeiffer, 1931.

5417 Friedrich Hauck, *Das Evangelium nach Markus*. Synoptiker I. Theologischer Handkommentar zum Neuen Testament mit Text und Paraphrase, 2. Leipzig: Deichert, 1931.

5418 James A. Kleist, *The Memoirs of St. Peter, or The Gospel according to St. Mark Translated into English Sense-Lines*. Milwaukee: Bruce, 1932.

5419 Louis Pirot, *Évangiles de S. Matthieu et de S. Marc*. La Sainte Bible. Texte latin et traduction française d'après les textes originaux avec un commentaire exégétique et théologique, 9. Paris: Letouzey et Ané, 1935.

5420 James A. Kleist, *The Gospel of Saint Mark Presented in Greek Thought-Units and Sense-Lines. With a Commentary.* New York: Bruce, 1936.

5421 Willibold Lauck, *Das Evangelium des hl. Matthäus und des hl. Markus.* II. Herders Bibelkommentar. Die Heilige Schrift für das Leben erklärt, 11/2. Freiburg: Herder, 1936.

5422 Josef Dillersberger, *Markus: Das Evangelium des heiligen Markus in theologisch und heilsgeschichtlich vertiefter Schau.* 5 vols. Salzburg: Muller, 1937.

5423 A. W. F. Blunt, *The Gospel according to Saint Mark in the Revised Version with Introduction and Commentary.* The Clarendon Bible. Oxford: Clarendon, 1947.

5424 R. H. Lightfoot, *The Gospel Message of St. Mark.* London: Oxford University Press, 1950.

5425 Ronald Knox, *A Commentary on the Gospels.* New York: Sheed & Ward, 1952.

5426 John A. O'Flynn, "The Gospel of Jesus Christ according to St. Mark," in Bernard Orchard, et al., eds., *A Catholic Commentary on Holy Scripture.* Edinburgh: Nelson, 1953. Pp. 905-34.

5427 Eduard Lohse, *Mark's Witness to Jesus Christ.* Stephen Neill, trans. New York: Association Press, 1955.

5428 C. C. Martindale, *The Gospel according to Saint Mark.* Stonyhurst Scripture Manuals. Westminster MD: Newman Press, 1956.

5429 Ralph Earle, *The Gospel according to Mark.* The Evangelical Commentary on the Bible. Grand Rapids: Zondervan, 1957.

5430 Richard Glover, *Teacher's Commentary on the Gospel of St. Mark.* London: Marshall, Morgan and Scott, 1957.

5431 Joseph Huby, "The Gospel according to Saint Mark," in *The Word of Salvation.* Milwaukee: Bruce, 1957. Pp. 503-923.

5432 C. Leslie Mitton, *The Gospel according to St. Mark*. Epworth Preacher's Commentaries. London: Epworth Press, 1957.

5433 Curtis Beach, *The Gospel of Mark: Its Making and Meaning*. New York: Harper, 1959.

5434 Philip Carrington, *According to Mark: A Running Commentary on the Oldest Gospel*. Cambridge/New York: Cambridge University Press, 1960.

5435 Sherman E. Johnson, *A Commentary on the Gospel According to St. Mark*. Black's/Harper's New Testament Commentary. London: A. and C. Black, 1960.

5436 Gerard S. Sloyan, *The Gospel of Saint Mark. Introduction and Commentary*. New Testament Reading Guide. Collegeville MN: Liturgical Press, 1960.

5437 Ralph Earle, *The Gospel of Mark*. Grand Rapids: Baker Book House, 1961.

5438 K. Hennig, *Das Markus-Evangelium*. Stuttgarter Bibelhefte. 3rd ed. Stuttgart: Quell Verlag, 1961.

5439 Joseph Huby and Pierre Benoit, *L'Évangile selon Saint Marc. Traduction introduction et notes*. 3rd. rev. ed. La Sainte Bibie traduite en français sous la direction de l'École Biblique de Jérusalem. Paris: Cerf, 1961.

5440 J. W. Beardslee, *Mark: A Translation with Notes*. New Brunswick NJ: The Theological Seminary, 1962.

5441 F. C. Grant, *New Testament: Matthew-Acts*. Nelson's Bible Commentary Based on the Revised Standard Version, 6. New York: Nelson, 1962.

5442 Paul S. Minear, *The Gospel according to Mark*. The Layman's Bible Commentary 17. Richmond: John Knox Press, 1962.

5443 Ernest T. Thompson, *The Gospel according to Mark and Its Meaning for Today*. Rev. ed. Richmond: John Knox Press, 1962.

5444 C. E. B. Cranfield, *The Gospel according to St. Mark: An Introduction and Commentary*. 10th ed. Cambridge Greek Testament Commentary. New York: Cambridge University Press, 1963.

5445 Alexander Jones, *The Gospel according to St. Mark. A Text and Commentary for Students*. New York: Sheed and Ward, 1963.

5446 D. E. Nineham, *The Gospel of St. Mark*. Pelican Commentary. Harmondsworth: Penguin Books, 1963.

5447 B. Harvie Branscomb, *The Gospel of St. Mark*. Moffatt New Testament Commentary. London: Hodder & Stoughton, [1937] 1964.

5448 F. Earle, *Matthew, Mark, Luke*. Beacon Bible Commentary 6. Kansas City MO: Beacon Hill, 1964.

5449 Rudolf Grob, *Einführung in das Markus Evangelium*. Zürich: Zwingli-Verlag, 1965.

5450 Ingo Hermann, *Das Markusevangelium. Erster Teil (1,1-8,26)*. Die Welt der Bibel, Kleinkommentare zur Heiligen Schrift, KK 5/1. Düsseldorf: Patmos-Verlag, 1965.

5451 C. F. D. Moule, *The Gospel according to Mark*. Cambridge Bible Commentary on the New English Bible. Cambridge: University Press, 1965.

5452 Henri Troadec, *Évangile selon S. Marc*. Commentaires sur les Évangiles. Paris: Mame, 1965.

5453 William Hamilton, *The Modern Reader's Guide to the Gospels: Mark*. The Modern Reader's Guide to the Gospels. London: Darton, Longman & Todd, 1966.

5454 Marie-Joseph Lagrange, *Évangile selon Saint Marc*. Études Bibliques. 4th ed. Paris: Gabalda, 1966.

5455 Vincent Taylor, *The Gospel according to St. Mark. The Greek Text with Introduction, Notes and Indexes*. 2nd ed. New York: Macmillan, 1966.

5456 F. M. Uricchio and G. M. Stano, *Vangelo secondo S. Marco*. La Sacra Bibbia. Turin/Rome: Marietti, 1966.

5457 Christian P. Ceroke, "The Gospel according to St. Mark," in *New Catholic Encyclopedia*. New York/London: McGraw-Hill, 1967. 9:233-40.

5458 Ingo Hermann, *Das Markusevangelium. Zweiter Teil (8,27-16,20)*. Die Welt der Bibel, Kleinkommentare zur Heiligen Schrift, KK 5/2. Düsseldorf: Patmos-Verlag, 1967.

5459 A. M. Hunter, *The Gospel according to Saint Mark: A Commentary*. Torch Bible Commentaries. 2nd ed. New York: Collier Books, 1967.

5460 Ernst Lohmeyer, *Das Evangelium des Markus übersetzt und erklärt*. Kritisch-exegetischer Kommentar über das Neue Testament I/2. 17th ed. Göttingen: Vandenhoeck & Ruprecht, 1967.

5461 I. Howard Marshall, *St. Mark*. Scripture Union Bible Study Books. Grand Rapids: Eerdmans, 1967.

5462 Karl Staab, *Das Evangelium nach Markus und Lukas*. Das Neue Testament #5. 2nd ed. Würzberg: Echter-Verlag, 1967. Pp. 1-94.

5463 Harold A. Guy, *The Gospel of Mark*. London/New York: Macmillan/St. Martin's Press, 1968.

5464 Ernst Haenchen, *Der Weg Jesu: Eine Erklärung des Markus-Evangeliums und der kanonischen Parallelen*. De Gruyter Lehrbuch. 2nd ed. Berlin: de Gruyter, 1968.

5465 Meinrad Limbeck, *Das Evangelium Jesu Christ nach Markus*. Kleiner Kommentar zum Neuen Testament II/1-2. 4th ed. Stuttgart: Katholisches Bibelwerk, 1968.

5466 Edward J. Mally, "The Gospel According to Mark," in Raymond E. Brown, Joseph A. Fitzmyer, and Roland E. Murphy, eds., *The Jerome Biblical Commentary II*. Englewood Cliffs NJ: Prentice-Hall, 1968. Pp. 21-61.

5467 Rudolf Pesch, *Naherwartungen. Tradition und Redaktion in Mk 13. Kommentare und Beiträge zum Alten und Neuen Testament*. Düsseldorf: Patmos, 1968.

5468 John Hargreaves, *A Guide to St. Mark's Gospel*. Rev. ed. Theological Educational Fund Study Guide 2. London: SPCK, 1969.

5469 Josef Schmid, *The Gospel according to Mark: A Version and Commentary*. Kevin Condon, trans. The Regensburg New Testament. Staten Island NY: Alba House, 1969.

5470 Henry Wansbrough, "St. Mark," in *New Catholic Commentary on Holy Scripture*. New York: Nelson, 1969. Pp. 954-85.

5471 Bertil E. Gärtner, *Markus evangelium*. Tolkning av Nya Testamentet II. Stockholm: Verbum, 1970.

5472 Herschel H. Hobbs, *An Exposition of the Gospel of Mark*. Grand Rapids: Baker Book House, 1970.

5473 Eduard Schweizer, *The Good News According to Mark*. Donald H. Madvig, trans. Richmond: John Knox Press, 1970.

5474 E. G. Swift, "Mark," in *New Bible Commentary Revised*, Donald Guthrie, et al., eds. 3rd ed. London: InterVarsity Press, 1970. Pp. 851-86.

5475 E. Warmers, ed., *Markus-Evangelium*. Schriftauslegung für Predigt, Bibelarbeit, Unterricht 7. Stuttgart: Klotz, 1970.

5476 Wolf-Dieter Zimmermann, *Markus über Jesus. Das Evangelium für unsere Tage interpretiert*. Gütersloh: G. Mohr, 1970.

5477 Robert A. Cole, *The Gospel according to St. Mark*. Tyndale Bible Commentary New Testament 2. London: Tyndale, 1971.

5478 Sean Freyne, "Mark," in Sean Freyne and Henry Wansbrough, eds., *Mark and Matthew*. Scripture Discussion

Commentary 7. London: Sheed and Ward; Chicago: ACTA Foundation, 1971. Pp. 1-136.

5479 Erich Klostermann, *Das Markusevangelium*. 5th ed. Handbuch zum Neuen Testament 3. Tübingen: Mohr, 1971.

5480 Alfred Loisy, *Les évangiles synoptiques*. 2 vols. Frankfurt on Main: Minerva, 1971.

5481 Lindsey P. Pherigo, "The Gospel according to Mark," in C. M. Layman, ed., *The Interpreter's One Volume Commentary on the Bible*. Nashville TN: Abingdon, 1971. Pp. 644-71.

5482 Rudolf Schnackenburg, *The Gospel according to St. Mark*. Werner Kruppa, trans. 2 vols. New Testament for Spiritual Reading 3. London/New York: Sheed & Ward/Herder & Herder, 1971.

5483 Pierre Mourlon Beernaert, *La bonne nouvelle selon Marc: Lecture continue et texte de travail*. Brussells: Institut d'Études Théologiques, 1972.

5484 K. S. L. Clark, *The Gospel according to St. Mark, with Notes and Commentary*. London: Darton, 1973.

5485 E. McMillan, *The Gospel according to Mark*. The Living Word Commentary #3. Austin TX: Sweet Publications, 1973.

5486 Thomas J. Smith, *The Mighty Message of Mark*. Winona MN: St. Mary's College Press, 1973.

5487 David E. Hiebert, *Mark: A Portrait of the Servant. A Commentary*. Chicago: Moody Press, 1974.

5488 William L. Lane, *The Gospel according to Mark: The English Text with Introduction. Exposition and Notes*. New International Commentary on the New Testament 2. Grand Rapids: Eerdmans, 1974.

5489 Jean Radermakers, *La bonne nouvelle selon saint Marc*: 1. Texte; 2. Lecture continue. Brussels: Institut d'Études Théologiques, 1974.

5490 Fritz Rienecker, *Das Evangelium des Markus, erklärt.* Wuppertaler Studienbibel. 5th ed. Wuppertal: R. Brockhaus, 1974.

5491 Paul J. Achtemeier, *Mark.* Proclamation Commentaries 1. Philadelphia: Fortress Press, 1975.

5492 William Barclay, *The Gospel of Mark.* Rev. ed. Philadelphia: Westminster Press, 1975.

5493 Robert Crotty, *Good News in Mark.* Mark in Today's English Version. Cleveland: Collins & World/Fount Books, 1975.

5494 C. E. W. Dorris, *A Commentary on the Gospel according to Mark.* New Testament Commentaries 2. 2nd ed. Nashville: Gospel Advocate Co., 1975.

5495 H. B. Green, *The Gospel according to Mark.* Oxford: University Press, 1975.

5496 Manford G. Gutzke, *Plain Talk on Mark.* Grand Rapids: Zondervan, 1975.

5497 William Hendriksen, *New Testament Commentary: Exposition of the Gospel According to Mark.* Grand Rapids: Baker, 1975.

5498 Bruno Maggioni, *Il racconto di Marco.* Come leggere il Vangelo. Assisi: Cittadella Editrice, 1975.

5499 Ralph P. Martin, *New Testament Foundations: A Guide for Christian Students.* 1. *The Four Gospels.* Grand Rapids MI: Eerdmans, 1975.

5500 D. E. Nineham, "The Order of Events in St. Mark's Gospel. An Examination of Dr. Dodd's Hypothesis," in D. E. Nineham, ed., *Studies in the Gospels: Essays in Honor of R. H. Lightfoot,* Oxford: Blackwell, 1975. Pp. 223-40.

5501 Hugh Anderson, *The Gospel of Mark.* New Century Bible. London: Oliphants, 1976.

5502 Mario Galizzi, *Un uomo che sa scegliere: Vangelo second Marco I. Voi l'avete ucciso: Vangelo secondo Marco II*. Commento al Novo Testamento. Leumann (Torino): Elle Di Ci, 1976.

5503 G. Campbell Morgan, *Gospel according to Mark*. London: Marshall, Morgan & Scott, 1976.

5504 Rudolf Pesch, *Das Markusevangelium. I. Teil: Einleitung und Kommentar zu Kap. 1,1-8,26*. Theologischer Kommentar zum Neuen Testament 2/1. Freiburg: Herder, 1976.

5505 Rudolf Pesch and R. Kratz, *So liest man synoptisch. Anleitung und Kommentar zum Studium der synoptischen Evangelien. II. Wundergeschichten, Teil I: Exorzismen—Heilungen—Totenerweckungen. III. Wundergeschichten, Teil II: Rettungswunder—Geschenkwunder—Normenwunder—Fernheilungen*. Frankfurt: Knecht, 1976.

5506 J. B. Phillips, *Peter's Portrait of Jesus: A Commentary on the Gospel of Mark and the Letters of Peter*. London/Glasgow/Cleveland: Collins & World, 1976.

5507 R. C. Stedman, *The Servant Who Rules*.. Waco TX: Word Books, 1976.

5508 R. C. Stedman, *The Servant Who Serves*. Waco TX: Word Books, 1976.

5509 T. Beck, *Una comunità legge il vangelo di Marco*. 2 vols. Bologna: Dehoniane, 1976-1978.

5510 Walter Grundmann, *Das Evangelium nach Markus*. Rev. ed. Theologischer Handkommentar zum Neuen Testament 2. Berlin: Evangelische Verlagsanstalt, 1977.

5511 Hugolinus Langkammer, *Ewangelia wedlug św Marka. Wstep—przeklad z oryginalu—komentarz*. Pismo Swiete Nowego Testamentu 3/2. Warsaw: Pallottinum, 1977.

5512 Rudolf Pesch, *Das Markusevangelium. II. Teil: Kommentar zu Kap. 8,27-16,20*. Theologischer Kommentar zum Neuen Testament 2/2. Freiburg/Basel/Vienna: Herder, 1977.

5513 Thomas J. Smith, *Good News about Jesus as told by Mark*. Atlanta: John Knox Press, 1977.

5514 Paul J. Achtemeier, *Invitation to Mark: A Commentary on the Gospel of Mark with Complete Text from the Jerusalem Bible*. Garden City NY: Doubleday, 1978.

5515 Joachim Gnilka, *Das Evangelium nach Markus. 1. Teilband: Mk 1,1-8,26*. Evangelisch-Katholischer Kommentar zum Neuen Testament 2/1. Zürich/Einsiedeln/Cologne: Benziger, 1978; Neukirchen-Vluyn: Neukirchener Verlag, 1978.

5516 A. Elwood Sanner, *Mark*. Beacon Bible Expositions #2. Kansas City MO: Beacon Hill Press, 1978.

5517 Howard F. Vos, *Mark*. A Study Guide Commentary. Grand Rapids: Zondervan, 1978.

5518 Joachim Gnilka, *Das Evangelium nach Markus. 2. Teilband: Mk 8,27-16,20*. Evangelisch-Katholischer Kommentar zum Neuen Testament 2/2. Zürich: Benziger, 1979.

5519 Johnnie C. Godwin, *Mark*. Layman's Bible Book Commentary. Nashville: Broadman, 1979.

5520 W. J. Harrington, *Mark*. New Testament Message 4. Wilmington DE: Glazier, 1979.

5521 Rudolf Pesch, *Das Evangelium der Urgemeinde. Wiederher gestellt und erläutert*. Herderbücherei 748. Freiburg/Basel/Vienna: Herder, 1979.

5522 Walter Schmithals, *Das Evangelium nach Markus*. 2 vols. Ökumenischer Taschenbuchkommentar zum Neuen Testament 2/1 and 2/2. Gütersloh: Echter-Verlag, 1979.

5523 Willard M. Swartley, *Mark: The Way for all Nations*. Scottdale PA: Herald Press. 1979.

5524 M. Fallon, *The Four Gospels: An Introductory Commentary*. The Winston Commentary on the Gospels. Minneapolis MN: Winston Press, 1980.

5525 J. F. Pécriaux Landier and D. Pizivin, *Avec Marc. Pour accompagner une lecture de l'Évangile de Marc*. Paris: Ouvrières, 1980.

5526 Terrence J. Keegan, *A Commentary on the Gospel of Mark*. New York: Paulist Press, 1981.

5527 Jack D. Kingsbury, *Jesus Christ in Matthew, Mark and Luke*. Proclamation Commentaries: The New Testament Witnesses for Preaching. Philadelphia: Fortress Press, 1981.

5528 Ralph P. Martin, *Mark*. Knox Preaching Guides. Atlanta: John Knox Press, 1981.

5529 George T. Montague, *Mark: Good News for Hard Times. A Popular Commentary on the Earliest Gospel*. Ann Arbor MI: Servant Books, 1981.

5530 David L. McKenna, *Mark*. Communicator's Commentary #2. Waco TX: Word Books, 1982.

5531 Alfred Plummer, *The Gospel according to St. Mark*. Cambridge Greek Testament for Schools and Colleges. Grand Rapids: Baker, 1982.

5532 Morna D. Hooker, *The Message of Mark*. London: Epworth, 1983.

5533 Benoît Standaert, *L'évangile selon Marc: Commentaire*. Lire la Bible #61. Paris: Cerf, 1983.

5534 Philip van Linden, *The Gospel according to Mark*. Collegeville Bible Commentary #2. Collegeville MN: Liturgical Press, 1983.

5535 Enzo Bianchi, *Evangelo secondo Marco: commento esegetico-spirituale*. Magnano: Qiqajon, 1984.

5536 Michel Quesnel, *Comment lire un évangile: Saint Marc*. Paris: Seuil, 1984.

5537 Joachim Gnilka, *El Evangelio según San Marcos*. 2 vols. Salamanca: Ediciones Sigueme, 1986.

5538 Meinrad Limbeck, *Markus-Evangelium*. Stuttgarter Kleiner Kommentar, Neues Testament, 2. 3rd ed. Stuttgart: Katholisches Bibelwerk, 1986.

5539 Jean Valette, *L'évangile de Marc: Parole de puissance, message de vie*. 3 vols. Paris: Bergers, 1986.

5540 Augustine Stock, *The Method and Message of Mark*. Wilmington DE: Glazier, 1986.

5541 Samuel T. Lachs, *A Rabbinic Commentary on the New Testament: The Gospels of Matthew, Mark and Luke*. Hoboken NJ: KTAV, 1987.

5542 J. M. González-Ruiz, *Evangelio segun Marcos: Introducción, traducción, comentario*. Pamplona: Verbo Divino, 1988.

5543 Aage Pilgaard, *Kommentar til Markusevangeliet*. Aarhus: Universitetsforlaget, 1988.

5544 Jakob van Bruggen, *Marcus: Het evangelie volgens Petrus*. Commentaar op het Nieuwe Testament, III/2. Kampen: Kok, 1988.

5545 Robert A. Guelich, *Mark 1-8:26*. Word Biblical Commentary. Dallas TX: Word, 1989.

5546 Larry W. Hurtado, *Mark*. New International Biblical Commentary #2. Peabody MA: Hendrickson, 1989.

5547 Daniel J. Harrington, "The Gospel according to Mark," in Raymond E. Brown, et al., eds., *The New Jerome Biblical Commentary*. Englewood Clifss NJ: Prentice Hall, 1990. Pp. 596-629.

5548 Daryl D. Schmidt, *Mark Reader: Dual Language Edition, with Introduction and Notes*. Sonoma CA: Polebridge Press, 1990.

5549 J. A. Brooks, *Mark*. New American Commentary #23. Nashville: Broadman Press, 1991.

5550 Robert W. Funk and M. H. Smith, *The Gospel of Mark: Red Letter Edition.* The Jesus Seminar. Sonoma CA: Polebridge, 1991.

5551 Daryl D. Schmidt, *The Gospel of Mark: With Introduction, Notes, and Original Text Featuring the New Scholars Version Translation.* The Scholars Bible #1. Sonoma CA: Polebridge Press, 1991.

5552 R. Strelan, *Crossing the Boundaries: A Commentary on Mark.* Adelaide: Lutheran Publishing Company, 1991.

5553 Robert H. Gundry, *Mark: A Commentary on His Apology for the Cross.* Grand Rapids: Eerdmans, 1993.

5554 John P. Heil, *The Gospel of Mark as a Model for Action: A Reader-Response Commentary.* Mahwah NJ: Paulist Press, 1993.

Author Index

Aalders, G. C., 2420
Aalen, Sverre, 3945
Abogunrin, Samuel O., 0217, 4481, 4565, 4883, 5173
Achtemeier, Paul J., 0251, 0388, 0920, 0921, 0933, 1695, 1723, 2051, 3039, 3147, 3867, 4157, 4164, 4172, 5491, 5514
Addis, W. E., 5079
Adinolfi, Marco, 2032
Adloff, Kristlieb, 1382
Aerts, Theo, 3239, 5370
Agnew, F., 3210
Ahern, B. M., 4013
Aichele, George, 0883, 1149, 3782, 4366
Aichinger, Hermann, 0523, 1701
Ajuria, J., 4305
Akande, Samuel T. O., 3320
Aland, Kurt, 3594, 4692, 5243, 5249
Albrecht, Evelin, 0247, 0565
Alegre, Xavier, 0950, 2232
Aletti, Jean-Noël, 0988, 4168, 4501, 5116
Alexander, William M., 3199
Alexandre, Jean, 4328
Alfaric, Prosper, 5413
Alfaro, Juan I., 0207
Allan, Johan A., 3465
Allen, J. E., 4416
Allen, W. C., 5080
Allen, Willougby C., 540
Allison, Dale C., 1099, 1680, 1740, 3006, 4502, 4826, 4891, 5140
Allsop, J. S., 0235, 0925, 1162
Almeida, Yvan, 4784
Alonso Díaz, José, 0463, 0625, 0685, 1356, 2563, 3103, 3559, 4015, 4065, 4830, 5100
Alsup, John E., 0179, 4869, 4870
Althaus, Paul, 3365, 3545
Althausen, Johannes, 1527
Ambrozic, Alousius M., 4059
Ambrozic, Aloysius M., 0244, 0282, 3164, 4297, 4684
Amerio, Maria L., 2641
Ammassari, Antonio, 2301, 2917, 4865
Amphoux, C.-B., 0330
Andersen, Francis L., 0082, 3934
Anderson, Charles P., 0382, 4507
Anderson, Hugh, 4778, 5501
Angelini, Cesae, 3175
Annen, Franz, 0987, 3197, 3434
Anthonysamy, Joseph, 3424, 4211, 4212
Anzalone, V., 2112, 2165
Apparicio, M., 3166
Arai, Sasagu, 1138
Aranda Pérez, Gonzalo, 1475
Arbeitman, Yoël, 0613, 2527
Arens, Edmund, 4347
Arens, Eduardo, 5380
Argebti, Cyrille, 0976
Argyle, A. W., 0264, 0281, 1284, 1372, 2662
Arichea, Daniel C., 3367
Armbruster, C. J., 4400
Armstrong, D. H. S., 4298
Armstrong, Edward A., 4299
Arnold, D. S., 1002
Arnold, Gerhard, 0035
Arnott, Arthur G., 2539

Arvedson, Tomas, 1557
Asensio, Félix, 3002, 5371
Ashby, Eric, 4949
Atkinson, David, 2852
Au, Wilkie, 3243
Auer, Alfons, 0372
Aune, David E., 4109, 5174
Auneau, Joseph, 3698
Aurelio, Tullio, 0965, 4333
Aus, Roger D., 1145
Avanzo, Martin, 0627, 0689, 1078
Baarda, Tjitze J., 1015, 1755, 1800, 2528, 3000
Baarlink, Heinrich, 0182, 0184, 3025, 3026, 3783, 4590
Bächli, Otto, 0274, 1020
Backhaus, Knut, 0491, 1135, 1147, 2197, 2971
Bacon, B. W., 3501, 5408
Bader, Günter, 4488
Badia, Leonard F., 4037, 4636
Baer, Y., 1286
Baer, Yitshak, 4749
Bailey, Ivor, 0391, 4197
Bailey, J. W., 4822
Bailey, James L., 1048, 3748
Bailey, Kenneth E., 2803
Bailey, T., 1520
Baillet, Maurice, 0887, 1254, 1262, 2292
Baird, J. Arthur, 0815, 0915, 3960
Baird, Michael W., 4793
Baird, Tom, 1397
Bajsić, Alois, 2789
Baker, Robert E., 3452
Bakken, Norman K., 0087, 0136, 0201, 3534
Balaguer, Vicente, 4277
Baldermann, Ingo, 0748, 0749, 0878
Baldi, Donato, 1348
Balentine, George L., 4767
Baljon, J. M. S., 5398
Baltensweiler, Heinrich, 0869, 1778, 5098
Baly, D., 1657
Bammel, Ernst, 1858, 2774, 2818, 3307, 3381, 3935, 4495, 4496, 4580, 4831, 4832, 5396
Bammel, W., 2246
Banks, Robert, 0480, 5124
Barag, D., 2942
Barbaglio, Giuseppe, 1368, 2558
Barbour, R. S., 2617, 3444, 3466, 3612, 4415
Barclay, William, 3555, 3579, 3644, 4018, 4302, 4395, 5492
Barkey Wolf, A. G., 1508
Barnard, L. W., 2256, 3560
Barr, A., 4375
Barr, David L., 3415
Barrett, C. K., 1588, 2013, 2025, 2159, 3813, 4738
Barrick, W. Boyd, 2653, 4464
Barsi, Istvun B., 1908
Bartelmus, Rüdiger, 0552
Barth, Gerhard, 0109, 1696, 1872, 2178, 3003
Bartholomew, Gilbert L., 2979
Bartina, Sebastián, 0221, 2299, 2812
Bartlett, David L., 3357
Bartlett, James V., 5410
Bartnicki, R., 2084, 2089, 2090
Barton, Stephen C., 2511, 3382, 4191
Bartsch, H.-W., 0459, 0461, 0658, 0774, 2180, 2918, 3614, 4397, 4401
Bäschlin, K., 3565
Bassin, François, 3734
Bassin, Marcel, 1552, 1731, 1974
Bassler, Jouette M., 1194, 3383
Bastin, Marcel, 4449
Batdorf, I. W., 3485
Batey, Richard A., 0478, 1094
Bauckham, Richard, 0911, 4355
Bauckham, Richard J., 2151, 2477, 5215
Baudler, Georg, 2284
Bauer, Gerhard, 2229
Bauer, Johannes B., 0859, 0960, 1542, 1576, 1805, 2516
Bauer, Walter, 2096
Baumbach, Günther, 2816
Baumeister, Andreas, 2361
Baumgarten, Albert I., 1325, 3983
Bayer, Hans F., 4896
Beach, Curtis, 3535, 4588, 5433
Beale, G. K., 3335
Beardslee, J. W., 5440
Beardslee, W. A., 1579
Beardslee, William A., 2008, 4263
Beare, Francis W., 3214, 4209, 4910, 5120
Beasley-Murray, George R., 0204, 1593, 2445, 2733, 2735, 3296, 3297, 3303, 3324, 3328, 3329, 3968, 4985
Beauchamp, Paul, 0724, 3386, 3973, 4809
Beauvery, R., 1466

Beavis, Mary Ann, 0810, 1052, 1370, 1385, 2371, 2509, 2689, 3370, 4514, 4652, 4918, 5354
Beck, B., 4522
Beck, Norman A., 1449, 4022
Beck, T., 5509
Beck, W. F., 3893
Becker, Jürgen, 2043, 2561
Becquet, Gilles, 3010
Bednarz, M., 4422
Bedouelle, Guy, 1879
Beguer, R., 2470
Beirnaert, Louis, 0989, 4169
Belcher, F. W., 2659
Bellshaw, J. G., 3298
Belo, Fernando, 4647
Bennett, W. J., 0580, 1551, 1685, 2279, 3464, 3866, 4409, 4976
Bennett, William H., 5400
Benoit, Pierre, 0888, 1255, 1278, 2293, 2747, 4623, 4630, 5028, 5439
Berg, Ludwig, 2319
Berg, Temma F., 3784
Berger, Klaus, 0279, 0720, 1128, 1571, 1670, 1840, 1851, 2228, 2710, 2778, 2783, 2798, 2817, 2920, 2993, 4779
Berger, P.-R., 0667, 2650, 2708, 2853
Berkey, Robert F., 0197, 5366
Bernardi, Jean, 4624
Bernardin, J. B., 5304
Bernoulli, C. A., 5092
Bertrand, Daniel A., 3059
Best, Ernest, 0273, 0598, 0635, 0640, 0676, 0688, 0806, 0842, 1112, 1463, 1486, 1572, 1757, 1758, 1761, 1860, 1870, 1946, 1954, 1967, 2009, 2109, 2175, 2183, 2425, 3221, 3223, 3241, 3265, 3360, 3680, 3707, 4173, 4270, 4274, 4404, 4547, 4555, 5013, 5220
Best, Thomas F., 5333
Betz, Hans Dieter, 1702, 2052, 3409, 4174
Betz, Otto, 0050, 0158, 0231, 0605, 0879, 1080, 1228, 2274, 2350, 2682, 3116, 4097, 4637
Bianchi, Enzo, 0256, 0444, 0693, 1057, 1233, 1519, 5535
Bickerman, Elias J., 4134
Biehl, Peter, 3477
Bieringer, R., 3814
Biguzzi, Giancarlo, 2182, 2705, 4557
Bilde, Per, 3036
Bilezikian, Gilbert G., 3546, 3660
Billerbeck, Paul, 4757
Binder, Hermann, 3681
Binz, S. J., 4527, 4905
Bird, C. H., 5360
Birdsall, J. Neville, 1682, 2546, 2720, 2765, 3389, 4966, 5241
Biser, Eugen, 4294
Bishop, Eric F. F., 0780, 0849, 0932, 1239, 1316, 2198, 3366, 3507, 4376, 5358
Bishop, Jonathan, 0383, 4354
Bissoli, Cesare, 0346
Bjerkelund, C. J., 5209
Black, C. Clifton, 3342, 3777, 4728
Black, David A., 0398, 0961, 1018, 1154, 1937
Black, Matthew, 0195, 1393, 1671, 1730, 2737, 3785, 4411, 4639, 4777, 4965
Blackman, E. Cyril, 4301
Blackwell, John N., 3699, 4267, 4508
Blaiklock, Edward M., 3566, 3580
Blair, H. A., 3595, 5043
Blanchard, J., 3627
Blank, Josef, 0293, 1033, 1366, 2219, 2587, 4549
Blaser, Klauspeter, 0017, 3942
Blatherwick, David, 3613
Blenker, Alfred, 0370
Blessing, Kamila, 1022
Blevins, James L., 3140, 4117, 4127
Bligh, John, 0974, 2634, 3304, 3427, 4854
Bligh, P. H., 2870
Blinzler, Josef, 0698, 1090, 1888, 2889, 2894, 3030, 3551, 4381, 4618
Blocher, G., 5375
Blomberg, Craig L., 0948, 1217, 2123
Blunt, A. W. F., 5423
Bobb, Victor, 0956
Bockmuehl, Markus N. A., 5217
Bode, Edward L., 2909, 3923, 4859, 4860
Boers, Hendrikus, 1506, 3700, 4136
Boesak, Allan, 1948
Bogert, Elizabeth A., 0733, 4289
Boismard, M.-É., 0053, 0324, 0588, 4694, 4816, 5008, 5028, 5103, 5138, 5175
Bollmann, Kaj, 2074
Boman, Thor, 2639
Bombet, G., 4783
Bombo, C., 0146
Bonnard, P.-E., 1167, 1206, 1377
Bonnet, Christian, 5386

Bonora, Adalberto, 3327
Bonsirven, Joseph, 1344
Boobyer, George H., 0416, 0707, 1231, 1232, 2648, 3422, 3517, 4095, 4140, 4141, 4142
Boomershine, Thomas E., 2978, 2979, 3786, 4438, 4515, 4868
Borgen, Peder, 0384, 0529, 2560, 4390
Borger, Rykle, 1158, 1821, 5273
Boring, M. Eugene, 0016, 0663, 0665, 0671, 0675, 1113, 1615, 2388, 3156, 3157, 3596, 3661, 3969
Bornkamm, Günther, 1600, 1693, 3313, 3478, 3480
Borsch, Frederick H., 2730, 4953, 4958, 4967
Bosch, David, 2406, 2553
Botha, F. J., 0085, 5359
Botha, Pieter J. J., 3235, 3927, 4282
Boucher, Madeleine I., 0715, 0760, 2241, 2547, 4334
Bouhours, Jean F., 5117
Boulton, P. H., 5365
Bouman, W. R., 5287
Bourke, Myles M., 4158
Bouttier, Michel, 3653, 4313
Bover, J. M., 0, 0508
Bowker, John W., 0741, 4320, 4981
Bowman, D. J., 4848
Bowman, John W., 4748, 5223
Boyd, W. J. P., 1468, 2762, 4537
Boythe, D., 0254
Bracewell, Ronald E., 4236
Bracht, Werner, 3247
Bradshaw, John, 1098
Brady, David, 4558
Brand, Richard C., 1304, 1329, 2508
Brandle, Max, 4851
Brandon, S. G. F., 3044, 3372, 3373, 3548, 4423, 5394, 5395
Branscomb, Harvie, 0402, 5447
Bratcher, Robert G., 0456, 2097, 2652, 2868, 3540, 3550, 3701
Braumann, Georg, 1062, 2003, 2071, 2699, 2779, 2843, 3306
Braun, Herbert, 0095, 0196, 0454, 0520, 1894
Braun, W., 1453
Bravo-Gallardo, Carlos, 4834
Breech, Earl, 3956, 4336
Breen, A. E., 3499
Bretscher, P. G., 0130, 1664
Breymayer, Reinhard, 2264
Breytenbach, Cilliers, 1721, 2512, 3735, 4266
Brezine, D. F., 3045
Brickham, Nelson H., 2505, 2687, 4723
Brière, Jean, 0172, 0243, 1722
Briggs, R. C., 3541
Brindle, W. A., 4940
Brinktrine, Johannes, 1258
Bristol, L. O., 3835
Broadhead, Edwin K., 0313, 0364, 0534, 0558, 2176, 2492, 3168, 4243
Brocke, Edna, 2229
Brocklehurst, Judith, 1647
Brodie, Louis T., 1810
Broer, Ingo, 2935, 4855
Brooke, George J., 0532, 4644, 4810
Brooks, J. A., 3080, 5549
Brooks, K. L., 3561
Brooten, Bernadette J., 1853, 1854
Brower, Kent E., 1612, 2855, 4192, 4467, 4489, 4785, 4797
Brown, Dale W., 3345
Brown, J. P., 3547, 4599
Brown, John P., 1285, 1559, 1762, 2016, 4982
Brown, Raymond E., 0140, 1509, 2612, 2615, 2697, 2895, 2940, 2999, 3719, 4017, 4146, 4503, 4523, 4550, 4909, 5162
Brown, Schuyler, 0641, 0818, 3952
Browne, Gerald M., 2100, 5251, 5254, 5268
Brox, Norbert, 3479
Bruce, F. F., 2258, 3637, 3736, 4394, 4766, 4786, 4833, 4989
Bruce, Willard L., 5343
Bruckmoser, J., 2825
Brueggemann, Walter, 2061, 4193, 4794
Bruners, Wilhelm, 1432
Buby, Bertrand, 0690, 1082, 3148
Buchanan, George W., 1324, 1441, 2133, 2134, 2147, 2692, 5199, 5200, 5205
Budesheim, Thomas L., 4753
Buetubela, Balembo, 0081, 0440, 1362, 2589, 3939, 5296
Bulckens, Jozef, 0937
Bultmann, Rudolf, 0758
Bundy, Walter E., 3504, 3828
Bunker, Michael, 4835
Burchard, Christoph, 2494, 2850, 4048
Burdette, M., 1003

Burdon, Christopher, 3371
Burgers, Wim, 3207
Burillo, J. Garcia, 3469
Burke, Clarence B., 3204
Burkill, T. A., 0238, 0493, 0584, 1019, 1024, 1208, 1350, 1351, 1352, 1353, 1500, 1602, 1629, 1639, 1844, 2072, 3024, 3092, 3556, 3557, 3620, 3621, 3708, 3928, 4057, 4091, 4092, 4096, 4143, 4215, 4218, 4285, 4386, 4388, 4950, 5188, 5189, 5190, 5191
Burks, Robert E., 3526, 3818
Burrows, Edward W., 5109, 5126
Buscemi, A. Marcello, 0575
Buse, Ivor, 3377, 3876, 4387, 4734, 5206
Bush, Roger A., 2980
Bussby, Frederick, 1556
Busse, Ulrich, 0258, 0769, 4200
Busslinger, H., 1703
Buth, Randall, 0606
Butler, B. C., 1735, 5021, 5094, 5096
Butterworth, Robert, 3179
Butts, James R., 3233
Buzzetti, Carlo, 0064, 0125, 0224, 0294, 0379, 0470, 0860, 2658
Byrd, Robert O., 4434
Cabaniss, Allen, 0365
Cain, Marvin F., 0004, 5111
Caird, George B., 1118, 1636, 3408, 4237, 4707, 5032, 5306
Callan, C. J., 3500
Calloud, Jean, 0361, 0472, 0990, 4783, 5048
Calmet, A., 1764
Camery-Hoggatt, Jerry A., 3817
Campbell, D. B. J., 3597
Cancik, Hubert, 3702, 3737
Canfora, Giovanni, 4544
Cantinat, Jean, 2656, 2698, 2750, 4875, 4876, 4877
Caragounis, Chrys C., 0656, 3974, 3980, 5006
Cárdenas-Pallares, José, 3764, 4350
Carl, William J., 1915, 1951, 2559
Carlston, Charles E., 1336, 3984, 4326, 4844, 5309
Carmignac, Jean, 3709, 3720, 4188
Carr, D., 4482
Carré, Henry B., 3992
Carrington, Philip, 3510, 3519, 3528, 5434
Carroll, Kenneth L., 3525
Carroll, William D., 3850
Carson, D. A., 4913
Cartledge, Samuel A., 3527
Cartlidge, David R., 3628, 3689, 5338
Carton, Giles, 0098
Carton, Gilles, 2298
Casá, Félix, 0828, 4329
Casalegno, Alberto, 0907
Casalis, Georges, 0249, 0995, 1363, 1704, 1909
Casciaro Ramírez, J. M., 0547, 0812, 1862, 2571, 3280, 5002
Casey, P. Maurice, 0424, 0531, 0554, 0666, 2030, 2550, 2581, 4978, 4995
Casey, Robert P., 3511
Cashwell, Thomas L., 4828
Cassel, Jay, 4483
Castellino, Georgius R., 0684
Catchpole, David R., 1515, 1744, 1828, 2086, 2741, 3244, 3925, 3986, 4064, 4421, 4497, 4983, 5123
Cavallin, Hans C., 2312
Cave, C. H., 0322, 0705, 3355, 4178
Caza, Lorraine, 2836
Celada Abad, Benito, 1899, 1934
Ceresa-Gastaldo, Aldo, 2854
Cerfaux, Lucien, 0582, 1104, 1207, 3484
Ceroke, Christian P., 0418, 3102, 3905, 5457
Ceulemans, Frans C., 5415
Chadwick, Henry, 1917
Chapalain, Claude, 2056
Chapman, J., 3503
Charles, J. D., 0089
Check, J. L., 4840
Chevalier, Max A., 0731
Chico, G., 0646
Chilton, Bruce D., 0153, 0255, 0648, 1611, 1613, 1643, 2357, 3348, 3908, 3970, 3971, 5010, 5332
Choroat, J.-L., 3841
Christ, Felix, 3113
Christensen, Jens, 2548, 3122, 4947
Christensen, W., 3122
Chronis, Harry L., 2857, 3153
Chu, Sumuel, 1708
Chung, Lee Oo, 3369
Church, I. F., 3654
Cignelli, Lino, 0576, 0597, 0959, 1152, 1212, 1428, 1936, 2340
Cirillo, Luigi, 3765
Clarence, R. J. D., 5269
Clark, David J., 0349

Clark, K. S. L., 5484
Clark, K. W., 5381
Clark, Kenneth W., 0338, 2986, 5236
Claudel, Gérard, 1531
Clavier, Henri, 1175, 1418, 1956
Clements, Ronald E., 2426, 3042
Clevenot, Michel, 2931
Coakley, J. F., 2510, 4744
Cockerill, Gareth L., 1928
Cohn, Haim H., 2849, 3886, 3932
Cohn-Sherbok, Dan M., 2311, 4758, 4884, 4922
Coiner, H. G., 1850
Coke, Paul T., 2446, 4210
Cole, Robert A., 5477
Colino, F. R., 2987
Collange, J.-F., 1471
Collin, M., 2307
Collins, Adela Y., 3421, 5003
Collins, R. F., 1321, 1384, 1705, 1924, 3897, 3918
Collins, Raymond F., 1321, 1924
Colpe, Carsten, 0421, 0674, 1548, 1684, 1724, 1970, 4988
Colunga, J. A., 2614
Colwell, Ernest C., 0029, 0075, 0092, 0975, 2796, 2983, 5224, 5229, 5231, 5242
Combet-Galland, Corina, 1163, 2230, 4278, 4356
Combrink, H. J. B., 2020
Comiskey, J. P., 3193
Condon, Kevin, 4074
Congar, Yves, 3091
Connick, C. Milo, 0935, 1538
Connolly-Weinert, Frank, 2703, 4528
Conzelmann, Hans, 4417
Cook, Donald E., 0, 0538, 3860, 4759
Cook, John G., 3749
Cook, Michael J., 4756
Cook, R. R. E., 4645
Cooke, Bernard, 4012
Cooke, F. A., 2132
Coover, G. D., 3098
Cope, Lamar, 0610, 5027, 5145
Coppens, Joseph, 4695, 4974
Cordoba, A., 2891
Cornette, A., 2227
Cornillon, Michel, 0216, 0595
Corsani, Bruno, 3467
Cortés, Enric, 2115, 2173
Cosby, Michael R., 2671, 4265
Costoya, Rafael Silva, 5313
Cotter, Wendy J., 2130, 3396
Couchoud, P.-L., 3502
Coulot, Claude, 0218, 4566
Coune, Michel, 1631, 3057, 4418, 5318, 5323
Countryman, L. W., 1451
Cousin, Hugues, 2116, 2166
Coutts, John, 0786, 2164, 3205, 3872
Cowling, C. C., 5362
Craghan, John, 3426
Cranfield, C. E. B., 0096, 3875, 5444
Cranmer, David, 3738
Crawford, Barry S., 1616, 2462, 2588
Cremer, Franz G., 0500, 0503
Crockett, Benny R., 0309, 1252, 1720, 2629
Crosby, Jeremiah, 0226, 3240
Crossan, John Dominic, 0622, 1075, 1874, 1883, 2101, 2102, 2157, 2158, 2186, 2214, 2249, 2270, 2480, 2602, 2882, 2921, 2924, 3901, 3924, 4271, 4306, 4314, 4685
Crotty, Robert, 5493
Crouch, William H., 3523, 3912
Crowder, William J., 3027
Cuba, Edward J., 3127
Cullmann, Oscar, 0078, 1799, 3209, 4286
Culpepper, R. Alan, 2068, 2141, 3672, 4468, 4878
Cunningham, Douglas, 2144
Cunningham, Scott, 1386, 4201
Curry, Michael S., 3274
Cuviller, Elian, 1301, 1555, 4731
Czalkowski, Michal F., 0066
Czerski, Janusz, 3475, 4000, 4450
Dahl, Nils A., 0864, 3536
Dahm, C., 4818
Dahmus, Joseph, 3750
Daily, Eugene W., 3090
Daly, Robert J., 4039, 5292
Dambricourt, G., 3604
Dambrine, Liliane, 1030
Daniel, C., 1457
Daniel, Constantin, 0579, 2114, 2117, 2278
Daniel, Felix H., 1626
Daniels, Jon B., 0331, 1317, 2277, 5276
Danker, Frederick W., 0339, 1425, 2403, 2486, 2842, 4220, 4222, 4419
Dannemann, Ruth, 1494
Danove, Paul L., 4283
Darby, Robert R., 3904
Darù, J., 3794
Dattler, Frederico, 0495, 1302, 2342, 2404

Daube, David, 2202, 2635
Daumoser, Innozenz, 5280
Dausch, Petrus, 5407
Dautzenberg, Gerhard, 0010, 0011, 0728, 1333, 2409, 2880, 3416, 3868, 3977, 4367, 4609, 4803
David, P. T., 1354
Davidsen, Ole, 3162
Davies, M., 5171
Davies, Paul E., 2012, 2027, 2566, 3827
Davies, William D., 3529
Davis, Charles T., 3721
Davis, Philip G., 3144, 3165
de Burgos Nuñez, Miguel, 0236, 0245, 0985, 1942, 2302, 2809, 3137, 3287, 3433, 4469, 4885
de Gopegui, Juan A. Ruiz, 2934
de Jonge, Marinus, 2358, 2434, 2675, 2771, 2785, 2862, 3344, 4811, 4941
de Klerk, J. C., 3770
de la Calle, Francisco, 3249, 3645
de la Potterie, Ignace, 1142, 1187, 1197, 1409, 1423, 1502, 3569
De Maat, Paul, 0455, 1884
de Mello, M., 0977, 3192, 3428
de Q. Robin, A., 3390
de Ru, G., 2019
de Solages, Bruno, 3629, 5097
de Tuya, Manuel, 2552, 2613
Dearing, Vinton A., 5135
Debergé, P., 1986
Deenick, J. W., 4773
Degenhardt, J. J., 1923
Dehandschutter, B., 2220, 4321
Dehn, Günther, 3096
Deibler, E. W., 1148
Deichgräber, R., 2517, 4619
Dekker, W., 0128, 1663, 2252
del Auga-Pérez, Augustin, 0057, 0112
del Mago, Claudino, 2034
del Valle, J. Alfaro, 1932
Delclaux, Adrien, 3697
Delebecque, Édouard, 1119
Delgado, J., 4118
Delling, Gerhard, 1856, 2000
Delorme, Jean, 0120, 0188, 0362, 0363, 1050, 1054, 1107, 1201, 1379, 1681, 1768, 1823, 2537, 2583, 2908, 2910, 3622, 3638, 3682, 3921, 3922, 4001, 4504, 4783, 4856, 4857, 5017, 5283
Deming, Will, 1781, 4081
den Heyer, Cornelis J., 0012, 2044, 2128, 2487, 3751
Denaux, Adelbert, 1496, 1503, 3176, 4439, 4551
Denis, A.-M., 1160, 1161, 1240, 3226, 5307
Denker, Jürgen, 1985, 4992
Depasse-Livet, Jeanine, 2976
Dermience, Alice, 1361, 4710, 5195
Derrett, J. Duncan M., 0222, 0521, 0571, 0649, 0846, 0882, 0993, 1032, 1100, 1236, 1332, 1429, 1461, 1567, 1659, 1783, 1784, 1788, 1789, 1875, 1950, 1998, 2087, 2118, 2138, 2148, 2181, 2209, 2257, 2261, 2305, 2366, 2452, 2499, 2540, 2670, 2760, 3436, 3438, 3752, 3910, 3985, 3987, 3988, 3998, 4054, 4183, 4343, 4424, 4574, 4755, 4886, 5163, 5194, 5202, 5211
Descamps, Albert L., 0212, 0436, 1736, 1815, 1900, 2900, 4068, 4696
Devisch, Michel, 4603
Dewar, Francis, 4396
Dewey, Joanna, 0347, 0351, 3088, 3227, 3248, 4005, 4657, 5058, 5063, 5164
Dewey, K. E., 2690, 2753, 2756, 4451, 4553, 4559
Dhanis, Édouard, 2881, 4100
Di Marco, A.-S., 1510, 2039
Di Pinto, Luigi, 0214
Dibelius, Martin, 3615
Dicharry, W., 3795
Dideberg, Dany, 0239
Diderichsen, Børge K., 3605
Didier, Marcel, 0736, 2201
Dietzfelbinger, Christian, 0568, 0739, 2906
Díez-Macho, Alexandro, 1595
Diezinger, Walter, 2324
Dihle, Albrecht, 3809
Dillersberger, Josef, 5422
Dillmann, Rainer, 0312
Dillon, Gerald F., 5310
Dillon, James T., 3820
Dillon, R. J., 3414
Dinter, P. E., 4675
Dobládez, Juan, 0051, 1608
Doble, Peter, 0139
Dockx, Stanislas, 2544, 3739, 3740
Dodd, C. H., 0133, 0452, 0756, 0885, 0900, 1225, 1249, 1424, 1454, 1575, 1577, 1635, 1711, 1765, 1766,

2208, 2393, 2422, 2474, 2498, 2530, 2772, 2799, 2904, 3007, 3011, 3520, 3552, 3894
Doeve, Jan W., 0403, 0467, 0541, 0856, 1651, 2076, 2647, 4391
Dombois, Hans, 2211
Domeris, William R., 0265, 0277, 0283, 0316, 4640
Dominic, Paul A., 1811
Domon, Jean, 1337
Donahue, John R., 0445, 0721, 2231, 2268, 2428, 2450, 2455, 2478, 3141, 3258, 3930, 3931, 4337, 4435, 4452, 5000
Donaldson, James, 0213, 1108, 3245, 4754
Dondorp, A., 0138
Donfried, Karl P., 1172, 1412, 3380, 4085, 4181
Donne, Brian K., 3015
Doohan, Leonard, 3895, 4529
Dooley, J., 3570
Dormeyer, Detlev, 0041, 0629, 0631, 0694, 3476, 3796, 4259, 4440, 4697
Dörrfuss, Ernst M., 0126
Dorris, C. E. W., 5494
Doty, William G., 1004, 4279, 4307
Doudna, John C., 3453
Doughty, Darrell J., 0354, 4991
Dowd, Sharyn E., 0618, 2177, 2630
Dowda, Robert E., 2137
Down, M. J., 3909, 4079
Downing, F. Gerald, 0782, 2309, 4887, 5165, 5182
Dows, Hope B., 5227
Dozzi, D. E., 0805
Drews, Arthur, 5409
Dreyfus, F.-P., 2310, 4841
Dross, R., 1181
Drury, John, 0015, 0202, 0740, 2216, 3067, 3771, 3941, 4315, 4348, 5052
du Plessis, J. G., 2240
du Roy, J.-B., 2554
Duff, Paul B., 2077
Dufton, Francis, 1371, 5198
Duling, Dennis C., 1484, 2049, 2355, 2736
Dungan, David L., 0233, 1827, 3606, 3628, 3689, 3906, 4058, 4698, 5146, 5152, 5158
Dunkerley, Ruderic, 0497
Dunn, James D. G., 0355, 0457, 0664, 1305, 1341, 1836, 3058, 3948, 3990, 3991, 4112
Duplacy, Jacques, 0417
Duplantier, Jean P., 2233, 4359
Dupont, Jacques, 0142, 0843, 0863, 0868, 0870, 0876, 0902, 1084, 1093, 1543, 1727, 1976, 2058, 2062, 2382, 2401, 2454, 2481, 3315, 4019, 4052, 4303
Duprez, Antoine, 0515
Durrwell, Françiois-Xavier, 4843
Dwyer, T. R., 4256
Dziuba, Andrzej F., 3012
Earle, F., 5448
Earle, Ralph, 5387, 5429, 5437
Easton, B. S., 5303
Eckel, Paul T., 1813
Eckstein, Richard, 0871, 2476
Edanad, Anthony, 4036
Edelsheim, Fery voo, 5416
Edwards, George R., 2203
Edwards, James R., 0115, 0556, 0745, 1037, 1105, 2111, 2491, 3167, 3884, 4275
Edwards, Richard A., 3607
Edwards, Walter R., 4575
Efird, James M., 1069, 4780
Egelkraut, Helmut L., 0296, 1785, 1797, 1822, 1852, 1863, 2079, 2179, 2321
Egger, Wilhelm, 0585, 1905, 1907, 3655, 3673
Ehrman, B. D., 3810
Ellena, Domenico, 0757, 0874, 0905
Ellington, John, 1474, 2599, 5385
Ellingworth, Paul, 0074, 0124, 0223, 0401, 0501, 1151, 1660, 1716, 1820, 1839, 1848, 2150, 5384
Elliott, J. K., 0072, 0315, 0340, 0341, 0465, 1375, 1812, 2362, 2465, 3061, 3292, 3815, 3870, 4156, 4175, 5183, 5259, 5345, 5382
Elliott, John H., 3282, 3722, 4560, 4968
Ellis, E. Earle, 4621
Ellis, P. F., 5061
Ellis, Terence B., 3891
Emden, Cecil S., 3450, 3518, 4536
Emerton, J. A., 0031, 2014, 2015, 2572, 2573, 2574, 5233, 5234, 5361
Emslie, B. L., 3253
Engelbrecht, J., 4135, 4186
Englezakis, B., 4322
English, E. Schuyler, 1182, 1421, 4152
Enslin, Morton S., 3034, 5305
Eppstein, Victor, 5208
Erlangen, Gerhard F., 4149

Erler, Rolf J., 1718
Ernst, Josef, 1504, 2316, 2694, 2754, 4476, 4561, 4563, 4712
Essame, W. G., 0845, 0857, 0884, 0913
Estrada Díaz, J. A., 3851
Evans, Christopher F., 3586
Evans, Craig A., 0545, 0744, 0825, 2160, 2226, 2711, 2925, 3023, 4352, 4534, 4564, 4791, 4792, 4801, 5009, 5216
Evans, G. R., 3723
Evans, Owen E., 5346
Fabris, Rinaldo, 0185, 2622, 4567
Fahner, Christian, 5077
Faierstein, Morris M., 1926, 2327
Fairweather, I. C. M., 1921, 2318
Fallon, M., 5524
Falusi, G. K., 0794
Fanin, Luciano, 0484
Fann, Delbert G., 3300
Fannon, Patrick, 3553, 3571
Faricy, Robert, 3874
Farla, P. J., 2045
Farmer, Ronald Lynn, 5335
Farmer, William R., 2991, 5038, 5104, 5112
Farrer, Austin M., 1173, 1417, 2405, 3508, 5026
Fascher, Erich, 2469, 2472, 3838
Fatum, Lone, 1040, 3108, 5356
Faw, C. E., 3530, 3537
Fay, Greg, 0725, 5070
Fee, Gordon D., 1270, 2417, 5131, 5260, 5266, 5267
Feldmeier, Reinhard, 2631, 3448, 4524
Fendler, Folkert, 3811
Feneberg, Wolfgang, 0573, 2541, 9030
Fenton, John C., 4086, 4389, 4509, 4823, 4839, 5012, 5239
Fernández y Fernández, Juan, 0475
Ferraro, Giuseppe, 5376
Feuillet, André, 0037, 0097, 0141, 0414, 0492, 1638, 1991, 2018, 2726, 3063, 3878, 4407, 4453, 4465, 4852
Fiebig, Paul, 5091
Fields, Weston W., 1803
Figueira, Dorothy, 1005
Finkelstein, Roberta, 1770, 3363
Fischer, Bonifatius, 0429, 1389, 1893, 2551
Fischer, Karl M., 1902
Fisher, Eugene, 0889, 1263, 4625
Fisher, K. M., 0926, 4184
Fitzmyer, Joseph A., 0890, 1264, 1323, 1677, 2103, 2352, 2811, 4470, 4600, 4635, 4804, 4984
FitzPatrick, Michael, 0123, 1296, 4129
Flammer, Barnabas, 1359, 5192
Flanagan, Neal M., 5076, 5210
Fleddermann, Harry T., 1256, 1528, 1739, 2363, 2669, 3142, 3255, 4919
Flender, Helmut, 3587
Fletcher, D. R., 3238
Florival, Ephren, 1912
Flowers, H. J., 0262
Flückiger, Felix, 4676
Flusser, David, 0044, 0154, 0512, 2748, 4025, 4425, 4477, 4631
Focant, Camille, 1272, 1885, 4705
Ford, Desmond, 2423, 3330
Ford, J. M., 2154, 4448, 4961, 5201
Fortna, Robert T., 4516, 4554, 4899
Fossion, André, 0323
Foulon-Piganiol, C.-I., 2792
Fowler, Robert M., 1200, 1422, 1450, 3753, 3787, 4128, 4180, 4484, 4648, 4649, 4650, 4658, 5153
Fox, Ruth, 4569
France, Richard T., 0021, 1546, 1683, 1729, 1969, 2021, 2078, 2575, 3914, 3917, 5213
Frankemölle, Hubert, 1529, 3149
Fredriksen, Paula, 4836, 5204
Freed, Edwin D., 3228, 3229
Frein, Brigid C., 4007
Freyne, Sean, 3211, 5478
Fridrichsen, Anton, 2011, 3512
Frieden, Ken, 1006, 3203, 3439
Friedrich, Gerhard, 1210, 1419
Friedrich, Martin, 2801
Friedrichsen, Timothy A., 5154, 5167, 5168
Frieling, Rudolf, 0377, 0945, 1383, 2224, 2757
Frizzi, Giuseppe, 1205
Fuchs, Albert, 0026, 0292, 0386, 0951, 1642
Fuchs, Ernst, 0897, 0903, 1601, 1712, 1919, 2458
Fuchs, Ottmar, 1906
Fuller, Reginald H., 1843, 4098, 4147, 4148, 4812, 5255
Funk, Robert W., 0692, 0906, 4525, 5550
Furnish, Victor P., 2142, 2295
Fürst, H., 1960
Fusco, Vittorio, 0325, 0717, 0726, 0820, 3975, 4360

Gaboury, Antonio, 0131, 5110
Gaechter, Paul, 0682
Gagg, Robert P., 2349
Gaide, Gilles, 0320, 0369, 0479, 0616
Gain, D. B., 5261
Galbiati, Enrico, 2905
Galizzi, Mario, 0033, 0038, 0065, 2618, 4486, 5502
Galot, Jean, 1648, 1655, 1939, 2578
Galvin, John P., 4904, 5005
Gamba, G. G., 0367, 0434, 0524, 0569
Gamwell, Franklin I., 0620
Gannon, P. J., 0623
Garafalo, R., 3903
Garcia Burillo, J., 1957
Garland, David E., 0237, 3087, 4530
Garnet, Paul, 0108, 0761, 0829
Garofalo, Salvatore, 1775
Gártner, Bertil E., 5471
Gatzweiler, Karl, 0980
Geddert, Timothy J., 3340
Geerlings, Jacob, 5240
Geischer, H.-J., 0759
Genest, Olivette, 2676
Gennarini, S., 5320
Géoltrain, Pierre, 0562
George, Augustin, 0498, 0753, 1978, 2022, 2215, 2262, 2584
Gerber, Wolfgang, 1652, 5314
Gerhardsson, Birger, 0143, 0708
Gero, Stephen, 0107, 3882
Gertner, M., 0732
Gese, Hartmut, 2834, 4772
Gewalt, Dietfried, 1617, 2755, 4556
Ghiberti, Giuseppe, 1153, 2330, 4871, 4888
Giavini, Giovanni, 1178, 1403, 2914
Gibbs, John M., 0008
Giblet, Jean, 2625
Giblin, Charles H., 2291, 3094
Gibson, Jeffrey B., 1435, 1443, 1452, 4202
Gideon, V. E., 3402, 5024
Giesen, Heinz, 0257, 1619, 2120, 2174, 2463, 2936, 3674, 3961, 4900
Gill, Athol, 1524, 5353
Gilmore, A., 4014
Gils, Félix, 0546, 0549, 4094, 4540, 4845
Girard, René, 1007
Giroud, Jean-Claude, 0727, 3976, 4276
Gittins, Anthony, 4213
Giuliano, Raffaele, 0219
Glasson, Thomas F., 1490, 2725, 2871, 5235, 5237
Glasswell, Mark E., 0034, 3778, 4150, 4743
Glaube, Paul, 0861, 2427, 2745, 2833
Globe, Alexander, 0039, 4938
Glover, Richard, 5430
Glusman, E. F., 3662, 3675
Gnilka, Joachim, 0835, 1143, 2394, 2677, 2840, 3341, 3349, 4531, 5515, 5518, 5537
Goan, S., 0798
Godwin, Johnnie C., 5519
Goldberg, A. M., 2727, 4747
Goldingay, John, 5293
Gollwitzer, Helmut, 0117, 0227
González-Faus, J., 0144, 0267, 0991, 1700
González-Ruiz, J. M., 5542
Good, R. S., 0489
Goodspeed, Edgar J., 4659
Goppelt, Leonhard, 2288, 2290
Gottschalk, Ingeborg, 0788, 0872
Goulder, Michael D., 0060, 0208, 0395, 0601, 0799, 1071, 1086, 1665, 2743, 2777, 2897, 2944, 4872
Gourbillon, J.-G., 3513
Gourgues, Michel, 0150, 0530, 1036, 2627, 2953
Graham, A. A. K., 3588
Graham, H. H., 3278, 3656
Graham, Helen R., 2396, 2397, 4510
Grández, R. M., 2832
Grant, F. C., 3521, 5441
Grässer, Erich, 0164, 1073, 3336, 4674
Grassi, Joseph A., 0518, 1198, 1230, 2643, 4028, 4204
Graudin, A. F., 3819
Grayston, Kenneth, 3358, 4378, 5073
Green, Barbara, 4082
Green, H. B., 5495
Greenlee, J. Harold, 0285, 0600, 1023, 2412, 2479, 2523, 5256
Greeven, Heinrich, 1141, 1609, 2199, 5258
Greig, James C. G., 0198, 3018
Grelot, Pierre, 1318, 2414, 2644
Griesbach, J., 5262
Griffiths, J. G., 1564
Grill, S., 0604
Grimm, Werner, 2023
Grob, Rudolf, 5449
Groenewald, E. P., 3630
Groff, Kent I., 2668, 2952
Gros-Louis, Kenneth R. R., 3639
Grossouw, Willem K., 2335
Grundmann, Walter, 5510

Guelich, Robert A., 0013, 0014, 3420, 4798, 5545
Guerra, Eduardo, 4102
Guichard, Daniel, 2805
Guillemette, Pierre, 0250, 0275, 0996, 1364, 1715, 3361, 3854
Guillet, Jacques, 4441
Gundry, Robert H., 2746, 5553
Gunther, John J., 2416, 3710
Gutbrod, Karl, 3608
Gutiérrez, Gustavo, 0189
Güttgemanns, Erhardt, 2217, 2912
Guttler, M., 3859
Gutzke, Manford G., 5496
Guy, Harold A., 2418, 2872, 3524, 4931, 5463
Haacker, Klaus, 0817, 2273, 2782, 2793, 2821, 5245
Haapa, Esko, 3514
Habener, Ivan, 3271
Haefner, A. E., 4764
Haenchen, Ernst, 1376, 3589, 5464
Hahn, Ferdinand, 0510, 0768, 0836, 2322, 2328
Haleblian, Krikor, 5066
Halkin, François, 3572, 3578
Hall, James L., 4837
Hall, Lemuel, 3823
Hall, Stuart G., 1632, 5339
Hall, T. C., 3822
Hallbäck, Geert, 1034, 2389
Hamann, H. P., 1526, 5113
Hamilton, J., 2332, 3683, 4714
Hamilton, N. Q., 2136, 3173, 4849
Hamilton, William, 5453
Hanson, A. T., 3406, 4799
Hare, Douglas R. A., 4993
Hargreaves, John, 0509, 0779, 5468
Harner, Philip B., 2874
Harnisch, Wolfgang, 1913
Harrington, Daniel J., 3084, 3724, 5547
Harrington, Wilfrid J., 1688, 1826, 2210, 2448, 3158, 3554, 3646, 4055, 4290, 5288, 5520
Harris, Michael A., 5053
Harrisville, Roy A., 1357, 2413, 3581
Harsch, Helmut, 0992, 3435
Hart, H. St. J., 2271
Hartdegen, Stephen J., 3711
Harter, W. H., 3562
Hartin, Patrick J., 0751, 0830, 3189, 4370
Hartlich, Christian, 0970, 1245
Hartman, Lars, 0101, 0199, 0423, 3060, 3128
Harvey, A. E., 3690
Hashimoto, S., 4775
Haskin, Richard W., 1916
Hasler, J. I., 1326, 5187
Hatton, Howard A., 0853
Hauck, Friedrich, 5417
Haufe, Günter, 0808
Haverly, Thomas P., 3725
Hawkin, David J., 3797, 4686, 4711, 5062, 5075
Hawkins, John C., 5081, 5082
Hawthorn, T., 0966
Hay, L. S., 0420, 0553, 4103, 4929, 4969
Head, Peter M., 0045, 4921, 5279
Heawood, Percy J., 1674
Hebert, Gabriel, 2902, 4842, 4846
Hedinger, Ulrich, 2006, 2495, 2794
Hedrick, Charles W., 3741, 4269, 5067
Heil, John P., 1247, 2484, 4185, 4372, 5072, 5554
Hein, Kenneth, 4023
Heising, Alkuin, 1220, 1221, 1420
Held, Heinz J., 3150, 3288
Hellestam, Sigvard, 1808
Helmbold, Heinrich, 1747, 1864, 2191
Helzle, Eugen, 2985
Hemelsoet, Ben, 0151, 3663, 4069
Hemer, Colin J., 1271, 4626, 4634
Hempelmann, Heinzpeter, 4610, 5166
Henaut, Barry W., 4897
Hendrickx, Herman, 3664, 4879
Hendriks, W. M. A., 4699
Hendriksen, William, 5497
Hengel, Martin, 1095, 1310, 2212, 3754, 3755, 3842, 4933, 5372
Hennelly, Alfred T., 0971, 3191
Hennig, K., 5438
Henshaw, Thomas, 3515
Herbert, Gabriel A., 1179
Héring, Jean, 2616, 3442
Hermann, Ingo, 2377, 5450, 5458
Hermant, Dominique, 0332, 1045, 1725, 1753, 3798
Herranz, A., 4284
Herrenbrück, Fritz, 0446, 0447
Herron, Robert W., 1817, 2696, 2758, 2761, 4076
Hertzsch, H.-P., 0904
Herz, Johannes, 0505, 0657, 0754, 0865, 2207, 2453

Hess, H. Harwood, 3461
Hiebert, David E., 5487
Hiers, Richard H., 1977, 2080, 2380, 2501, 2633, 3195, 3392, 3946, 3949, 3954, 4030
Higgins, A. J. B., 4008, 4955
Higgins, Martin J., 0430, 0592, 0633, 0914, 1719, 2784
Hill, David, 1074, 1257, 3843, 3958
Hill, Robert, 0821
Hindley, J. C., 3451, 3549
Hinlicky, Paul R., 3726, 4248
Hinz, Christoph, 4912
Hirt, Oscar H., 1487, 4726
Hobbs, Edward C., 3492, 4765
Hobbs, Herschel H., 5472
Hodges, Zane C., 2937, 3403, 4853
Hoefelmann, Verner, 0360, 4511
Hoffmann, Gottfried, 1880, 3068
Hoffmann, Jean G. H., 3582
Hoffmann, N., 2033, 2577
Hoffmann, Paul, 0079, 1550
Hofius, Otfried, 0378
Hogarth, Henry, 3626
Hollenbach, Bruce, 3816
Hollenbach, Paul W., 3200
Holman, Charles L., 1606, 2408, 3321
Holmes, Zan, 1014
Holst, Robert, 0672, 2522
Holtzmann, Oskar, 5412
Hommel, Hildebrecht, 1794, 1959
Honey, T. E. Floyd, 4596
Honoré, A. M., 5108
Hook, Norman, 3907
Hooker, Morna D., 1627, 4119, 4805, 4959, 5011, 5184, 5340, 5532
Hope, C., 4377, 4838
Horman, John, 0747
Horsley, Richard A., 1136
Horstmann, Maria, 1489
Horton, Fred L., 1396, 4194
Horvath, Tibor, 1776, 2915
Hostetler, M. S., 1745, 4517, 4901
Howard, F. D., 4296
Howard, George, 0297, 0425, 0589, 0700, 1582, 1786, 1837, 2695
Howard, J. K., 1469, 3311, 3362
Howard, Virgil, 3887
Howe, Allan H., 3143
Hoyer, George W., 2325
Hubaut, Michel, 0809, 4323, 4330
Hübner, Hans, 1290
Huby, Joseph, 5431, 5439
Hudson, D. F., 0263
Huffman, Norman, 5019, 5226
Hug, Joseph, 2994
Hull, R., 3391
Hultgren, Arland J., 0519, 2320, 3187
Humphrey, Hugh M., 3082, 4252
Hunter, A. M., 5459
Hurault, B., 3691
Hurtado, Larry W., 3086, 3799, 5244, 5270, 5546
Huston, H. W., 5228
Hutchinson, N. W., 3106
Igarashi, Peter H., 0802, 4586
Ilan, Tal, 4820
Inrig, J. G., 1751
Ireland, W. J., 4244
Isenberg, W. W., 3181
Jacks, Clive F., 3573
Jackson, David R., 1622, 4996, 4998
Jackson, Henry L., 5078
Jackson, Howard M., 2858, 3892, 4518, 4902
Jacob, René, 5136
Jacquemin, Edmond, 0077
Janowski, B., 1585, 2037
Janssen, Friedrich, 3180
Janzen, J. Gerald, 2313, 4892
Jason, Heda, 2294
Jasper, David, 1008, 3440, 3498
Jay, Bernard, 0522, 1914
Jenkins, Allan K., 2954
Jenkins, L. H., 1209
Jensen, I. L., 3623
Jeremias, Joachim, 0767, 1547, 2017, 2149, 2368, 2500, 2524, 2568, 2637, 3831, 4032, 5105
Jérôme, S., 2135
Jervell, Jakob, 1125, 1456
Jett, Billy C., 3353
Jewell, A. J., 3574
John, H. S., 3531
Johns, Eric, 3692
Johnson, David W., 4827
Johnson, Earl S., 1467, 2053, 2878, 3073, 3160, 4179, 4519
Johnson, James H., 3354
Johnson, S. Lewis, 0099, 1640
Johnson, Sherman E., 5435
Johnson, William A., 4761
Johnston, Edwin D., 4733
Jones, Alexander, 1089, 3295, 5445

Jones, Cecil W., 4945
Jones, G. V., 0787, 4291
Jones, I. H., 4353
Jones, M. W., 3505
Jones, Peter R., 4338, 4344, 4349
Jones, Ray C., 2591, 4046
Jonge, Marinus de, 2865
Jordan, Lynn M., 4795, 5336
Josuttis, M., 2826
Joüon, Paul, 5414
Juel, Donald H., 0043, 0067, 0116, 0187, 2683, 2685, 2773, 3885, 3933
Jüngel, Eberhard, 1930
Kafka, Gustav, 1746, 1782
Kahlefeld, Heinrich, 3206
Kähler, Martin, 3836
Kahmann, J. J. A., 0178, 1563, 2958
Kahn, J. G., 2172
Kaiser, Walter C., 1686, 4796
Kalin, E. R., 3647
Kallas, James, 4589
Kallikuzhuppil, John, 2379, 3289, 3963
Kanijirakompil, D. C., 5391
Kapolyo, J. M., 3231
Karavidopoulos, Johannes D., 2815
Karnetzki, Manfred, 4662, 4663, 4709
Käsemann, Ernst, 1586, 3837
Katz, Peter, 1857
Kaye, Bruce N., 1841
Kazmierski, Carl, 0335, 1558, 4206, 4715, 4935
Kea, Perry V., 0240, 0795, 3962, 4132
Kealy, Seán P., 3473, 3712, 3713, 3846
Keck, Leander E., 0006, 0583, 3105, 4466, 5044
Kee, Alistair, 3374, 4304
Kee, Howard Clark, 1590, 1865, 3161, 3356, 3470, 3665, 3742, 3788, 4680, 4776, 5031, 5321
Keegan, Terrence J., 5526
Keifert, Patrick R., 0043, 0067, 0187, 3714
Kelber, Werner H., 2619, 2623, 3117, 3219, 3316, 3445, 3852, 3947, 3950, 3955, 4272, 4426, 4454, 4455, 4456, 4979, 5297, 5302
Keller, Joseph, 0406, 3375
Keller, Walter E., 0345
Kellogg, Frederick R., 1288
Kelly, H. A., 3190
Kempthorne, Renatus, 2688, 2732
Kennard, J. Spencer, 2287, 2892, 3825
Kennedy, C. A., 4030
Kenny, Anthony, 1637
Ker, R. E., 1065
Kermode, Frank, 3684
Kern, Walter, 0252
Kernaghan, Ronald J., 0352, 4124, 4716
Kertelge, Karl, 0422, 2028, 2331, 2344, 3213, 4024, 4038, 4677, 4802
Kevil, Timothy J., 4273
Kieffer, René, 0084, 0160, 1246, 4745
Kilgallen, John J., 1618, 4122
Killunen, Jarmo, 0357, 2333
Kilmartin, E. J., 4026
Kilpatrick, George D., 0129, 0343, 0344, 0466, 0590, 0957, 1338, 1754, 2400, 2402, 2519, 2820, 3423, 3454, 3455, 3462, 3542, 3993, 5277, 5377, 5392
Kim, Deuk J., 4880
Kim, Sangbok D., 5129
Kingsbury, Jack D., 3050, 3152, 3155, 3188, 3472, 4936, 5527
Kio, Stephen Hre, 3397
Kirby, M. F., 3224
Kirchschlager, Walter, 0307
Kirk, J. A., 3118, 5221
Kirkland, J. R., 0792, 4335
Kistemaker, S. J., 2846
Kittel, Ronald A., 3938
Kittlaus, Lloyd R., 4739, 4740, 4742
Klassen, William, 2886, 5351
Klauck, Hans-Josef, 0376, 2213, 4260
Klausner, Joseph, 3826
Klein, Günter, 1866, 1868, 4539, 4545
Klein, Hans, 1507, 4570
Kleist, James A., 5418, 5420
Klemm, Hans G., 2269
Klijn, A. F. J., 1897
Kline, C. Benton, 1835, 4071
Klinger, H. E., 0680
Kloppenborg, John S., 0076, 1855, 2438, 3350, 4083, 4613, 5185
Klostermann, Erich, 5479
Klumbies, P.-G., 0574, 4198
Knackstedt, Joseph, 1088, 1402
Knigge, H.-D., 3590
Knight, George W., 4436
Knopp, R., 3861
Knox, John, 2666
Knox, Ronald, 5425
Knox, Wilfred L., 5022
Kobayashi, Teruo, 4541
Köbert, R., 1947

Koch, Dietrich-Alex, 0441, 1491, 3131, 3132, 3727
Koch, W., 4405
Koester, Helmut, 0762, 1793, 2225, 3497, 3728, 3789, 3800, 4616, 4617
Kolenkow, A. B., 2081, 2140, 4167, 4457
Kollmann, B., 0280
Konings, Johan, 4700
Kopas, Jane, 5352
Koppen, Klaus-Peter, 0161, 3919
Körtner, Ulrich H. J, 1193, 4562
Kosch, D., 4614, 5041
Kosmala, Hans, 0840, 1763, 2391, 2766, 2767, 2962, 4622
Kowalski, T. W., 0298
Kraeling, Carl H., 1523
Krass, Alfred, 1530
Kratz, R., 5505
Krause, Gerhard, 4225
Kraybill, D. B., 3978
Kremer, Jacob, 1242, 2192, 2709, 4412
Krieger, K.-S., 1127, 1460
Krijger, A., 2673, 2951
Kruse, Heinz, 5289
Kuby, Alfred, 3543
Küchler, Max, 2592
Kugelman, Richard, 3616, 4737
Kuhn, Heinz-Wolfgang, 2926, 3617, 3833, 4681
Kuhn, Karl G., 4379
Kuld, L., 0252
Kümmel, W. G., 1591, 2244, 2247, 4316, 5159
Künzi, Martin, 1610, 2460
Kürzinger, Josef, 3404, 3666
Kuss, Otto, 0896, 0898, 1445, 1999
Kuthirakkattel, Scaria, 0169, 3898
López-Dóriga, Enrique, 1067
Lach, Jan, 4182
Lachs, Samuel T., 0336, 3936, 5541
Lackey, James E., 3076
Ladd, George Eldon, 3308, 4721
Lafon, Guy, 0687
Lafontaine, René, 1488
Lagrange, Marie-Joseph, 5403, 5454
LaHurd, Carol S., 1009, 1010, 3364, 3441, 4655
Lahutsky, Nadia M., 3801
Lake, Silva T., 5225
Lamarche, Paul, 0032, 0435, 0437, 0938, 0972, 2680, 2740, 2863, 4170, 4228, 4230, 4542
Lamberigts, Sylvester, 1101, 2059, 2488
Lambiasi, F., 3772
Lambrecht, Jan, 0018, 0451, 0614, 0615, 0973, 1291, 1561, 3123, 3693, 3902, 3943, 3989, 4300, 4327, 4606, 4615, 4664, 4665, 4666, 4701, 4732, 5042
Lampe, G. W. H., 4548
Lampe, Peter, 0789
Lancellotti, Angelo, 0288, 0431, 0628, 0691, 0801, 1756, 1849, 4724
Lane, William L., 3081, 3129, 3471, 3598, 3694, 3802, 4670, 5379, 5488
Lang, F. G., 1388, 1699, 1903, 3182
Langevin, P.-É., 0177, 0875, 3078
Langkammer, Hugolinus, 0009, 3133, 3323, 4690, 5511
Lapointe, Roger, 3033
Larocco, Steven M., 3779
Lattanzi, Hugo, 2378
Lattey, Cuthbert, 2611
Lattke, Michael, 1807
Lauck, Willibold, 5421
Laufen, Rudolf, 5139
Laursen, Elizabeth, 1633
Lausberg, Heinrich, 0055
LaVerdiere, Eugene A., 0042, 0047, 0093, 0165, 0168, 0170, 0359, 0513, 0619, 0722, 1038, 1085, 1102, 1110, 1131, 1146, 1227, 1238, 1298, 1299, 1349, 1415, 1433, 1462, 1465, 1541, 1818, 1819, 1847, 2002, 2369, 2769, 2955, 2969, 3019, 3020
Lawrence, Walter S., 2593, 4656
Laws, Sophie, 3035
Leaney, A. R. C., 1121
Leder, H. G., 3491
Lee, E. K., 4735
Lee, G. M., 0469, 1117, 1477, 1933, 2764, 2768, 2791, 2806, 2856, 4410, 4576
Lee, J. A. L., 0775
Lee, Young-Heon, 2190
Lee-Pollard, Dorothy A., 4245
Leenhardt, Franz J., 0981, 3430, 4385
Lefevre, Frans, 2529
Légasse, Simon, 0090, 0659, 1748, 1898, 1904, 1910, 1941, 1992, 2005, 2323, 2334, 2864, 3883, 4578, 4770
Legault, André, 2496, 3877, 4858
Legrand, Lucien, 0891, 1114, 1265, 4214, 4898

Leitch, James W., 1398, 1532, 3567, 4911
Leivestad, Ragnar, 1596
Lekai, Emery A., 4227
Leloir, Louis, 1392
Lemcio, Eugene E., 0743, 1328, 1448, 1767, 3640, 4591, 5064
Lenhardt, P., 2307
Lentzen-Deis, Fritzleo, 0730, 2490, 4371
Léon-Dufour, Xavier, 2029, 2586, 4392, 4393, 4472, 5311
Leonardi, Giovanni, 1869
Lescow, Theodor, 3443
Leslie Mitton, C., 1458
Levie, Jean, 0560, 1174, 1691, 1734, 5095
Levison, John R., 2399
Lewis, Jack P., 1889
Lewis, James N., 3284
Lewis, P. B., 5033
Liefeld, Walter L., 5325
Lightenstern, H. H., 3506
Lightfoot, R. H., 0303, 2594, 5424
Lillie, William, 1156, 2956, 4850
Limbeck, Meinrad, 0632, 0652, 0697, 0831, 0952, 1300, 1710, 3196, 5465, 5538
Lincoln, Andrew T., 2961
Lindars, Barnabas, 1342, 1594, 2036, 3146, 4807, 4977, 4986, 5016
Lindberg, Carter, 2564, 4041
Lindemann, Andreas, 0186, 0525, 1876, 2928, 3496, 3965
Linden, Philip Van, 4229
Lindeskog, Gösta, 2860, 5219
Lindsey, Robert L., 3599, 5344
Linmans, A. J. M., 0943, 3410, 5047
Linnemann, Eta, 3600, 4420, 4543
Linton, Olof, 0908, 1436, 3585, 3929
Lipp, Wolfgang, 0380, 0946, 1706
Little, James C., 0710, 4691
Liuzza, Roy M., 0269, 0302, 5275
Livio, J. B., 0157, 0229
Ljungvik, Herman, 0071, 0122, 0171, 0397, 0426, 0837, 1476
Loader, W. R. G., 2359, 2714, 3016
Locatelli, Aldo, 2957
Lockman, Jan M., 3601
Lode, Lars, 0225, 0326, 0381, 0432, 0526, 0572, 0650, 1426, 1787, 4264
Loewen, Grant, 1580
Lohfink, Gerhard, 0763, 0764, 0765, 1199, 3387, 3964, 3979
Lohfink, N., 2338, 2339
Lohmeyer, Ernst, 2204, 5460
Lohse, Eduard, 0517, 0706, 1949, 3114, 5427
Loisy, Alfred, 5404, 5480
Long, Thomas G., 2105
Longenecker, R. N., 4110
Longstaff, Thomas R. W., 0287, 0566, 1769, 2139, 2535, 3151, 4873, 5130
Lorenzen, Dortee, 4473
Lorenzen, Thorwald, 2601, 2664, 2966
Lorenzmeier, Theodor, 0118, 1931
Losada, Diego A., 0714, 1144, 1327, 3037
Loslie, L. A., 2121, 2168, 3393
Louw, J. P., 0967
Lövestam, Evald, 0668, 0669, 2067, 2351, 2459, 2461, 2475, 2716, 3331, 3848, 4066
Lovin, Robin W., 1987
Lowe, Malcolm, 1314, 5141
Lownds, F. E., 3053
Lubsczyk, Hans, 3138
Luck, Ulrich, 0413, 4813
Luck, W. F., 4080
Lüderitz, Gert, 0028, 0299, 0409, 0947, 2390, 3743
Ludlum, J. H., 5099
Lührmann, Dieter, 1345, 2700, 3047, 3715, 3790, 4611
Lull, David J., 2040, 3889
Luz, Ulrich, 1505, 3844
Luzarraga, Jesús, 2974
Lynch, W. E., 4016
Maartens, Pieter J., 0487, 0854, 2738, 3337, 3858, 5001
McArthur, Harvey K., 0474, 1334, 2206, 2723, 4084, 4308
MacCaffrey, James, 4583
McCasland, S. Vernon, 2638
McCaughey, J. D., 4060
McCloskey, Liz L., 1039
Maccoby, Hyam Z., 2787
McCombie, F., 5015
McCool, Francis J., 0, 0834
McCormick, Michael, 0852, 0955, 5263
McCurley, Foster R., 1653
McDermott, J. E., 5046
McDermott, John M., 0203, 3966, 4937
McDonald, Charles C., 0734
McDonald, J. I. H., 1738, 1892, 3348, 3971, 4906
McDonnell, J. J., 5169
McEleney, N. J., 1289, 2759
McGann, Diarmuid, 3756

McGinlay, Hugh, 3716
McGuckin, John A., 0839, 3040
McHardy, W. D., 1312
McHugh, John J., 3631
McIndoe, J. H., 2950, 3920
Mack, Burton L., 3972
McKenna, David L., 5530
McKenzie, R. A., 4893
McKinnis, Ray, 1971
McKinnon, Donald M., 0152
Mackowski, Richard M., 5373
MacLaurin, E. C. B., 0230, 0653, 3198
McLoughlin, Swithun, 5106
McMillan, E., 5485
McNamara, Elmer A., 1355
McNicol, Allan, 2451, 3394
Macomber, W. F., 5264
MacRae, George W., 4061
McRuer, J., 4402
McVann, Mark F. S. C., 0928, 0929, 0930, 0963, 2654, 2660, 3071, 3290, 4205, 4526
Maddox, Robert J., 0368, 0660, 1540, 1672, 4964
Madore, Marian, 4231
Maggioni, Bruno, 3865, 5498
Magne, Jean, 0443, 0458
Magness, James L., 5068
Mahoney, Matthew, 2411, 2813
Maisch, Ingrid, 0371
Major, David, 3692
Makrides, V. N., 2195
Malbon, Elizabeth Struthers, 0462, 2372, 3049, 3259, 3474, 3667, 3766, 3856, 4581, 4651, 5049, 5065, 5389
Mally, Edward J., 5466
Malone, David, 1940
Maloney, Elliott C., 3460
Mánek, Jindrich, 0228, 1447
Mangatt, George, 3134, 3729, 3926
Manicardi, Ermenegildo, 2830
Manno, B. V., 3246, 3845
Manns, Frédéric, 1155
Mansfield, Mecklin R., 4246
Manson, T. W., 0548, 2131, 2901, 4090, 5020
Manson, William, 0784, 1259, 2392, 3839
Mantey, Julius R., 2837
Manus, Chris U., 2877
Marcello Buscemi, A., 0276, 0850, 1059
Marcheselli, C. C., 0234, 0718, 3318, 3951
Marco, M. H., 0321, 1584, 2248, 3609, 4427, 4916
Marconcini, Benito, 0557, 4678
Marcus, Joel, 0205, 0796, 1678, 2719, 3070, 3967, 4351, 4942
Mariadasan, V., 2085
Mariani, Bonaventura, 3031
Marin, Louis, 4478
Marlow, Ransom, 4957
Marrion, Malachy, 2167
Marshall, Christopher D., 4253
Marshall, I. Howard, 0132, 0419, 0752, 1545, 2549, 2728, 3109, 4040, 4930, 4956, 4970, 5155, 5461
Martin, François, 0080, 2004, 3780
Martin, Ralph P., 3593, 3632, 5290, 5499, 5528
Martin, Raymond A., 4133
Martindale, C. C., 5428
Martinez, Ernest R., 3130
Martínez Dalmau, Eduardo, 5101
Martini, Carlo M., 0460, 1501
Martucci, Jean, 1046, 1061, 1170
Marucci, Corrado, 2196
Marxsen, Willi, 1027, 4009, 4661, 4671, 4861
Maser, Peter, 2440
Massaux, Edouard, 3803
Masson, Charles, 0318, 0968, 1072, 1446, 1624, 2893, 3591, 5312
Mastin, Brian A., 1096, 1427, 2083, 2565
Masuda, Sarrae, 1191, 1413
Mateos, Juan, 0832, 0833, 0862, 1478, 1554, 5383
Matera, Frank J., 0049, 1122, 2828, 3717, 3773, 3864, 3890, 4234, 4505, 4669, 5036
Maunder, C. J., 2525, 3412
Maurer, Christian, 3097, 4106, 4380, 4927
Mauser, Ulrich W., 0156, 4219
May, David M., 0617, 1958, 4247
Mayer, Bernhard, 1081
Maynard, Arthur H., 4741
Mays, James L., 0175, 1492
Mead, R. T., 0366, 4144
Meagher, J. C., 3407, 3411, 4706, 4718
Mearns, Chris L., 0800, 3343, 4999
Mehlmann, J., 2888, 2941
Meinertz, Max, 1439, 2467
Meli, A., 2497
Melick, George F., 5137
Menken, M. J. J., 2054, 4176

Mentz, Hermann, 3767
Mercurio, Roger, 0683
Merendino, R. P., 0052, 0712, 0713
Merkel, Helmut, 1335, 5030
Merklein, Helmut, 4033
Merli, Dino, 1442, 2218, 4154
Merritt, Robert L., 2788
Mesa, José L., 2110
Metz, José B., 1536, 1537
Metzger, Bruce, 3293
Meye, Robert P., 0804, 0922, 2975, 3212, 4104, 4177, 4862
Meyer, Ben F., 4049, 4249
Meyer, Dieter, 5367
Meyer, Marvin W., 1522, 2674
Meyer, Paul W., 3100
Meynet, Roland, 0644
Michaels, J. R., 2869
Michaud, Jean-Paul, 1354
Michaux, J. W., 3177
Michel, Otto, 1549, 3302, 4752
Michie, D., 4262
Michl, Johann, 0400
Miguéns, Manuel, 2336
Milavec, Aaron A., 2234, 2239, 2243, 4361, 4362, 4368
Miller, Dale, 3641, 3804
Miller, J. I., 1479
Miller, Johnny V., 4490
Miller, Patricia, 3804
Miller, Robert J., 2152
Milling, F. H., 4408
Milne, Douglas J. W., 3275
Minear, Paul S., 2439, 3046, 3283, 5442
Minette de Tillesse, Gaëtan, 0058, 1124, 4107
Minnerath, Roland, 0284, 0599, 2200
Mirecki, Paul A., 2998, 3013, 3186, 4729, 5300
Mirro, Joseph A., 2057
Mitchell, Curtis C., 0155, 0490
Mitton, C. Leslie, 1792, 3652, 5432
Mizell, Edgar S., 4208
Moeller, Henry B., 5230
Mohn, Werner, 2621, 3446
Mohrlang, Roger, 4708
Moir, I. A., 1607, 5250
Moiser, Jeremy, 1068, 1658
Molitor, Joseph, 1790, 2946
Molland, Einar, 0917
Moloney, Francis J., 0215, 0442, 0594, 1211, 1416, 2543, 4051, 4790, 4987
Moltmann, Jürgen, 1497, 1537
Moltmann-Wendel, Elisabeth, 1497
Montagninni, Felice, 2947
Montague, George T., 5529
Montefiore, Claude G., 5401
Montefiore, Hugh W., 1204, 2345
Montgomery, R. B., 2156
Moo, Douglas J., 0555
Moore, A. L., 3312
Moore, C. A., 0824
Moore, D. R., 2992
Moore, Stephen D., 4006, 5054
Moore, W. Ernest, 2001, 4242
Morag, S., 1395
Morey, A.-J., 1011, 4280
Morgan, C. S., 0543, 3022
Morgan, G. Campbell, 5503
Moriconi, Bruno, 2356
Morin, J.-A., 0607, 2526
Morlet, Michel, 4309
Morosco, Robert E., 3230
Morrice, William G., 1773, 2070, 2250, 2254, 2663
Moseley, Fred B., 3899, 4944
Moser, Theresa, 3648
Mosetto, Francesco, 0927
Mosley, A. W., 3994
Motyer, S., 2866, 3488
Moulder, W. J., 2031
Moule, A. W. H., 5114
Moule, C. F. D., 0737, 2973, 4120, 4582, 4598, 4832, 5451
Mourlon Beernaert, Pierre, 0239, 0348, 0389, 0407, 1488, 2542, 3757, 4693, 5483
Mouson, Jean, 2155
Mowery, Robert L., 3405, 3487, 3791, 4751
Muddiman, John B., 0483, 0485, 1993, 1995, 3234
Mueller, James R., 1816
Mueller, T., 0073
Mulholland, Morton R., 3668
Müller, H.-P., 5308
Müller, Klaus W., 2651
Müller, Mogens, 4994
Müller, Ulrich B., 0353, 0997, 1390, 3124, 3338
Mullins, T. Y., 3657
Mündelein, Gerhard, 2113
Munn, G. L., 3676
Muñoz León, Domingo, 1620, 2609, 2972
Munro, Winsome, 2504, 5349

Muraoka, Takumitsu, 3457
Murphy, C. M., 3242
Murphy-O'Connor, Jerome, 5341
Murray, D. J., 3062
Murray, Gregory, 0308, 0337, 0392, 1012, 1041, 1109, 1297, 1438, 1929, 2329, 2370, 3021, 3730, 3744, 3774
Mussner, Franz, 0180, 0190, 0191, 0271, 0851, 0899, 2300, 2437, 2464, 2712, 3309, 4287, 4620
Muszyński, Henryk, 0147
Myers, Ched, 0295, 0923, 1464, 2073, 2482, 3268, 3339, 3385, 3398, 4195
Myers, William R., 0783
Myhre, Klara, 2579
Myre, André, 4113
Nardoni, Enrique, 1614, 2557, 4722, 5329
Nauck, Wolfgang, 1796
Navone, John, 4050, 4235, 4498
Negōitā, Athanase, 1457
Neil, William, 0766, 4295
Neirynck, Frans, 0002, 0054, 0148, 0327, 0427, 0494, 0550, 0612, 1132, 1139, 1202, 1737, 2749, 2929, 2948, 3332, 3685, 3995, 3996, 3997, 4, 4607, 4687, 4719, 4746, 4762, 5035, 5039, 5121, 5122, 5147, 5156, 5176, 5179, 5390
Neri, Paolo, 1472
Nesbitt, Charles F., 2095, 2108, 2514
Nestle, Dieter, 1056
Neugebauer, Fritz, 1195, 2354, 3384
Neumann, Gerhart J., 5025
Neusner, Jacob, 2145, 2146, 3768, 5203, 5298
Nevius, Richard C., 4223, 4257, 4258
Newell, J. E., 4311
Newell, R. R., 4311
Newman, Barclay M., 2995
Newman, Robert G., 3568
Neyrey, Jerome H., 2597, 4241
Nicholls, R., 3805
Nickelsburg, George W. E., 4479
Nicklin, T., 0094
Nicoll, Maurice, 4363
Nida, Eugene A., 3550
Niederwimmer, Kurt, 3051
Niedner, Frederick A., 3064
Nielsen, Helge K., 0248, 0962, 2055
Niemann, F.-J., 2927
Nineham, D. E., 3169, 5446, 5500
Nissen, Johannes, 3333
Nkwoka, Anthony O., 0611, 1881
Noble, David F., 5057
Nolan, Brian M., 2457
Nolting, William C., 0673
Noorda, Sijbolt J., 1083
Nortje, S. J., 1133, 1525, 1690
Nützel, Johannes M., 1129, 1676, 3325, 5324
Oakman, Douglas E., 0645
Obeng, E. A., 1598, 2646, 3489, 4584
Oberliner, Lorenz, 0626, 1077, 2883, 2943
Obermüller, Rudolph, 0819
O'Callaghan, D., 4062
O'Callaghan, José, 0428, 0496, 0504, 0772, 0778, 0848, 0892, 1266, 1275, 1583, 1661, 1944, 1996, 2010, 4632, 5246
O'Collins, Gerald, 1646, 2899, 2981, 4087, 4458, 4571, 4903, 5355
O'Day, Gail R., 0964, 1709, 4250
Odenkirchen, P. Cornelius, 2604, 2963
O'Donnell, Desmond, 3855
O'Flynn, John A., 4011, 5426
Ogle, Arthur, 2259, 3095
O'Grady, John F., 3418, 3703, 3869, 4196, 4480
O'Hara, John, 0476, 1250, 1473
O'Hara, M. L., 1925
Oke, C. Clare, 1675
Olbricht, Thomas H., 3853
Olson, Stanley N., 0528
O'Mahony, Gerald, 3806, 4339, 4881
Omanson, Roger L., 0609, 5252, 5278
O'Neill, J. C., 0499, 0677, 2717, 2742
Ong, Walter J., 3775
Oppermann, Ralf, 2960
Orchard, John B., 5127
Ordon, Hubert, 1513
O'Rourke, J. J., 5368
Orsatti, Mauro, 3959
Ortega, Alfonso, 0063
Ory, G., 1184, 1404
Osborn, Henry, 2098
Osborne, B. A. E., 3194
Osborne, Grant R., 1248, 4717, 4725, 4890
Osborne, William L., 3862
Osburn, Carroll D., 3458, 5271
Oswald, Julius, 4474, 4787
Outler, Albert C., 3695, 3731
Overstreet, R. L., 4471
Owen, H. P., 1587, 2430, 2724, 3301
Pace, Giuseppe, 0909, 1190

Paci, I., 1380, 5074
Packer, James I., 2296
Page, S. H. T., 2035
Palmer, D. W., 2585, 2949, 4063
Pangritz, Andreas, 1171, 1294
Panier, Louis, 2242
Parker, George G., 3583
Parker, Pierson, 3052, 3603, 4627, 4736, 4943, 5023, 5034, 5148
Parker, S. Thomas, 1025, 1387
Parkin, Vincent, 0797, 3686
Parlier, Isabelle, 0387, 4207
Patrick, M. W., 2337
Patsch, Hermann, 4428
Patte, Daniel, 1877, 5050, 5051
Patten, Priscilla C., 3038
Patterson, Leon Bell, 3944
Paul, André, 0319, 2047, 2088, 3642
Paul, M. J., 5177
Paulsen, Henning, 2930
Pavelsky, R. L., 3916
Pavur, Claude N., 0880, 4357
Payne, P. B., 4340, 4342, 4345
Peabody, David B., 3776, 5132, 5149
Peacock, H. F., 3251, 5281
Pécriaux Landier, J. F., 5525
Pedersen, Sigfred, 0113, 0711, 0770, 1625
Peisker, C. H., 0823
Pella, G., 2829
Pelletier, André, 2861
Pelser, G. M. M., 4824
Percy, Ernst, 0704, 0813
Pérez, Gonzalo Aranda, 5274
Pérez Gordo, Angel, 4459, 4460
Perrin, Norman, 1140, 1493, 1605, 2713, 2729, 3115, 3174, 3493, 3495, 3658, 4312, 4461, 4962, 4963
Perrot, Charles, 1076, 1867, 2376
Persson, Lennart, 1281
Pesch, Rudolf, 0007, 0023, 0211, 0242, 0304, 0448, 0453, 0978, 0982, 1047, 1303, 1330, 1346, 1511, 1592, 1911, 2442, 2502, 2532, 2533, 2596, 2693, 2752, 3429, 3431, 3888, 4034, 4042, 4447, 4491, 5467, 5504, 5505, 5512, 5521
Pesch, Wilhelm, 1574, 1952, 1990, 2245
Petersen, K. Weinholt, 3110
Petersen, Norman R., 0702, 3294, 3677
Pettem, Michael, 1203, 4044
Petzke, Gerd, 1698, 2265, 3359
Pezzella, Sosio, 2468
Phelan, John E., 1166, 4203
Pherigo, Lindsey P., 5481
Phillips, Gary A., 5045
Phillips, J. B., 5506
Phillips, John A., 4928
Pickering, S. R., 4645
Pigulla, Wilfried, 2576
Pilch, John J., 0328, 1830, 4072, 4190
Pilgaard, Aage, 3957, 4187, 5543
Pili, F., 1431
Pimentel, Peter, 0268, 1001, 1369, 1707, 3202, 4642
Piper, O. A., 4384
Pirot, Louis, 5419
Pizivin, D., 5525
Platt, E. E., 4088
Plumley, J. M., 5257
Plummer, Alfred, 5531
Pobee, John, 2873
Poeppig, F., 3111
Pohl, Adolf, 3769
Poirier, C. A., 3055
Pokorn, Petr, 3669
Pollard, Vincent K., 1237
Potin, Jean, 1029
Pousset, Édouard, 3678
Powell, Ivor, 3758
Powell, W., 1066
Powley, Brian G., 3704, 4108, 4126, 4130
Prast, Franz, 2326
Prete, Benedetto, 2707
Price, Norman D., 3896
Procter, David I., 4727
Pryke, E. J., 4713
Pryor, J. W., 4310, 4683
Pudussery, Paul S., 0206, 1495, 2398, 2441, 3254, 3272
Queckc, Hans, 5247, 5248
Quesnel, Michel, 5536
Quesnell, Quentin, 1276
Rabacchi, S., 3745
Rabinowitz, Isaac, 1391, 1394
Radaelli, A., 0027
Radcliffe, Timothy, 3041
Radermakers, Jean, 1982, 4866, 5060, 5489
Ragot, A., 1656
Rahmani, L. Y., 2286
Räisänen, Heikki, 0621, 1339, 1340, 4121, 4138, 4317
Raiser, Konrad, 1216, 3379
Ramaroson, Leonard, 3649
Ramsauer, H., 2046

Ramsey, A. M., 4398
Rank, R. G., 4972
Rao, O. M., 3575
Rasco, Emilio, 0394
Rauch, C., 5222
Ravarotto, Efrem, 4546
Rawlinson, A. E. J., 5411
Read, David H. C., 2838
Reardon, Patrick H., 1989, 3285, 4535
Rebell, Walter, 1581
Reed, Harold, 4374
Reedy, C. J., 1533
Reese, James M., 3849
Rehm, Martin, 2839
Reicke, Bo, 0375, 2395, 5037
Reid, Barbara E., 1628, 3807, 5342
Reiser, Marius, 0405, 1229, 2304, 2859
Reist, John S., 1055
Rengstorf, Karl H., 2365, 4769
Renié, J., 1260
Reploh, Karl-Georg, 0176, 3624, 4672
Repo, Eero, 1180, 1234
Reumann, John H., 0173, 2844, 4782
Reynolds, S. M., 1064, 1309, 1311, 3456, 5369, 5374
Rhoads, David, 4261, 4262
Riach, John L., 3830
Ricca, Paolo, 2569, 4043
Rice, George E., 0642, 0643, 1961, 1963, 2970, 5272
Richards, John R., 4932, 4975
Richardson, Alan, 1219
Richter, George, 0105
Ricoeur, Paul, 4281, 4533, 4997
Riddle, D. W., 0703, 5055, 5093
Riddle, Douglas D. J., 5291
Rienecker, Fritz, 5490
Riesenfeld, Harald, 1692, 1983, 3610, 4660
Riesner, Rainer, 0291, 0486, 0958, 1814
Riga, P. J., 1920
Rigato, M. L., 0290
Rigaux, Béda, 0816, 2419, 3576, 4552
Rigg, H. A., 3532
Riley, Harold, 3792, 5170
Riley, Mark, 2645, 3447
Rinaldi, Bonaventura, 2347, 2814, 2831
Rinaldi, G., 1279
Ringe, Sharon H., 3159, 3346, 5299
Ringshausen, Gerhard, 1886
Riquelme, J., 3881
Rist, John M., 5133
Ritt, Hubert, 1244, 2933
Ritter, Adolf M., 4577
Rivera, L. F., 0919, 3077, 3618, 3879, 4667, 4673, 5315
Robbins, Vernon K., 0019, 0174, 0507, 1051, 1752, 1759, 1779, 1878, 1882, 2048, 2534, 3072, 3089, 3419, 3705, 3857, 4160, 4926, 5378
Roberts, C. H., 0893, 1267, 4628, 5257
Roberts. "Galilean Resurrecti, J., 1130
Robertson, A. T., 3544
Robinson, James M., 1644, 3178, 3481, 3482, 3533, 4702
Robinson, John A. T., 0539, 1687, 2255, 2722, 3299, 4325
Robinson, T. H., 3834
Robinson, W. C., 4116
Rodd, Cyril S., 0561, 1287
Ródenas, Angel, 2066
Rodgers, P., 2819
Rodríguez Carmona, Antonio, 3291, 3679
Roe, William W., 3871
Rogers, Alan D., 0540
Roggenbuck, Clemens, 0781
Rohrhirsch, Ferdinand, 1274, 4643, 4646
Rohrig, Byron L., 0679
Rolland, Philippe, 0149, 0333, 0334, 0411, 0412, 0488, 0655, 0807, 0954, 1103, 1134, 1218, 1713, 1760, 2282, 2410, 2432, 2435, 2538, 2808, 2938, 3732
Roloff, Jürgen, 2026, 3483
Romaniuk, Kazimierz, 0826, 2119, 4825
Ronen, Yochanan, 1292
Roosa, William V., 3352
Rose, A., 4847
Rose, Jean-Baptiste, 5397
Rosenbaum, Hans-Udo, 1273, 4641
Ross, J. M., 0061, 1157, 1313, 1480, 1597, 1774, 1795, 2099
Ross, Ronald, 0410
Roth, Cecil, 5207
Roth, W., 4808, 4821
Roulin, Placide, 0098
Roure, Damià, 0536
Rousseau, Robert P., 3135, 3937
Rowe, Robert D., 3154
Rowland, Christopher, 2275
Rubinkiewicz, Ryszard, 2848
Ruckstuhl, Eugen, 0110, 3065, 3486, 4800, 4939
Ruddick, C. T., 0059
Ruegg, Ulrich, 0942, 1381

Rüger, Hans P., 0163, 0260, 0858, 3459
Ruhland, Maria, 4520
Runnalls, Donna, 4238
Russell, E. A., 0516, 1365, 1771, 2266, 3759
Ryrie, Charles C., 0317, 1845, 4077
Saayman, Willem A., 2570, 4045
Sabbe, Maurits, 4703
Sabin, Marie, 4373, 4763
Sabourin, Léopold, 0266, 0374, 0563, 0567, 0791, 0894, 0941, 0986, 1031, 1043, 1063, 1222, 1243, 1268, 1360, 1411, 1514, 2715, 3746, 4111, 4162, 4165, 4331, 4629, 4788
Sagne, Jean-Claude, 2851
Sahlin, Harald, 0022, 0603, 0777, 0838, 0877, 0969, 1060, 1280, 1343, 1347, 1512, 1521, 1962, 2375, 2447, 2503, 2823, 2847, 2922, 3425
Salas, Antonio, 1092
Saldarini, Anthony J., 3048, 4760
Saltet, Louis, 2610
Salvoni, Faustino, 0670
Samuel, S. Johnson, 3808
Sand, Alexander, 3032
Sanday, William, 5083
Sanders, E. P., 1901, 4602, 5119, 5160, 5171
Sanders, I. L., 4948
Sandmel, Samuel, 3172, 4954
Sanner, A. Elwood, 5516
Sauer, Jürgen, 0570, 1873
Saunderson, Barbara, 3449
Sauser, Ekkart, 0686
Sawyerr, Harry, 5056
Saydon, Patrick P., 2649
Scattolon, Alfredo, 0134, 1666, 2253
Schaberg, Jane, 2739, 4814, 5007
Schabert, Arnold, 3563
Schäfer, Karl T., 0502
Schaller, Berndt, 1859, 4056
Schauch, Werner, 2094, 2386, 2598
Scheifler, José R., 2804
Schelkle, K. H., 0790
Schenk, Wolfgang, 1694, 3760, 3940, 4240, 4442, 4443, 4605, 4688
Schenke, Hans M., 2672, 5337
Schenke, Ludger, 2489, 2907, 4163, 4224, 4429, 4444
Schenker, Adrian, 2038, 4035
Scherer, P. E., 1358
Schick, Edwin A., 3305
Schierse, Franz J., 3119
Schille, Gottfried, 0477, 0482, 0934, 1137, 1518, 2890, 3413, 3538, 4216, 4221, 4704
Schilling, F. A., 1891
Schlarb, Robert, 0306, 0630, 0695, 1430, 2161, 2260, 2493, 2959
Schlatter, Adolf, 3747
Schlier, Heinrich, 2911, 4445
Schlosser, Jacques, 1772, 2169, 2188, 2383, 2384, 2822, 3395, 5218
Schmahl, Günther, 3215, 3217
Schmid, Josef, 1282, 1444, 1498, 1669, 1824, 2163, 4382, 5469
Schmidt, Daryl D., 5548, 5551
Schmietenkoff, M., 2046
Schmithals, Walter, 0924, 1697, 3216, 3761, 5322, 5522
Schmitt, John J., 5348
Schnackenburg, Rudolf, 0210, 1106, 1215, 1535, 1732, 1749, 2193, 3633, 4781, 5482
Schneider, Gerhard, 0135, 0847, 1378, 1834, 2353, 2360, 2655, 2678, 2679, 2775, 2781, 2827, 2876, 3004, 4433, 4499
Schnell, C. W., 3770
Schnellbächer, Ernst L., 0114, 1634, 1654, 2879, 4239, 5388
Schnider, Franz, 0949, 2506
Schoeps, H.-J., 0537, 0578, 1283, 1825, 3028
Scholz, Günter, 2790, 2896
Schott, E., 1070
Schottroff, Luise, 0527, 0535, 0551, 2513, 2884, 2932, 4914
Schramm, Tim, 5115
Schreiber, Johannes, 2718, 2786, 2802, 3101, 3107, 4413, 4485, 4668
Schroeder, R. P., 2603
Schroer, Silvia, 0121, 1120
Schubert, Kurt, 1517, 2681, 2701, 4917
Schüling, Joachim, 0046, 0647, 1573, 1623
Schultze, Bernhard, 0901, 3279
Schulz, Anselm, 0637, 0701, 0803, 1972, 1980, 1981, 2885
Schulz, Siegfried, 4601, 4768, 5294
Schulze, W. A., 0162
Schüngel, P. H., 4446
Schürmann, Heinz, 2556, 2562, 4020
Schüssler Fiorenza, Elisabeth, 3236, 5350
Schützeichel, Heribert, 2835
Schwank, Benedikt, 2285

Schwartz, Daniel R., 0654, 1295
Schwartz, Jacques, 1123
Schwarz, Günther, 0232, 0310, 0399, 0591, 1021, 1373, 1566, 1569, 1802, 1806, 2126, 2129, 2171, 2184, 5196, 5265
Schweizer, Eduard, 0003, 0272, 0735, 0742, 3139, 3252, 3314, 4101, 4882, 4952, 5282, 5473
Scippa, Vincenzo, 1035
Scott, Bernard B., 0750, 0866, 0867, 2235, 2449, 2456
Scott, M. Philip, 0699, 4004
Scroggs, Robin, 0662, 2668, 2952
Seal, Welton O., 3334
Secco, David P., 1568, 3232, 4512
Seeley, David, 2042, 3821, 4532, 4612, 5172
Segalla, Giuseppe, 0102, 1938, 2189, 2317, 2471
Seim, Jürgen, 1649
Seim, T. K., 0738
Seitz, J. F., 0005, 1589, 2444, 2731, 2763, 4990
Sellen, Gerhard, 0716
Sellew, Philip H., 0729, 3793, 3911, 5040, 5178
Sellin, Gerhard, 0111, 0719, 0811, 0916, 2251, 3066, 4137
Selvidge, Marla J., 1049, 1053, 1973, 5347
Senior, Donald P., 1192, 1414, 2531, 2657, 3687, 4500
Sergeant, John, 3781
Setzer, J. S., 3120, 3319
Sevenster, Jan N., 2289
Shae, G. S., 2194, 3873
Shaw, Alan, 1177, 1401, 4145
Shaw, R. H., 2421, 3310
Shepherd, Tom, 1042, 5180
Sibinga, J. Smit, 0564
Sicre, José L., 2104
Sidebottom, E. M., 0404, 1777
Siegman, E. F., 0785
Sigal, Phillip, 1293, 5150, 5151
Silva Costoya, Rafael, 1630
Simon, Louis, 2024, 2367
Simonis, Walter, 2306, 4815
Simonsen, Hejne, 1482, 4114, 4689
Simpson, Patrick, 0167
Simpson, R. T., 5102
Sinclair, Scott G., 3075, 4139
Sint, Josef A., 2903
Skeat, T. C., 1315, 5393
Slomp, J., 0036, 4934
Sloyan, Gerard S., 3079, 3170, 4430, 5436
Slusser, Dorothy M., 3840, 4155
Slusser, Gerald H., 3840
Slusser, Michael, 1322
Smalley, Stephen S., 1603
Smart, James D., 1984
Smit, J. A., 1319
Smith, C. W. F., 2127, 3388
Smith, Charles L., 4217, 5357
Smith, D. Moody, 2898, 3706, 4923
Smith, Karen E., 2632
Smith, M. H., 0696, 4889, 5550
Smith, Marion, 3185
Smith, Morton, 1213, 3634, 3635, 3915, 5253, 5331
Smith, Robert, 1621, 2913, 4437
Smith, Stephen H., 2064, 2381, 4254, 5071
Smith, Thomas J., 5486, 5513
Smith, William T., 3237
Smylie, James H., 1780, 1887
Smyth-Florentin, Françoise, 0137
Snape, H. C., 3611
Snodgrass, Klyne R., 0056, 2221
Snoy, Thierry, 1241, 1253, 1434, 2433
Snyman, A. H., 1534
Soards, Marion L., 2807, 4506, 5301
Soares Prabhu, G. M., 0944
Soares-Prabhu, George M., 2343
Söding, Thomas, 2628, 3262, 4730
Soldatelli, A., 0822
Songer, Harold S., 4288
Soubigou, Louis, 1599, 3650, 5327
Soulen, Richard N., 1833, 4053
Sowers, Sidney G., 2415
Spadafora, Francesco, 0624, 0634, 0681
Sperber, Daniel, 2374, 5238
Spiegel, Egon, 2143
Sproule, John A., 0910, 4346
St. John, Harold, 3099
Staab, Karl, 5462
Stackpole, A. J., 3564
Stacy, Robert W., 4232
Stadelmann, L. I. J., 0261, 4492
Stagg, Frank, 3014, 4021
Stahl, Michael, 0746, 4369
Stählin, Gustav, 1440
Standaert, Benoît, 0358, 2636, 3417, 4268, 5533
Stanley, David M., 3043, 3171, 3256
Stano, G. M., 5456

Stanton, Graham N., 2429
Starobinski, Jean, 0979, 0983, 0984, 3432
Staudinger, Ferdinand, 0936
Stauffer, Ethelbert, 1091, 1223, 1459, 1689, 2007, 2272, 2520
Stedman, R. C., 0001, 1481, 5507, 5508
Stegemann, Ekkehard W., 0356, 0881, 4568
Stegemann, Wolfgang, 0527, 0535, 1953, 4914
Steichele, H. J., 4789
Stein, Dominique, 1714
Stein, Robert H., 0259, 1641, 1831, 2606, 2923, 2967, 4073, 4679, 4682, 4874, 5328
Steinbeck, J., 2555
Steinhauser, Michael G., 0511, 2063, 2069, 3074
Steinmetz, F. J., 4123
Steinseifer, Bernd, 2964
Stenger, Werner, 1861
Stephenson, A. M. G., 4598
Stern, David, 2236, 4364
Stern, Jay B., 2315
Sternheim, Arnold E., 4003
Stevens, Bruce A., 1553, 5004
Stock, Augustine, 0183, 0581, 1470, 1838, 2060, 2280, 2887, 3257, 3351, 4002, 4070, 5069, 5540
Stock, Klemens, 0181, 0301, 0636, 2875, 3218, 3718
Stoffel, Ernest Lee, 2050
Stöger, Alois, 0587, 1013, 4226
Stoldt, Hans-Herbert, 5134, 5142
Stonehouse, Ned B., 3832
Storch, Rainer, 2518
Storch, W., 1306, 5193
Stotzer-Klos, H., 0942, 1381
Strack, H. L., 4757
Straton, H. H., 4105, 4960
Strecker, Georg, 1544, 1728, 1968, 3625, 4099
Streeter, B. H., 4592, 4593, 4594, 4595, 5084, 5085, 5086, 5087, 5088, 5161
Strelan, R., 5552
Strijdom, J. M., 2939
Strobel, August, 2686, 2780, 4414
Strus, Andrea, 0998, 1750, 2222
Stuhlmacher, Peter, 2916
Stuhlmann, Rainer, 0200, 0873, 2431, 3008
Sturch, R. L., 1079, 4171
Styler, G. M., 5143
Sudbrack, J., 0596, 1578
Suggit, John N., 2065, 2507, 3277
Sugirtharajah, R. S., 1374, 2373, 2521
Suh, Joong S., 3266
Suhl, Alfred, 0253, 0289, 0651, 1028, 3201, 4771
Sulzbach, Maria F., 4951
Suriano, T. M., 0939, 1185, 1406, 3378
Swain, Lionel, 3125
Swartley, Willard M., 5059, 5523
Sweet, J. P. M., 4161, 4318
Sweetland, Dennis M., 3269
Swetnam, James, 0342, 1437, 4894
Swift, E. G., 5474
Synge, F. C., 0393, 0793, 0940, 1044, 1165, 2092, 2536, 2545, 2797, 2919, 4027, 5319
Szarek, Eugene C., 0586, 3286
Szarek, Gene, 2624, 3220, 4980
Tagawa, Kenzo, 2263, 3577, 3670
Tannehill, Robert C., 1565, 3145, 3222, 3250
Taylor, B. B., 3812
Taylor, Edward L., 3225
Taylor, J., 1679, 4819
Taylor, Robert H., 3913
Taylor, Vincent, 3516, 3539, 4089, 4093, 4383, 5455
Telford, William R., 2122, 3085, 3762, 4720, 5212
Tello, C. Castro, 3999
Ternant, Paul, 0024, 2364, 2607, 3009
Testa, E. N., 1097, 3005
Theissen, Gerd, 1367, 1955, 2704, 3183, 5197
Theobald, Michael, 0438, 3163
Thiede, Carsten P., 4638
Thien An Vo, N., 3468, 3494
Thiering, B. E., 2567
Thimmes, Pamela, 0953, 3863
Thissen, Werner, 0350
Thomas, John C., 2996, 3273
Thomas, Joseph, 2626
Thomas, Kenneth J., 2341
Thomas, R. L., 5128
Thompson, Ernest T., 5443
Thompson, James W., 2407
Thompson, William G., 3260, 3270
Thorley, John, 0408, 0577, 0771, 1116, 1331, 1570, 2283, 2348, 2436, 2795
Thouless, Robert H., 1058, 4153
Thrall, Margaret, 4774, 5316
Throckmorton, Burton H., 4597

Thyen, Hartwig, 0070
Tillard, J. M. R., 4579
Tinsley, E. J., 2721, 4946
Tipson, Baird, 0678
Tooley, Wilfred, 1224, 2600
Tosato, A., 0106
Tosatto, Giuseppe, 4487
Towner, W. Sibley, 2443
Towns, Elmer L., 3017
Trakatellis, Demetrios, 0449, 3263
Trémel, Y.-B., 5326
Treu, Kurt, 5232
Trevijano Etcheverría, Rámon, 0025, 0069, 0270, 1017, 1168, 1169, 1188, 1407, 1410, 1829, 3636, 3659, 4067
Trilling, Wolfgang, 4406
Trimaille, Michel, 2237, 4365
Trites, Allison A., 5330
Troadec, Henri, 0514, 1918, 5452
Trocmé, Étienne, 1604, 2153, 2314, 3112, 3126, 3643, 3651, 4332, 4493, 4920
Trompf, G. W., 2989, 2990, 4863
Trotti, John B., 2466
Trudinger, L. Paul, 0506, 2665, 2845
Tuckett, Christopher M., 0062, 0209, 0396, 0415, 0602, 0723, 1087, 1667, 1741, 2744, 2770, 2945, 4131, 4358
Turlington, Henry E., 3602
Turner, H. E. W., 4538, 5363
Turner, Nigel, 0542, 0773, 0841, 1111, 1539, 4010
Twelftree, Graham, 3276
Tyson, Joseph B., 1126, 3208
Ulansey, David, 0127, 2867
Uleyn, A. J. R., 0999, 1000, 3437, 3671
Uricchio, F. M., 3281, 5456
Urner, H., 1979
Vaganay, Léon, 0855, 1733, 1798, 3509
Valette, Jean, 5539
Van Aarde, A. G., 1196, 2238, 2939
van Bruggen, Jakob, 5544
van Cangh, Jean-Marie, 0119, 0192, 0314, 1183, 1186, 1405, 1408, 1726, 1922, 2605, 2965, 4029, 4159, 4971
van Daalen, D. H., 2308
van den Ende, T., 1560
van der Horst, P. W., 2977, 4125
van der Valk, M., 2984
van der Voort, A. J., 3522
van Eck, E., 2238
van Halsema, J. H., 0533, 0544, 1307, 1964, 2082
van Iersel, B. M. F., 0088, 0433, 0943, 1226, 1400, 1560, 1791, 2608, 2968, 3069, 3410, 3490, 3696, 3733, 4653, 4654, 5047, 5286
van Linden, Phillip, 3847, 5534
Van Oyen, Geert, 0166
van Ruler, Arnold A., 2485
van Tilborg, Sjef, 0994, 2223, 2267, 2620
van Unnik, W. C., 2640, 2684, 3558
van Veldhuizen, Adriaan, 5405
Van Vurst, James, 2346
vander Broek, Lyle D., 1516, 1988, 2124
Vanhoye, Albert, 2667, 4431
Vannorsdall, John, 0390
Vardaman, E. J., 0886, 1261, 4633
Vargas-Machuca, Antonio, 0104, 0145, 1832, 2734, 3880, 4075
Vassiliadis, Petros, 4604, 5029, 5125
Vattioni, Francesco, 1842
Vaughan, P., 3805
Veerkamp, Ton, 2385, 2824, 2997
Veldhurzen, A. van, 1804
Vellanickal, Matthew, 0193, 1485, 2483, 4494
Venetz, H.-J., 1483, 1927
Verheyden, Jozef, 0300, 1277
Via, Dan O., 1966, 3347, 4251
Viard, A., 0246
Vielhauer, Philip, 3104
Vierzig, Siegfried, 3584, 4432
Vignolo, Roberto, 2982, 4908
Villegas, Beltran, 0450, 0608
Vincent, John J., 0468, 2205, 3267, 3829
Vinson, Richard B., 5144, 5157
Vischer, Wilhelm, 2642
Visser 't Hooft, Willem A., 2091
Viviano, Benedict T., 1662, 2297, 2661
Vogels, Heinrich, 2582
Vogt, Ernst, 0895, 1269
Vögtle, Anton, 0103, 2706, 3001
Völkel, Martin, 0439
von der Osten-Sacken, Peter, 3136
von Heusinger, Mechthild, 0385
von Kienle, Bettina, 2125, 2170, 3401
von Loewenich, W., 0814
von Wahlde, Urban C., 1742, 3264
von Wahlde, W. C., 0926, 4184
Vorster, Willem S., 1150, 1562, 2387, 3184, 4572, 4817, 4907
Vos, Howard F., 5517
Voser, M., 0942, 1381
Vouga, François, 2303

Vrijdaghs, Bartholomeus, 1871
Wagenaars, Frans, 2988
Wagner, Günter, 3083
Wagner, Guy, 2093, 2162, 3399, 5214
Wagner, Walter, 1943, 5018
Waibel, Maria, 0473
Walker, Geoffrey, 4166
Walker, William O., 4973
Walsh, Richard G., 4255
Walter, Nikolaus, 1896, 3029, 4864
Wambacq, B. N., 1846, 4078
Wanamaker, C. A., 2187
Wansbrough, Henry, 0638, 5470
Warmers, E., 5475
Waterman, G. Henry, 3326
Watson, Francis, 0278
Watson, Nigel M., 1668, 4608, 4895
Waverly, Thomas P., 4573
Waybright, Gregory L., 3261
Weber, Anton, 3056
Weber, J. C., 3900
Weber, Leslie F., 4233
Weder, Hans, 0040, 0194
Weeden, Theodore J., 2800, 3592, 3619, 3688, 3953, 4341, 4462
Weeks, W. R., 0083
Wegner, Uwe, 2041, 2276, 2580, 4047, 4513
Weinacht, Harald, 3121
Weis, P. R., 1308, 5364
Weiser, Alfons, 3317
Weiss, Johannes, 5399
Wenham, David, 0639, 0709, 1743, 4319, 5118
Wenham, John W., 5181, 5186
Werner, Eric, 3824
West, Ralph L., 4585
Weyman, Volker, 1703
Whiston, Lionel A., 0918, 1809
White, J. L., 4521
White, K. D., 4292
White, O. G., 3322, 4867
Wichelhaus, Manfred, 0305
Wiggins, Daphne C., 2776
Wilcox, Max, 2595, 2751
Wilde, James, 4924, 4925
Wildens, Wilhelm, 1251
Wilder, A. N., 4324
Wilkens, Thomas G., 5295
Wilkens, Wilhelm, 0159, 4293
Wilkinson, John, 2841, 4151, 4403
Willaert, B., 1499
Willemse, J. J. C., 0020
Williams, Francis E., 5107
Williams, N. P., 5089
Williamson, Lamar, 1189
Wilson, W. A. A., 3463
Winandy, Jacques, 2473
Wink, Walter, 1164, 1645
Winnett, A. R., 4031, 4463
Winter, Paul, 2691, 2702, 4399
Wohlenberg, Gustav, 5402
Wojciechowski, Michal, 0329, 0776, 0827, 2107, 2590, 2810, 3400, 4199
Wolff, Christian, 0068
Wonderly, Daniel E., 4587
Wood, H. G., 5090
Wood, James E., 4829
Wormser, G., 2281, 3093
Wrede, William, 4115
Wretlind, D. O., 0311
Wright, George A., 3763
Wright, John, 0048, 4806
Wulf, Friedrich, 2515, 5285
Yates, J. E., 0086, 3054
Yonggi, Paul Cho, 3368
Zarrella, Pietro, 0091
Zeitlin, Solomon, 3981, 3982
Zeller, Dieter, 0100, 4475, 5284
Ziener, Georg, 1176, 1455, 3376
Ziesler, J. A., 0481, 5014, 5317
Ziffer, W., 4750
Zimmerli, Walther, 1895
Zimmermann, Heinrich, 1801
Zimmermann, Wolf-Dieter, 5476
Zorn, Walter D., 4915
Zuntz, Günther, 1994, 2424